ALICE IN BORDERLAND

STORY AND ART BY
HARO ASO

4

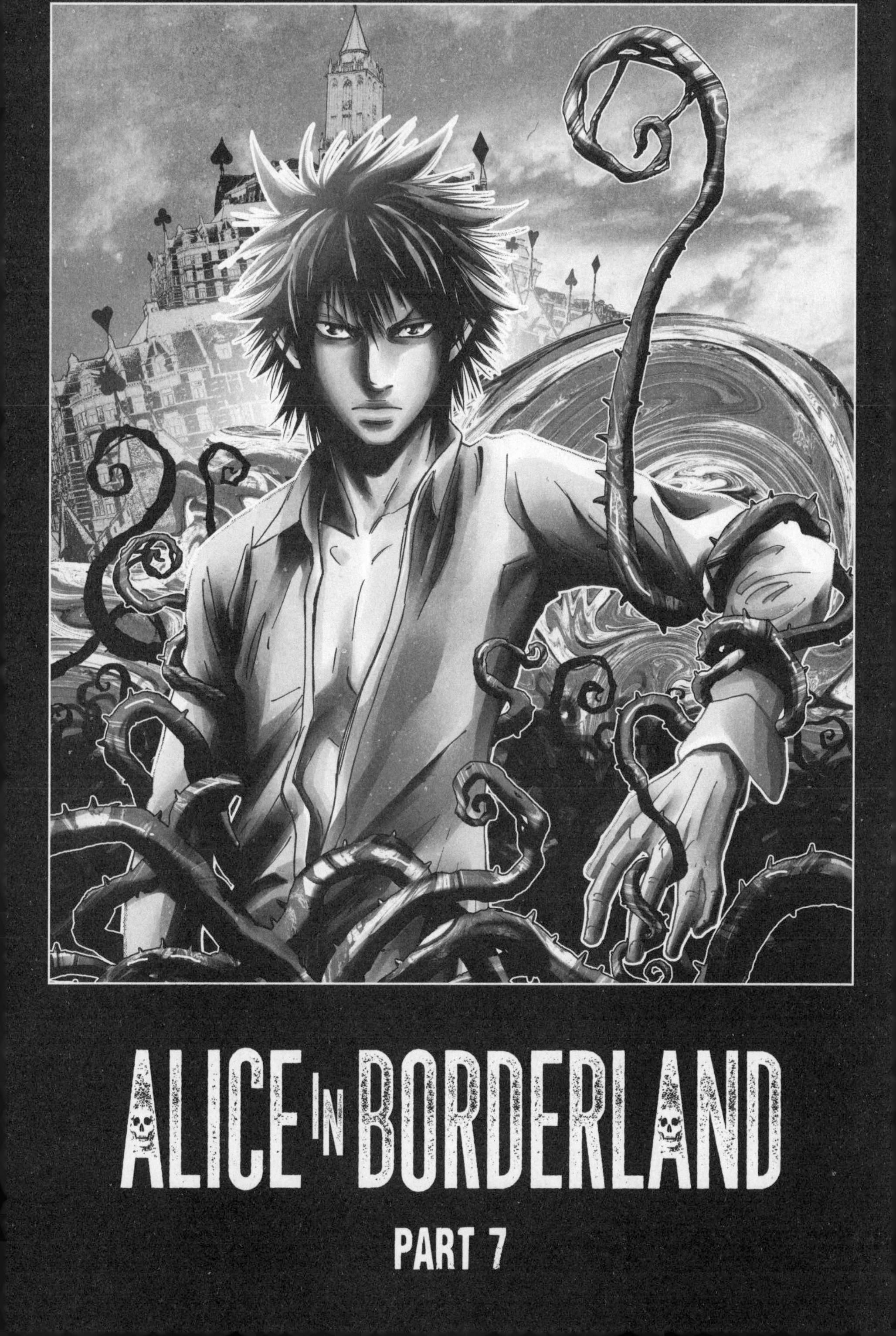

ALICE IN BORDERLAND

PART 7

ALICE IN BORDERLAND

PART 7

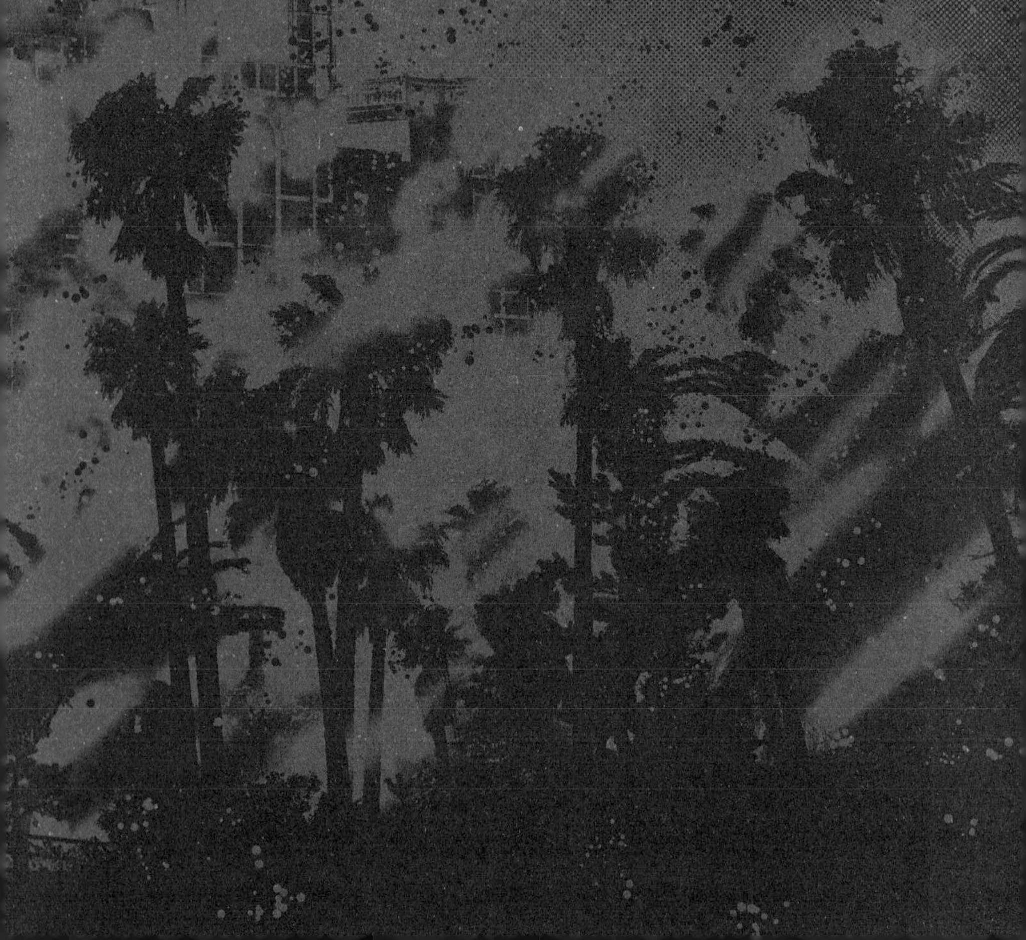

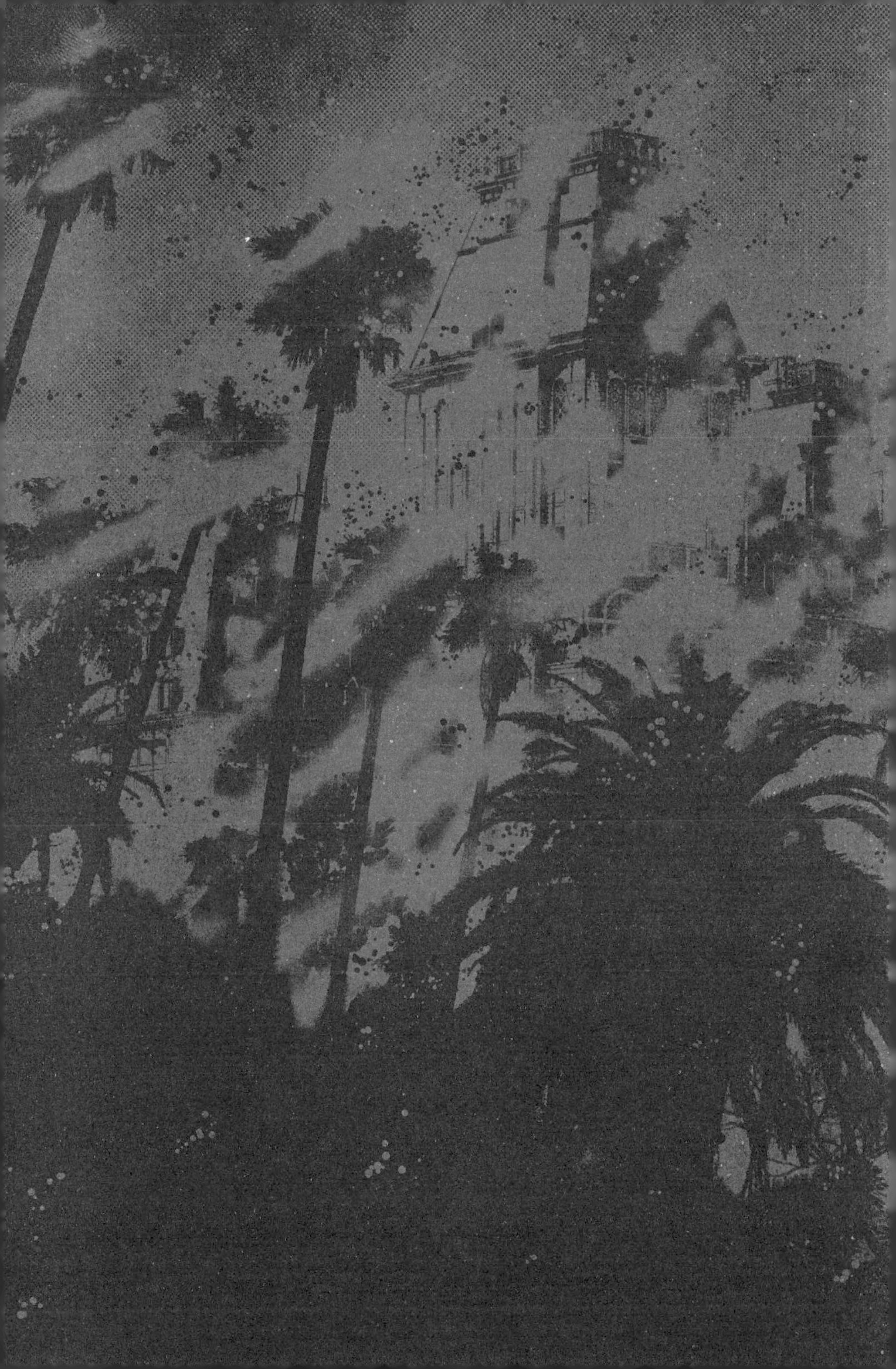

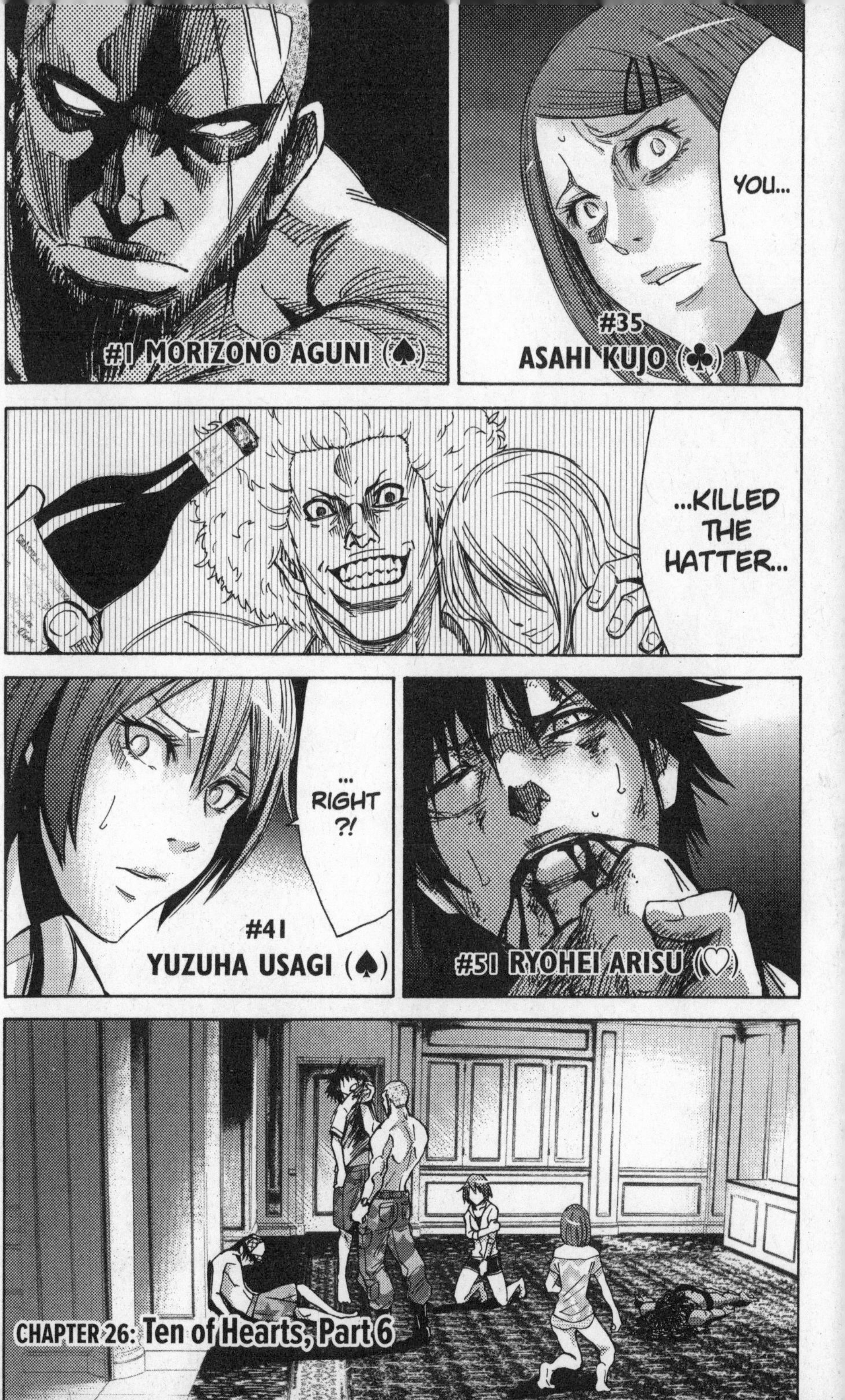
YOU...
#35
ASAHI KUJO (♣)
#1 MORIZONO AGUNI (♠)
...KILLED THE HATTER...
#51 RYOHEI ARISU (♡)
... RIGHT ?!
#41
YUZUHA USAGI (♠)
CHAPTER 26: Ten of Hearts, Part 6

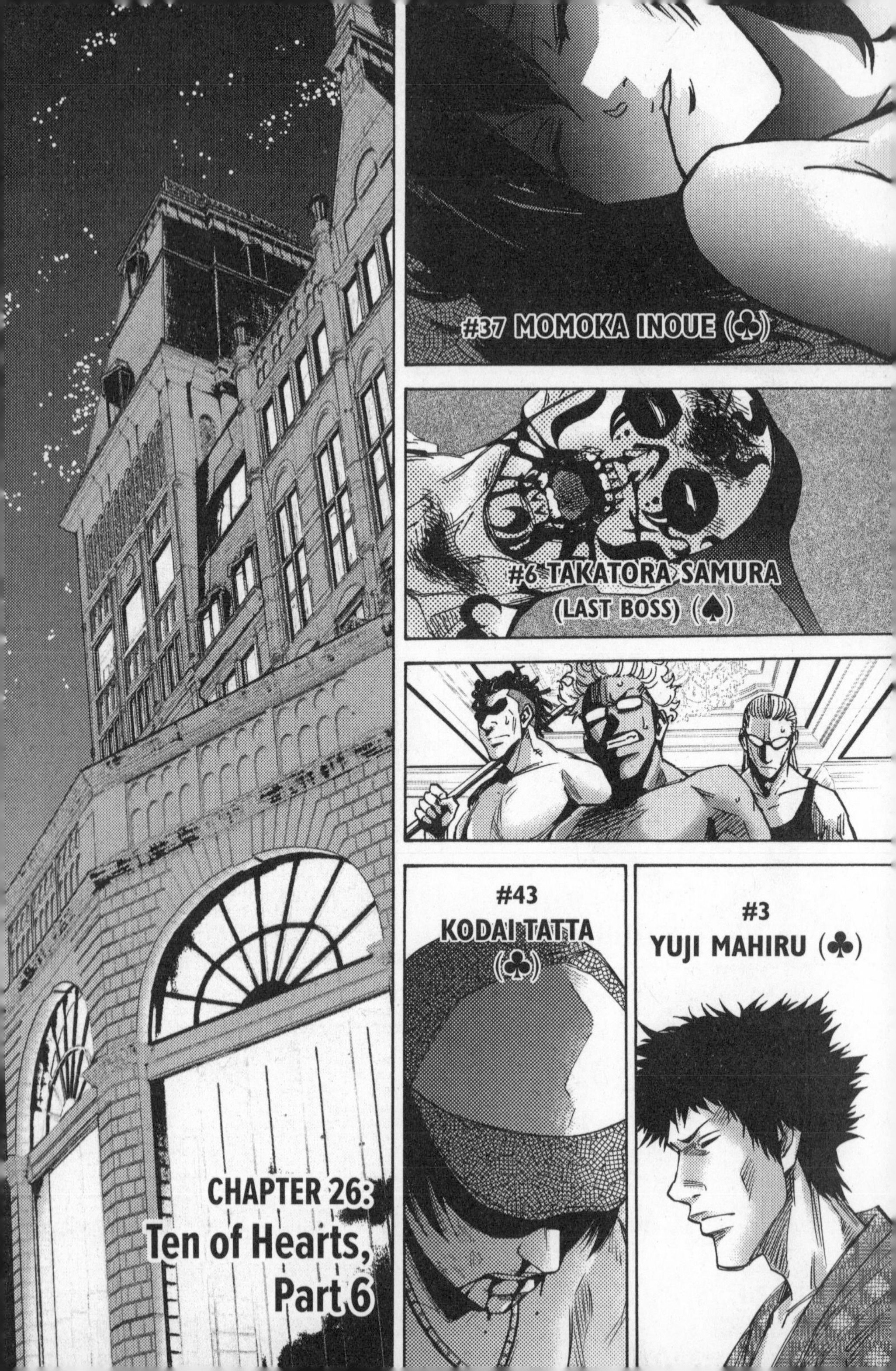
#37 MOMOKA INOUE (♧)
#6 TAKATORA SAMURA
(LAST BOSS) (♠)
#3
YUJI MAHIRU (♣)
#43
KODAI TATTA
(♧)
CHAPTER 26:
Ten of Hearts,
Part 6

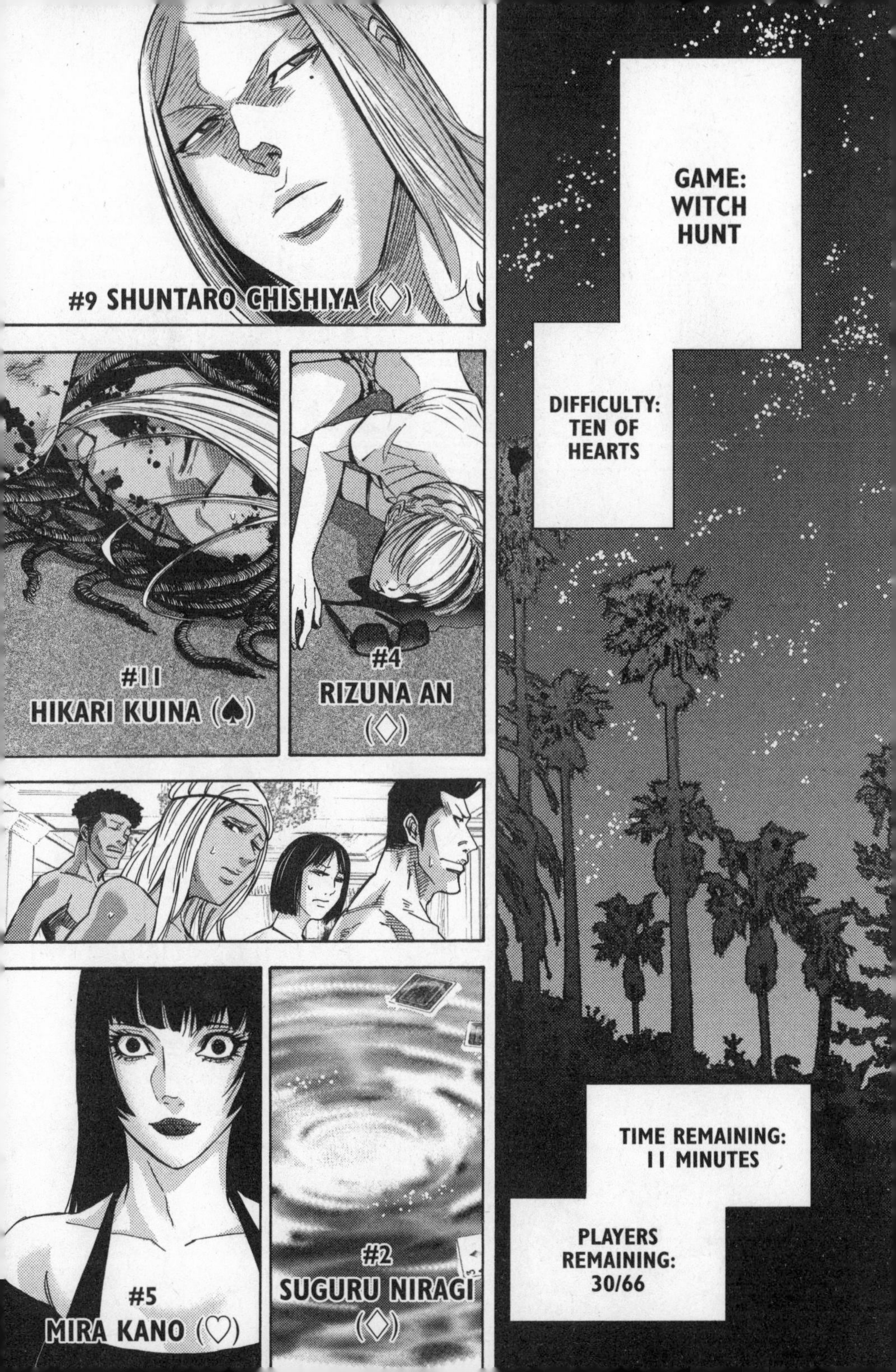
GAME: WITCH HUNT
DIFFICULTY: TEN OF HEARTS
TIME REMAINING: 11 MINUTES
PLAYERS REMAINING: 30/66
#9 SHUNTARO CHISHIYA (♢)
#4 RIZUNA AN (♢)
#11 HIKARI KUINA (♠)
#2 SUGURU NIRAGI (♢)
#5 MIRA KANO (♡)

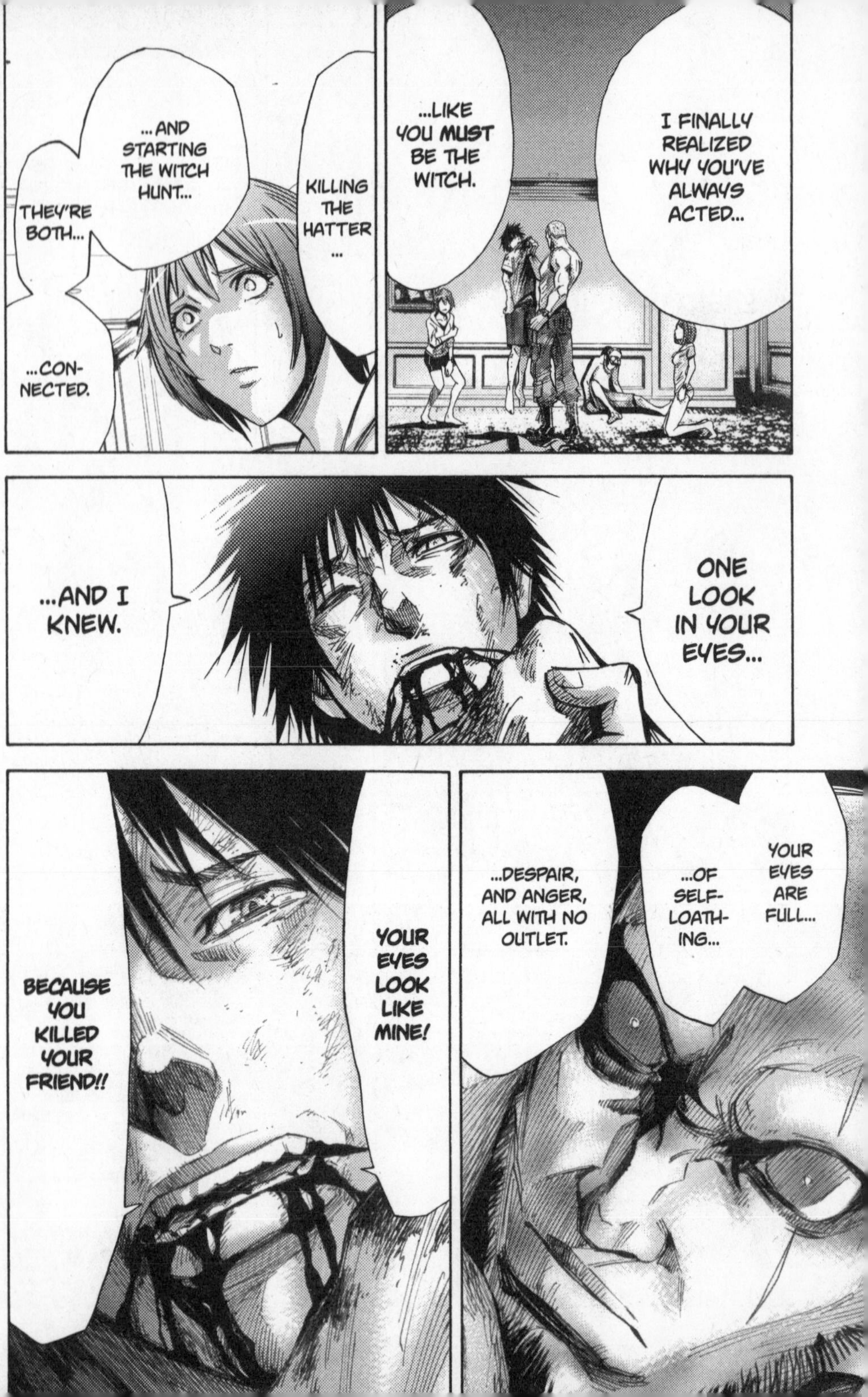
I FINALLY REALIZED WHY YOU'VE ALWAYS ACTED...
...LIKE YOU MUST BE THE WITCH.
KILLING THE HATTER ...
...AND STARTING THE WITCH HUNT...
THEY'RE BOTH...
...CON-NECTED.
ONE LOOK IN YOUR EYES...
...AND I KNEW.
YOUR EYES ARE FULL...
...OF SELF-LOATHING...
...DESPAIR, AND ANGER, ALL WITH NO OUTLET.
YOUR EYES LOOK LIKE MINE!
BECAUSE YOU KILLED YOUR FRIEND!!

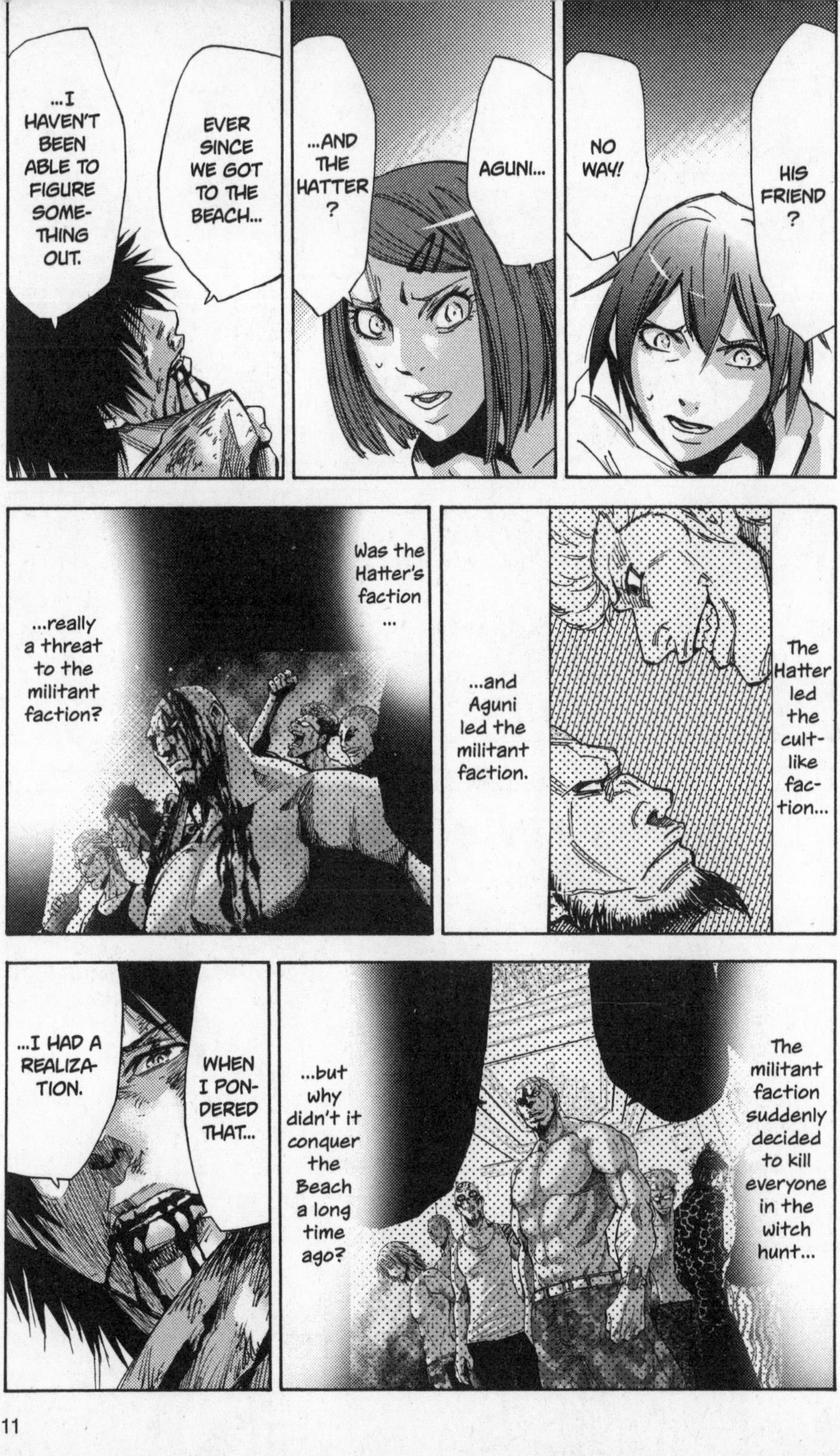
HIS FRIEND?
NO WAY!
AGUNI...
...AND THE HATTER?
EVER SINCE WE GOT TO THE BEACH...
...I HAVEN'T BEEN ABLE TO FIGURE SOME-THING OUT.
The Hatter led the cult-like fac-tion...
...and Aguni led the militant faction.
Was the Hatter's faction...
...really a threat to the militant faction?
The militant faction suddenly decided to kill everyone in the witch hunt...
...but why didn't it conquer the Beach a long time ago?
WHEN I PON-DERED THAT...
...I HAD A REALIZA-TION.

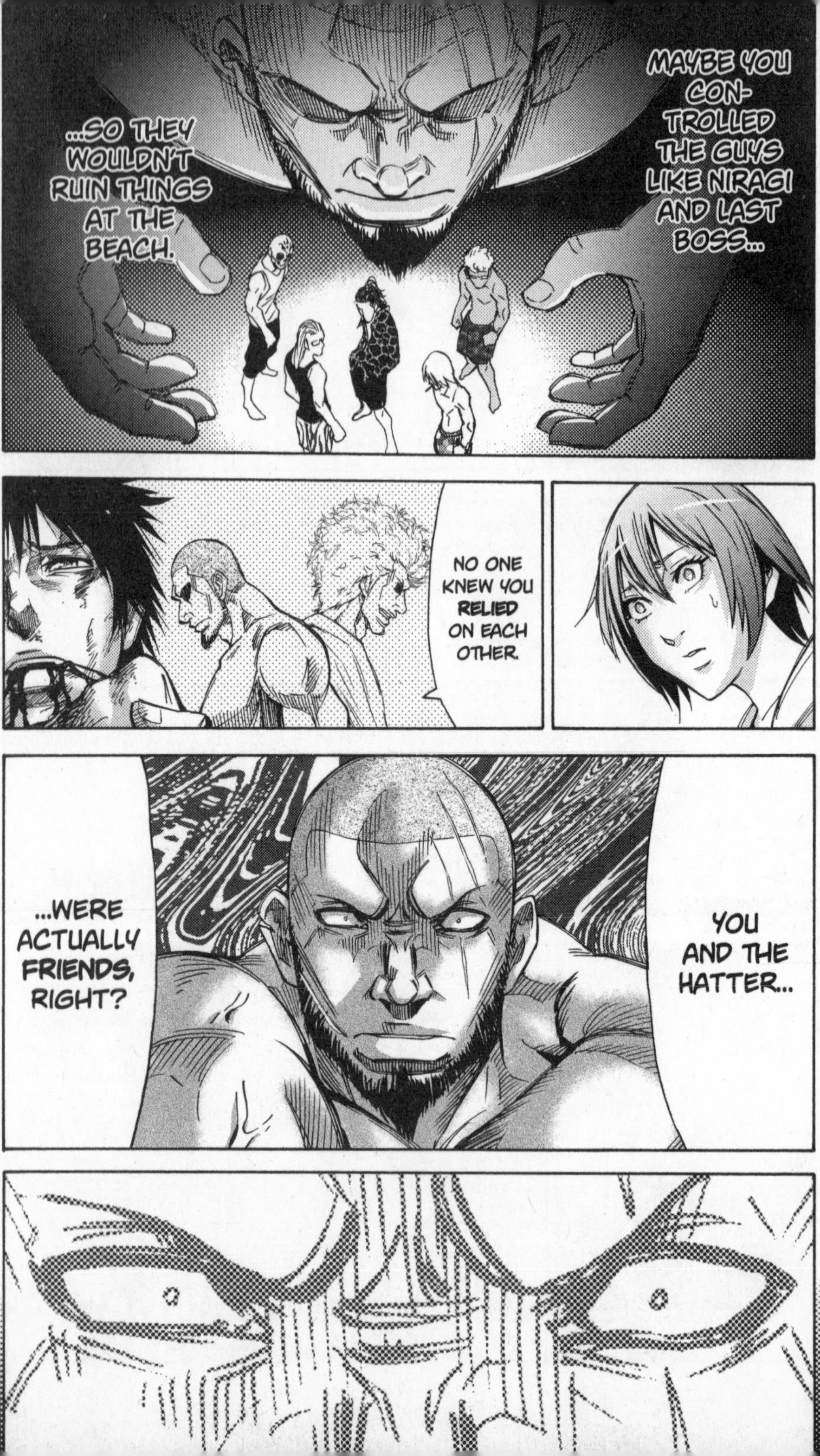
MAYBE YOU CON-TROLLED THE GUYS LIKE NIRAGI AND LAST BOSS...
...SO THEY WOULDN'T RUIN THINGS AT THE BEACH.
NO ONE KNEW YOU RELIED ON EACH OTHER.
YOU AND THE HATTER...
...WERE ACTUALLY FRIENDS, RIGHT?

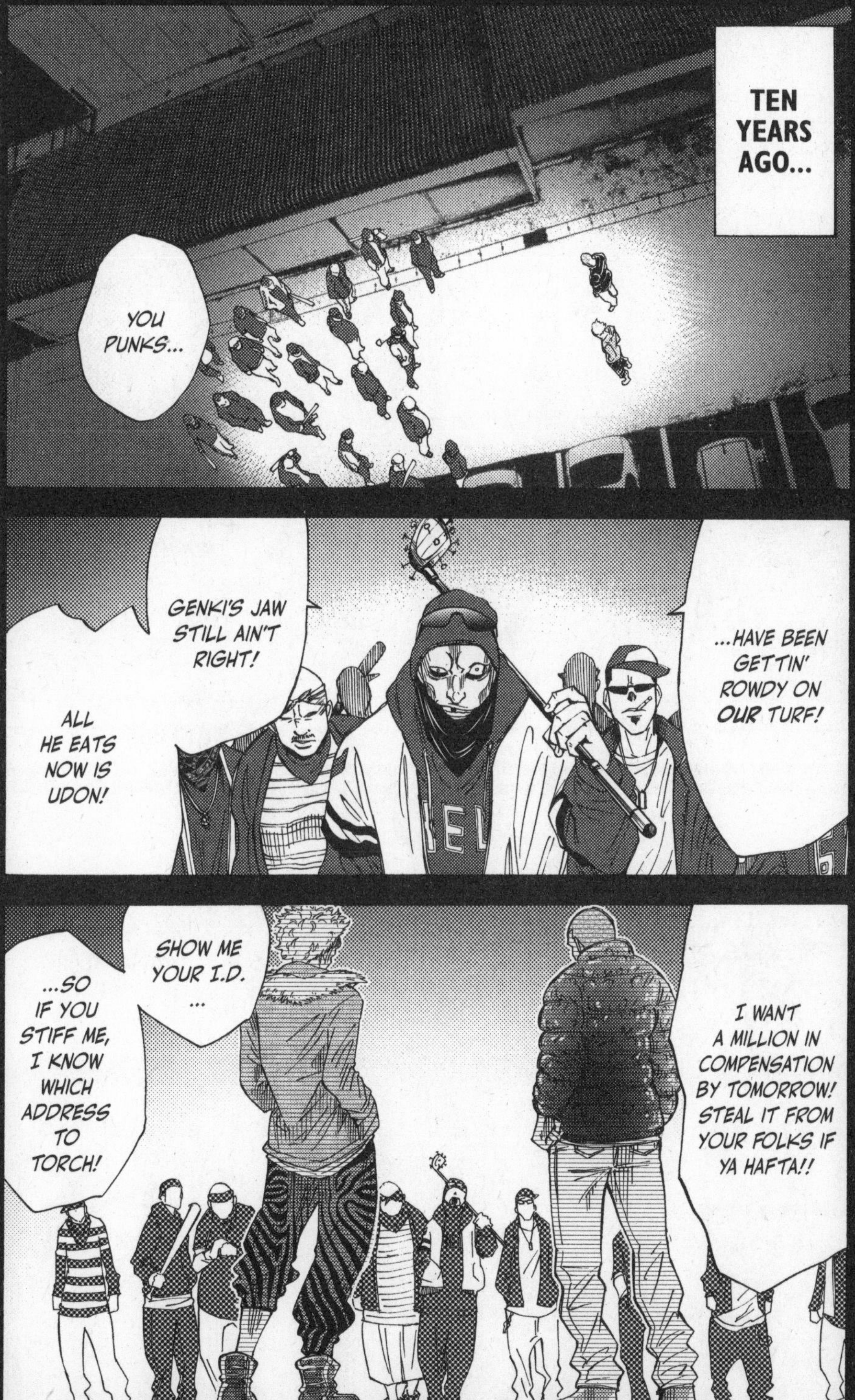
TEN YEARS AGO...
YOU PUNKS...
...HAVE BEEN GETTIN' ROWDY ON OUR TURF!
GENKI'S JAW STILL AIN'T RIGHT!
ALL HE EATS NOW IS UDON!
I WANT A MILLION IN COMPENSATION BY TOMORROW! STEAL IT FROM YOUR FOLKS IF YA HAFTA!!
SHOW ME YOUR I.D. ...
...SO IF YOU STIFF ME, I KNOW WHICH ADDRESS TO TORCH!

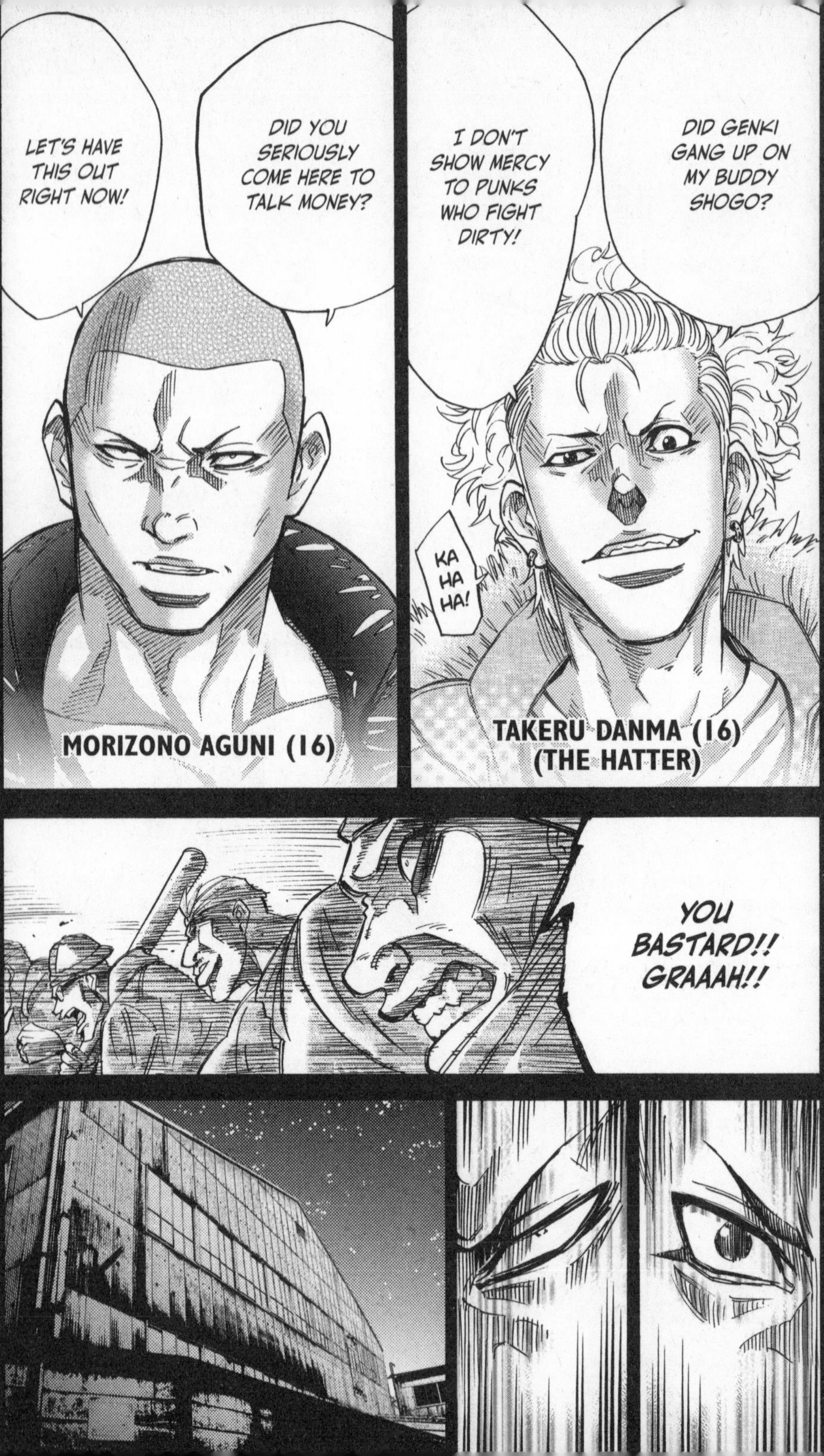
DID GENKI GANG UP ON MY BUDDY SHOGO?
I DON'T SHOW MERCY TO PUNKS WHO FIGHT DIRTY!
KA HA HA!
TAKERU DANMA (16) (THE HATTER)
DID YOU SERIOUSLY COME HERE TO TALK MONEY?
LET'S HAVE THIS OUT RIGHT NOW!
MORIZONO AGUNI (16)
YOU BASTARD!! GRAAAH!!

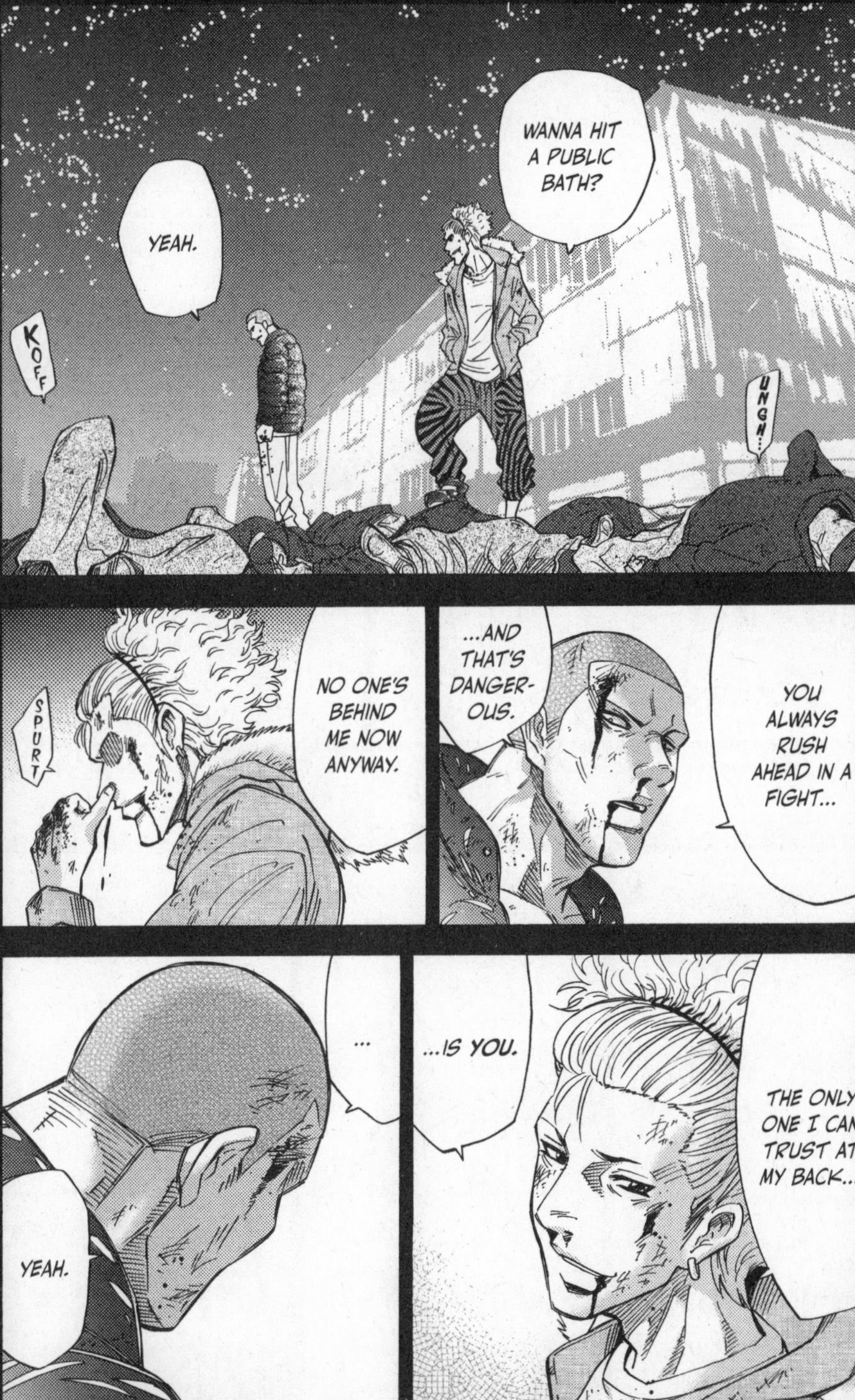
WANNA HIT A PUBLIC BATH?
UNGH...
YEAH.
KOFF
YOU ALWAYS RUSH AHEAD IN A FIGHT...
...AND THAT'S DANGER-OUS.
NO ONE'S BEHIND ME NOW ANYWAY.
SPURT
THE ONLY ONE I CAN TRUST AT MY BACK...
...IS YOU.
...
YEAH.

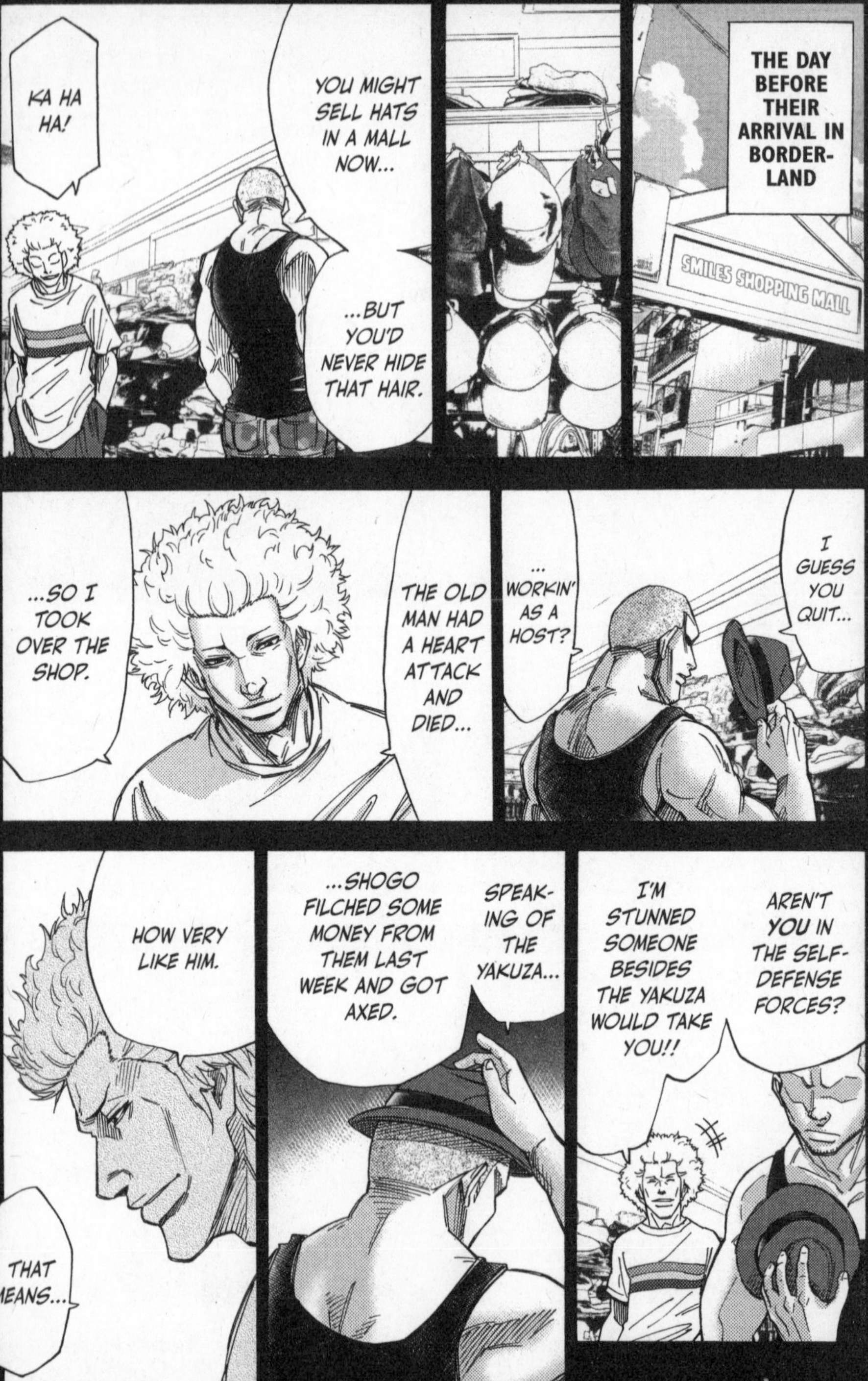
THE DAY BEFORE THEIR ARRIVAL IN BORDER-LAND
SMILES SHOPPING MALL
YOU MIGHT SELL HATS IN A MALL NOW...
...BUT YOU'D NEVER HIDE THAT HAIR.
KA HA HA!
I GUESS YOU QUIT...
...WORKIN' AS A HOST?
THE OLD MAN HAD A HEART ATTACK AND DIED...
...SO I TOOK OVER THE SHOP.
AREN'T YOU IN THE SELF-DEFENSE FORCES?
I'M STUNNED SOMEONE BESIDES THE YAKUZA WOULD TAKE YOU!!
SPEAK-ING OF THE YAKUZA...
...SHOGO FILCHED SOME MONEY FROM THEM LAST WEEK AND GOT AXED.
HOW VERY LIKE HIM.
THAT MEANS...

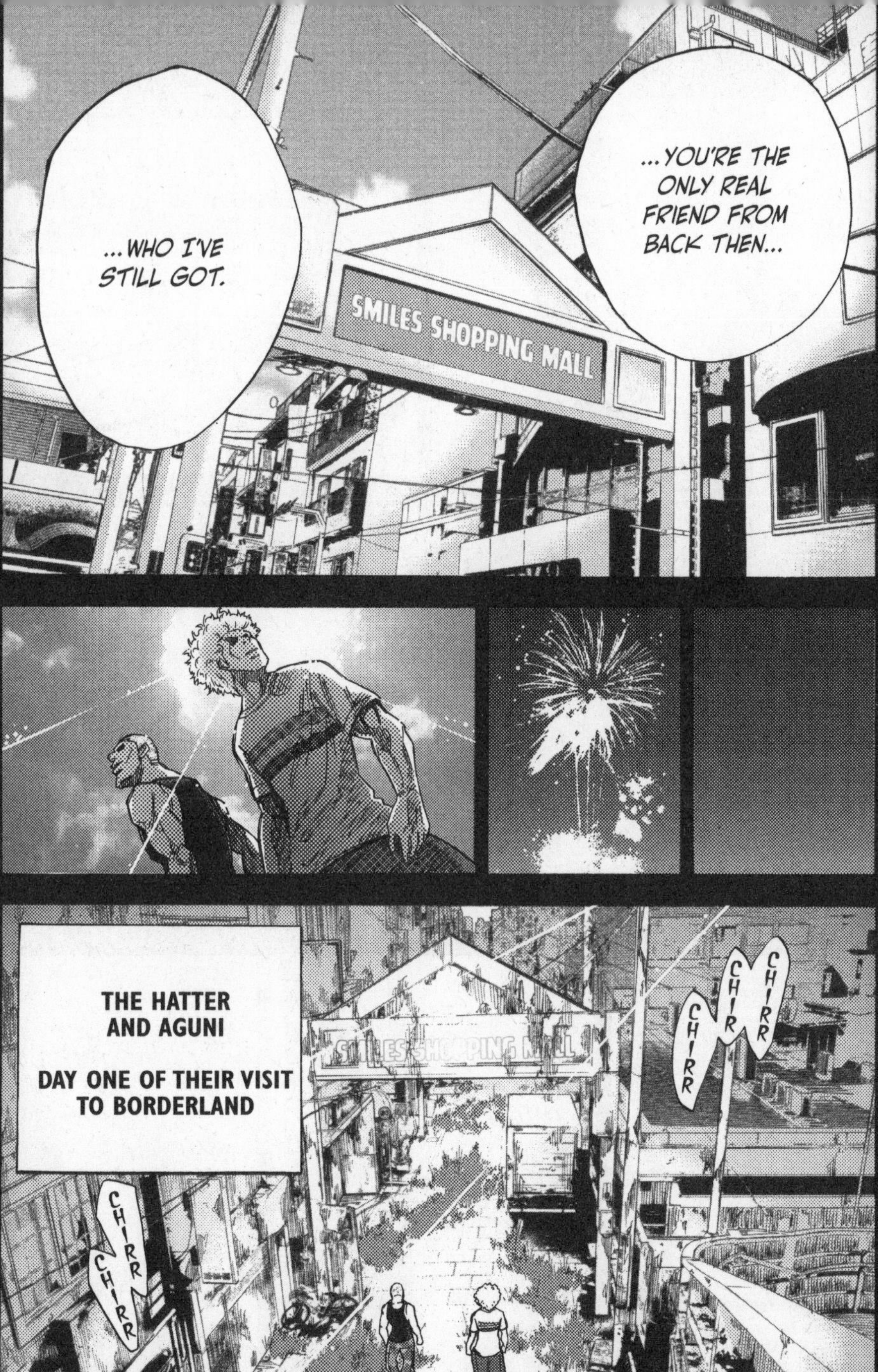
...YOU'RE THE ONLY REAL FRIEND FROM BACK THEN...
...WHO I'VE STILL GOT.
SMILES SHOPPING MALL
CHIRR
CHIRR
CHIRR
THE HATTER AND AGUNI

DAY ONE OF THEIR VISIT TO BORDERLAND
SMILES SHOPPING MALL
CHIRR
CHIRR

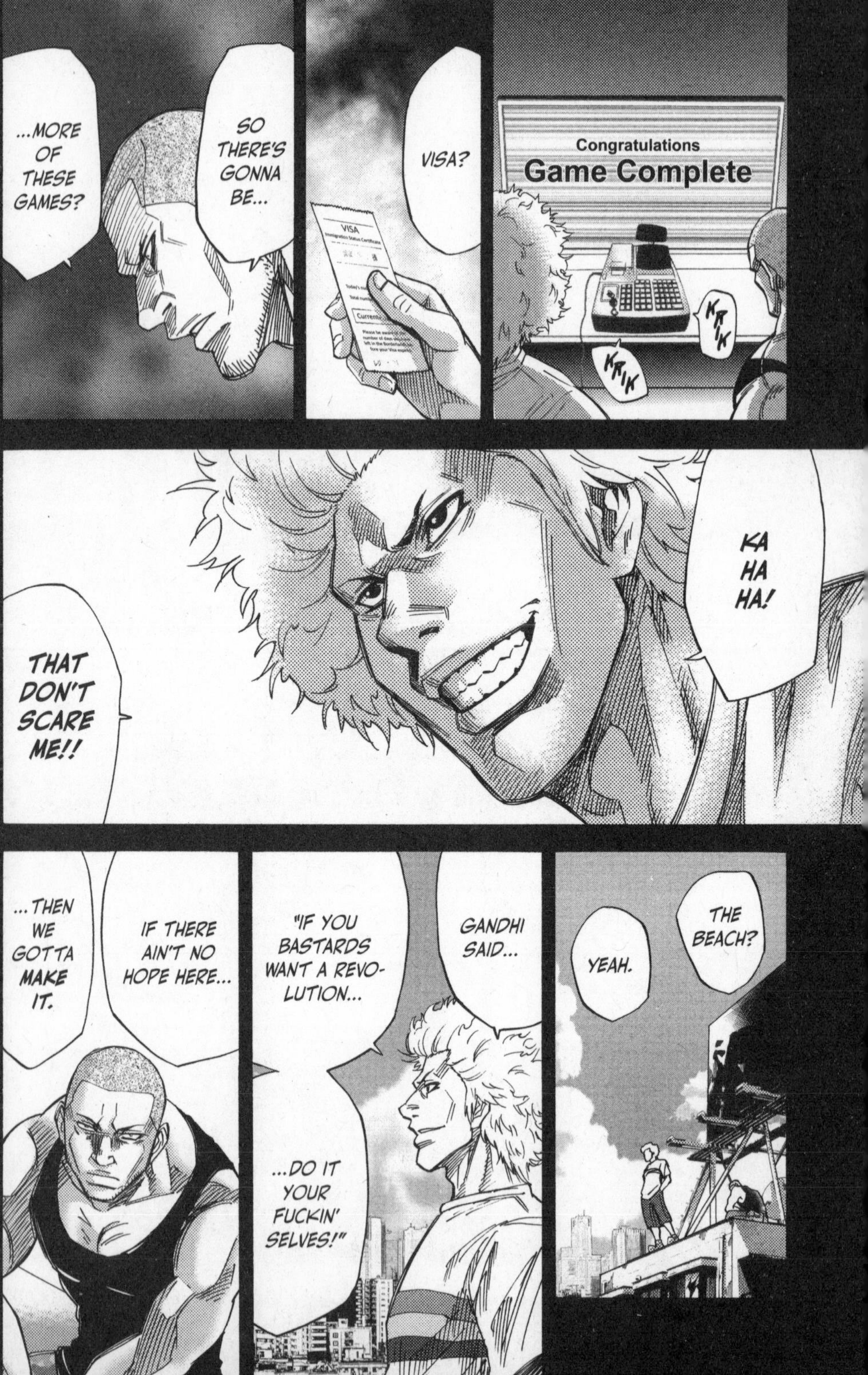
Congratulations
Game Complete
KRIK
KRIK
VISA
Immigration Status Certificate
VISA?
SO THERE'S GONNA BE...
...MORE OF THESE GAMES?
KA HA HA!
THAT DON'T SCARE ME!!
THE BEACH?
YEAH.
GANDHI SAID...
"IF YOU BASTARDS WANT A REVOLUTION...
...DO IT YOUR FUCKIN' SELVES!"
IF THERE AIN'T NO HOPE HERE...
...THEN WE GOTTA MAKE IT.

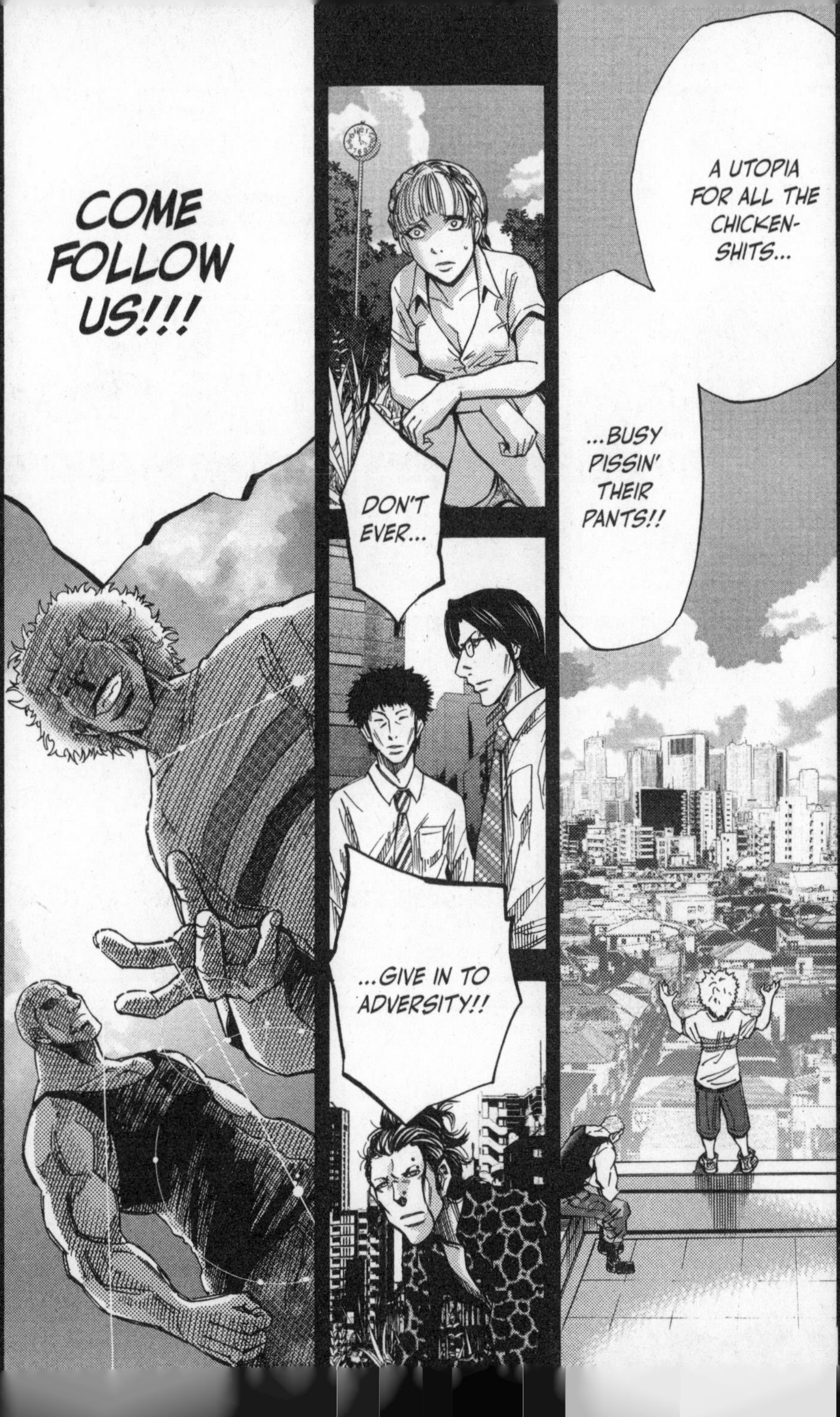
A UTOPIA FOR ALL THE CHICKEN-SHITS...
...BUSY PISSIN' THEIR PANTS!!
DON'T EVER...
...GIVE IN TO ADVERSITY!!
COME FOLLOW US!!!

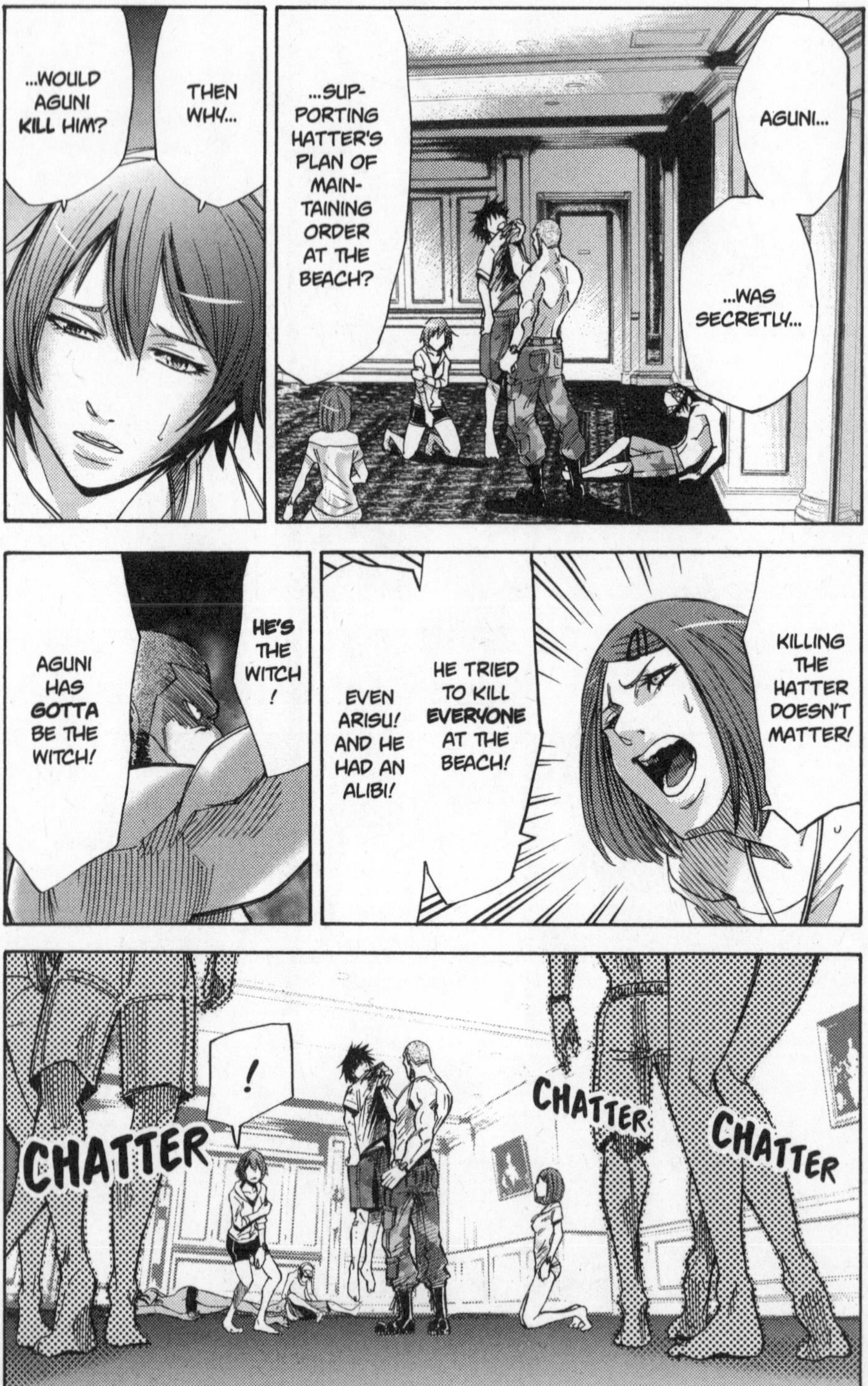
AGUNI...
...WAS SECRETLY...
...SUP-PORTING HATTER'S PLAN OF MAIN-TAINING ORDER AT THE BEACH?
THEN WHY...
...WOULD AGUNI KILL HIM?
KILLING THE HATTER DOESN'T MATTER!
HE TRIED TO KILL EVERYONE AT THE BEACH!
EVEN ARISU! AND HE HAD AN ALIBI!
HE'S THE WITCH!
AGUNI HAS GOTTA BE THE WITCH!
CHATTER
CHATTER
!
CHATTER

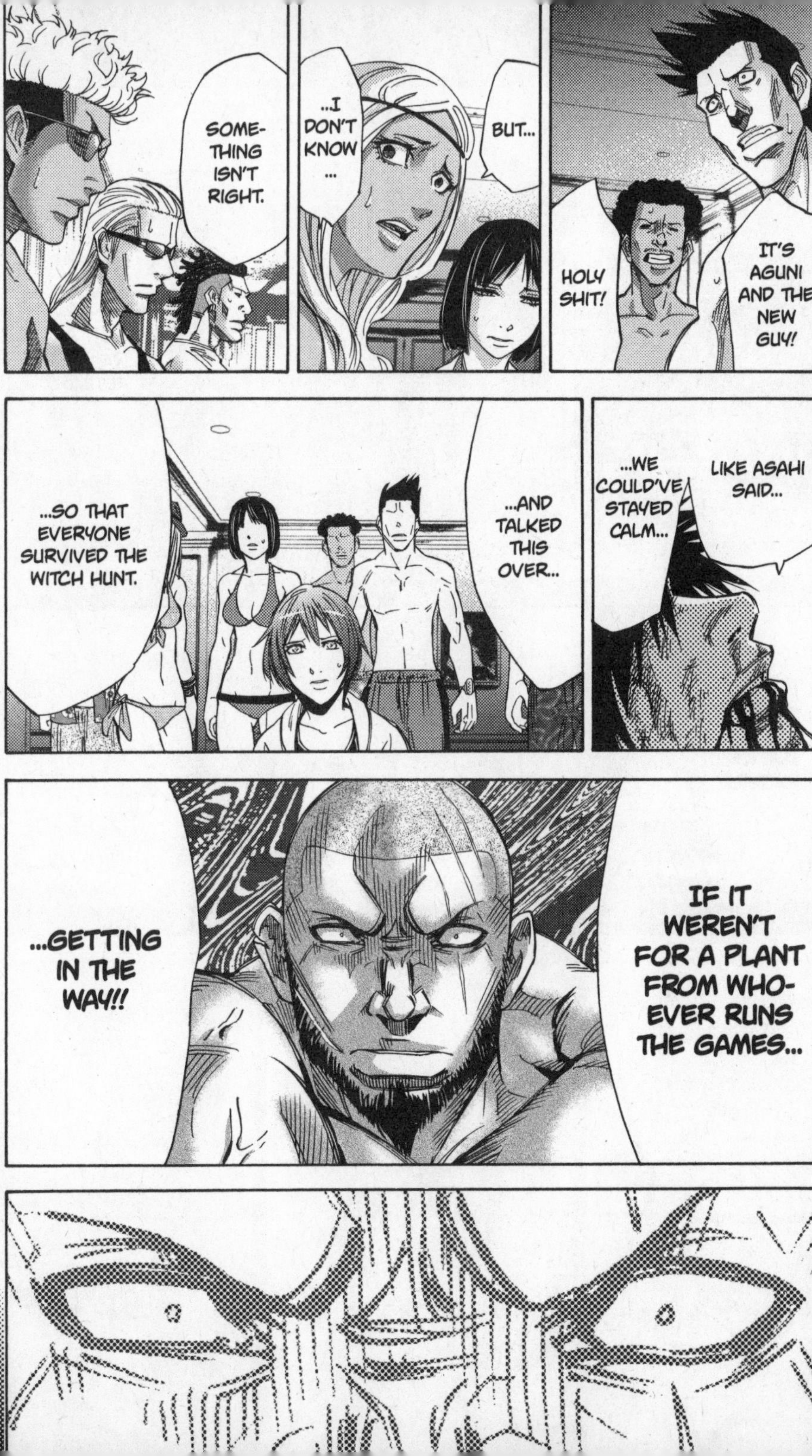
IT'S AGUNI AND THE NEW GUY!
HOLY SHIT!
BUT...
...I DON'T KNOW ...
SOME-THING ISN'T RIGHT.
LIKE ASAHI SAID...
...WE COULD'VE STAYED CALM...
...AND TALKED THIS OVER...
...SO THAT EVERYONE SURVIVED THE WITCH HUNT.
IF IT WEREN'T FOR A PLANT FROM WHO-EVER RUNS THE GAMES...
...GETTING IN THE WAY!!

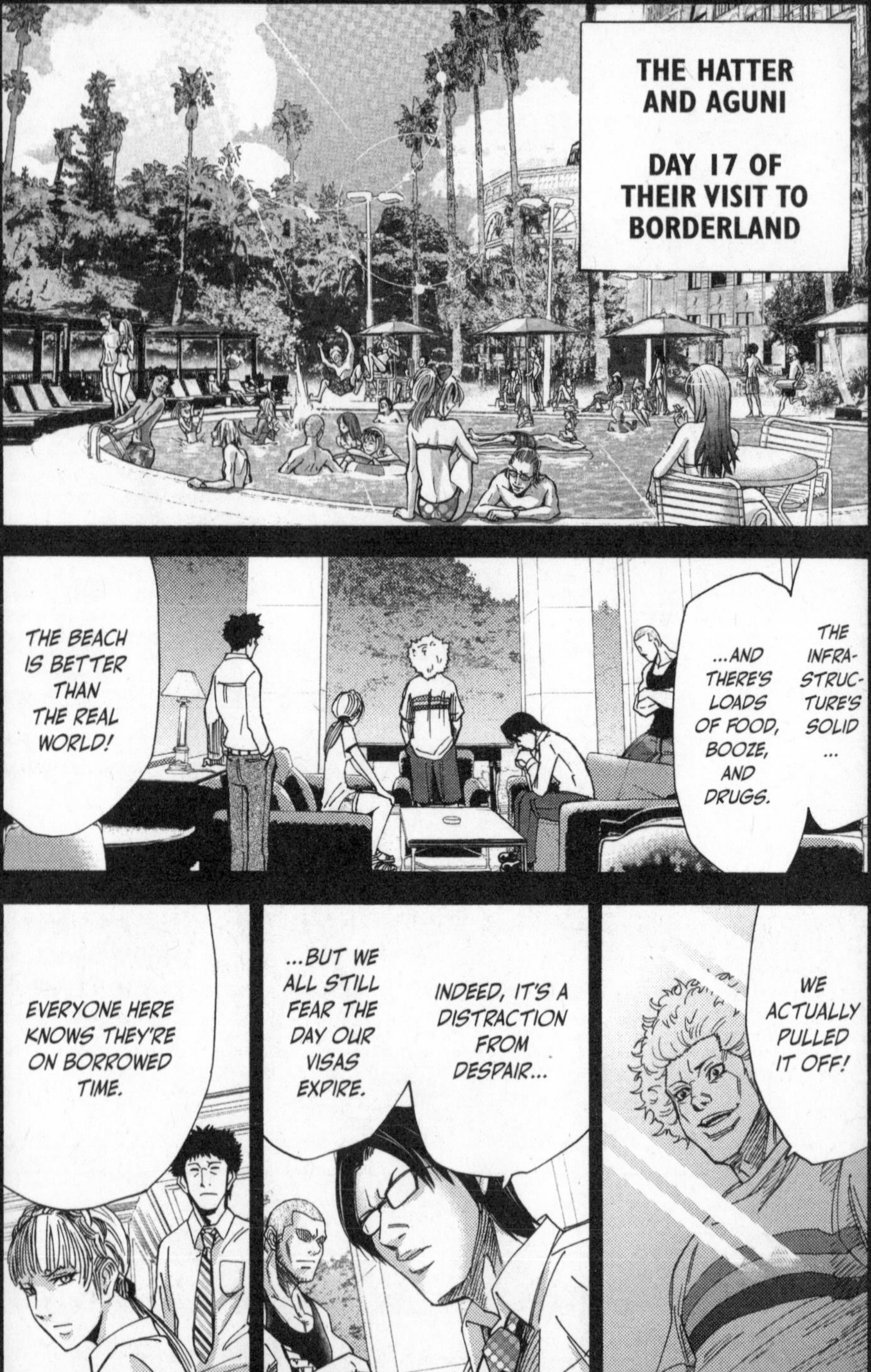
THE HATTER AND AGUNI

DAY 17 OF THEIR VISIT TO BORDERLAND
THE INFRA-STRUCTURE'S SOLID ...
...AND THERE'S LOADS OF FOOD, BOOZE, AND DRUGS.
THE BEACH IS BETTER THAN THE REAL WORLD!
WE ACTUALLY PULLED IT OFF!
INDEED, IT'S A DISTRACTION FROM DESPAIR...
...BUT WE ALL STILL FEAR THE DAY OUR VISAS EXPIRE.
EVERYONE HERE KNOWS THEY'RE ON BORROWED TIME.

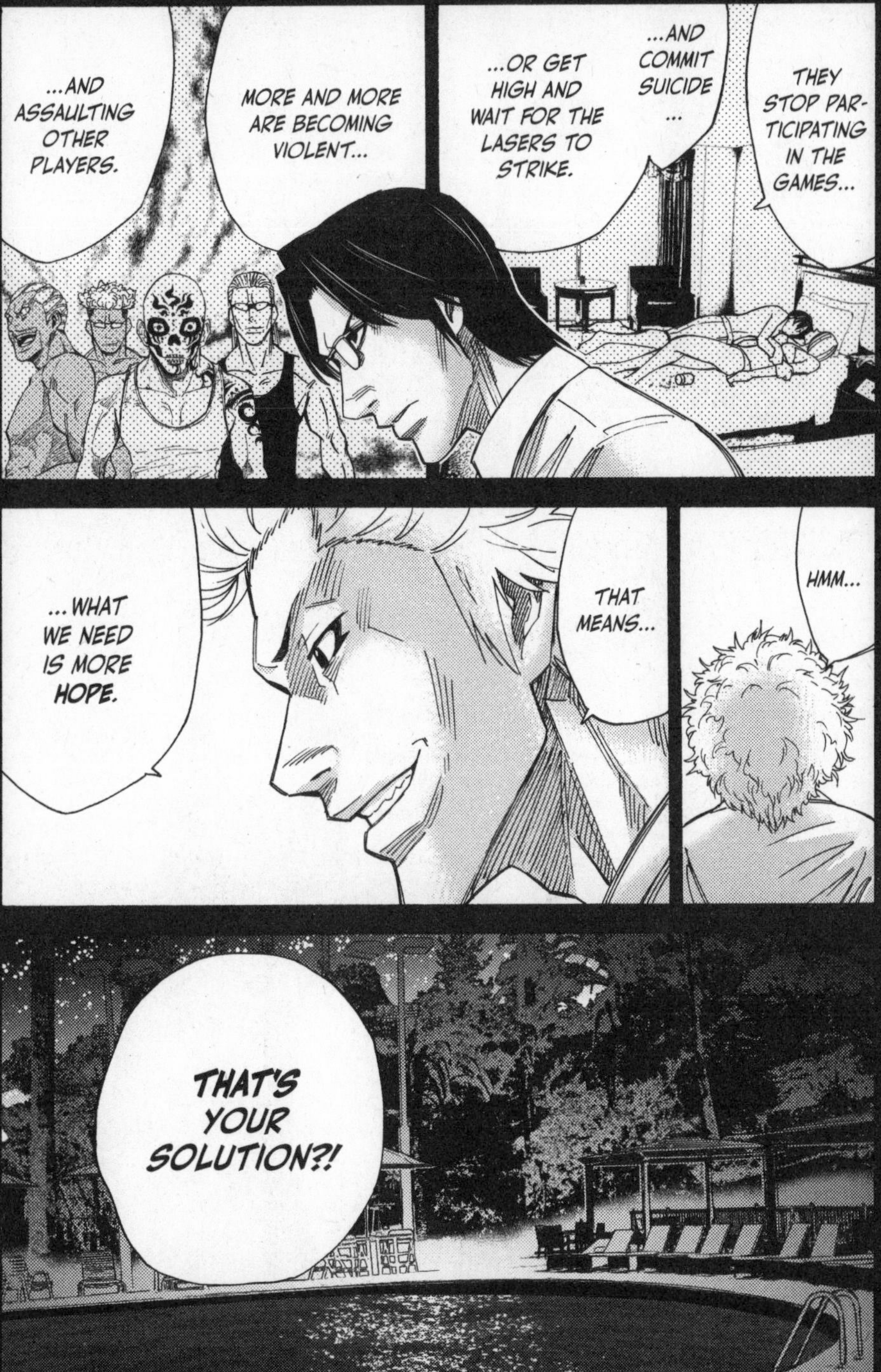
THEY STOP PAR-TICIPATING IN THE GAMES...
...AND COMMIT SUICIDE ...
...OR GET HIGH AND WAIT FOR THE LASERS TO STRIKE.
MORE AND MORE ARE BECOMING VIOLENT...
...AND ASSAULTING OTHER PLAYERS.
HMM...
THAT MEANS...
...WHAT WE NEED IS MORE HOPE.
THAT'S YOUR SOLUTION?!

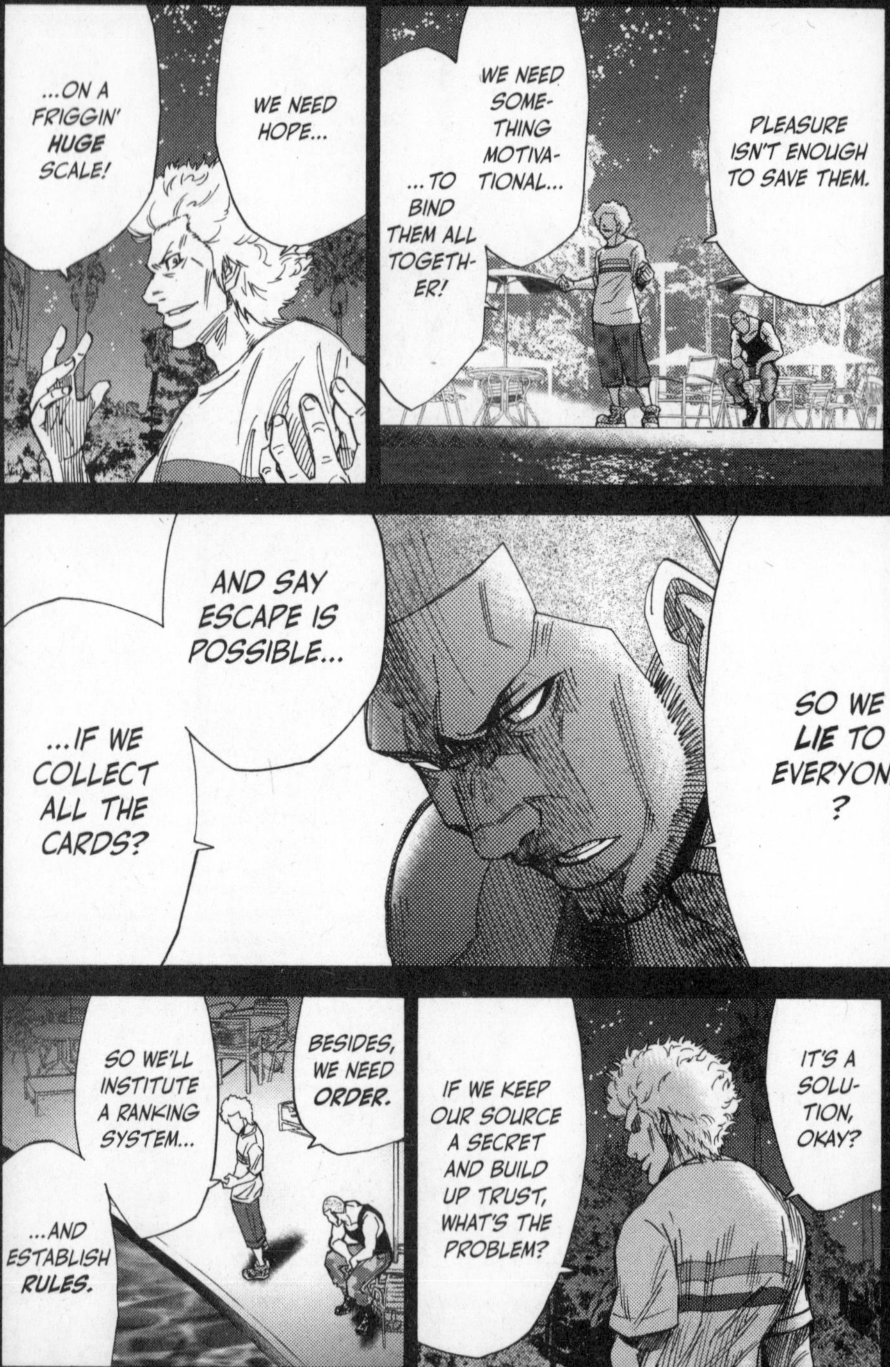
PLEASURE ISN'T ENOUGH TO SAVE THEM.
WE NEED SOMETHING MOTIVATIONAL...
...TO BIND THEM ALL TOGETHER!
WE NEED HOPE...
...ON A FRIGGIN' **HUGE** SCALE!
SO WE **LIE** TO EVERYONE?
AND SAY ESCAPE IS POSSIBLE...
...IF WE COLLECT ALL THE CARDS?
IT'S A SOLUTION, OKAY?
IF WE KEEP OUR SOURCE A SECRET AND BUILD UP TRUST, WHAT'S THE PROBLEM?
BESIDES, WE NEED **ORDER.**
SO WE'LL INSTITUTE A RANKING SYSTEM...
...AND ESTABLISH **RULES.**

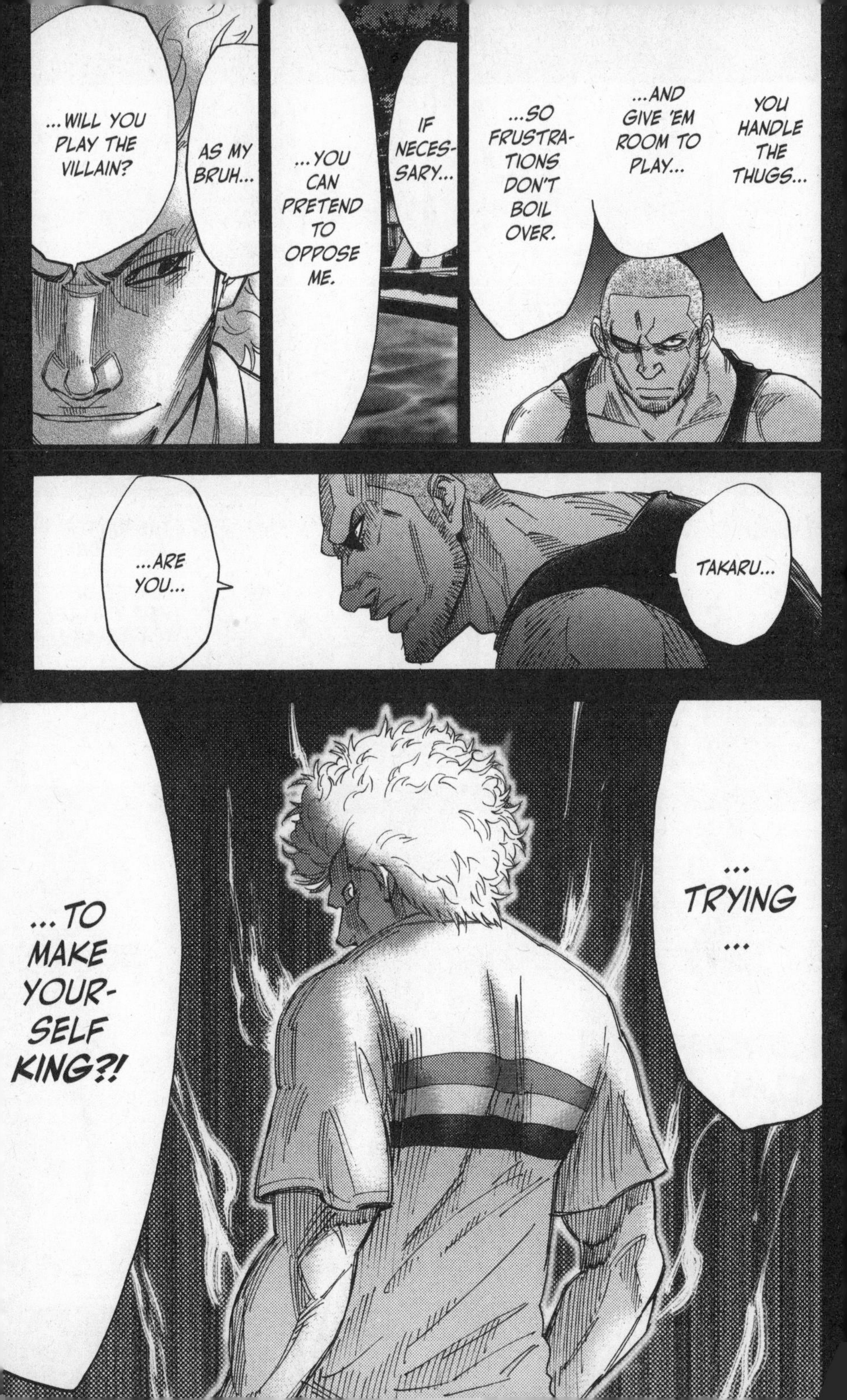
YOU HANDLE THE THUGS...
...AND GIVE 'EM ROOM TO PLAY...
...SO FRUSTRATIONS DON'T BOIL OVER.
IF NECESSARY...
...YOU CAN PRETEND TO OPPOSE ME.
AS MY BRUH...
...WILL YOU PLAY THE VILLAIN?
TAKARU...
...ARE YOU...
...TRYING...
...TO MAKE YOURSELF KING?!

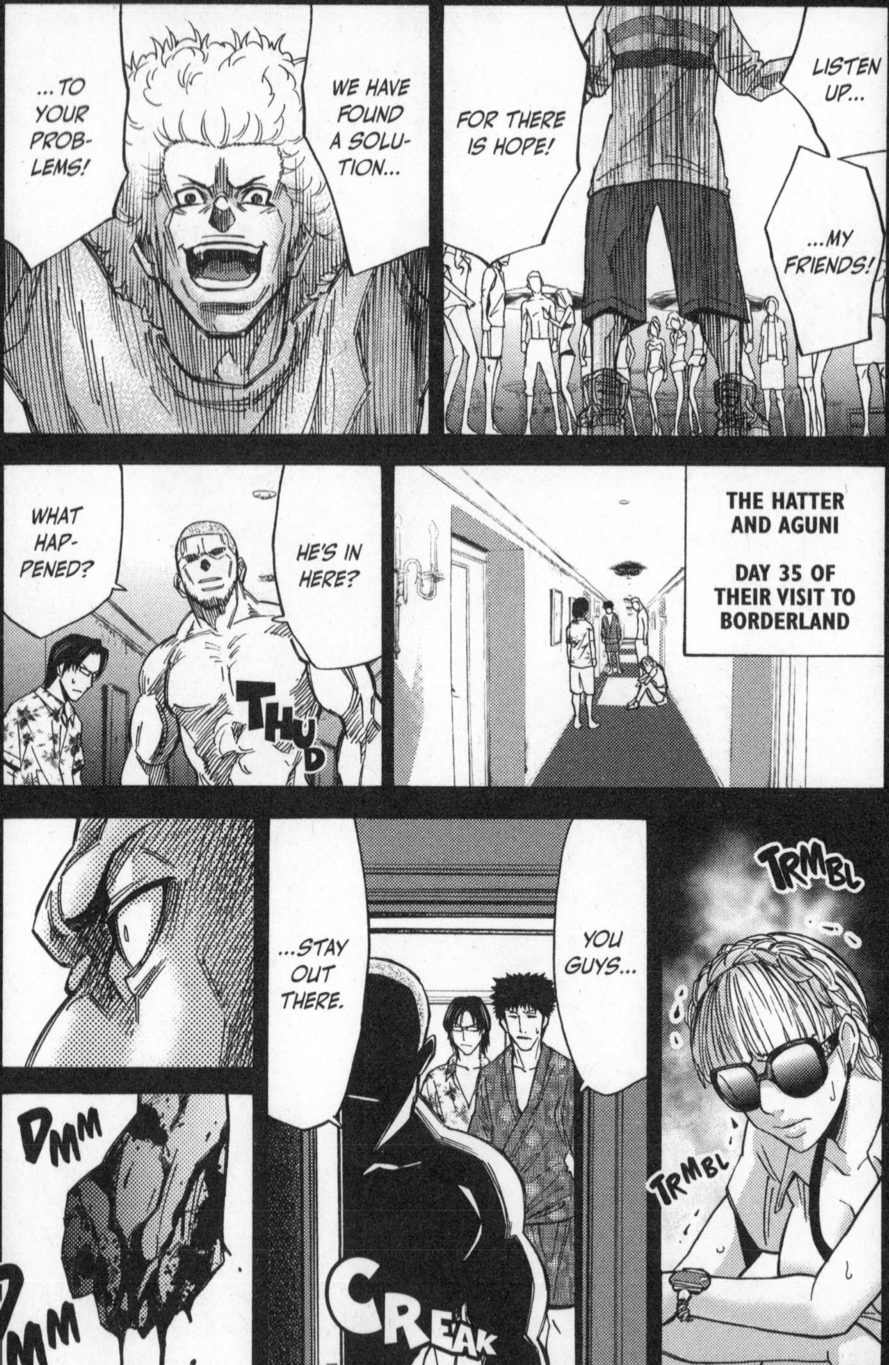
LISTEN UP...
...MY FRIENDS!
FOR THERE IS HOPE!
WE HAVE FOUND A SOLUTION...
...TO YOUR PROBLEMS!
THE HATTER AND AGUNI

DAY 35 OF THEIR VISIT TO BORDERLAND
HE'S IN HERE?
WHAT HAPPENED?
THUD
TRMBL
TRMBL
YOU GUYS...
...STAY OUT THERE.
CREAK
DMM
DMM

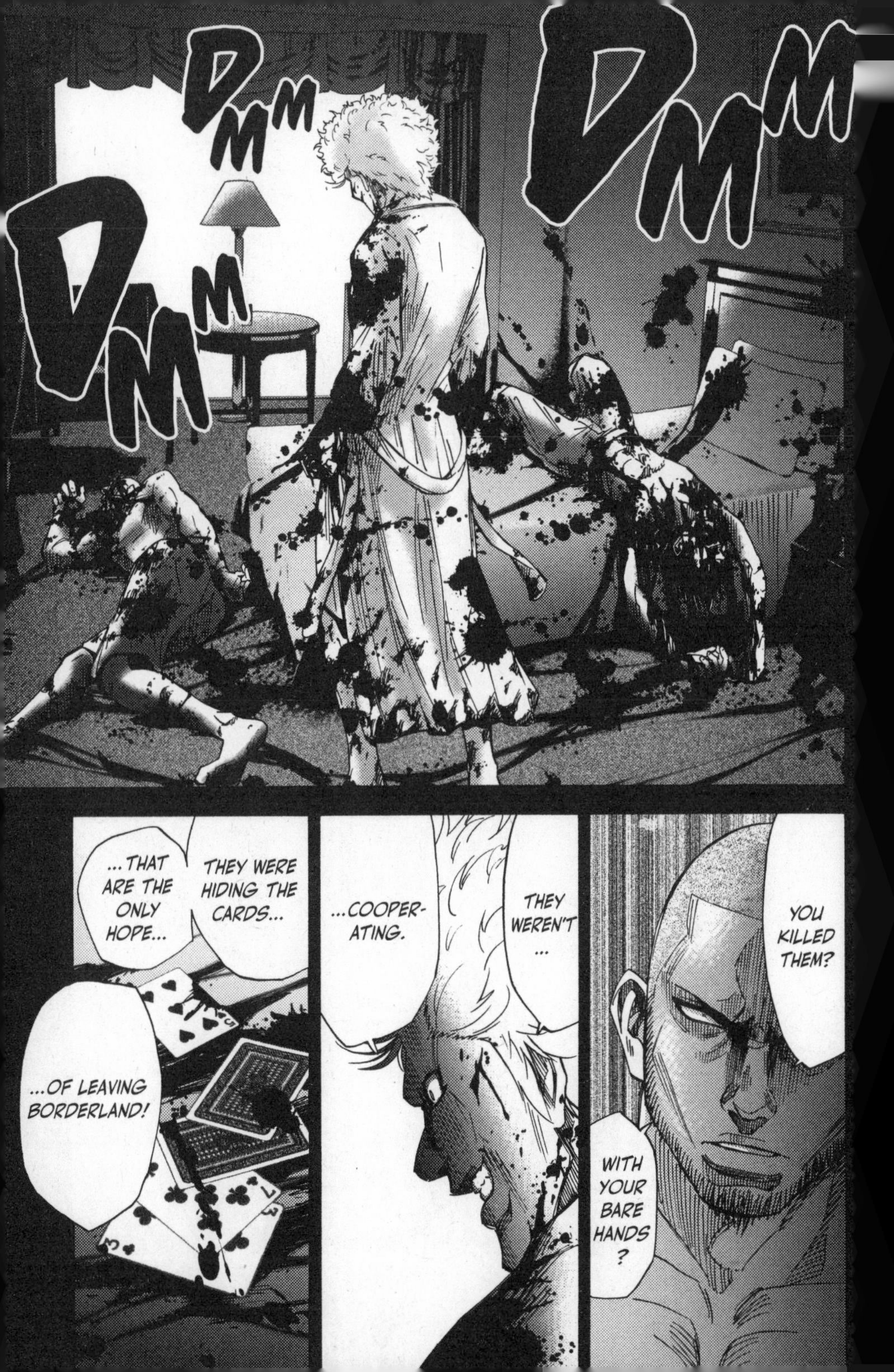
DMMM
DMMM
DMMM
YOU KILLED THEM?
WITH YOUR BARE HANDS?
THEY WEREN'T ...
...COOPERATING.
THEY WERE HIDING THE CARDS...
...THAT ARE THE ONLY HOPE...
...OF LEAVING BORDERLAND!

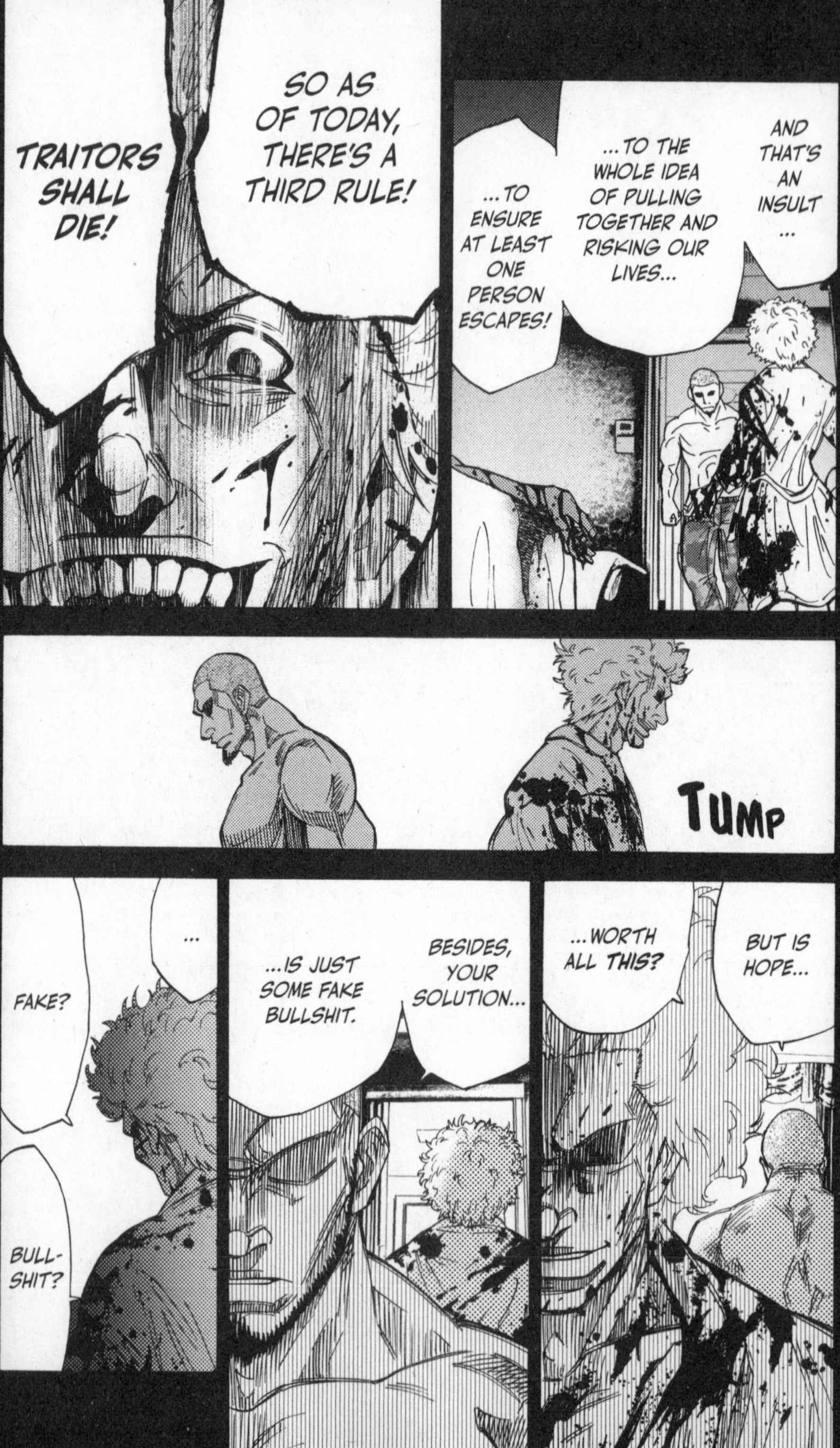
AND THAT'S AN INSULT...
...TO THE WHOLE IDEA OF PULLING TOGETHER AND RISKING OUR LIVES...
...TO ENSURE AT LEAST ONE PERSON ESCAPES!
SO AS OF TODAY, THERE'S A THIRD RULE!
TRAITORS SHALL DIE!
TUMP
BUT IS HOPE...
...WORTH ALL THIS?
BESIDES, YOUR SOLUTION...
...IS JUST SOME FAKE BULLSHIT.
...
FAKE?
BULL-SHIT?

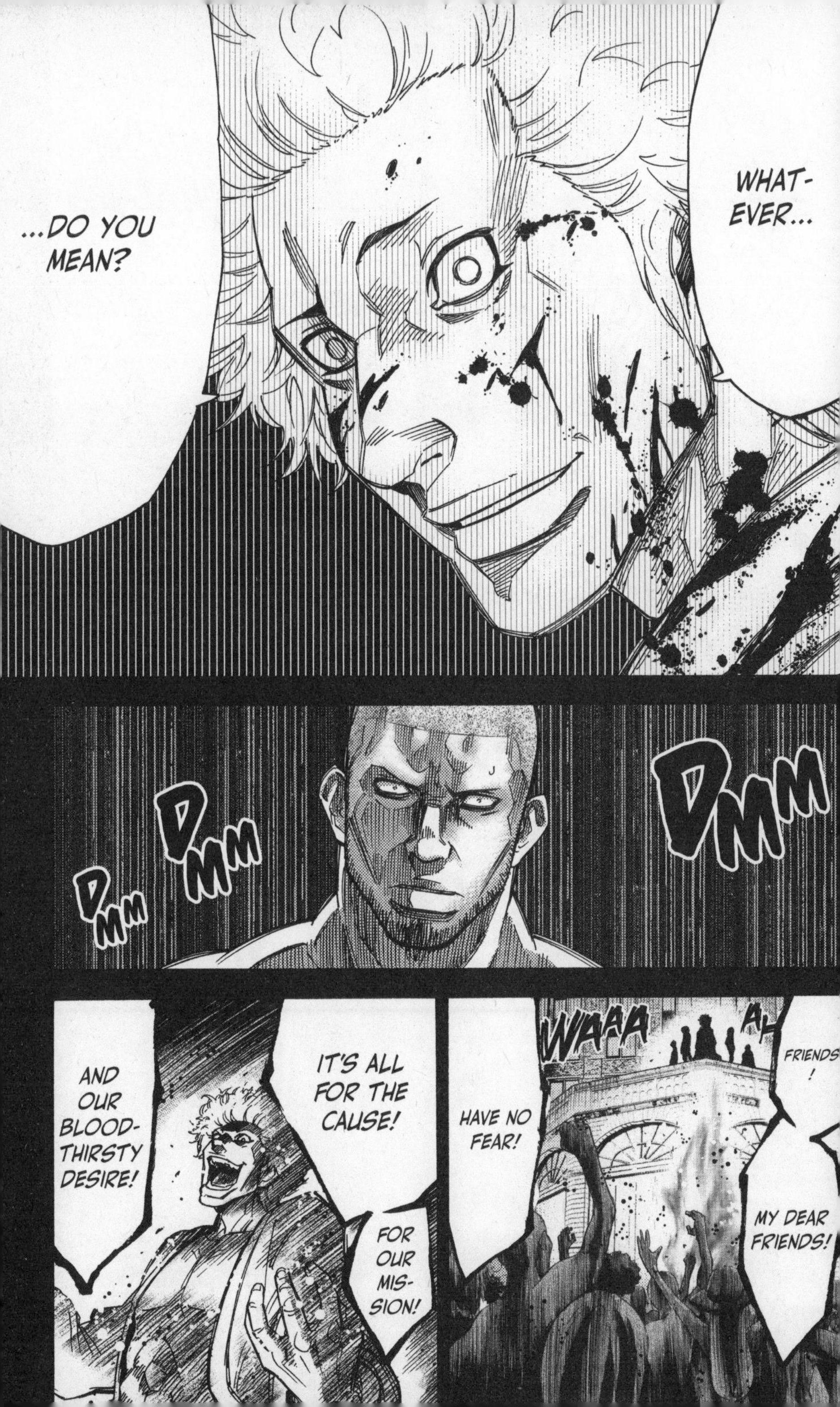
WHAT-EVER...
...DO YOU MEAN?
DMM
DMM
DMM
AH
WAAA
FRIENDS!
MY DEAR FRIENDS!
HAVE NO FEAR!
IT'S ALL FOR THE CAUSE!
FOR OUR MISSION!
AND OUR BLOOD-THIRSTY DESIRE!

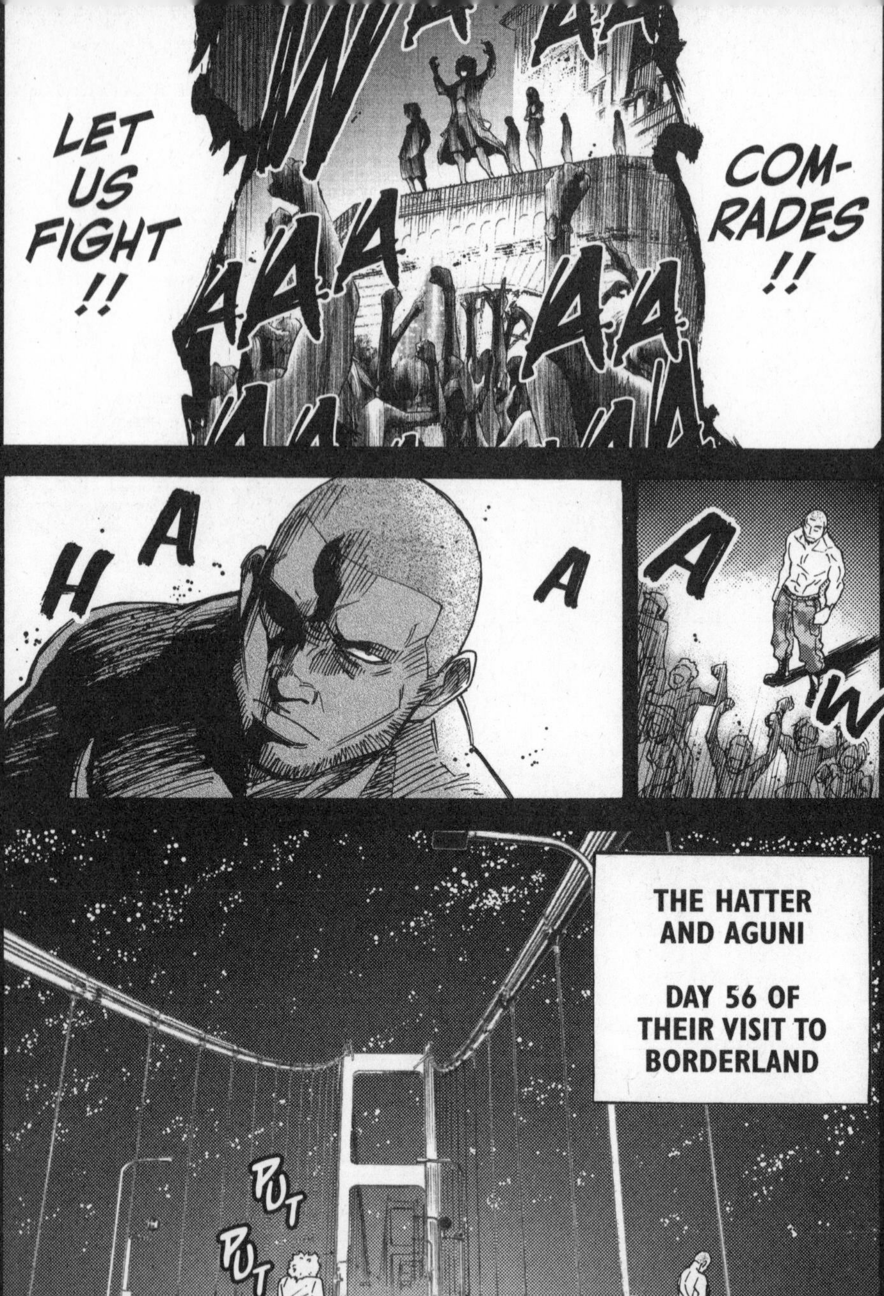
COMRADES!!
LET US FIGHT!!
WAAAAAAAAAAA
AW
HAA
THE HATTER AND AGUNI

DAY 56 OF THEIR VISIT TO BORDERLAND
PUT PUT
SKRK

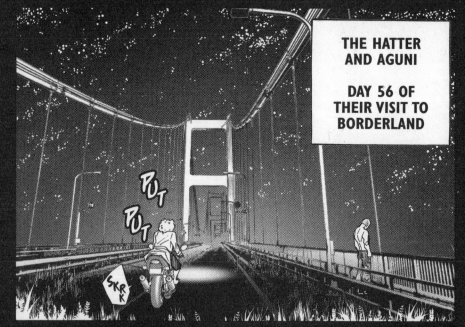

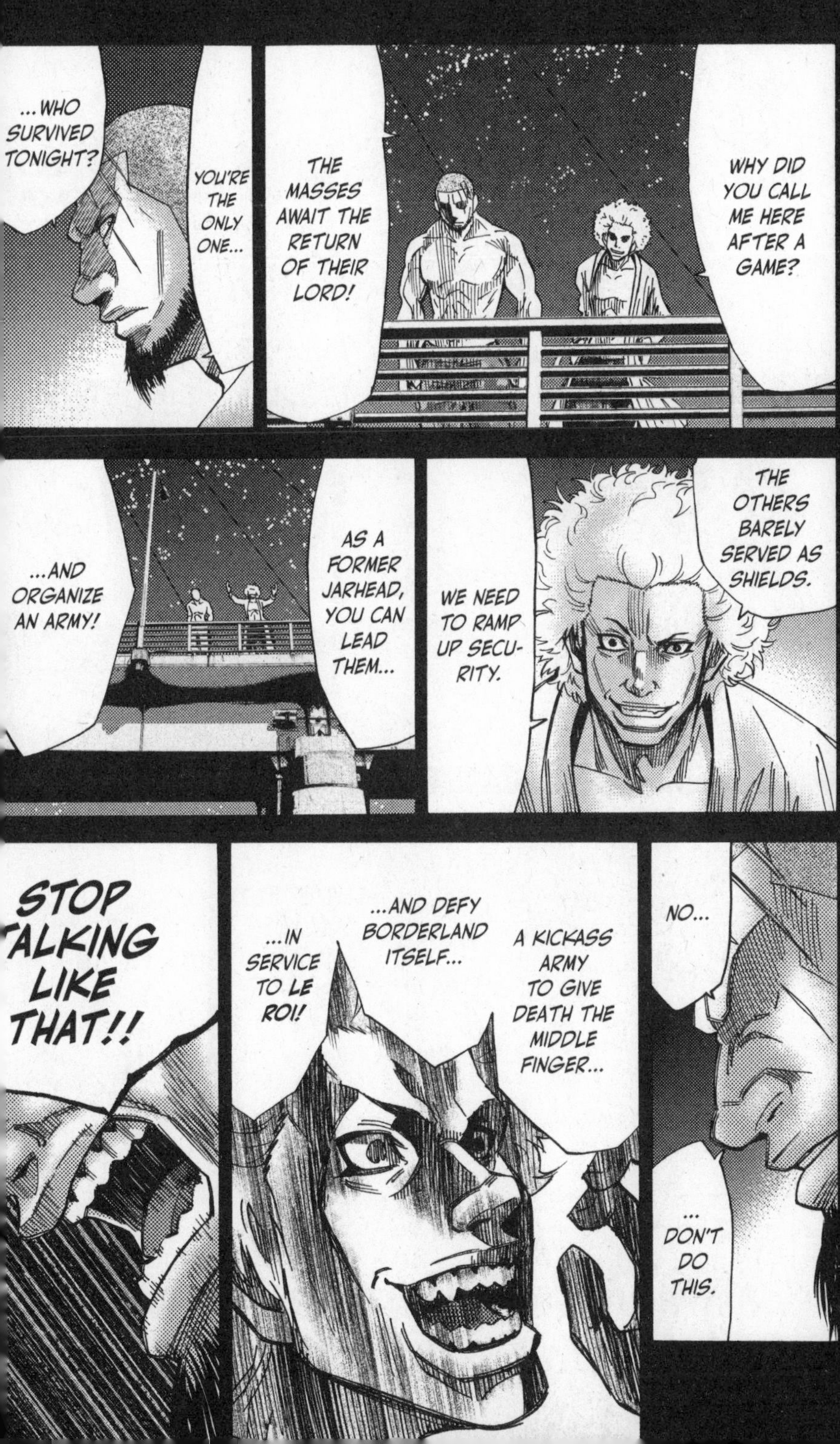
WHY DID YOU CALL ME HERE AFTER A GAME?
THE MASSES AWAIT THE RETURN OF THEIR LORD!
YOU'RE THE ONLY ONE...
...WHO SURVIVED TONIGHT?
THE OTHERS BARELY SERVED AS SHIELDS.
WE NEED TO RAMP UP SECU-RITY.
AS A FORMER JARHEAD, YOU CAN LEAD THEM...
...AND ORGANIZE AN ARMY!
NO...
...DON'T DO THIS.
A KICKASS ARMY TO GIVE DEATH THE MIDDLE FINGER...
...AND DEFY BORDERLAND ITSELF...
...IN SERVICE TO LE ROI!
STOP TALKING LIKE THAT!!

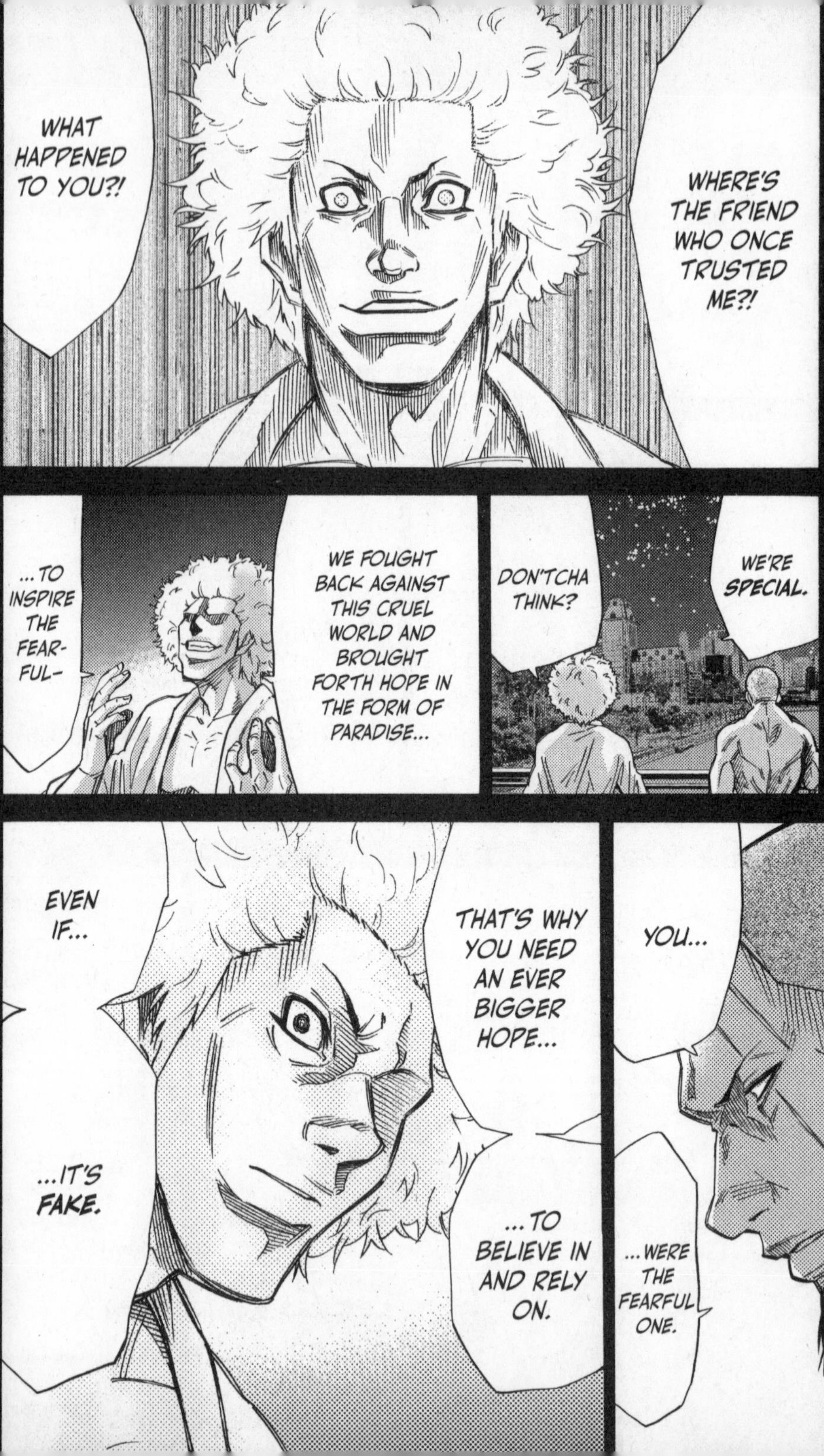
WHERE'S THE FRIEND WHO ONCE TRUSTED ME?!
WHAT HAPPENED TO YOU?!
WE'RE **SPECIAL.**
DON'TCHA THINK?
WE FOUGHT BACK AGAINST THIS CRUEL WORLD AND BROUGHT FORTH HOPE IN THE FORM OF PARADISE...
...TO INSPIRE THE FEAR-FUL-
YOU...
...WERE THE FEARFUL ONE.
THAT'S WHY YOU NEED AN EVER BIGGER HOPE...
...TO BELIEVE IN AND RELY ON.
EVEN IF...
...IT'S **FAKE.**

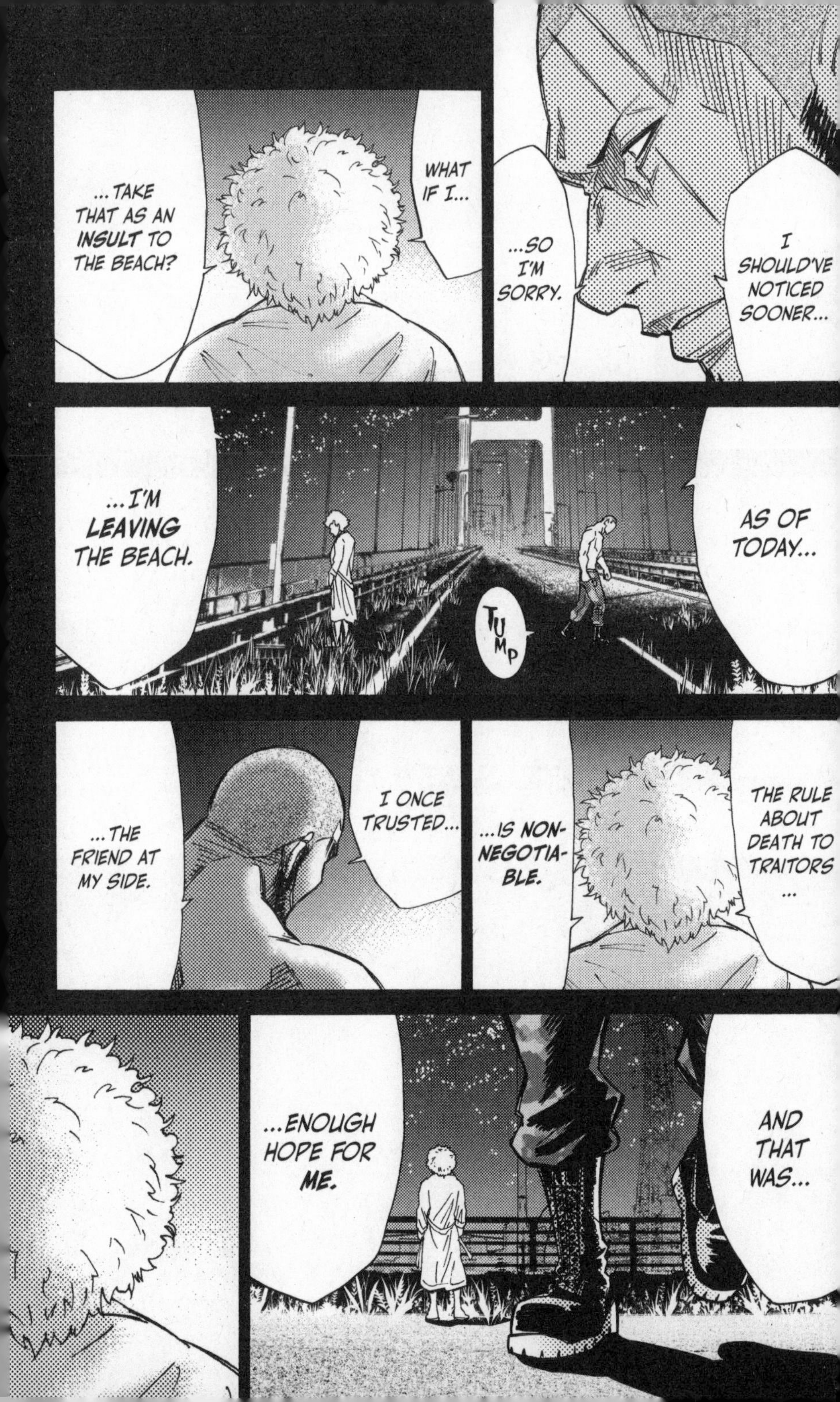
I SHOULD'VE NOTICED SOONER...
...SO I'M SORRY.
WHAT IF I...
...TAKE THAT AS AN **INSULT** TO THE BEACH?
AS OF TODAY...
TUMP
...I'M **LEAVING** THE BEACH.
THE RULE ABOUT DEATH TO TRAITORS ...
...IS **NON-NEGOTIABLE.**
I ONCE TRUSTED...
...THE FRIEND AT MY SIDE.
AND THAT WAS...
...ENOUGH HOPE FOR **ME.**

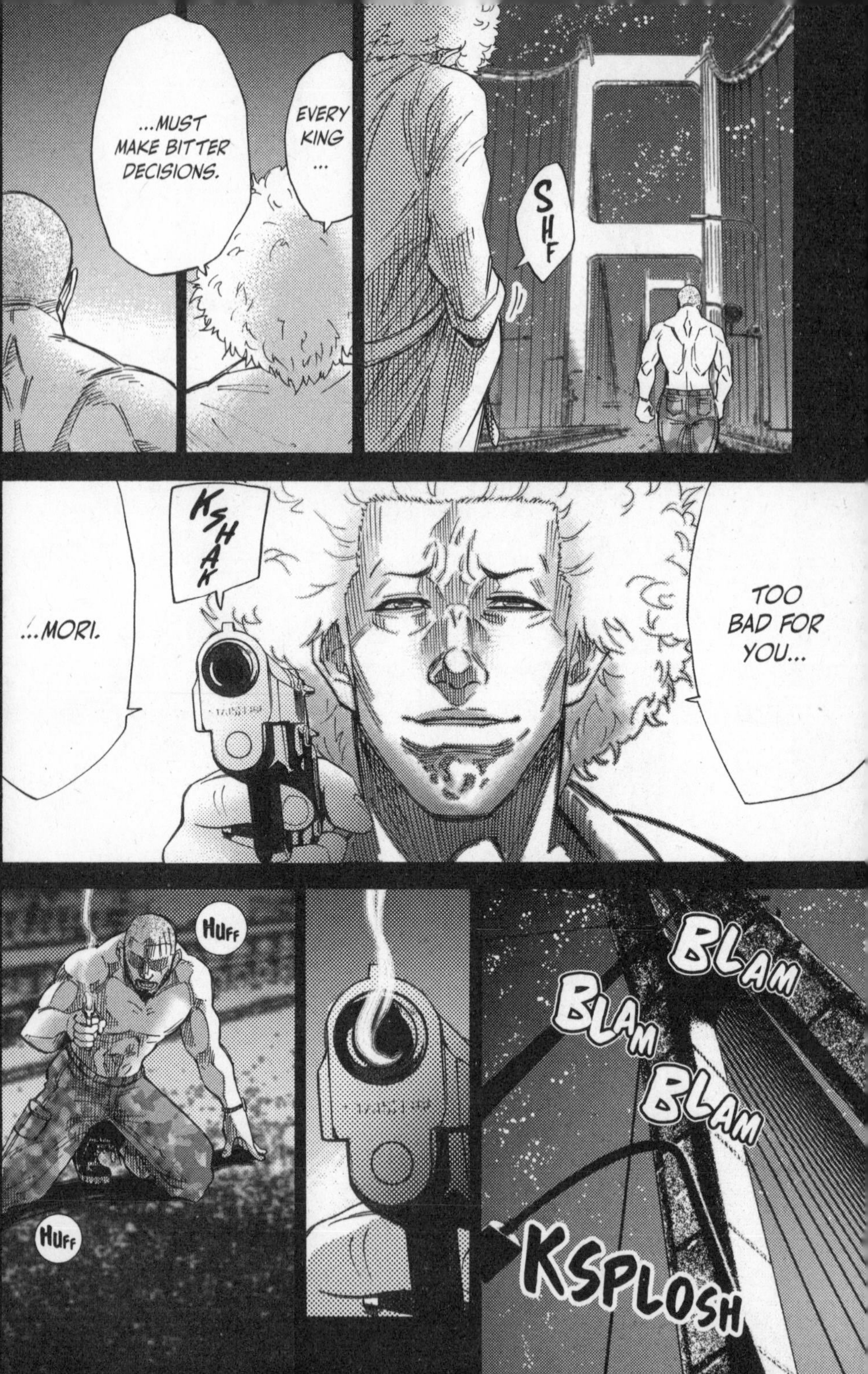
SHF
EVERY KING ...
...MUST MAKE BITTER DECISIONS.
TOO BAD FOR YOU...
KSHAK
...MORI.
BLAM
BLAM
BLAM
KSPLOSH
HUFF
HUFF

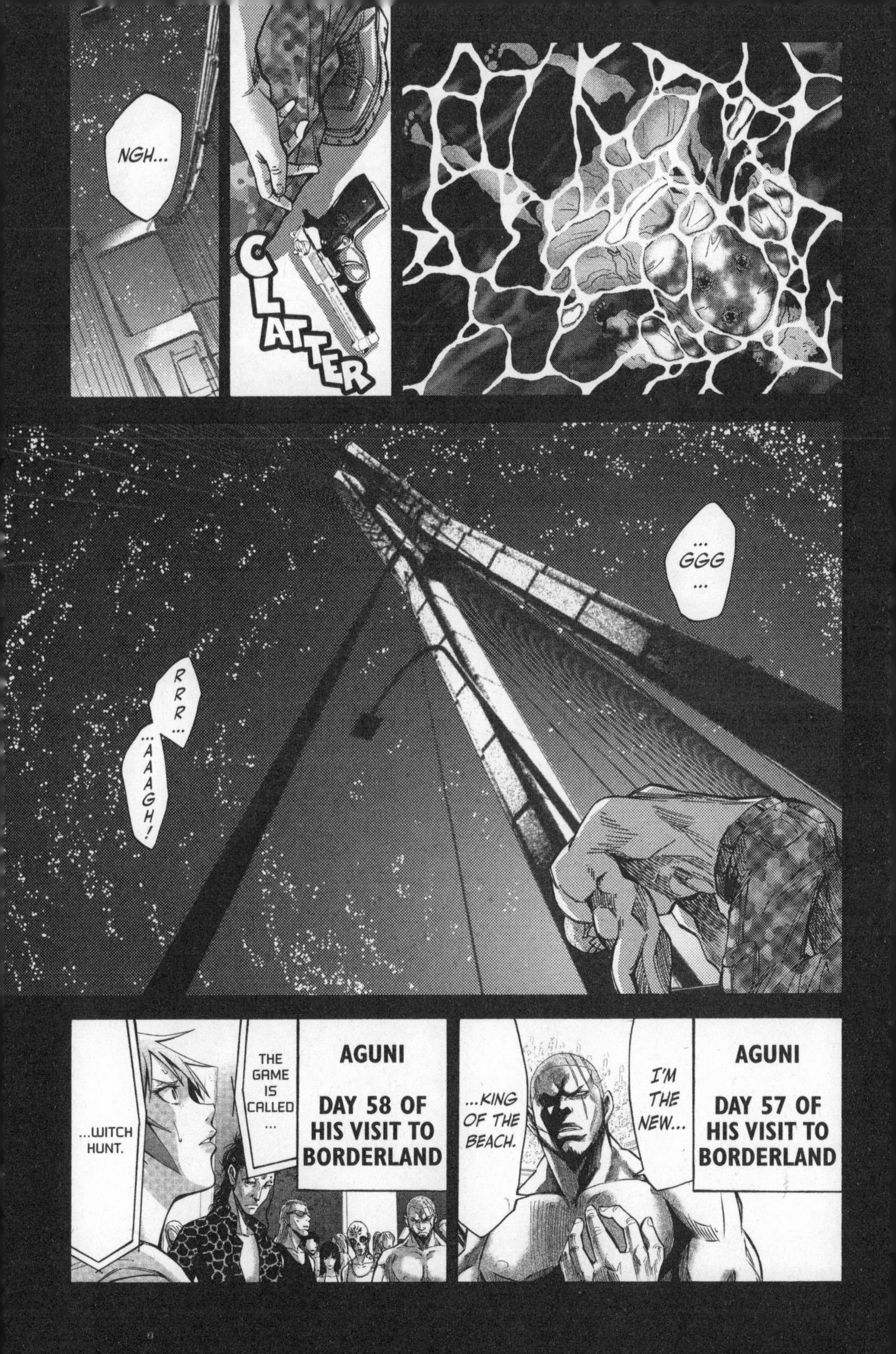
CLATTER
NGH...
...GGG...
RRR...
...AAAAGH!
AGUNI
DAY 57 OF HIS VISIT TO BORDERLAND
I'M THE NEW...
...KING OF THE BEACH.
AGUNI
DAY 58 OF HIS VISIT TO BORDERLAND
THE GAME IS CALLED...
...WITCH HUNT.

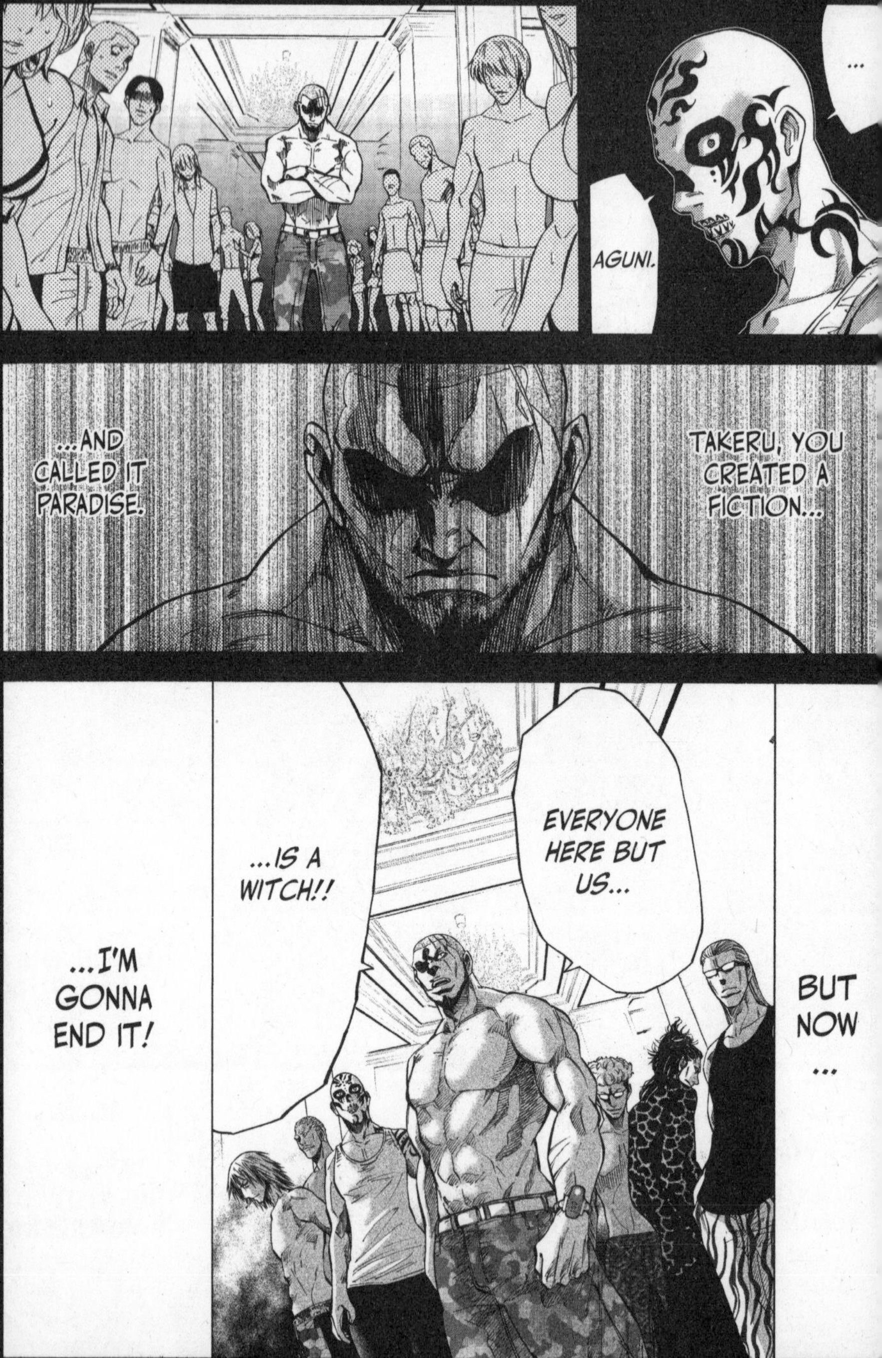
...
AGUNI.
TAKERU, YOU CREATED A FICTION...
...AND CALLED IT PARADISE.
BUT NOW ...
EVERYONE HERE BUT US...
...IS A WITCH!!
...I'M GONNA END IT!

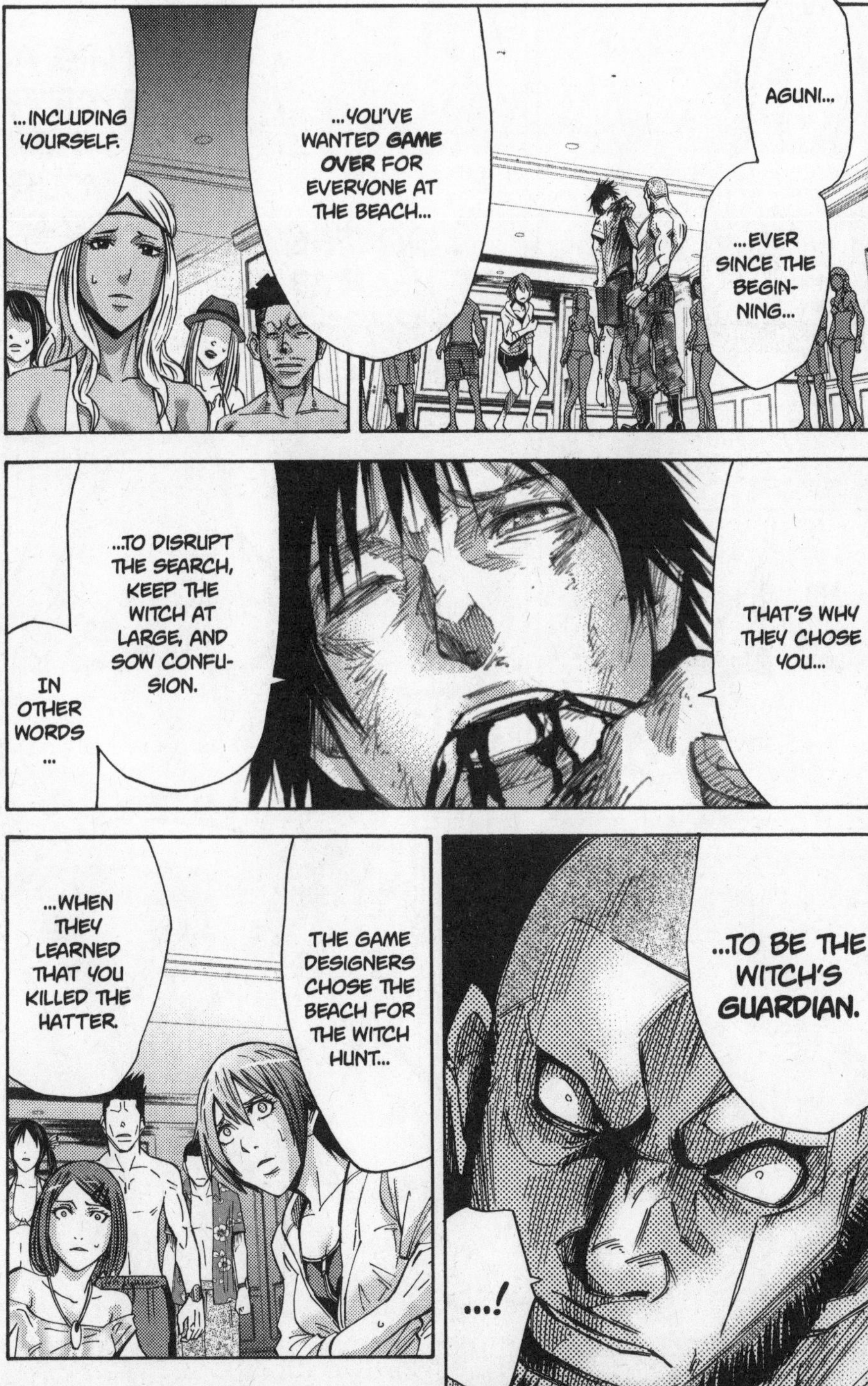
AGUNI...
...EVER SINCE THE BEGIN-NING...
...YOU'VE WANTED GAME OVER FOR EVERYONE AT THE BEACH...
...INCLUDING YOURSELF.
THAT'S WHY THEY CHOSE YOU...
IN OTHER WORDS ...
...TO DISRUPT THE SEARCH, KEEP THE WITCH AT LARGE, AND SOW CONFU-SION.
...TO BE THE WITCH'S GUARDIAN.
...!
THE GAME DESIGNERS CHOSE THE BEACH FOR THE WITCH HUNT...
...WHEN THEY LEARNED THAT YOU KILLED THE HATTER.

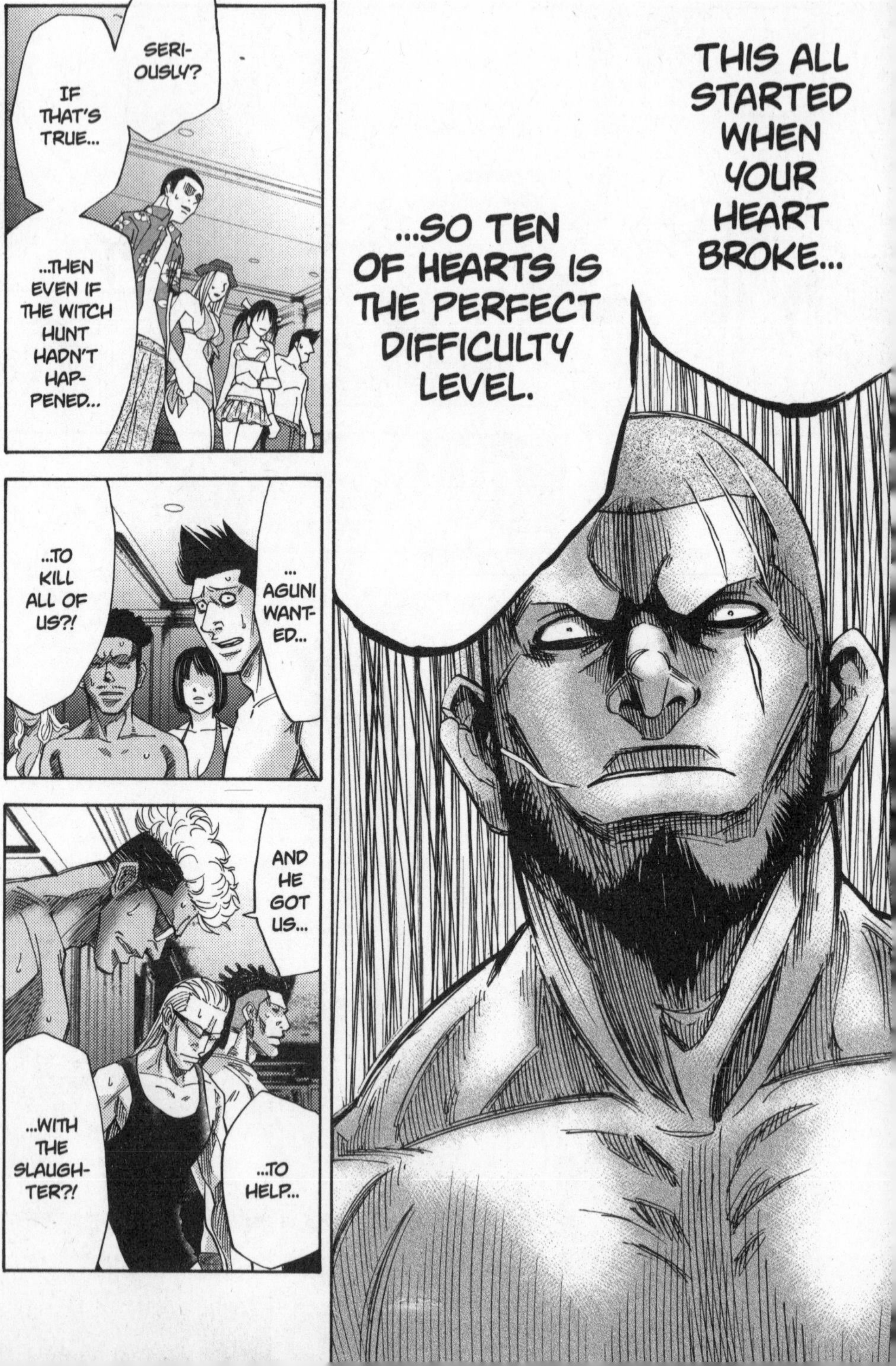

THIS ALL STARTED WHEN YOUR HEART BROKE...
...SO TEN OF HEARTS IS THE PERFECT DIFFICULTY LEVEL.
SERI-OUSLY?
IF THAT'S TRUE...
...THEN EVEN IF THE WITCH HUNT HADN'T HAP-PENED...
... AGUNI WANT-ED...
...TO KILL ALL OF US?!
AND HE GOT US...
...TO HELP...
...WITH THE SLAUGHTER?!

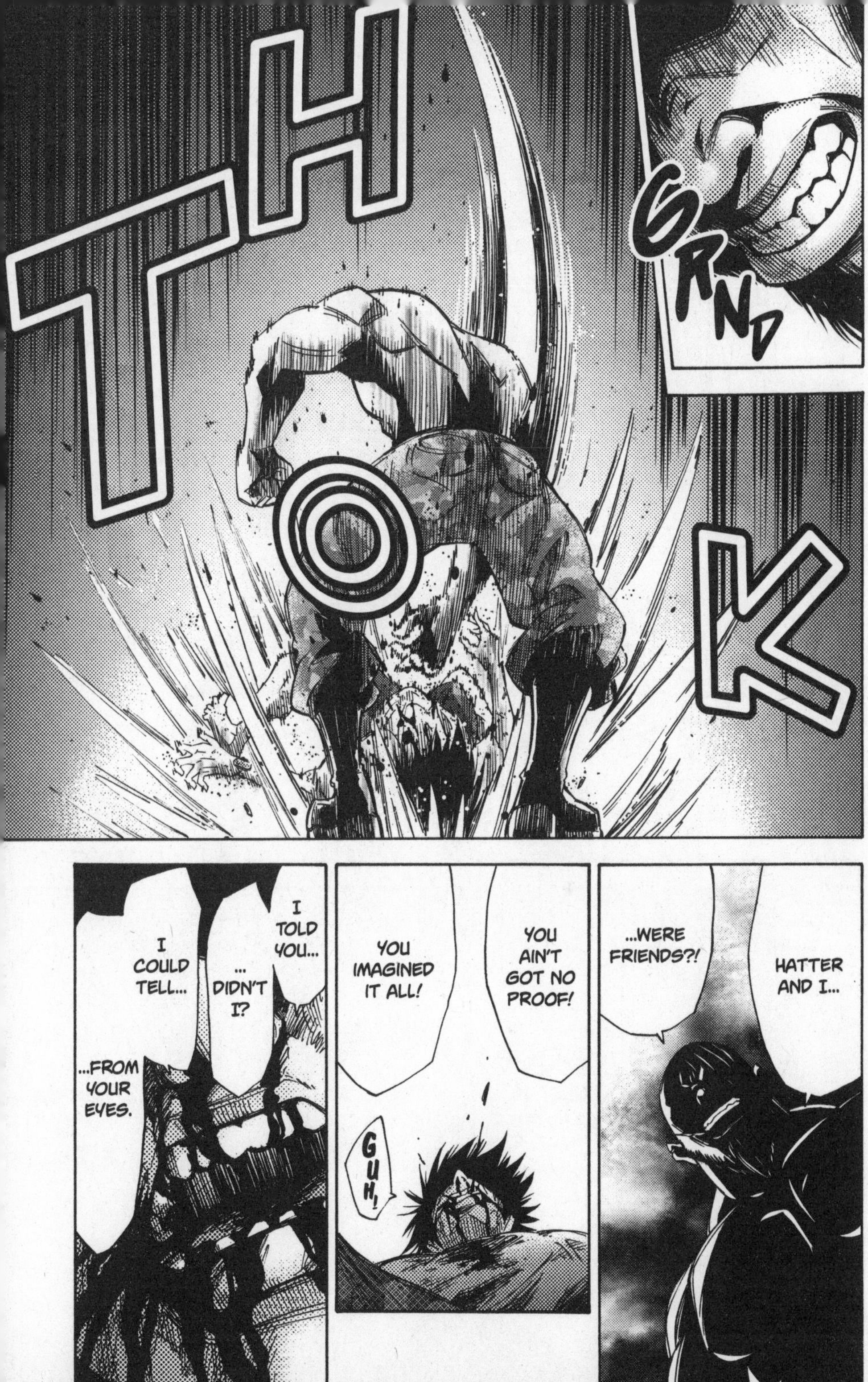
SGRND
THOK
HATTER AND I...
...WERE FRIENDS?!
YOU AIN'T GOT NO PROOF!
YOU IMAGINED IT ALL!
GUH!
I TOLD YOU...
...DIDN'T I?
I COULD TELL...
...FROM YOUR EYES.

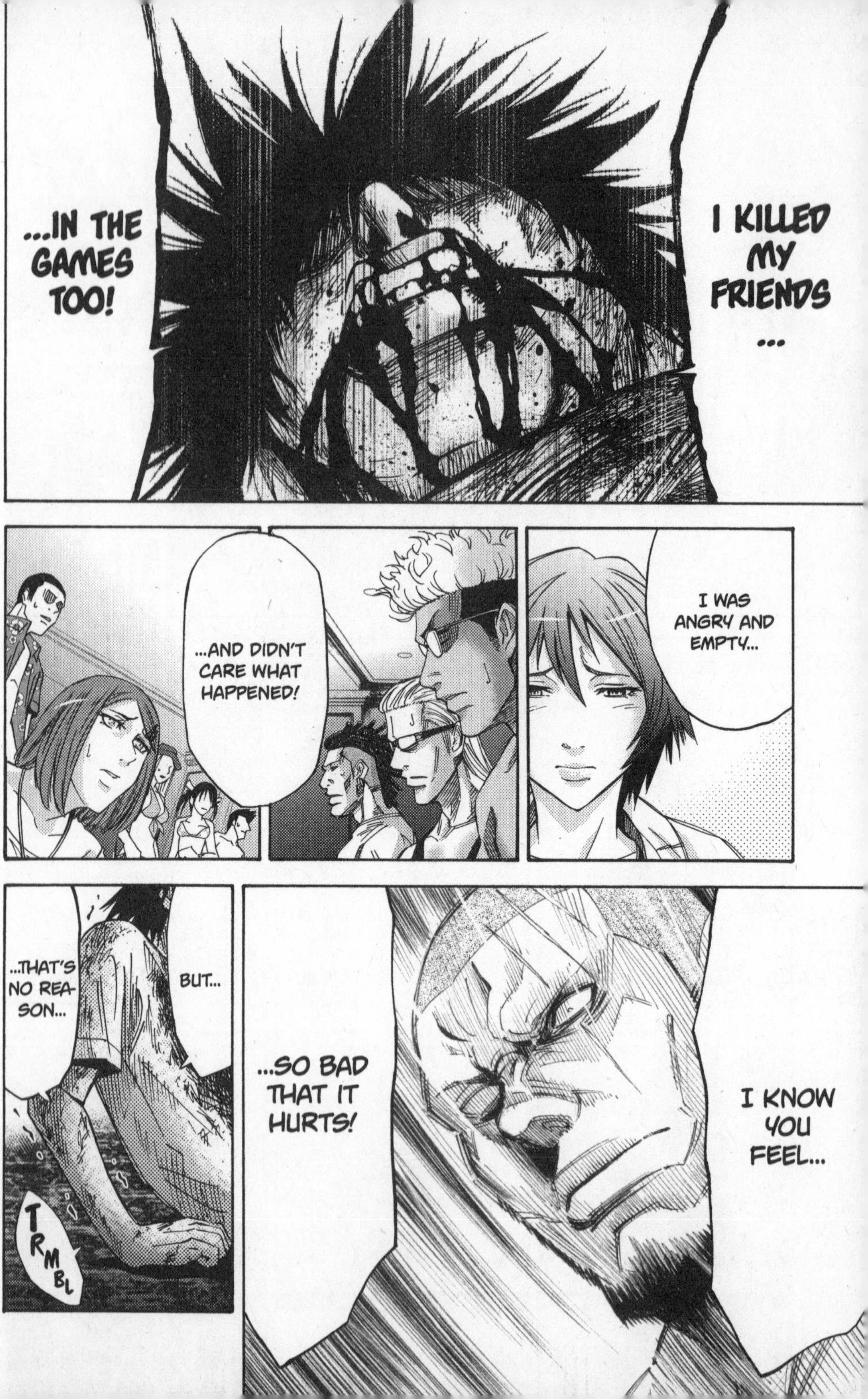
I KILLED MY FRIENDS...
...IN THE GAMES TOO!
I WAS ANGRY AND EMPTY...
...AND DIDN'T CARE WHAT HAPPENED!
I KNOW YOU FEEL...
...SO BAD THAT IT HURTS!
BUT...
...THAT'S NO REA-SON...
TRMBL

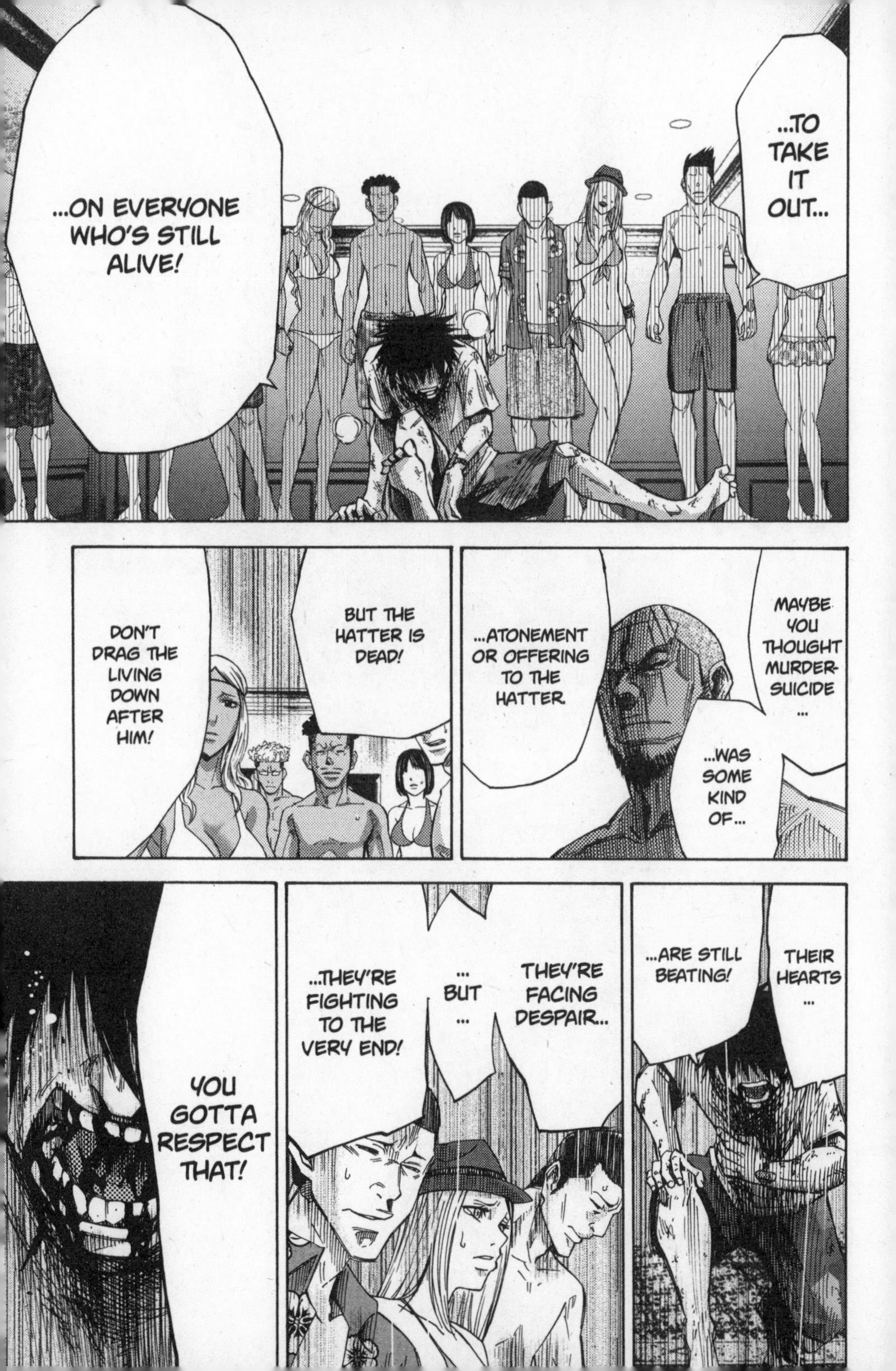
...TO TAKE IT OUT...
...ON EVERYONE WHO'S STILL ALIVE!
MAYBE YOU THOUGHT MURDER-SUICIDE ...
...WAS SOME KIND OF...
...ATONEMENT OR OFFERING TO THE HATTER.
BUT THE HATTER IS DEAD!
DON'T DRAG THE LIVING DOWN AFTER HIM!
THEIR HEARTS ...
...ARE STILL BEATING!
THEY'RE FACING DESPAIR...
... BUT ...
...THEY'RE FIGHTING TO THE VERY END!
YOU GOTTA RESPECT THAT!

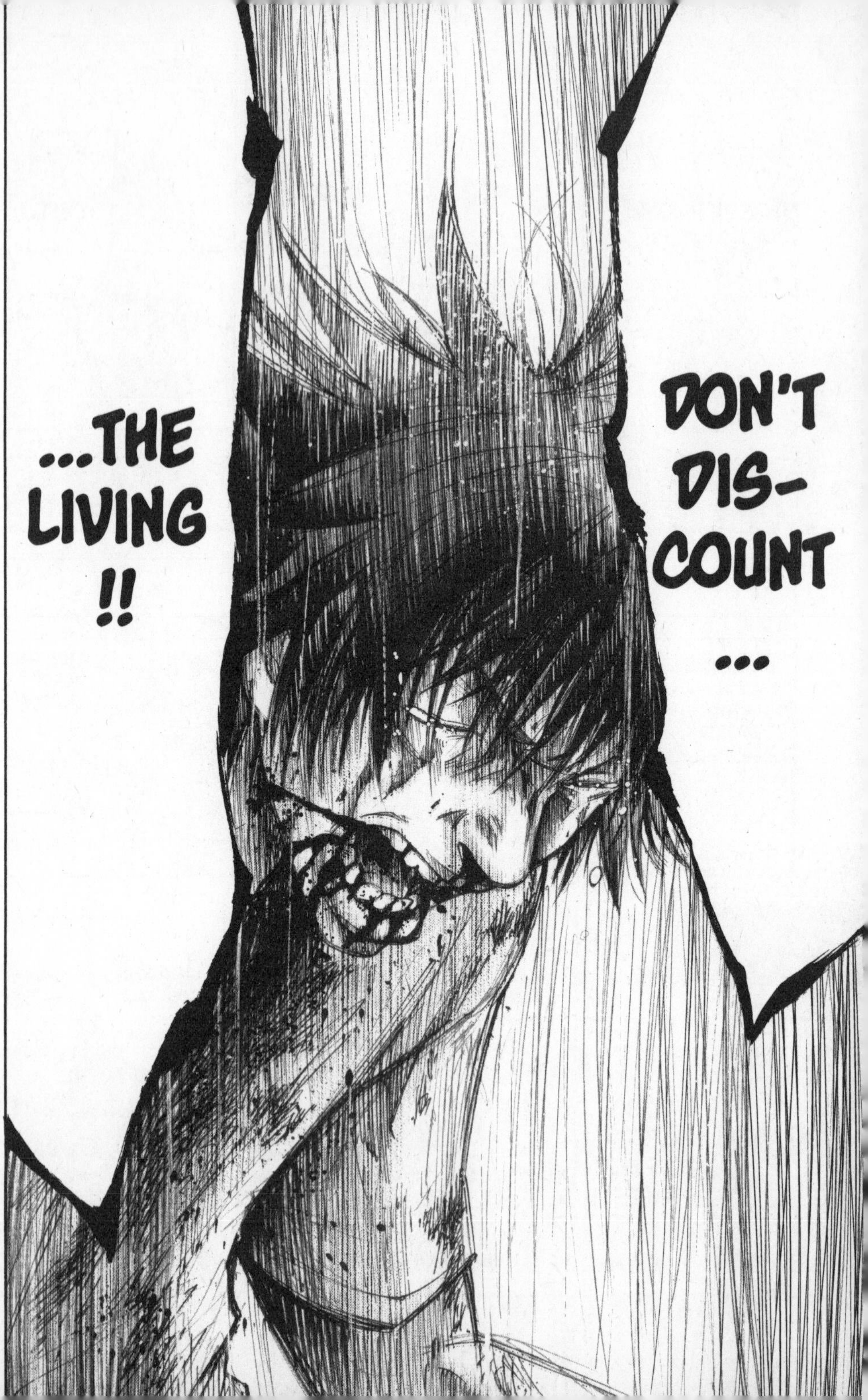
DON'T DIS-COUNT...
...THE LIVING!!

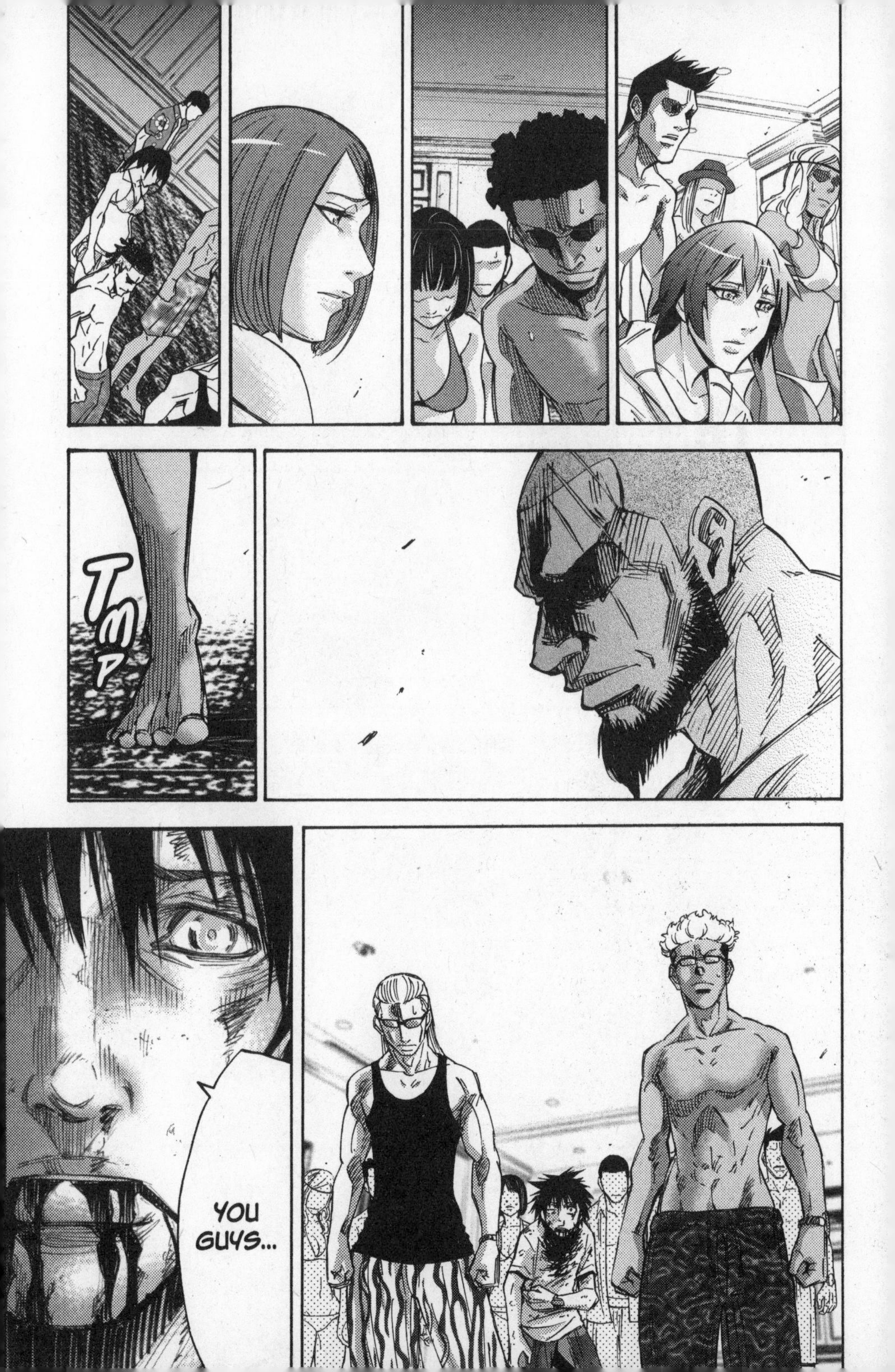
TMP
YOU GUYS...

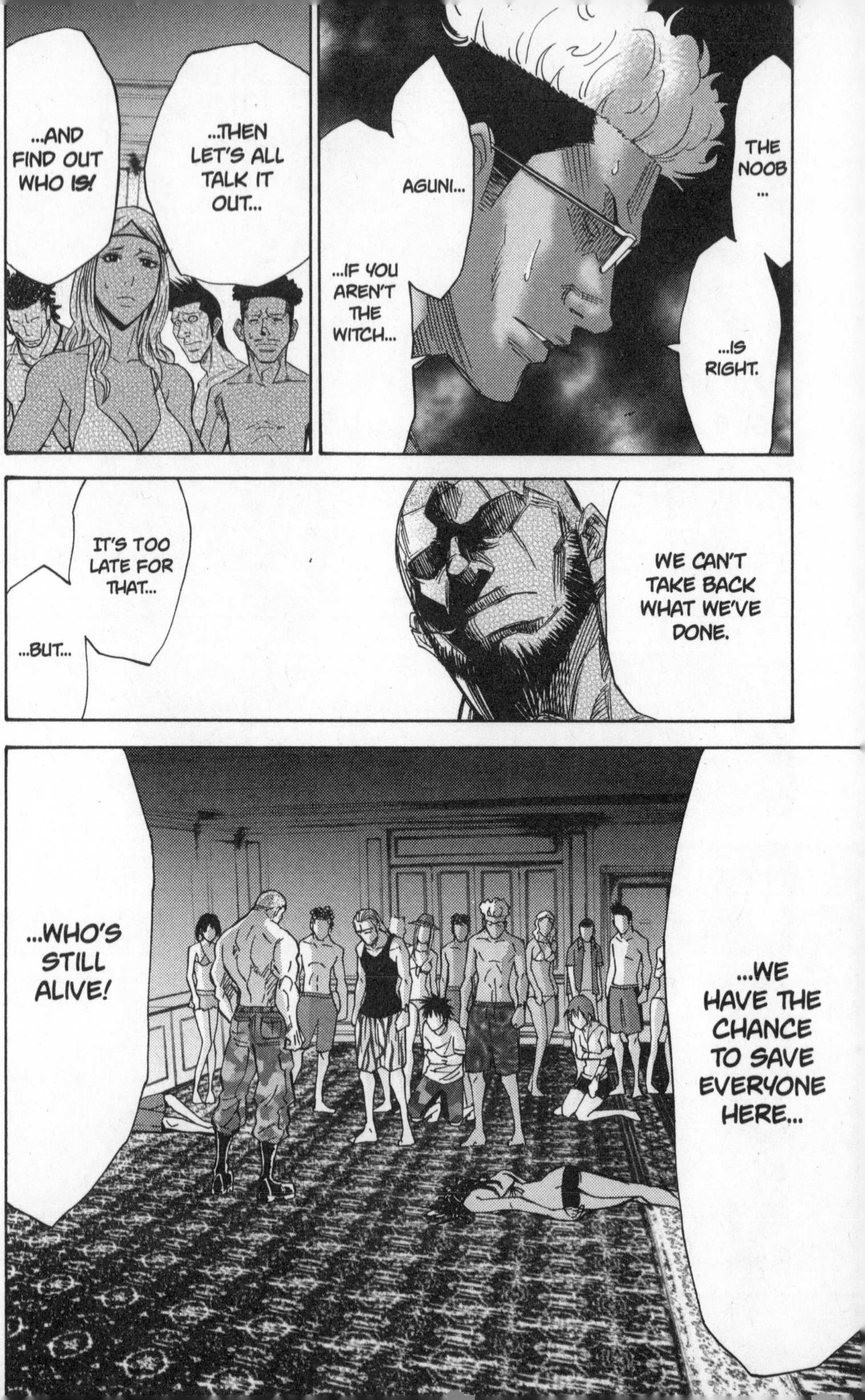
THE NOOB ...
...IS RIGHT.
AGUNI...
...IF YOU AREN'T THE WITCH...
...THEN LET'S ALL TALK IT OUT...
...AND FIND OUT WHO IS!
WE CAN'T TAKE BACK WHAT WE'VE DONE.
IT'S TOO LATE FOR THAT...
...BUT...
...WE HAVE THE CHANCE TO SAVE EVERYONE HERE...
...WHO'S STILL ALIVE!

CHAPTER 27: Ten of Hearts, Part 7

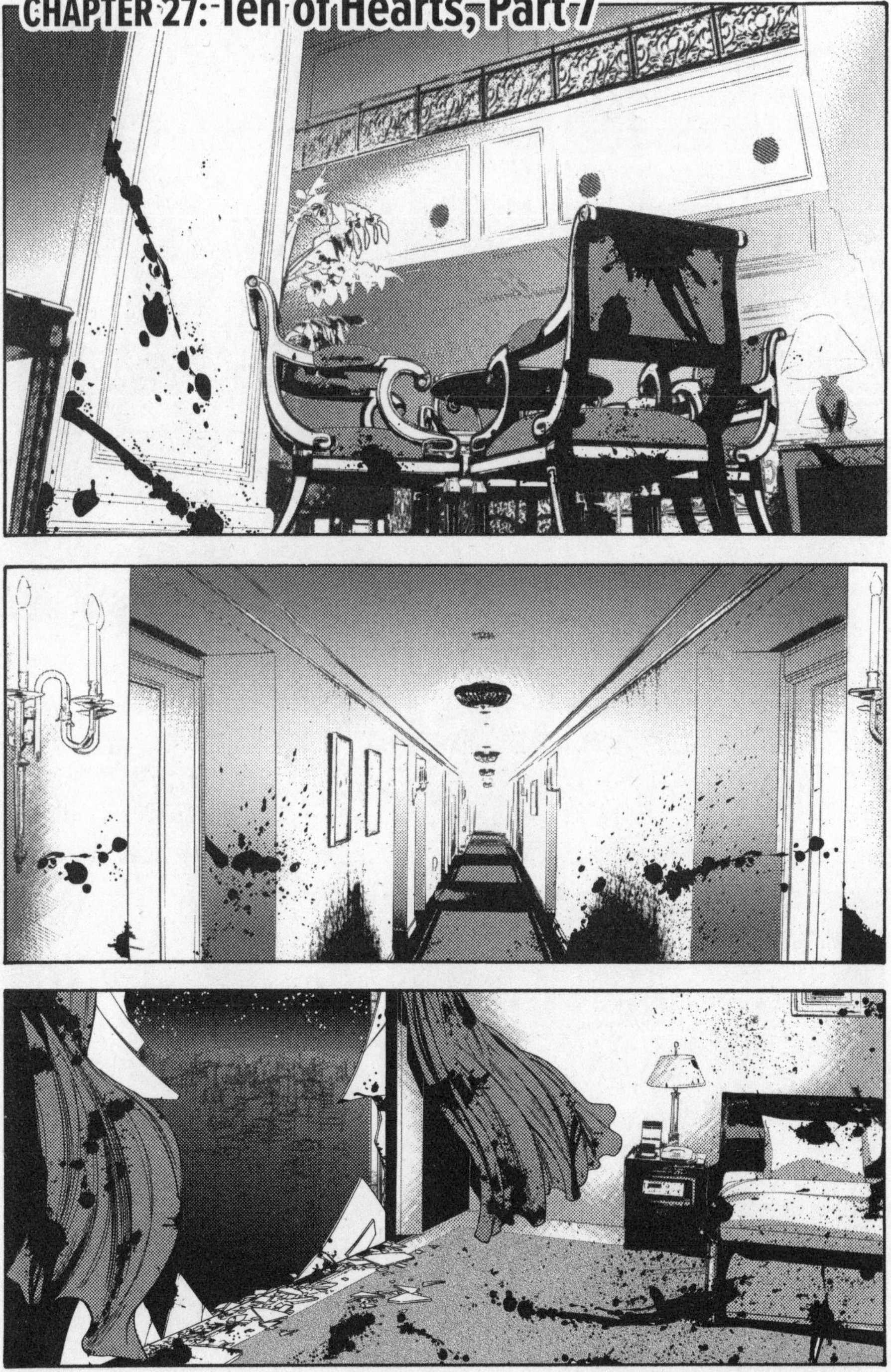

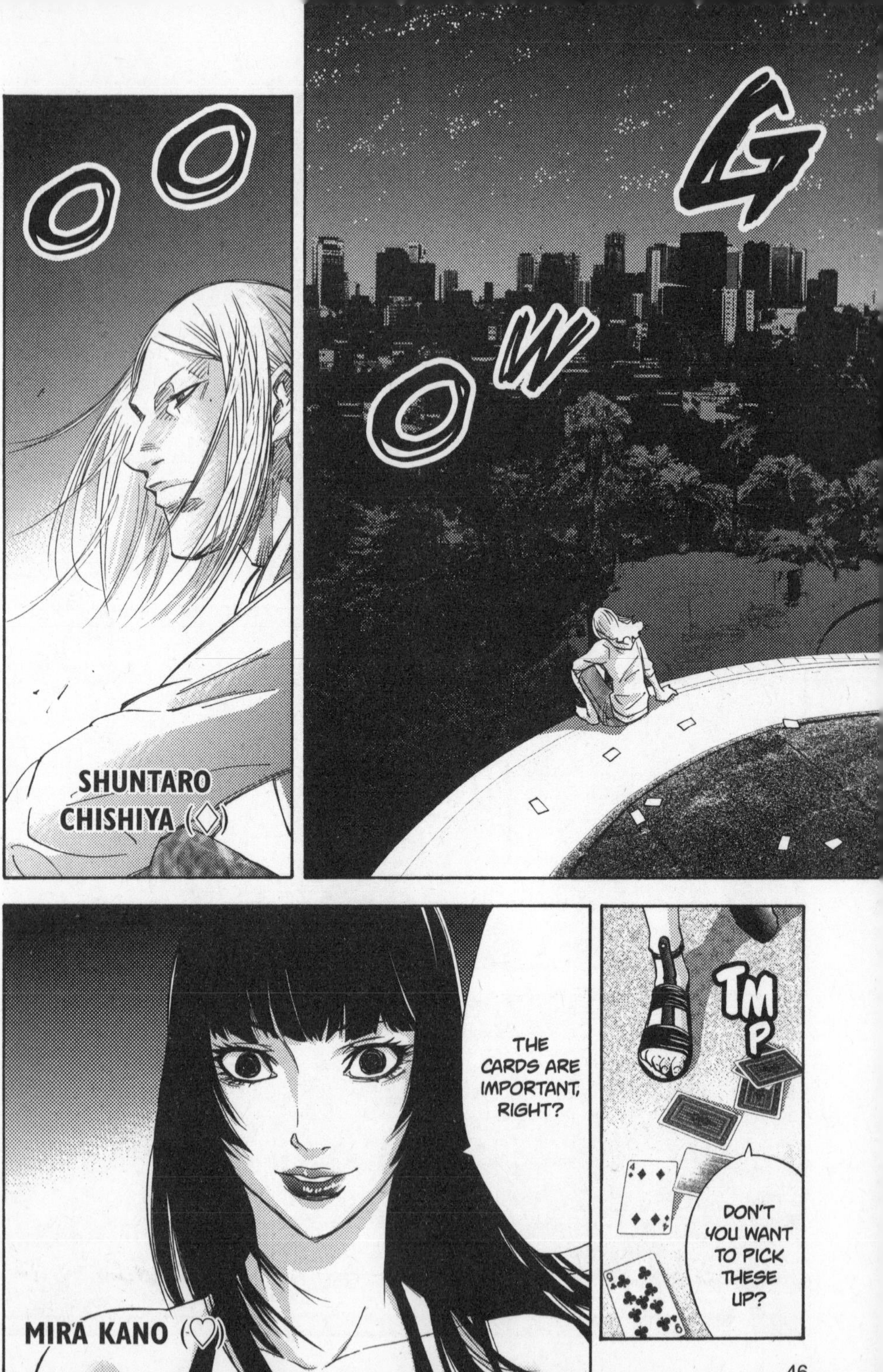
G
W
O
O O
SHUNTARO CHISHIYA (♢)
TMP
DON'T YOU WANT TO PICK THESE UP?
THE CARDS ARE IMPORTANT, RIGHT?
MIRA KANO (♡)

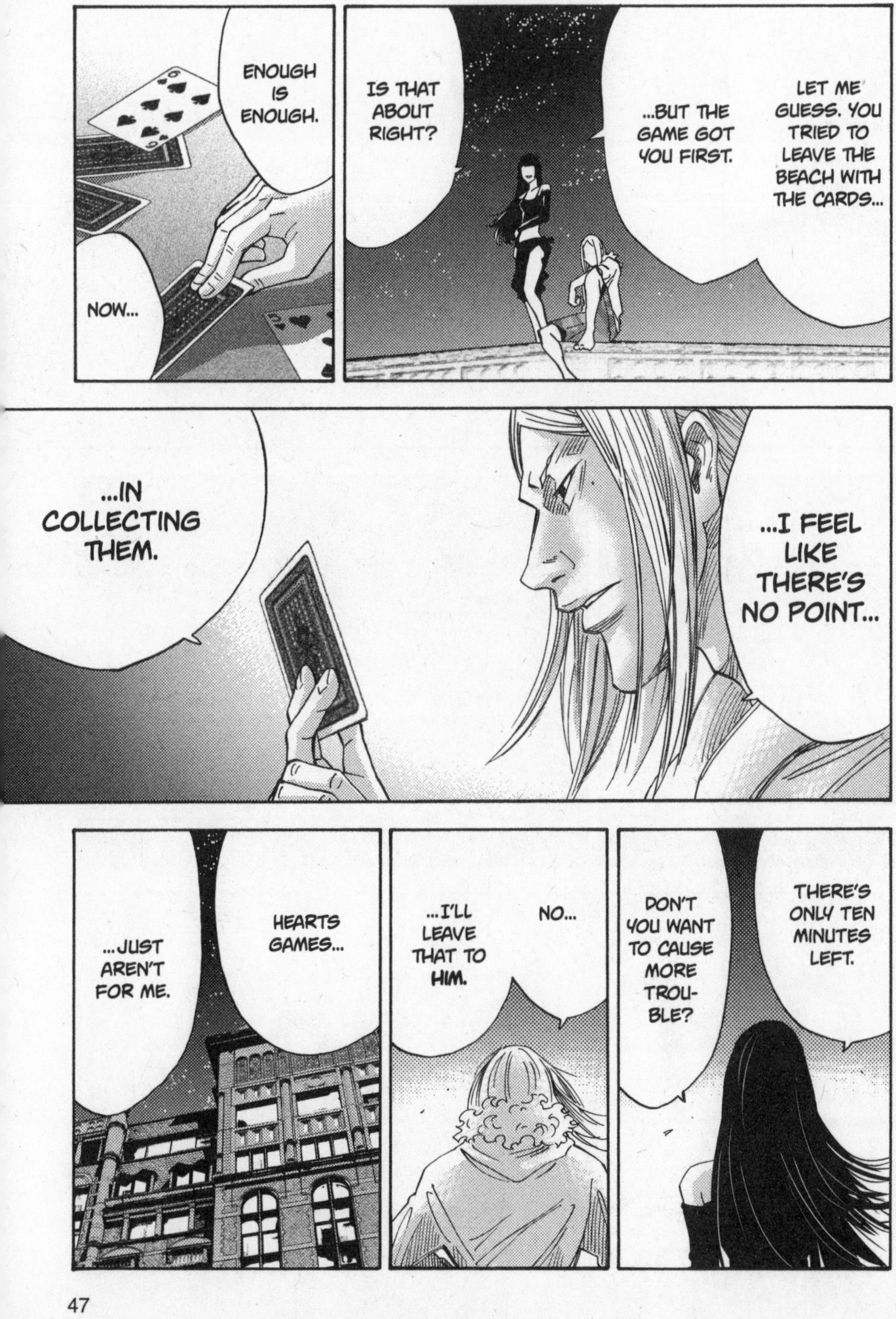
LET ME GUESS. YOU TRIED TO LEAVE THE BEACH WITH THE CARDS...
...BUT THE GAME GOT YOU FIRST.
IS THAT ABOUT RIGHT?
ENOUGH IS ENOUGH.
NOW...
...I FEEL LIKE THERE'S NO POINT...
...IN COLLECTING THEM.
THERE'S ONLY TEN MINUTES LEFT.
DON'T YOU WANT TO CAUSE MORE TROU-BLE?
NO...
...I'LL LEAVE THAT TO HIM.
HEARTS GAMES...
...JUST AREN'T FOR ME.

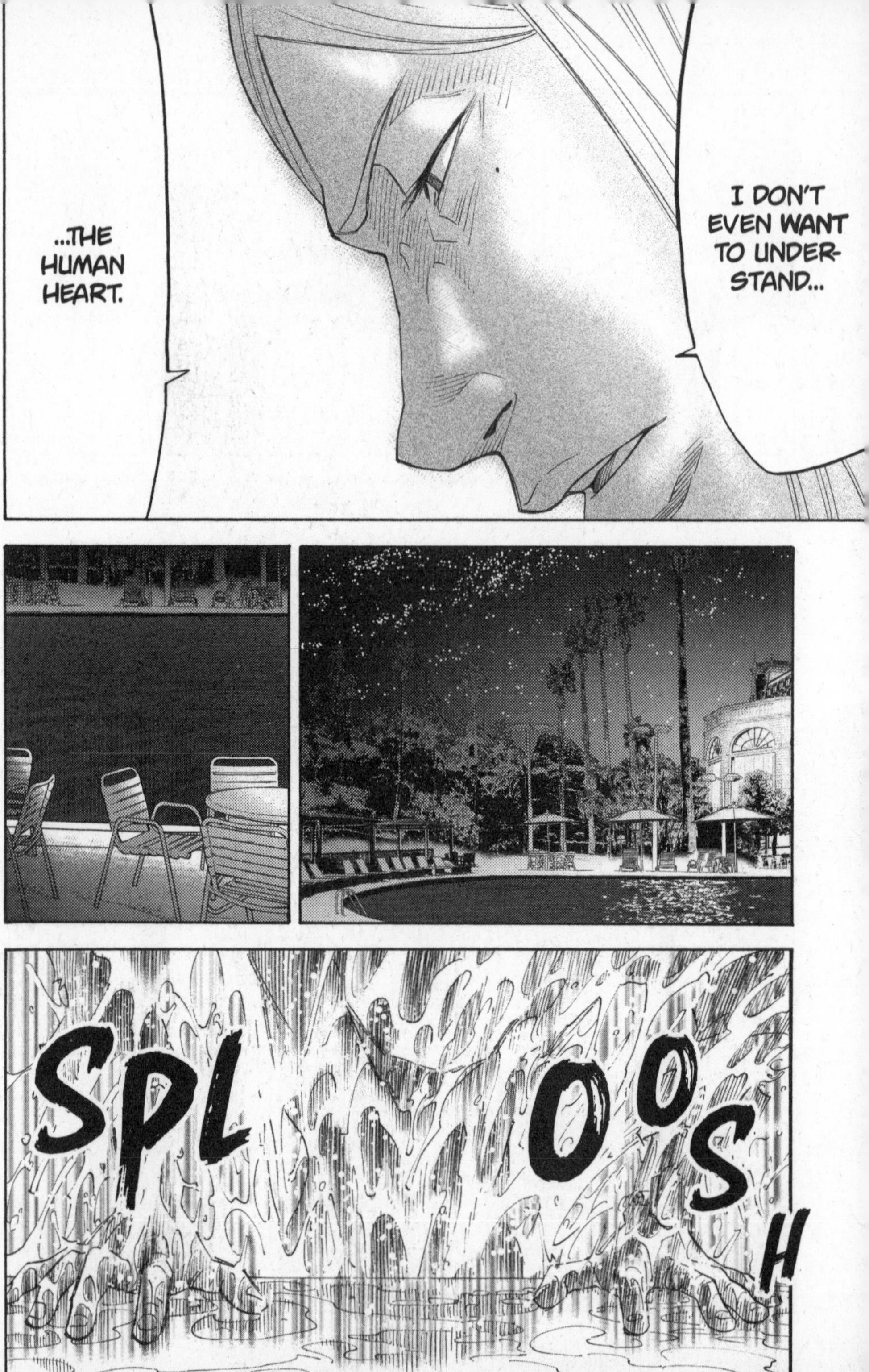
I DON'T EVEN WANT TO UNDER-STAND...
...THE HUMAN HEART.
SPLOOOSH

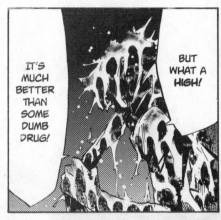

HYA HA! OW...
KOFF
HYA HA HA!
I'M IN SERIOUS PAIN!
KOFF
BUT WHAT A HIGH!
IT'S MUCH BETTER THAN SOME DUMB DRUG!
THE GAMES ...
...ARE AWE-SOME!!
SUGURU NIRAGI (◇)
...!
RIZUNA AN (◇)

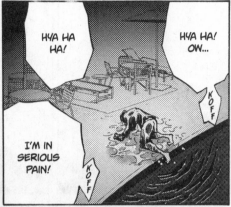

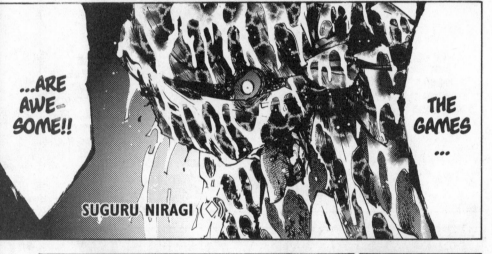

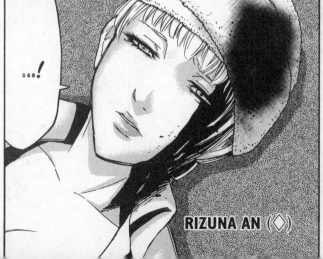

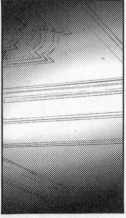

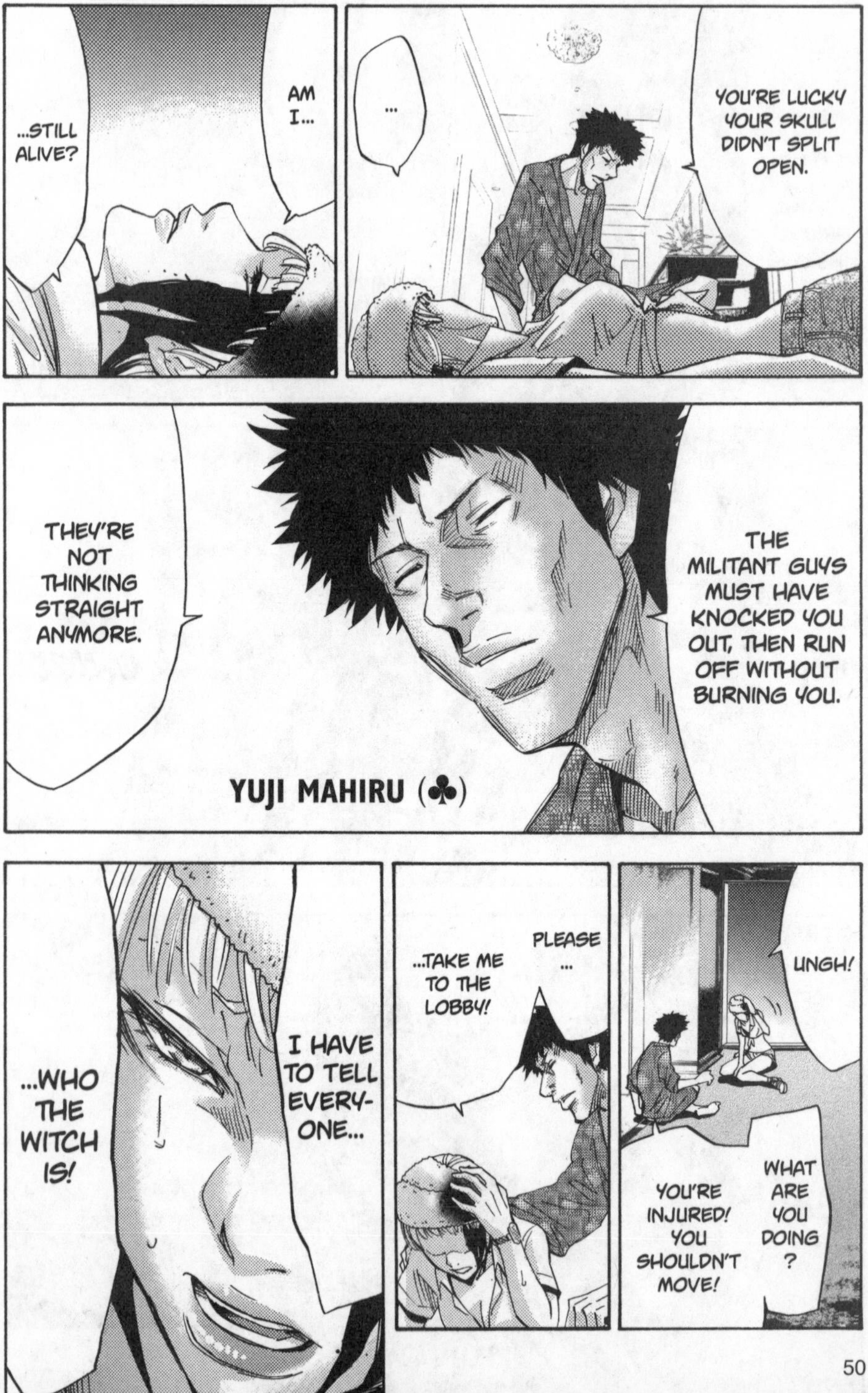
YOU'RE LUCKY YOUR SKULL DIDN'T SPLIT OPEN.
...
AM I...
...STILL ALIVE?
THE MILITANT GUYS MUST HAVE KNOCKED YOU OUT, THEN RUN OFF WITHOUT BURNING YOU.
THEY'RE NOT THINKING STRAIGHT ANYMORE.
YUJI MAHIRU (♣)
UNGH!
WHAT ARE YOU DOING?
YOU'RE INJURED! YOU SHOULDN'T MOVE!
PLEASE...
...TAKE ME TO THE LOBBY!
I HAVE TO TELL EVERY-ONE...
...WHO THE WITCH IS!

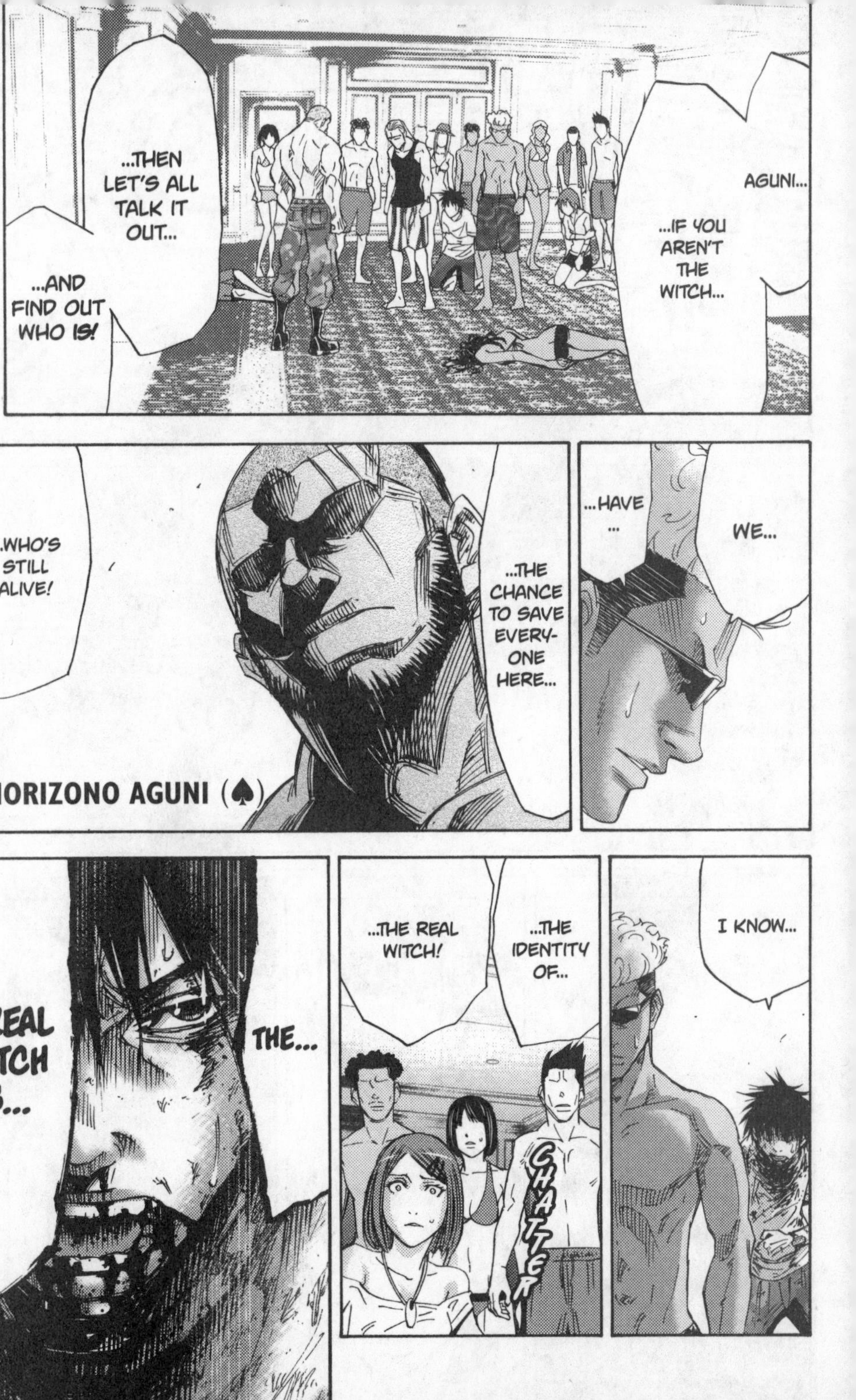
AGUNI...
...IF YOU AREN'T THE WITCH...
...THEN LET'S ALL TALK IT OUT...
...AND FIND OUT WHO IS!
WE...
...HAVE ...
...THE CHANCE TO SAVE EVERY-ONE HERE...
...WHO'S STILL ALIVE!
MORIZONO AGUNI (♠)
I KNOW...
...THE IDENTITY OF...
...THE REAL WITCH!
CHATTER
THE...
...REAL WITCH IS...

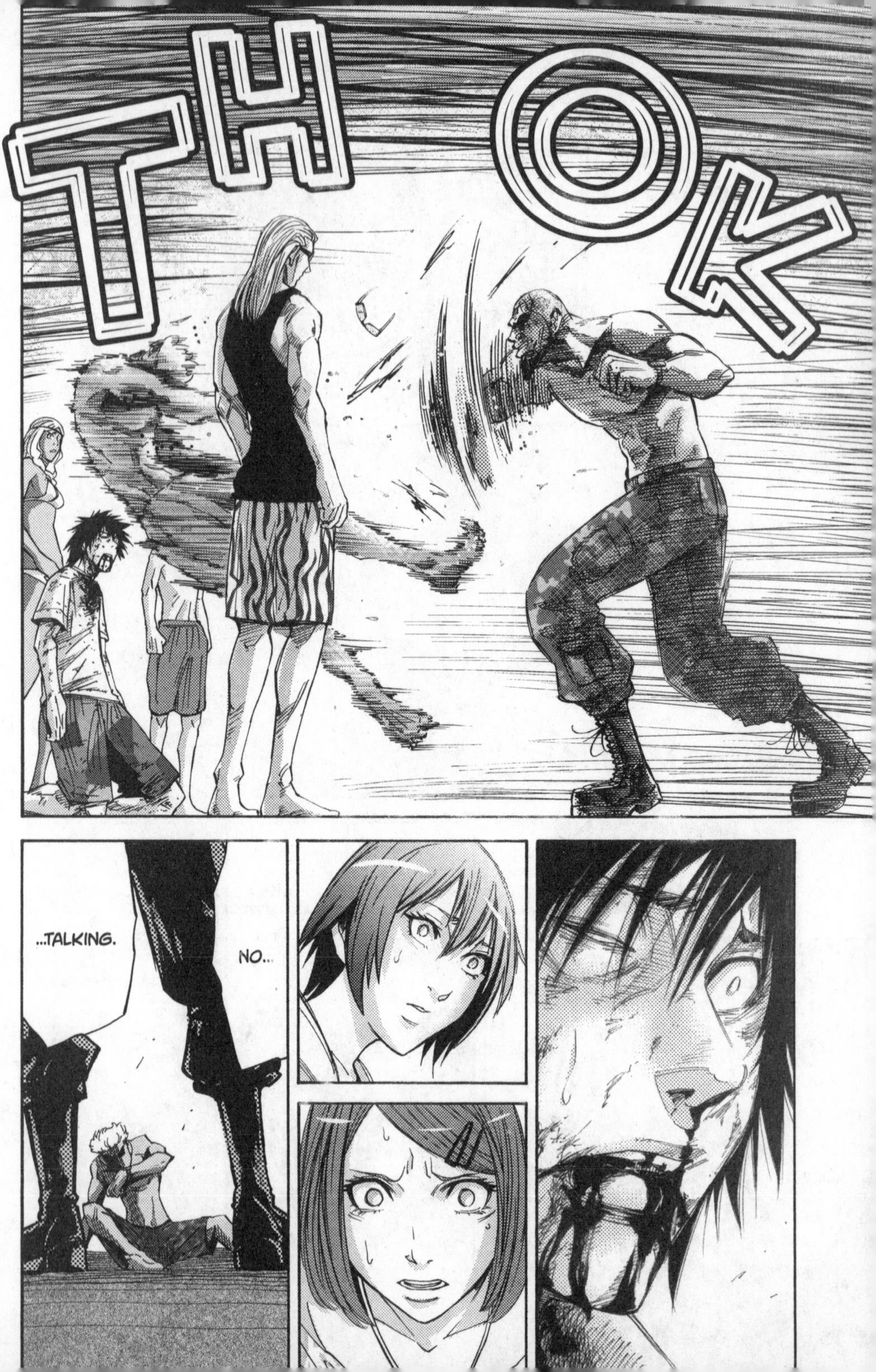
THOK
NO...
...TALKING.

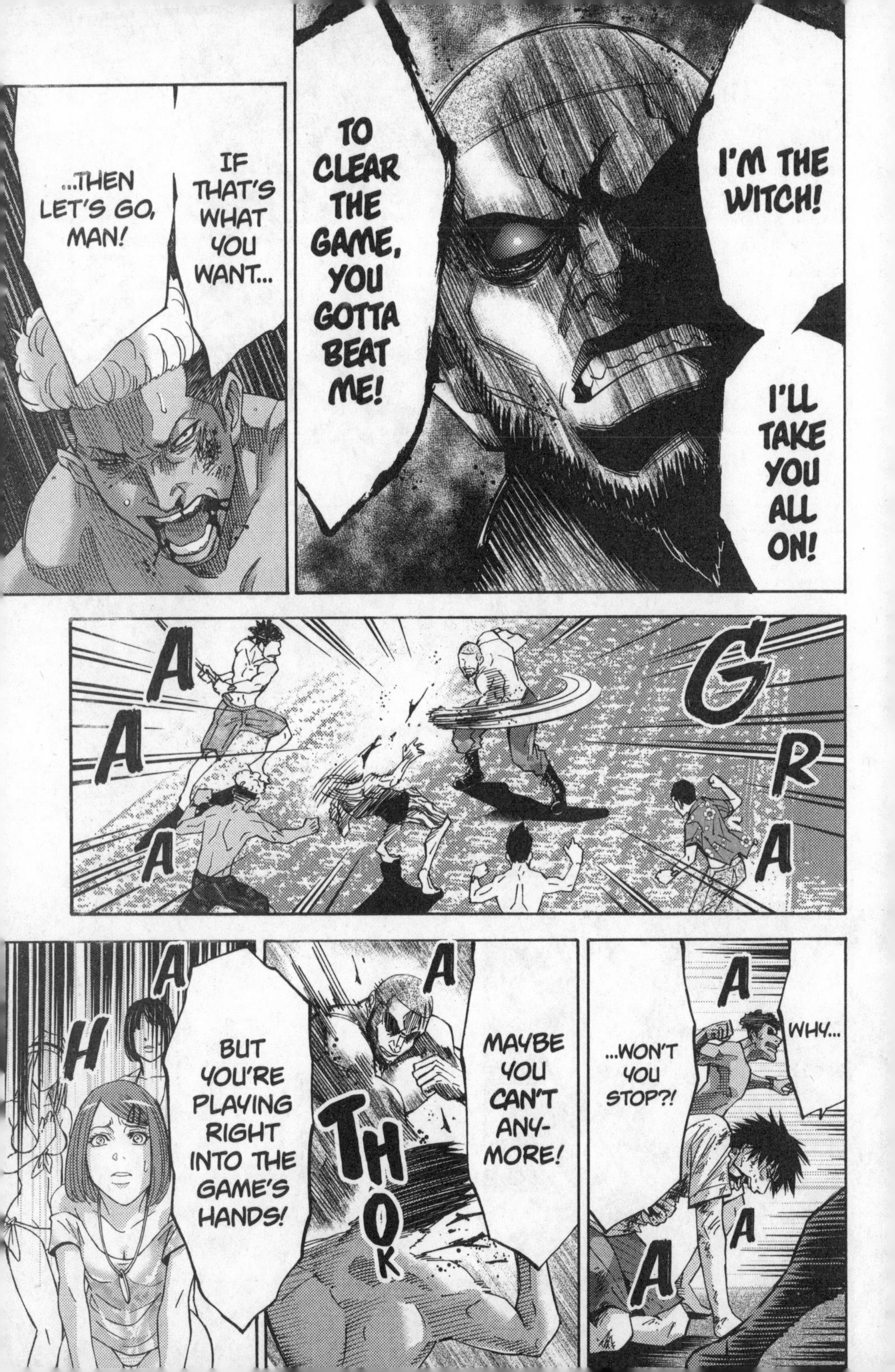
I'M THE WITCH!
TO CLEAR THE GAME, YOU GOTTA BEAT ME!
I'LL TAKE YOU ALL ON!
IF THAT'S WHAT YOU WANT...
...THEN LET'S GO, MAN!
GRA
AAA
WHY...
...WON'T YOU STOP?!
AAA
MAYBE YOU CAN'T ANYMORE!
A
THOK
BUT YOU'RE PLAYING RIGHT INTO THE GAME'S HANDS!
AH

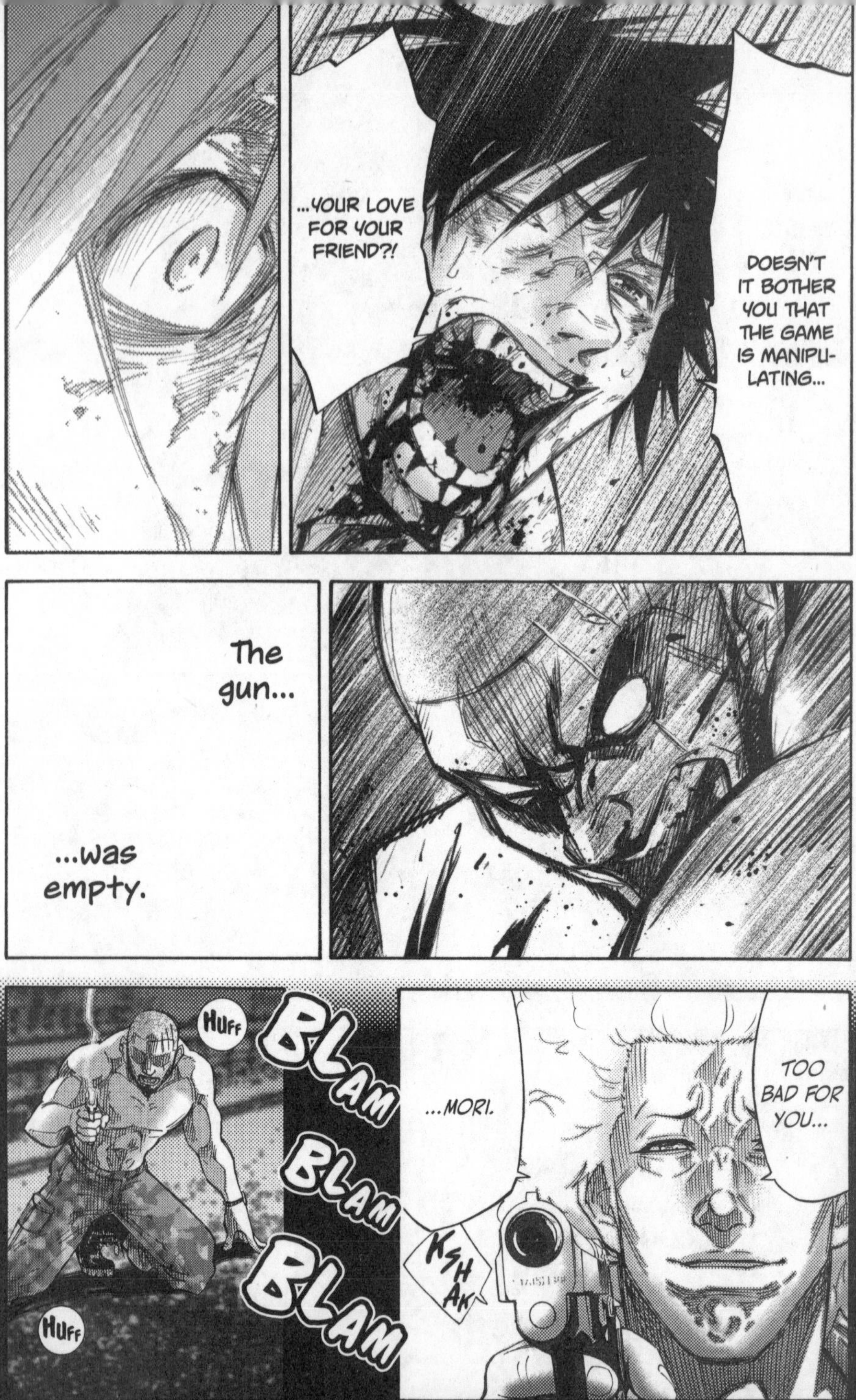
DOESN'T IT BOTHER YOU THAT THE GAME IS MANIPULATING...
...YOUR LOVE FOR YOUR FRIEND?!
The gun...
...was empty.
TOO BAD FOR YOU...
...MORI.
KSHAK
BLAM
BLAM
BLAM
HUFF
HUFF

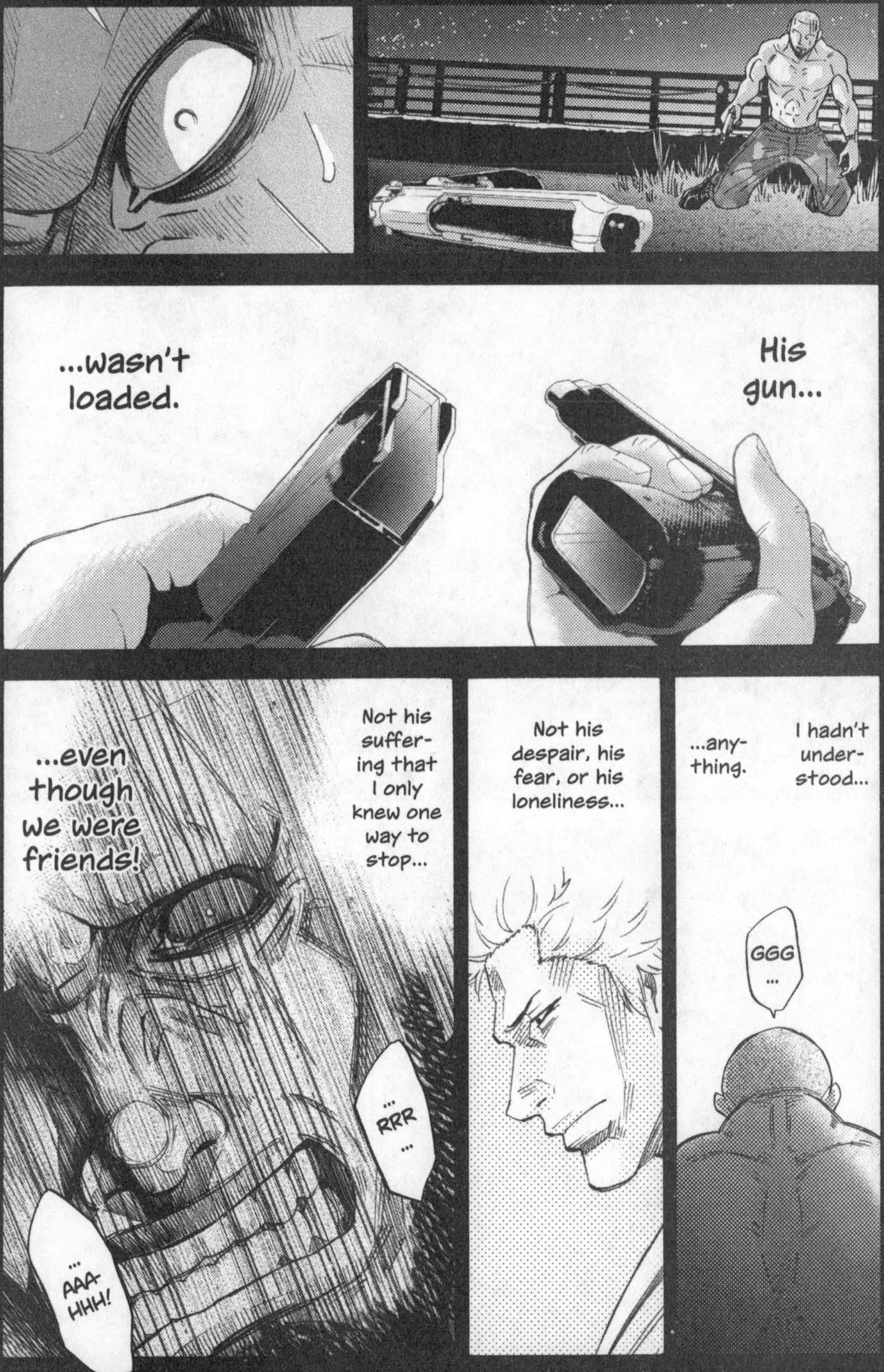
His gun...
...wasn't loaded.
I hadn't understood...
...anything.
GGG ...
Not his despair, his fear, or his loneliness...
Not his suffering that I only knew one way to stop...
...even though we were friends!
... RRR ...
... AAAHHH!

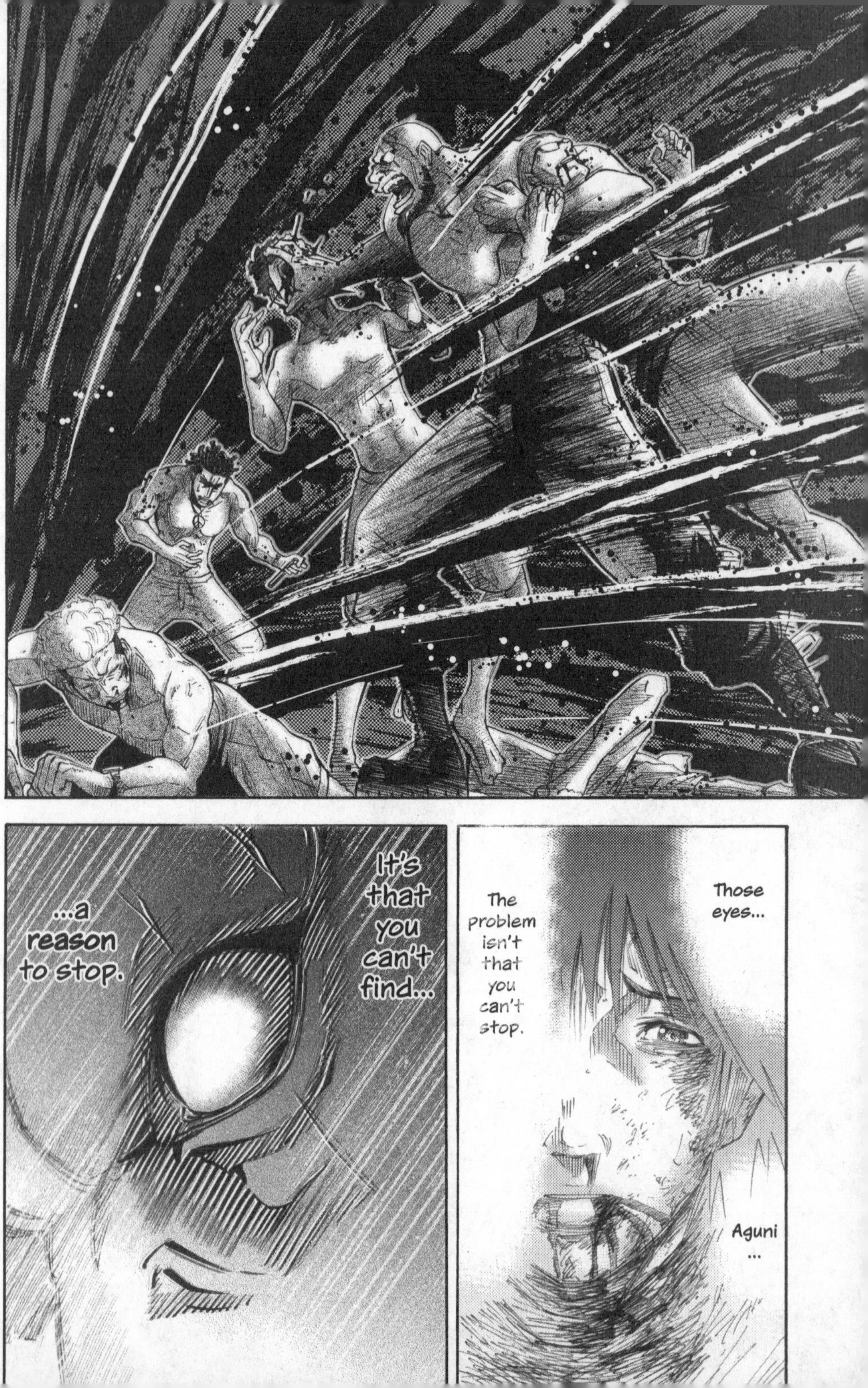
Those eyes...
The problem isn't that you can't stop.
Aguni...
It's that you can't find...
...a reason to stop.

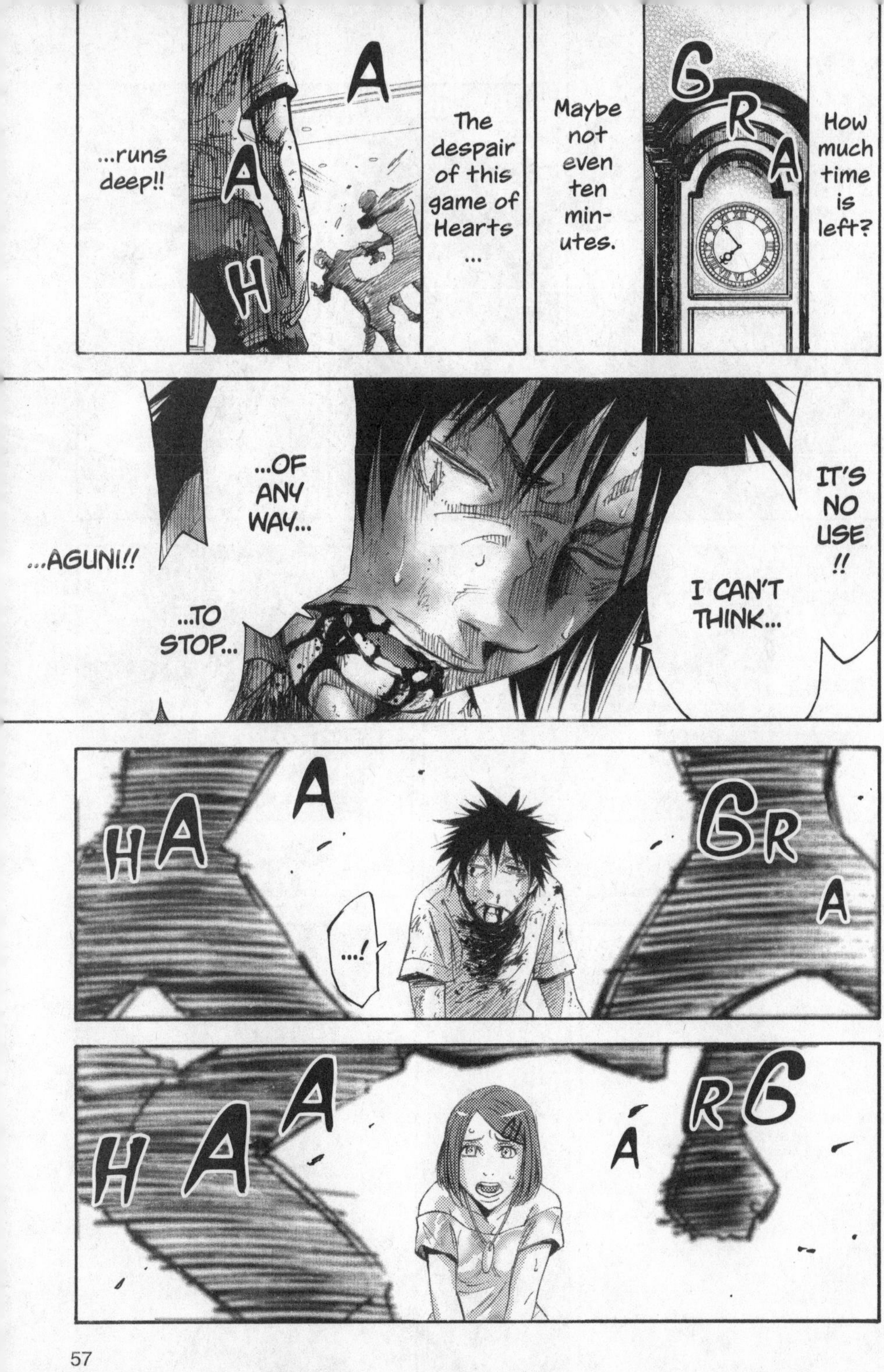
How much time is left?
GRA
Maybe not even ten minutes.
The despair of this game of Hearts...
A
AAH
...runs deep!!
IT'S NO USE!!
I CAN'T THINK...
...OF ANY WAY...
...TO STOP...
...AGUNI!!
GRA
A
...!
A
HA
G R
Á
A
A
HA

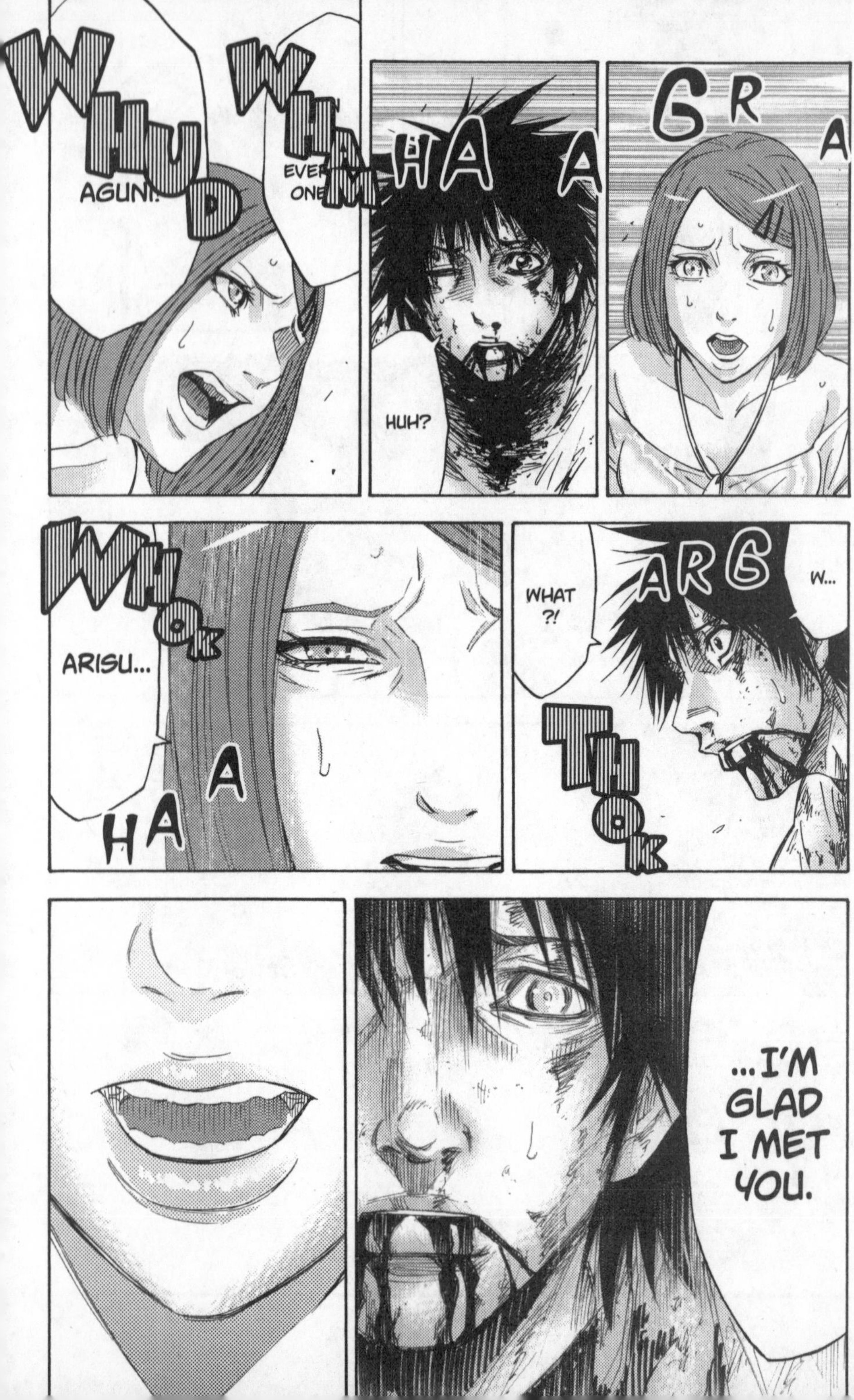
GRA A
HA A
HUH?
WHAM
EVERYONE
WHUD
AGUNI!
W...
ARG
WHAT?!
THOK
WHOK
ARISU...
HA A
...I'M GLAD I MET YOU.

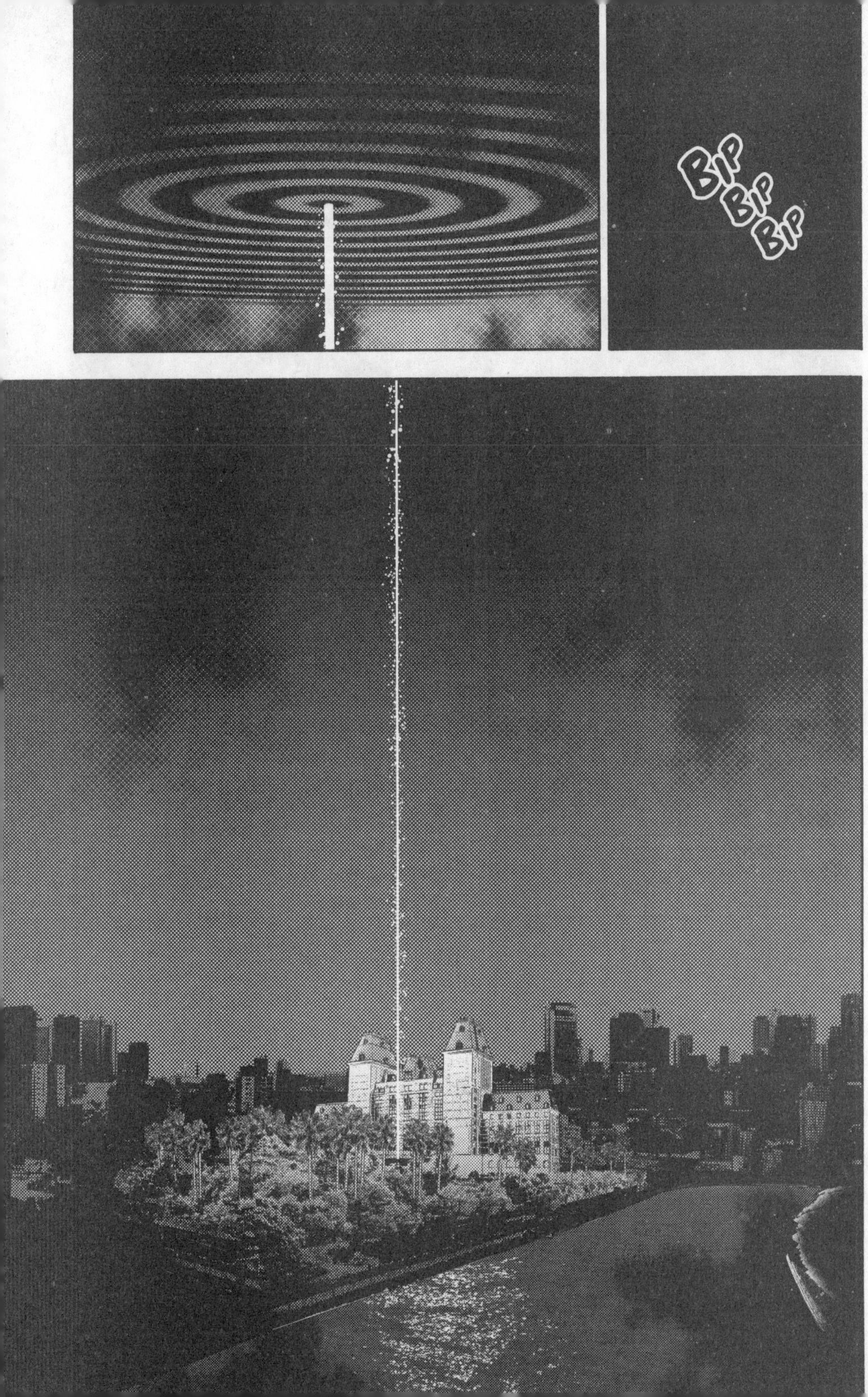
BIP
BIP
BIP

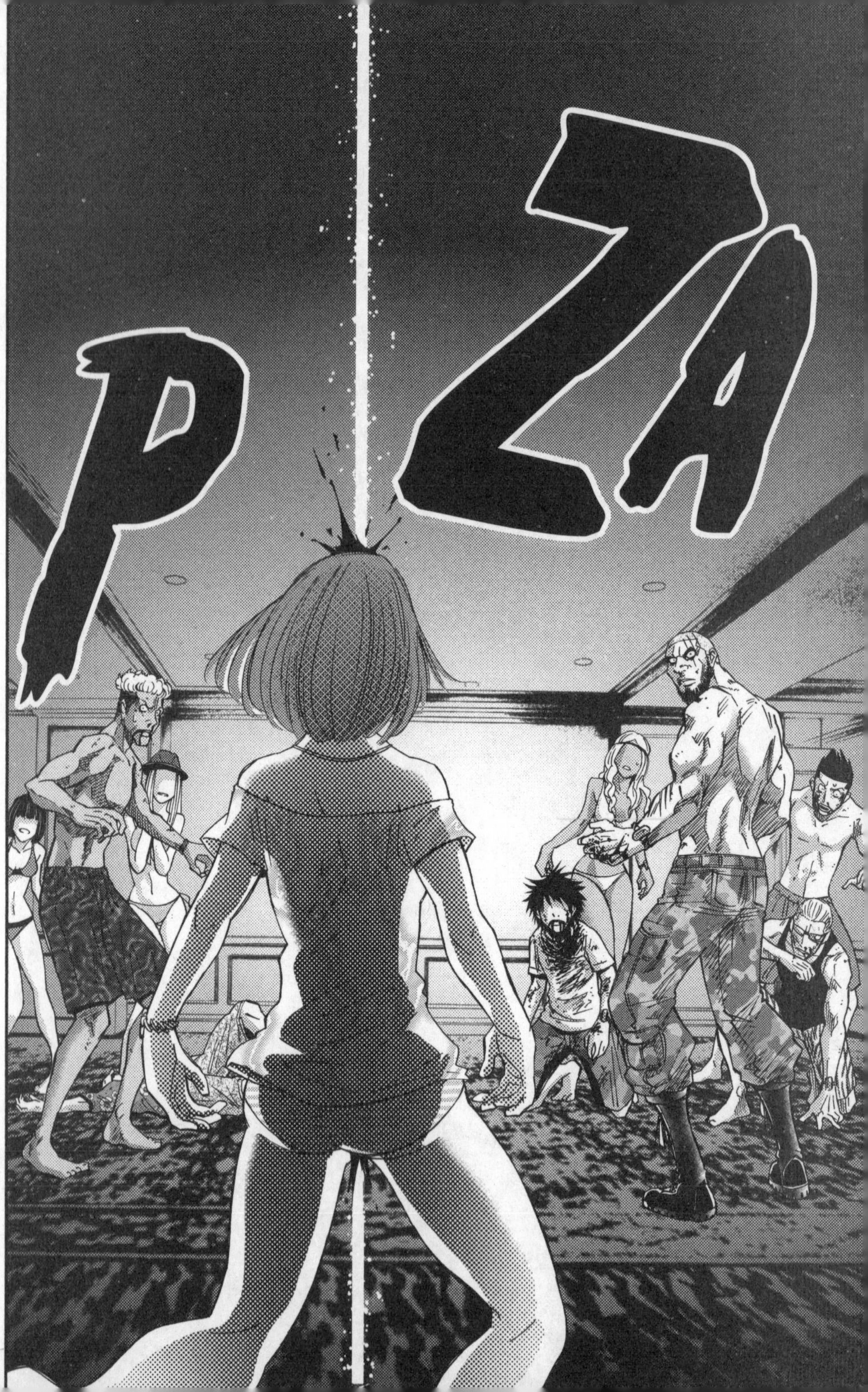
PZA

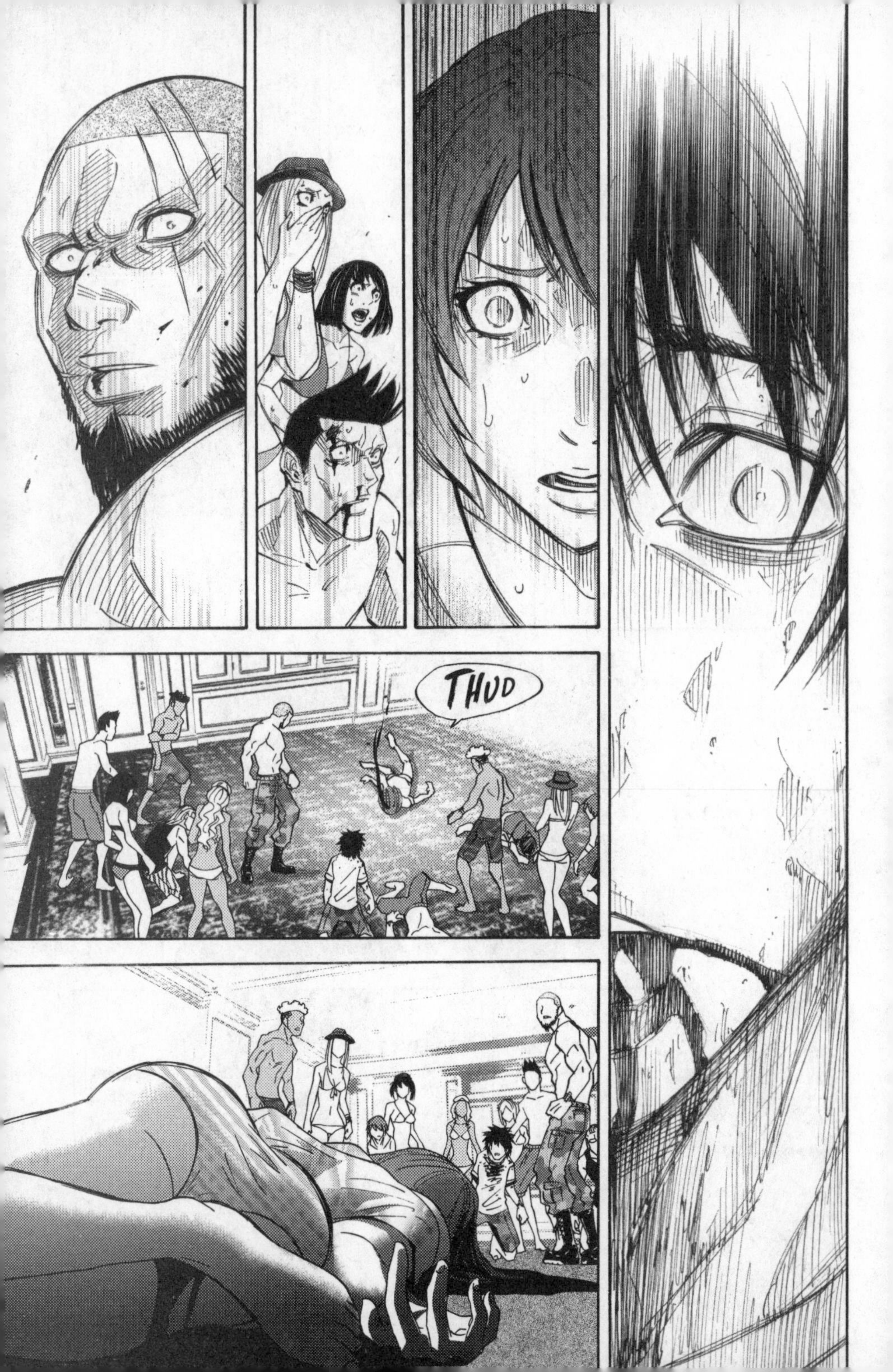
THUD

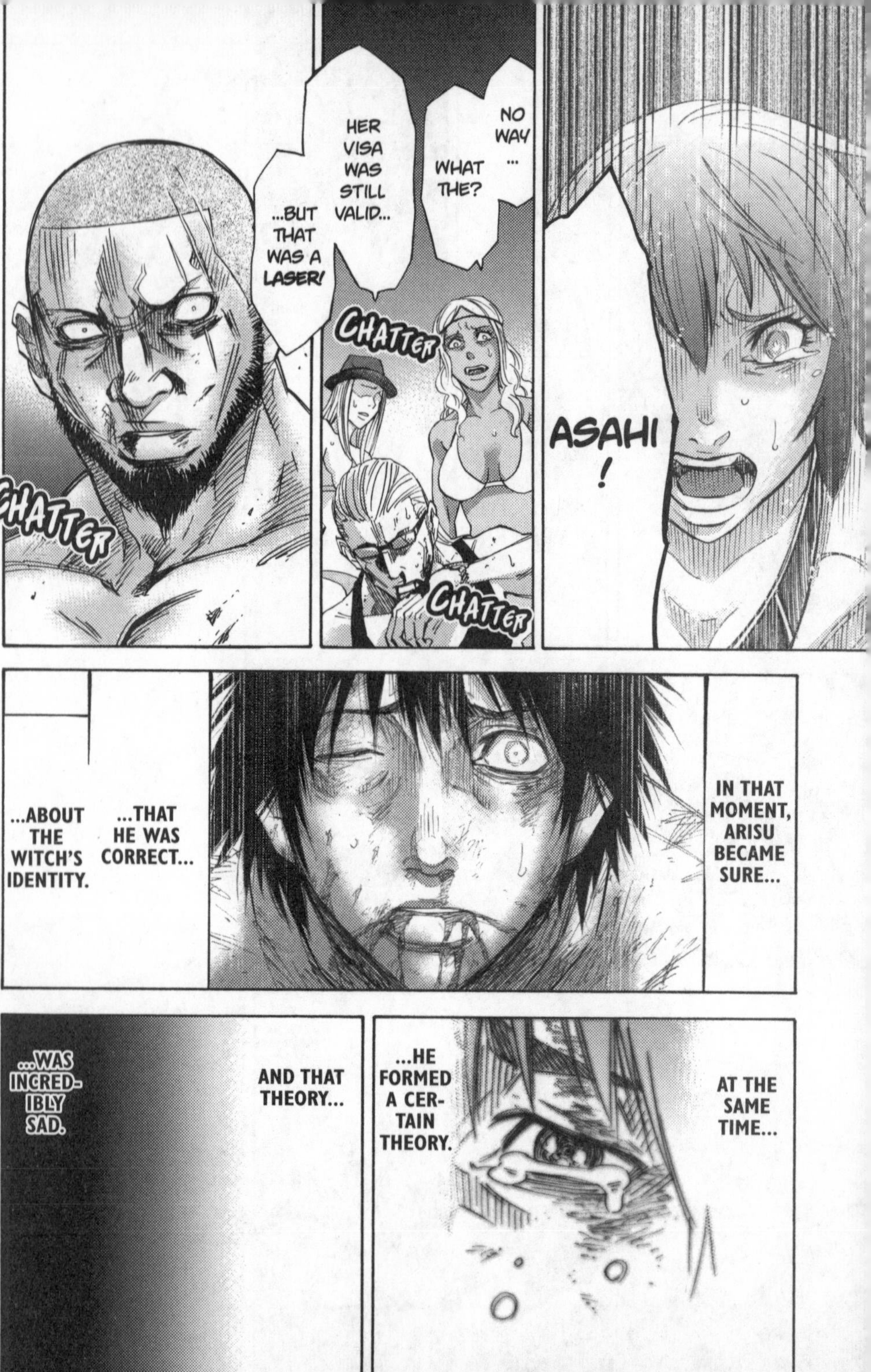
ASAHI!
NO WAY...
WHAT THE?
HER VISA WAS STILL VALID...
...BUT THAT WAS A LASER!
CHATTER
CHATTER
CHATTER
IN THAT MOMENT, ARISU BECAME SURE...
...THAT HE WAS CORRECT...
...ABOUT THE WITCH'S IDENTITY.
AT THE SAME TIME...
...HE FORMED A CERTAIN THEORY.
AND THAT THEORY...
...WAS INCREDIBLY SAD.

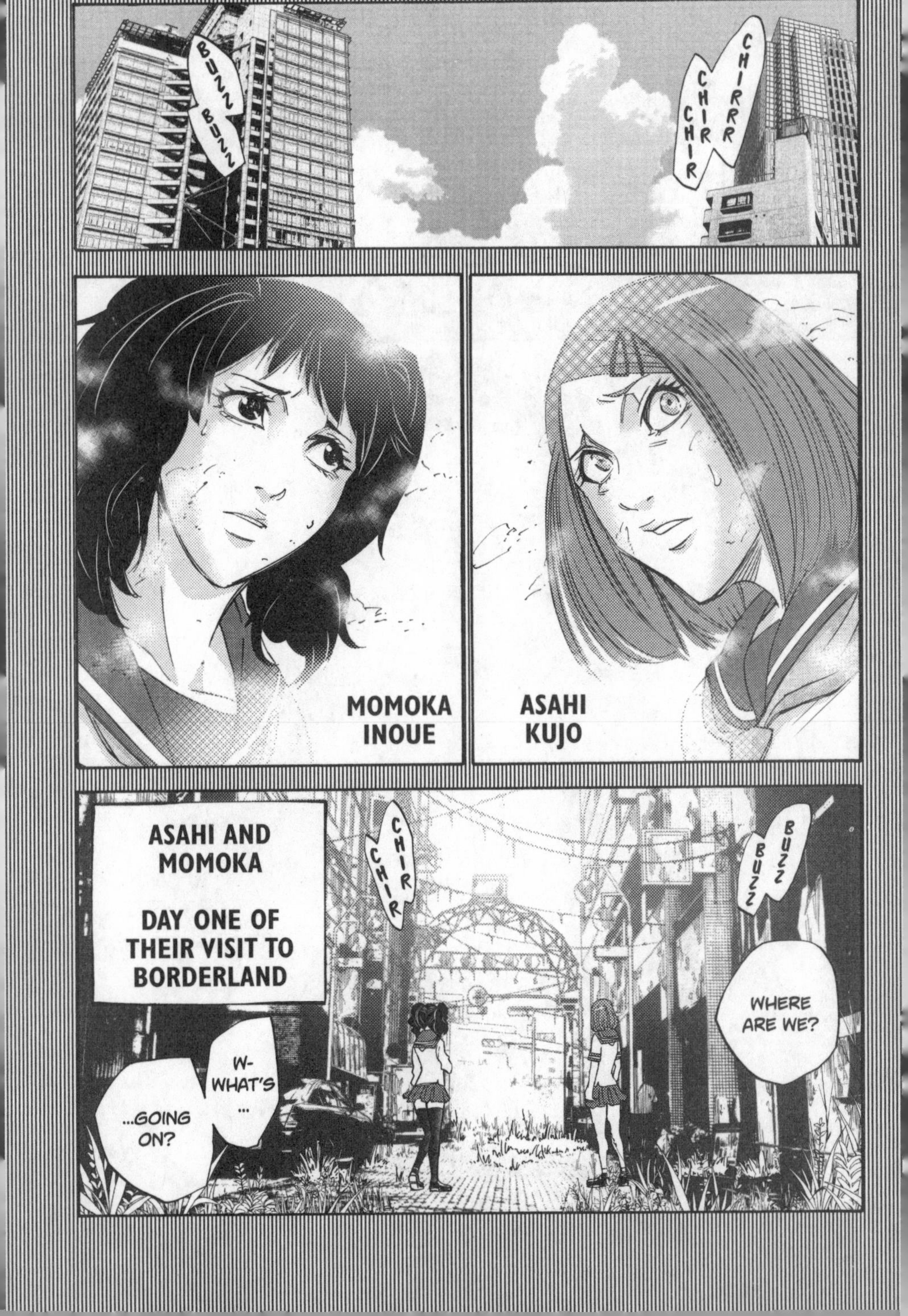
CHIR CHIR CHIRRR
BUZZ BUZZ
ASAHI KUJO
MOMOKA INOUE
BUZZ BUZZ
WHERE ARE WE?
CHIR CHIR
ASAHI AND MOMOKA

DAY ONE OF THEIR VISIT TO BORDERLAND
W- WHAT'S ...
...GOING ON?

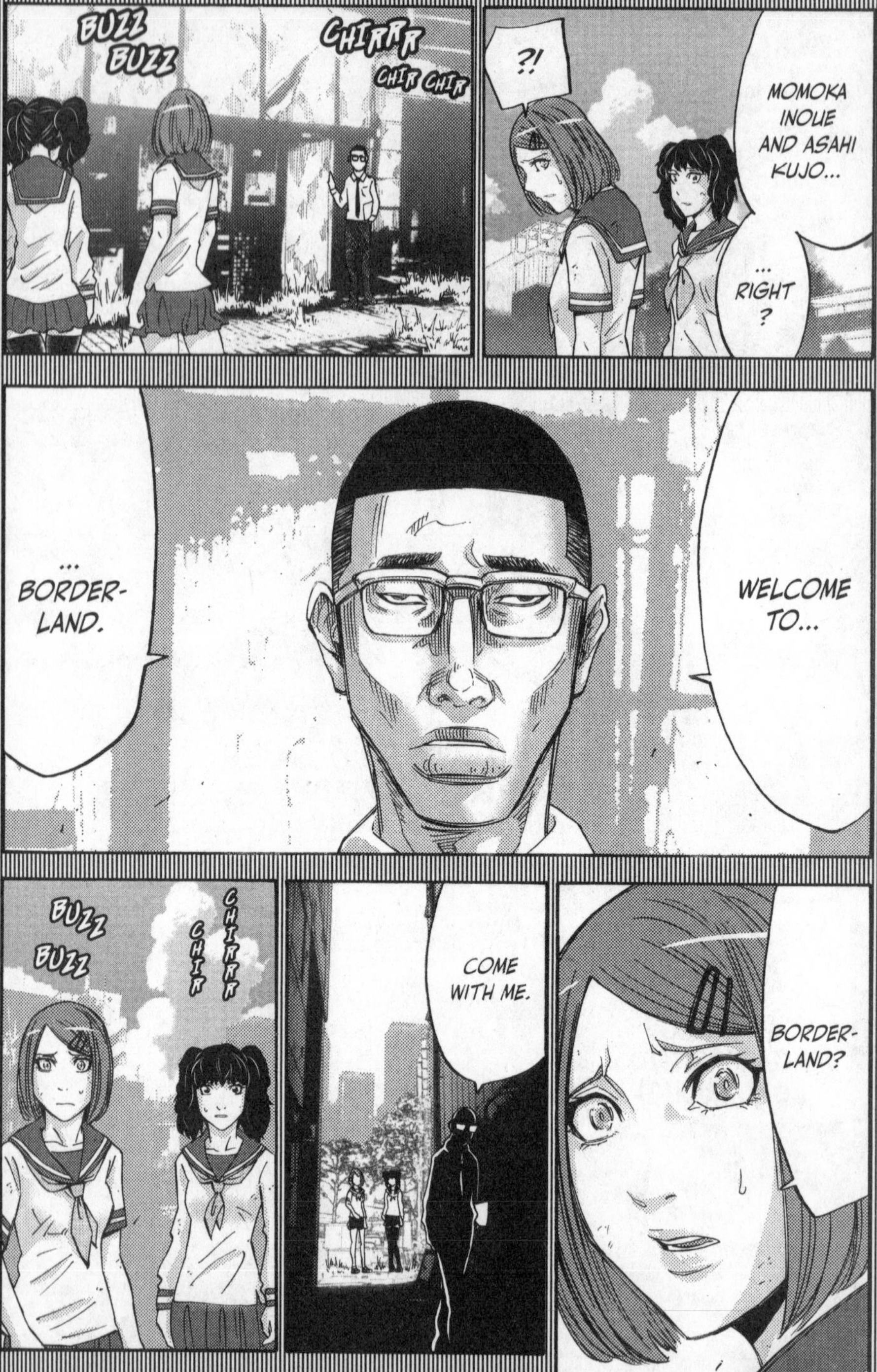
MOMOKA INOUE AND ASAHI KUJO...
...RIGHT?
?!
CHIRRR
CHIR CHIR
BUZZ BUZZ
WELCOME TO...
...BORDER-LAND.
BORDER-LAND?
COME WITH ME.
CHIRRR
CHIR
BUZZ BUZZ

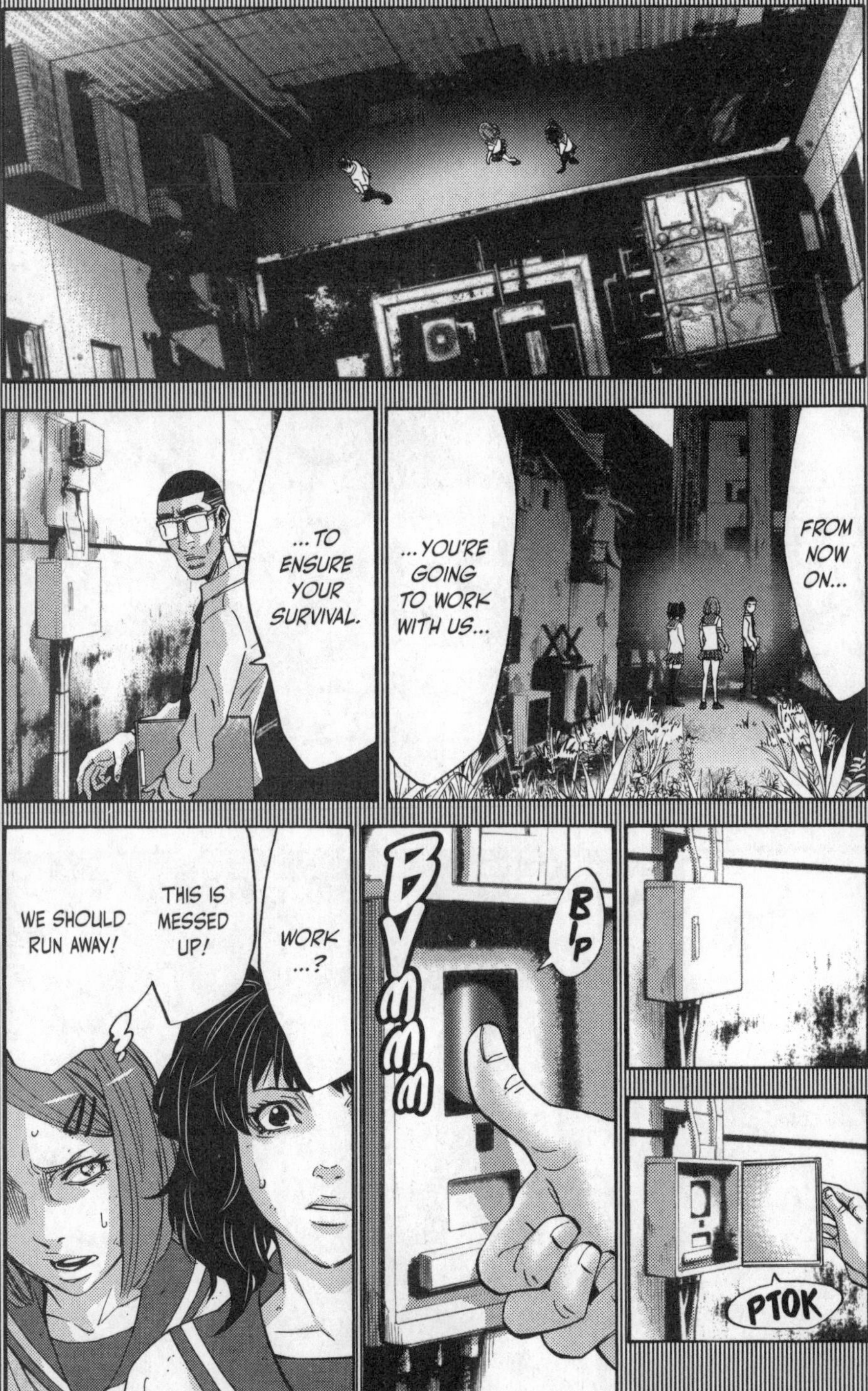
FROM NOW ON...
...YOU'RE GOING TO WORK WITH US...
...TO ENSURE YOUR SURVIVAL.
PTOK
BVMMM
BIP
WORK ...?
THIS IS MESSED UP!
WE SHOULD RUN AWAY!

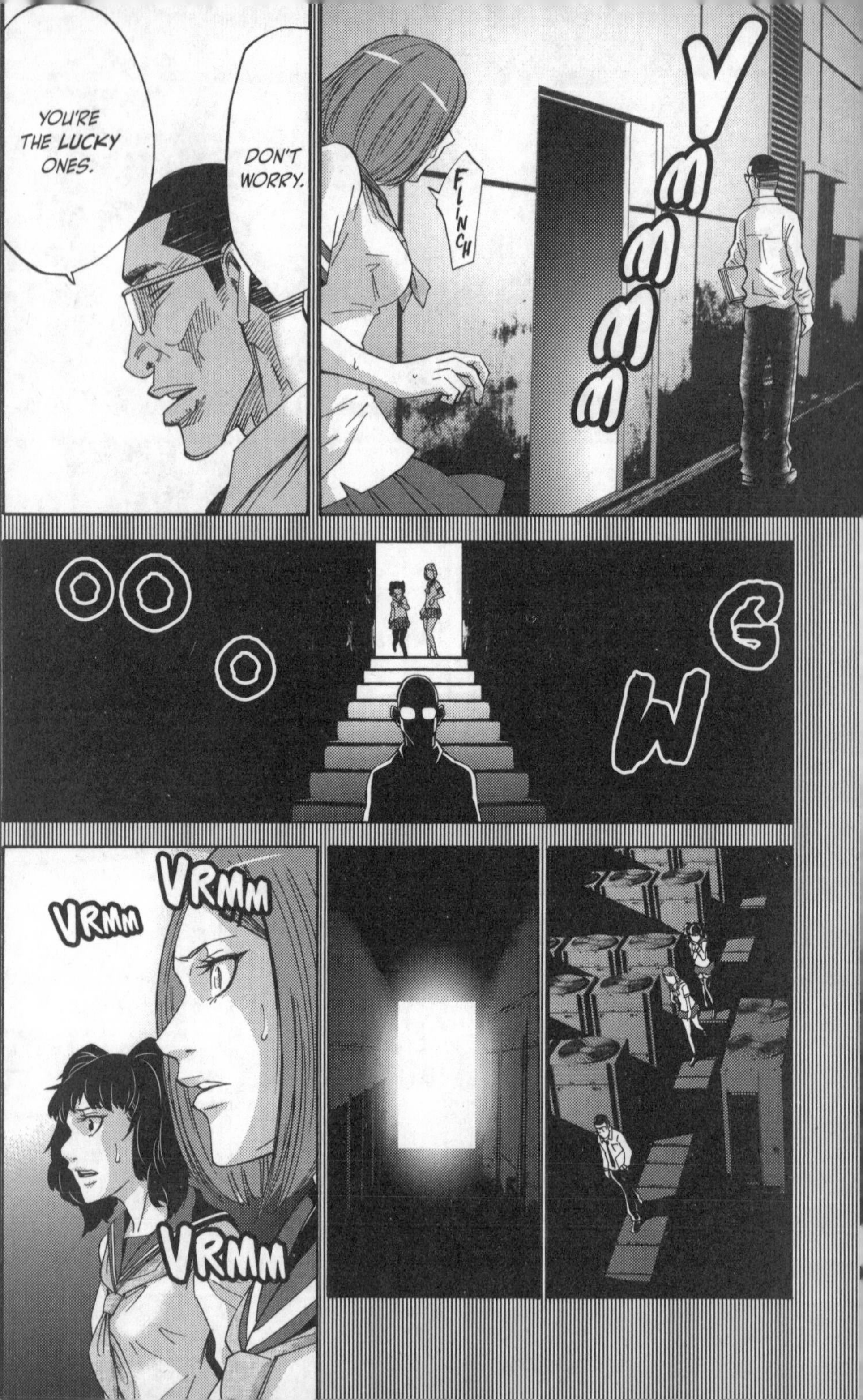
VMMMMMMM
FLINCH
DON'T WORRY.
YOU'RE THE LUCKY ONES.
GWOOO
VRMM
VRMM
VRMM

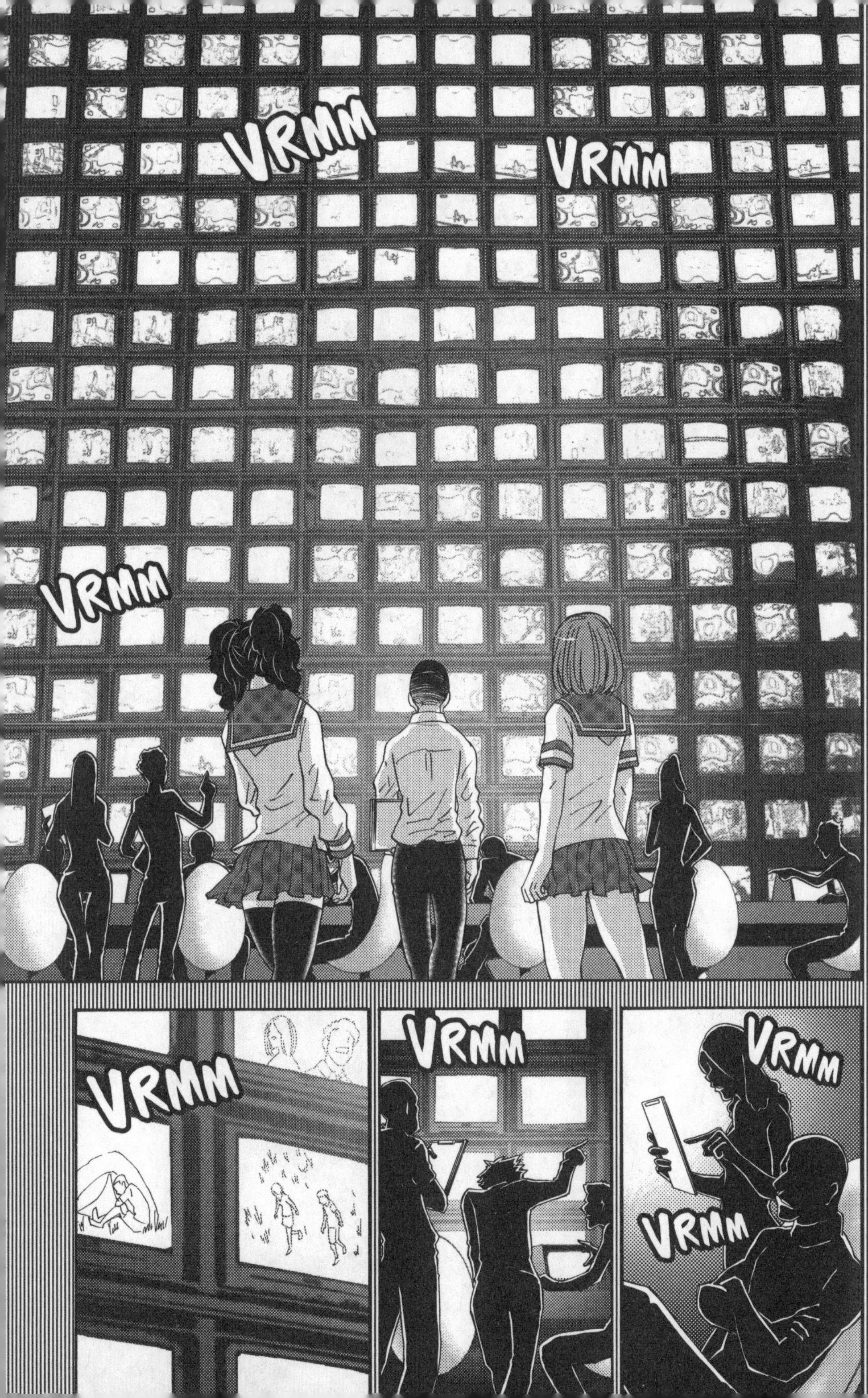
VRMM
VRMM
VRMM
VRMM
VRMM
VRMM
VRMM

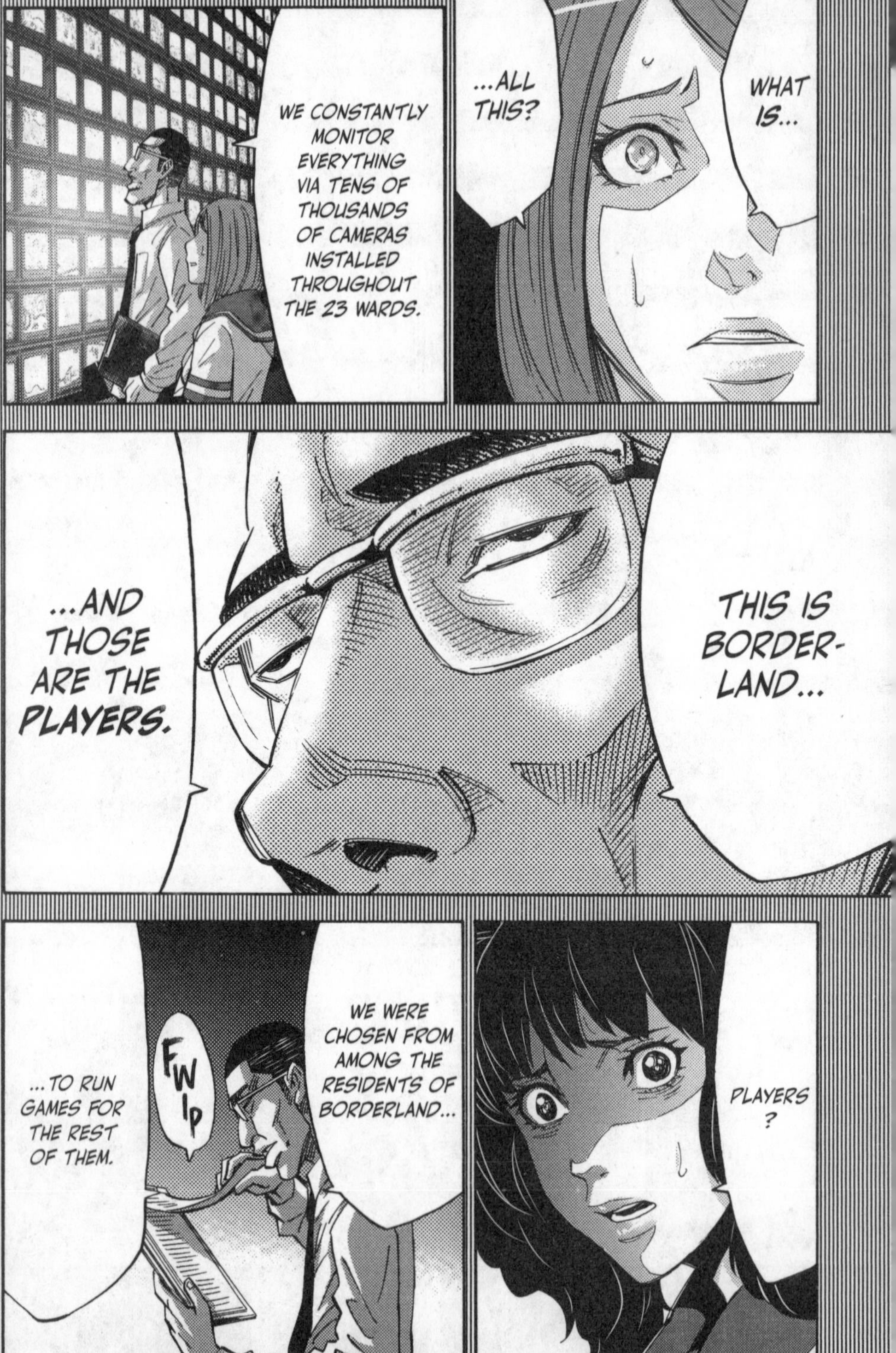
WHAT IS...
...ALL THIS?
WE CONSTANTLY MONITOR EVERYTHING VIA TENS OF THOUSANDS OF CAMERAS INSTALLED THROUGHOUT THE 23 WARDS.
THIS IS BORDERLAND...
...AND THOSE ARE THE PLAYERS.
PLAYERS ?
WE WERE CHOSEN FROM AMONG THE RESIDENTS OF BORDERLAND...
FWIP
...TO RUN GAMES FOR THE REST OF THEM.

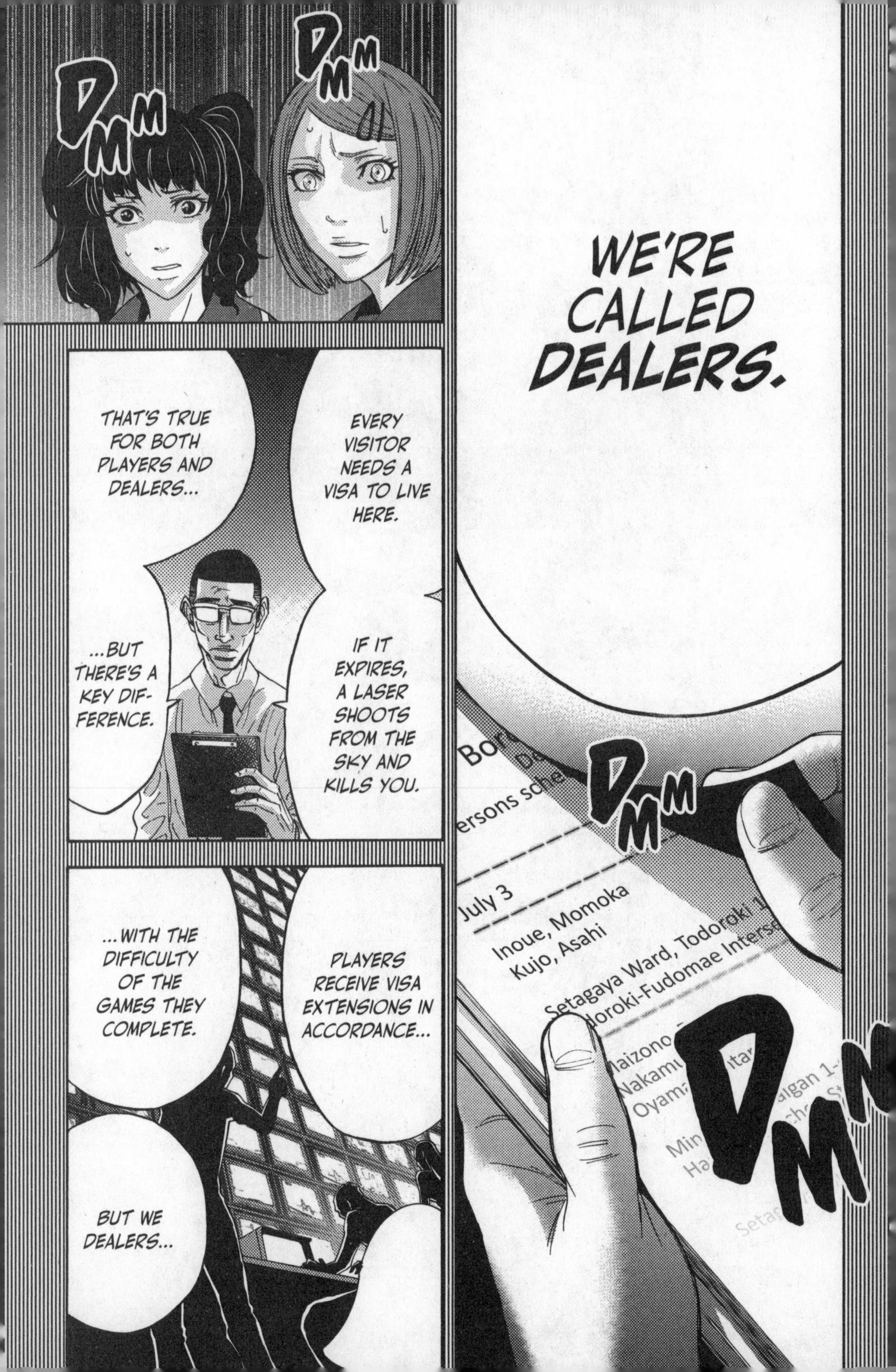

WE'RE CALLED DEALERS.
DMM
July 3
Inoue, Momoka
Kujo, Asahi
Setagaya Ward, Todoroki
DMM
DMM
DMM
EVERY VISITOR NEEDS A VISA TO LIVE HERE.
THAT'S TRUE FOR BOTH PLAYERS AND DEALERS...
IF IT EXPIRES, A LASER SHOOTS FROM THE SKY AND KILLS YOU.
...BUT THERE'S A KEY DIF-FERENCE.
PLAYERS RECEIVE VISA EXTENSIONS IN ACCORDANCE...
...WITH THE DIFFICULTY OF THE GAMES THEY COMPLETE.
BUT WE DEALERS...

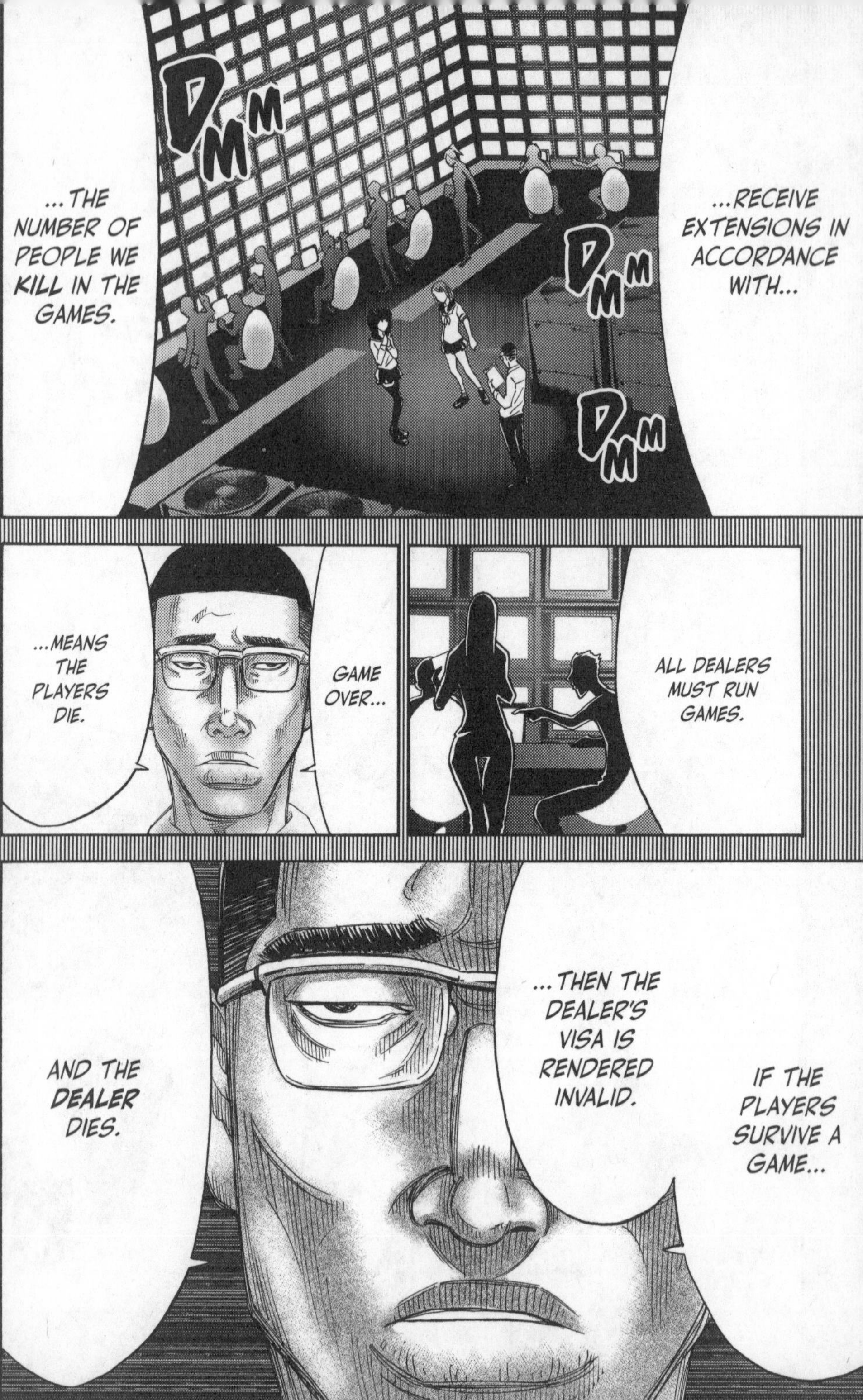
...RECEIVE EXTENSIONS IN ACCORDANCE WITH...
DMM
DMM
DMM
...THE NUMBER OF PEOPLE WE KILL IN THE GAMES.
ALL DEALERS MUST RUN GAMES.
GAME OVER...
...MEANS THE PLAYERS DIE.
IF THE PLAYERS SURVIVE A GAME...
...THEN THE DEALER'S VISA IS RENDERED INVALID.
AND THE DEALER DIES.

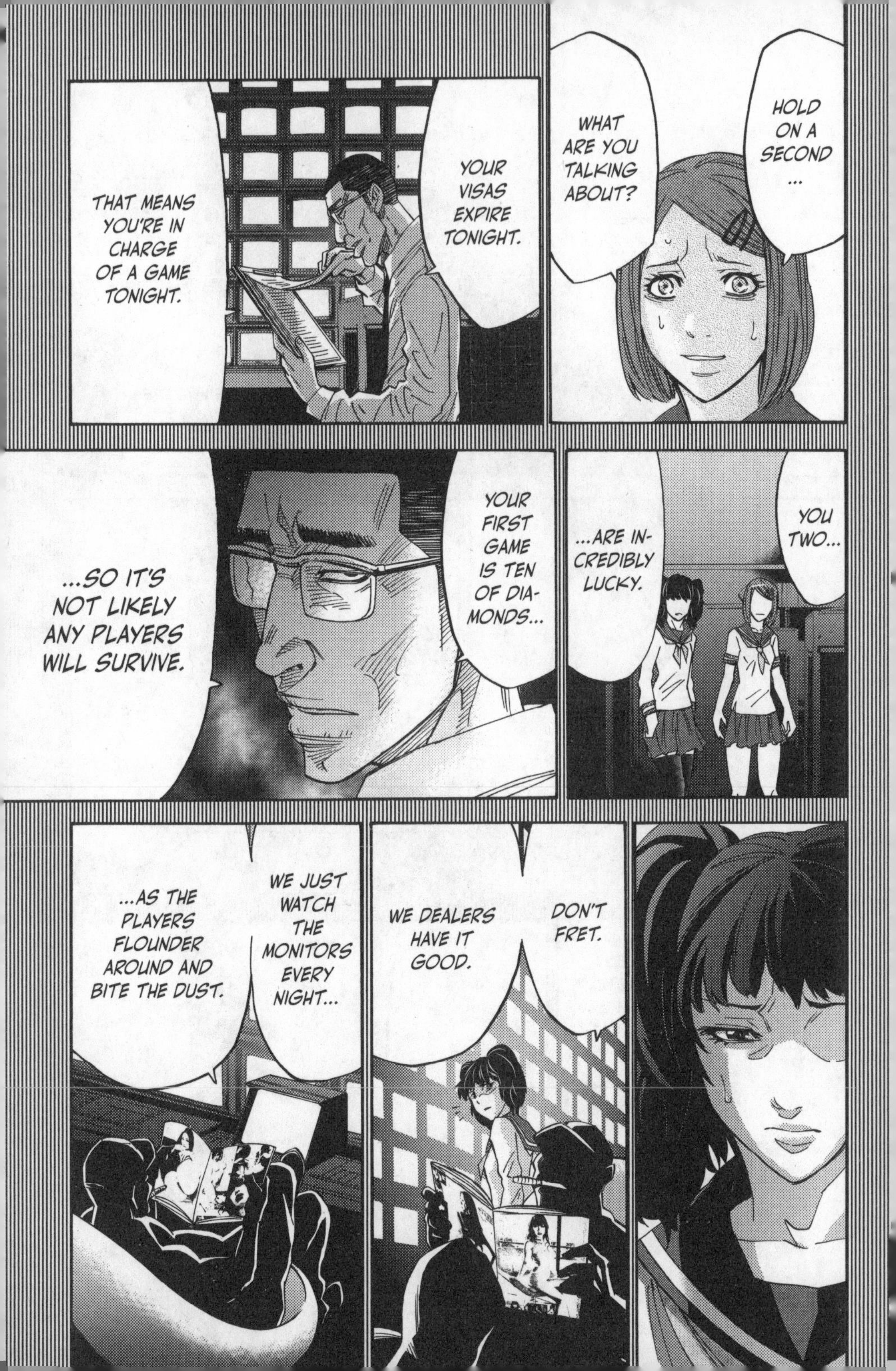
HOLD ON A SECOND ...
WHAT ARE YOU TALKING ABOUT?
YOUR VISAS EXPIRE TONIGHT.
THAT MEANS YOU'RE IN CHARGE OF A GAME TONIGHT.
YOU TWO...
...ARE INCREDIBLY LUCKY.
YOUR FIRST GAME IS TEN OF DIAMONDS...
...SO IT'S NOT LIKELY ANY PLAYERS WILL SURVIVE.
DON'T FRET.
WE DEALERS HAVE IT GOOD.
WE JUST WATCH THE MONITORS EVERY NIGHT...
...AS THE PLAYERS FLOUNDER AROUND AND BITE THE DUST.

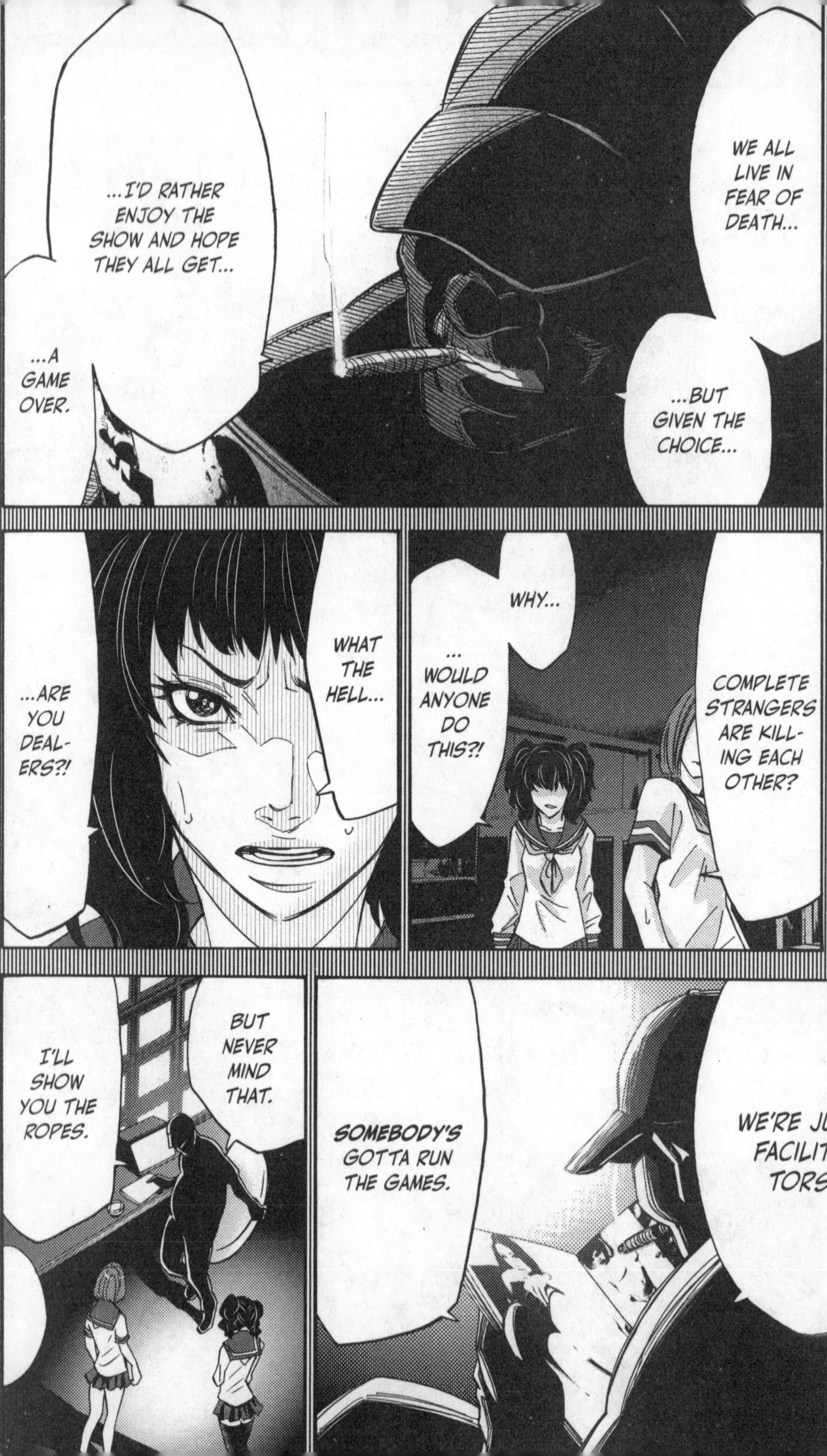
WE ALL LIVE IN FEAR OF DEATH...
...BUT GIVEN THE CHOICE...
...I'D RATHER ENJOY THE SHOW AND HOPE THEY ALL GET...
...A GAME OVER.
COMPLETE STRANGERS ARE KILL-ING EACH OTHER?
WHY...
...WOULD ANYONE DO THIS?!
WHAT THE HELL...
...ARE YOU DEAL-ERS?!
WE'RE JUST FACILITA-TORS.
SOMEBODY'S GOTTA RUN THE GAMES.
BUT NEVER MIND THAT.
I'LL SHOW YOU THE ROPES.

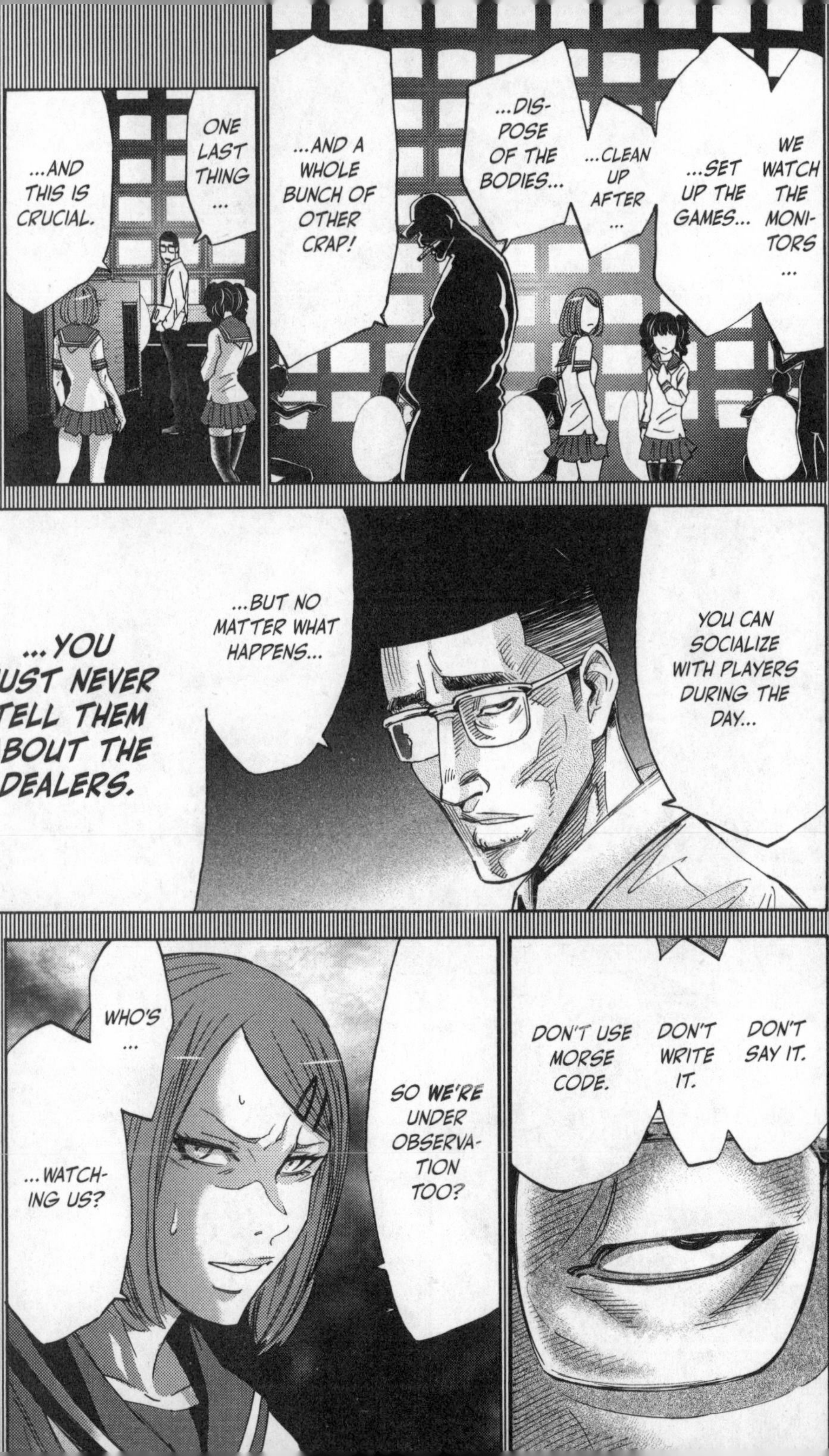
WE WATCH THE MONITORS...
...SET UP THE GAMES...
...CLEAN UP AFTER...
...DISPOSE OF THE BODIES...
...AND A WHOLE BUNCH OF OTHER CRAP!
ONE LAST THING...
...AND THIS IS CRUCIAL.
YOU CAN SOCIALIZE WITH PLAYERS DURING THE DAY...
...BUT NO MATTER WHAT HAPPENS...
...YOU MUST NEVER TELL THEM ABOUT THE DEALERS.
DON'T SAY IT.
DON'T WRITE IT.
DON'T USE MORSE CODE.
SO WE'RE UNDER OBSERVATION TOO?
WHO'S...
...WATCHING US?

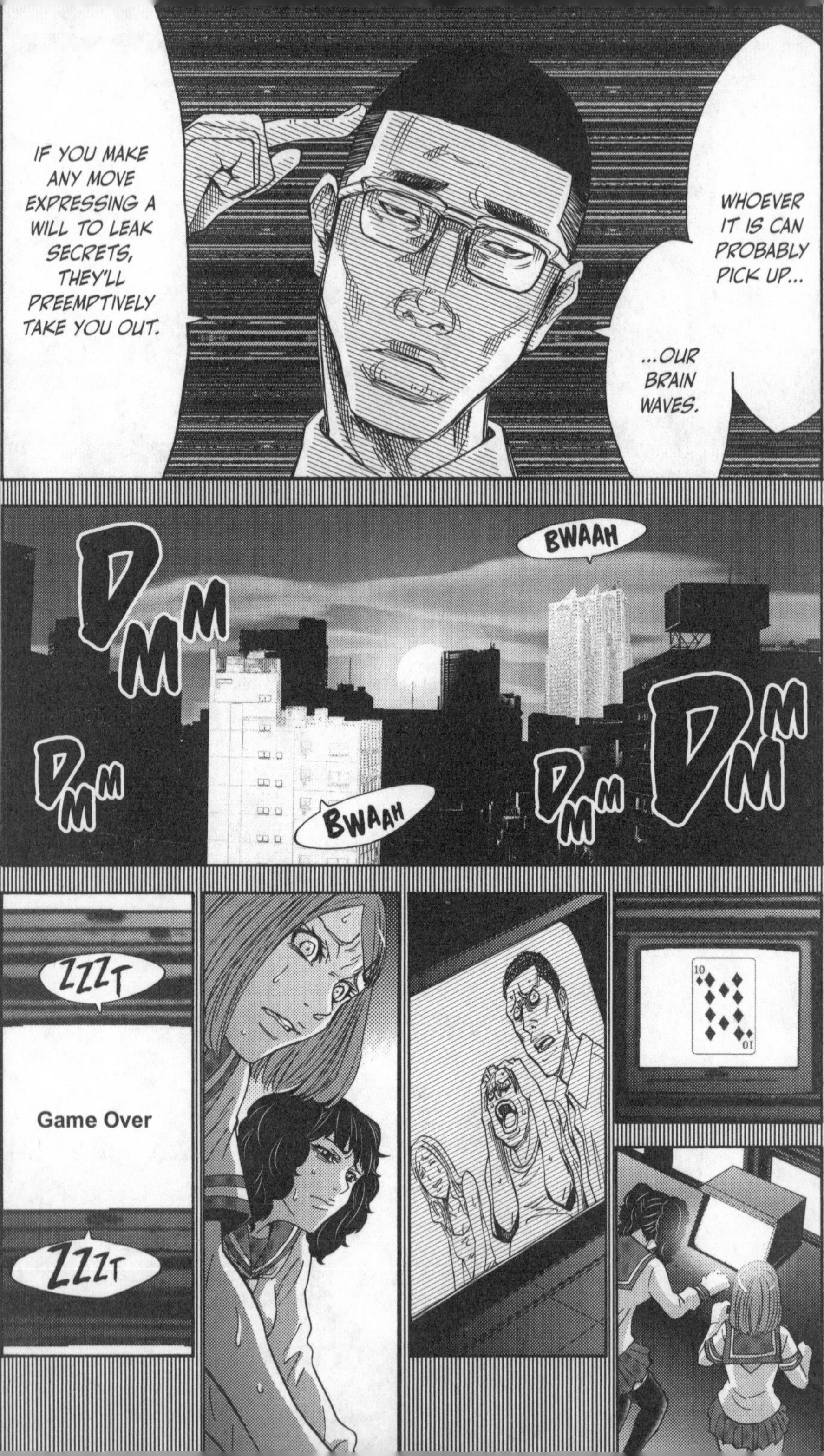
WHOEVER IT IS CAN PROBABLY PICK UP...
...OUR BRAIN WAVES.
IF YOU MAKE ANY MOVE EXPRESSING A WILL TO LEAK SECRETS, THEY'LL PREEMPTIVELY TAKE YOU OUT.
DMMM
DMMM
BWAAH
DMMM
BWAAH
DMMM
ZZZT
Game Over
ZZZT

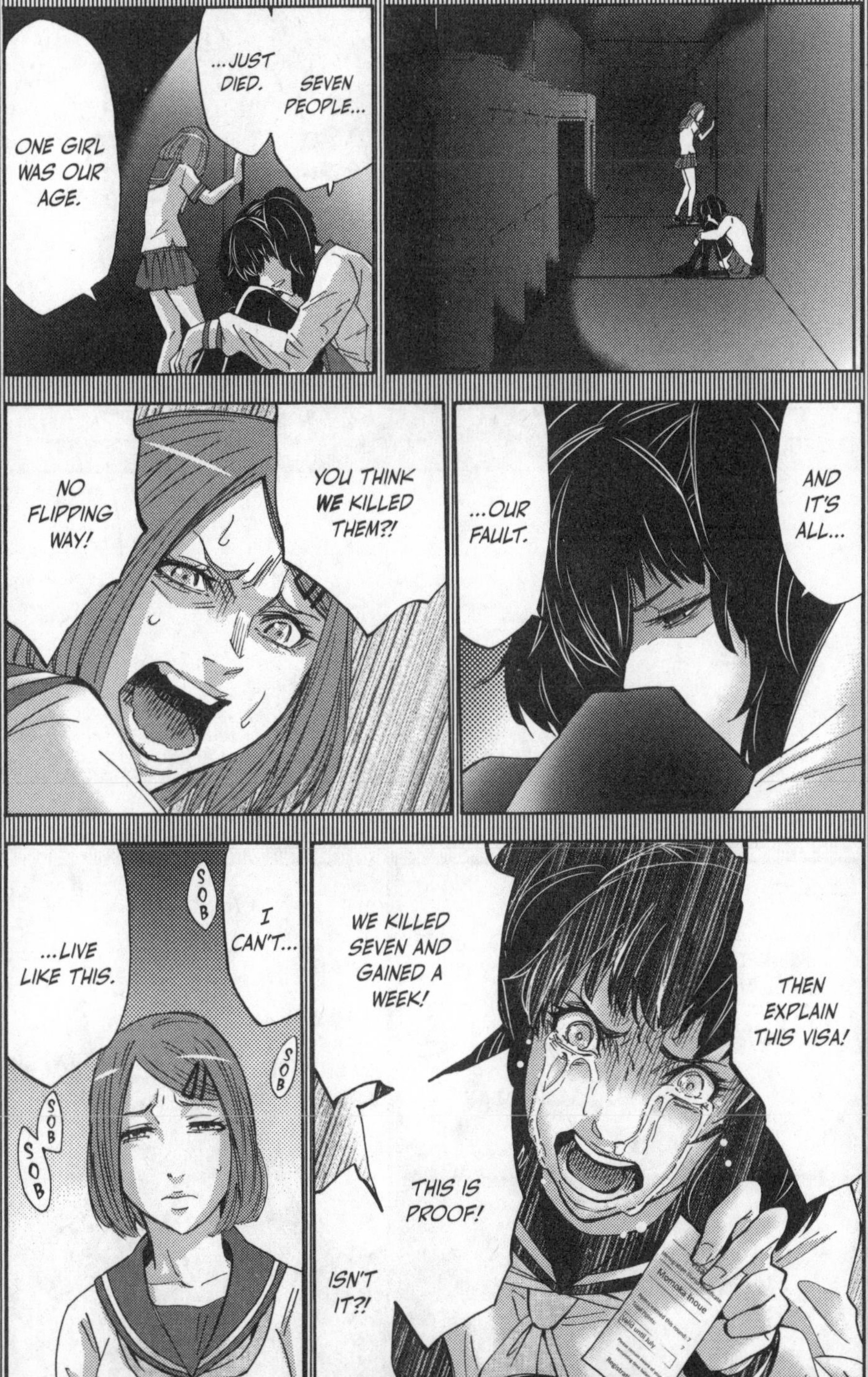
SEVEN PEOPLE...
...JUST DIED.
ONE GIRL WAS OUR AGE.
AND IT'S ALL...
...OUR FAULT.
YOU THINK WE KILLED THEM?!
NO FLIPPING WAY!
THEN EXPLAIN THIS VISA!
WE KILLED SEVEN AND GAINED A WEEK!
THIS IS PROOF!
ISN'T IT?!
Momoka Inoue
Valid until July
Registration: 010
SOB
SOB
SOB
SOB
I CAN'T...
...LIVE LIKE THIS.

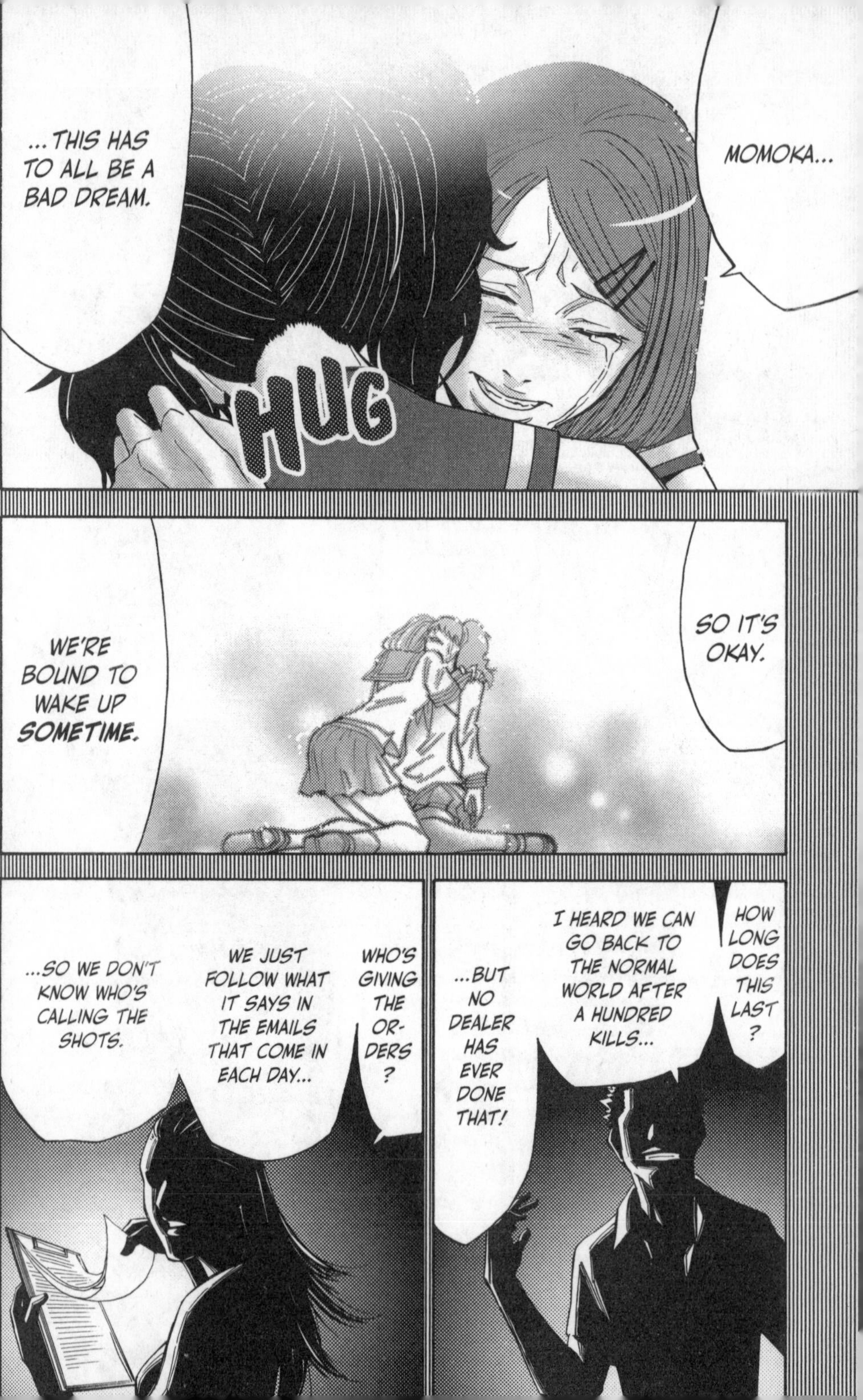
MOMOKA...
...THIS HAS TO ALL BE A BAD DREAM.
HUG
SO IT'S OKAY.
WE'RE BOUND TO WAKE UP SOMETIME.
HOW LONG DOES THIS LAST?
I HEARD WE CAN GO BACK TO THE NORMAL WORLD AFTER A HUNDRED KILLS...
...BUT NO DEALER HAS EVER DONE THAT!
WHO'S GIVING THE OR-DERS?
WE JUST FOLLOW WHAT IT SAYS IN THE EMAILS THAT COME IN EACH DAY...
...SO WE DON'T KNOW WHO'S CALLING THE SHOTS.

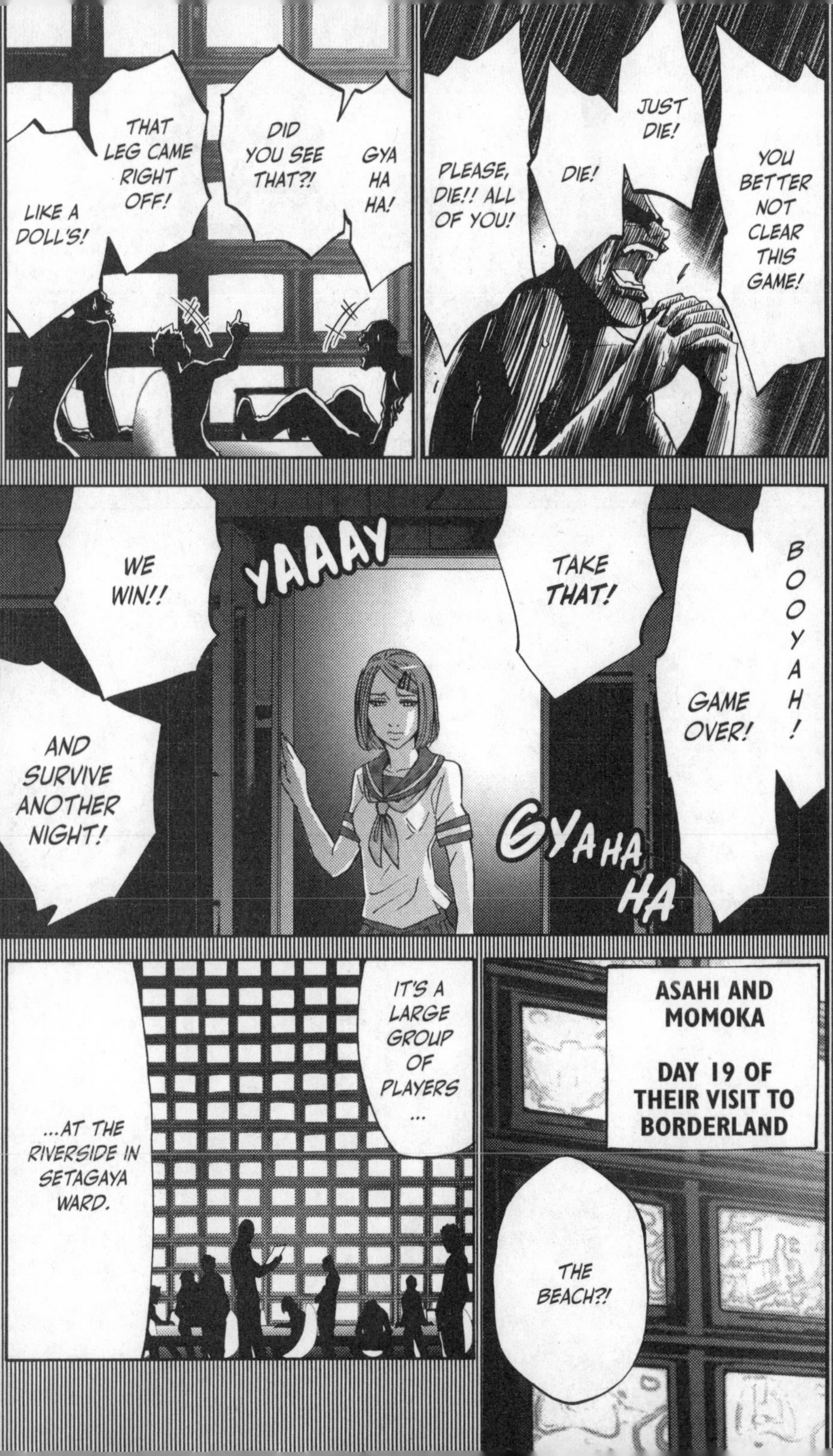
YOU BETTER NOT CLEAR THIS GAME!
JUST DIE!
DIE!
PLEASE, DIE!! ALL OF YOU!
GYA HA HA!
DID YOU SEE THAT?!
THAT LEG CAME RIGHT OFF!
LIKE A DOLL'S!
BOOYAH!
GAME OVER!
TAKE THAT!
GYAHAHA HA
YAAAY
WE WIN!!
AND SURVIVE ANOTHER NIGHT!
ASAHI AND MOMOKA
DAY 19 OF THEIR VISIT TO BORDERLAND
THE BEACH?!
IT'S A LARGE GROUP OF PLAYERS ...
...AT THE RIVERSIDE IN SETAGAYA WARD.

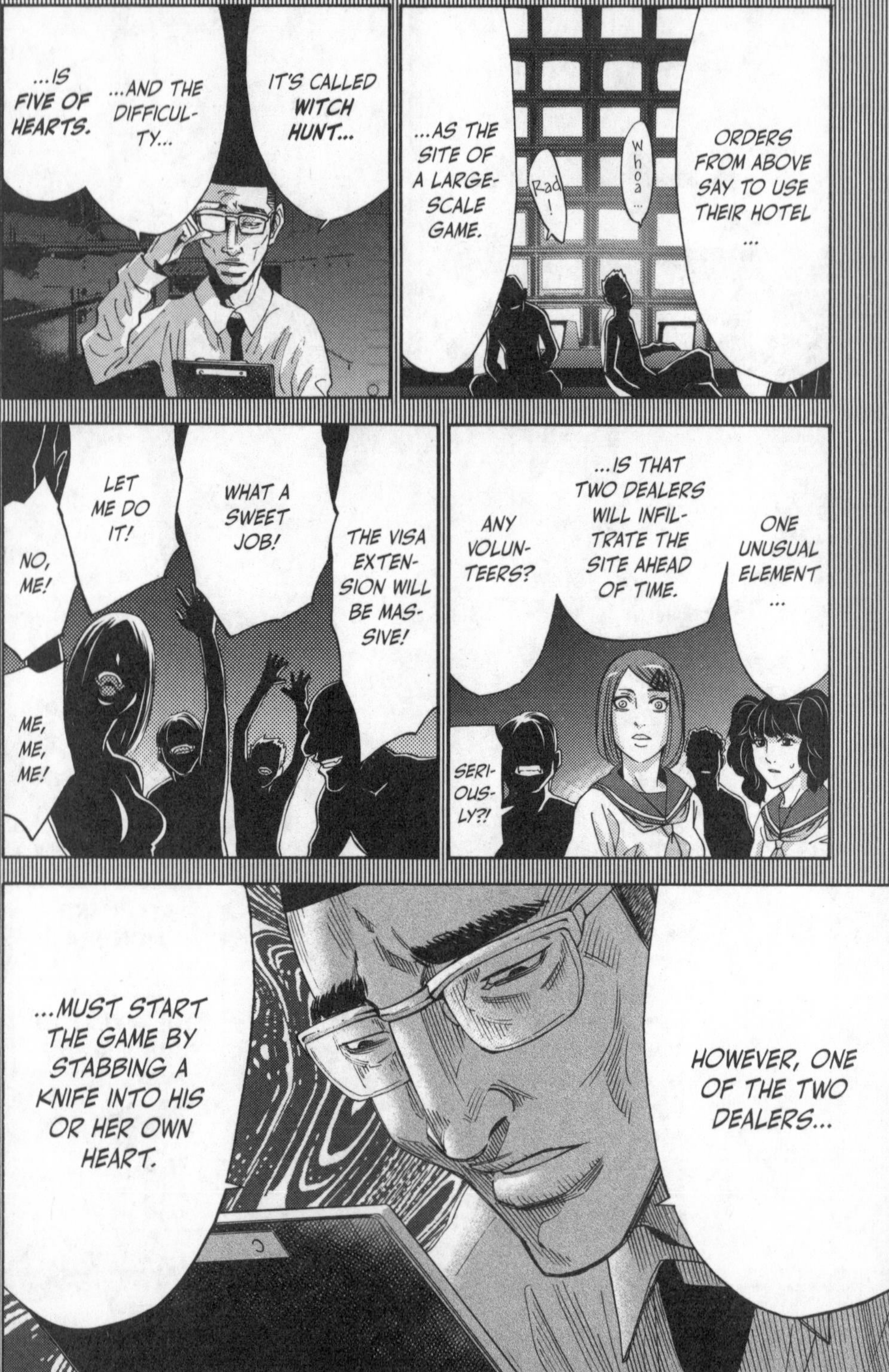

ORDERS FROM ABOVE SAY TO USE THEIR HOTEL ...
Whoa...
Rad!
...AS THE SITE OF A LARGE-SCALE GAME.
IT'S CALLED WITCH HUNT...
...AND THE DIFFICULTY...
...IS FIVE OF HEARTS.
ONE UNUSUAL ELEMENT ...
...IS THAT TWO DEALERS WILL INFILTRATE THE SITE AHEAD OF TIME.
ANY VOLUNTEERS?
SERIOUSLY?!
THE VISA EXTENSION WILL BE MASSIVE!
WHAT A SWEET JOB!
LET ME DO IT!
NO, ME!
ME, ME, ME!
HOWEVER, ONE OF THE TWO DEALERS...
...MUST START THE GAME BY STABBING A KNIFE INTO HIS OR HER OWN HEART.

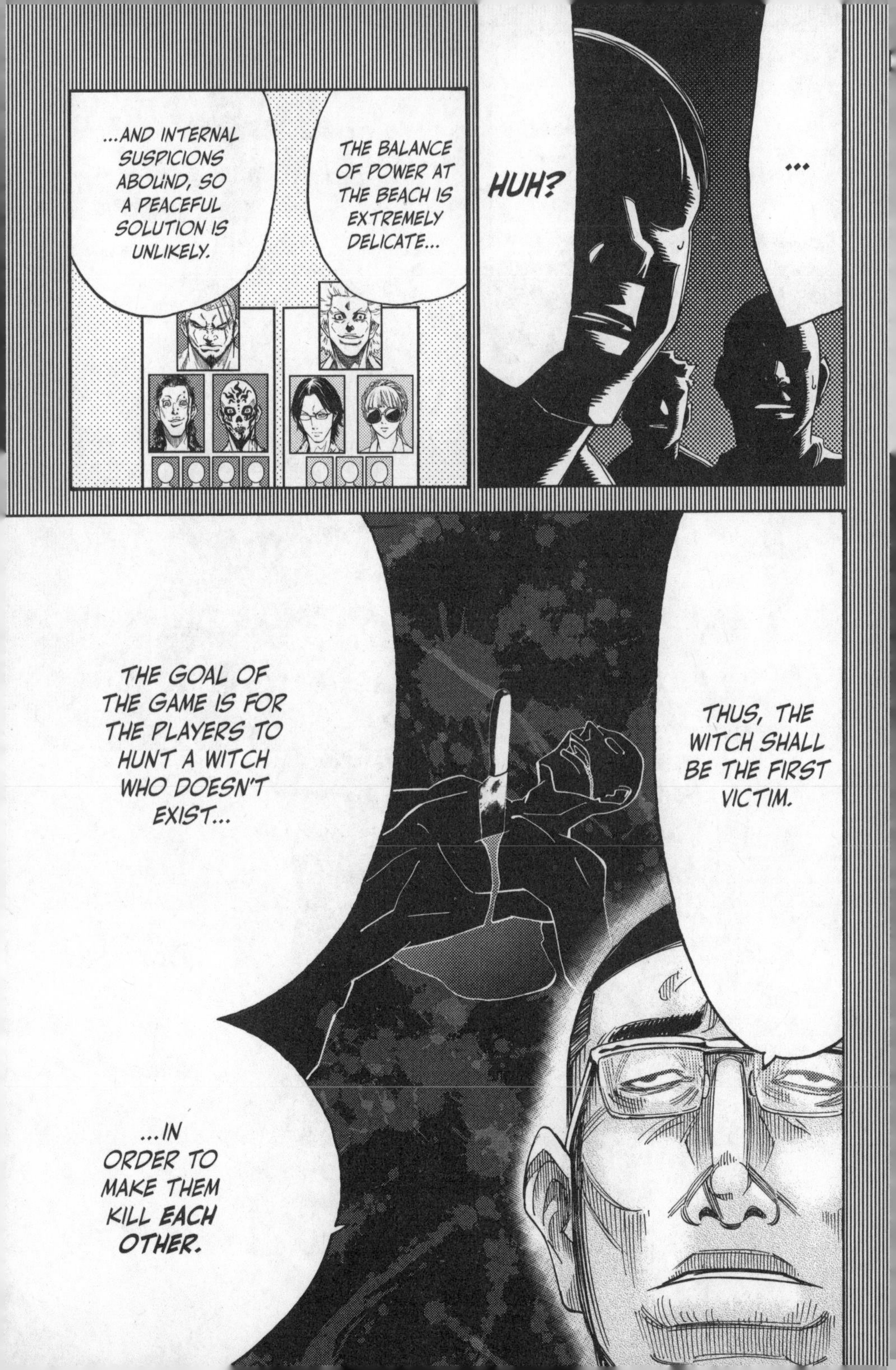
...
HUH?
THE BALANCE OF POWER AT THE BEACH IS EXTREMELY DELICATE...
...AND INTERNAL SUSPICIONS ABOUND, SO A PEACEFUL SOLUTION IS UNLIKELY.
THE GOAL OF THE GAME IS FOR THE PLAYERS TO HUNT A WITCH WHO DOESN'T EXIST...
...IN ORDER TO MAKE THEM KILL EACH OTHER.
THUS, THE WITCH SHALL BE THE FIRST VICTIM.

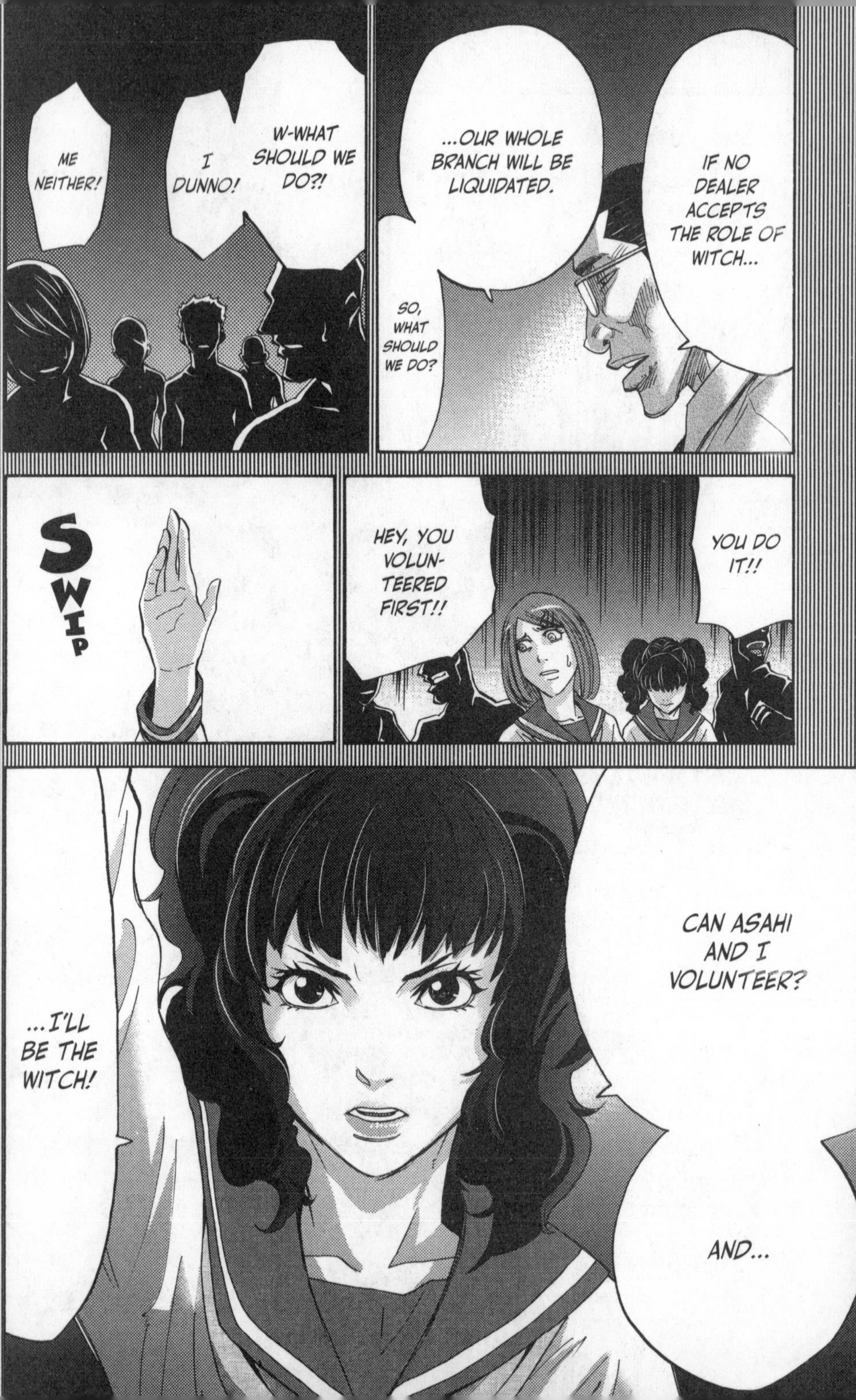
IF NO DEALER ACCEPTS THE ROLE OF WITCH...
...OUR WHOLE BRANCH WILL BE LIQUIDATED.
SO, WHAT SHOULD WE DO?
W-WHAT SHOULD WE DO?!
I DUNNO!
ME NEITHER!
YOU DO IT!!
HEY, YOU VOLUN-TEERED FIRST!!
SWIP
CAN ASAHI AND I VOLUNTEER?
AND...
...I'LL BE THE WITCH!

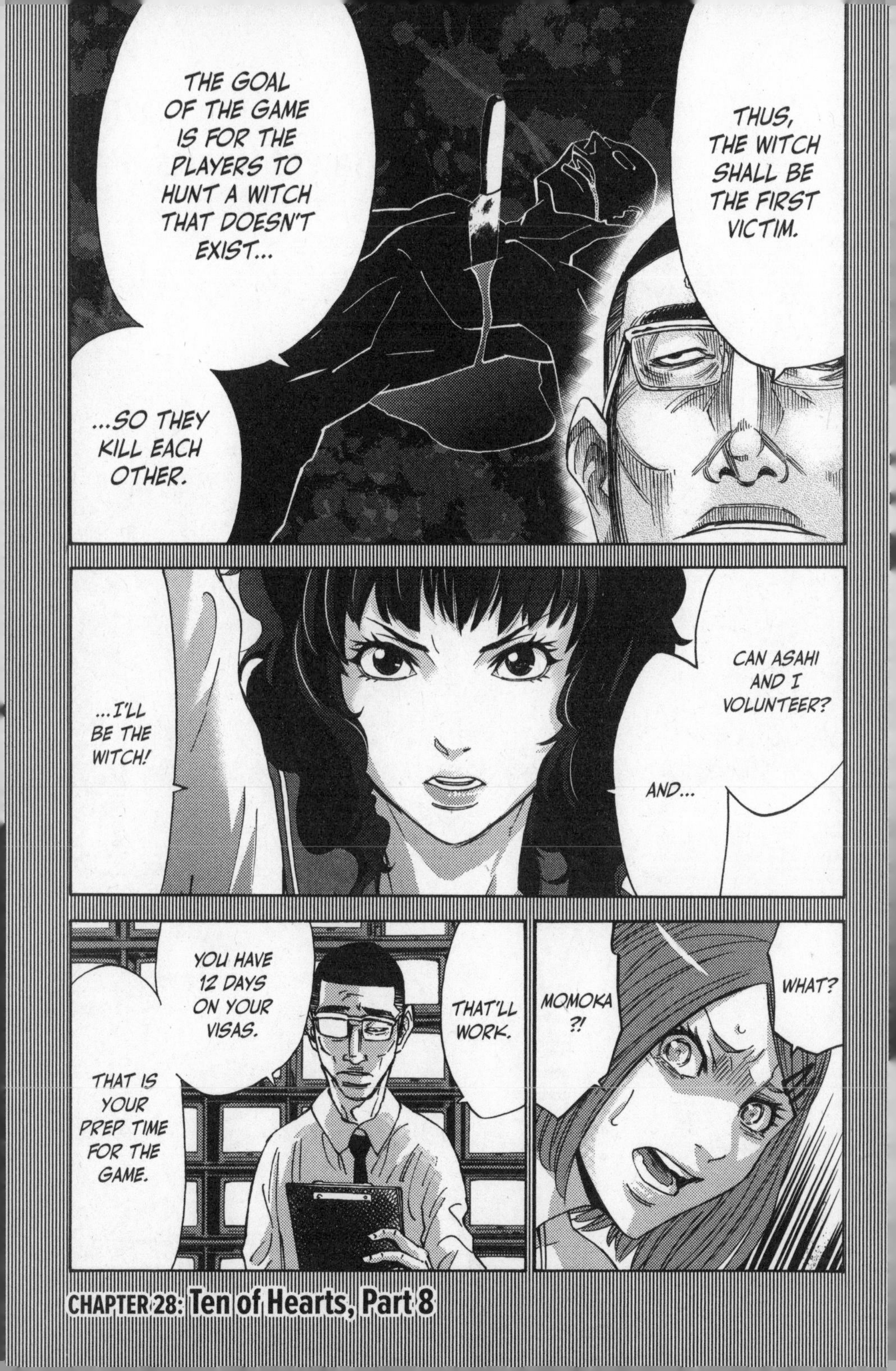
THUS, THE WITCH SHALL BE THE FIRST VICTIM.
THE GOAL OF THE GAME IS FOR THE PLAYERS TO HUNT A WITCH THAT DOESN'T EXIST...
...SO THEY KILL EACH OTHER.
CAN ASAHI AND I VOLUNTEER?
AND...
...I'LL BE THE WITCH!
WHAT?
MOMOKA ?!
THAT'LL WORK.
YOU HAVE 12 DAYS ON YOUR VISAS.
THAT IS YOUR PREP TIME FOR THE GAME.

CHAPTER 28: Ten of Hearts, Part 8

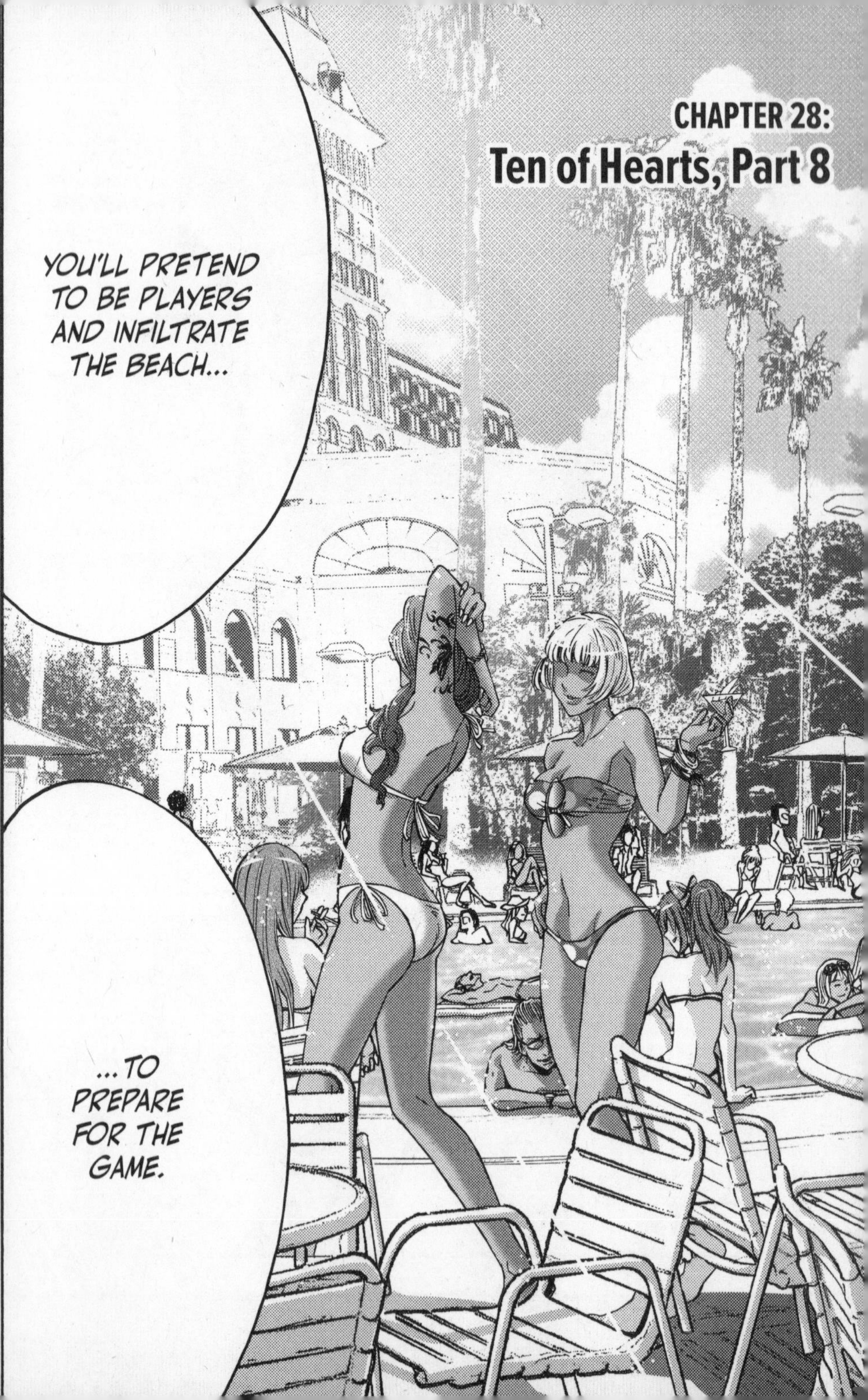
CHAPTER 28:
Ten of Hearts, Part 8
YOU'LL PRETEND TO BE PLAYERS AND INFILTRATE THE BEACH...
...TO PREPARE FOR THE GAME.

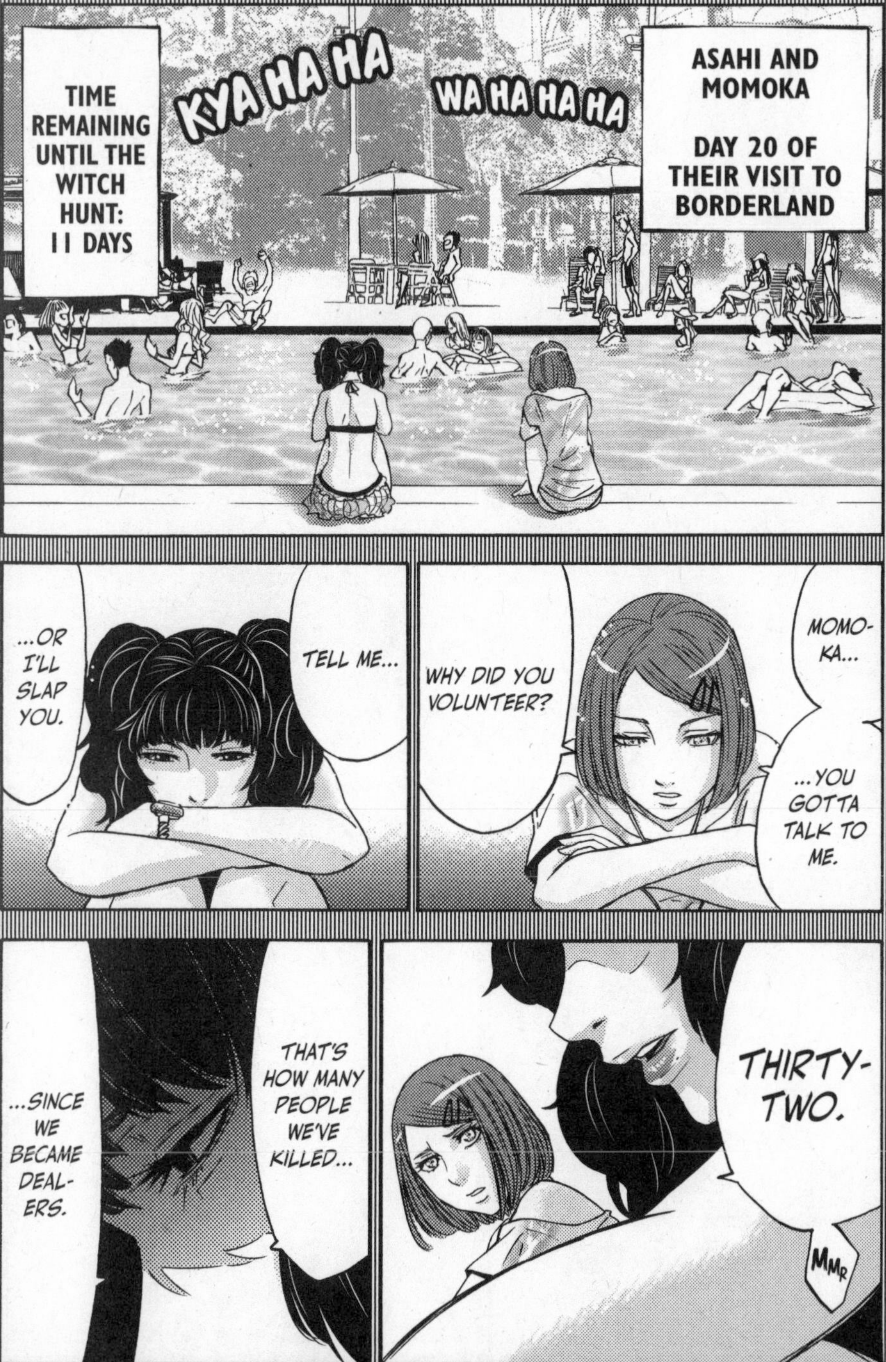
ASAHI AND MOMOKA
DAY 20 OF THEIR VISIT TO BORDERLAND
WA HA HA HA
KYA HA HA
TIME REMAINING UNTIL THE WITCH HUNT: 11 DAYS
MOMO-KA...
WHY DID YOU VOLUNTEER?
...YOU GOTTA TALK TO ME.
TELL ME...
...OR I'LL SLAP YOU.
THIRTY-TWO.
MMR
THAT'S HOW MANY PEOPLE WE'VE KILLED...
...SINCE WE BECAME DEAL-ERS.

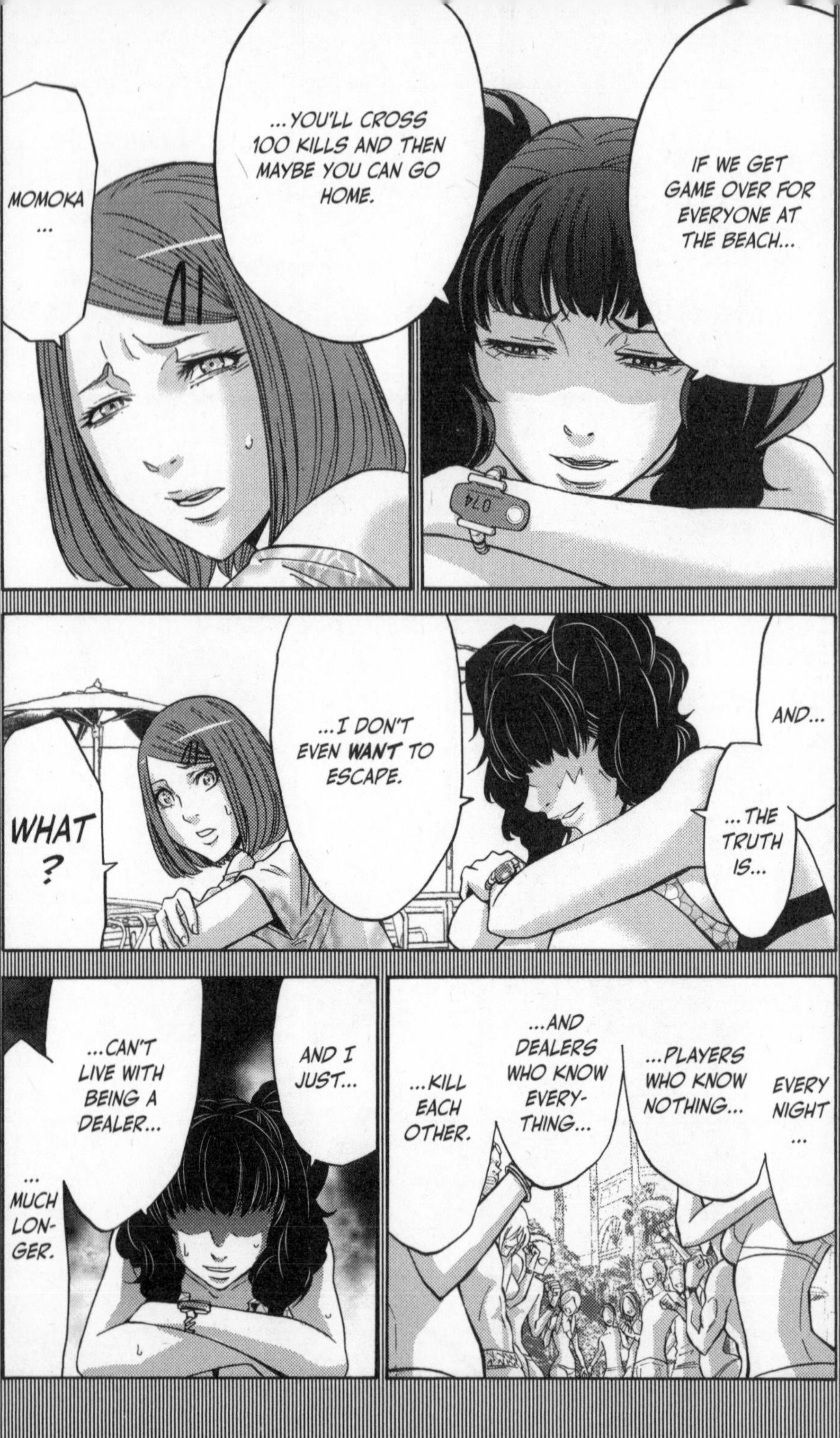
IF WE GET GAME OVER FOR EVERYONE AT THE BEACH...
...YOU'LL CROSS 100 KILLS AND THEN MAYBE YOU CAN GO HOME.
MOMOKA ...
AND...
...THE TRUTH IS...
...I DON'T EVEN WANT TO ESCAPE.
WHAT ?
EVERY NIGHT ...
...PLAYERS WHO KNOW NOTHING...
...AND DEALERS WHO KNOW EVERY-THING...
...KILL EACH OTHER.
AND I JUST...
...CAN'T LIVE WITH BEING A DEALER...
... MUCH LON-GER.

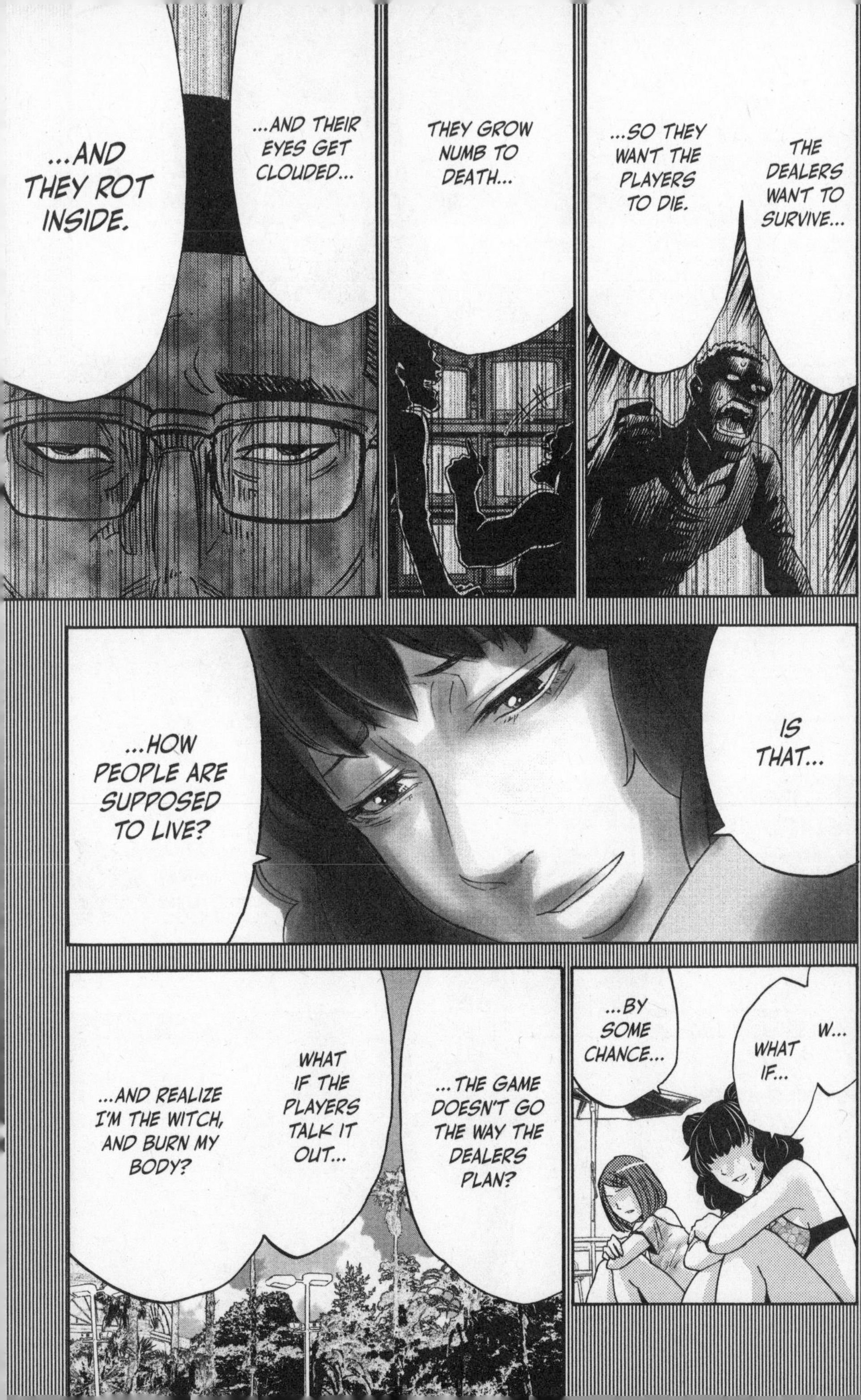

THE DEALERS WANT TO SURVIVE...
...SO THEY WANT THE PLAYERS TO DIE.
THEY GROW NUMB TO DEATH...
...AND THEIR EYES GET CLOUDED...
...AND THEY ROT INSIDE.
IS THAT...
...HOW PEOPLE ARE SUPPOSED TO LIVE?
W...
WHAT IF...
...BY SOME CHANCE...
...THE GAME DOESN'T GO THE WAY THE DEALERS PLAN?
WHAT IF THE PLAYERS TALK IT OUT...
...AND REALIZE I'M THE WITCH, AND BURN MY BODY?

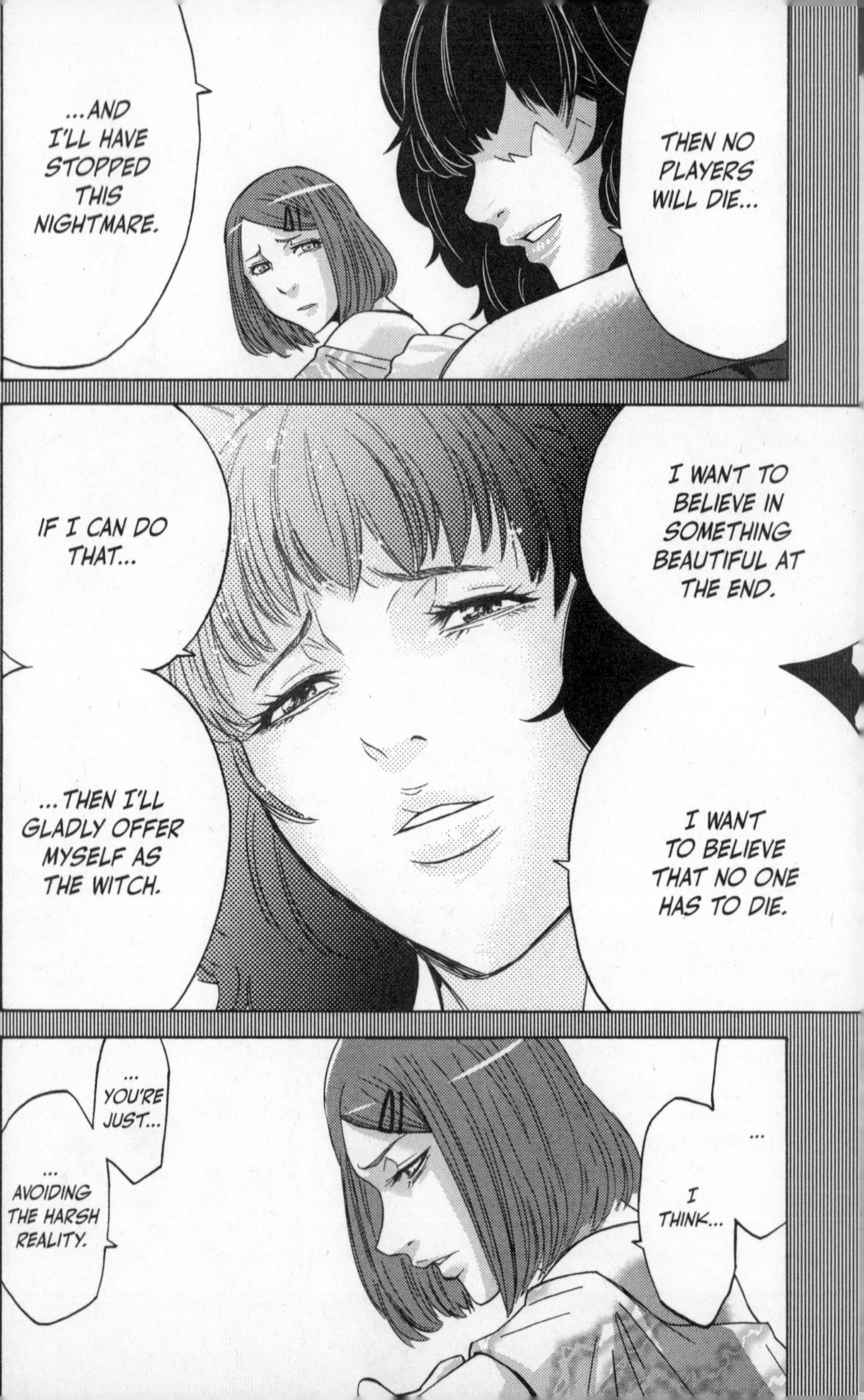
THEN NO PLAYERS WILL DIE...
...AND I'LL HAVE STOPPED THIS NIGHTMARE.
I WANT TO BELIEVE IN SOMETHING BEAUTIFUL AT THE END.
I WANT TO BELIEVE THAT NO ONE HAS TO DIE.
IF I CAN DO THAT...
...THEN I'LL GLADLY OFFER MYSELF AS THE WITCH.
... I THINK...
... YOU'RE JUST...
... AVOIDING THE HARSH REALITY.

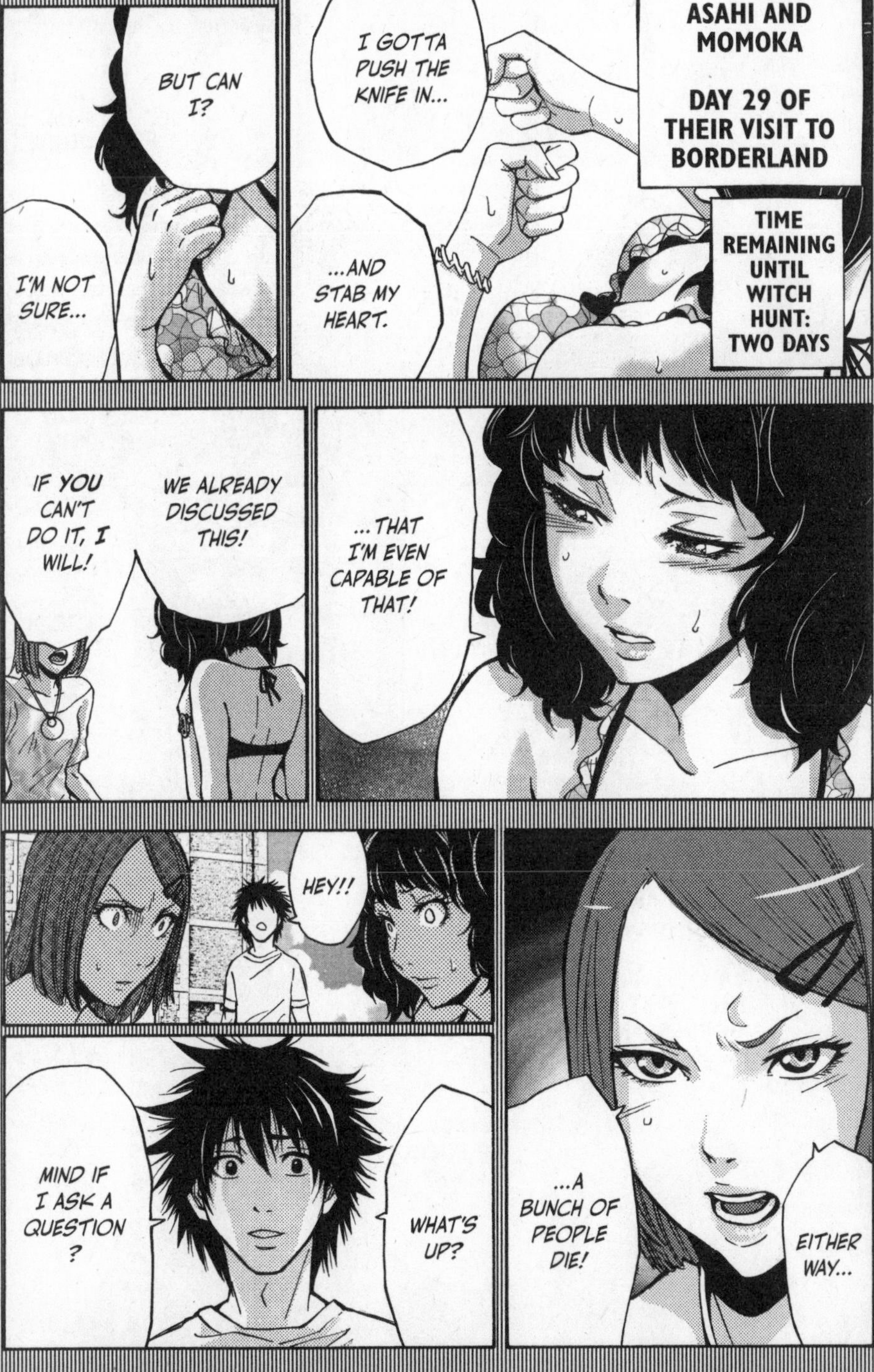
ASAHI AND MOMOKA
DAY 29 OF THEIR VISIT TO BORDERLAND
TIME REMAINING UNTIL WITCH HUNT: TWO DAYS
I GOTTA PUSH THE KNIFE IN...
...AND STAB MY HEART.
BUT CAN I?
I'M NOT SURE...
...THAT I'M EVEN CAPABLE OF THAT!
WE ALREADY DISCUSSED THIS!
IF YOU CAN'T DO IT, I WILL!
EITHER WAY...
...A BUNCH OF PEOPLE DIE!
HEY!!
WHAT'S UP?
MIND IF I ASK A QUESTION?

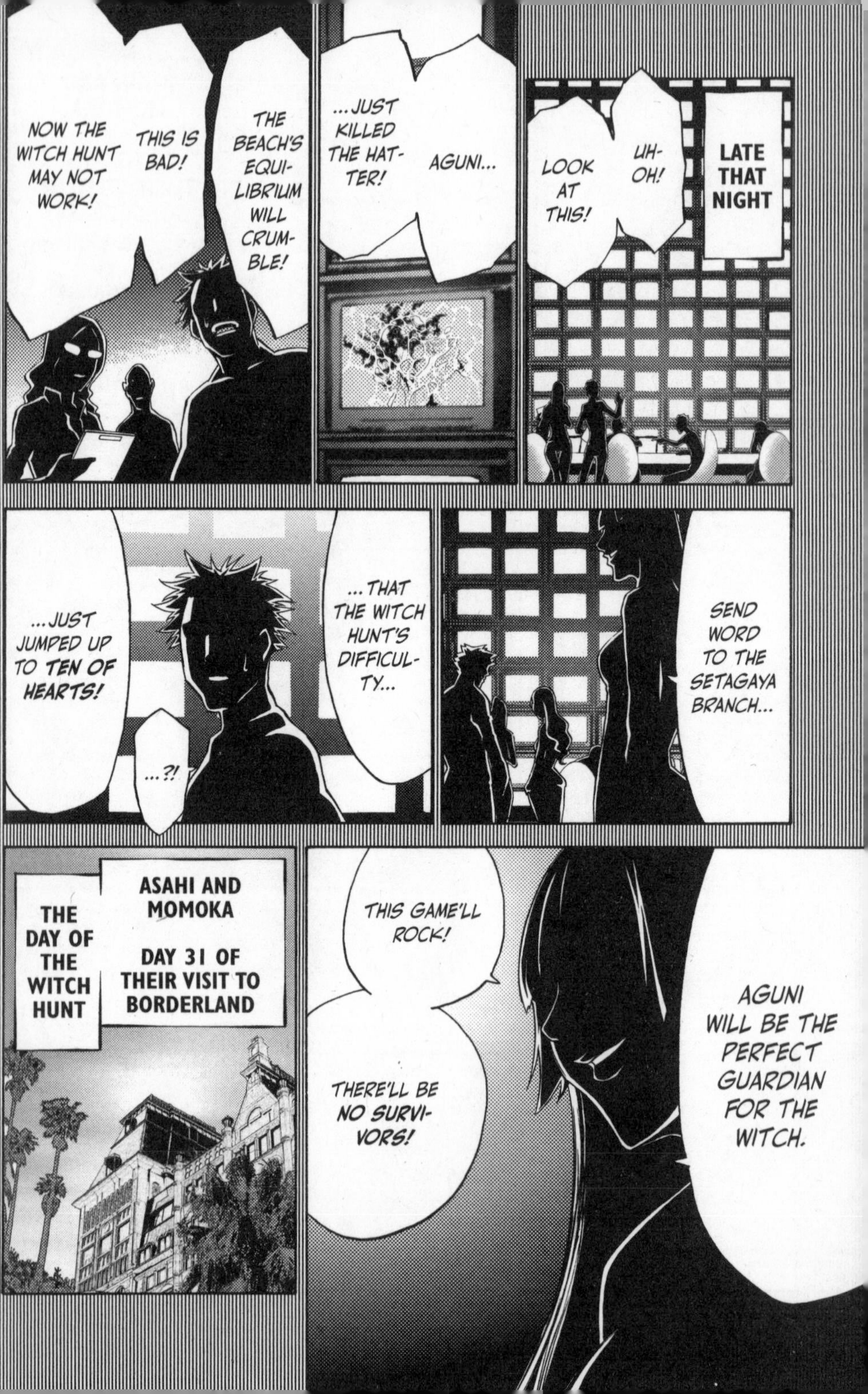
LATE THAT NIGHT
UH-OH!
LOOK AT THIS!
AGUNI...
...JUST KILLED THE HAT-TER!
THE BEACH'S EQUI-LIBRIUM WILL CRUM-BLE!
THIS IS BAD!
NOW THE WITCH HUNT MAY NOT WORK!
SEND WORD TO THE SETAGAYA BRANCH...
...THAT THE WITCH HUNT'S DIFFICUL-TY...
...JUST JUMPED UP TO TEN OF HEARTS!
...?!
AGUNI WILL BE THE PERFECT GUARDIAN FOR THE WITCH.
THIS GAME'LL ROCK!
THERE'LL BE NO SURVI-VORS!
ASAHI AND MOMOKA
DAY 31 OF THEIR VISIT TO BORDERLAND
THE DAY OF THE WITCH HUNT

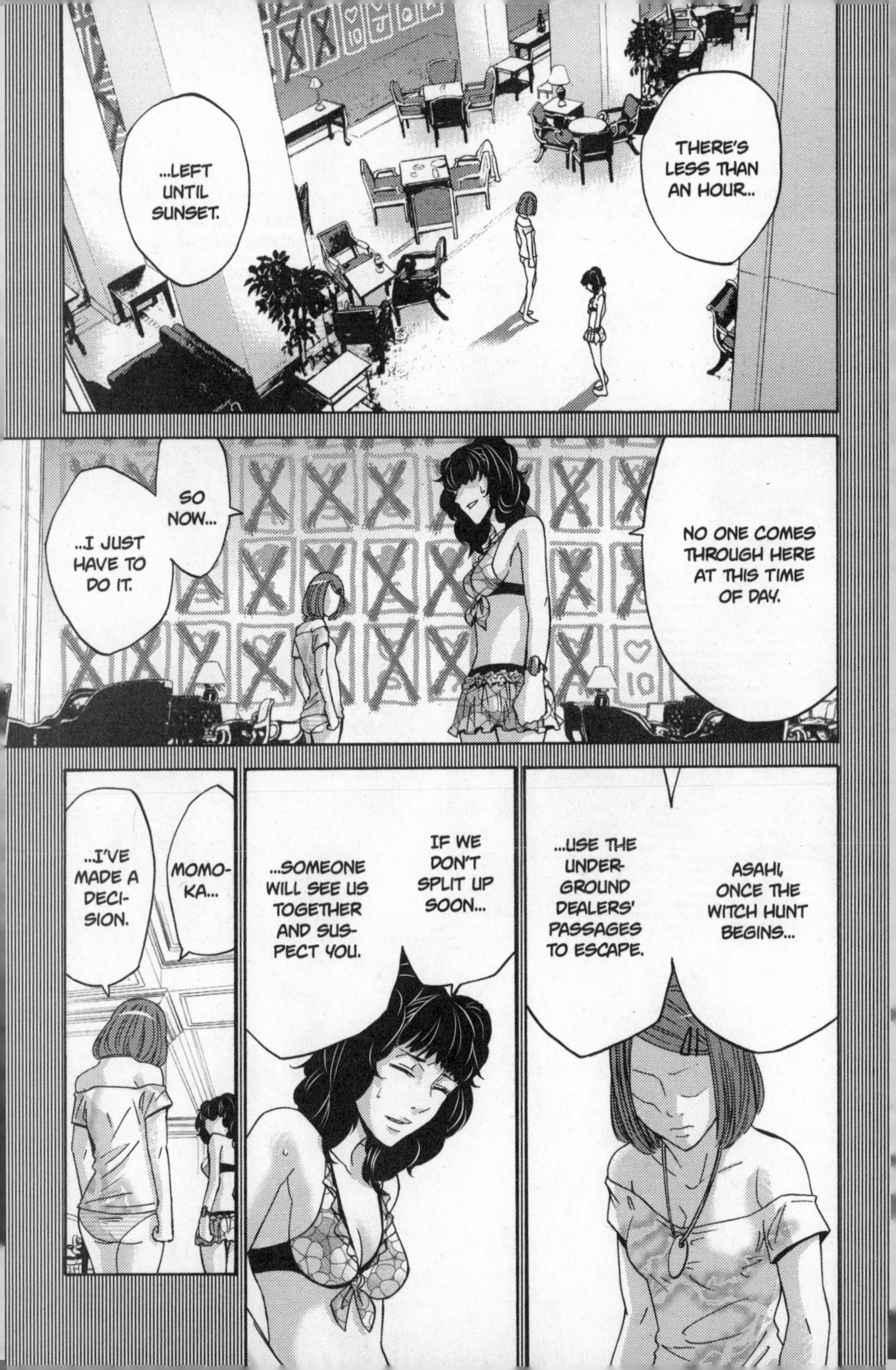
THERE'S LESS THAN AN HOUR...
...LEFT UNTIL SUNSET.
NO ONE COMES THROUGH HERE AT THIS TIME OF DAY.
SO NOW...
...I JUST HAVE TO DO IT.
ASAHI, ONCE THE WITCH HUNT BEGINS...
...USE THE UNDERGROUND DEALERS' PASSAGES TO ESCAPE.
IF WE DON'T SPLIT UP SOON...
...SOMEONE WILL SEE US TOGETHER AND SUSPECT YOU.
MOMOKA...
...I'VE MADE A DECISION.

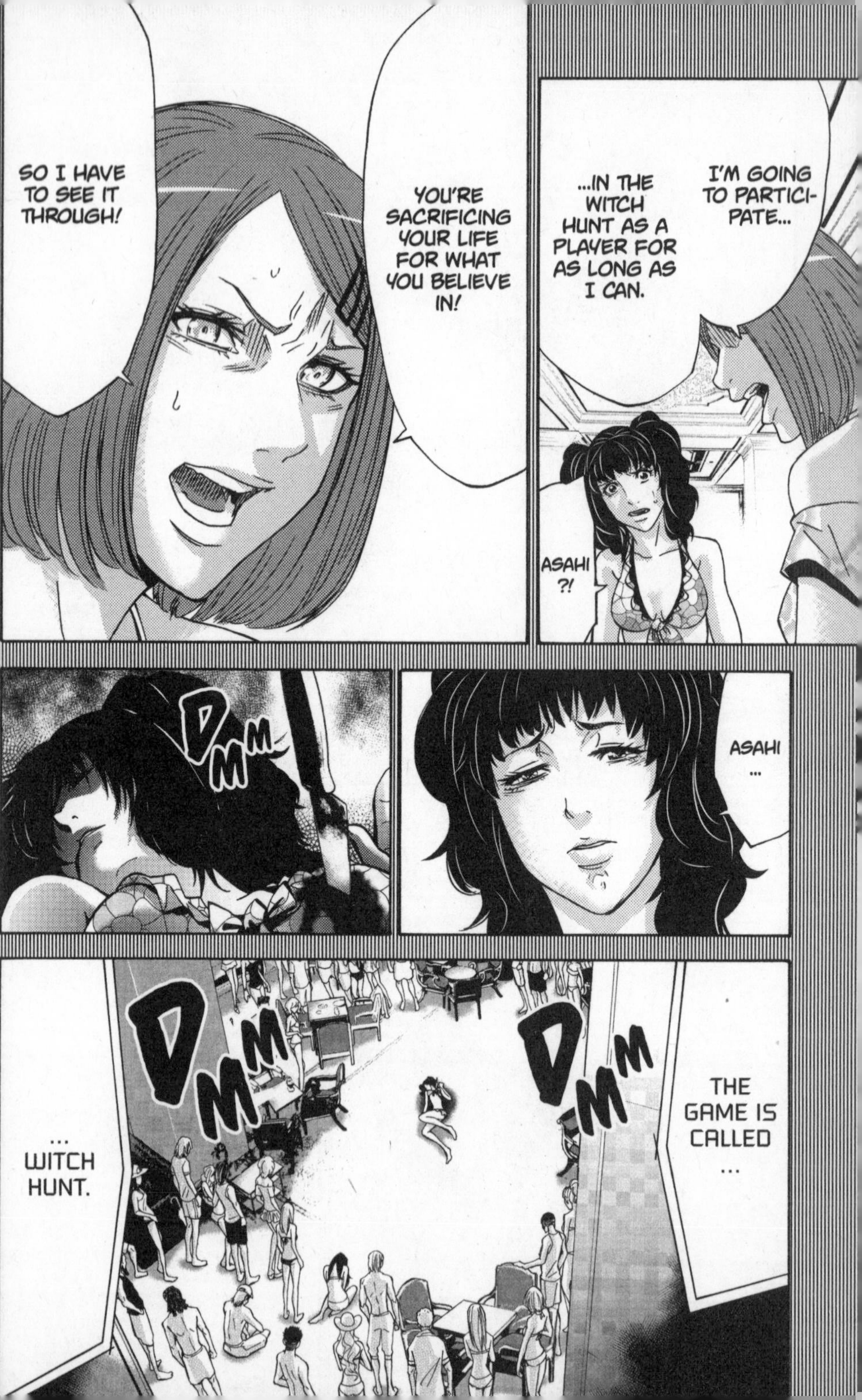
I'M GOING TO PARTICI- PATE...
...IN THE WITCH HUNT AS A PLAYER FOR AS LONG AS I CAN.
ASAHI ?!
YOU'RE SACRIFICING YOUR LIFE FOR WHAT YOU BELIEVE IN!
SO I HAVE TO SEE IT THROUGH!
ASAHI ...
DMM
THE GAME IS CALLED ...
DMM
DMM
... WITCH HUNT.

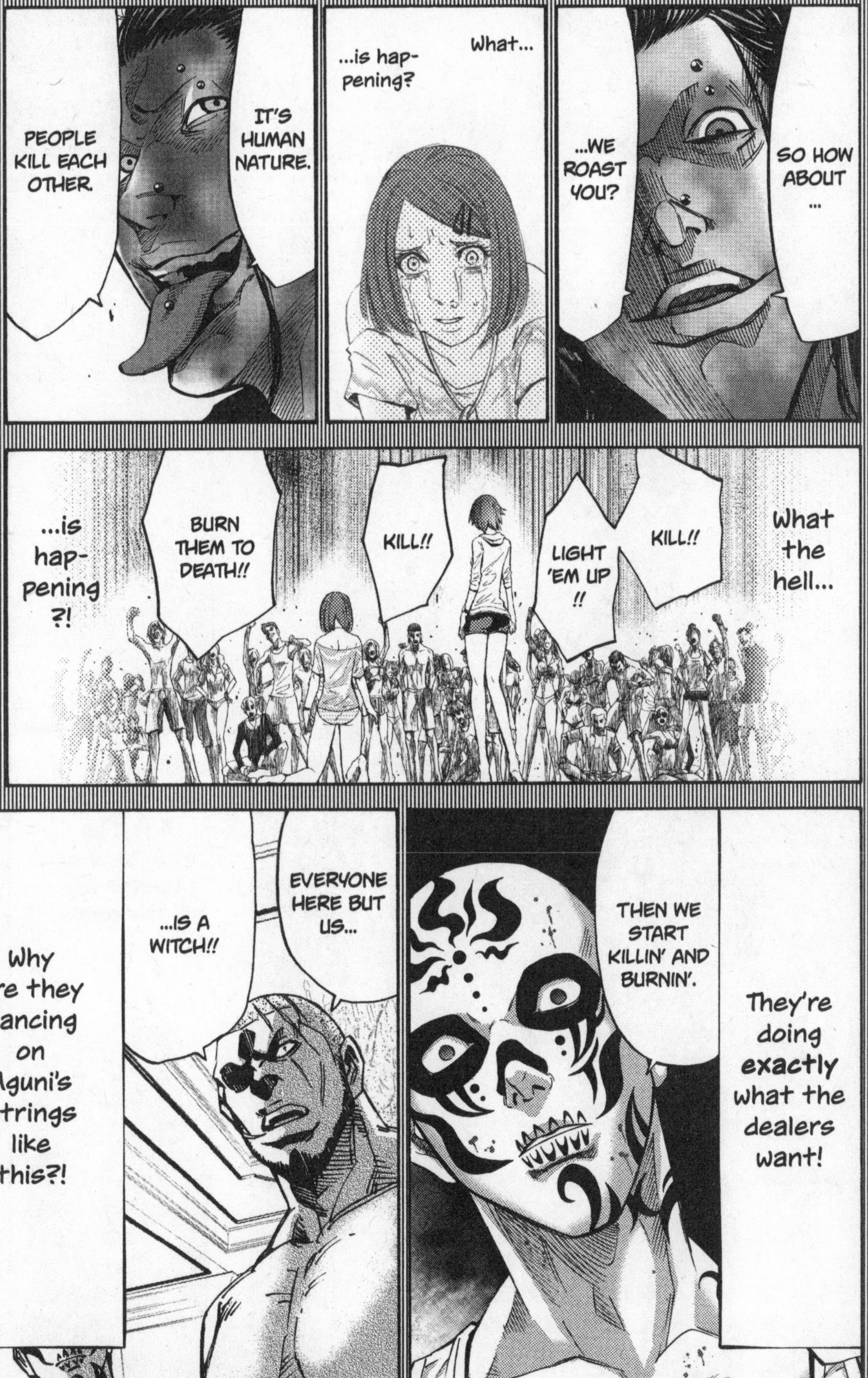
SO HOW ABOUT ...
...WE ROAST YOU?
What...
...is hap-pening?
IT'S HUMAN NATURE.
PEOPLE KILL EACH OTHER.
What the hell...
KILL!!
LIGHT 'EM UP !!
KILL!!
BURN THEM TO DEATH!!
...is hap-pening ?!
THEN WE START KILLIN' AND BURNIN'.
They're doing exactly what the dealers want!
EVERYONE HERE BUT US...
...IS A WITCH!!
Why are they dancing on Aguni's strings like this?!

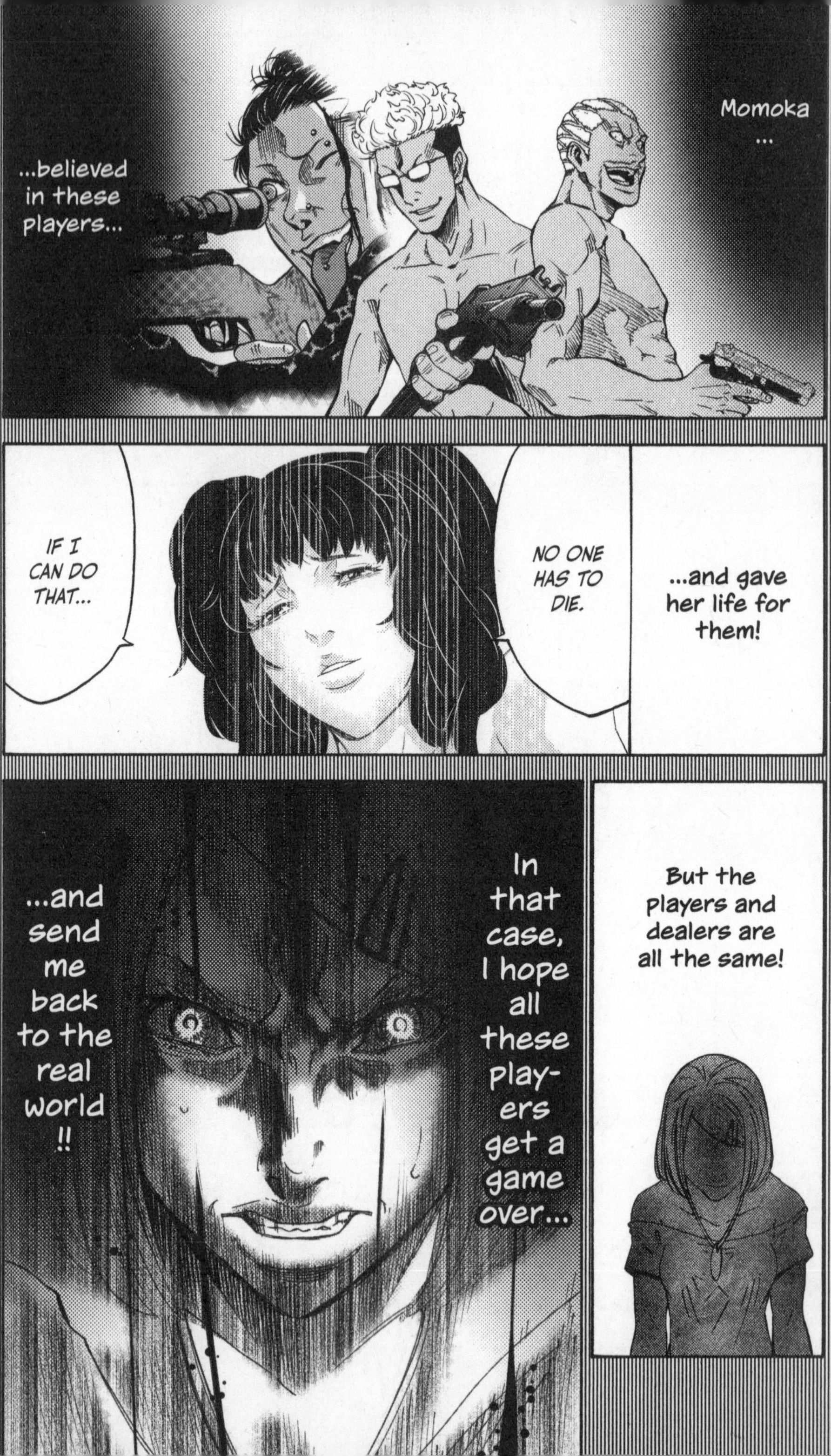
Momoka ...
...believed in these players...
...and gave her life for them!
NO ONE HAS TO DIE.
IF I CAN DO THAT...
But the players and dealers are all the same!
In that case, I hope all these play-ers get a game over...
...and send me back to the real world!!

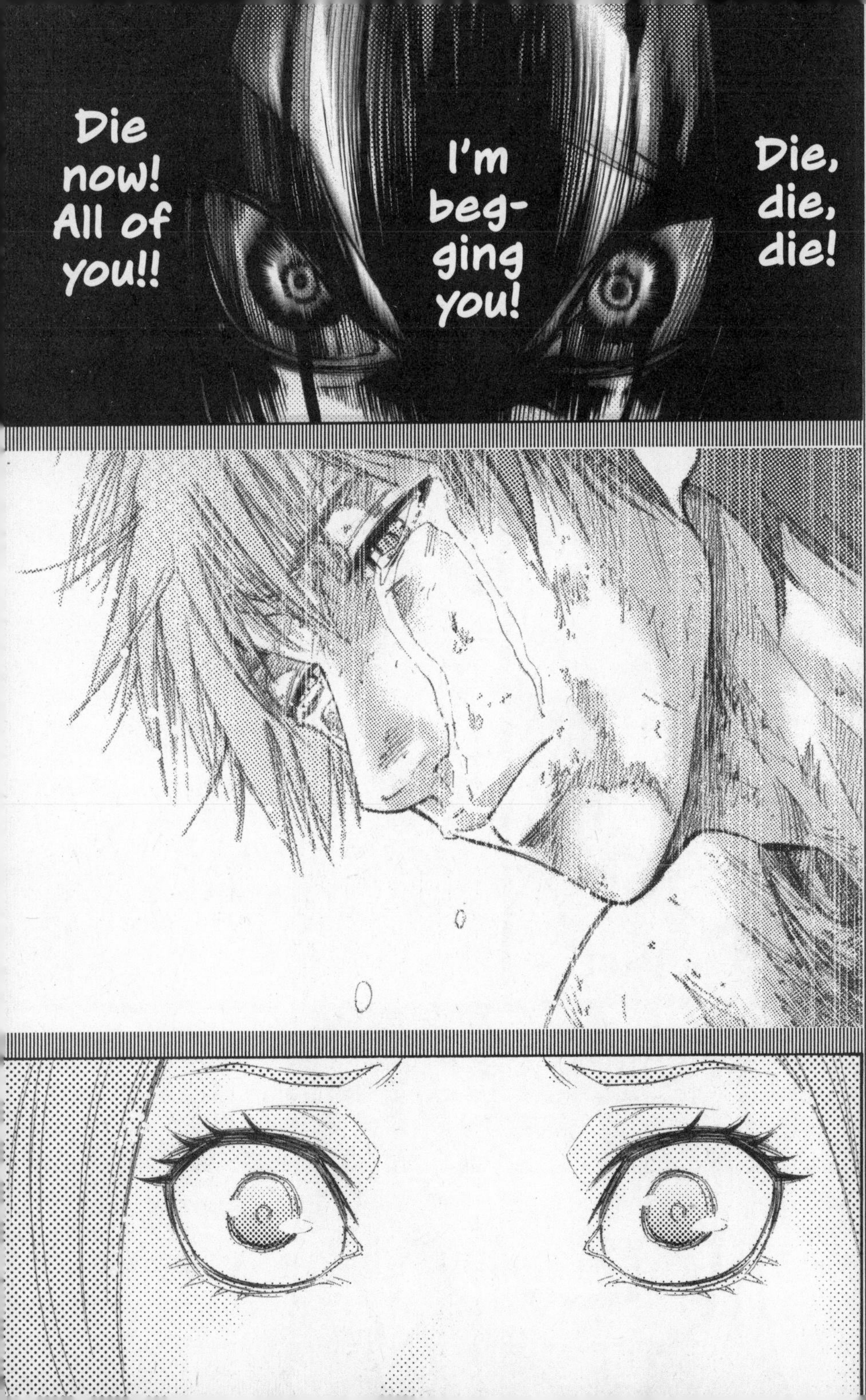
Die, die, die!
I'm beg-ging you!
Die now! All of you!!

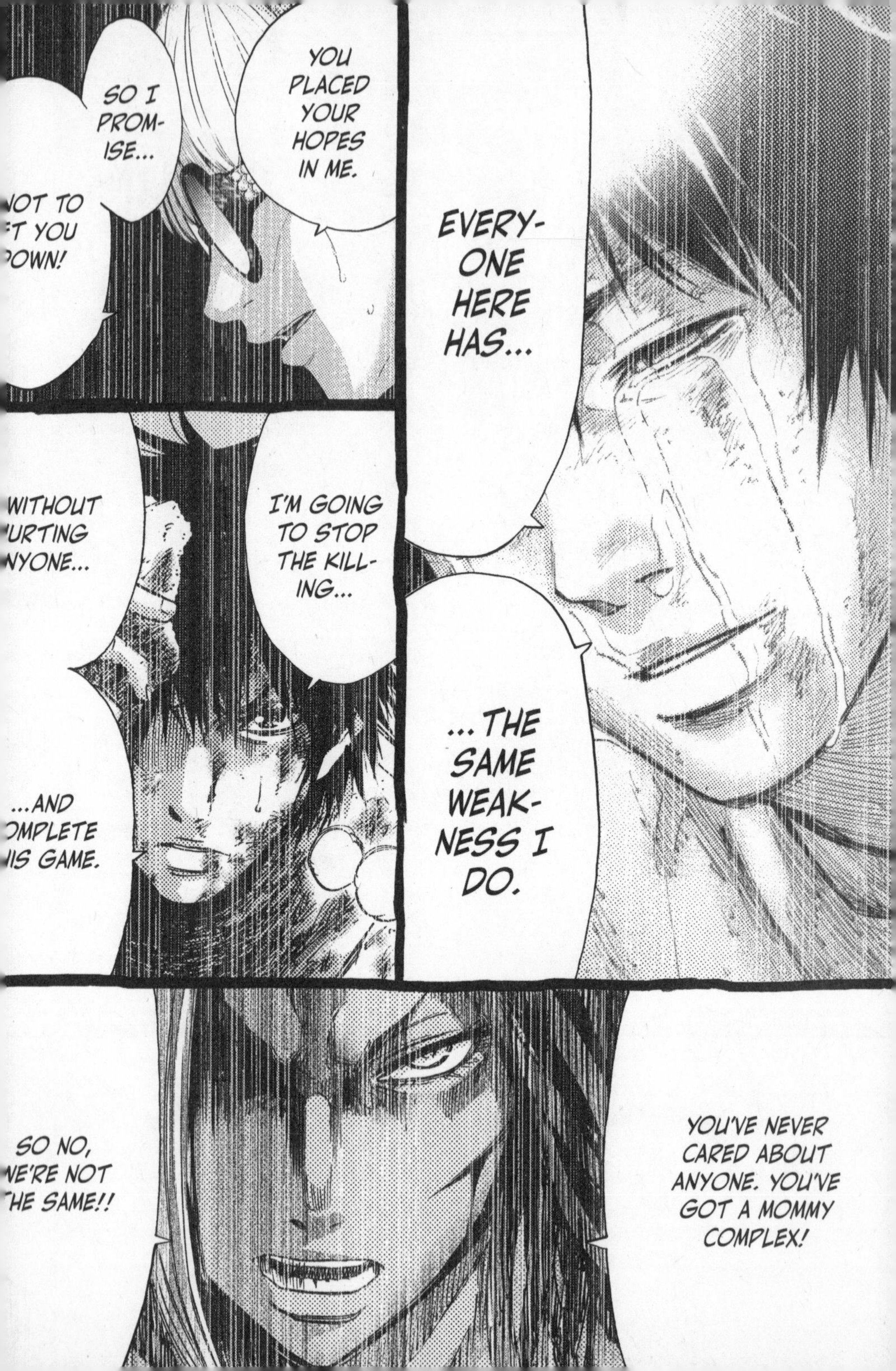
EVERY-ONE HERE HAS...
...THE SAME WEAK-NESS I DO.
YOU PLACED YOUR HOPES IN ME.
SO I PROM-ISE...
NOT TO T YOU OWN!
I'M GOING TO STOP THE KILL-ING...
WITHOUT URTING NYONE...
...AND OMPLETE IS GAME.
YOU'VE NEVER CARED ABOUT ANYONE. YOU'VE GOT A MOMMY COMPLEX!
SO NO, E'RE NOT HE SAME!!

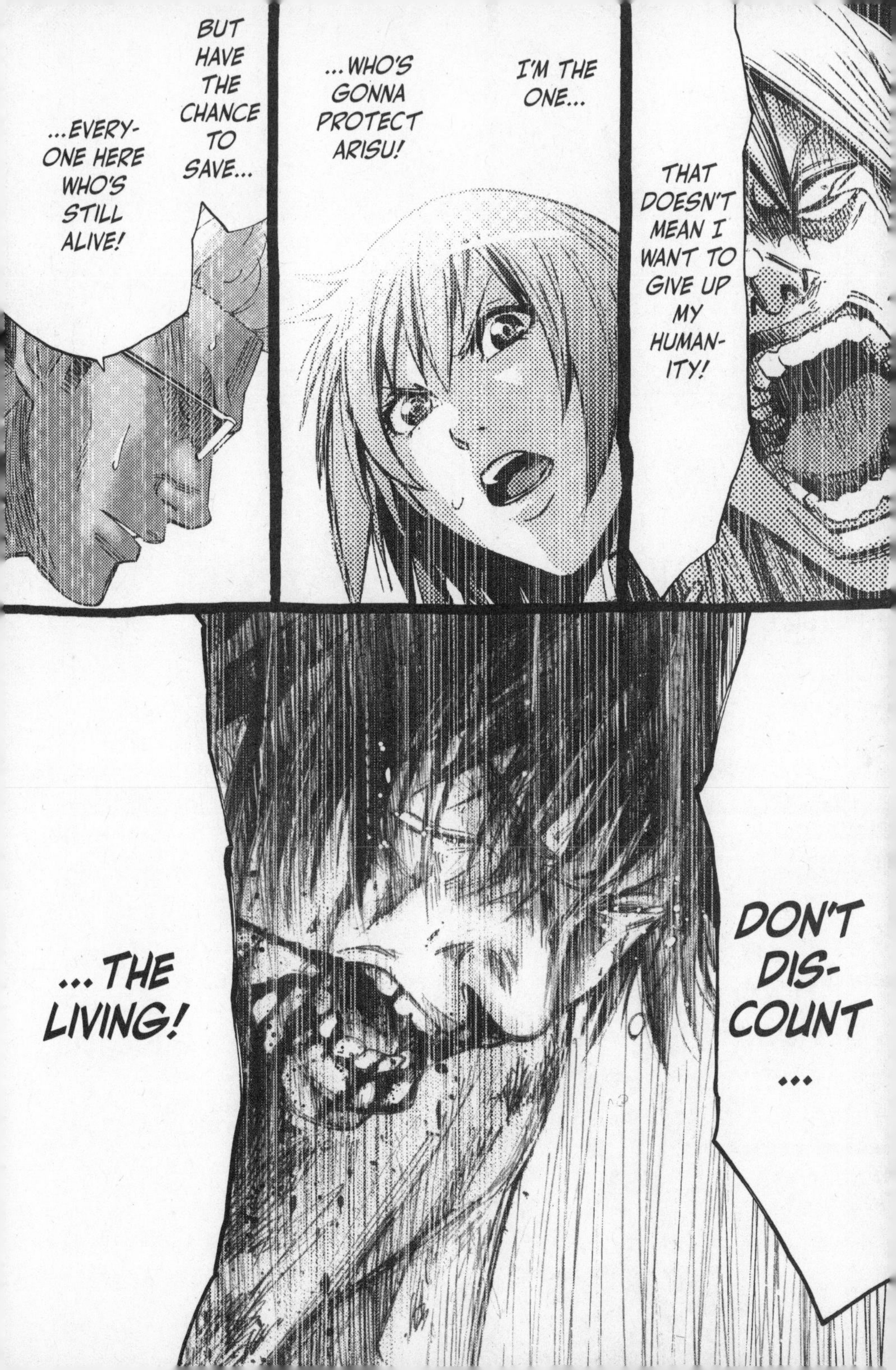
THAT DOESN'T MEAN I WANT TO GIVE UP MY HUMAN-ITY!
I'M THE ONE...
...WHO'S GONNA PROTECT ARISU!
BUT HAVE THE CHANCE TO SAVE...
...EVERY-ONE HERE WHO'S STILL ALIVE!
DON'T DIS-COUNT ...
...THE LIVING!

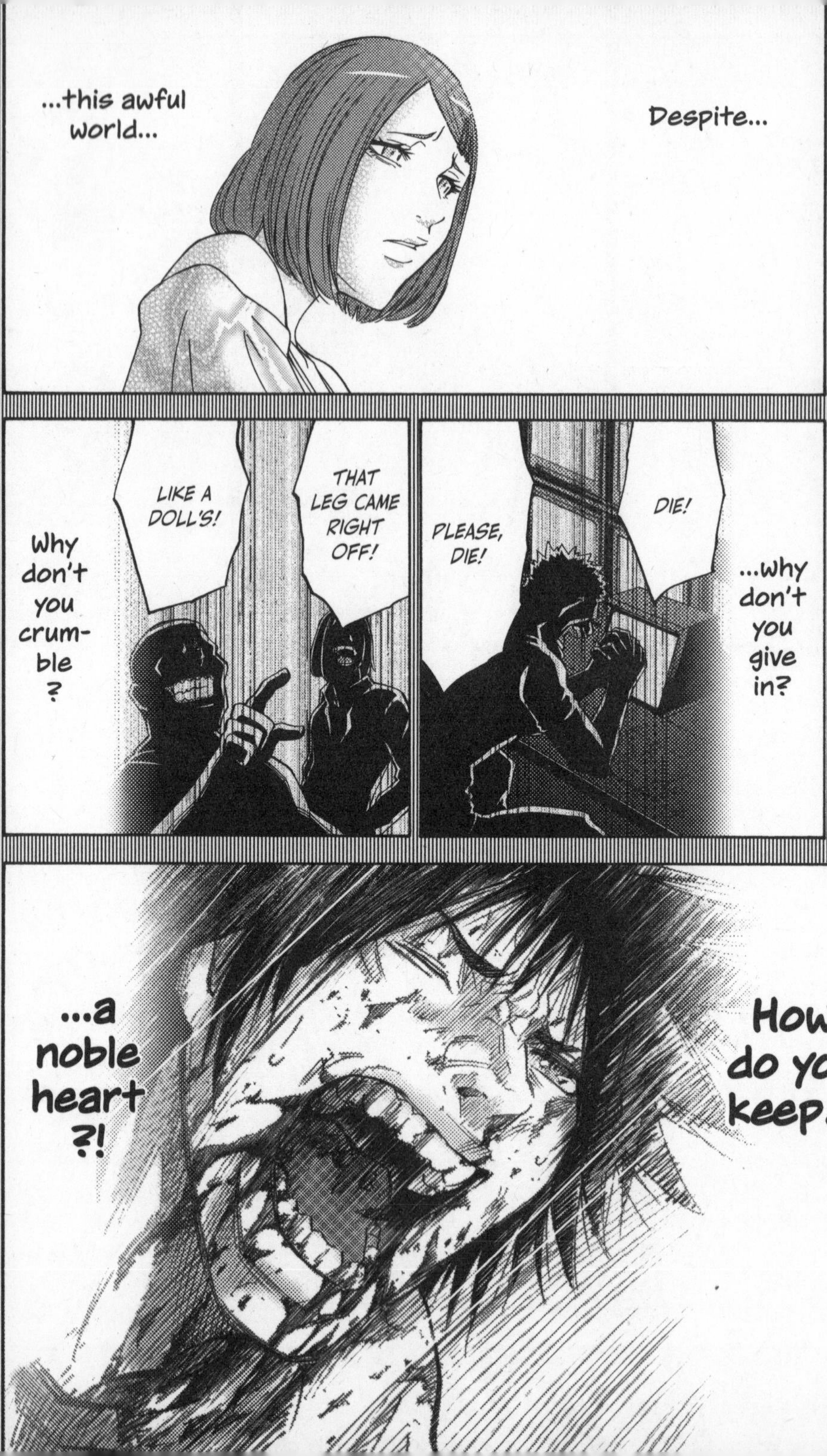
Despite...
...this awful world...
...why don't you give in?
DIE!
PLEASE, DIE!
THAT LEG CAME RIGHT OFF!
LIKE A DOLL'S!
Why don't you crum-ble?
How do you keep...
...a noble heart?!

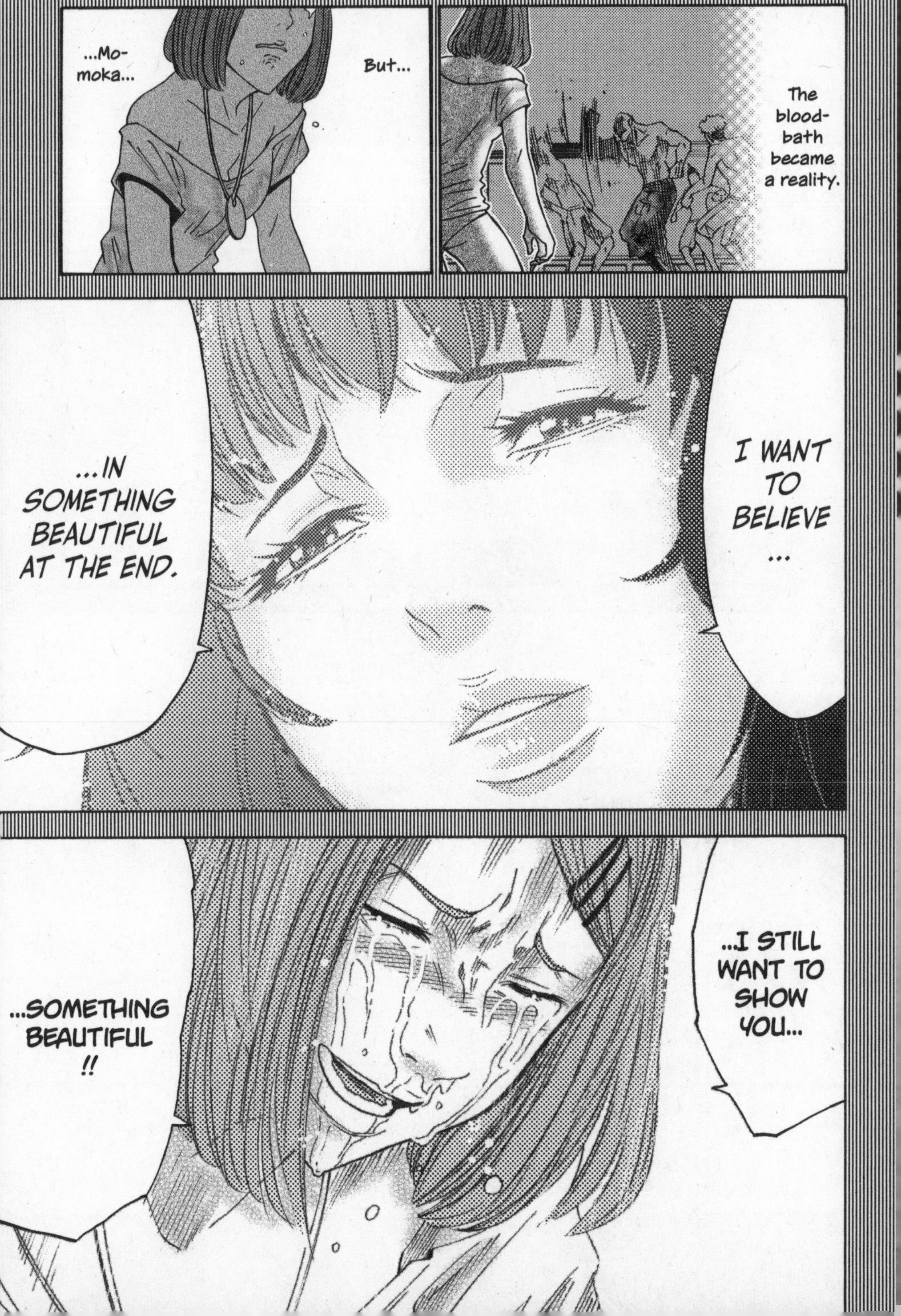
The blood-bath became a reality.
But...
...Mo-moka...
I WANT TO BELIEVE...
...IN SOMETHING BEAUTIFUL AT THE END.
...I STILL WANT TO SHOW YOU...
...SOMETHING BEAUTIFUL!!

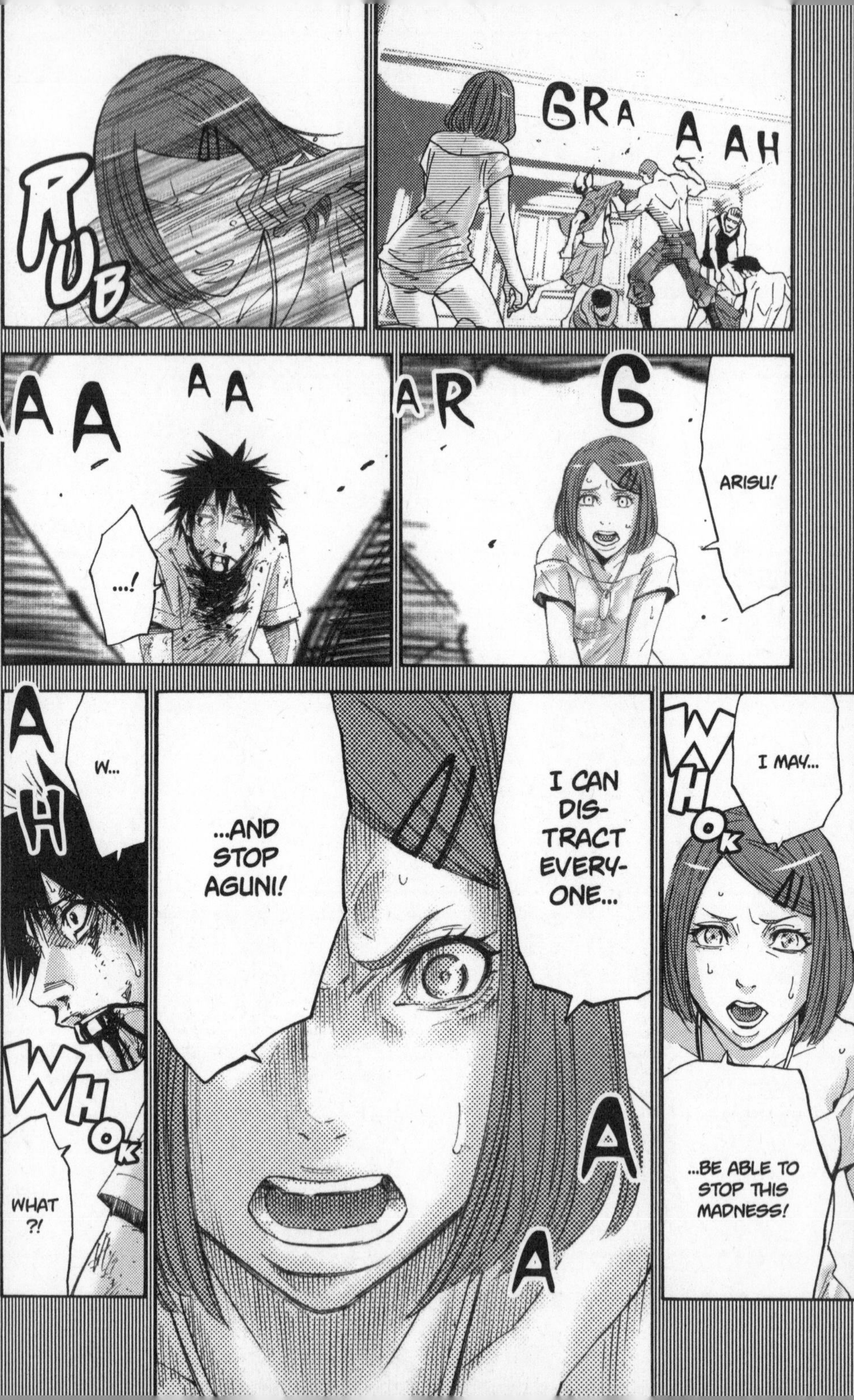
GRA AAH
RUB
ARISU!
AR G
AAA AA
...!
I MAY...
WHOK
...BE ABLE TO STOP THIS MADNESS!
I CAN DISTRACT EVERYONE...
...AND STOP AGUNI!
A A
W...
AHH
WHOK
WHAT?!

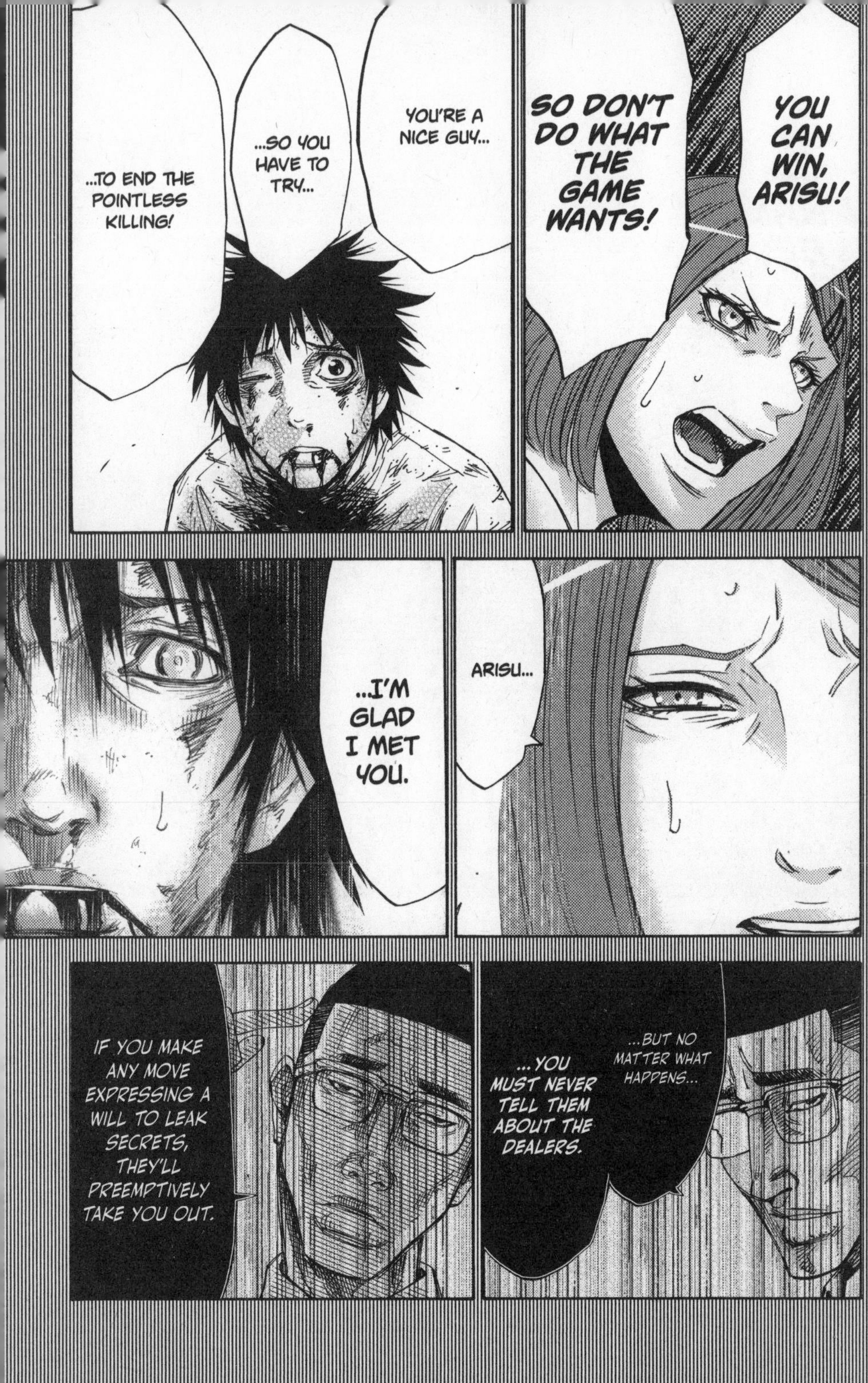
YOU CAN WIN, ARISU!
SO DON'T DO WHAT THE GAME WANTS!
YOU'RE A NICE GUY...
...SO YOU HAVE TO TRY...
...TO END THE POINTLESS KILLING!
ARISU...
...I'M GLAD I MET YOU.
...BUT NO MATTER WHAT HAPPENS...
...YOU MUST NEVER TELL THEM ABOUT THE DEALERS.
IF YOU MAKE ANY MOVE EXPRESSING A WILL TO LEAK SECRETS, THEY'LL PREEMPTIVELY TAKE YOU OUT.

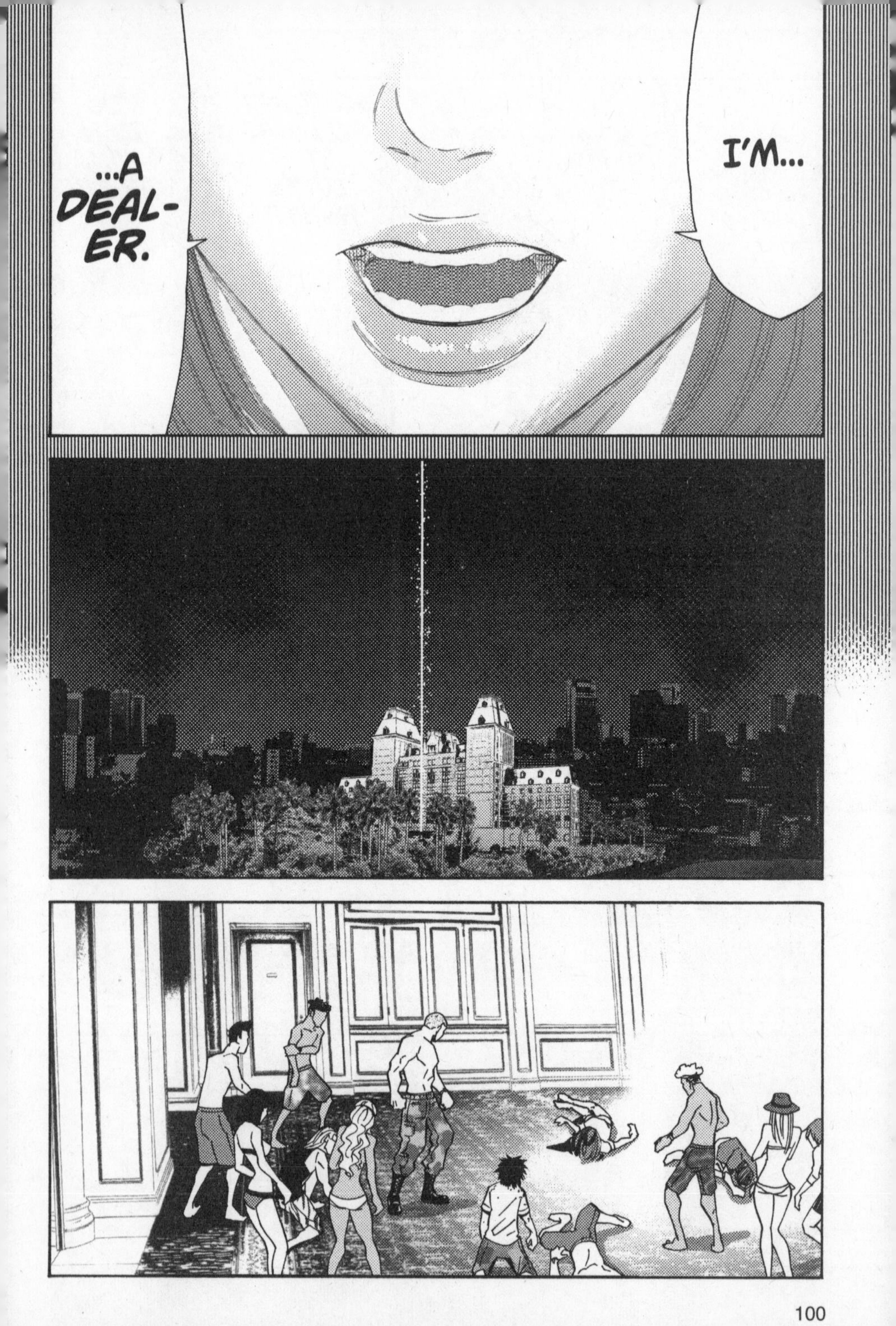
I'M...
...A DEAL-ER.

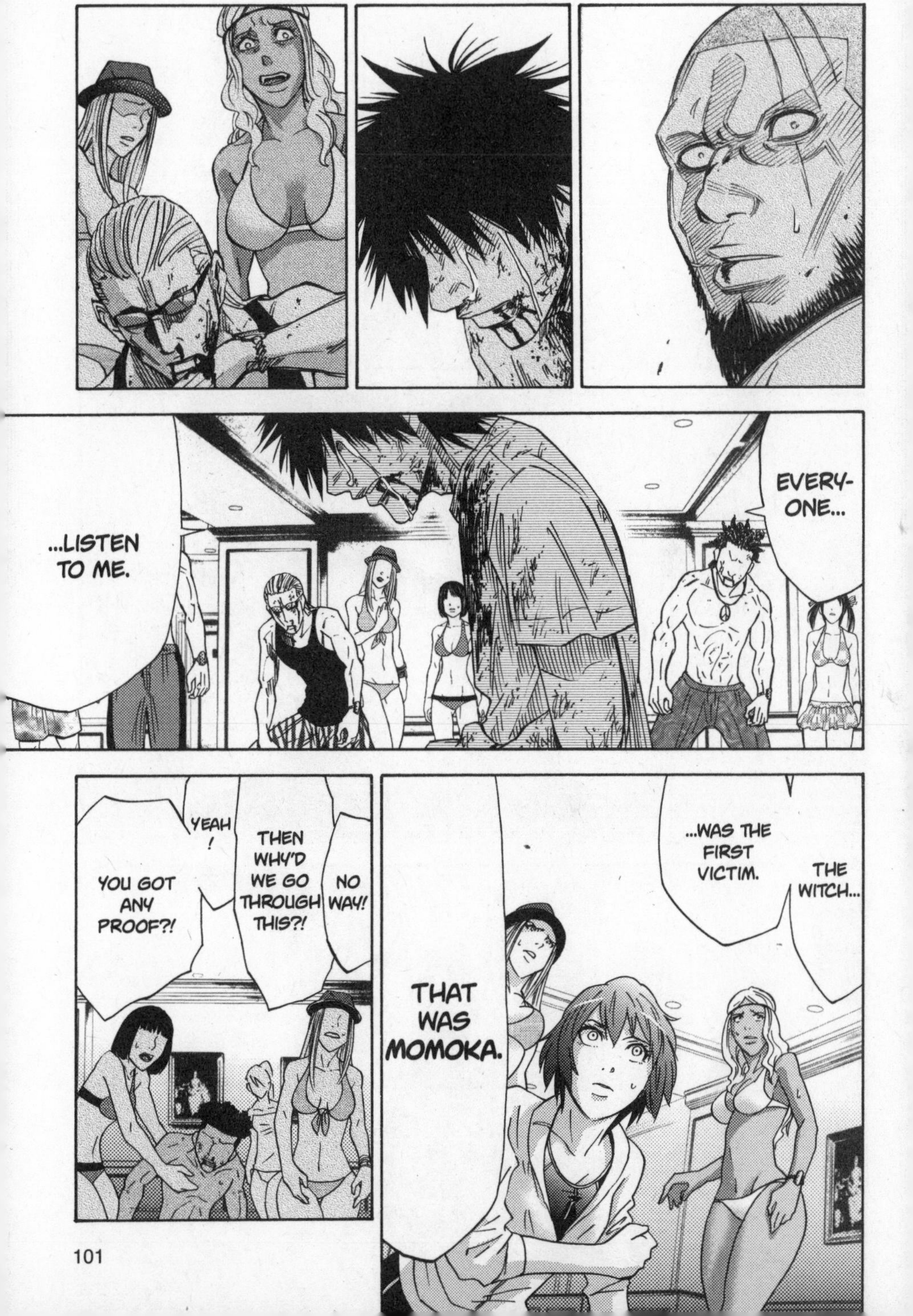
EVERY-ONE...
...LISTEN TO ME.
THE WITCH...
...WAS THE FIRST VICTIM.
THAT WAS MOMOKA.
NO WAY!
THEN WHY'D WE GO THROUGH THIS?!
YEAH!
YOU GOT ANY PROOF?!

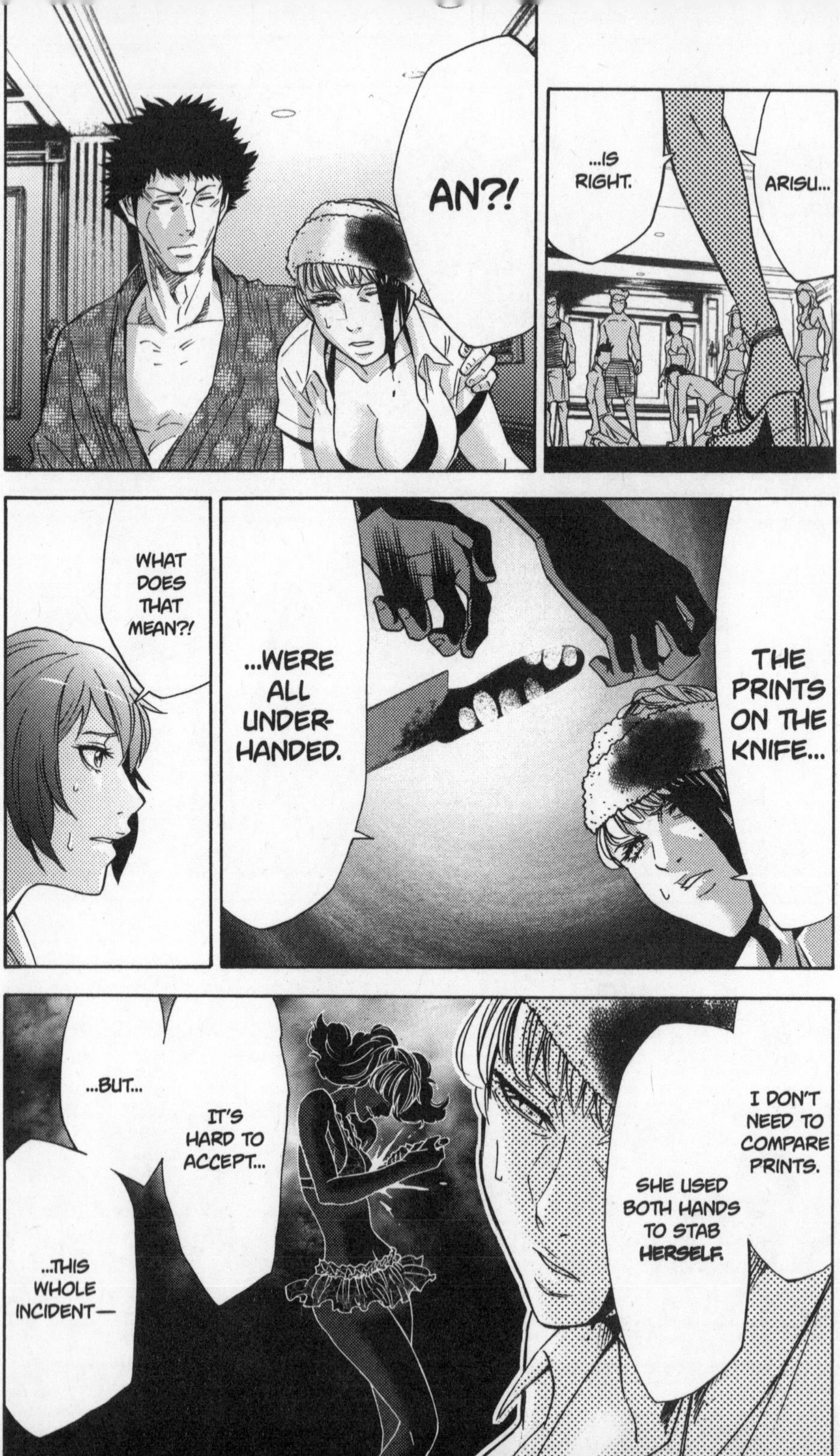
ARISU...
...IS RIGHT.
AN?!
THE PRINTS ON THE KNIFE...
...WERE ALL UNDER-HANDED.
WHAT DOES THAT MEAN?!
I DON'T NEED TO COMPARE PRINTS.
SHE USED BOTH HANDS TO STAB HERSELF.
IT'S HARD TO ACCEPT...
...BUT...
...THIS WHOLE INCIDENT—

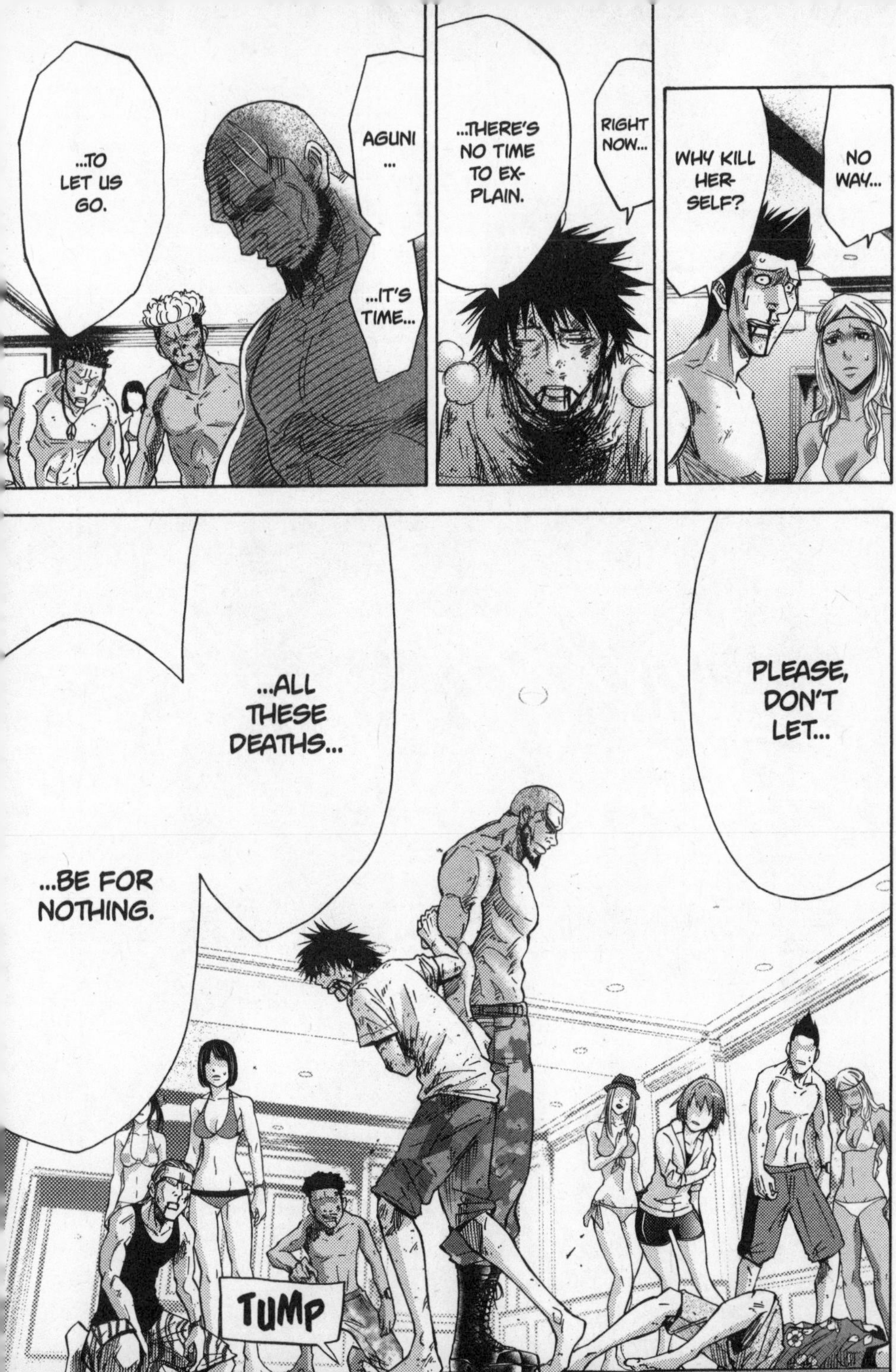
NO WAY...
WHY KILL HER-SELF?
RIGHT NOW...
...THERE'S NO TIME TO EX-PLAIN.
AGUNI ...
...IT'S TIME...
...TO LET US GO.
PLEASE, DON'T LET...
...ALL THESE DEATHS...
...BE FOR NOTHING.
TUMP

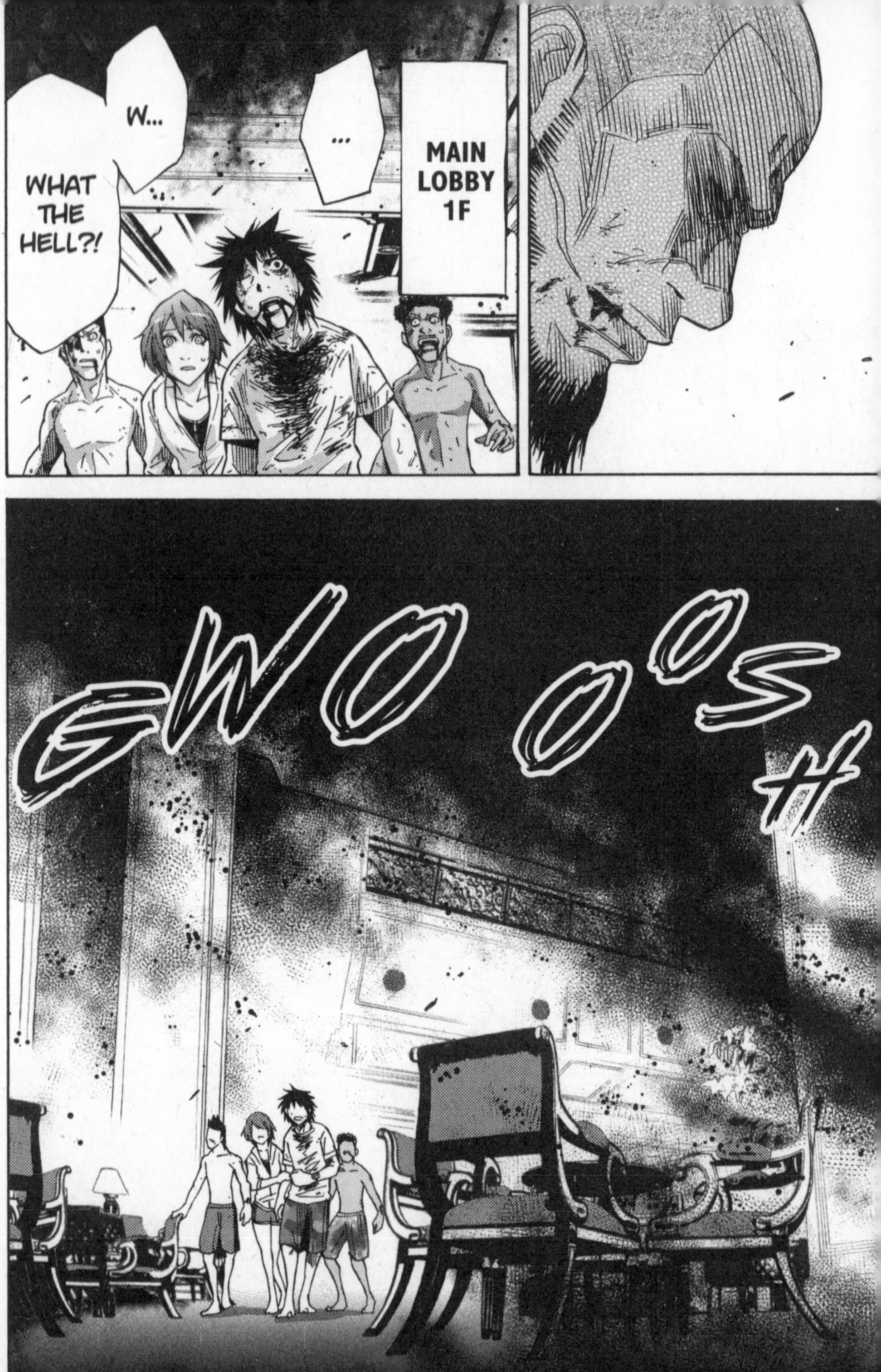
MAIN LOBBY 1F
...
W...
WHAT THE HELL?!
GWOOOSH

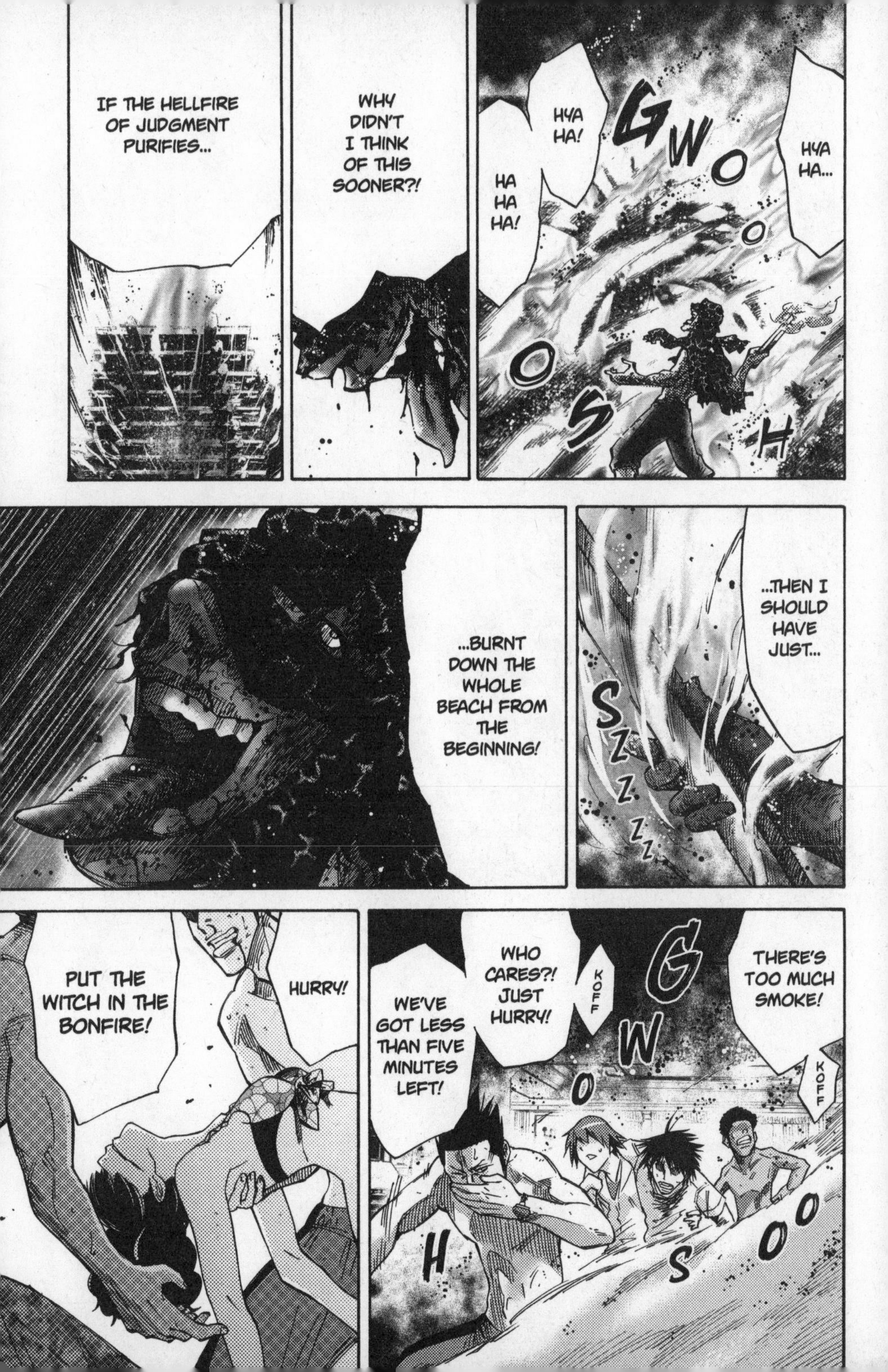
HYA HA...
GWOOOSH
HYA HA!
HA HA HA!
WHY DIDN'T I THINK OF THIS SOONER?!
IF THE HELLFIRE OF JUDGMENT PURIFIES...
...THEN I SHOULD HAVE JUST...
SZZZZZ
...BURNT DOWN THE WHOLE BEACH FROM THE BEGINNING!
THERE'S TOO MUCH SMOKE!
KOFF
GWOOOSH
KOFF
WHO CARES?! JUST HURRY!
WE'VE GOT LESS THAN FIVE MINUTES LEFT!
HURRY!
PUT THE WITCH IN THE BONFIRE!

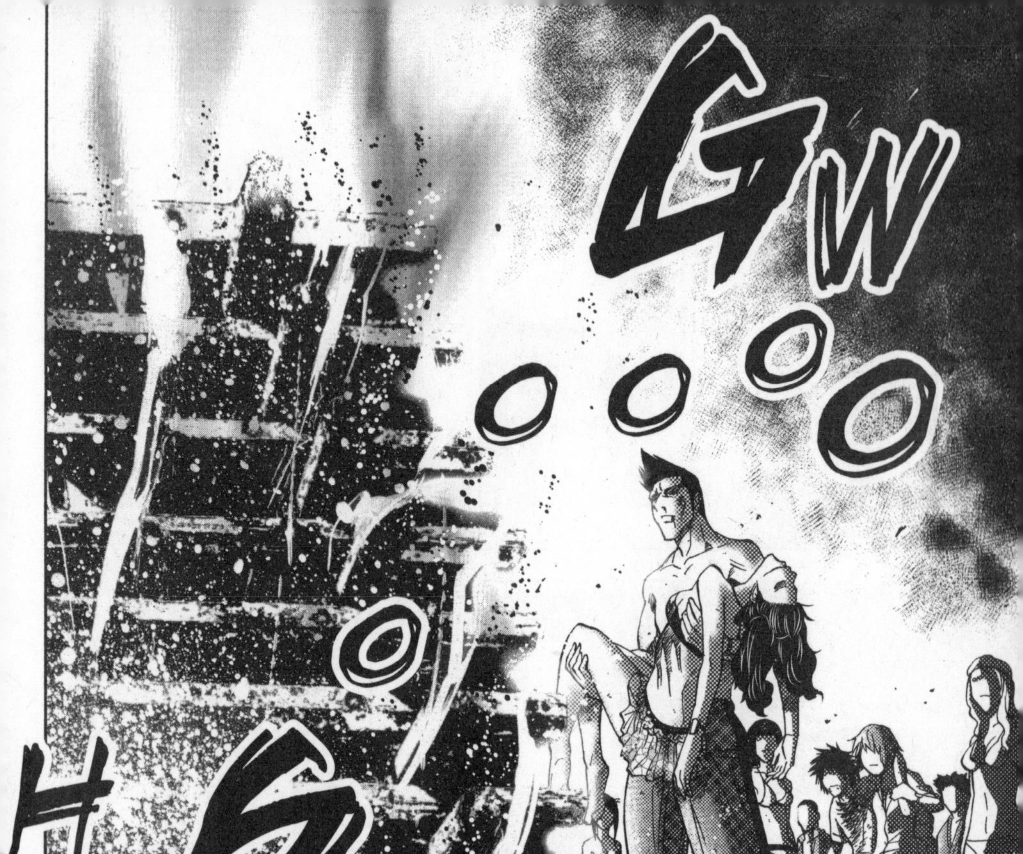
GWOOOOSH
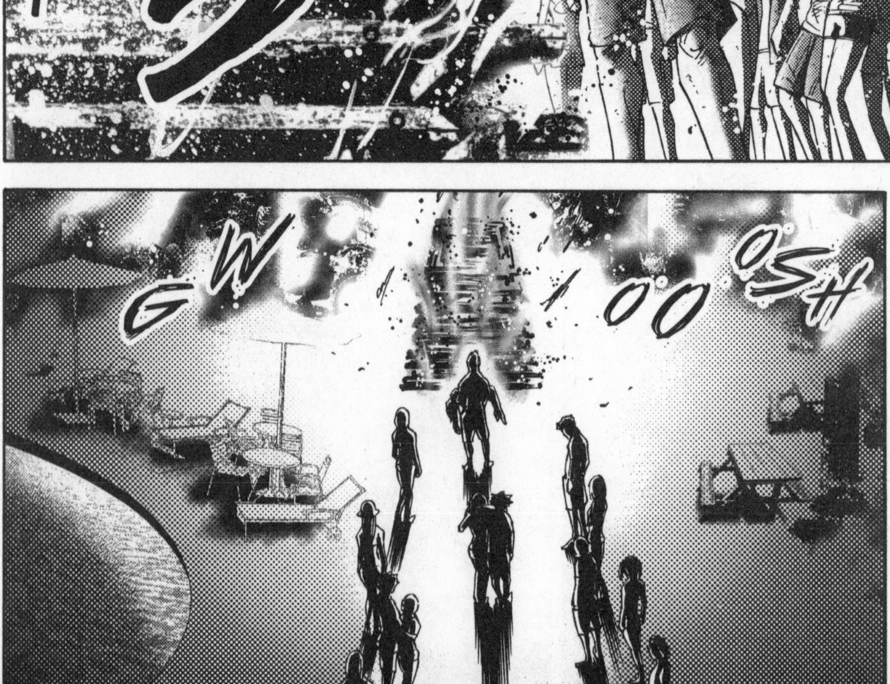
GWOOOSH

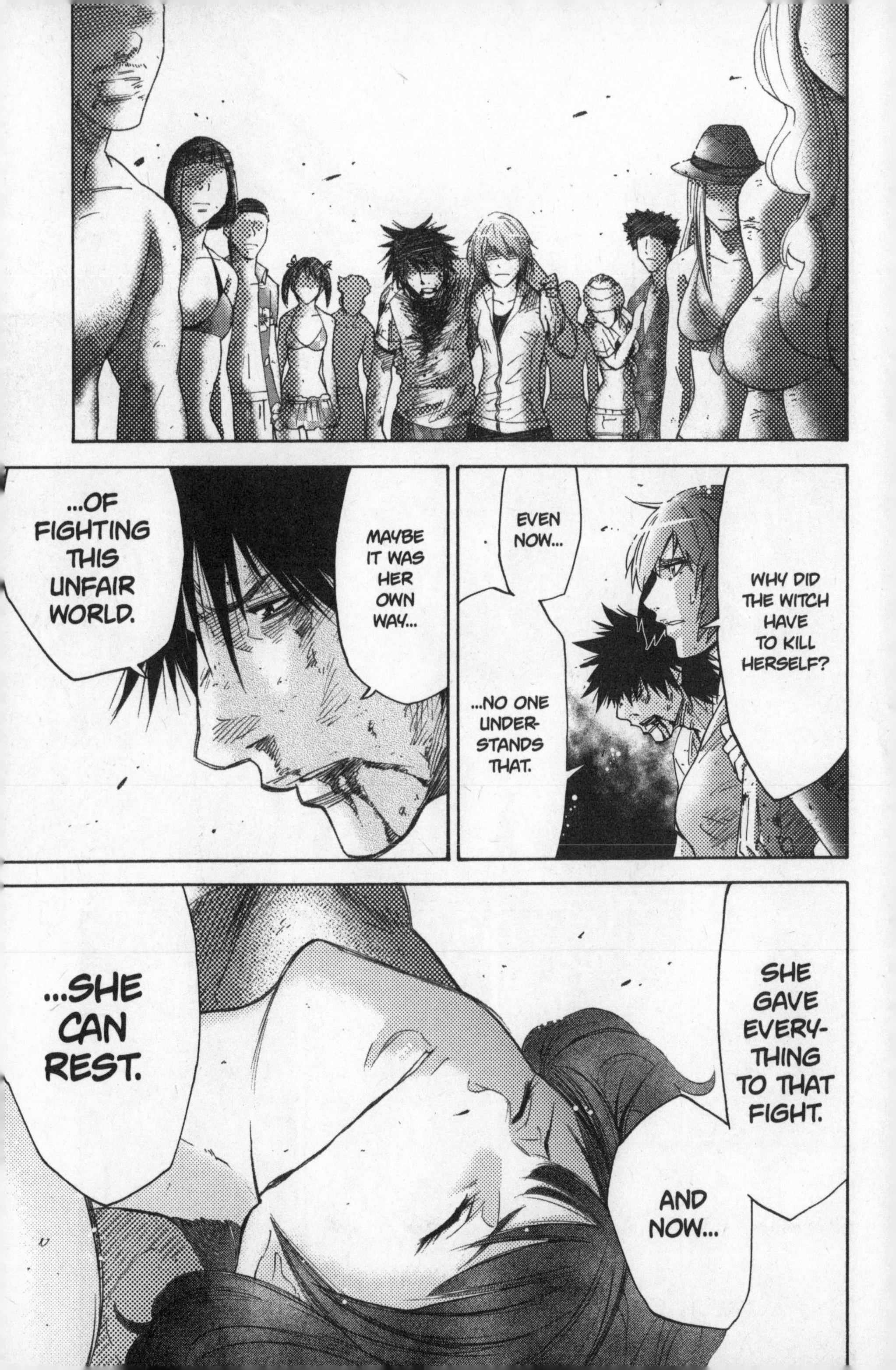
WHY DID THE WITCH HAVE TO KILL HERSELF?
EVEN NOW...
...NO ONE UNDERSTANDS THAT.
MAYBE IT WAS HER OWN WAY...
...OF FIGHTING THIS UNFAIR WORLD.
SHE GAVE EVERYTHING TO THAT FIGHT.
AND NOW...
...SHE CAN REST.

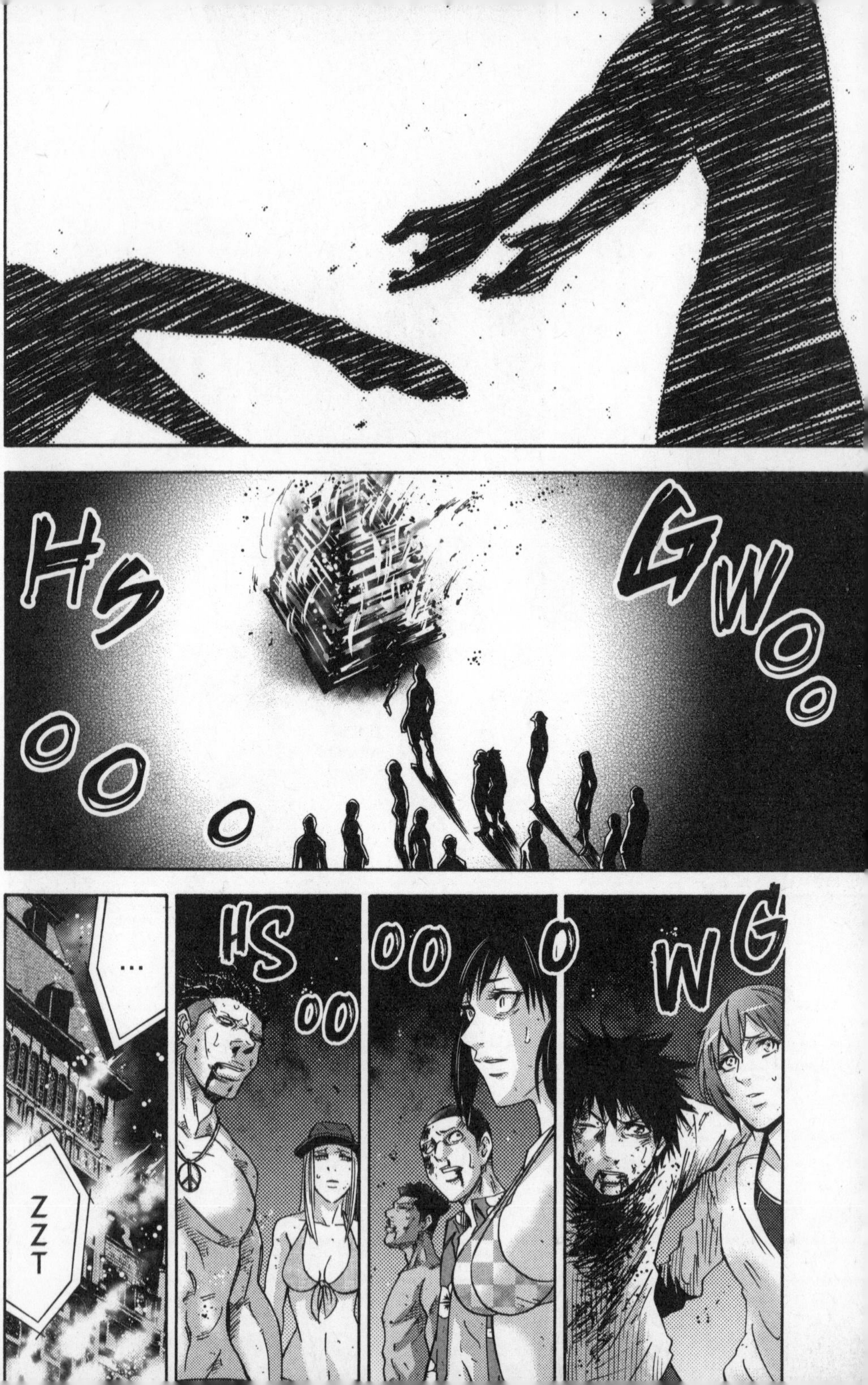
GWOOO
HSOOOO
WG
OOO
HSOO
...
ZZT

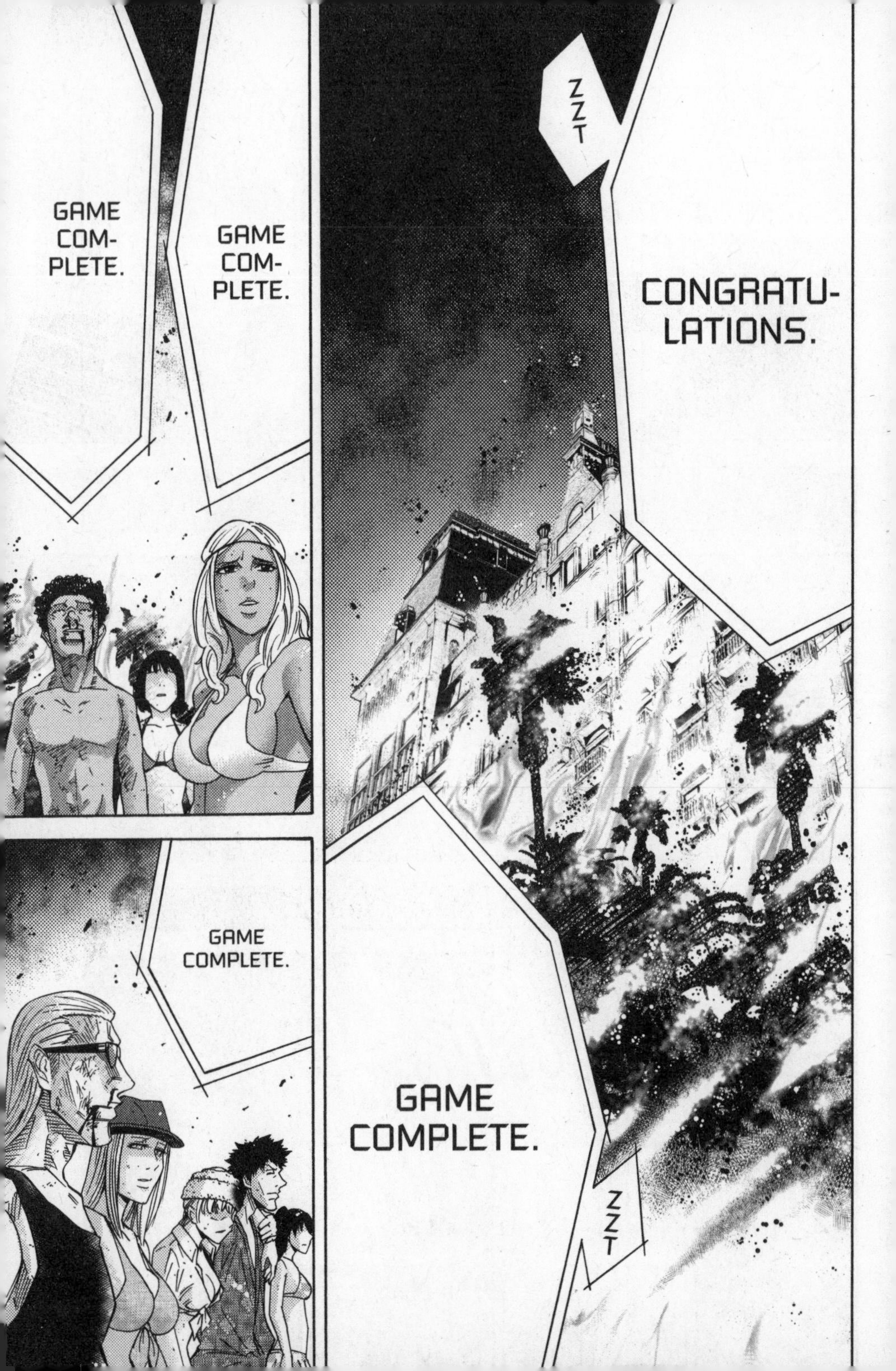
ZZT
CONGRATULATIONS.
GAME COMPLETE.
ZZT
GAME COMPLETE.
GAME COMPLETE.
GAME COMPLETE.

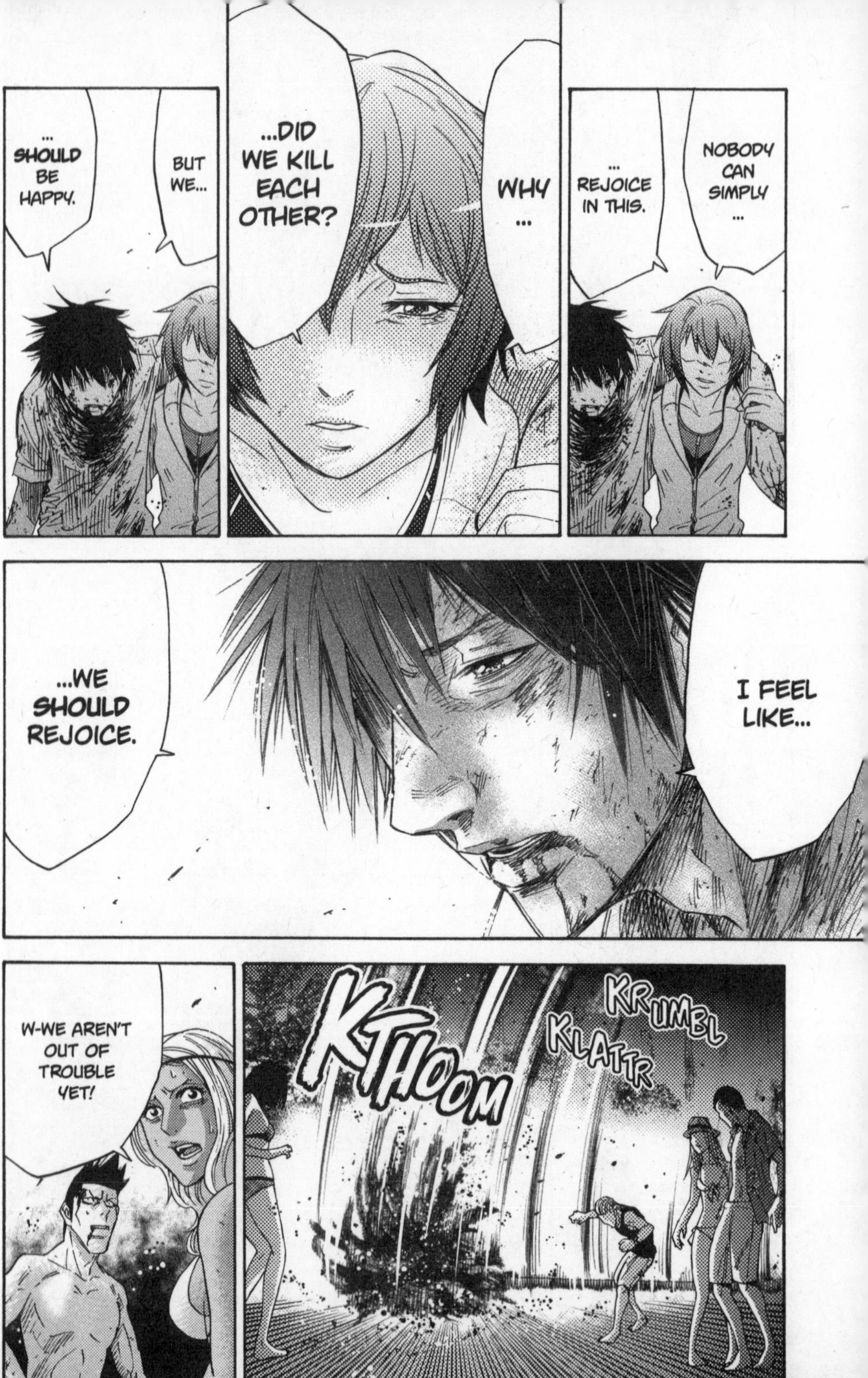
NOBODY CAN SIMPLY ...
... REJOICE IN THIS.
WHY ...
...DID WE KILL EACH OTHER?
BUT WE...
... SHOULD BE HAPPY.
I FEEL LIKE...
...WE SHOULD REJOICE.
KRUMBL
KLATTR
KTHOOM
W-WE AREN'T OUT OF TROUBLE YET!

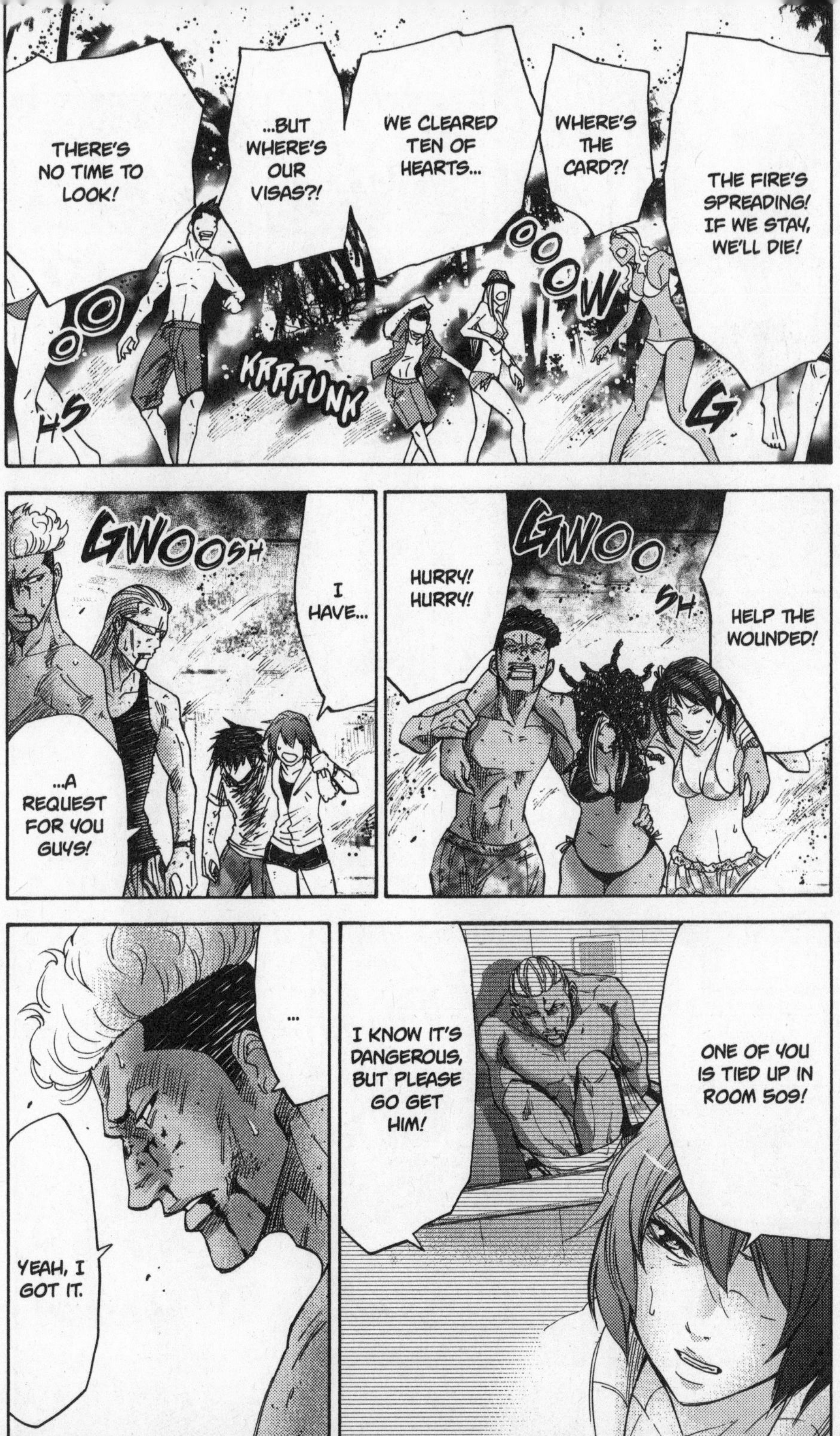
THE FIRE'S SPREADING! IF WE STAY, WE'LL DIE!
WHERE'S THE CARD?!
WE CLEARED TEN OF HEARTS...
...BUT WHERE'S OUR VISAS?!
THERE'S NO TIME TO LOOK!
KRRRUNK
HELP THE WOUNDED!
HURRY! HURRY!
GWOOSH
I HAVE...
...A REQUEST FOR YOU GUYS!
GWOOSH
ONE OF YOU IS TIED UP IN ROOM 509!
I KNOW IT'S DANGEROUS, BUT PLEASE GO GET HIM!
...
YEAH, I GOT IT.

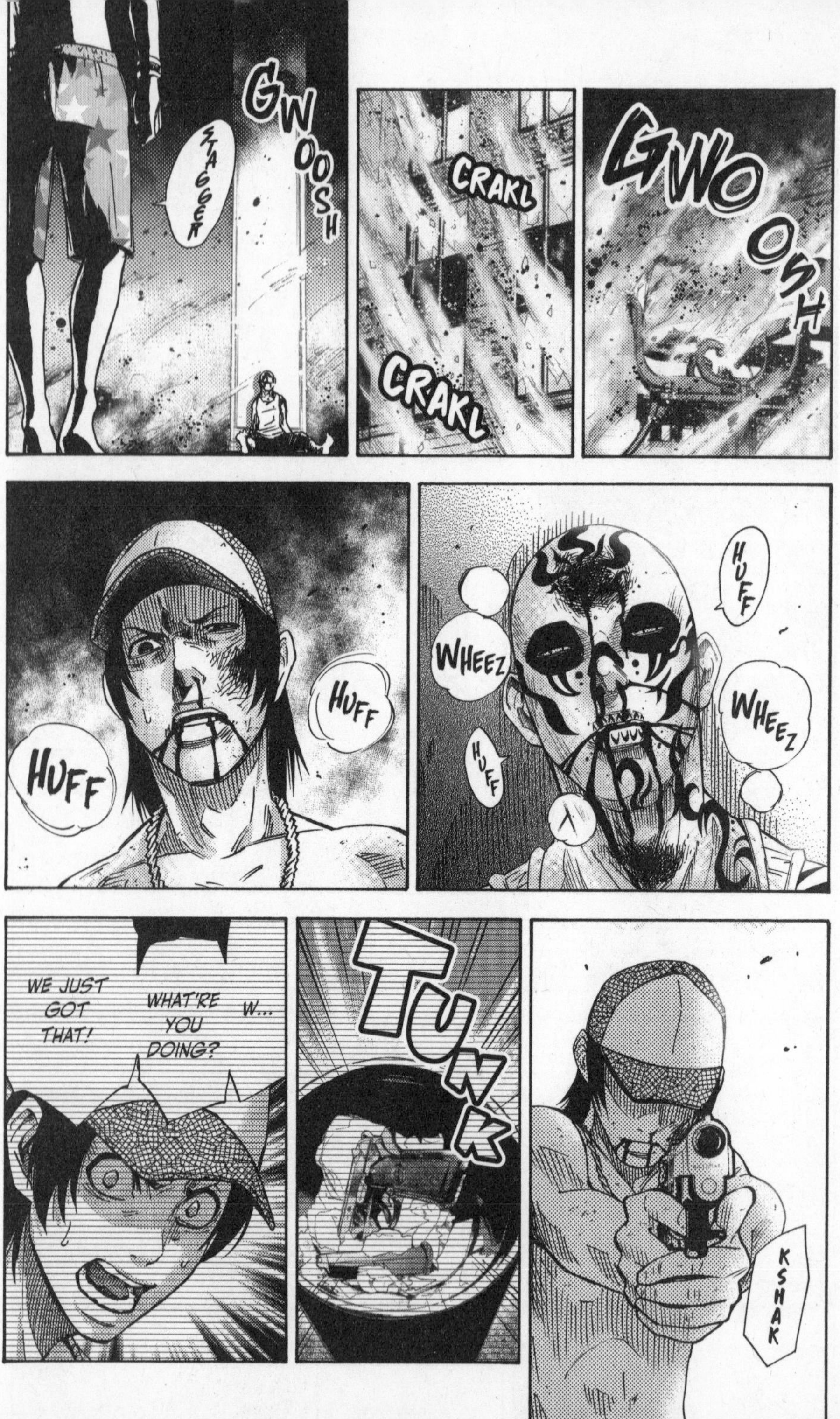
GWOOSH
CRAKL
CRAKL
GWOOSH
STAGGER
HUFF
WHEEZ
WHEEZ
HUFF
HUFF
HUFF
KSHAK
TUNK
W...
WHAT'RE YOU DOING?
WE JUST GOT THAT!

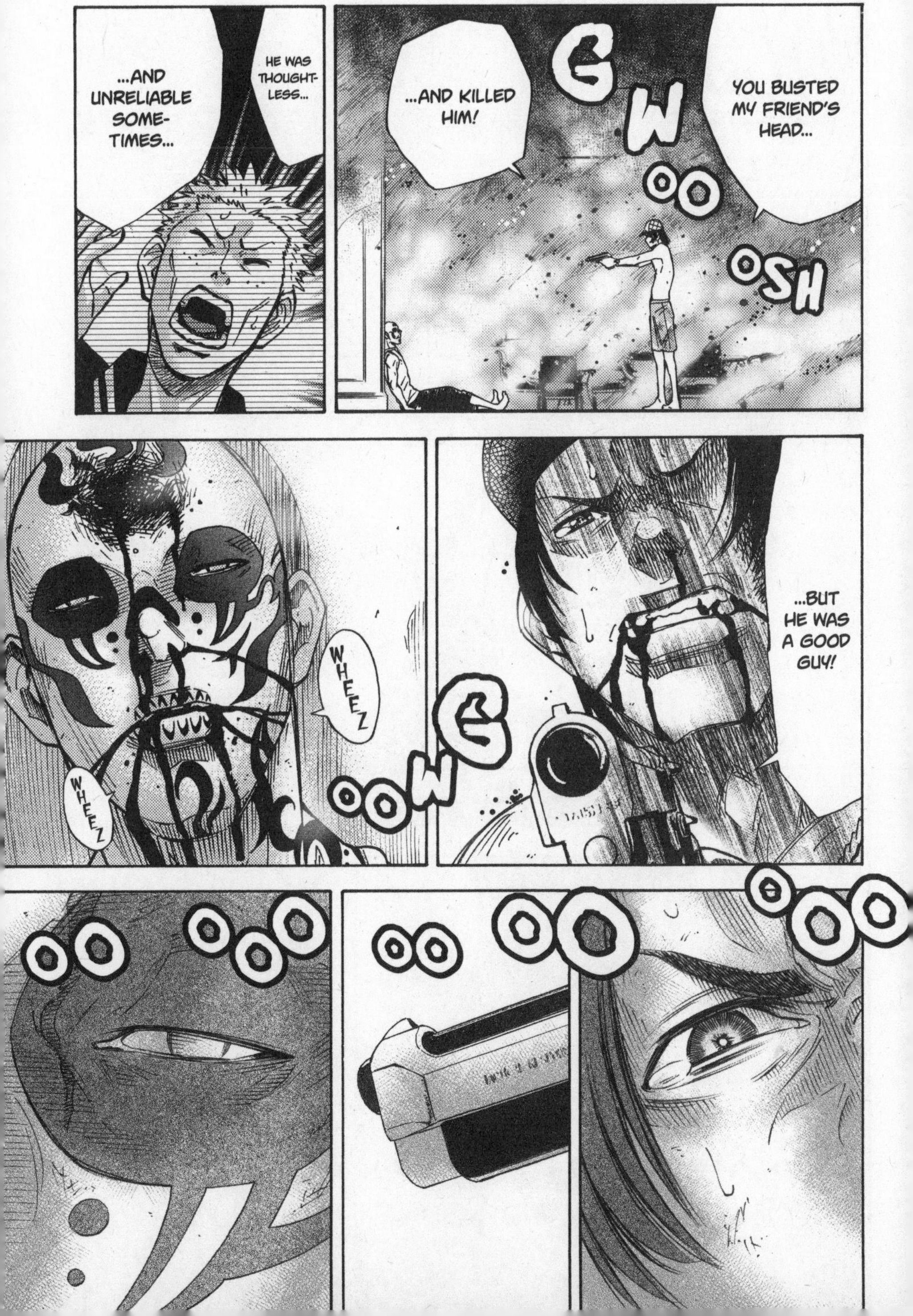
YOU BUSTED MY FRIEND'S HEAD...
...AND KILLED HIM!
GWOOOSH
HE WAS THOUGHTLESS...
...AND UNRELIABLE SOMETIMES...
...BUT HE WAS A GOOD GUY!
GOOOW
WHEEZ
WHEEZ
OOO
OO OO
OOOOO

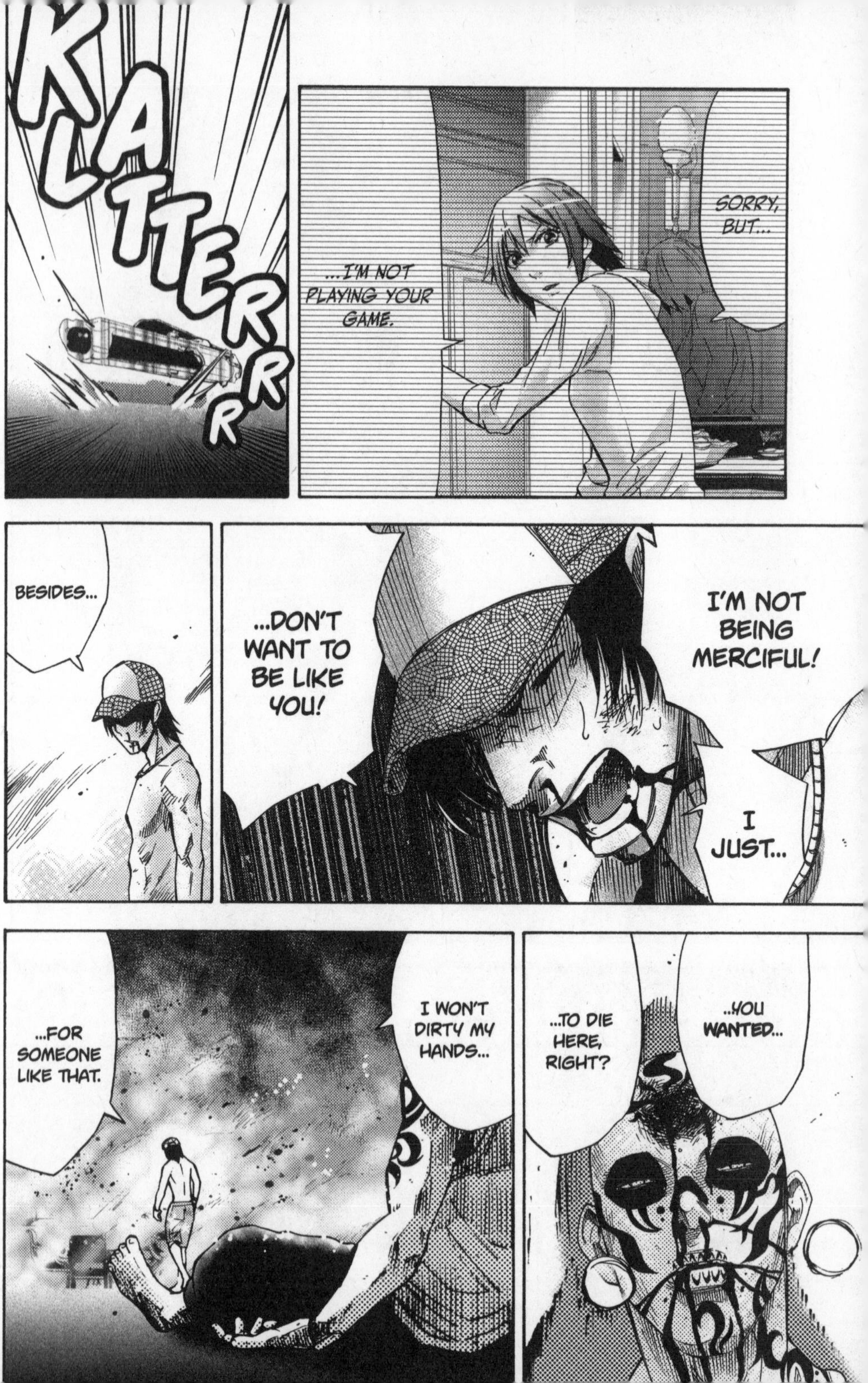
SORRY, BUT...
...I'M NOT PLAYING YOUR GAME.
KLATTERRR
I'M NOT BEING MERCIFUL!
I JUST...
...DON'T WANT TO BE LIKE YOU!
BESIDES...
...YOU WANTED...
...TO DIE HERE, RIGHT?
I WON'T DIRTY MY HANDS...
...FOR SOMEONE LIKE THAT.

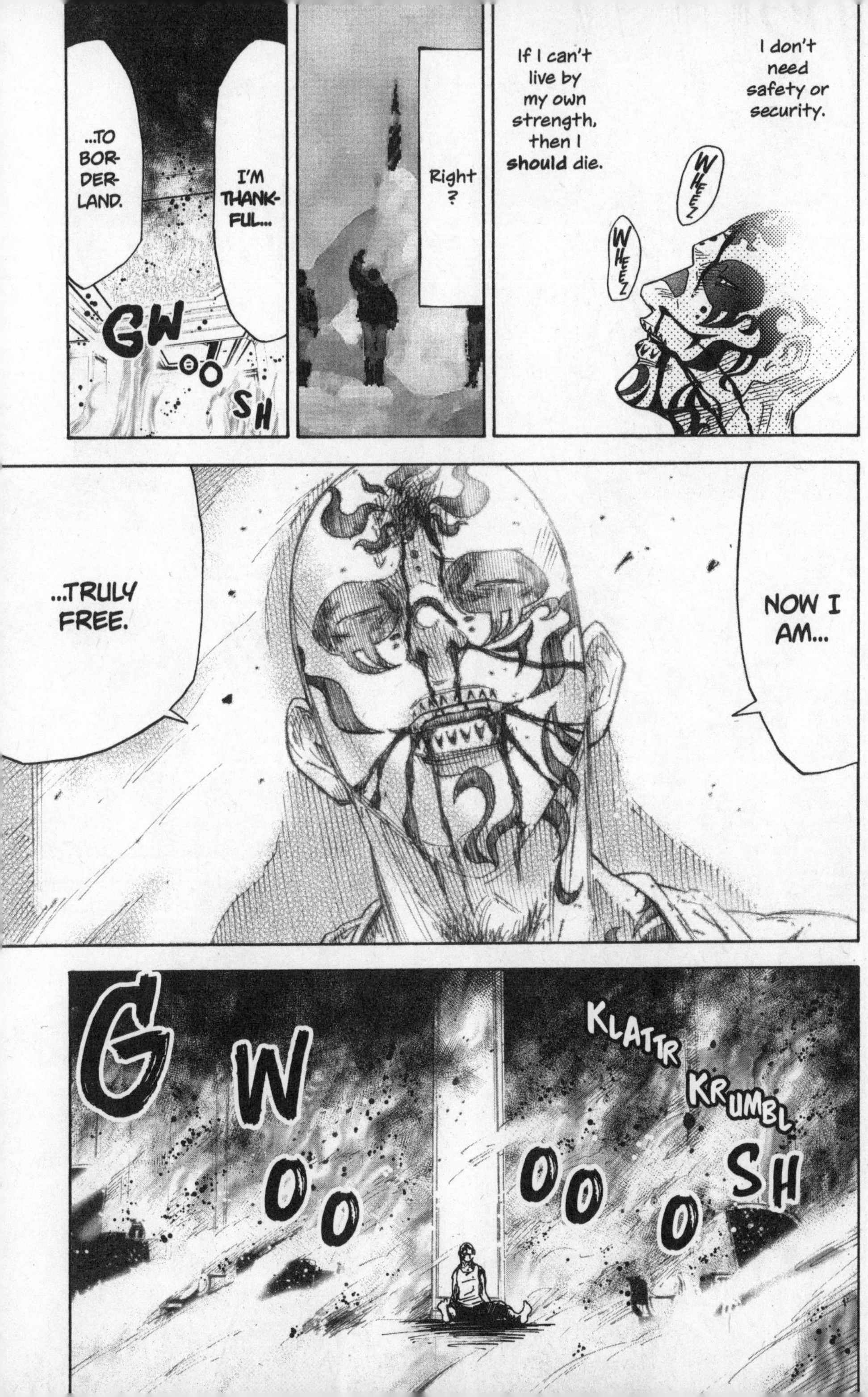
I don't need safety or security.
WHEEZ
WHEEZ
If I can't live by my own strength, then I should die.
Right?
I'M THANKFUL...
...TO BORDERLAND.
GWOOSH
NOW I AM...
...TRULY FREE.
KLATTR
KRUMBL
GWOOOOOSH

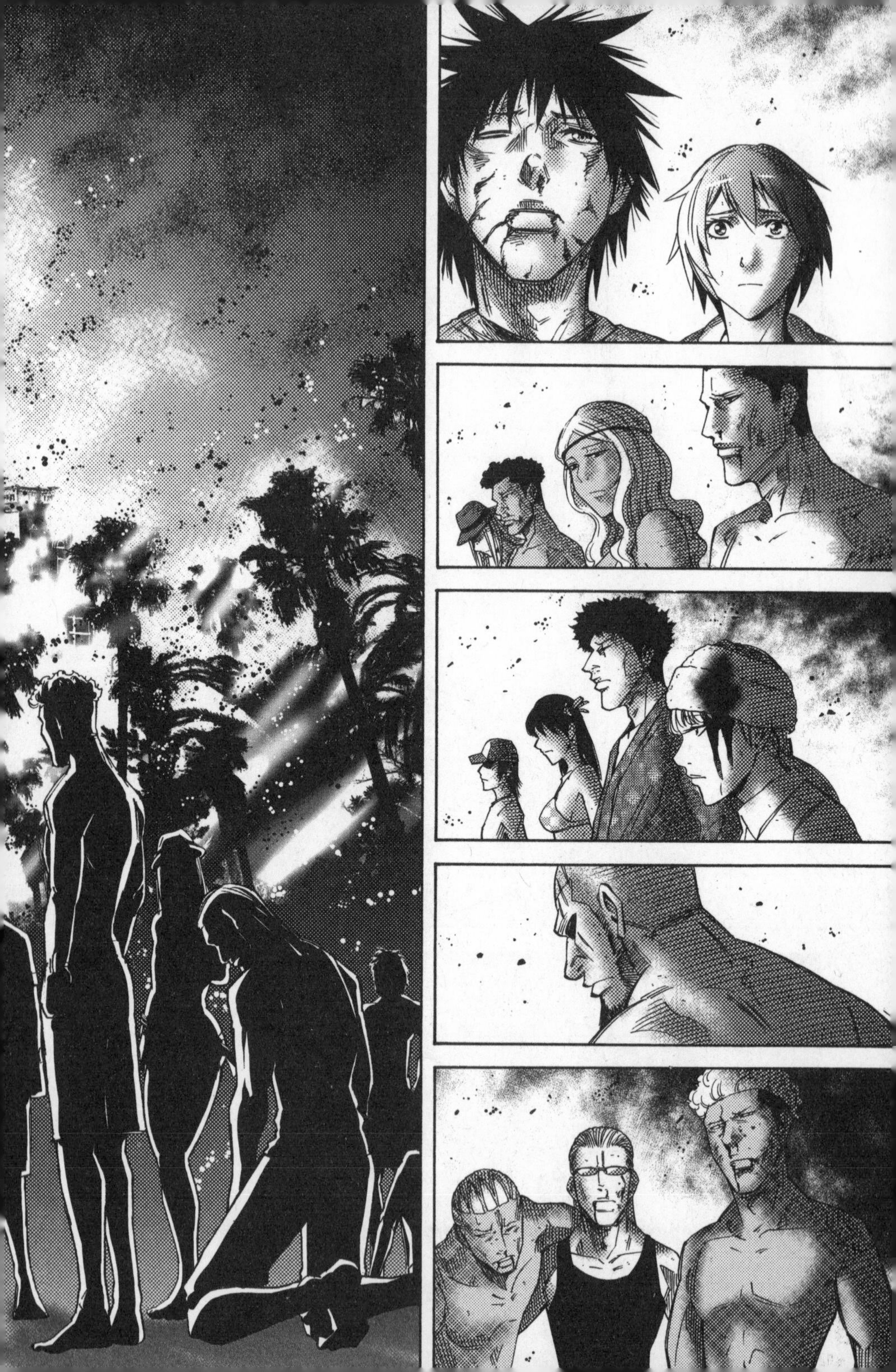

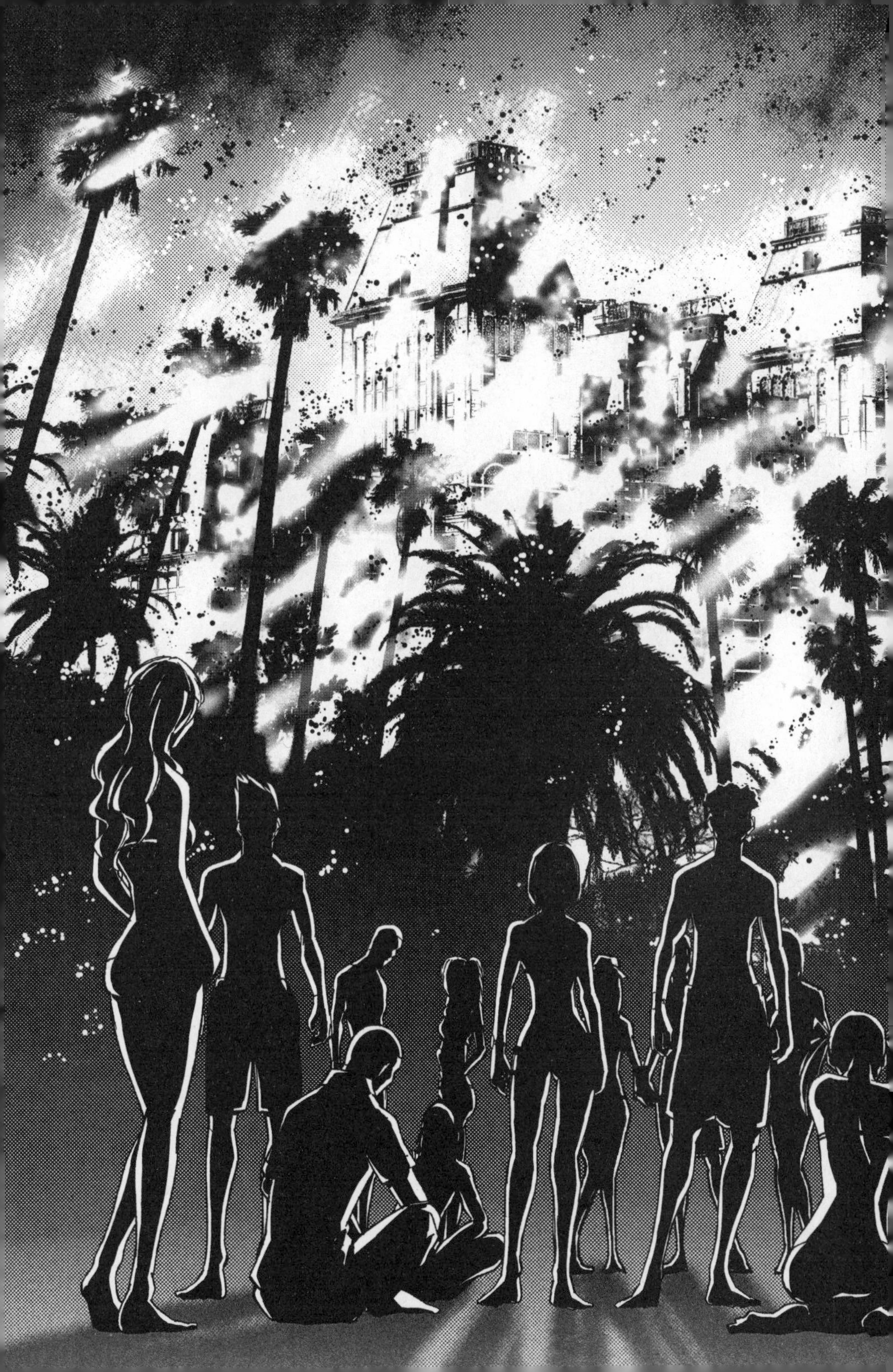

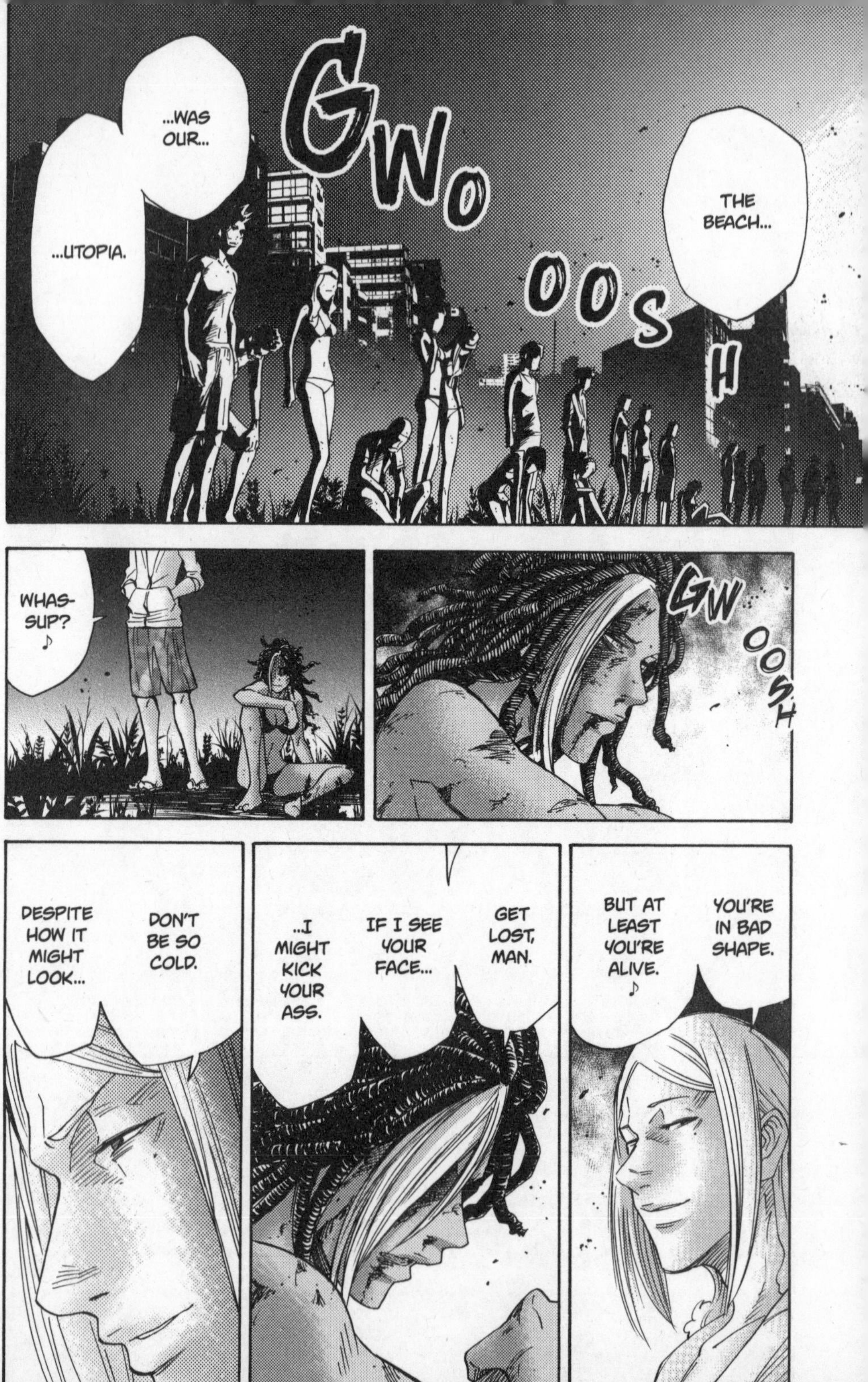
THE BEACH...
GWOOOSH
...WAS OUR...
...UTOPIA.
GWOOSH
WHAS-SUP? ♪
YOU'RE IN BAD SHAPE.
BUT AT LEAST YOU'RE ALIVE. ♪
GET LOST, MAN.
IF I SEE YOUR FACE...
...I MIGHT KICK YOUR ASS.
DON'T BE SO COLD.
DESPITE HOW IT MIGHT LOOK...

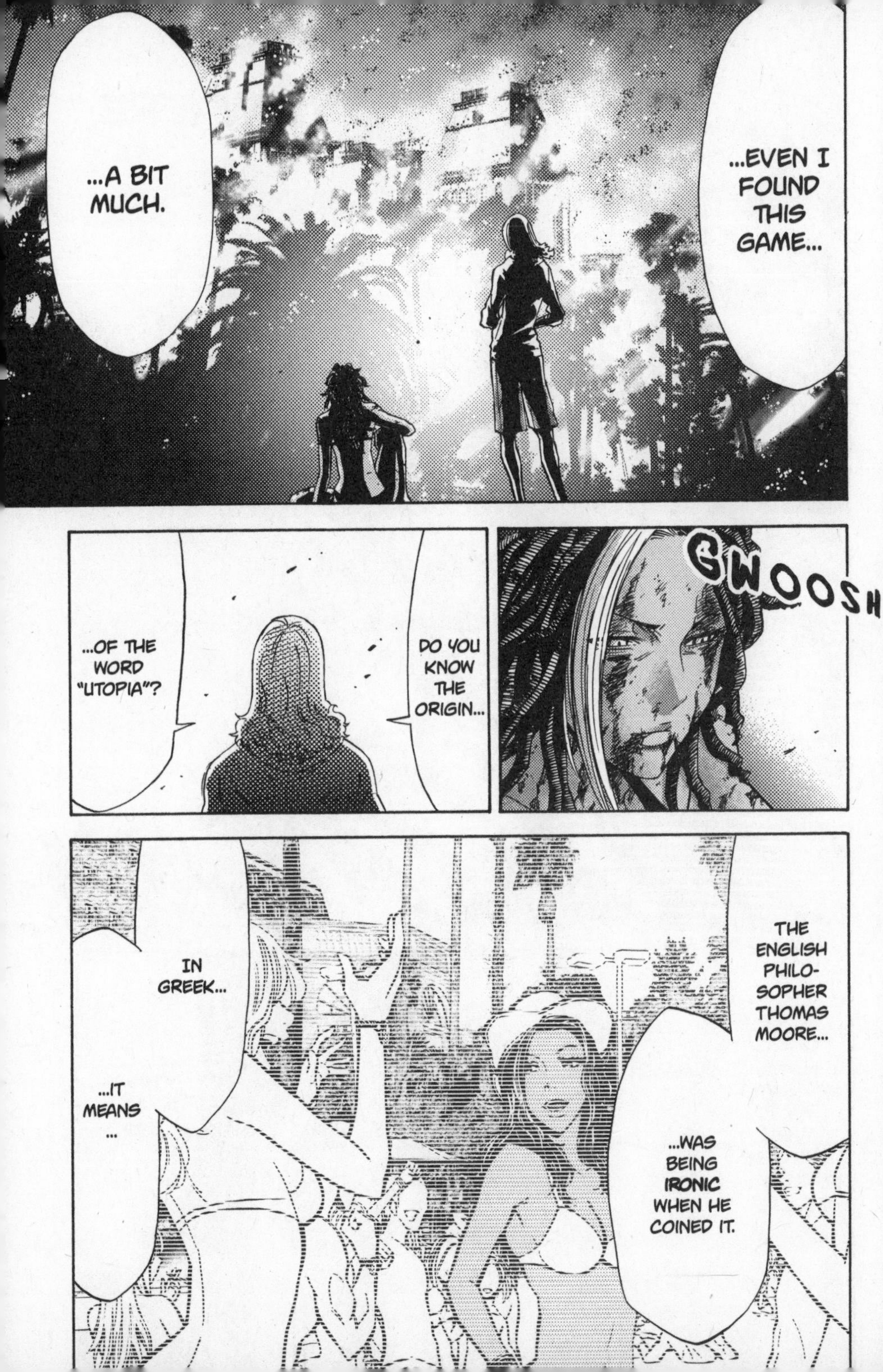
...EVEN I FOUND THIS GAME...
...A BIT MUCH.
GWOOSH
DO YOU KNOW THE ORIGIN...
...OF THE WORD "UTOPIA"?
THE ENGLISH PHILO-SOPHER THOMAS MOORE...
...WAS BEING **IRONIC** WHEN HE COINED IT.
IN GREEK...
...IT MEANS ...

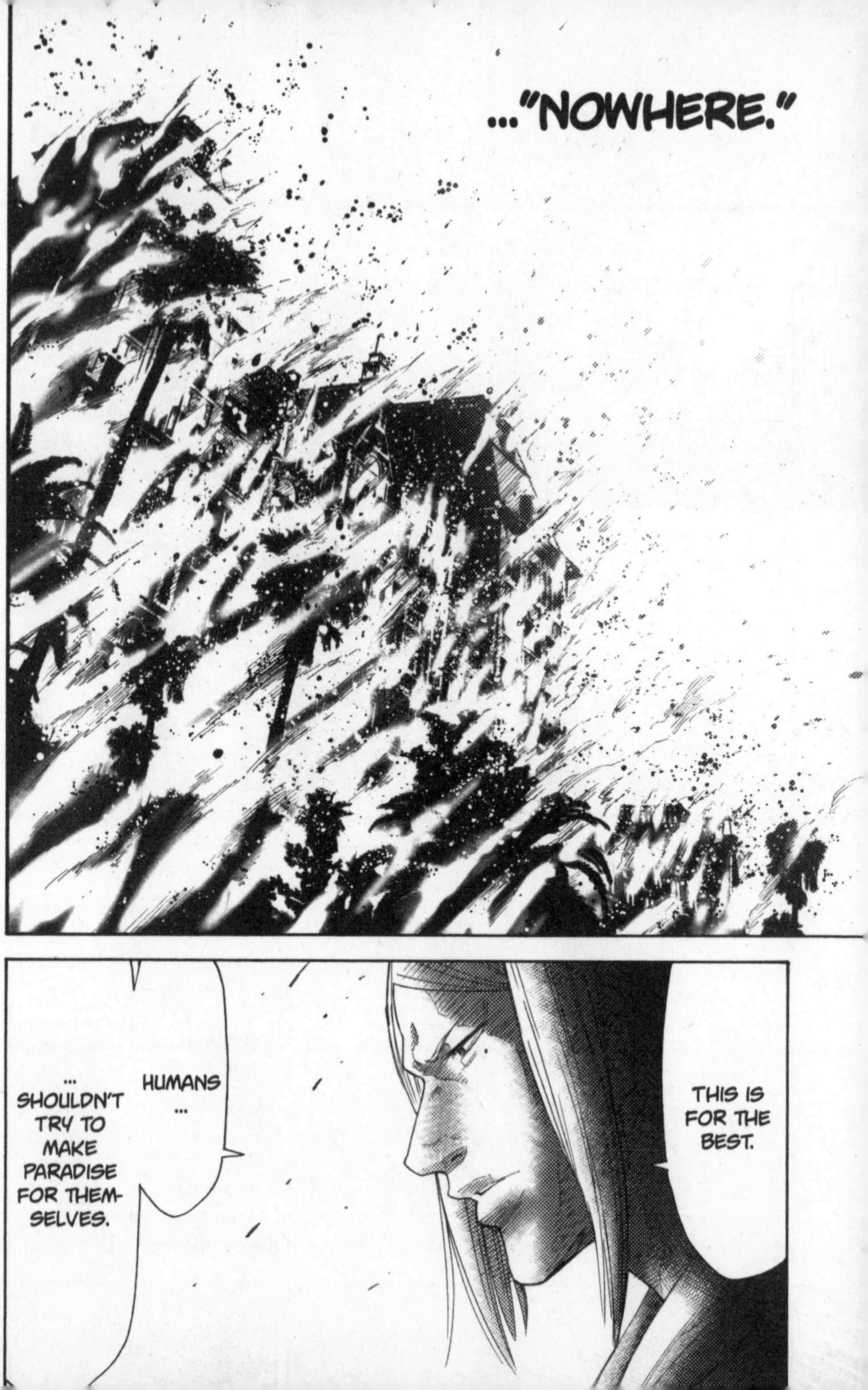
..."NOWHERE."
THIS IS FOR THE BEST.
HUMANS ...
... SHOULDN'T TRY TO MAKE PARADISE FOR THEM-SELVES.

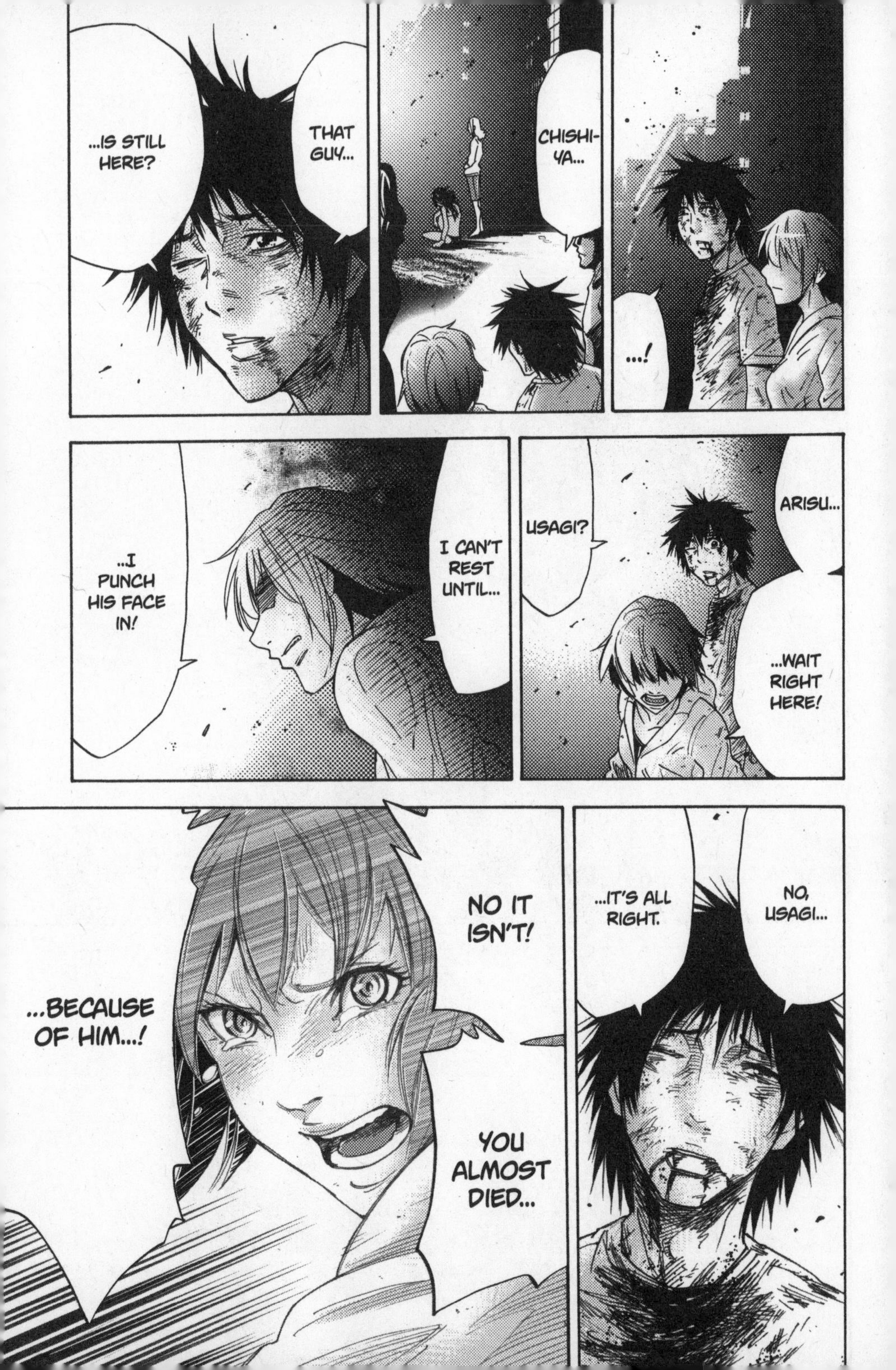
...!
CHISHI-YA...
THAT GUY...
...IS STILL HERE?
ARISU...
USAGI?
...WAIT RIGHT HERE!
I CAN'T REST UNTIL...
...I PUNCH HIS FACE IN!
NO, USAGI...
...IT'S ALL RIGHT.
NO IT ISN'T!
YOU ALMOST DIED...
...BECAUSE OF HIM...!

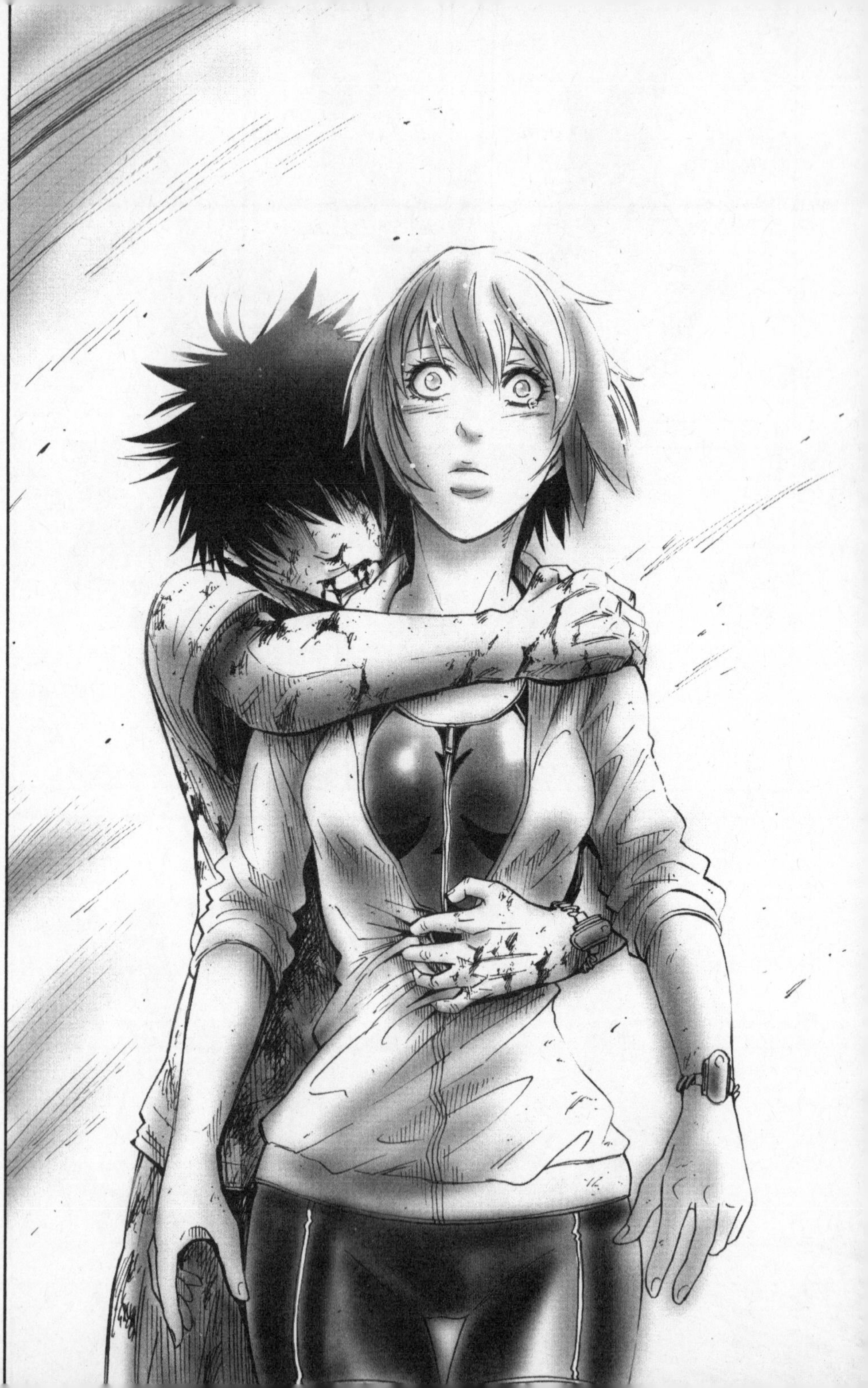

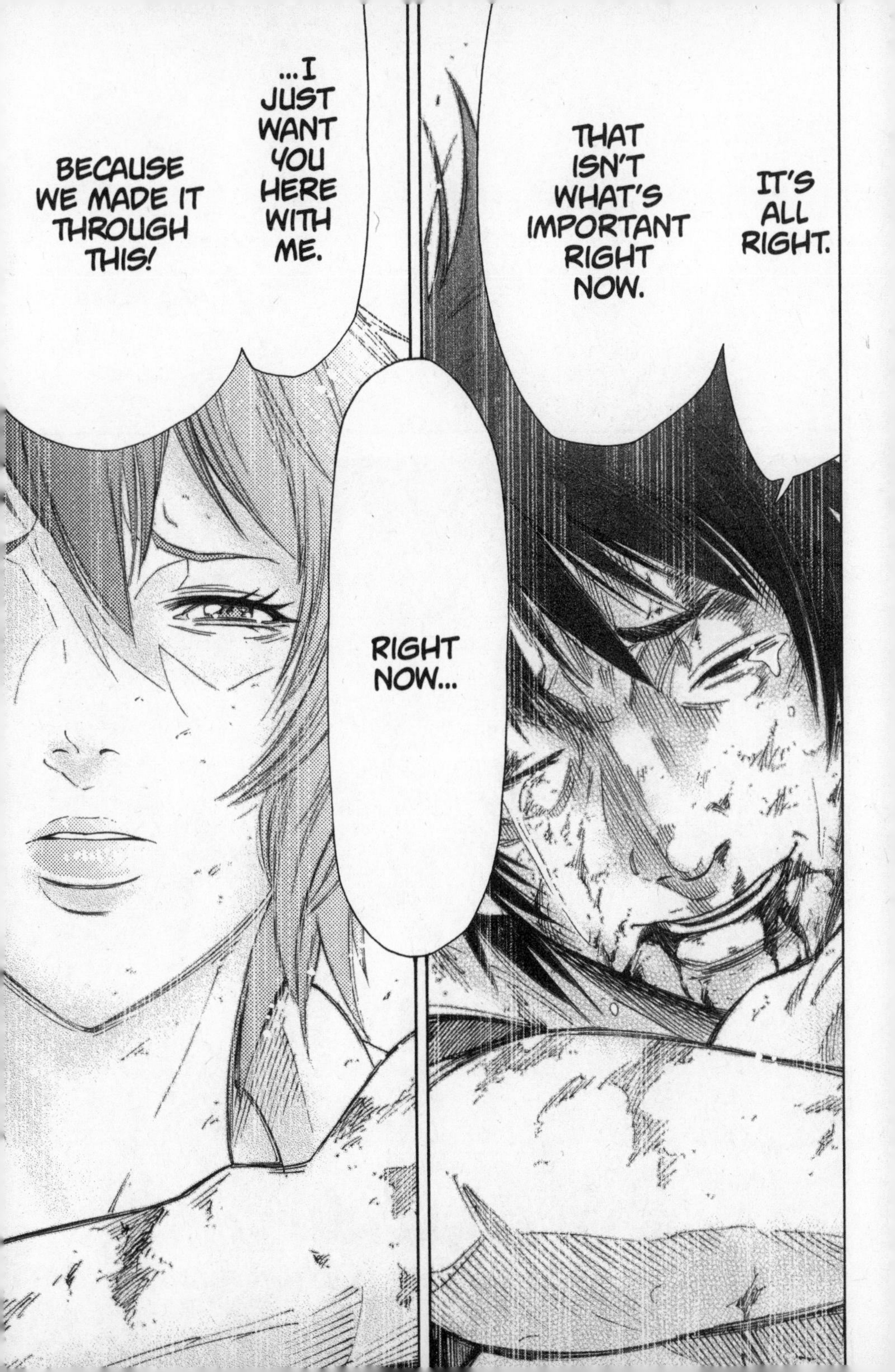
IT'S ALL RIGHT.
THAT ISN'T WHAT'S IMPORTANT RIGHT NOW.
RIGHT NOW...
...I JUST WANT YOU HERE WITH ME.
BECAUSE WE MADE IT THROUGH THIS!

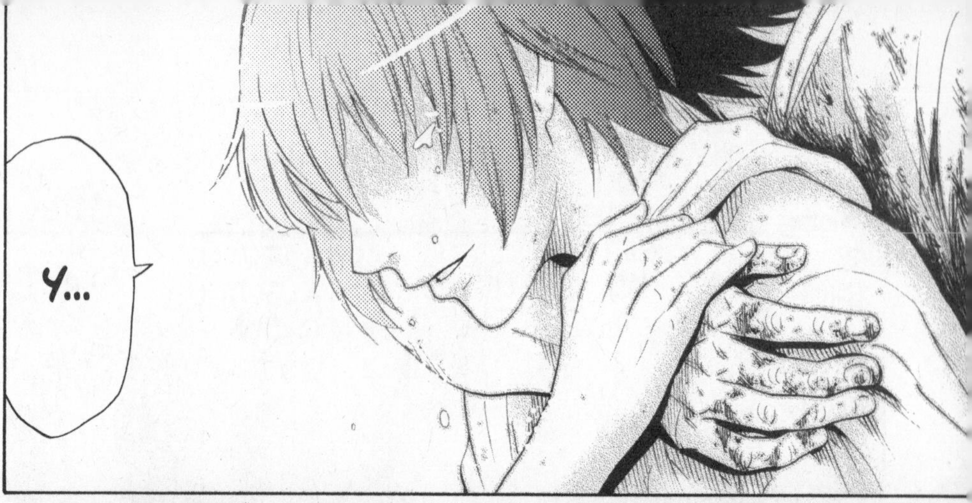
Y...

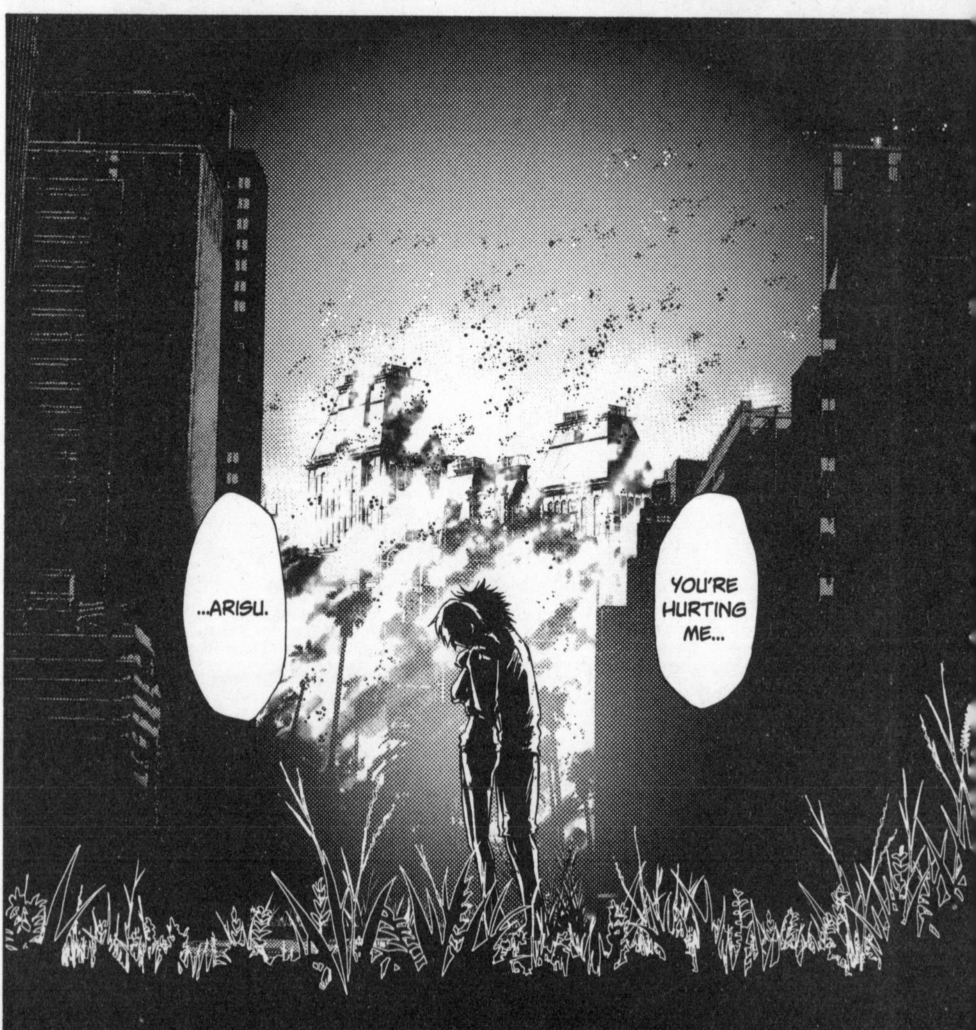
YOU'RE HURTING ME...
...ARISU.

CHAPTER 29: Day 11 of Our Visit

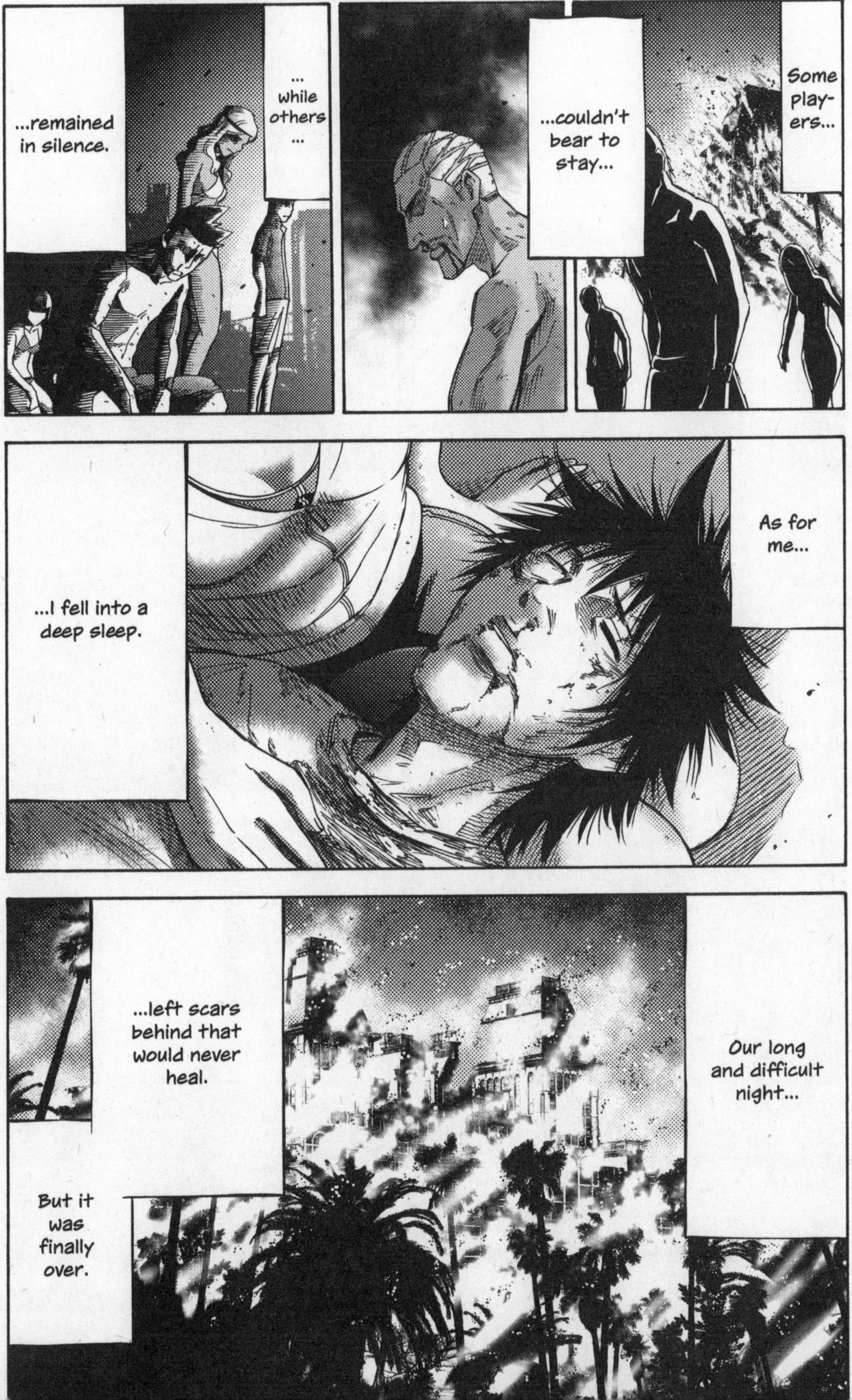
Some play-ers...
...couldn't bear to stay...
... while others ...
...remained in silence.
As for me...
...I fell into a deep sleep.
Our long and difficult night...
...left scars behind that would never heal.
But it was finally over.

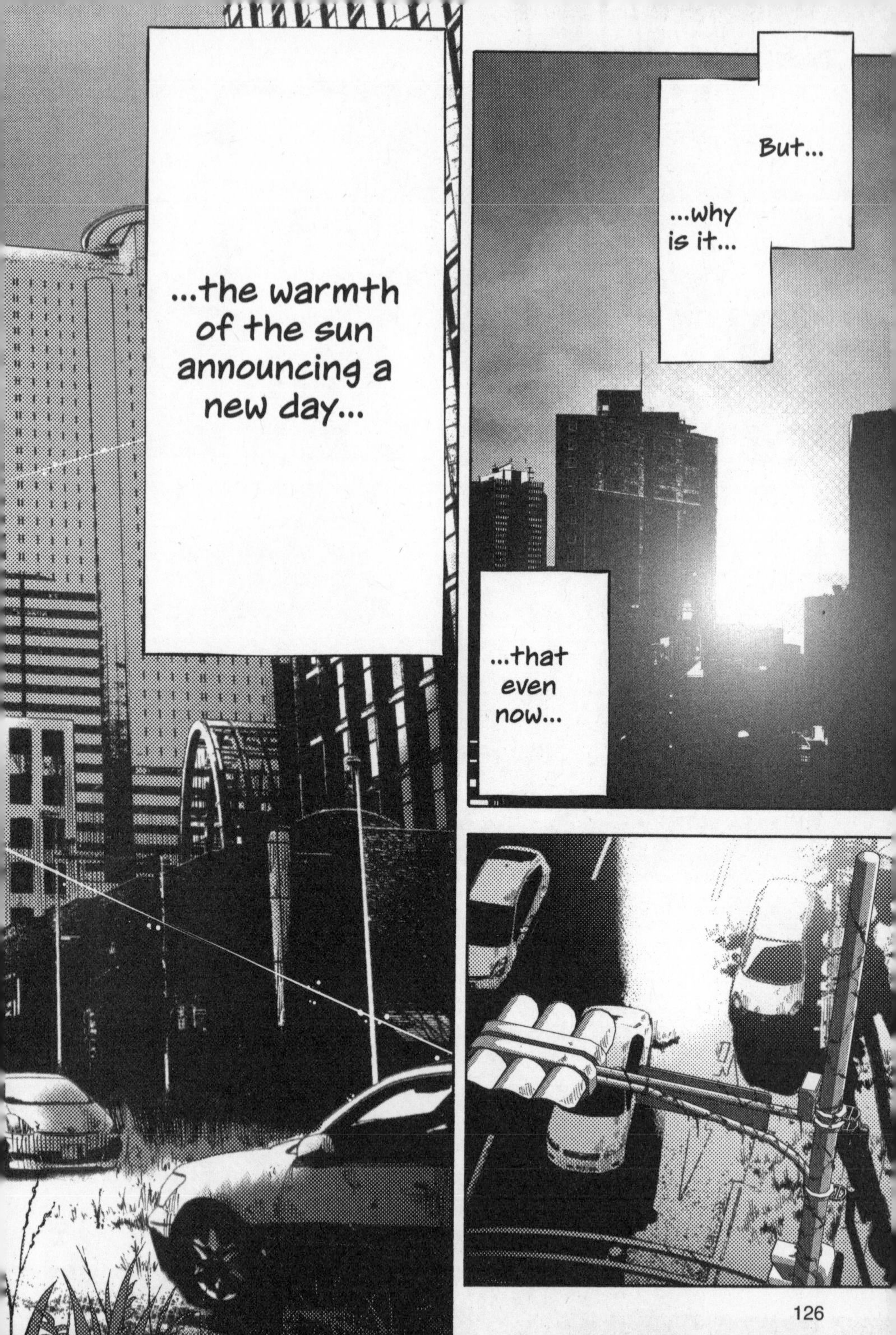
But...
...why is it...
...that even now...
...the warmth of the sun announcing a new day...

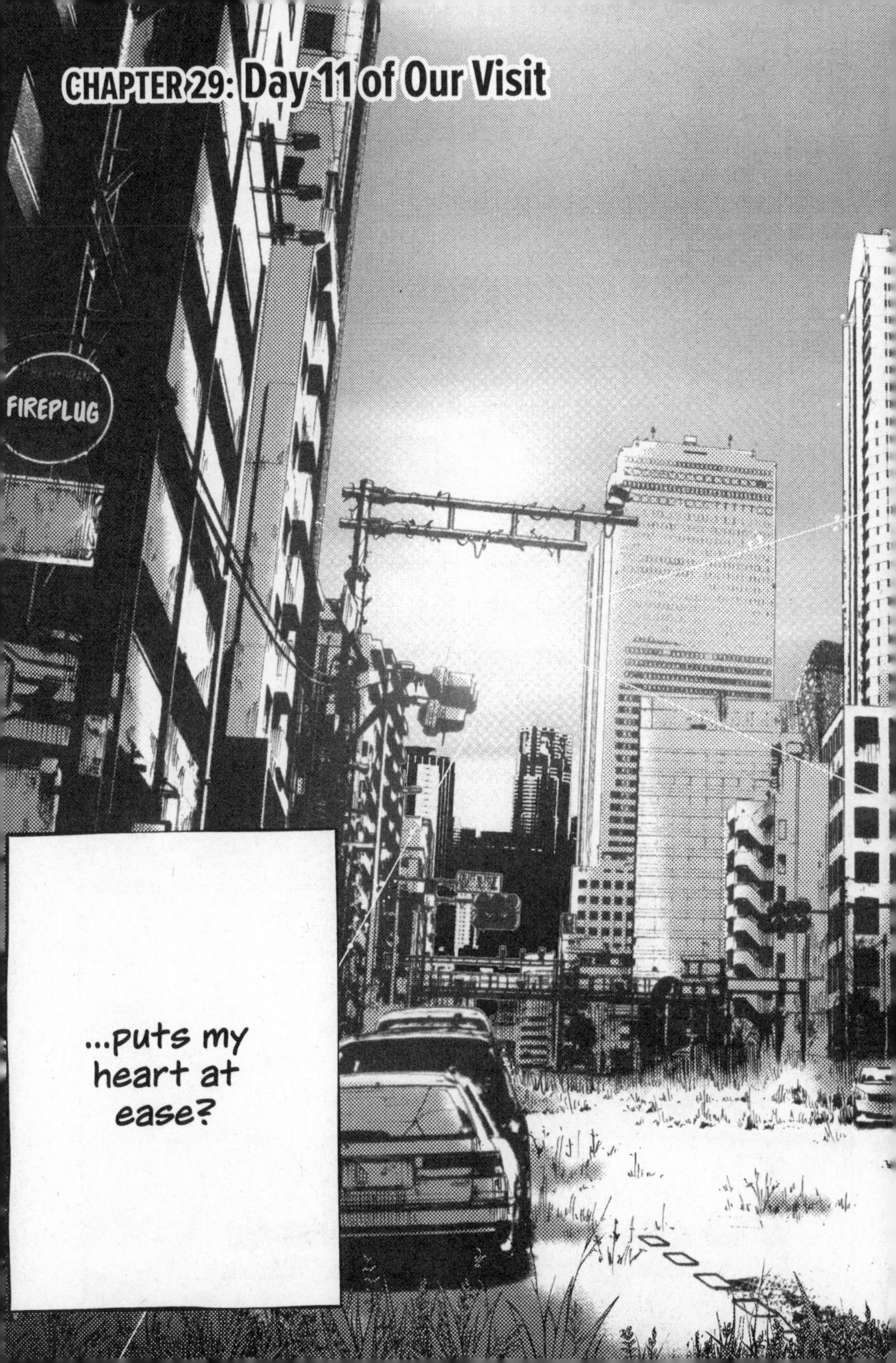
CHAPTER 29: Day 11 of Our Visit
FIREPLUG
...puts my heart at ease?

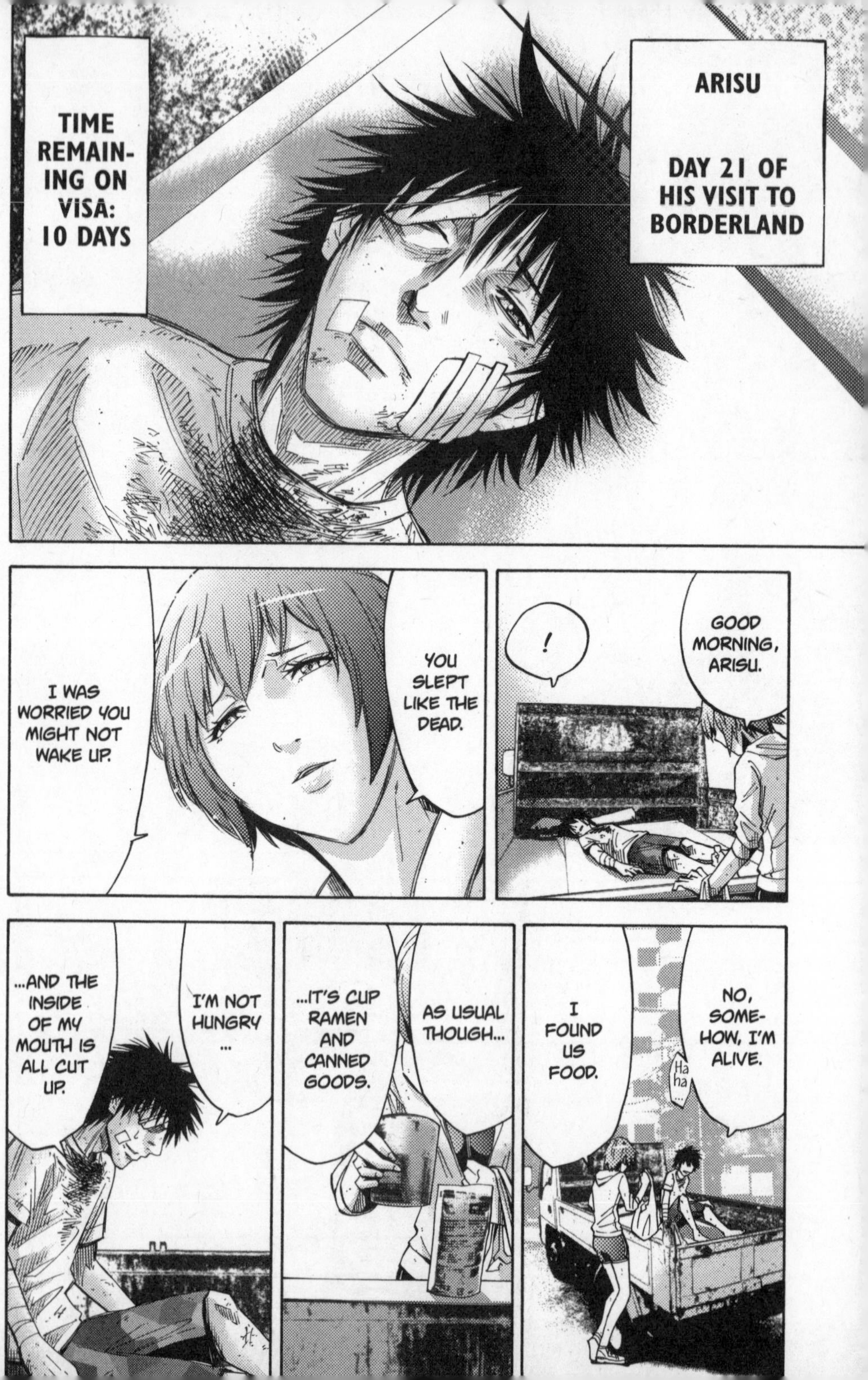
ARISU
DAY 21 OF HIS VISIT TO BORDERLAND
TIME REMAINING ON VISA: 10 DAYS
GOOD MORNING, ARISU.
!
YOU SLEPT LIKE THE DEAD.
I WAS WORRIED YOU MIGHT NOT WAKE UP.
NO, SOMEHOW, I'M ALIVE.
Ha ha ...
I FOUND US FOOD.
AS USUAL THOUGH...
...IT'S CUP RAMEN AND CANNED GOODS.
I'M NOT HUNGRY ...
...AND THE INSIDE OF MY MOUTH IS ALL CUT UP.

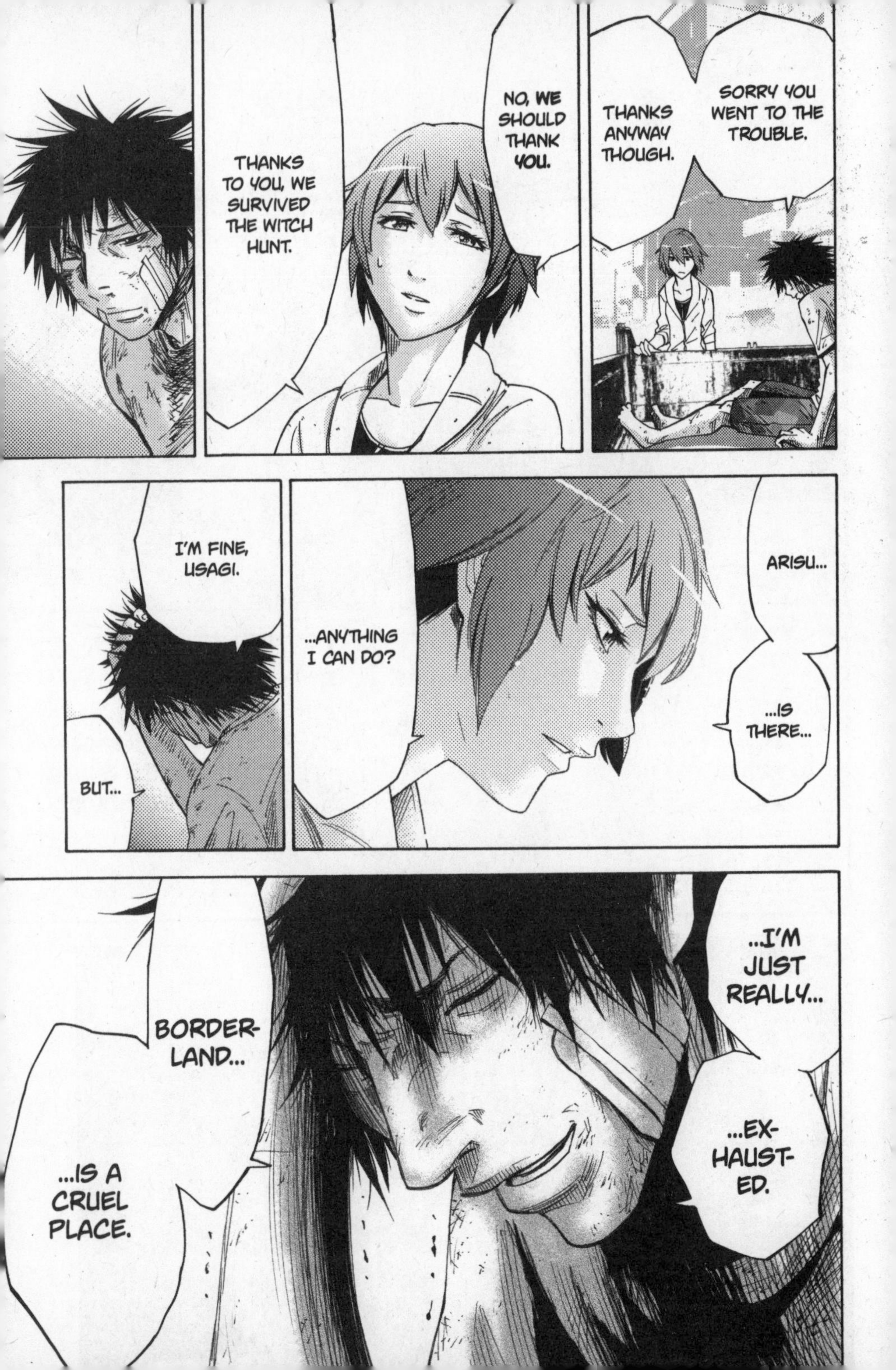
SORRY YOU WENT TO THE TROUBLE.
THANKS ANYWAY THOUGH.
NO, WE SHOULD THANK YOU.
THANKS TO YOU, WE SURVIVED THE WITCH HUNT.
ARISU...
...IS THERE...
...ANYTHING I CAN DO?
I'M FINE, USAGI.
BUT...
...I'M JUST REALLY...
...EX-HAUST-ED.
BORDER-LAND...
...IS A CRUEL PLACE.

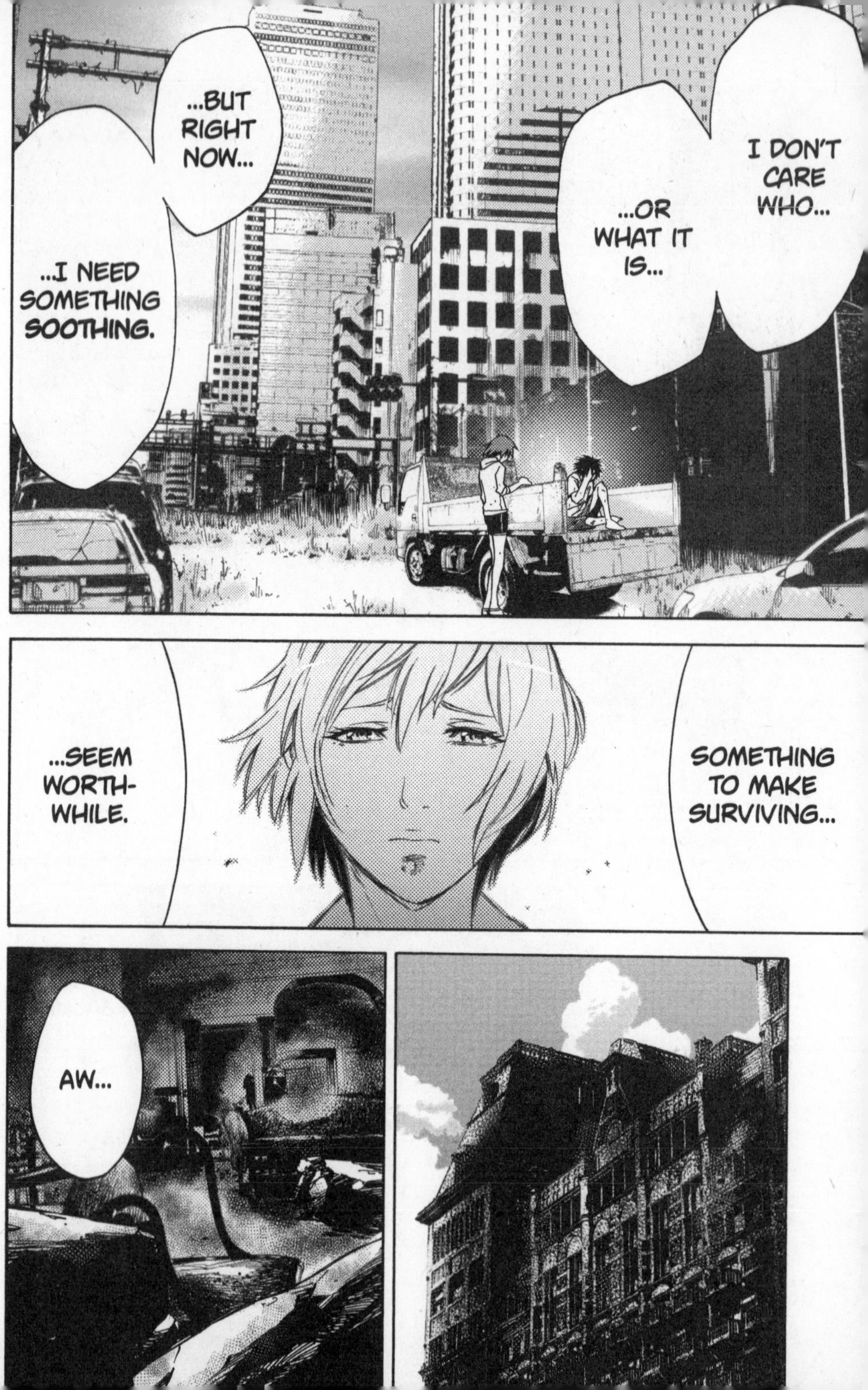
I DON'T CARE WHO...
...OR WHAT IT IS...
...BUT RIGHT NOW...
...I NEED SOMETHING SOOTHING.
SOMETHING TO MAKE SURVIVING...
...SEEM WORTH-WHILE.
AW...

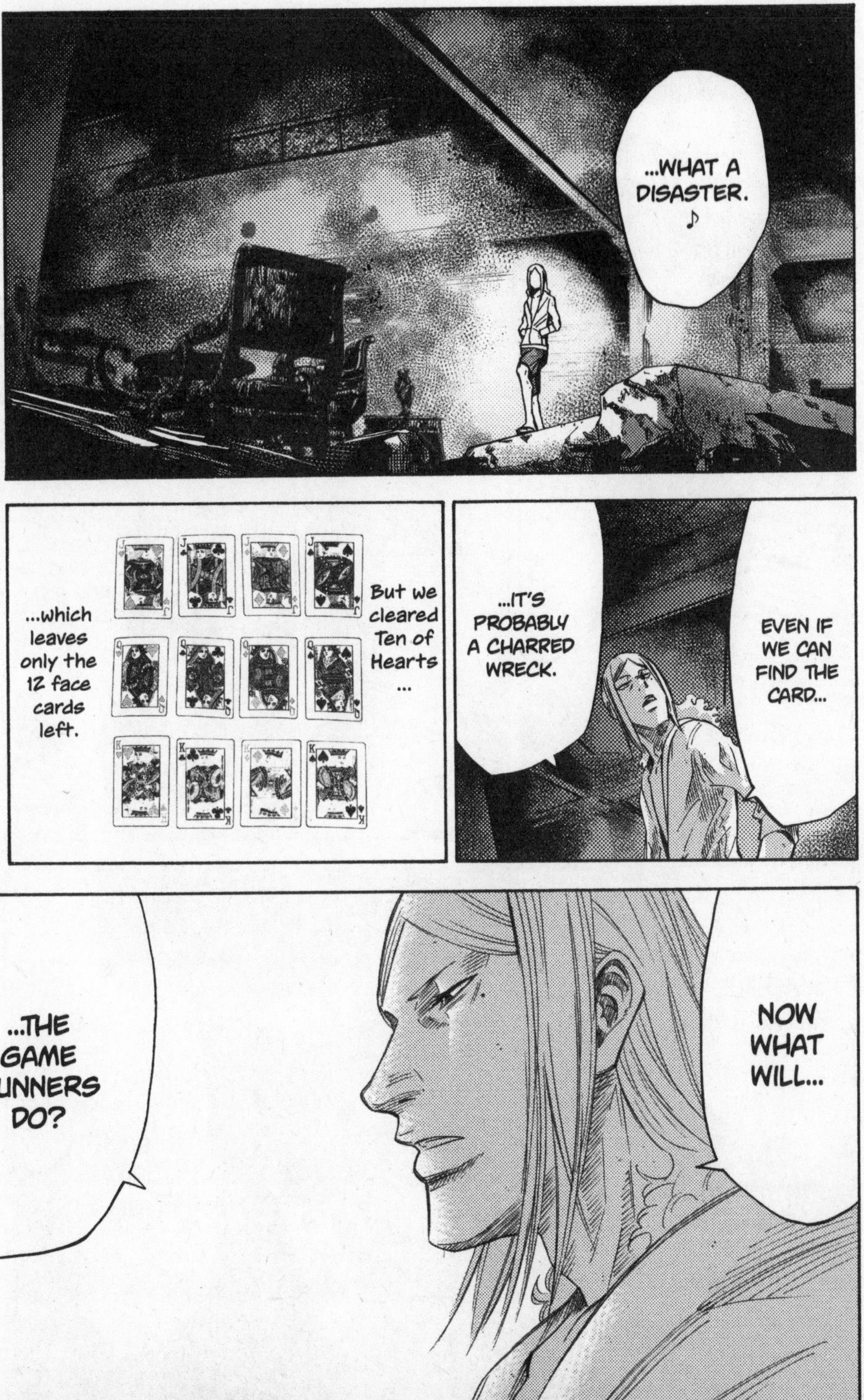
...WHAT A DISASTER. ♪
EVEN IF WE CAN FIND THE CARD...
...IT'S PROBABLY A CHARRED WRECK.
But we cleared Ten of Hearts ...
...which leaves only the 12 face cards left.
NOW WHAT WILL...
...THE GAME RUNNERS DO?

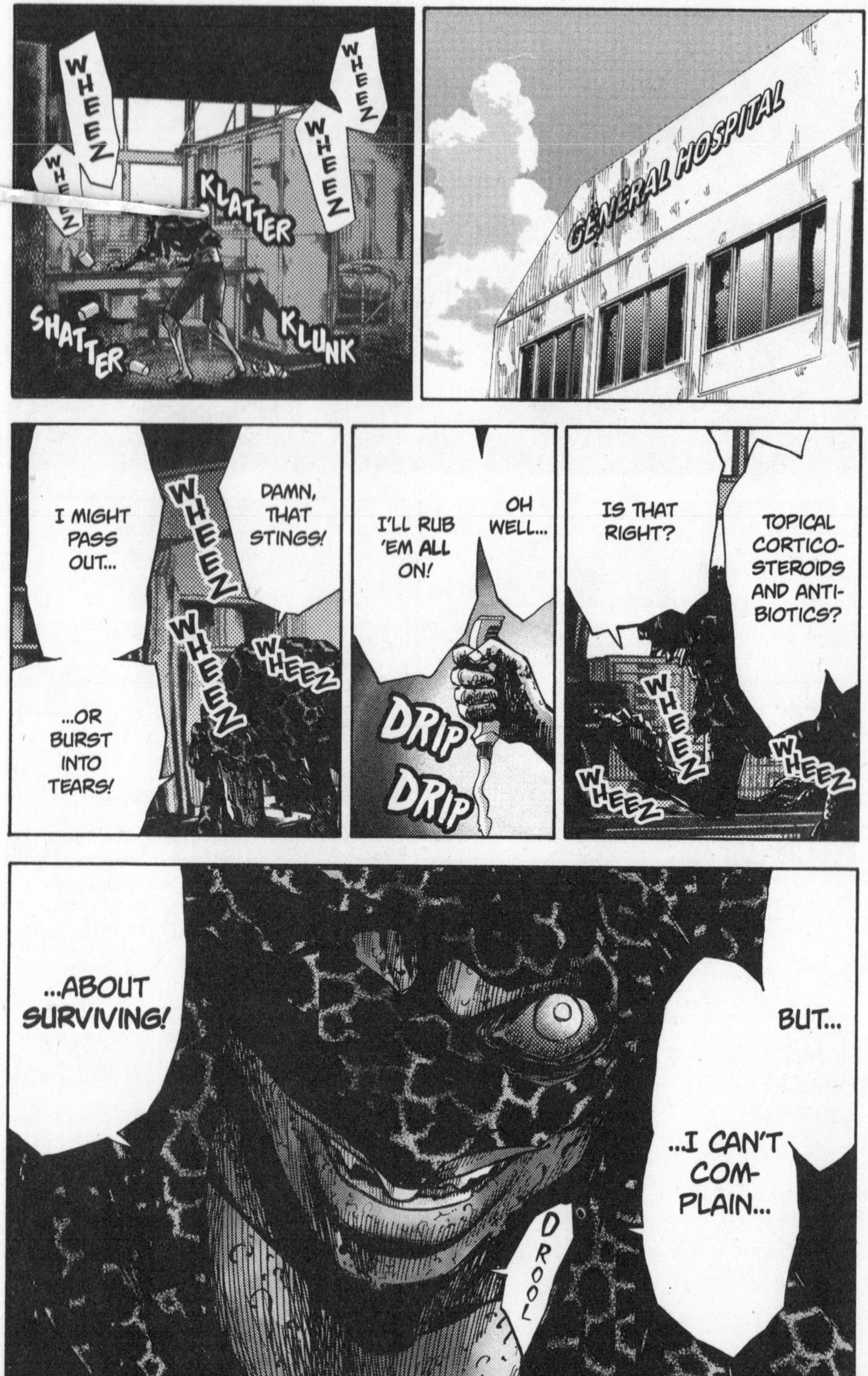
GENERAL HOSPITAL
WHEEZ
WHEEZ
KLATTER
WHEEZ
WHEEZ
SHATTER
KLUNK
TOPICAL CORTICO-STEROIDS AND ANTI-BIOTICS?
IS THAT RIGHT?
WHEEZ
WHEEZ
WHEEZ
OH WELL...
I'LL RUB 'EM ALL ON!
DRIP
DRIP
DAMN, THAT STINGS!
I MIGHT PASS OUT...
WHEEZ
WHEEZ
WHEEZ
...OR BURST INTO TEARS!
BUT...
...I CAN'T COM-PLAIN...
DROOL
...ABOUT SURVIVING!

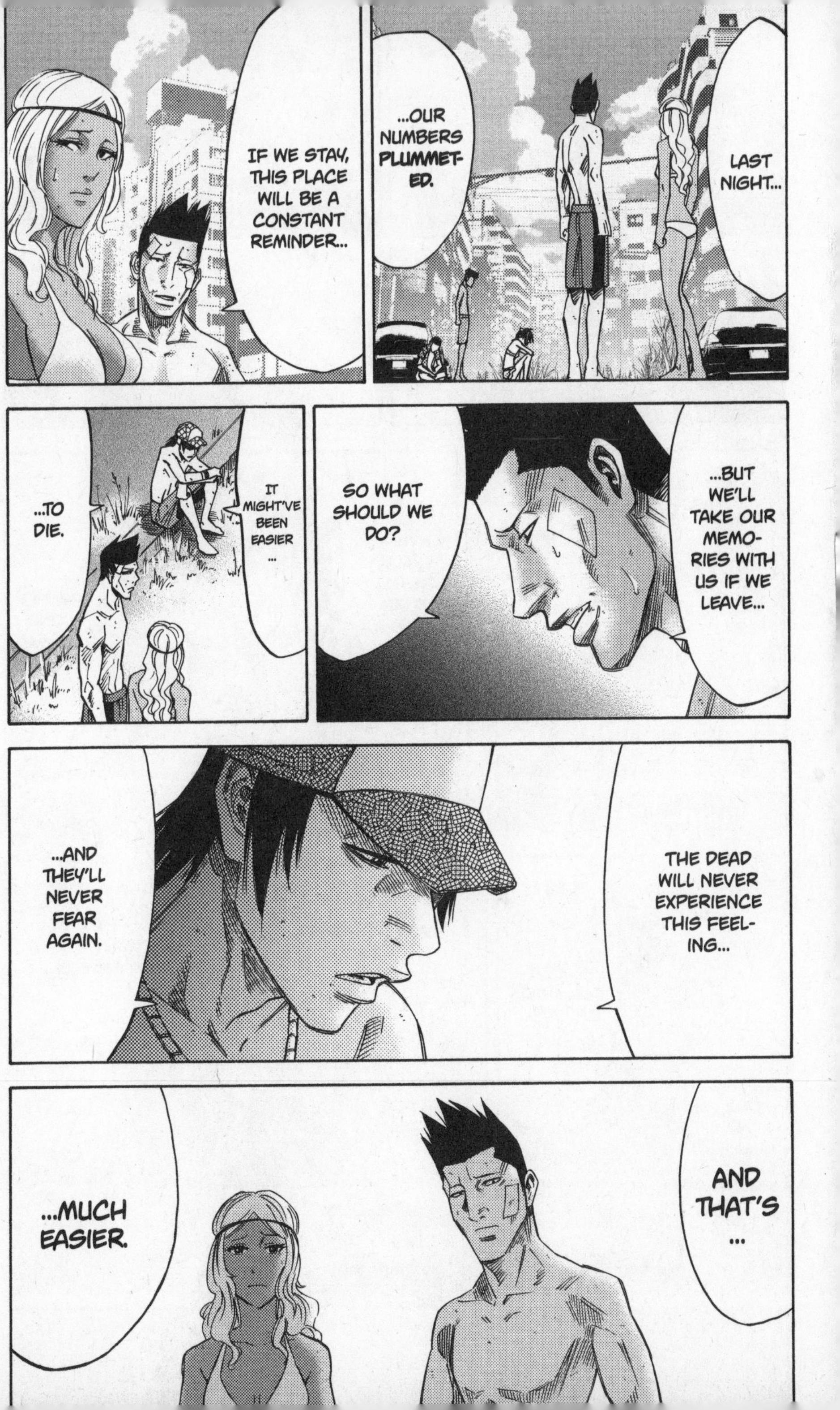
LAST NIGHT...
...OUR NUMBERS PLUMMET-ED.
IF WE STAY, THIS PLACE WILL BE A CONSTANT REMINDER...
...BUT WE'LL TAKE OUR MEMO-RIES WITH US IF WE LEAVE...
SO WHAT SHOULD WE DO?
IT MIGHT'VE BEEN EASIER ...
...TO DIE.
THE DEAD WILL NEVER EXPERIENCE THIS FEEL-ING...
...AND THEY'LL NEVER FEAR AGAIN.
AND THAT'S ...
...MUCH EASIER.

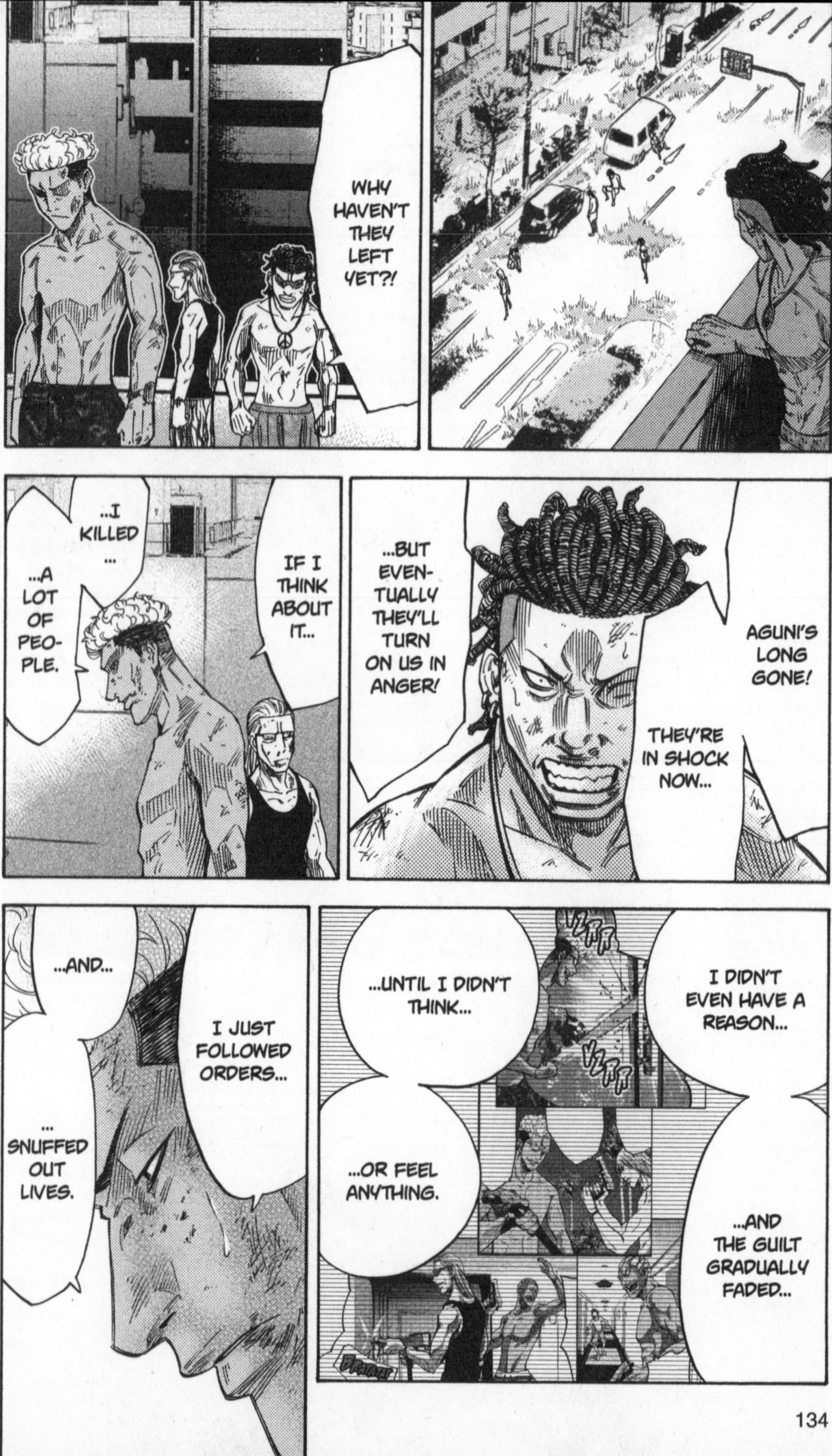
WHY HAVEN'T THEY LEFT YET?!
AGUNI'S LONG GONE!
THEY'RE IN SHOCK NOW...
...BUT EVEN-TUALLY THEY'LL TURN ON US IN ANGER!
IF I THINK ABOUT IT...
...I KILLED...
...A LOT OF PEO-PLE.
I DIDN'T EVEN HAVE A REASON...
...AND THE GUILT GRADUALLY FADED...
...UNTIL I DIDN'T THINK...
...OR FEEL ANYTHING.
I JUST FOLLOWED ORDERS...
...AND...
...SNUFFED OUT LIVES.

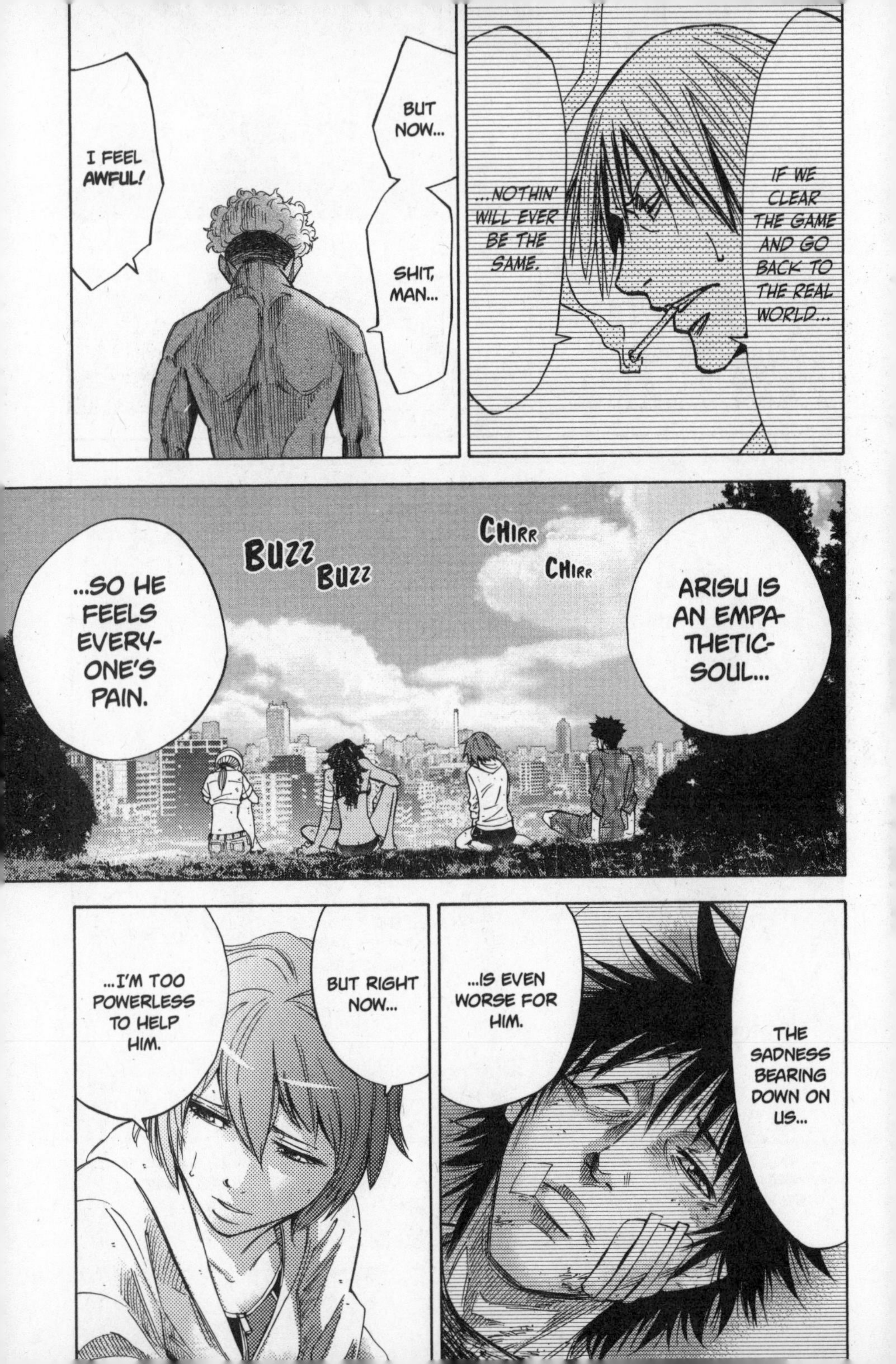
IF WE CLEAR THE GAME AND GO BACK TO THE REAL WORLD...
...NOTHIN' WILL EVER BE THE SAME.
BUT NOW...
SHIT, MAN...
I FEEL AWFUL!
ARISU IS AN EMPA-THETIC-SOUL...
CHIRR
CHIRR
BUZZ
BUZZ
...SO HE FEELS EVERY-ONE'S PAIN.
THE SADNESS BEARING DOWN ON US...
...IS EVEN WORSE FOR HIM.
BUT RIGHT NOW...
...I'M TOO POWERLESS TO HELP HIM.

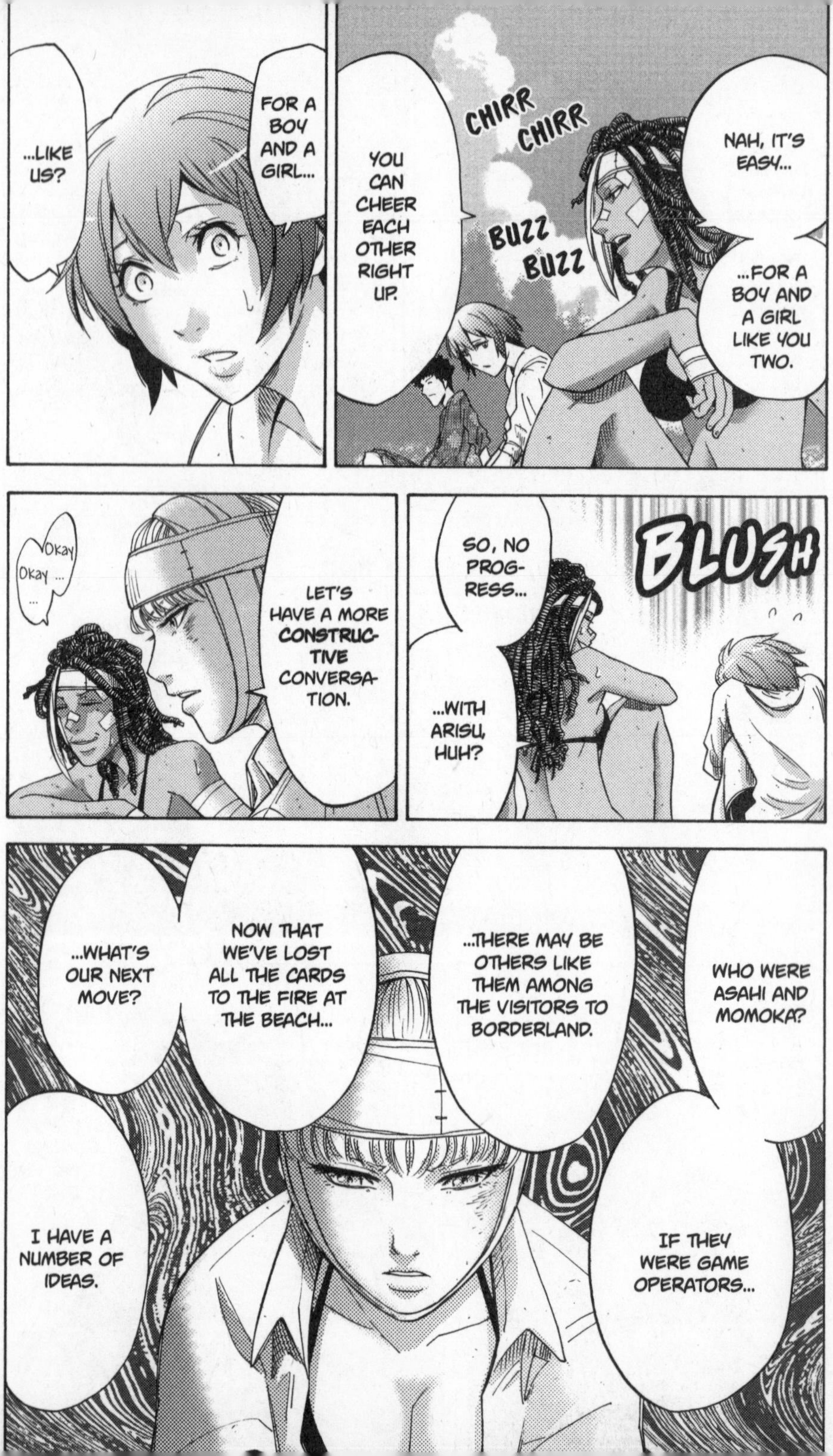
NAH, IT'S EASY...
...FOR A BOY AND A GIRL LIKE YOU TWO.
CHIRR CHIRR
BUZZ BUZZ
YOU CAN CHEER EACH OTHER RIGHT UP.
FOR A BOY AND A GIRL...
...LIKE US?
BLUSH
SO, NO PROGRESS...
...WITH ARISU, HUH?
LET'S HAVE A MORE **CONSTRUCTIVE** CONVERSATION.
Okay Okay ... ...
WHO WERE ASAHI AND MOMOKA?
...THERE MAY BE OTHERS LIKE THEM AMONG THE VISITORS TO BORDERLAND.
NOW THAT WE'VE LOST ALL THE CARDS TO THE FIRE AT THE BEACH...
...WHAT'S OUR NEXT MOVE?
IF THEY WERE GAME OPERATORS...
I HAVE A NUMBER OF IDEAS.

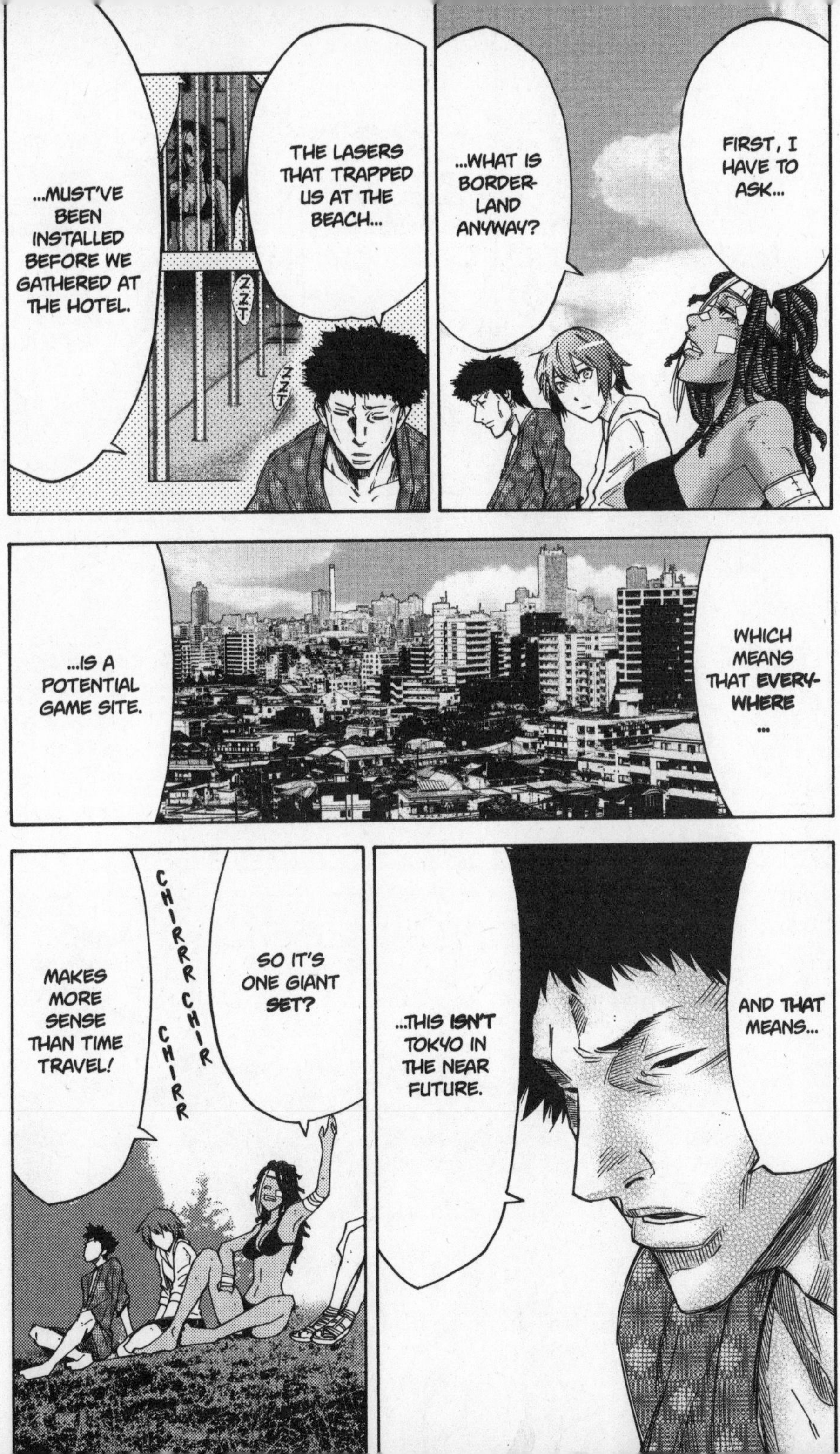
FIRST, I HAVE TO ASK...
...WHAT IS BORDER-LAND ANYWAY?
THE LASERS THAT TRAPPED US AT THE BEACH...
ZZT
ZZT
...MUST'VE BEEN INSTALLED BEFORE WE GATHERED AT THE HOTEL.
WHICH MEANS THAT EVERY-WHERE ...
...IS A POTENTIAL GAME SITE.
AND THAT MEANS...
...THIS ISN'T TOKYO IN THE NEAR FUTURE.
SO IT'S ONE GIANT SET?
CHIRRR CHIR
CHIRR
MAKES MORE SENSE THAN TIME TRAVEL!

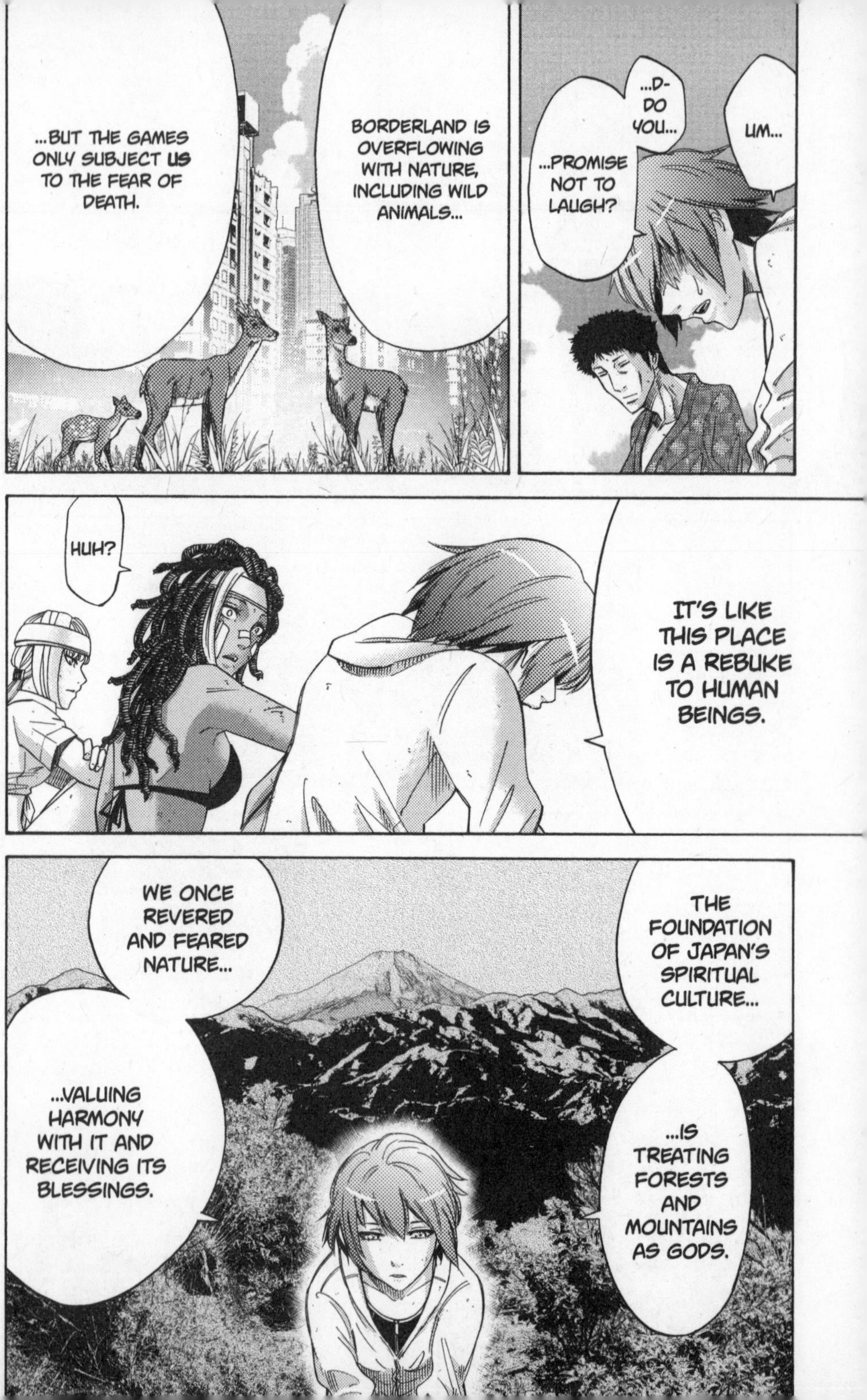
UM...
...D-DO YOU...
...PROMISE NOT TO LAUGH?
BORDERLAND IS OVERFLOWING WITH NATURE, INCLUDING WILD ANIMALS...
...BUT THE GAMES ONLY SUBJECT US TO THE FEAR OF DEATH.
IT'S LIKE THIS PLACE IS A REBUKE TO HUMAN BEINGS.
HUH?
THE FOUNDATION OF JAPAN'S SPIRITUAL CULTURE...
...IS TREATING FORESTS AND MOUNTAINS AS GODS.
WE ONCE REVERED AND FEARED NATURE...
...VALUING HARMONY WITH IT AND RECEIVING ITS BLESSINGS.

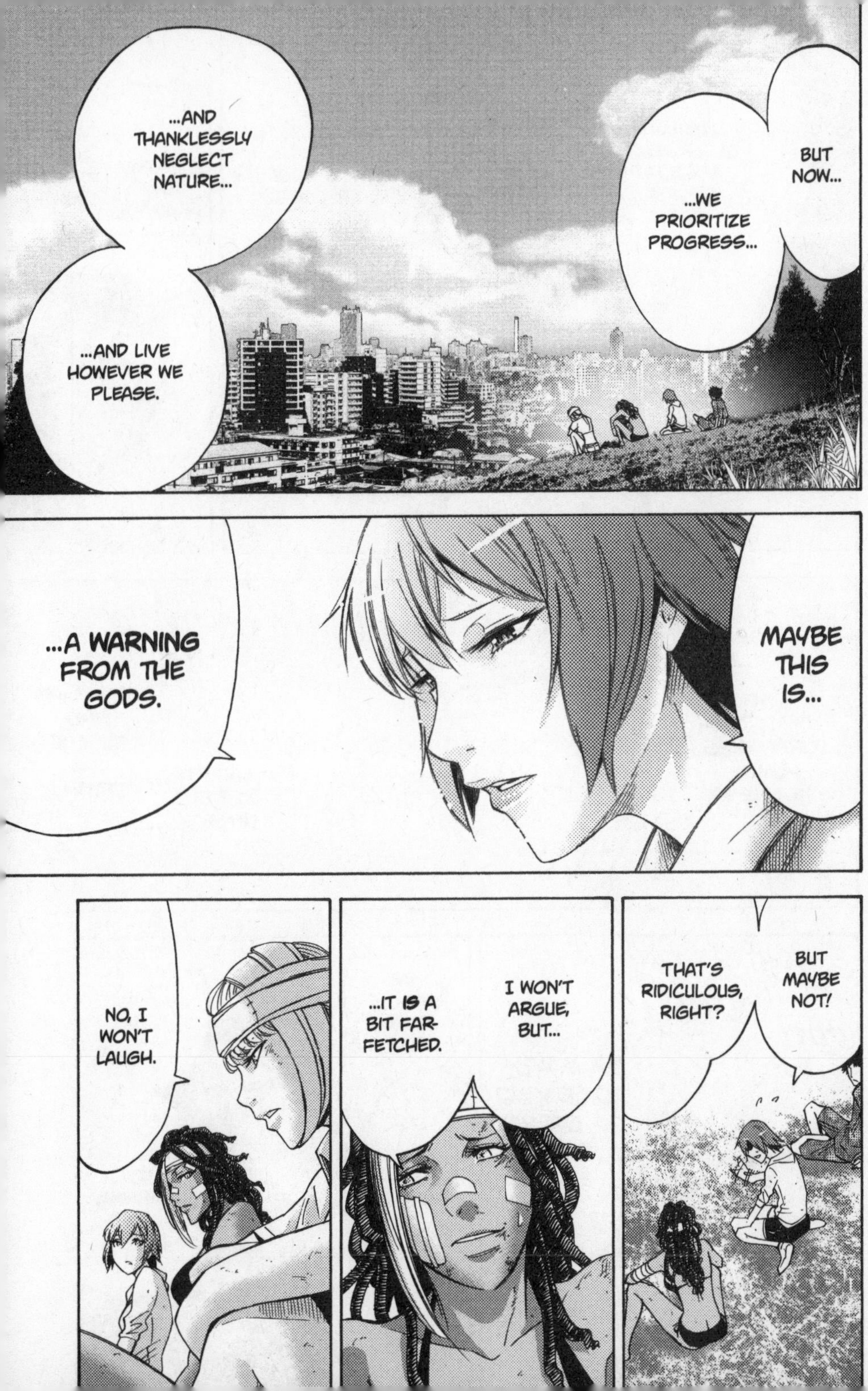
BUT NOW...
...WE PRIORITIZE PROGRESS...
...AND THANKLESSLY NEGLECT NATURE...
...AND LIVE HOWEVER WE PLEASE.
MAYBE THIS IS...
...A WARNING FROM THE GODS.
BUT MAYBE NOT!
THAT'S RIDICULOUS, RIGHT?
I WON'T ARGUE, BUT...
...IT IS A BIT FAR-FETCHED.
NO, I WON'T LAUGH.

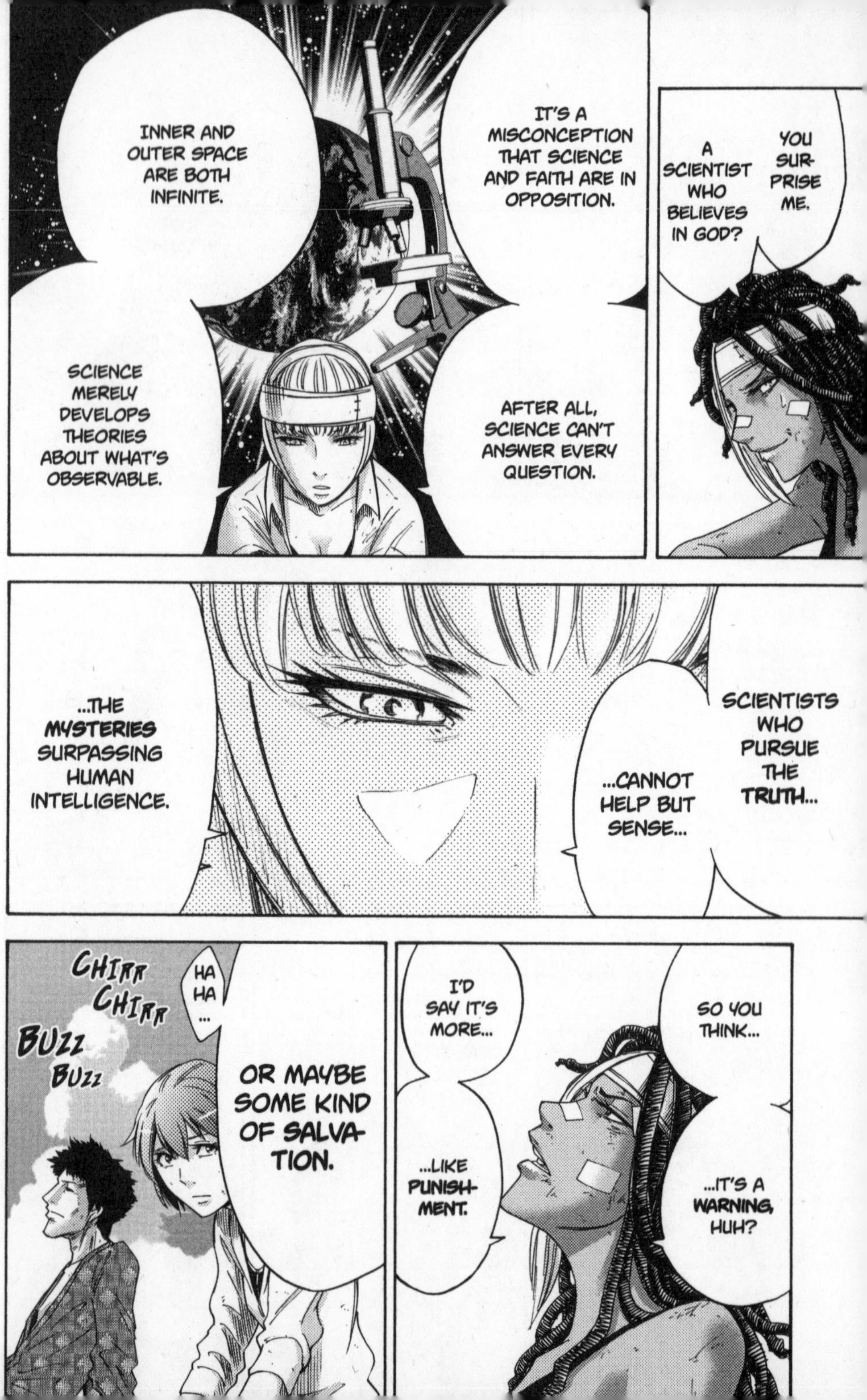
YOU SURPRISE ME.
A SCIENTIST WHO BELIEVES IN GOD?
IT'S A MISCONCEPTION THAT SCIENCE AND FAITH ARE IN OPPOSITION.
INNER AND OUTER SPACE ARE BOTH INFINITE.
AFTER ALL, SCIENCE CAN'T ANSWER EVERY QUESTION.
SCIENCE MERELY DEVELOPS THEORIES ABOUT WHAT'S OBSERVABLE.
SCIENTISTS WHO PURSUE THE TRUTH...
...CANNOT HELP BUT SENSE...
...THE MYSTERIES SURPASSING HUMAN INTELLIGENCE.
SO YOU THINK...
...IT'S A WARNING, HUH?
I'D SAY IT'S MORE...
...LIKE PUNISHMENT.
HA HA ...
OR MAYBE SOME KIND OF SALVATION.
CHIRR CHIRR
BUZZ BUZZ

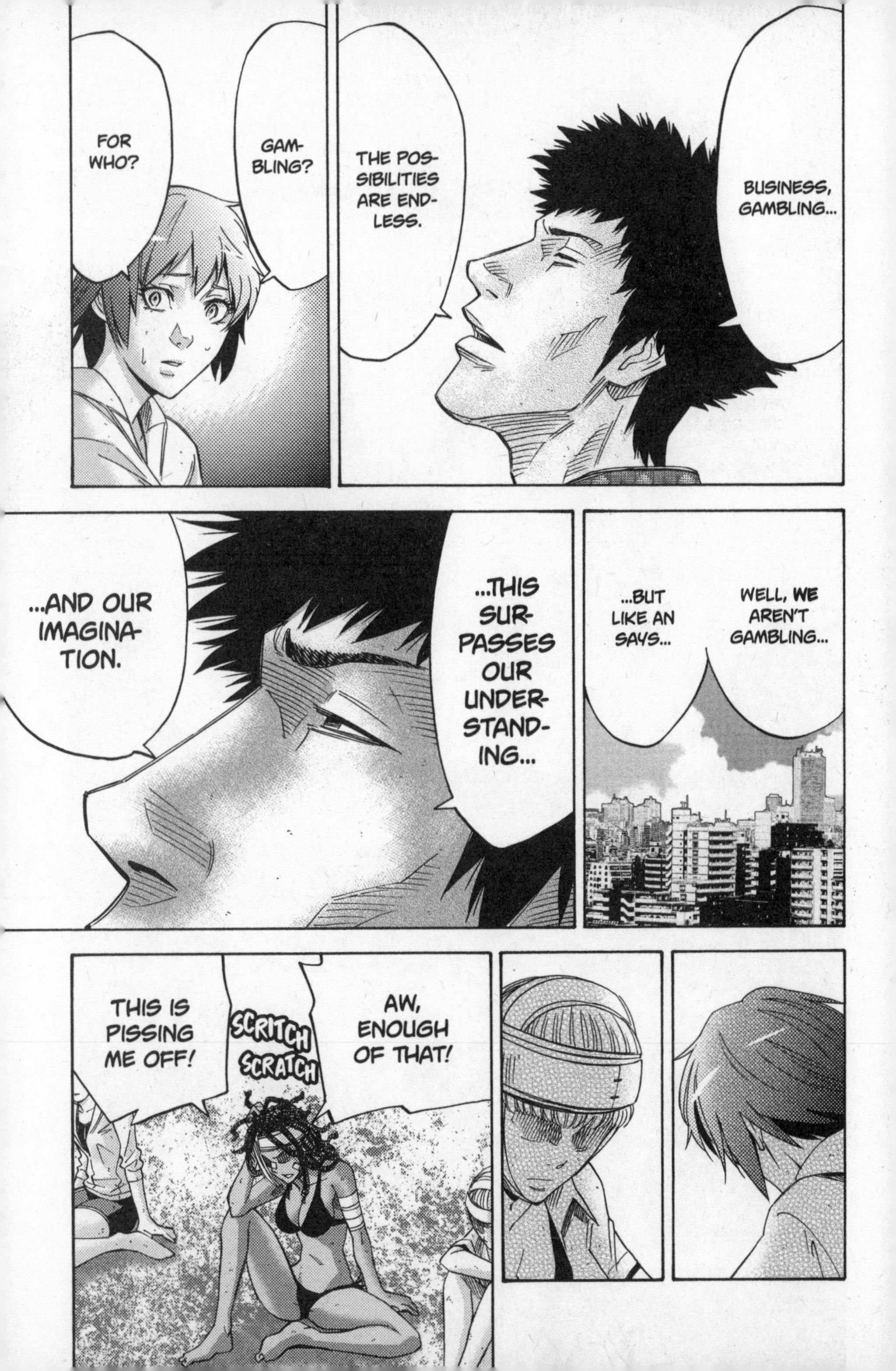
BUSINESS, GAMBLING...
THE POSSIBILITIES ARE ENDLESS.
GAMBLING?
FOR WHO?
WELL, WE AREN'T GAMBLING...
...BUT LIKE AN SAYS...
...THIS SURPASSES OUR UNDERSTANDING...
...AND OUR IMAGINATION.
AW, ENOUGH OF THAT!
SCRITCH SCRATCH
THIS IS PISSING ME OFF!

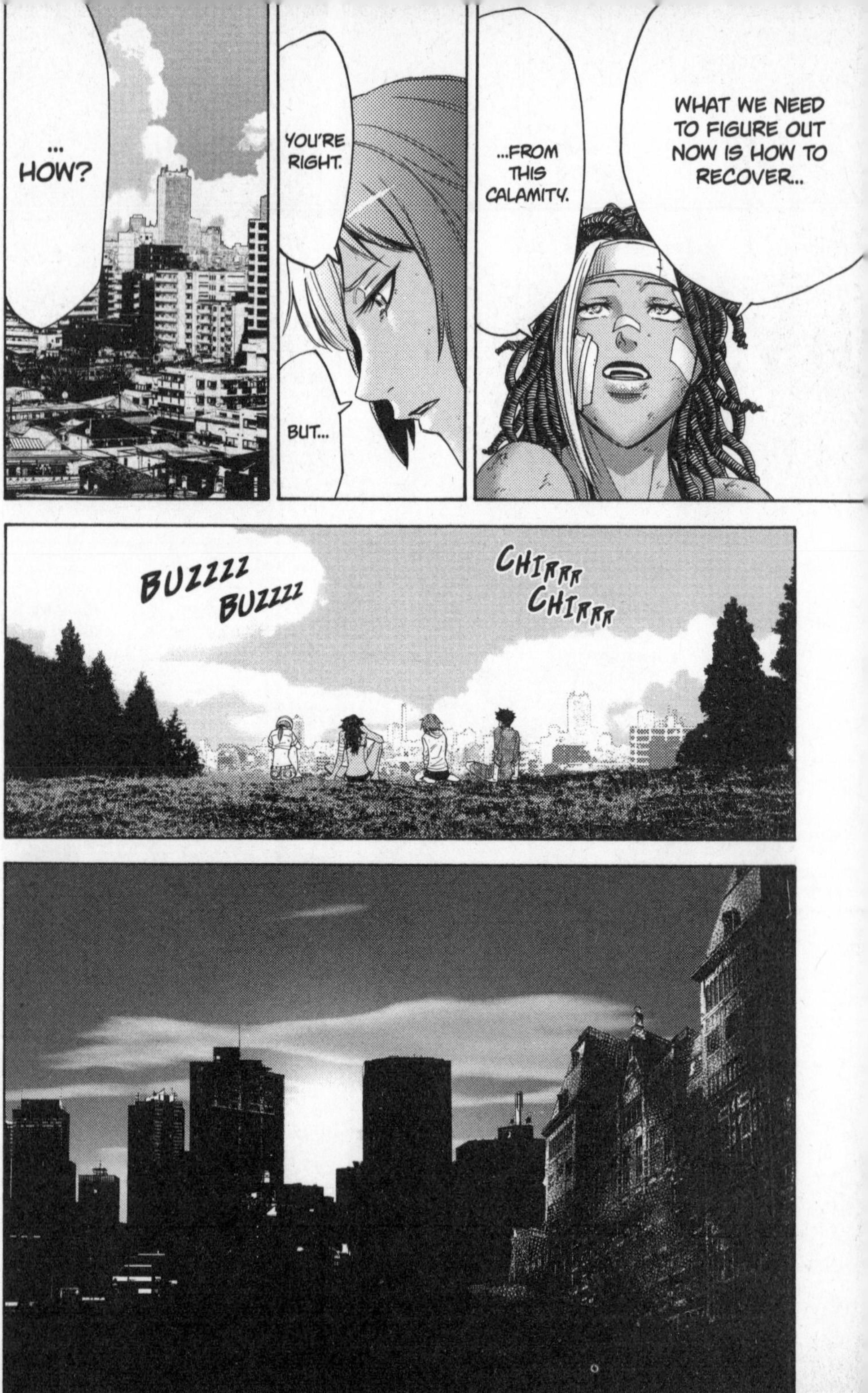
WHAT WE NEED TO FIGURE OUT NOW IS HOW TO RECOVER...
...FROM THIS CALAMITY.
YOU'RE RIGHT.
BUT...
... HOW?
CHIRRR CHIRRR
BUZZZZ BUZZZZ

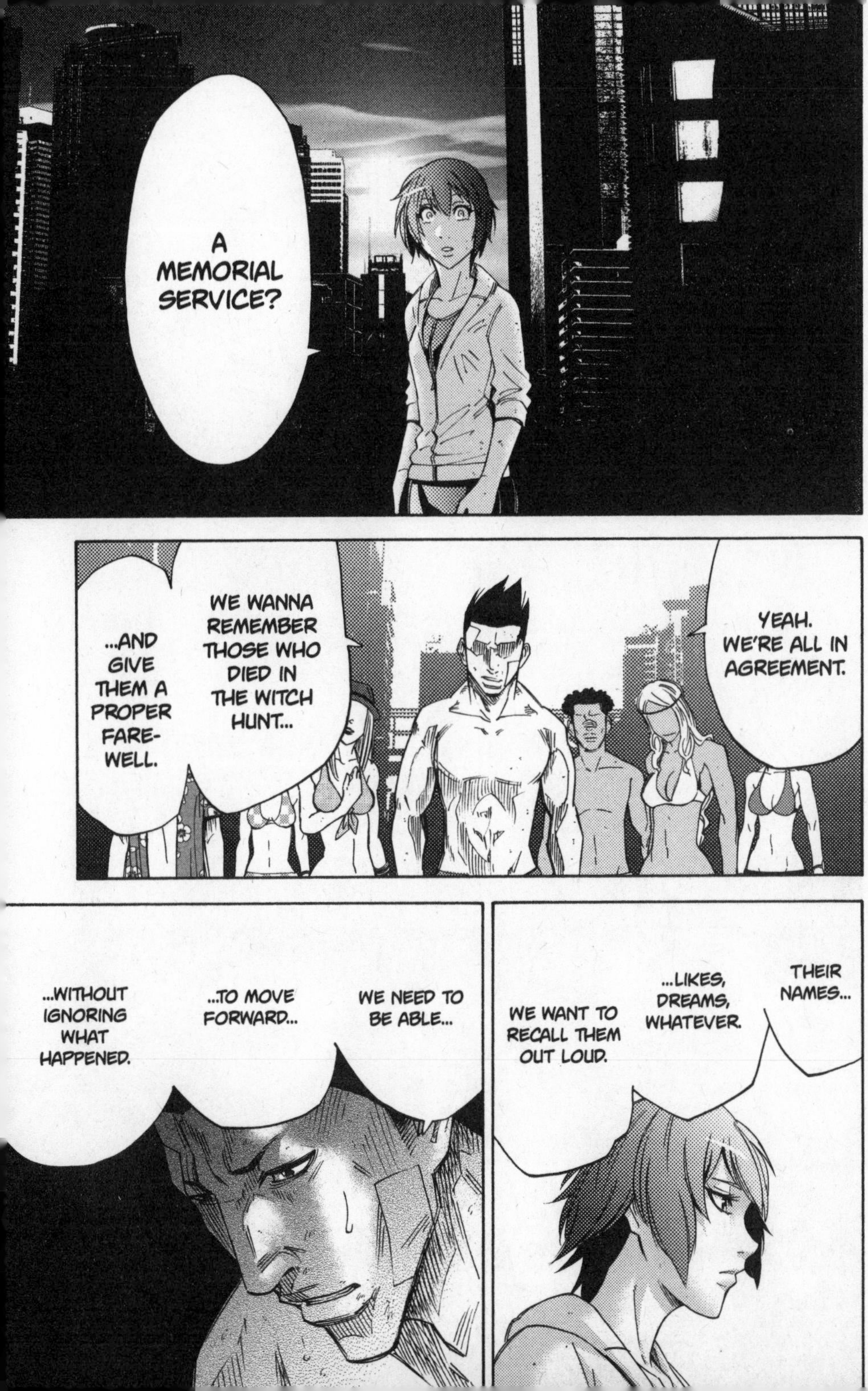
A MEMORIAL SERVICE?
YEAH. WE'RE ALL IN AGREEMENT.
WE WANNA REMEMBER THOSE WHO DIED IN THE WITCH HUNT...
...AND GIVE THEM A PROPER FARE-WELL.
THEIR NAMES...
...LIKES, DREAMS, WHATEVER.
WE WANT TO RECALL THEM OUT LOUD.
WE NEED TO BE ABLE...
...TO MOVE FORWARD...
...WITHOUT IGNORING WHAT HAPPENED.

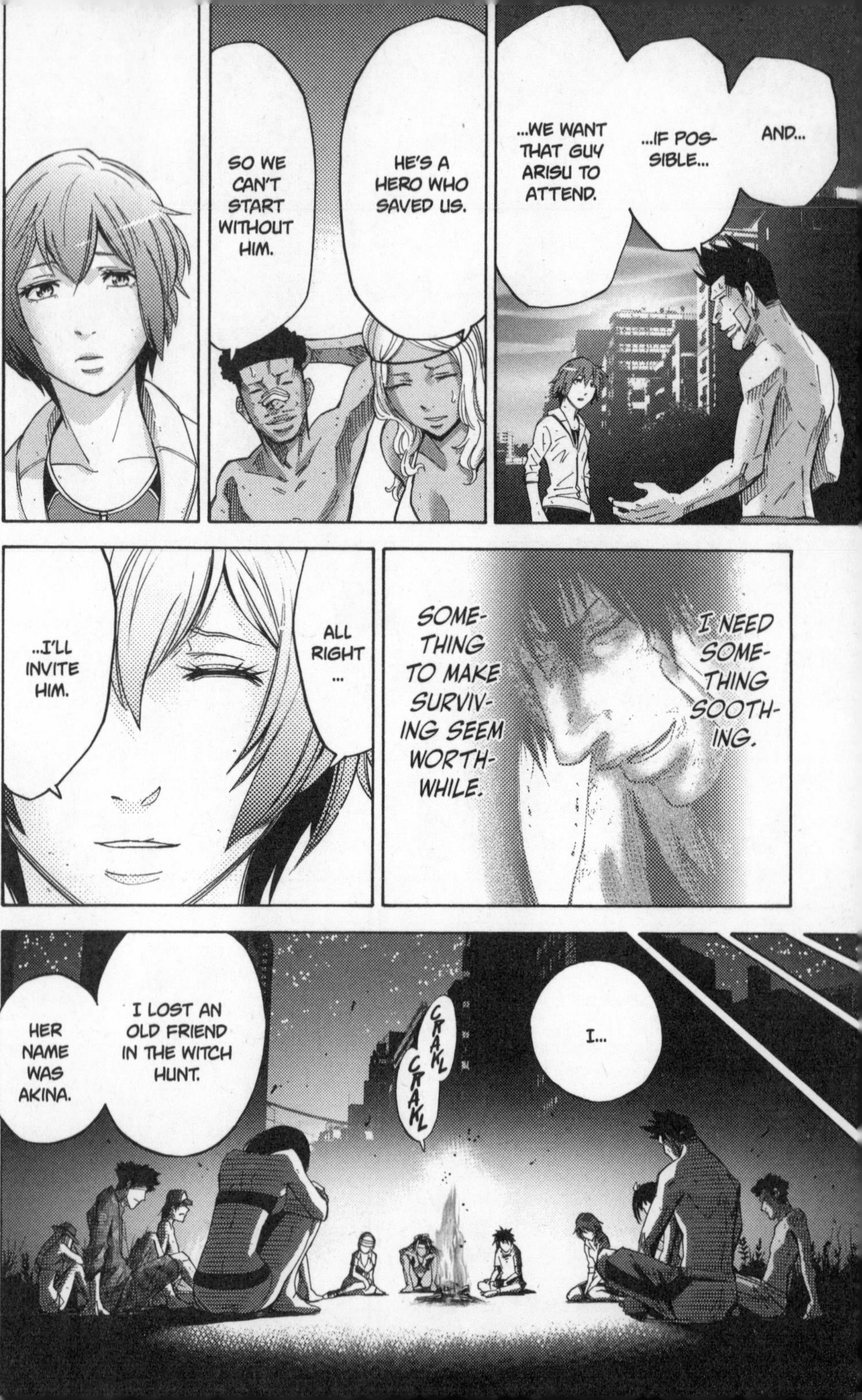
AND...
...IF POSSIBLE...
...WE WANT THAT GUY ARISU TO ATTEND.
HE'S A HERO WHO SAVED US.
SO WE CAN'T START WITHOUT HIM.
I NEED SOMETHING SOOTHING.
SOMETHING TO MAKE SURVIVING SEEM WORTHWHILE.
ALL RIGHT...
...I'LL INVITE HIM.
I...
CRAKL CRAKL
I LOST AN OLD FRIEND IN THE WITCH HUNT.
HER NAME WAS AKINA.

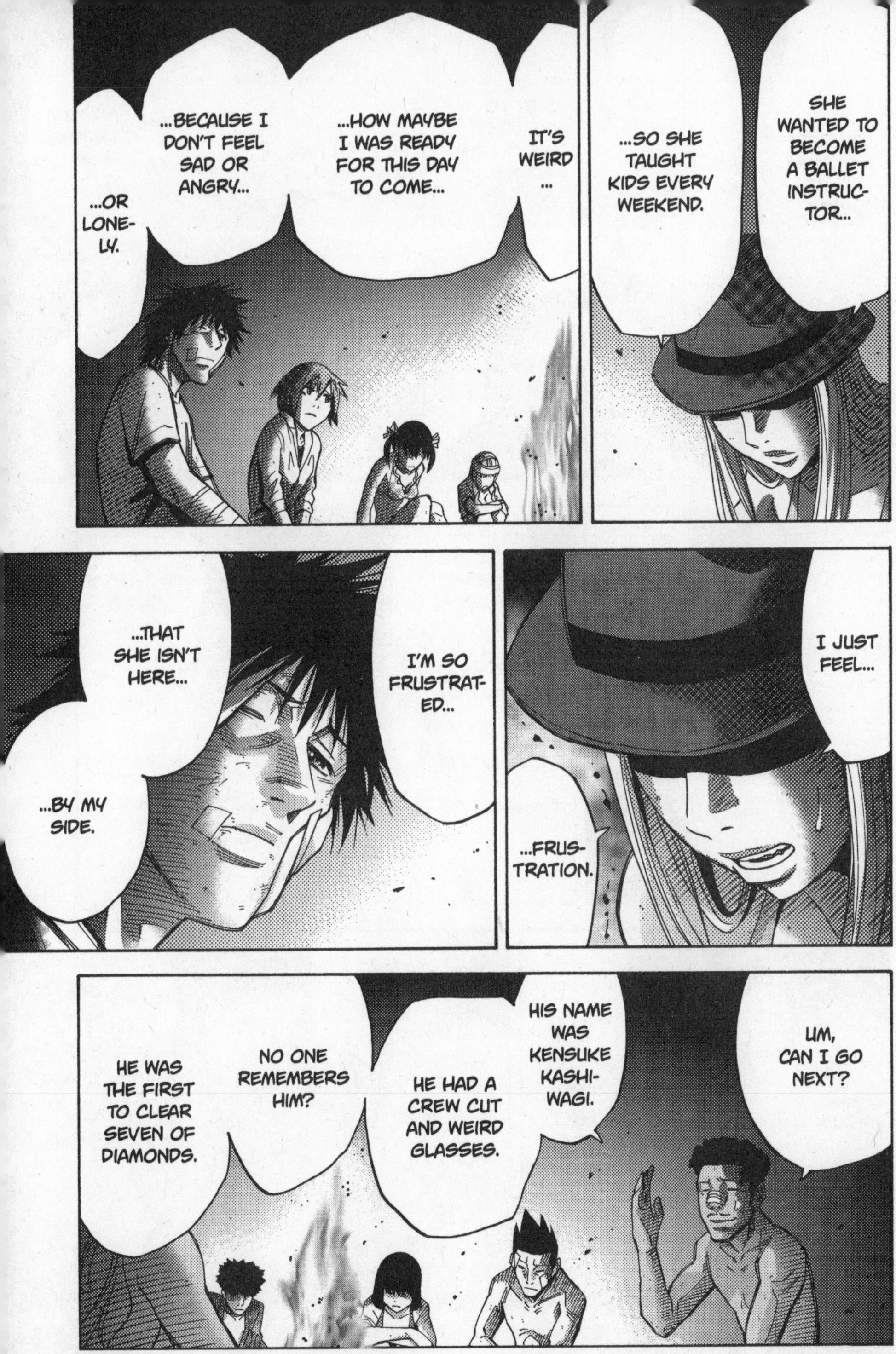
SHE WANTED TO BECOME A BALLET INSTRUCTOR...
...SO SHE TAUGHT KIDS EVERY WEEKEND.
IT'S WEIRD...
...HOW MAYBE I WAS READY FOR THIS DAY TO COME...
...BECAUSE I DON'T FEEL SAD OR ANGRY...
...OR LONELY.
I JUST FEEL...
...FRUSTRATION.
I'M SO FRUSTRATED...
...THAT SHE ISN'T HERE...
...BY MY SIDE.
UM, CAN I GO NEXT?
HIS NAME WAS KENSUKE KASHIWAGI.
HE HAD A CREW CUT AND WEIRD GLASSES.
NO ONE REMEMBERS HIM?
HE WAS THE FIRST TO CLEAR SEVEN OF DIAMONDS.

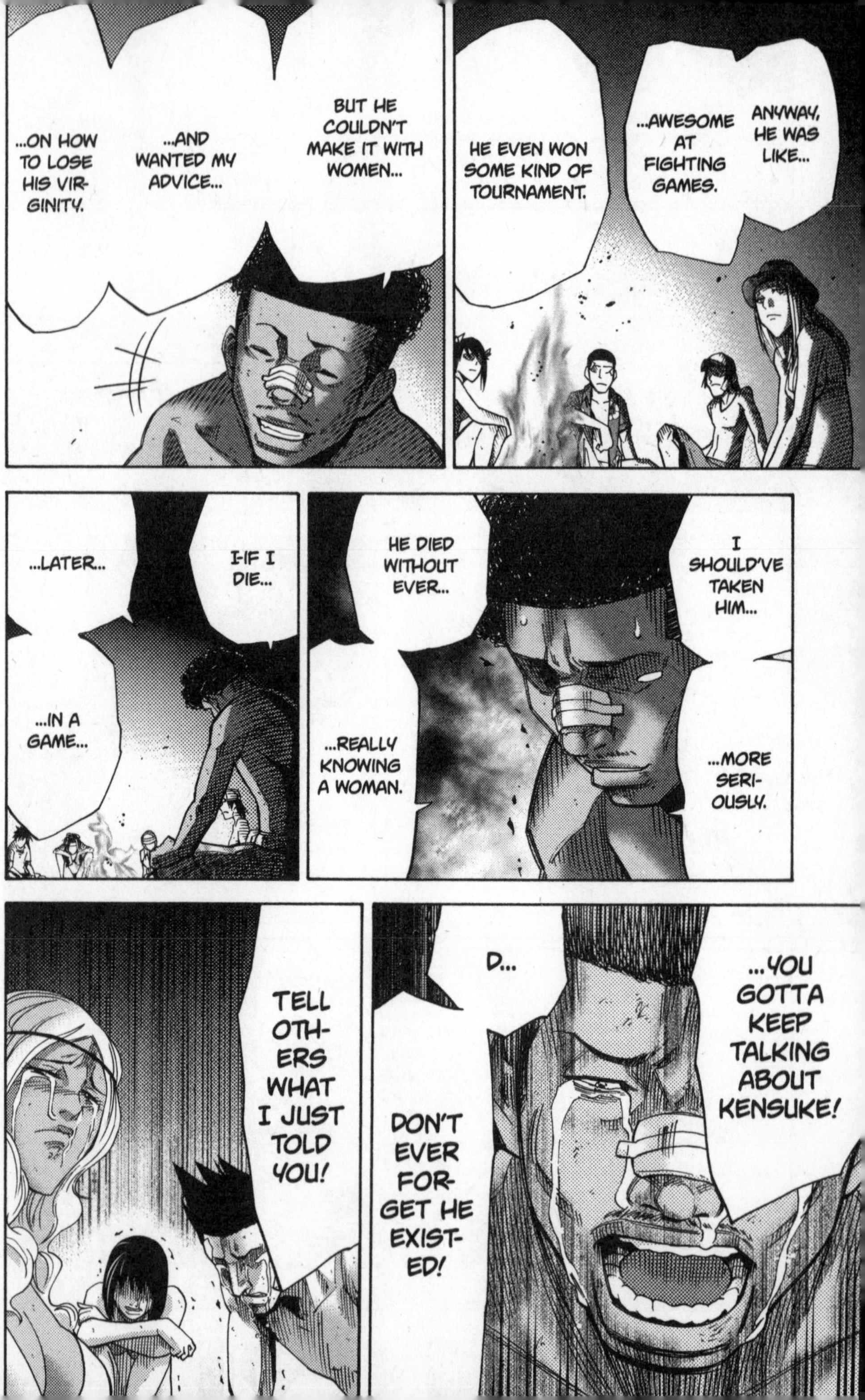
ANYWAY, HE WAS LIKE...
...AWESOME AT FIGHTING GAMES.
HE EVEN WON SOME KIND OF TOURNAMENT.
BUT HE COULDN'T MAKE IT WITH WOMEN...
...AND WANTED MY ADVICE...
...ON HOW TO LOSE HIS VIRGINITY.
I SHOULD'VE TAKEN HIM...
...MORE SERIOUSLY.
HE DIED WITHOUT EVER...
...REALLY KNOWING A WOMAN.
I-IF I DIE...
...LATER...
...IN A GAME...
...YOU GOTTA KEEP TALKING ABOUT KENSUKE!
D...
DON'T EVER FORGET HE EXISTED!
TELL OTHERS WHAT I JUST TOLD YOU!

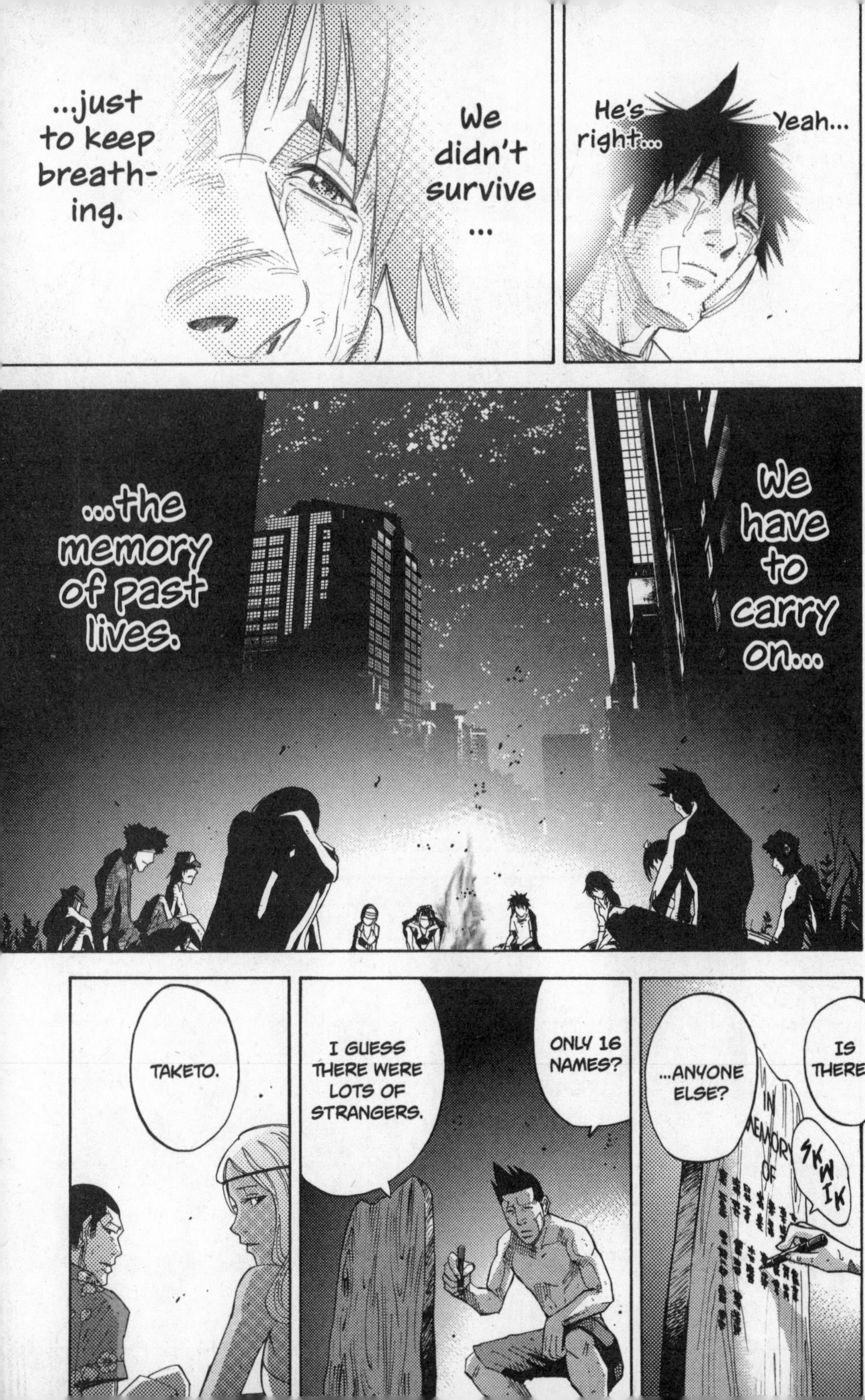
Yeah...
He's right...
We didn't survive ...
...just to keep breath-ing.
We have to carry on...
...the memory of past lives.
IS THERE...
...ANYONE ELSE?
SKWIK
IN MEMORY OF
ONLY 16 NAMES?
I GUESS THERE WERE LOTS OF STRANGERS.
TAKETO.

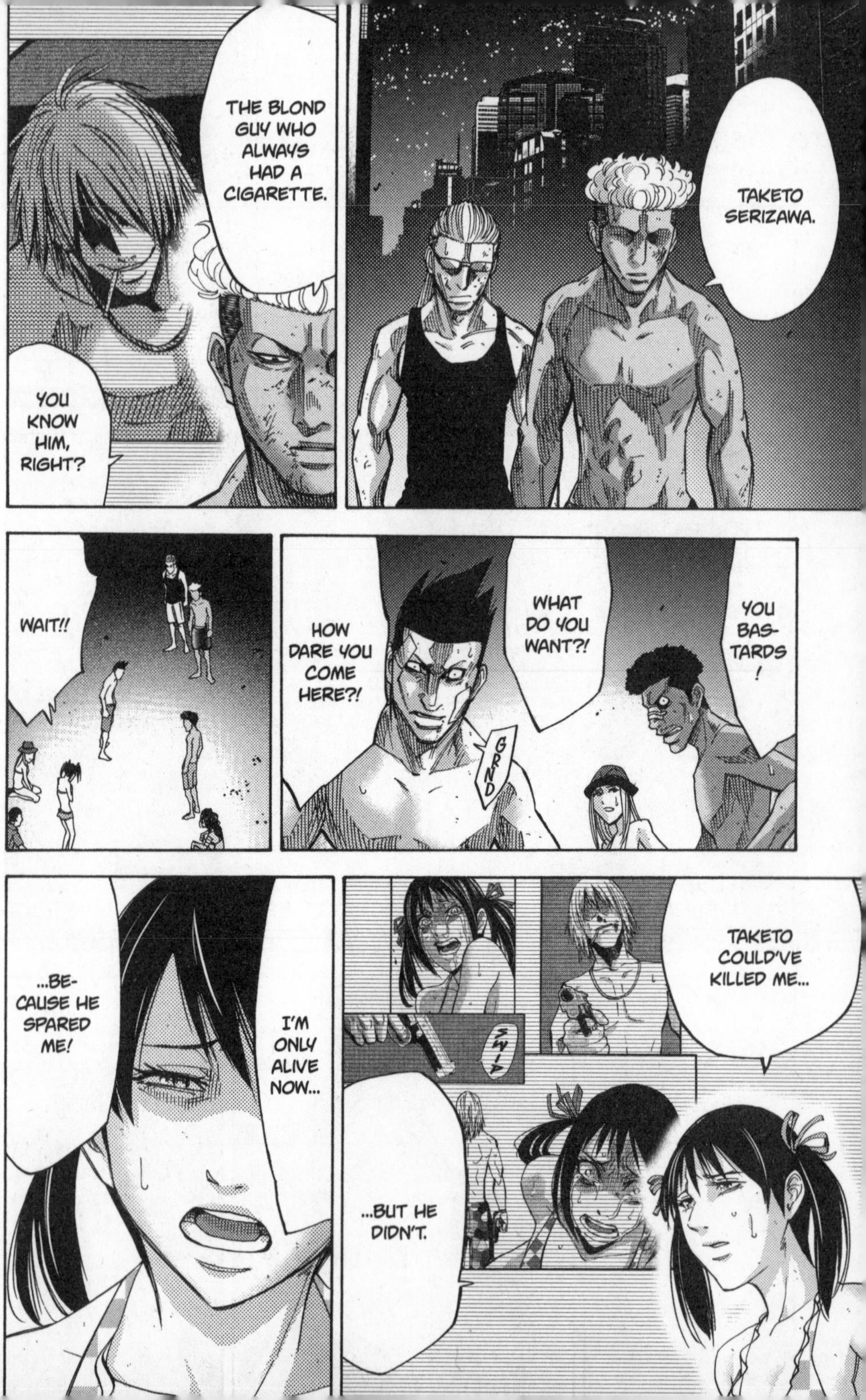
TAKETO SERIZAWA.
THE BLOND GUY WHO ALWAYS HAD A CIGARETTE.
YOU KNOW HIM, RIGHT?
YOU BAS-TARDS!
WHAT DO YOU WANT?!
HOW DARE YOU COME HERE?!
GRND
WAIT!!
TAKETO COULD'VE KILLED ME...
SWIP
...BUT HE DIDN'T.
I'M ONLY ALIVE NOW...
...BE-CAUSE HE SPARED ME!

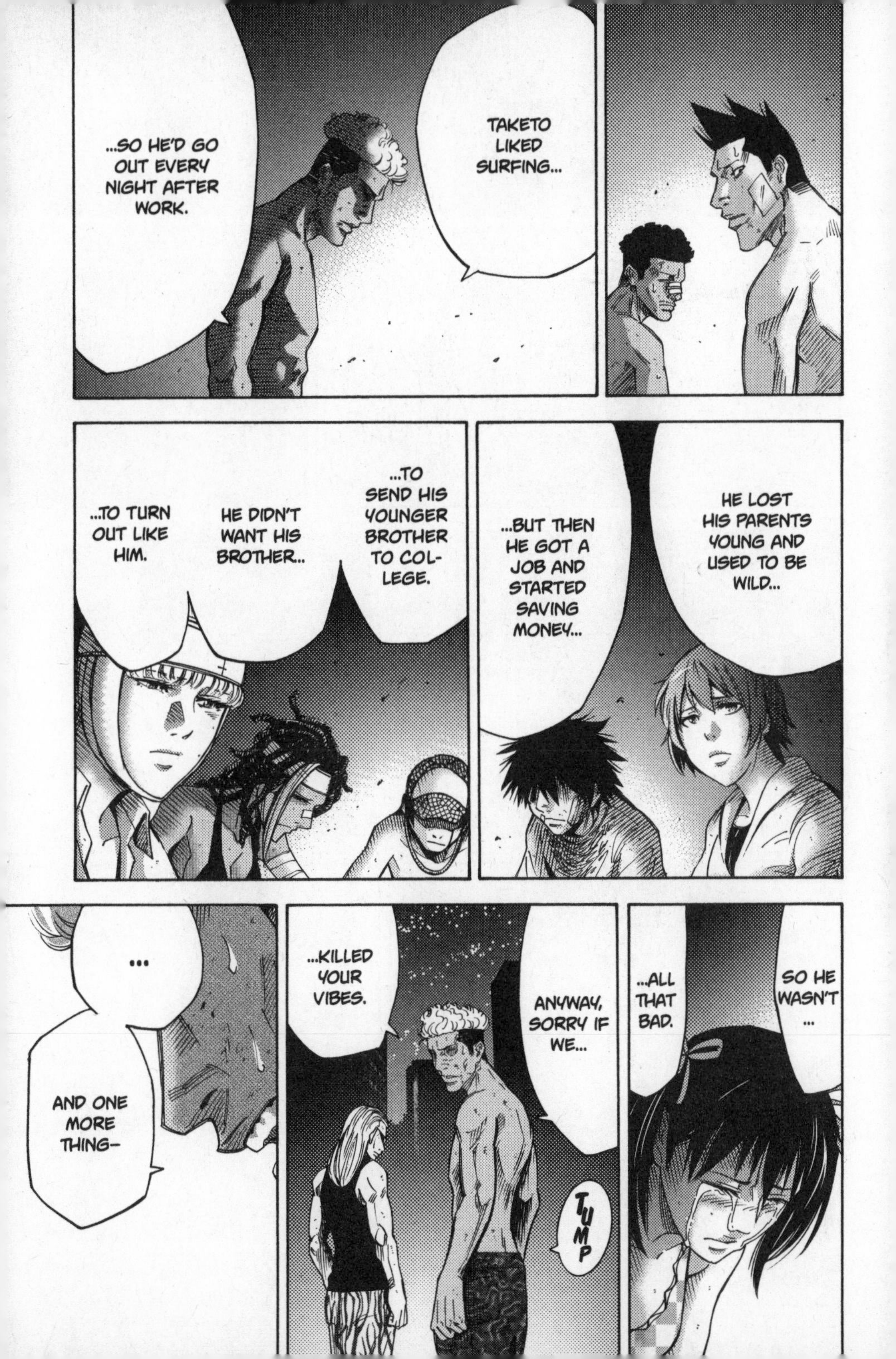
TAKETO LIKED SURFING...
...SO HE'D GO OUT EVERY NIGHT AFTER WORK.
HE LOST HIS PARENTS YOUNG AND USED TO BE WILD...
...BUT THEN HE GOT A JOB AND STARTED SAVING MONEY...
...TO SEND HIS YOUNGER BROTHER TO COL-LEGE.
HE DIDN'T WANT HIS BROTHER...
...TO TURN OUT LIKE HIM.
SO HE WASN'T ...
...ALL THAT BAD.
ANYWAY, SORRY IF WE...
...KILLED YOUR VIBES.
TUMP
...
AND ONE MORE THING–

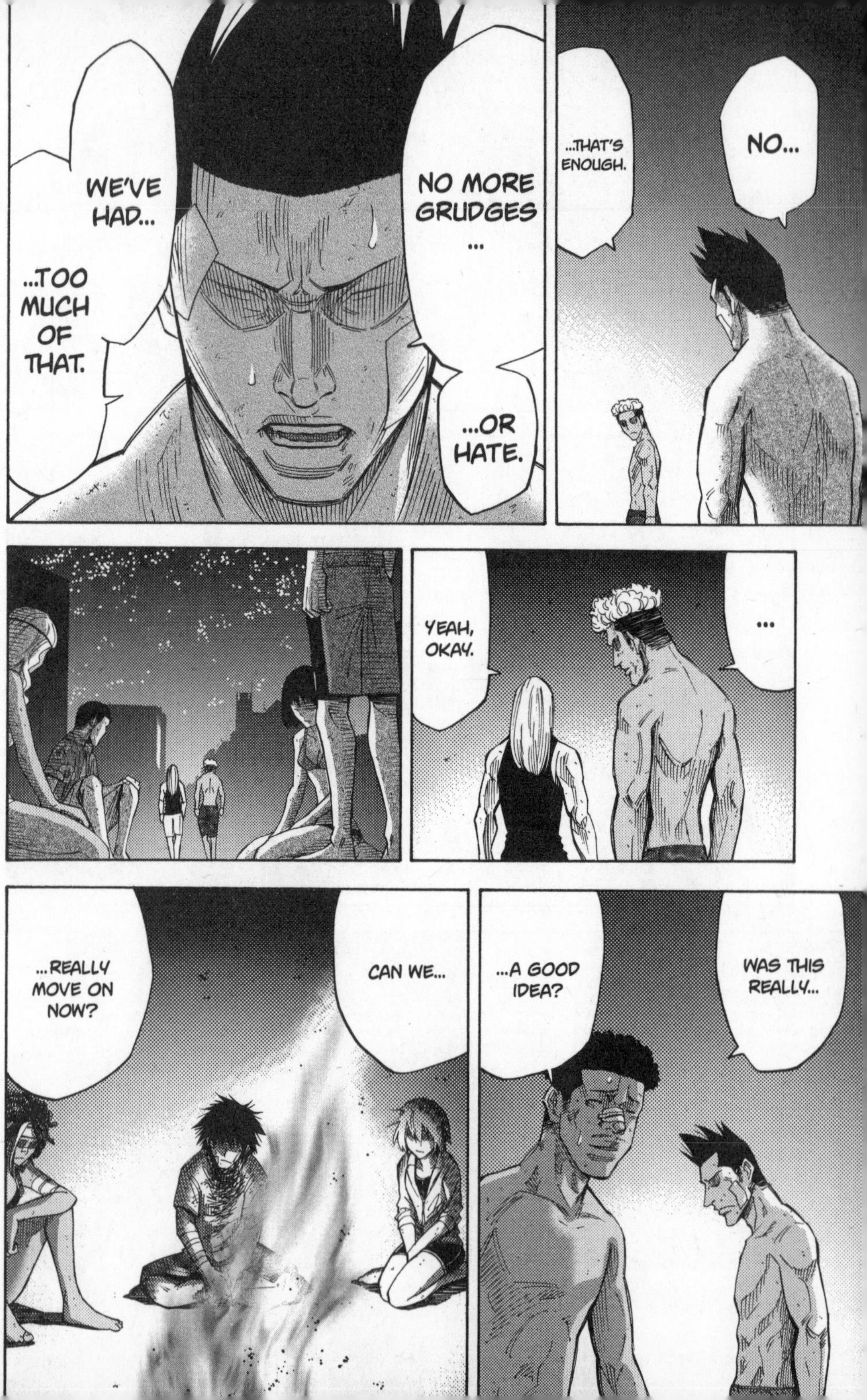
NO...
...THAT'S ENOUGH.
NO MORE GRUDGES ...
...OR HATE.
WE'VE HAD...
...TOO MUCH OF THAT.
...
YEAH, OKAY.
WAS THIS REALLY...
...A GOOD IDEA?
CAN WE...
...REALLY MOVE ON NOW?

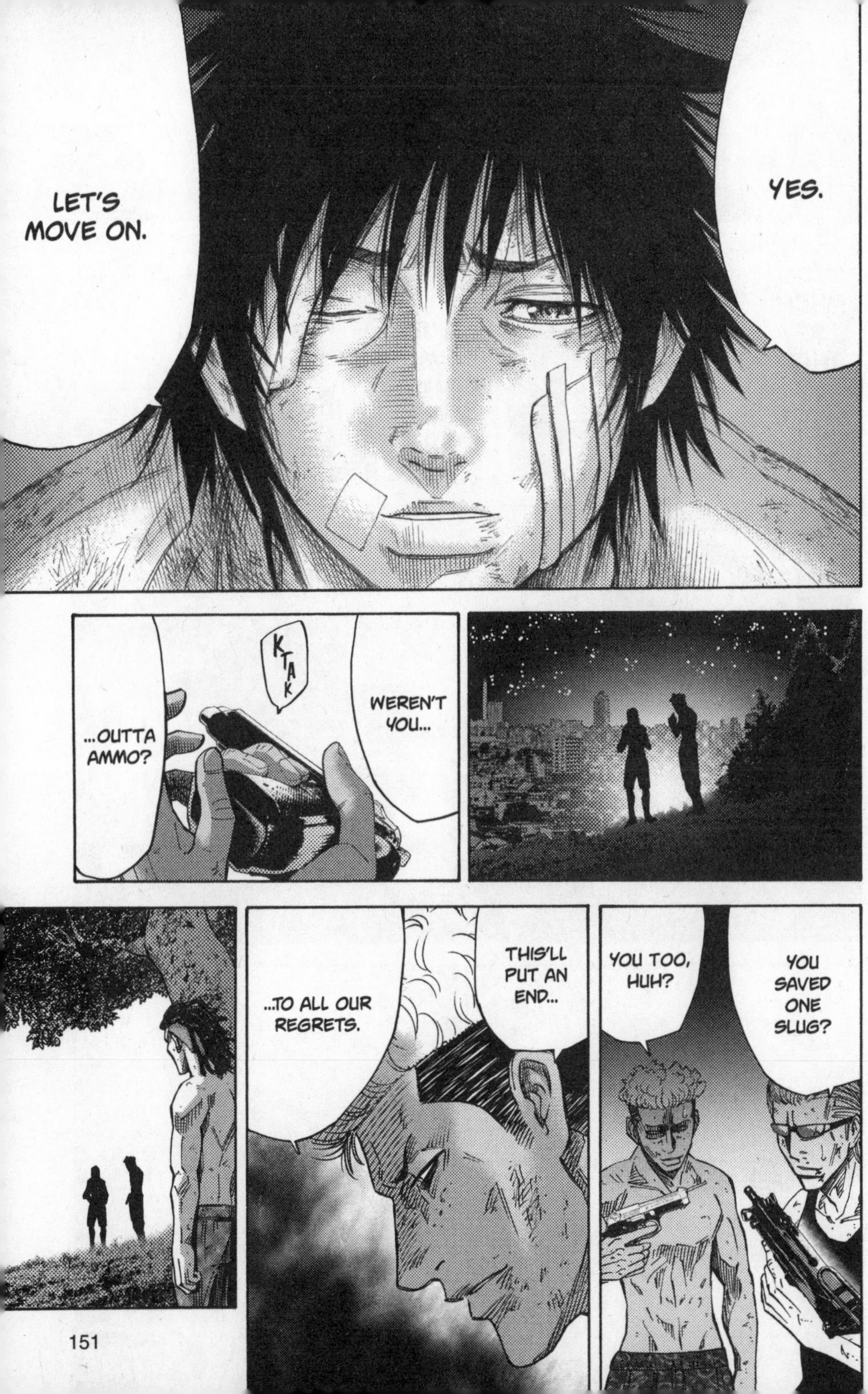

YES.
LET'S MOVE ON.
WEREN'T YOU...
KTAK
...OUTTA AMMO?
YOU SAVED ONE SLUG?
YOU TOO, HUH?
THIS'LL PUT AN END...
...TO ALL OUR REGRETS.

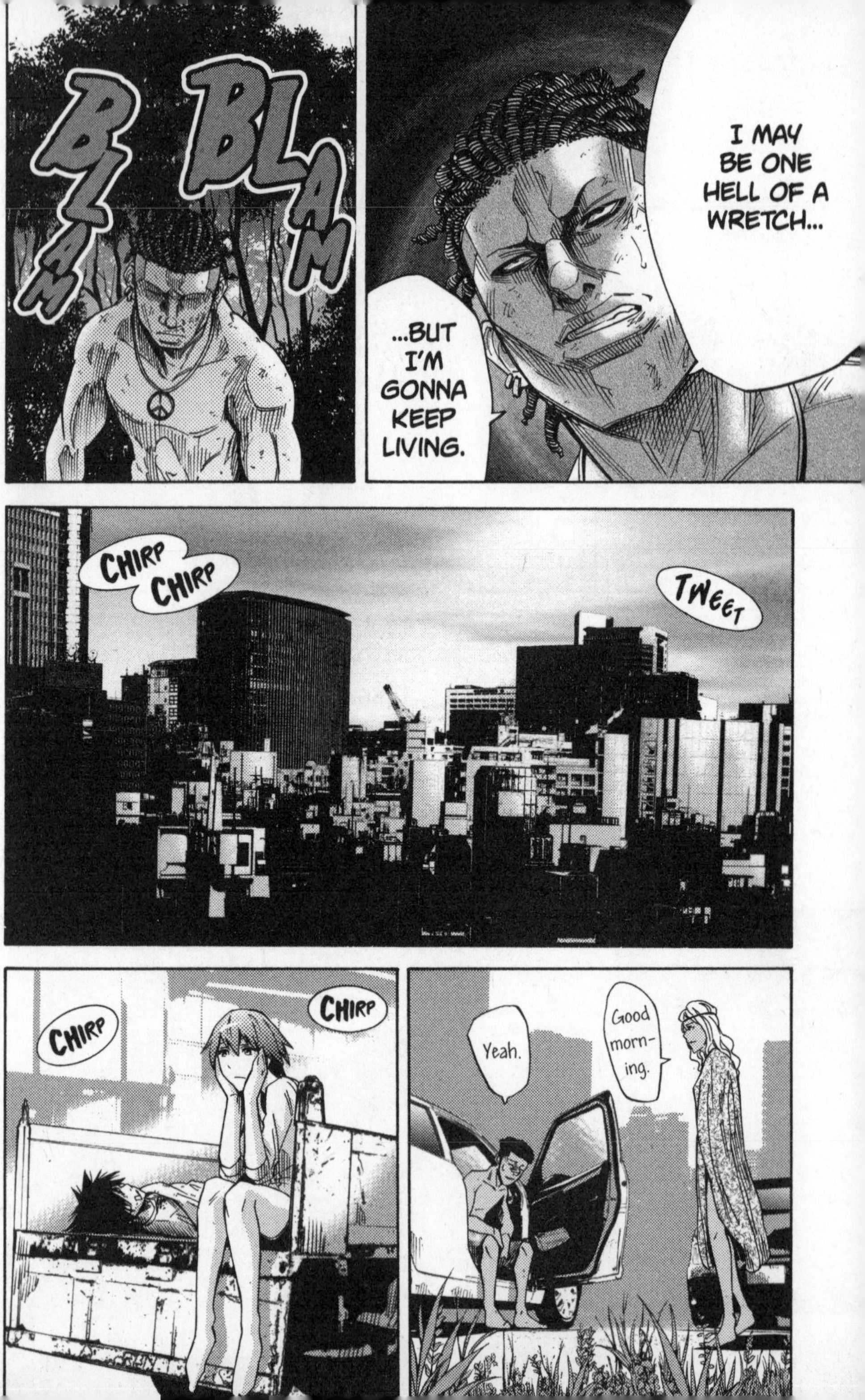
I MAY BE ONE HELL OF A WRETCH...
...BUT I'M GONNA KEEP LIVING.
BLAM
BLAM
TWEET
CHIRP CHIRP
Good morning.
Yeah.
CHIRP
CHIRP

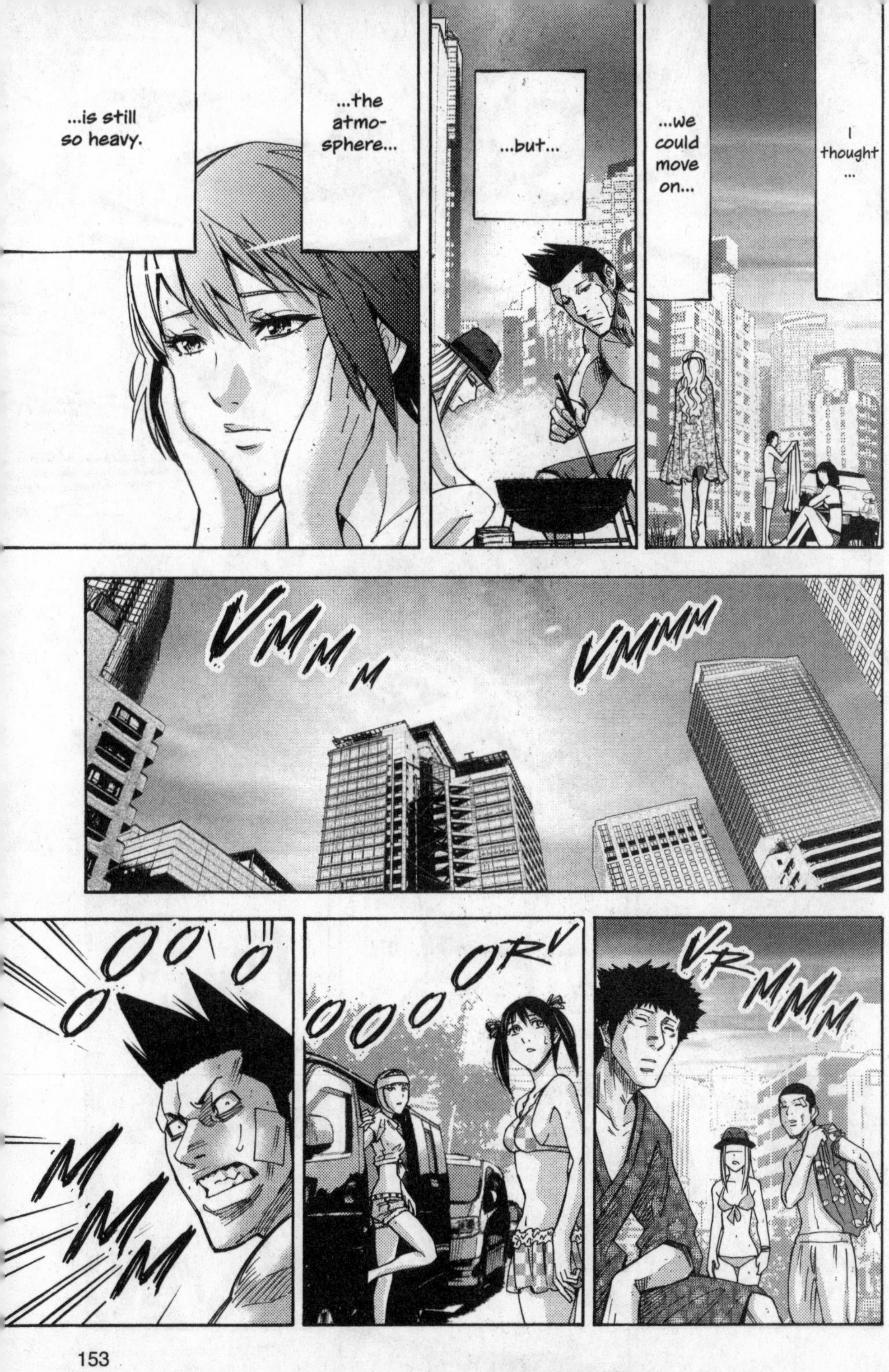

I thought...
...we could move on...
...but...
...the atmo-sphere...
...is still so heavy.
VMMMM
VMMMM
VRMMMM
OOOOOORV
OOOOO
MMMM

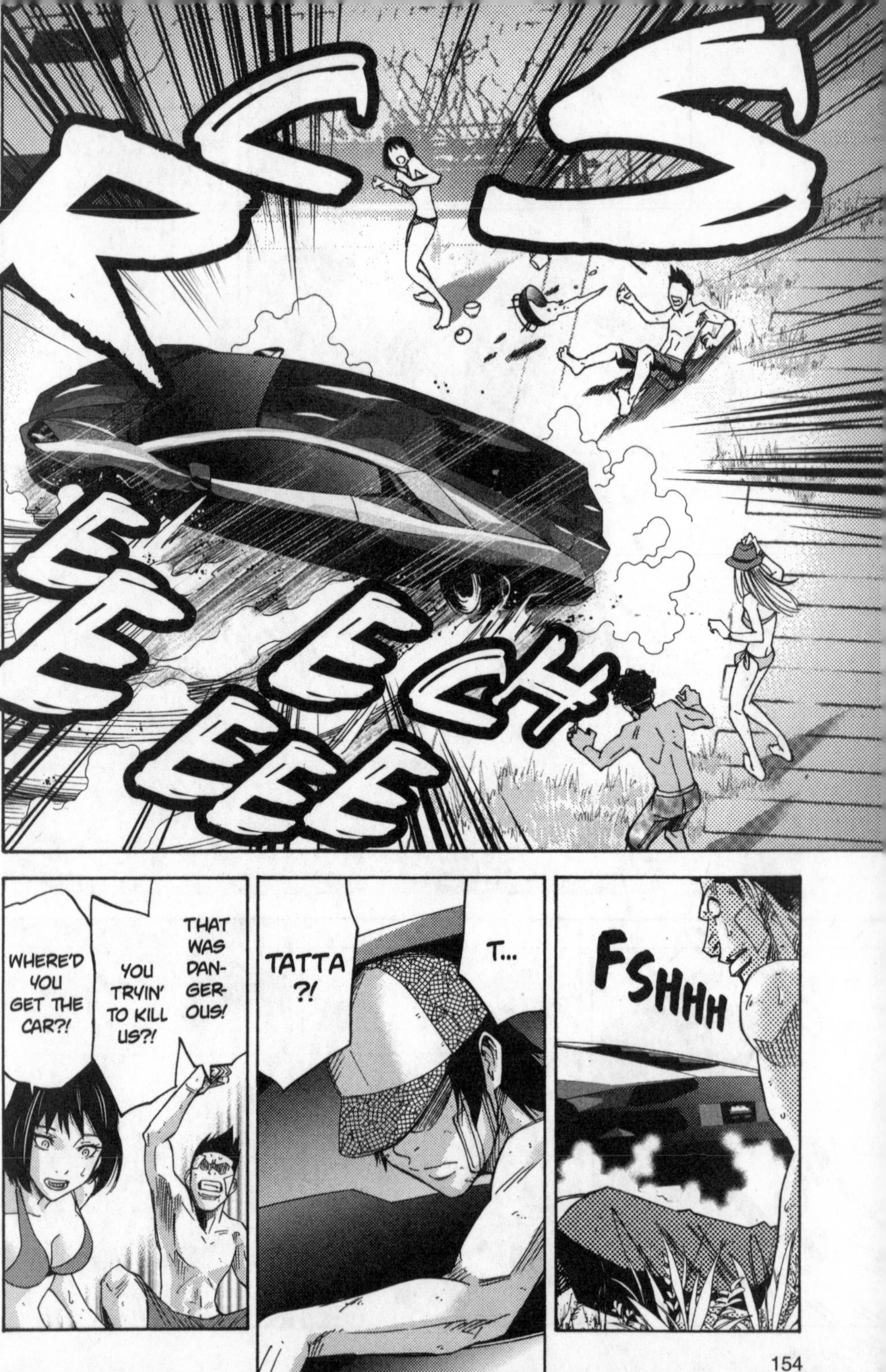
FSHHH
T...
TATTA ?!
THAT WAS DAN-GER-OUS!
YOU TRYIN' TO KILL US?!
WHERE'D YOU GET THE CAR?!

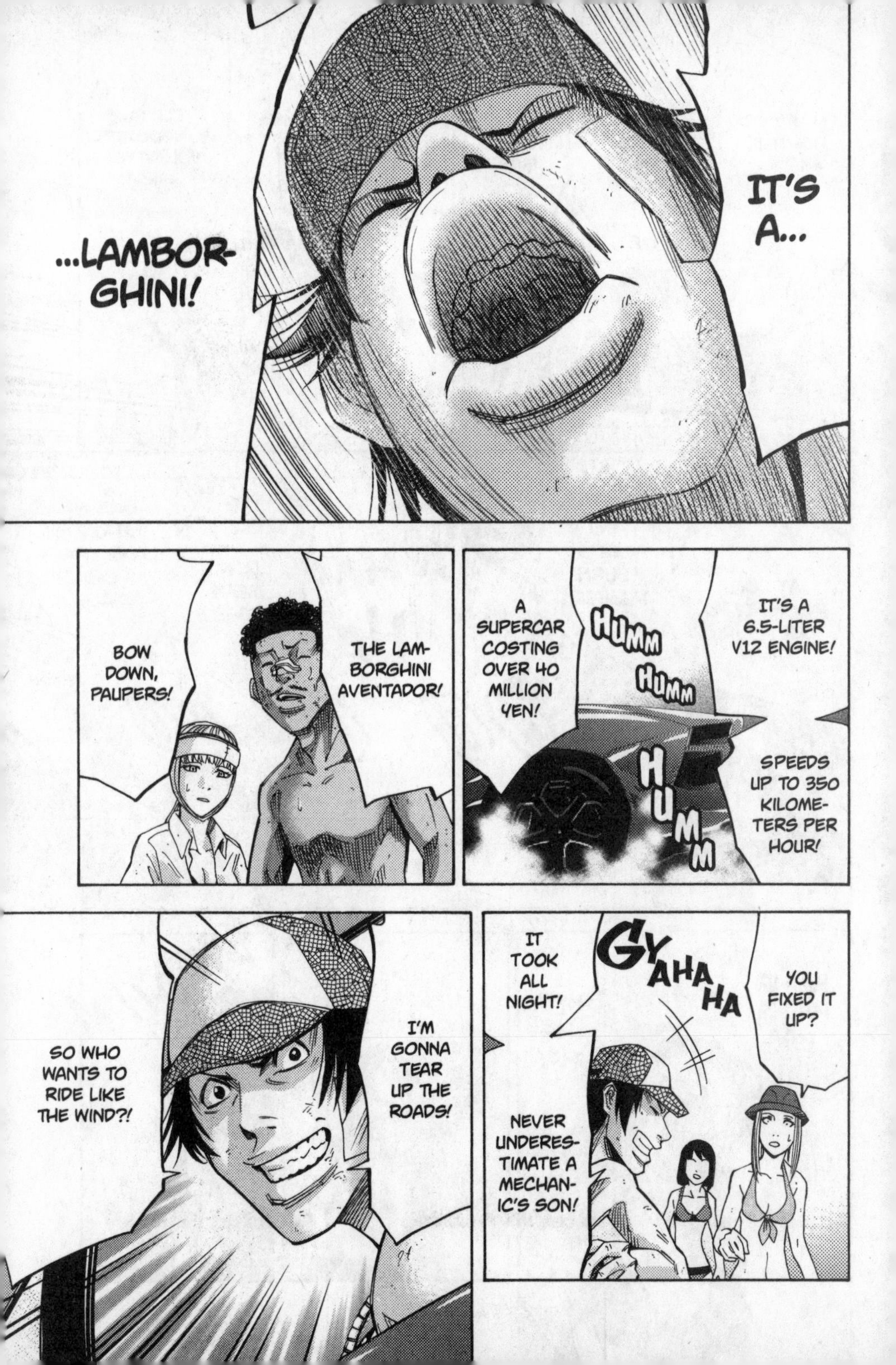
IT'S A...
...LAMBORGHINI!
IT'S A 6.5-LITER V12 ENGINE!
SPEEDS UP TO 350 KILOMETERS PER HOUR!
HUMM HUMM HUMM
A SUPERCAR COSTING OVER 40 MILLION YEN!
THE LAMBORGHINI AVENTADOR!
BOW DOWN, PAUPERS!
YOU FIXED IT UP?
GYAHAHA
IT TOOK ALL NIGHT!
NEVER UNDERESTIMATE A MECHANIC'S SON!
I'M GONNA TEAR UP THE ROADS!
SO WHO WANTS TO RIDE LIKE THE WIND?!

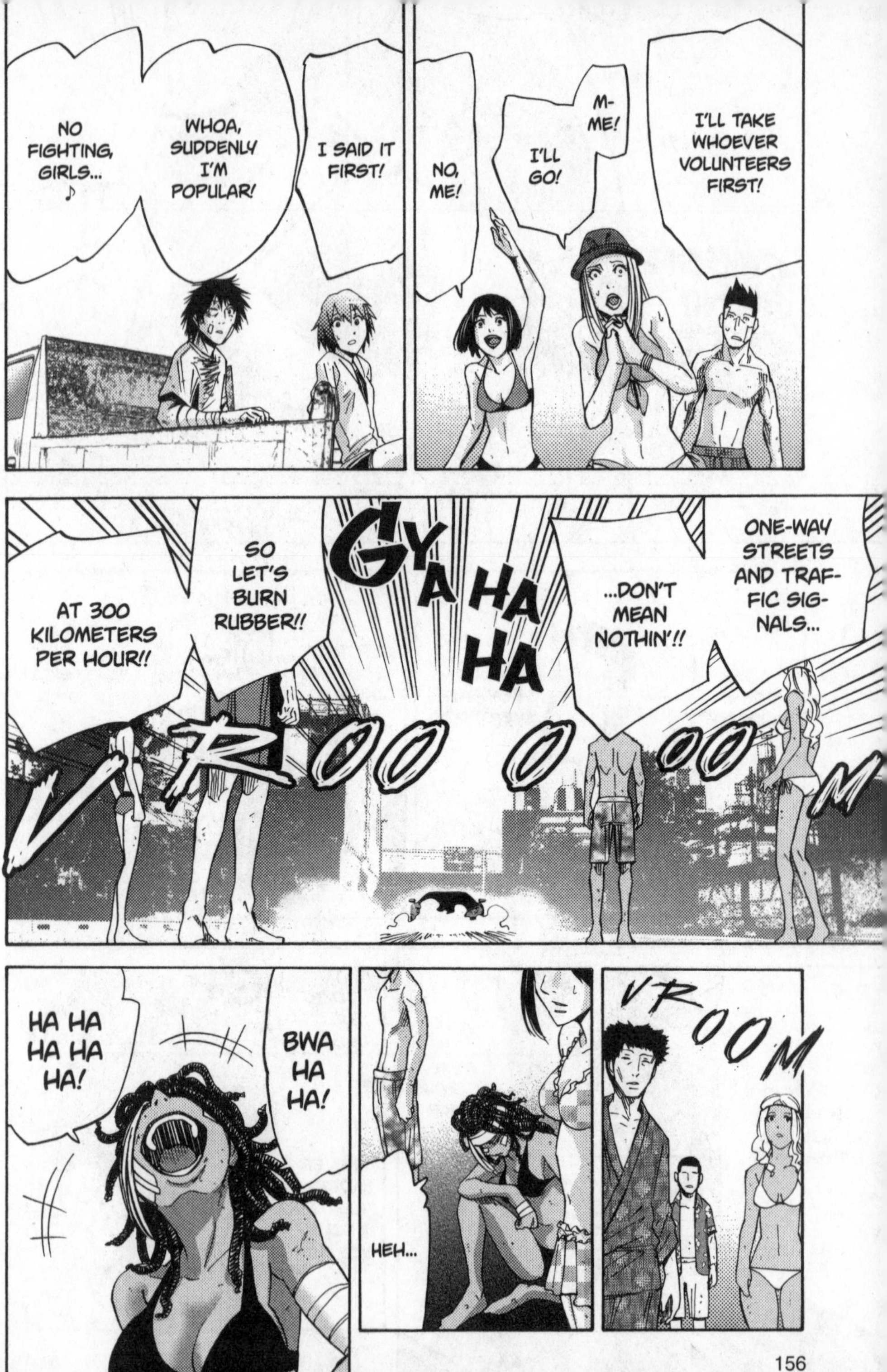
I'LL TAKE WHOEVER VOLUNTEERS FIRST!
M-ME!
I'LL GO!
NO, ME!
I SAID IT FIRST!
WHOA, SUDDENLY I'M POPULAR!
NO FIGHTING, GIRLS... ♪
ONE-WAY STREETS AND TRAF-FIC SIG-NALS...
...DON'T MEAN NOTHIN'!!
GYAHAHAHA
SO LET'S BURN RUBBER!!
AT 300 KILOMETERS PER HOUR!!
VROOOOOOOM
VROOOM
HEH...
BWA HA HA!
HA HA HA HA HA!

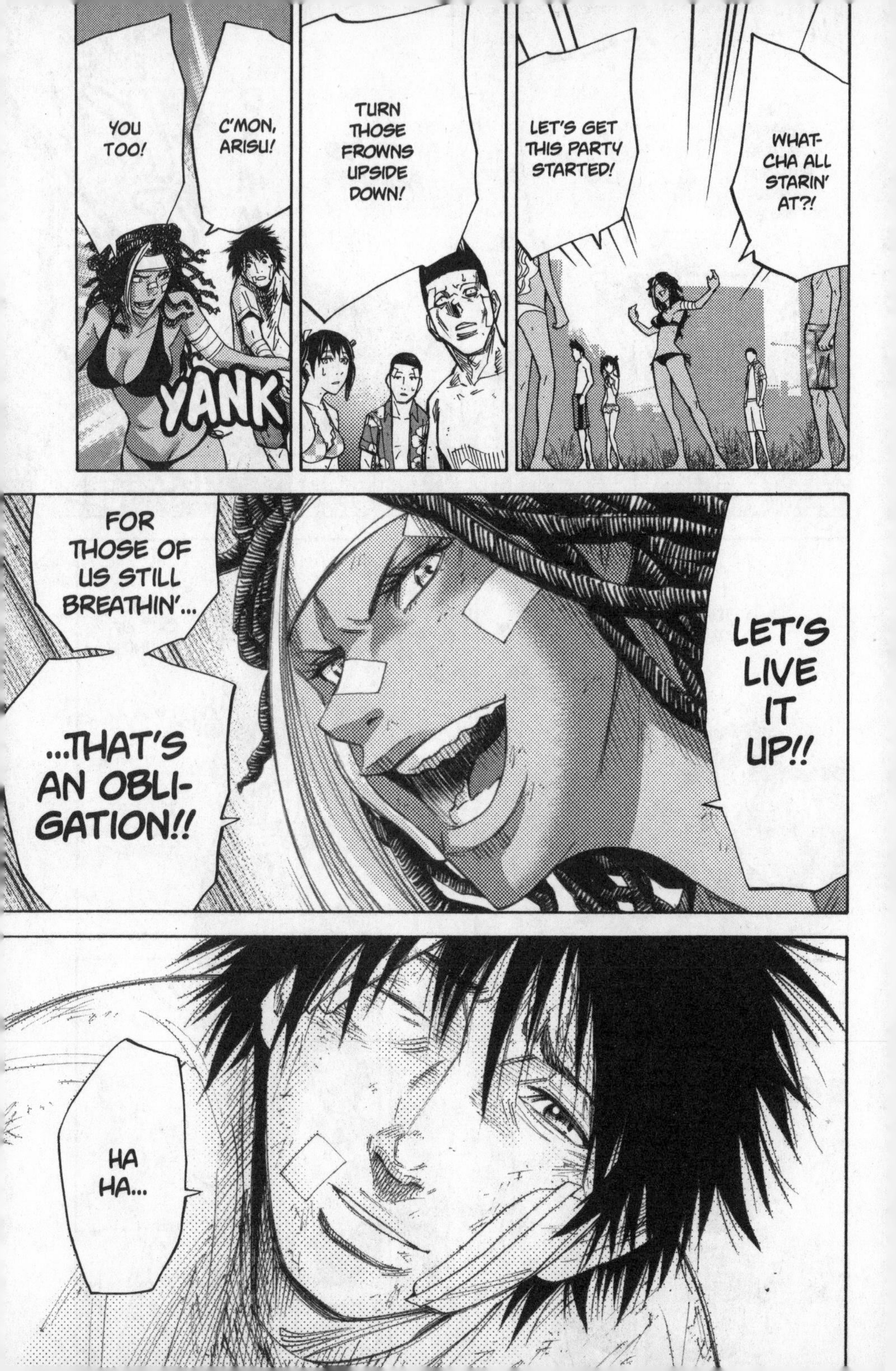
WHAT-CHA ALL STARIN' AT?!
LET'S GET THIS PARTY STARTED!
TURN THOSE FROWNS UPSIDE DOWN!
C'MON, ARISU!
YOU TOO!
YANK
LET'S LIVE IT UP!!
FOR THOSE OF US STILL BREATHIN'...
...THAT'S AN OBLIGATION!!
HA HA...

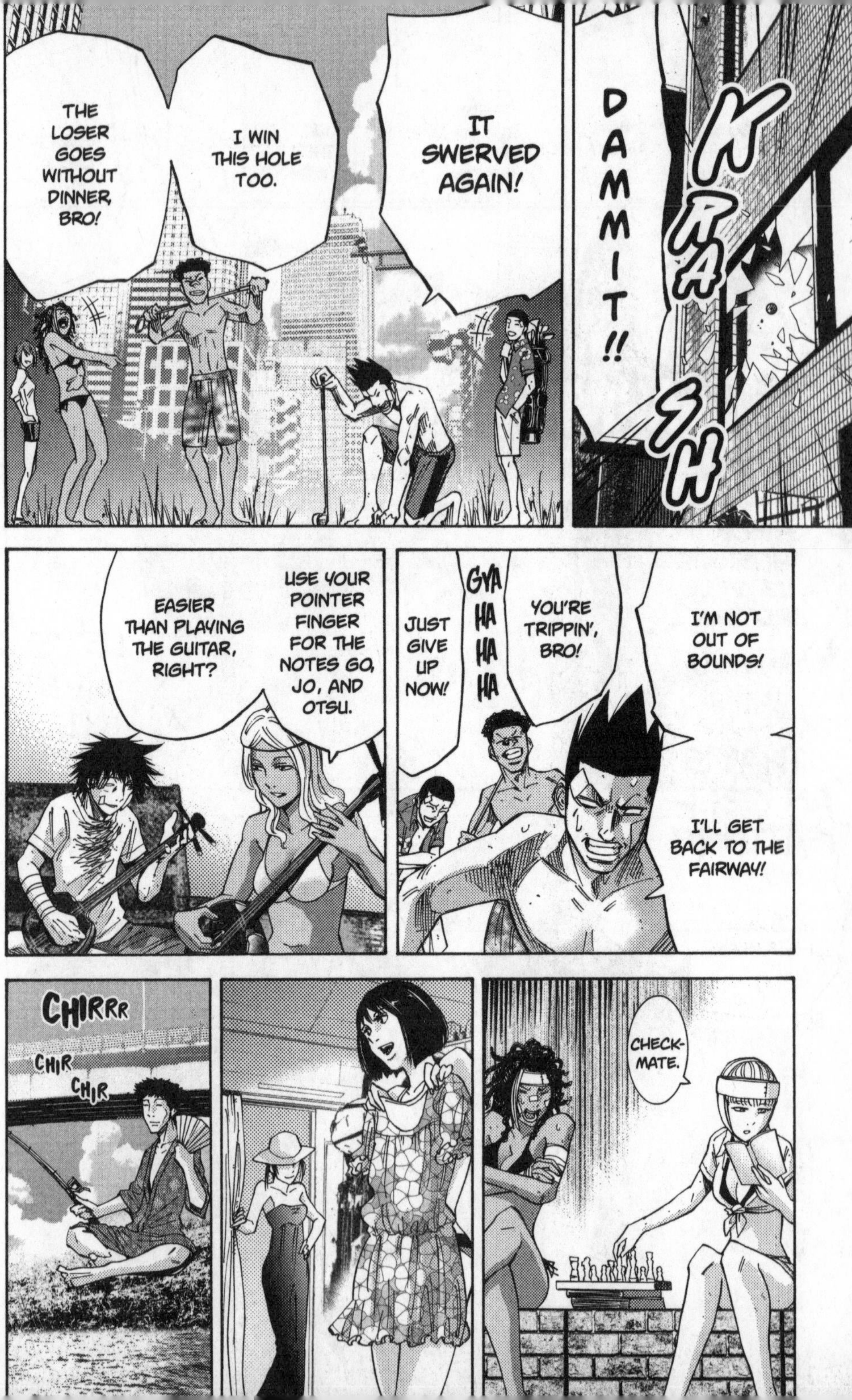
KRASH
DAMMIT!!
IT SWERVED AGAIN!
I WIN THIS HOLE TOO.
THE LOSER GOES WITHOUT DINNER, BRO!
I'M NOT OUT OF BOUNDS!
I'LL GET BACK TO THE FAIRWAY!
YOU'RE TRIPPIN', BRO!
GYA HA HA HA
JUST GIVE UP NOW!
USE YOUR POINTER FINGER FOR THE NOTES GO, JO, AND OTSU.
EASIER THAN PLAYING THE GUITAR, RIGHT?
CHECK-MATE.
CHIRRR
CHIR
CHIR

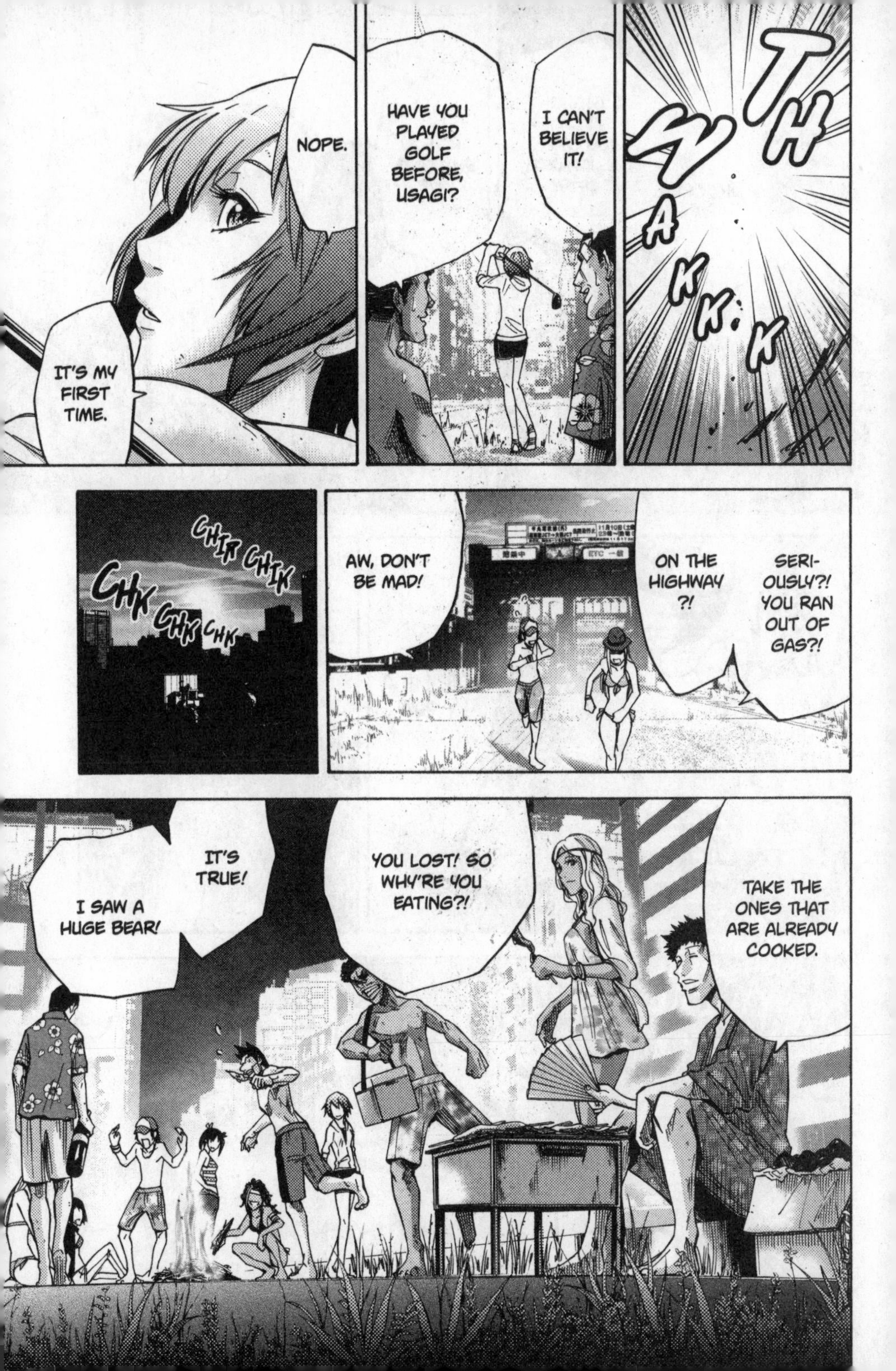
THWAKKK
I CAN'T BELIEVE IT!
HAVE YOU PLAYED GOLF BEFORE, USAGI?
NOPE.
IT'S MY FIRST TIME.
SERI-OUSLY?! YOU RAN OUT OF GAS?!
ON THE HIGHWAY ?!
AW, DON'T BE MAD!
CHIR CHIK
CHK CHK CHK
TAKE THE ONES THAT ARE ALREADY COOKED.
YOU LOST! SO WHY'RE YOU EATING?!
IT'S TRUE!
I SAW A HUGE BEAR!

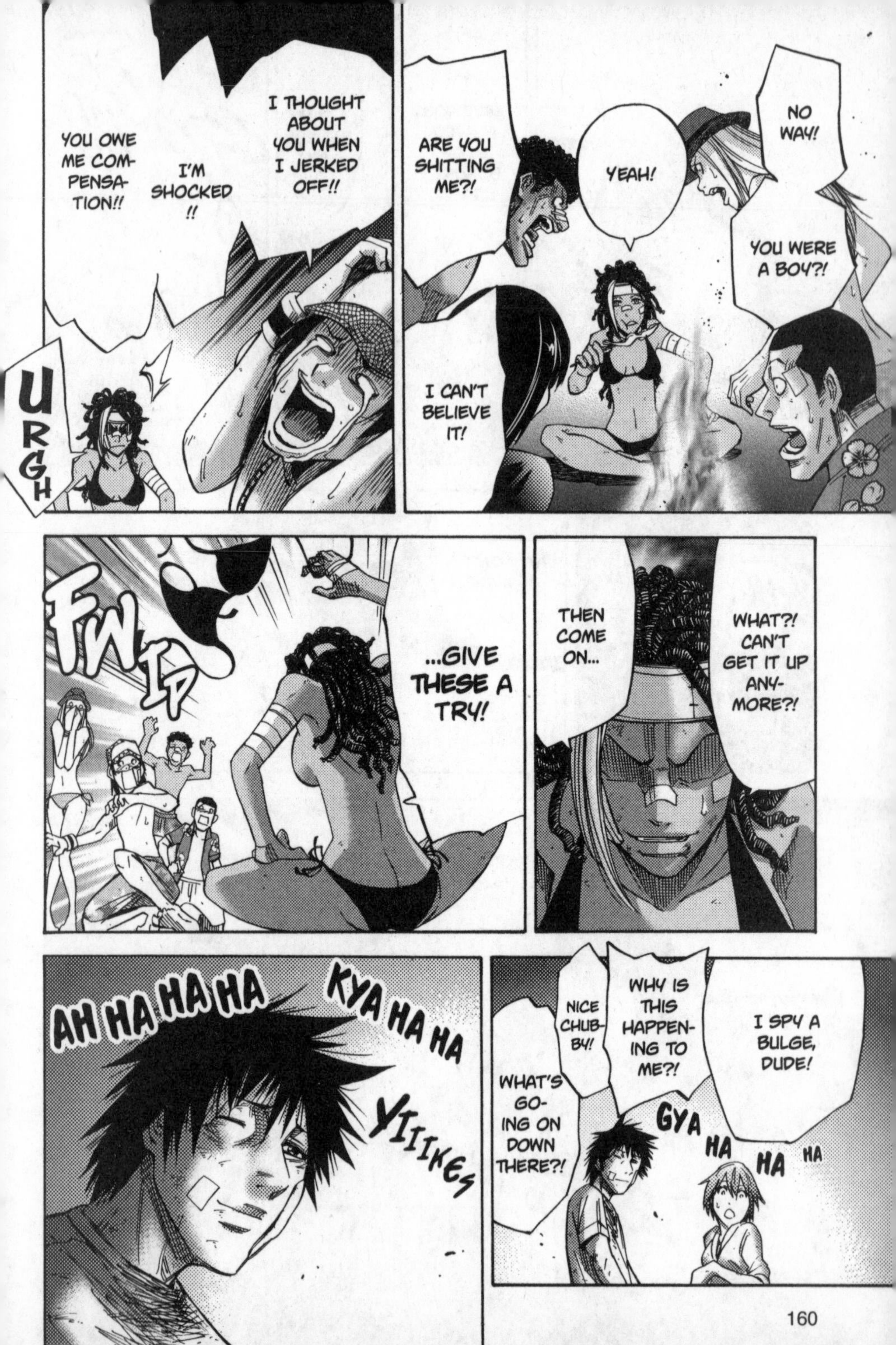
NO WAY!
YOU WERE A BOY?!
YEAH!
ARE YOU SHITTING ME?!
I CAN'T BELIEVE IT!
I THOUGHT ABOUT YOU WHEN I JERKED OFF!!
I'M SHOCKED!!
YOU OWE ME COMPENSATION!!
URGH
WHAT?! CAN'T GET IT UP ANYMORE?!
THEN COME ON...
...GIVE THESE A TRY!
FWIP
I SPY A BULGE, DUDE!
WHY IS THIS HAPPENING TO ME?!
NICE CHUBBY!
GYA HA HA HA
WHAT'S GOING ON DOWN THERE?!
KYA HA HA
AH HA HA HA
YIIIKES

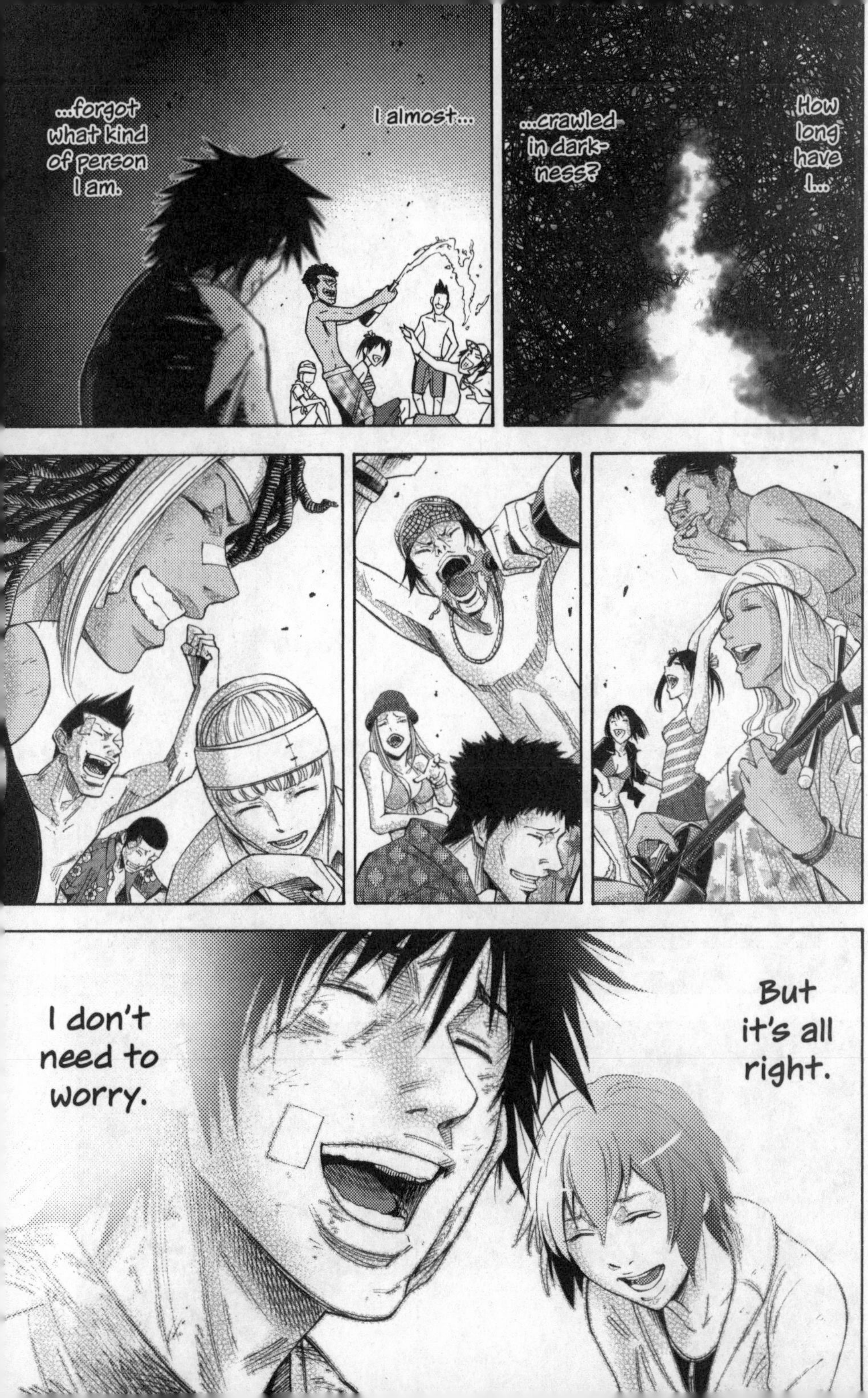
How long have I...
...crawled in dark-ness?
I almost...
...forgot what kind of person I am.
But it's all right.
I don't need to worry.

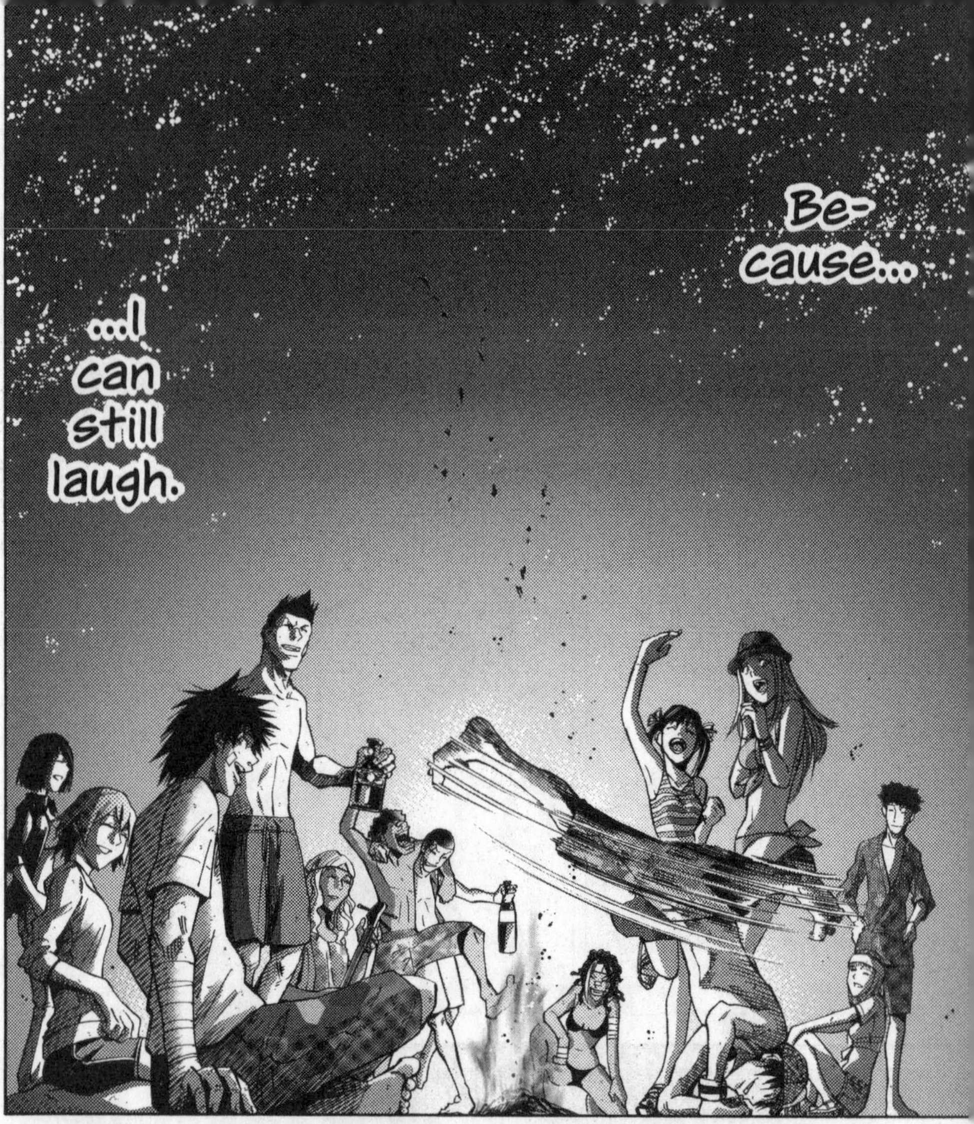
Be-cause...
...I can still laugh.

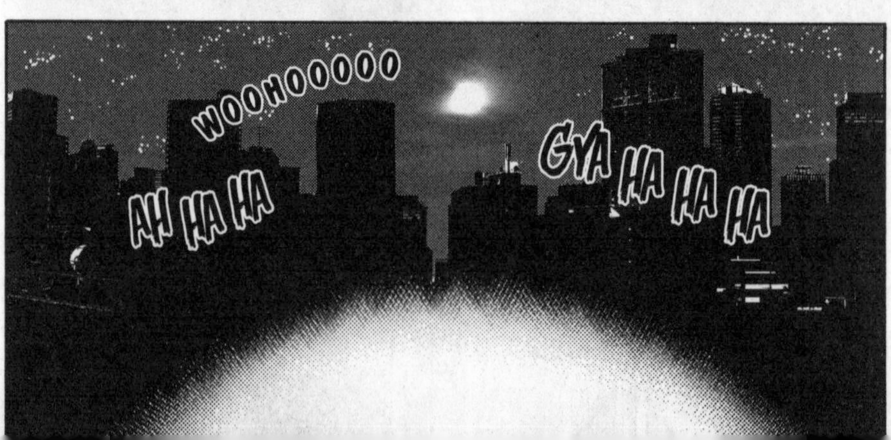
GYA HA HA HA HA
WOOHOOOOOO
AH HA HA

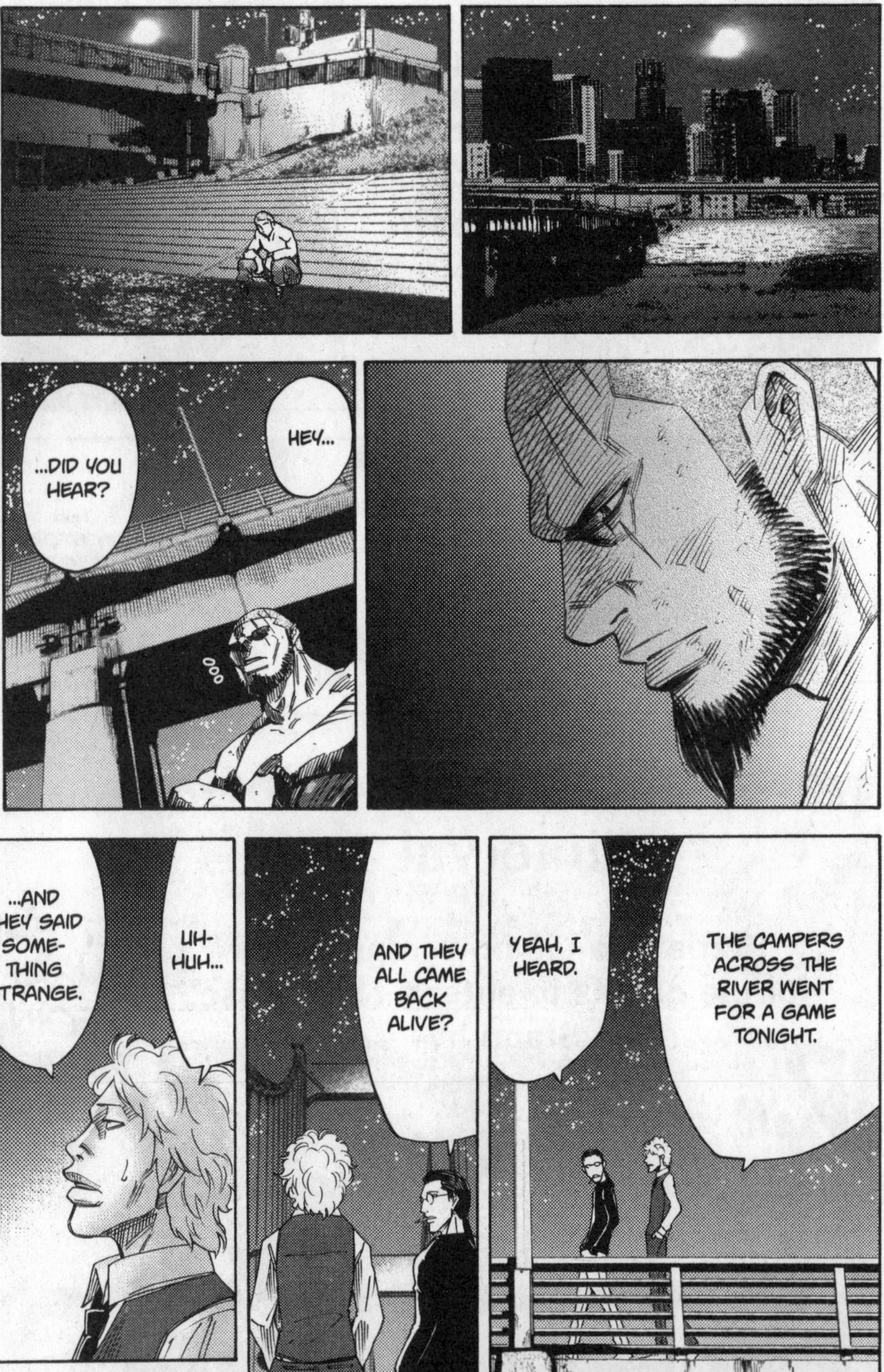
HEY...
...DID YOU HEAR?
THE CAMPERS ACROSS THE RIVER WENT FOR A GAME TONIGHT.
YEAH, I HEARD.
AND THEY ALL CAME BACK ALIVE?
UH-HUH...
...AND THEY SAID SOME-THING STRANGE.

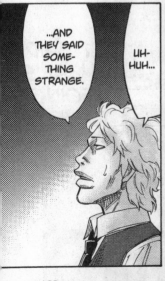

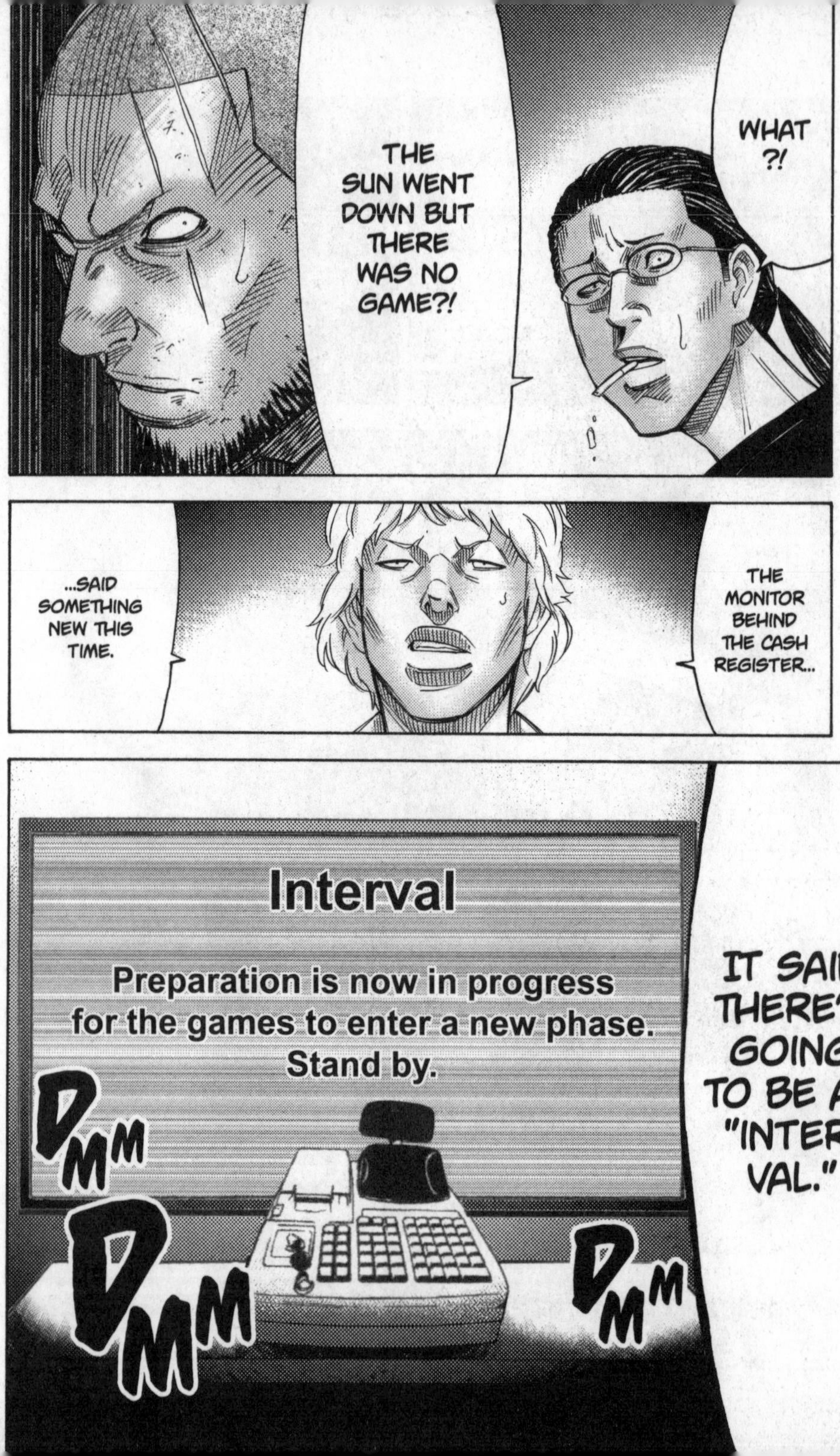
WHAT ?!
THE SUN WENT DOWN BUT THERE WAS NO GAME?!
THE MONITOR BEHIND THE CASH REGISTER...
...SAID SOMETHING NEW THIS TIME.
IT SAID THERE'S GOING TO BE AN "INTER-VAL."
Interval
Preparation is now in progress for the games to enter a new phase. Stand by.
DMMM
DMMM
DMMM

I've traveled to all sorts of places inside and outside of the country. Maybe there was even a time when I was searching for paradise. But now I know paradise isn't a place.

— HARO ASO

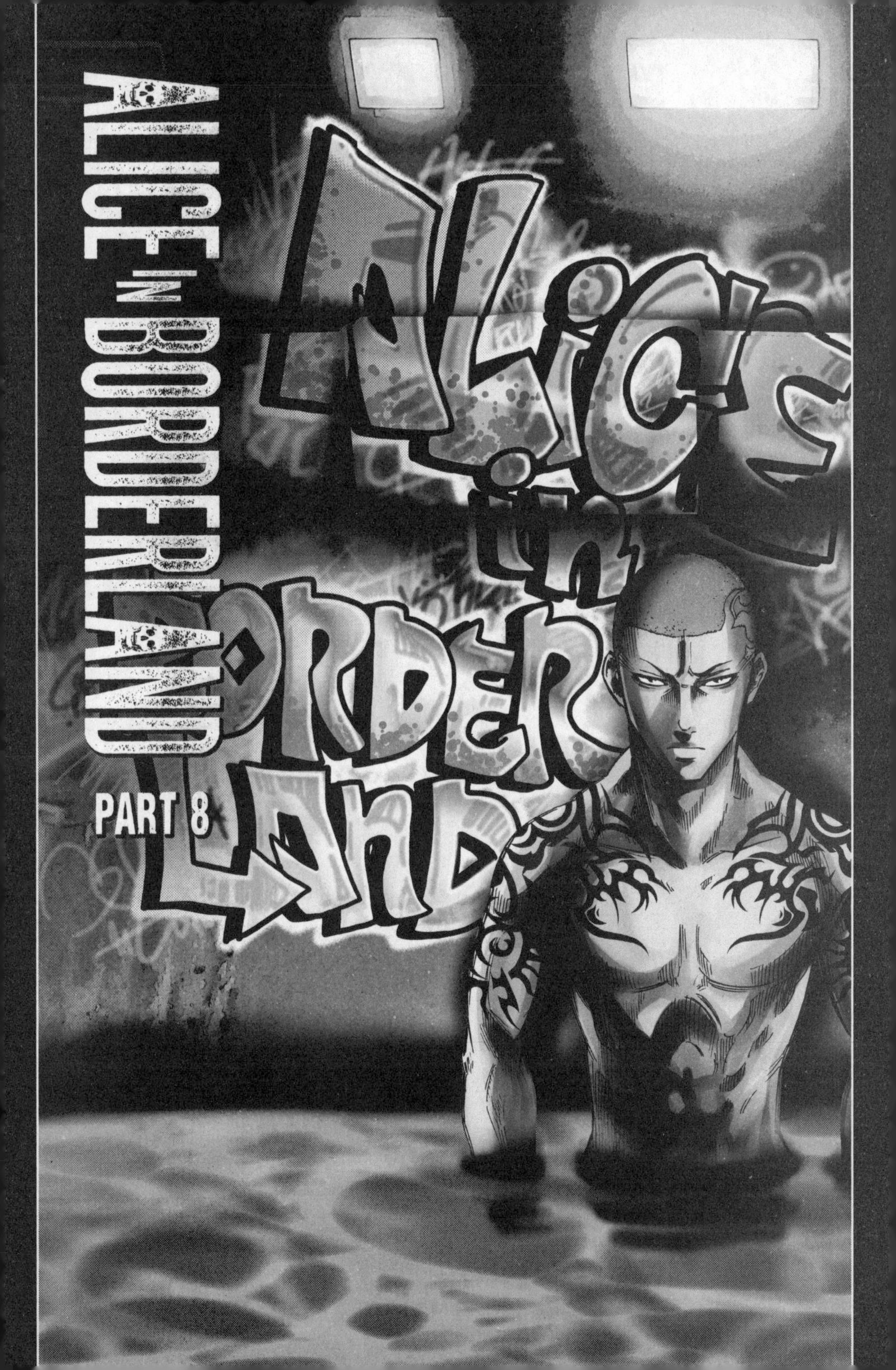
ALICE IN BORDERLAND
PART 8

ALICE IN BORDERLAND

PART 8

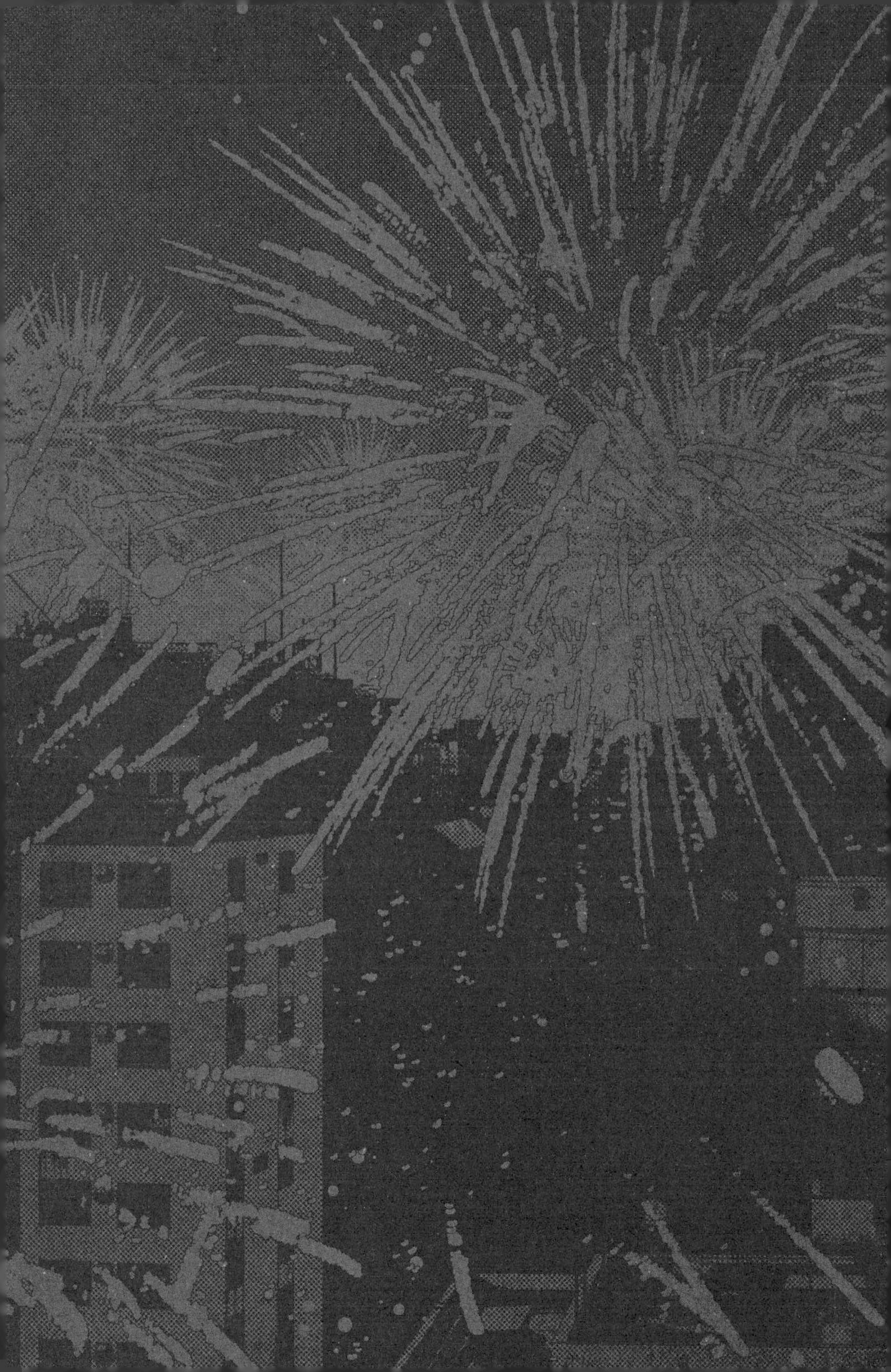

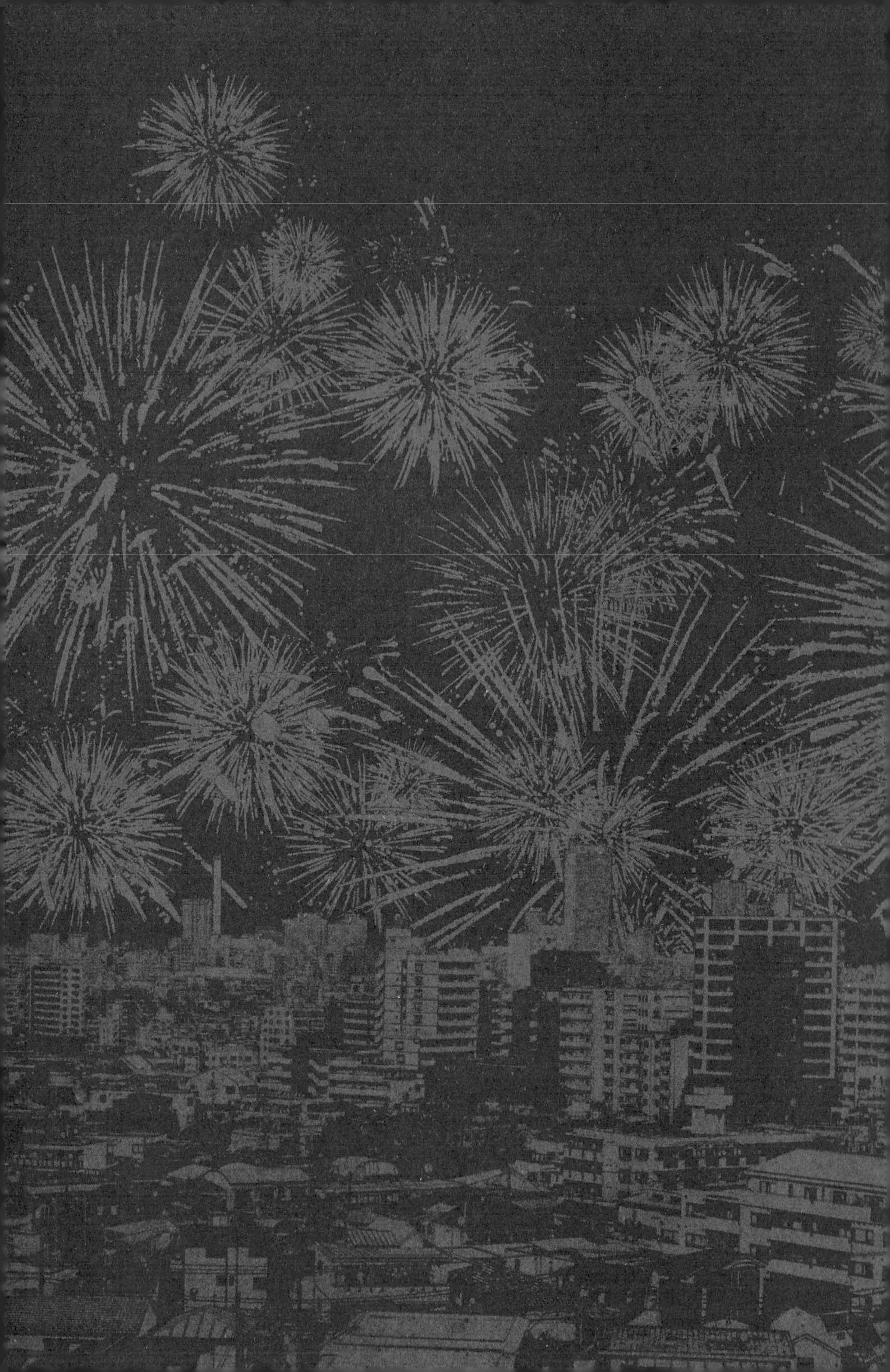

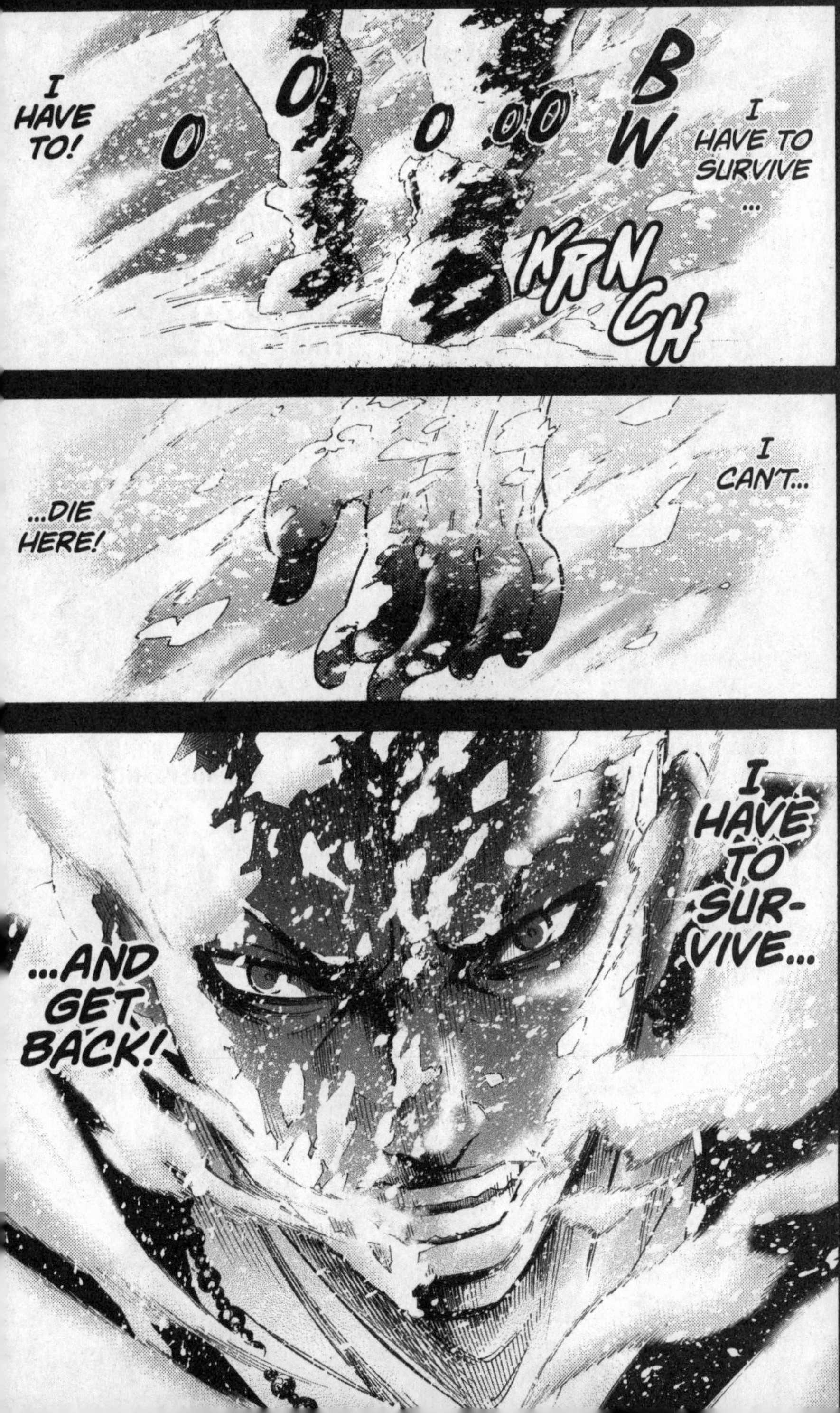
I HAVE TO SURVIVE ...
BWOOOOO
KRNCH
I HAVE TO!
I CAN'T...
...DIE HERE!
I HAVE TO SURVIVE...
...AND GET BACK!

BORDERLAND...

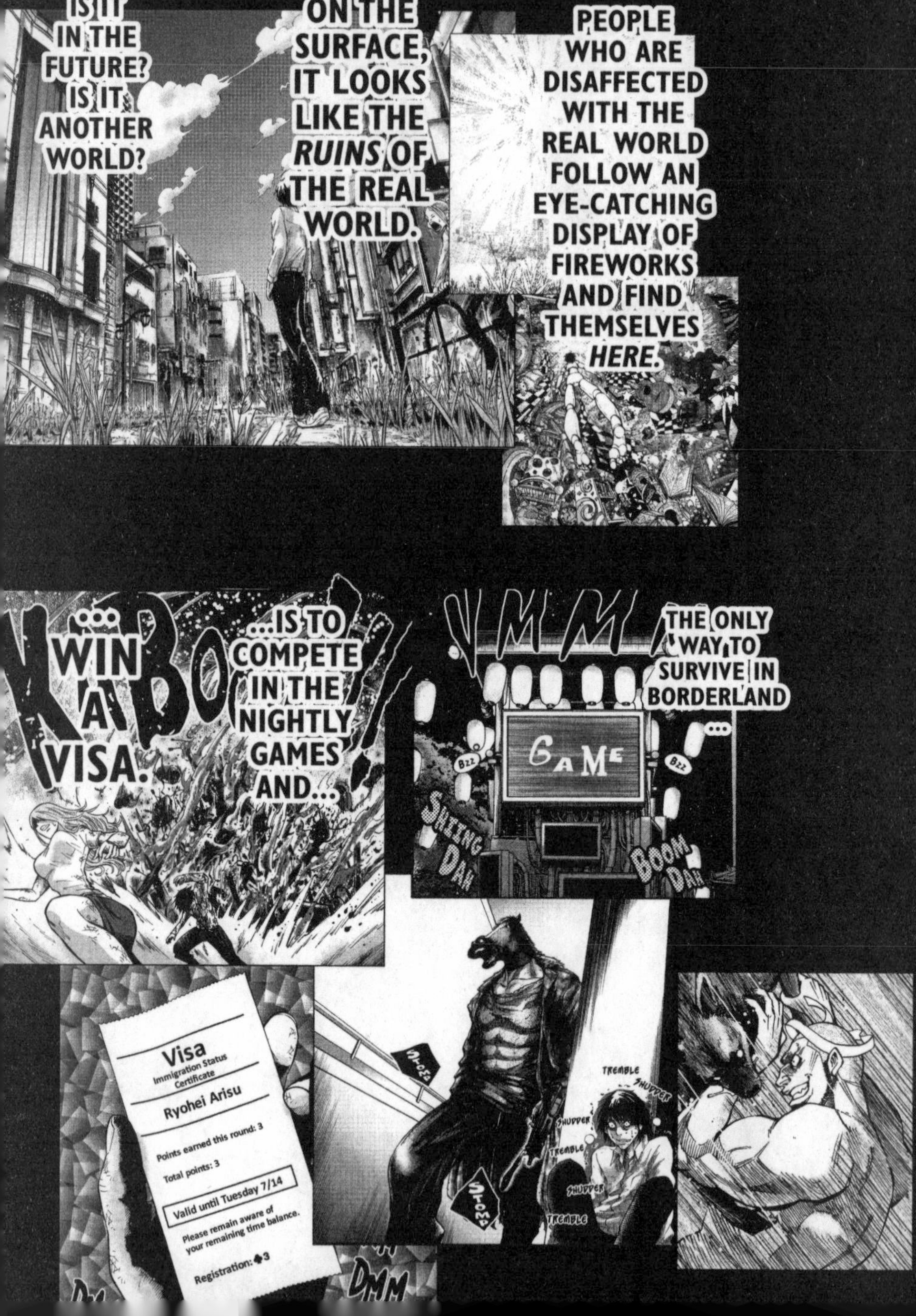
PEOPLE WHO ARE DISAFFECTED WITH THE REAL WORLD FOLLOW AN EYE-CATCHING DISPLAY OF FIREWORKS AND FIND THEMSELVES *HERE.*
ON THE SURFACE, IT LOOKS LIKE THE *RUINS* OF THE REAL WORLD.
IS IT IN THE FUTURE? IS IT ANOTHER WORLD?
THE ONLY WAY TO SURVIVE IN BORDERLAND...
GAME
Bzz
Bzz
SHING DAH
BOOM DAH
...IS TO COMPETE IN THE NIGHTLY GAMES AND...
...WIN A VISA.
TREMBLE
SHUDDER
SHUDDER
TREMBLE
SHUDDER
TREMBLE
STOMP
STOMP
Visa
Immigration Status Certificate
Ryohei Arisu
Points earned this round: 3
Total points: 3
Valid until Tuesday 7/14
Please remain aware of your remaining time balance.
Registration: ♣3
DMM

...AND AN EXPIRED VISA RESULTS IN A FORCED REMOVAL.

A GAME OVER EQUALS DEATH...

Game over

ROARR

ROAR

DO NOT OPEN

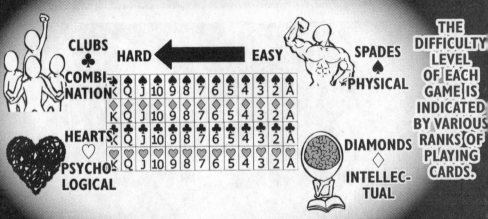

THE DIFFICULTY LEVEL OF EACH GAME IS INDICATED BY VARIOUS RANKS OF PLAYING CARDS.

CLUBS ♣ COMBI-NATION

HARD ← EASY

SPADES ♠ PHYSICAL

HEARTS ♡ PSYCHO-LOGICAL

DIAMONDS ♦ INTELLEC-TUAL

♠	K	Q	J	10	9	8	7	6	5	4	3	2	A
♦	K	Q	J	10	9	8	7	6	5	4	3	2	A
♣	K	Q	J	10	9	8	7	6	5	4	3	2	A
♡	K	Q	J	10	9	8	7	6	5	4	3	2	A

TONIGHT, SIX STRANGERS WILL PARTICIPATE IN A NEW GAME.

IS THERE A WAY TO RETURN TO THE REAL WORLD?

WILL THERE EVER BE AN END TO THESE CRUEL GAMES?

NO ONE KNOWS.

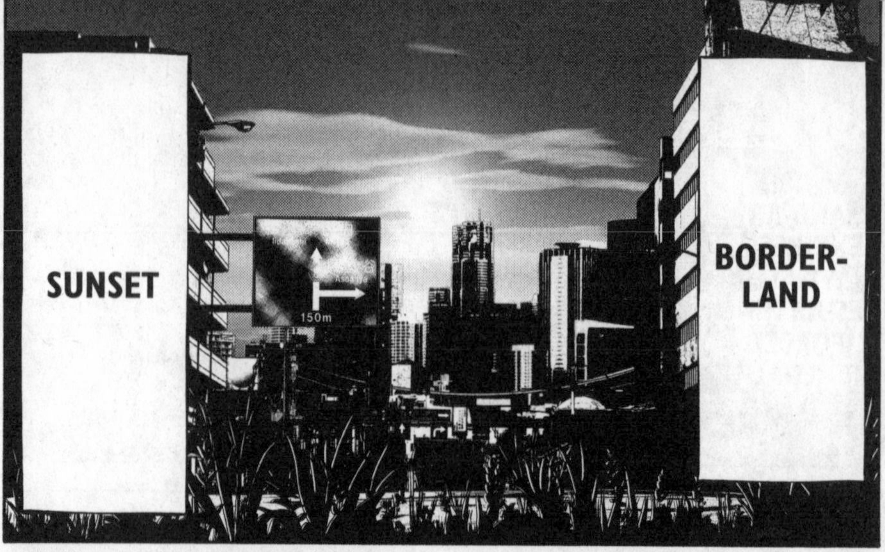
BORDER-LAND
150m
SUNSET

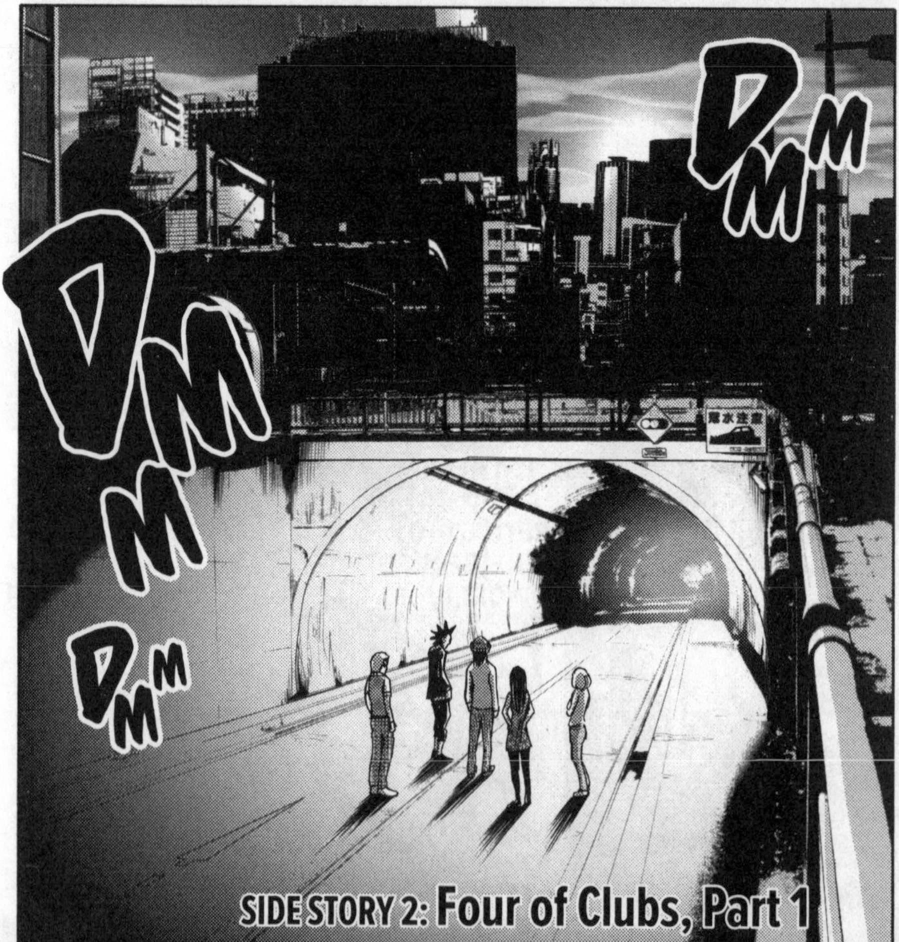
DMM
DMMMM
DMM

SIDE STORY 2: Four of Clubs, Part 1

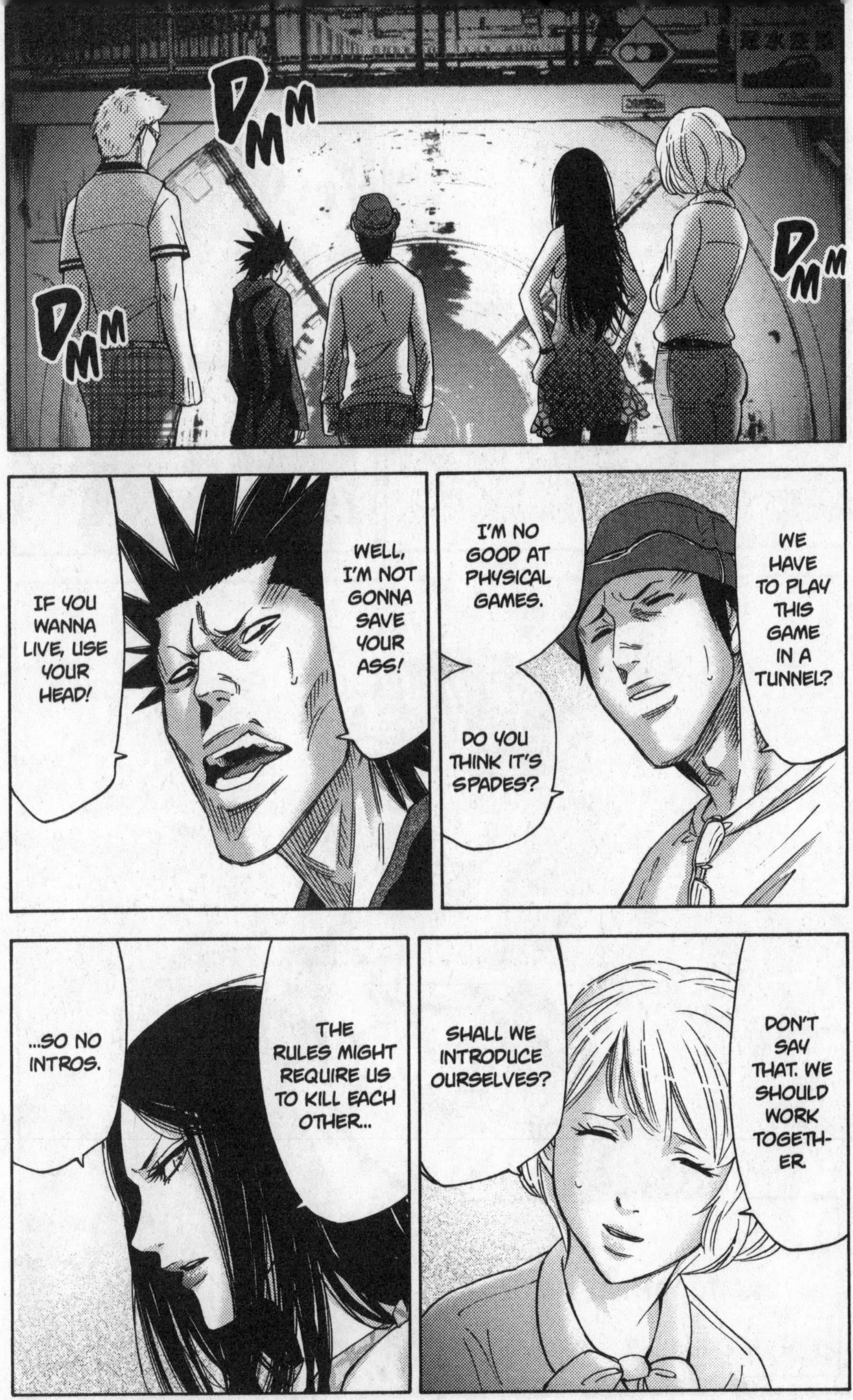
DMM
DMM
DMM
WE HAVE TO PLAY THIS GAME IN A TUNNEL?
I'M NO GOOD AT PHYSICAL GAMES.
DO YOU THINK IT'S SPADES?
WELL, I'M NOT GONNA SAVE YOUR ASS!
IF YOU WANNA LIVE, USE YOUR HEAD!
DON'T SAY THAT. WE SHOULD WORK TOGETHER.
SHALL WE INTRODUCE OURSELVES?
THE RULES MIGHT REQUIRE US TO KILL EACH OTHER...
...SO NO INTROS.

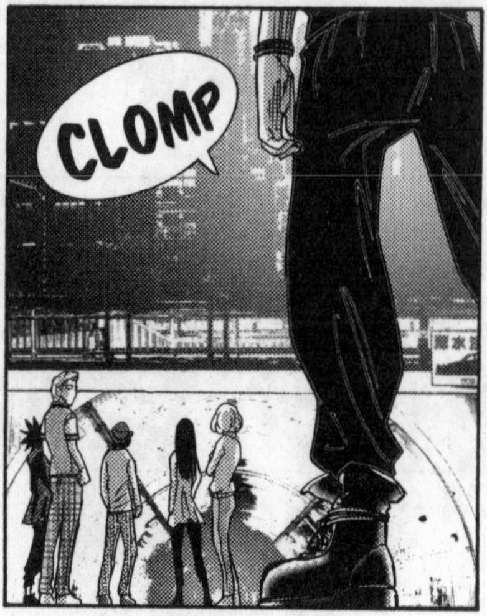
CLOMP

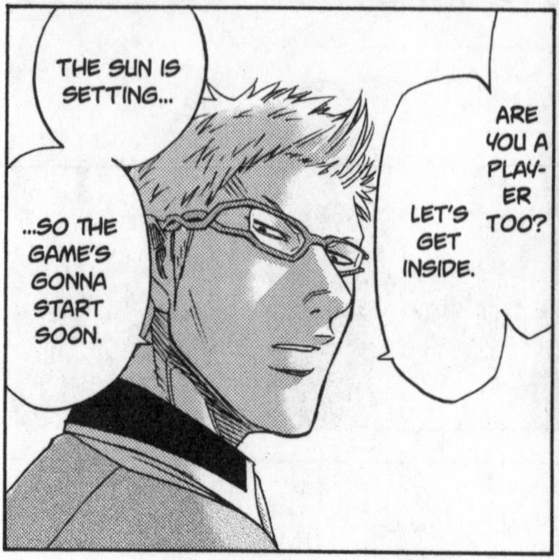
ARE YOU A PLAYER TOO?
LET'S GET INSIDE.
THE SUN IS SETTING...
...SO THE GAME'S GONNA START SOON.

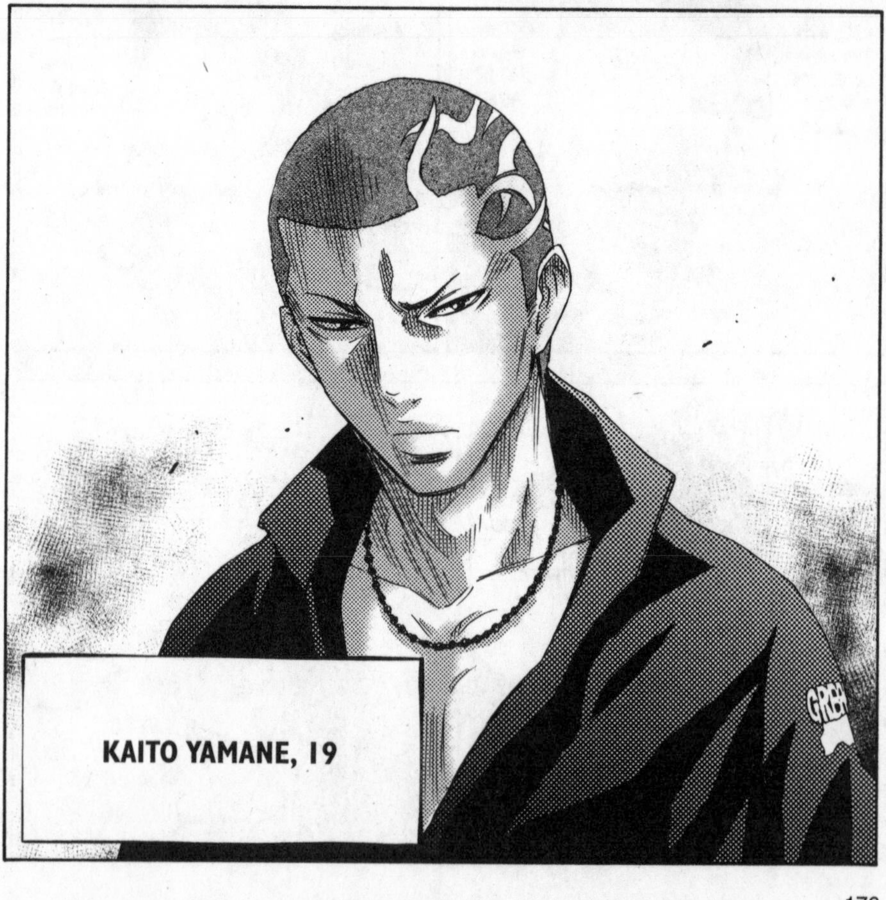
KAITO YAMANE, 19

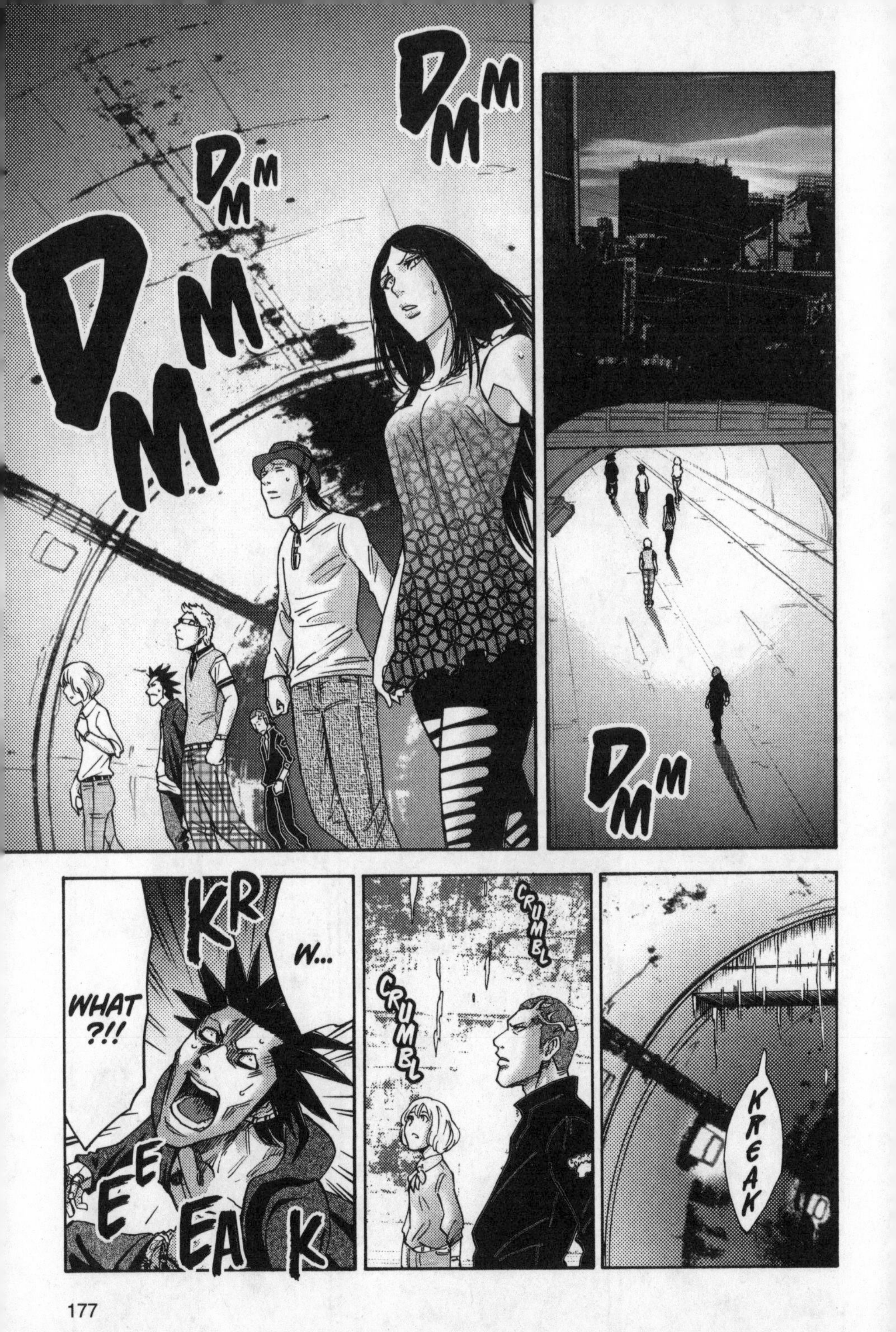
DMM
DMM
DMM
DMMM...
KREAK
CRUMBL
CRUMBL
KR
W...
WHAT?!!
EEEEAK

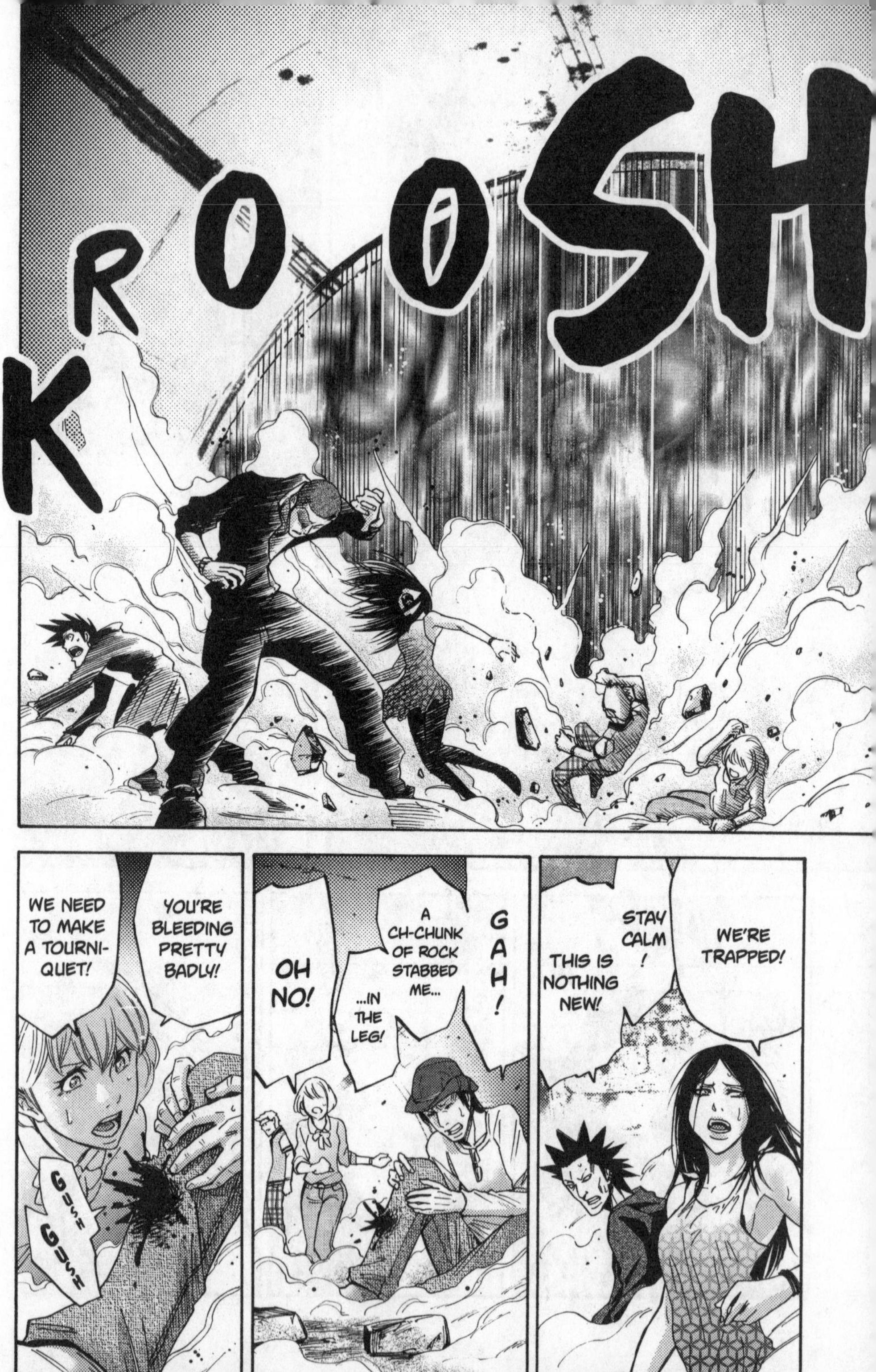
KROOSH
WE'RE TRAPPED!
STAY CALM! THIS IS NOTHING NEW!
GAH!
A CH-CHUNK OF ROCK STABBED ME...
...IN THE LEG!
OH NO!
YOU'RE BLEEDING PRETTY BADLY!
WE NEED TO MAKE A TOURNIQUET!
GUSH GUSH

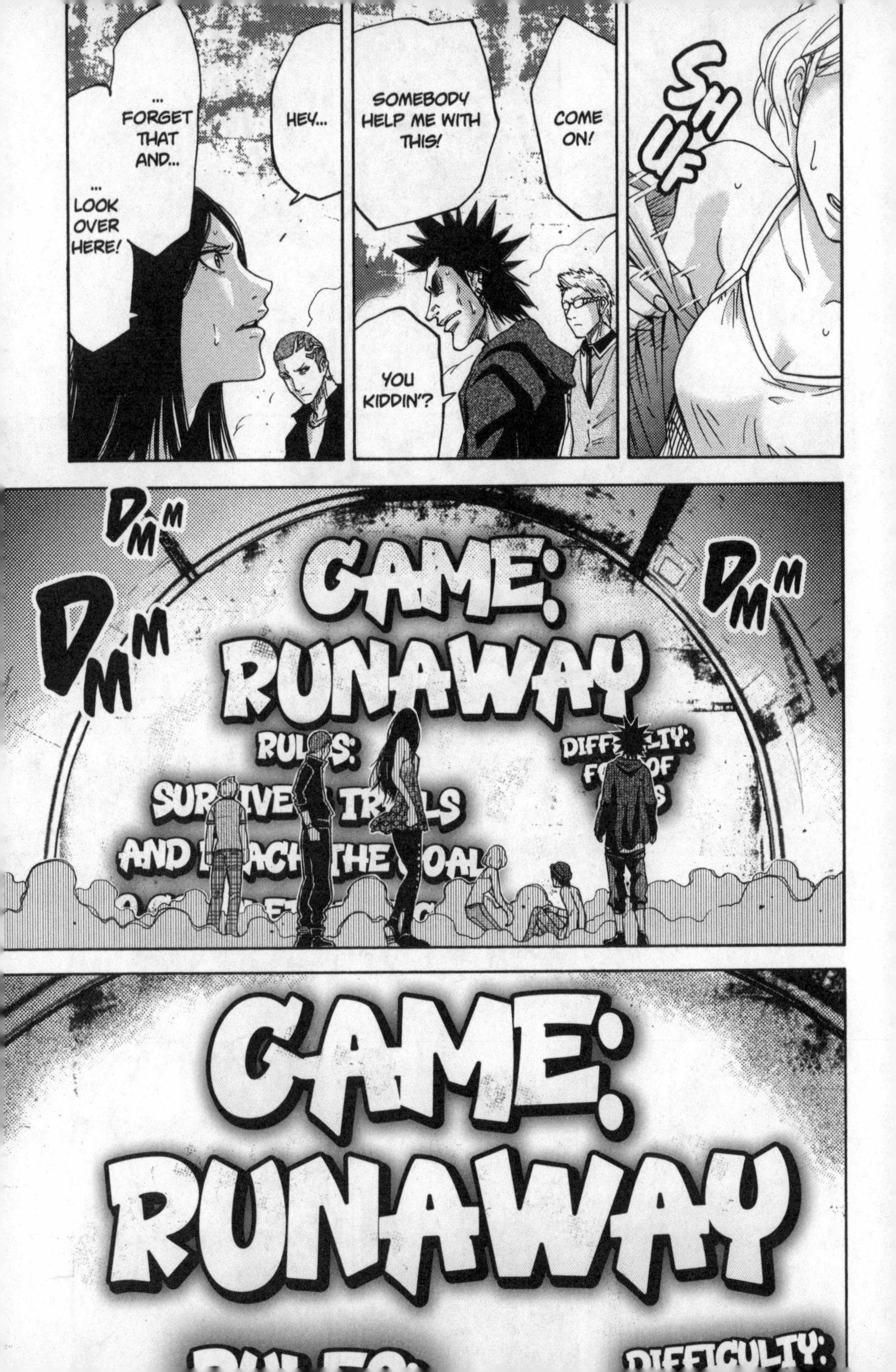
SHUF
COME ON!
SOMEBODY HELP ME WITH THIS!
YOU KIDDIN'?
HEY...
... FORGET THAT AND...
... LOOK OVER HERE!
DMM
DMM
DMM
GAME: RUNAWAY
GAME: RUNAWAY
DIFFICULTY:

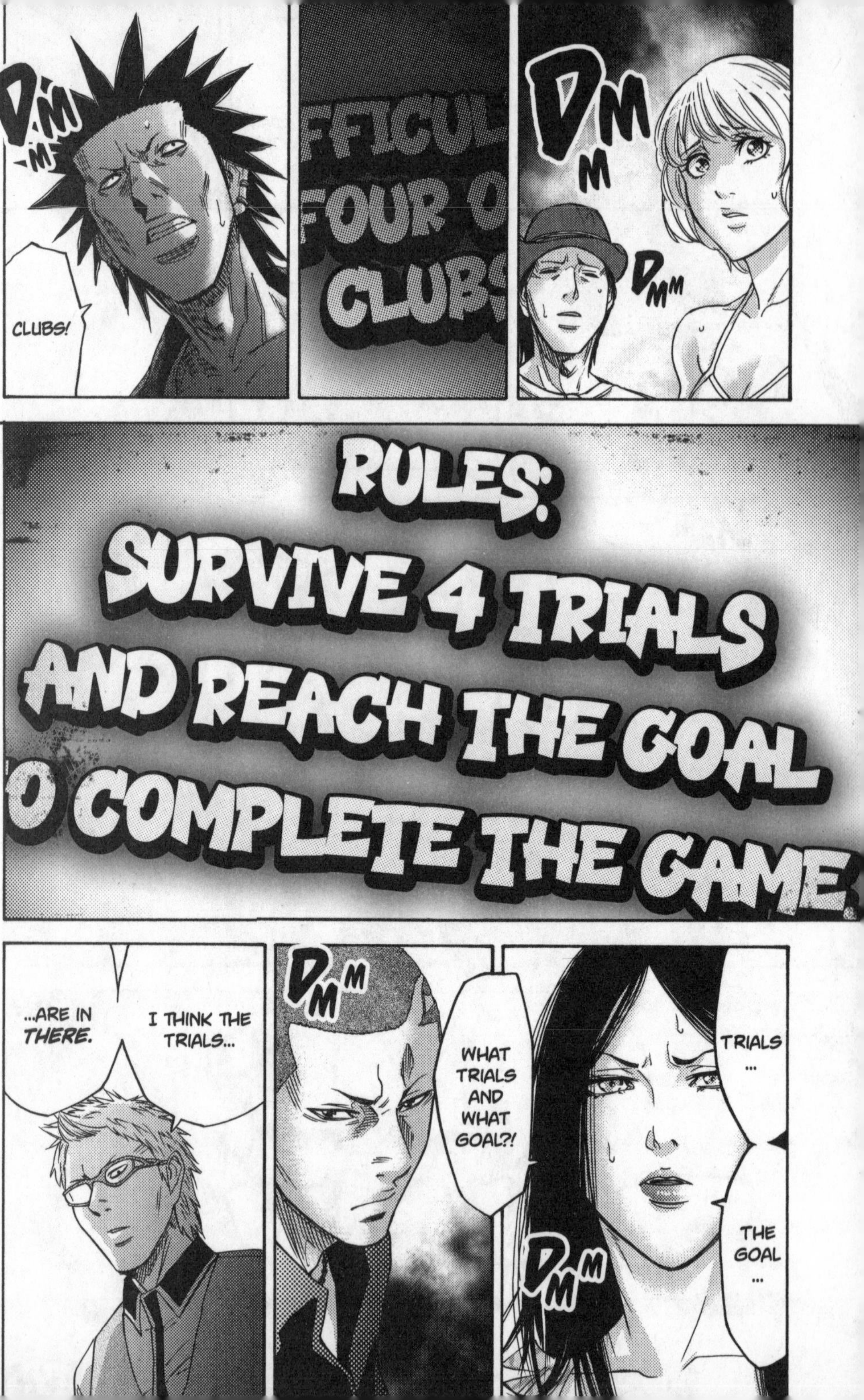
DMM
DMM
FFICUL
FOUR O
CLUBS
DMM
CLUBS!
RULES:
SURVIVE 4 TRIALS
AND REACH THE GOAL
O COMPLETE THE GAME.
TRIALS ...
THE GOAL ...
DMM
WHAT TRIALS AND WHAT GOAL?!
DMM
I THINK THE TRIALS...
...ARE IN THERE.

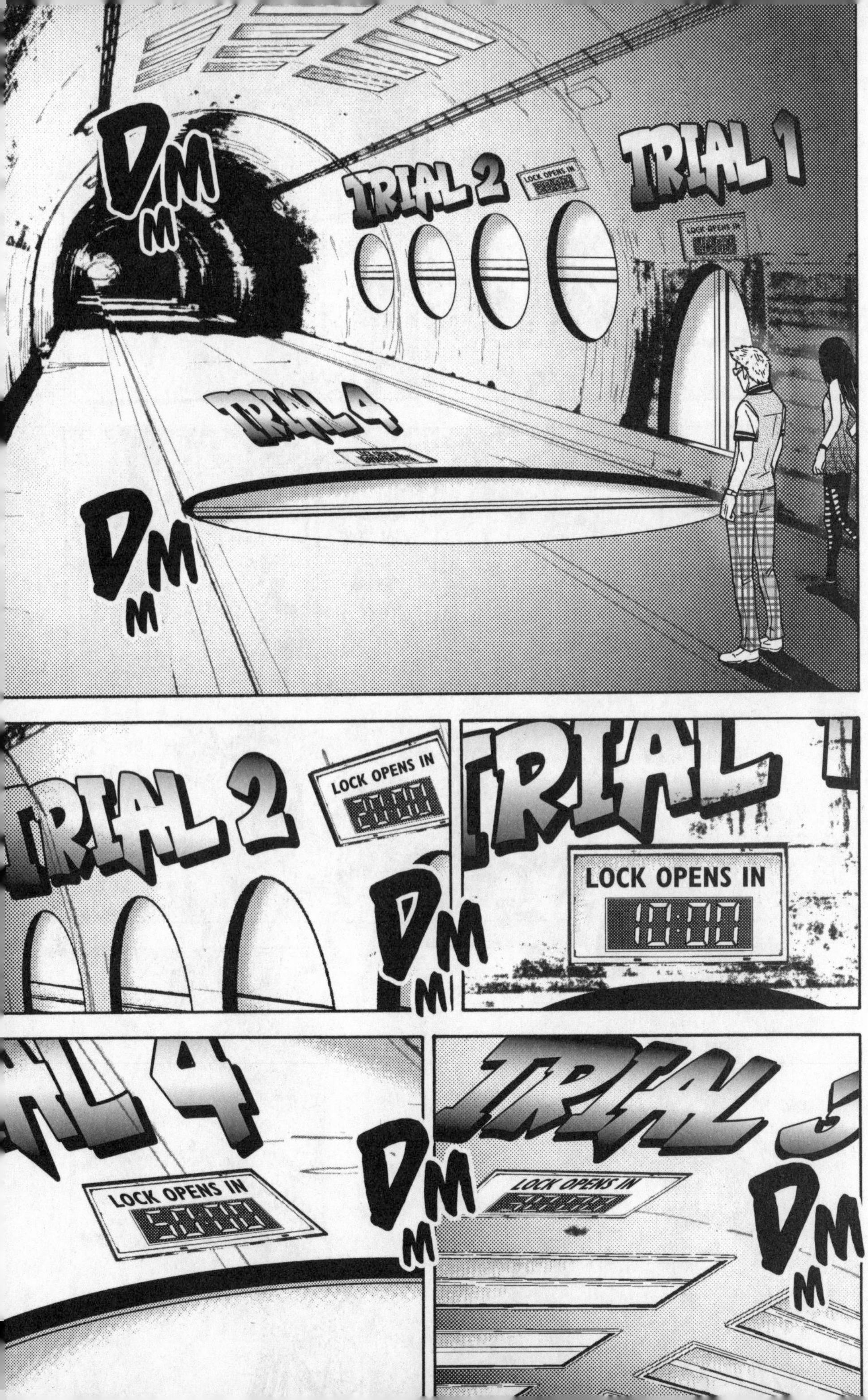

TRIAL 1
LOCK OPENS IN
TRIAL 2
LOCK OPENS IN
DMM
TRIAL 4
DMM
RIAL
LOCK OPENS IN
10:00
DMM
RIAL 2
LOCK OPENS IN
TRIAL
LOCK OPENS IN
DMM
DMM
AL 4
LOCK OPENS IN

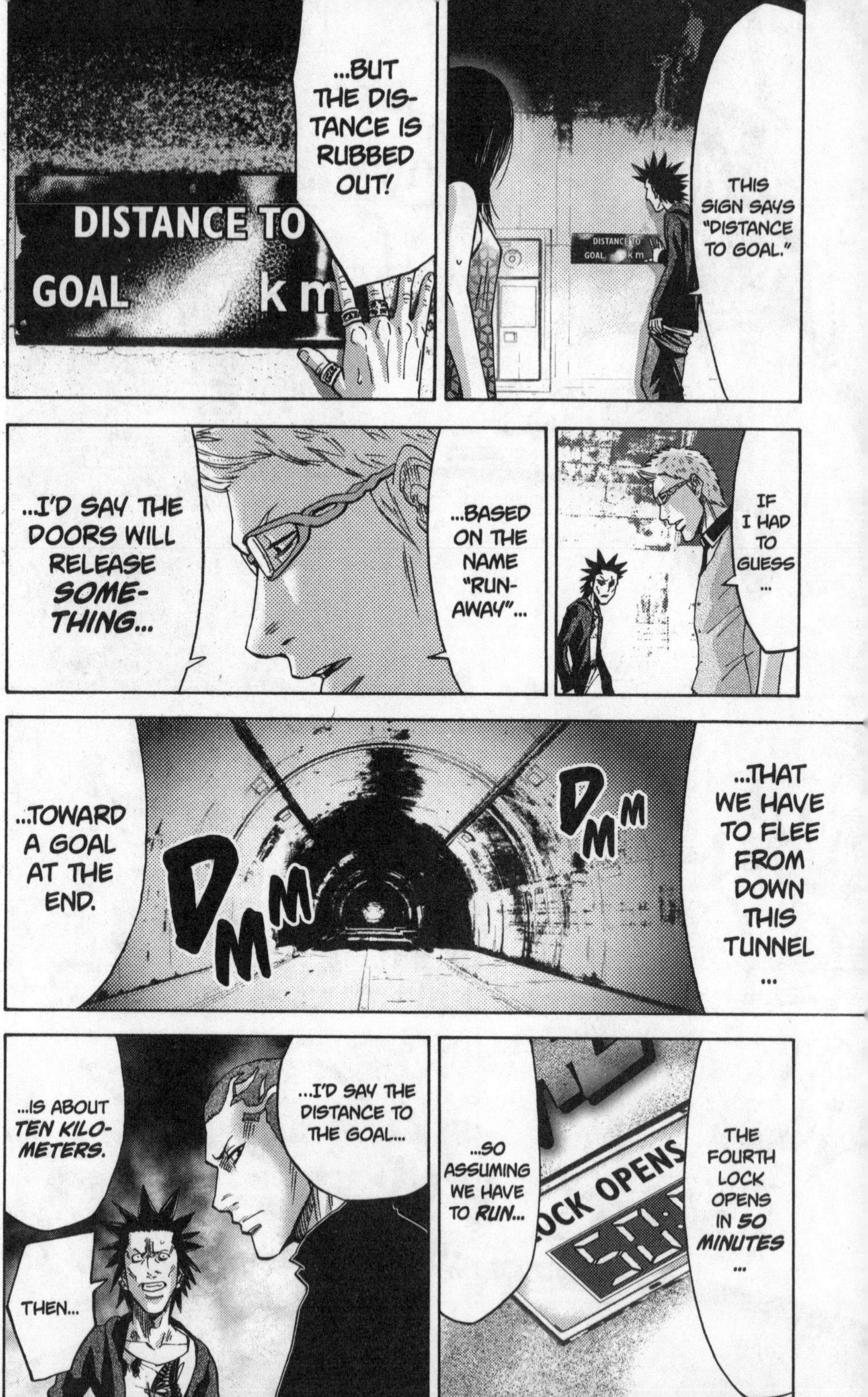
THIS SIGN SAYS "DISTANCE TO GOAL."
DISTANCE TO GOAL km
...BUT THE DISTANCE IS RUBBED OUT!
DISTANCE TO GOAL km
IF I HAD TO GUESS...
...BASED ON THE NAME "RUN-AWAY"...
...I'D SAY THE DOORS WILL RELEASE *SOMETHING*...
...THAT WE HAVE TO FLEE FROM DOWN THIS TUNNEL...
DMM
DMM
...TOWARD A GOAL AT THE END.
THE FOURTH LOCK OPENS IN *50 MINUTES*...
LOCK OPENS
...SO ASSUMING WE HAVE TO *RUN*...
...I'D SAY THE DISTANCE TO THE GOAL...
...IS ABOUT *TEN KILOMETERS.*
THEN...

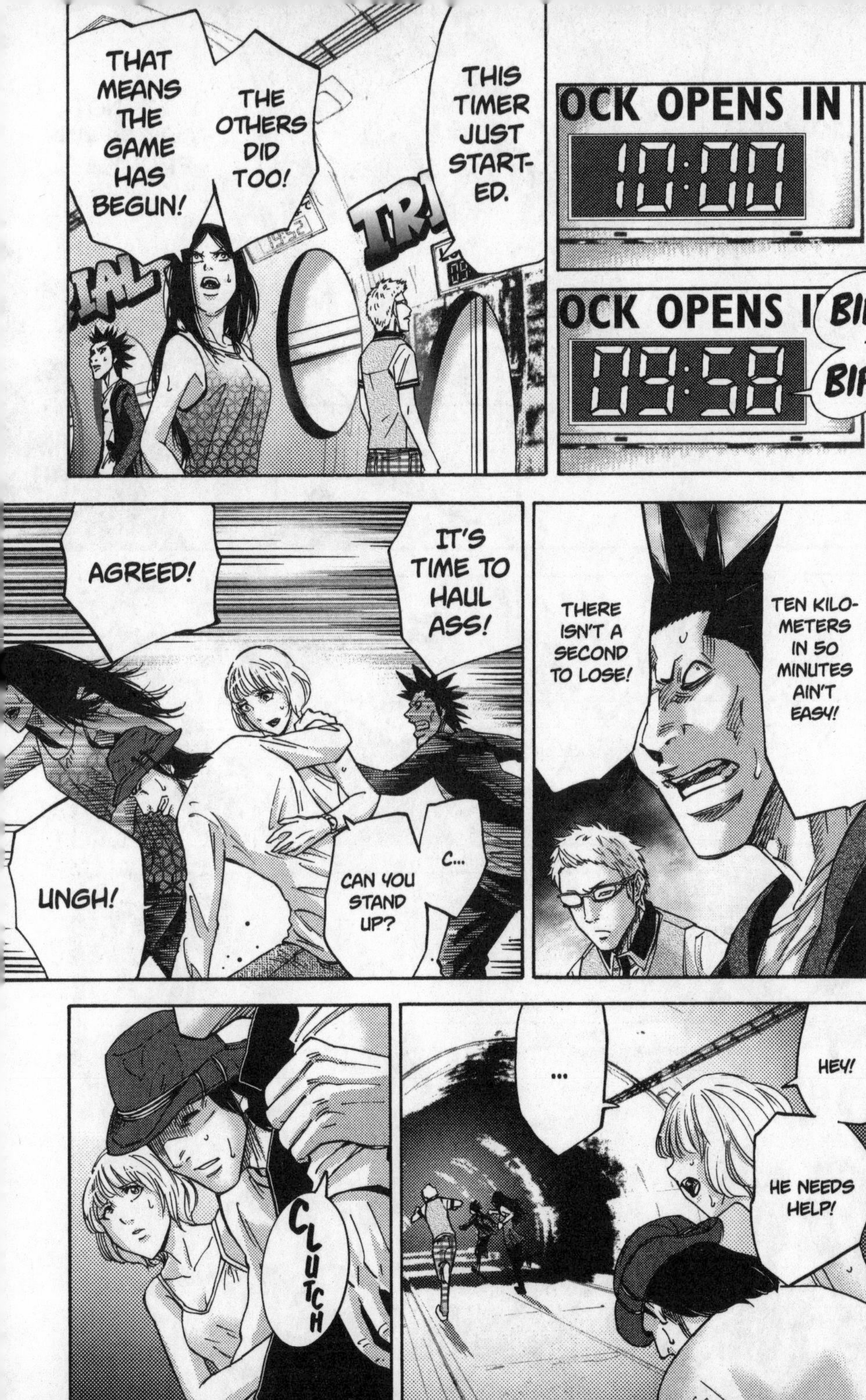
OCK OPENS IN
10:00
OCK OPENS IN
09:58
BIP
BIP
THIS TIMER JUST START-ED.
THE OTHERS DID TOO!
THAT MEANS THE GAME HAS BEGUN!
TEN KILO-METERS IN 50 MINUTES AIN'T EASY!
THERE ISN'T A SECOND TO LOSE!
IT'S TIME TO HAUL ASS!
AGREED!
C...
CAN YOU STAND UP?
UNGH!
HEY!
HE NEEDS HELP!
...
CLUTCH

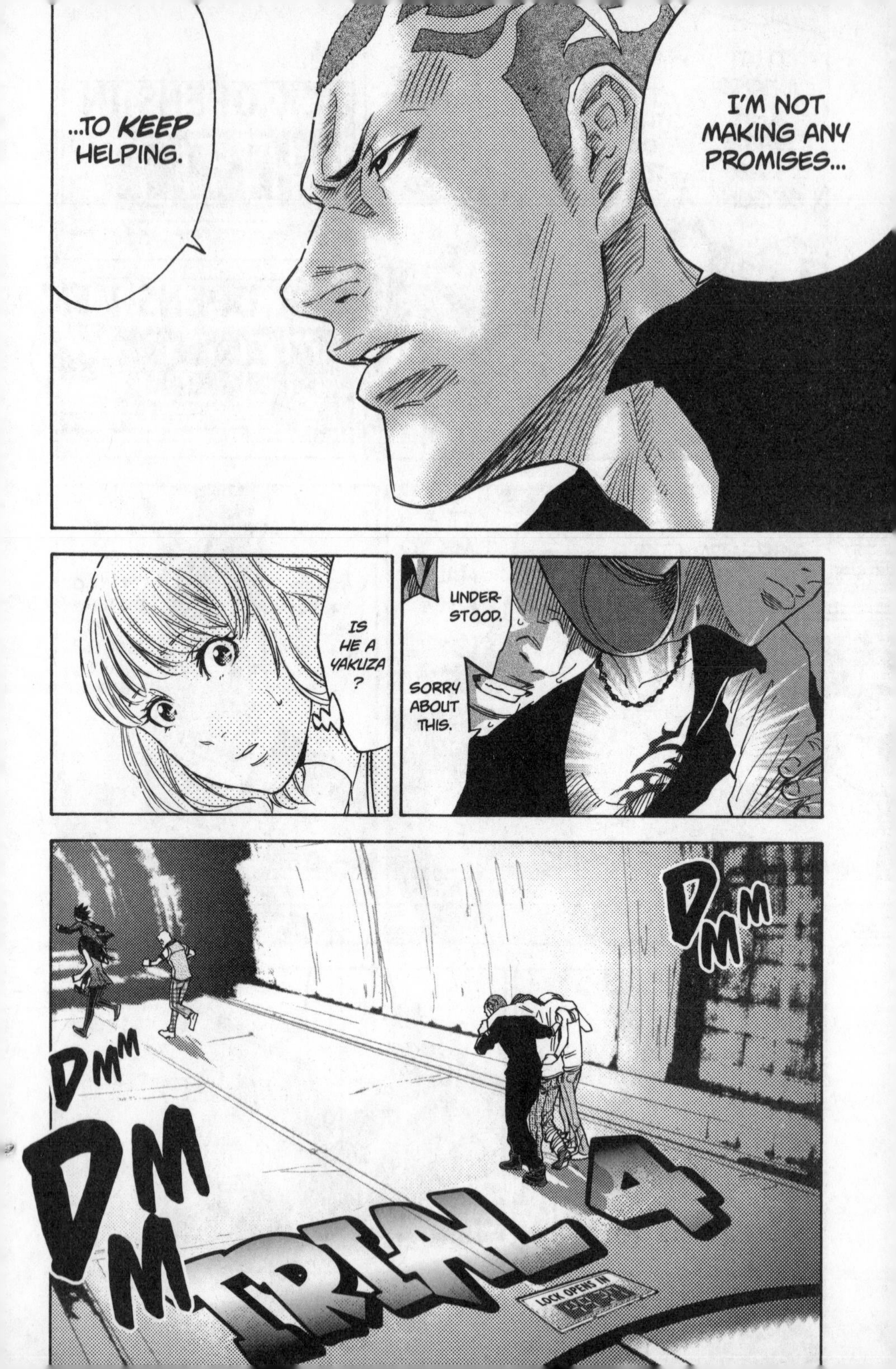
I'M NOT MAKING ANY PROMISES...
...TO KEEP HELPING.
UNDER-STOOD.
SORRY ABOUT THIS.
IS HE A YAKUZA?
DMM
DMM
DMM
TRIAL 4
LOCK OPENS IN

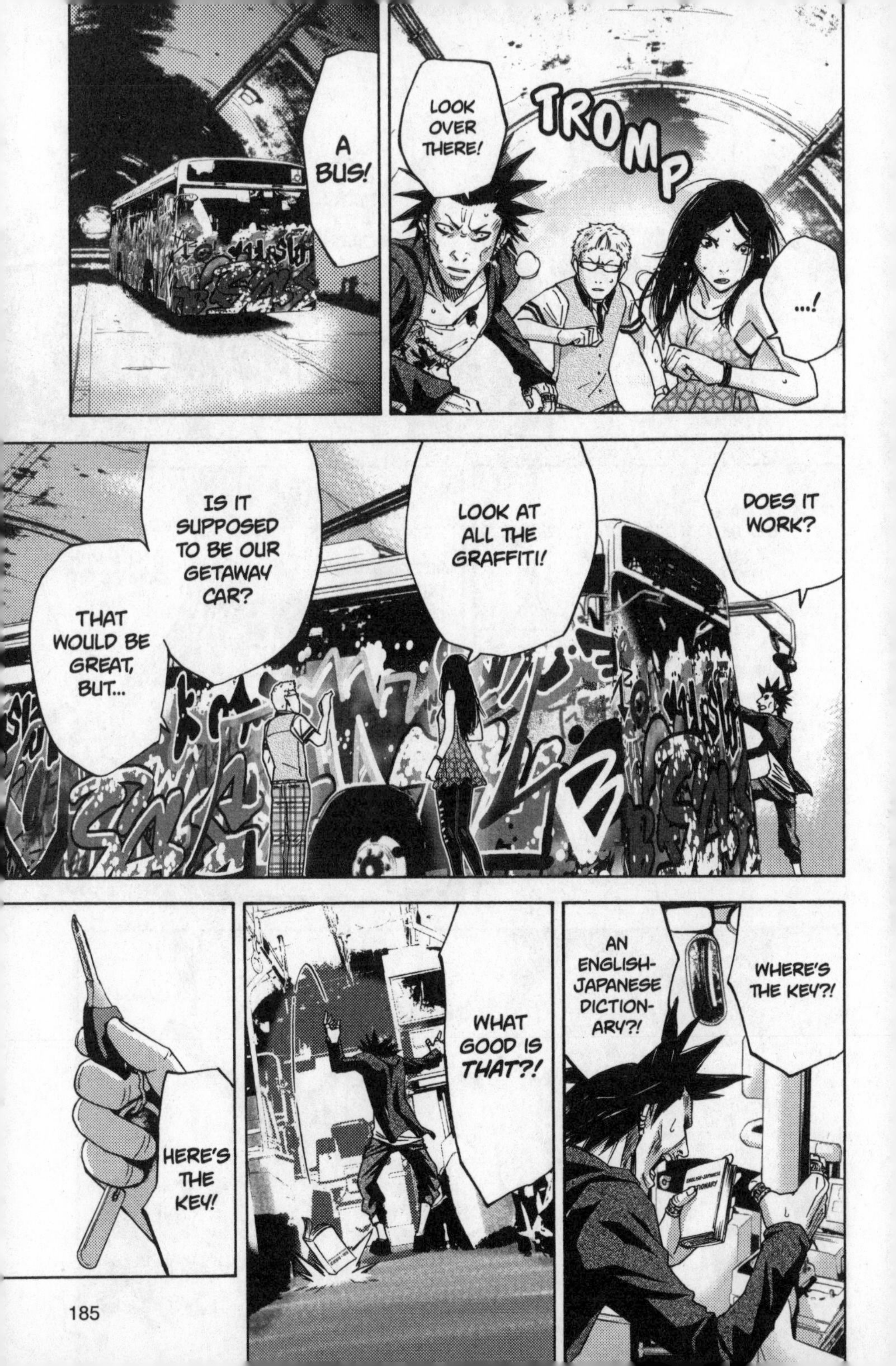
TROMP
LOOK OVER THERE!
...!
A BUS!
DOES IT WORK?
LOOK AT ALL THE GRAFFITI!
IS IT SUPPOSED TO BE OUR GETAWAY CAR?
THAT WOULD BE GREAT, BUT...
WHERE'S THE KEY?!
AN ENGLISH-JAPANESE DICTION-ARY?!
WHAT GOOD IS THAT?!
HERE'S THE KEY!

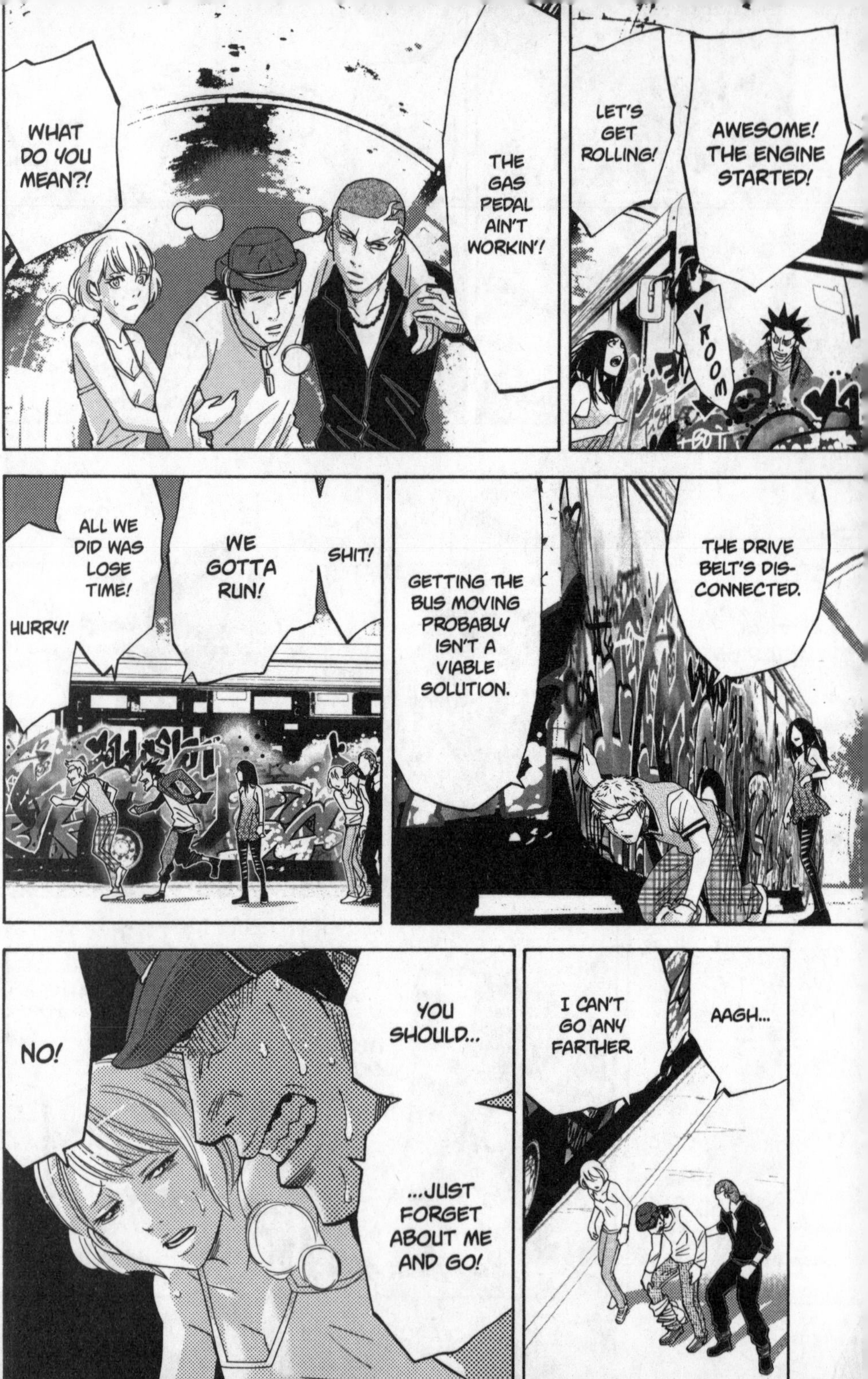
AWESOME! THE ENGINE STARTED!
LET'S GET ROLLING!
VROOM
THE GAS PEDAL AIN'T WORKIN'!
WHAT DO YOU MEAN?!
THE DRIVE BELT'S DIS-CONNECTED.
GETTING THE BUS MOVING PROBABLY ISN'T A VIABLE SOLUTION.
SHIT!
WE GOTTA RUN!
ALL WE DID WAS LOSE TIME!
HURRY!
AAGH...
I CAN'T GO ANY FARTHER.
YOU SHOULD...
...JUST FORGET ABOUT ME AND GO!
NO!

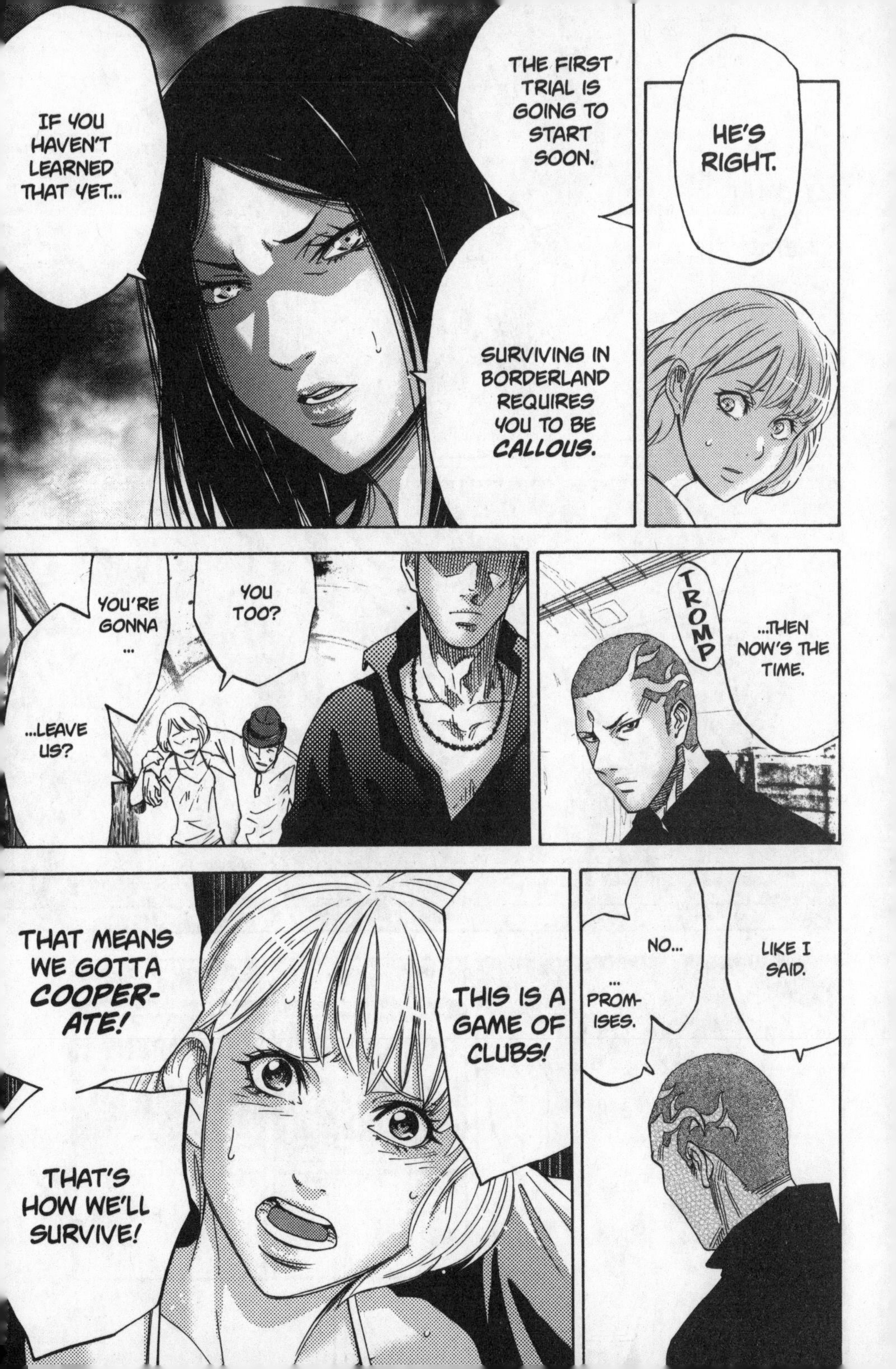
HE'S RIGHT.
THE FIRST TRIAL IS GOING TO START SOON.
SURVIVING IN BORDERLAND REQUIRES YOU TO BE *CALLOUS.*
IF YOU HAVEN'T LEARNED THAT YET...
TROMP
...THEN NOW'S THE TIME.
YOU TOO?
YOU'RE GONNA ...
...LEAVE US?
LIKE I SAID.
NO...
...PROMISES.
THIS IS A GAME OF CLUBS!
THAT MEANS WE GOTTA *COOPERATE!*
THAT'S HOW WE'LL SURVIVE!

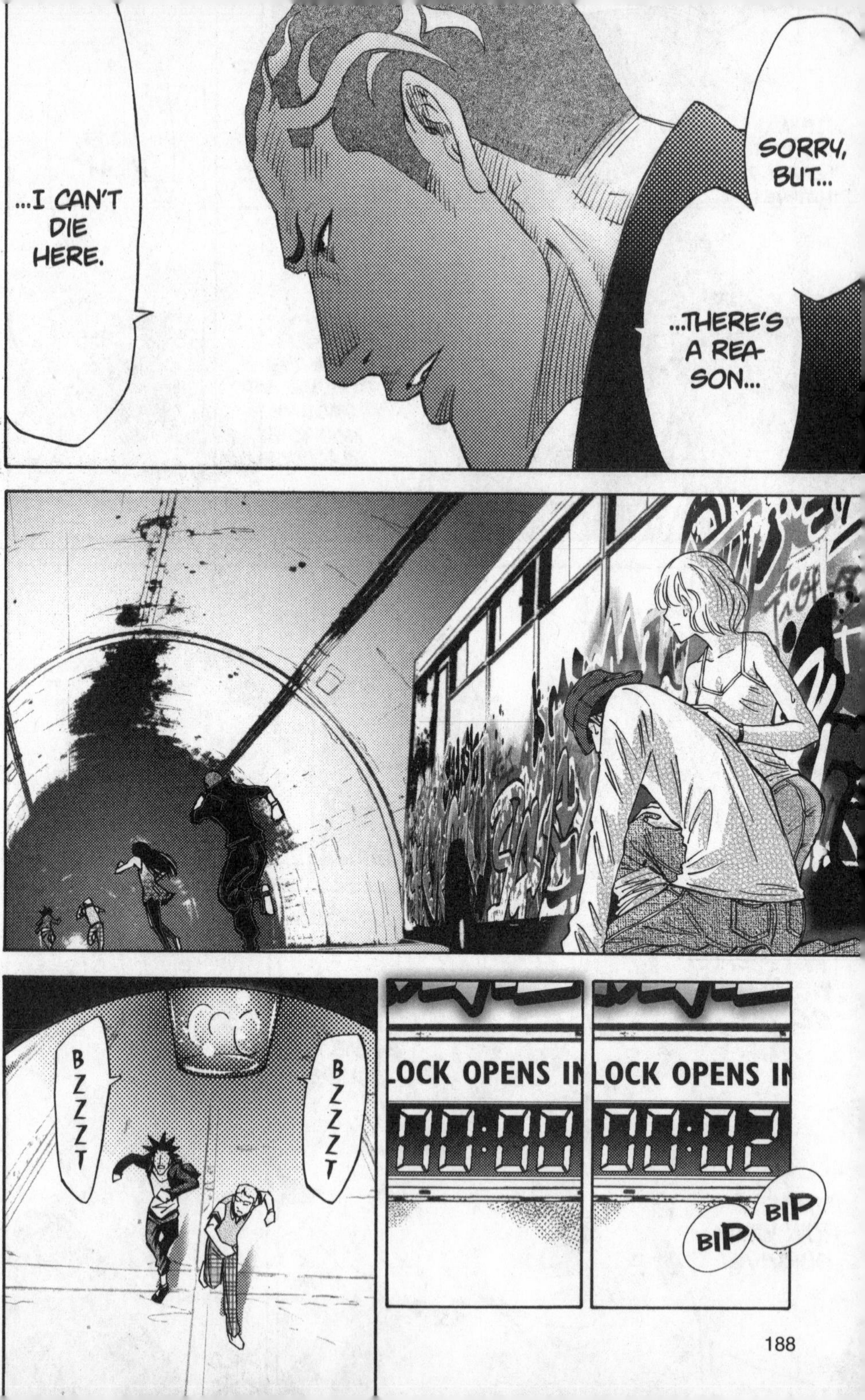
SORRY, BUT...
...THERE'S A REA SON...
...I CAN'T DIE HERE.
LOCK OPENS IN
00:02
BIP
BIP
LOCK OPENS IN
00:00
BZZZT
BZZZT

BZZZT

THE TRIAL...

...IS STARTING!

LOCK OPENS IN

RRMBL

THAT WAS FAST!

BZZZT

BZZZZT

IT'S ALREADY BEEN TEN MINUTES?!

...AAAAAHH!

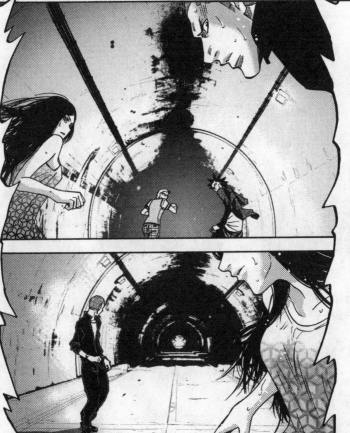

GYAAAAA...

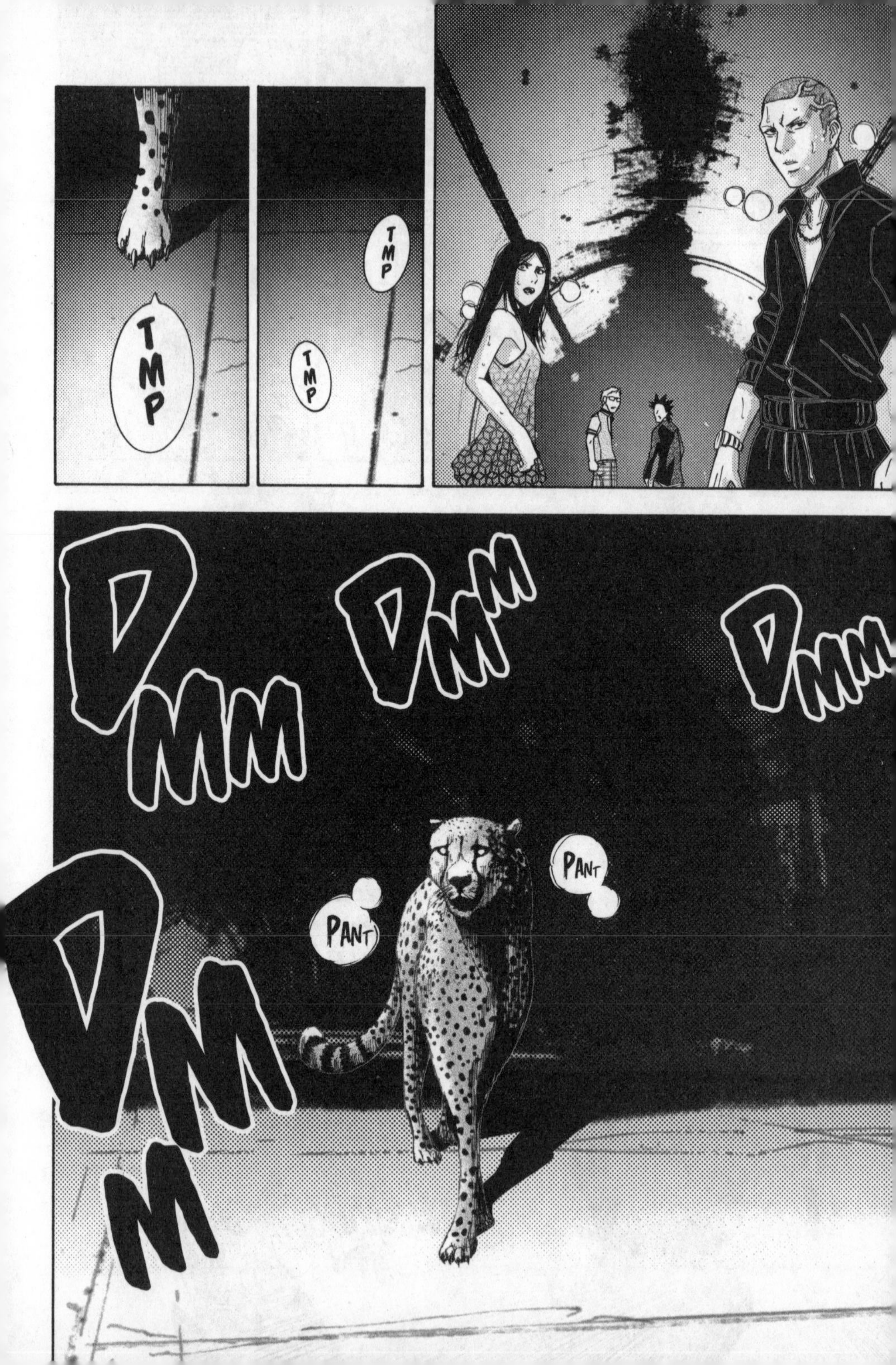
TMP
TMP
TMP
DMMM
DMMM
DMMM
PANT
PANT
DMMM

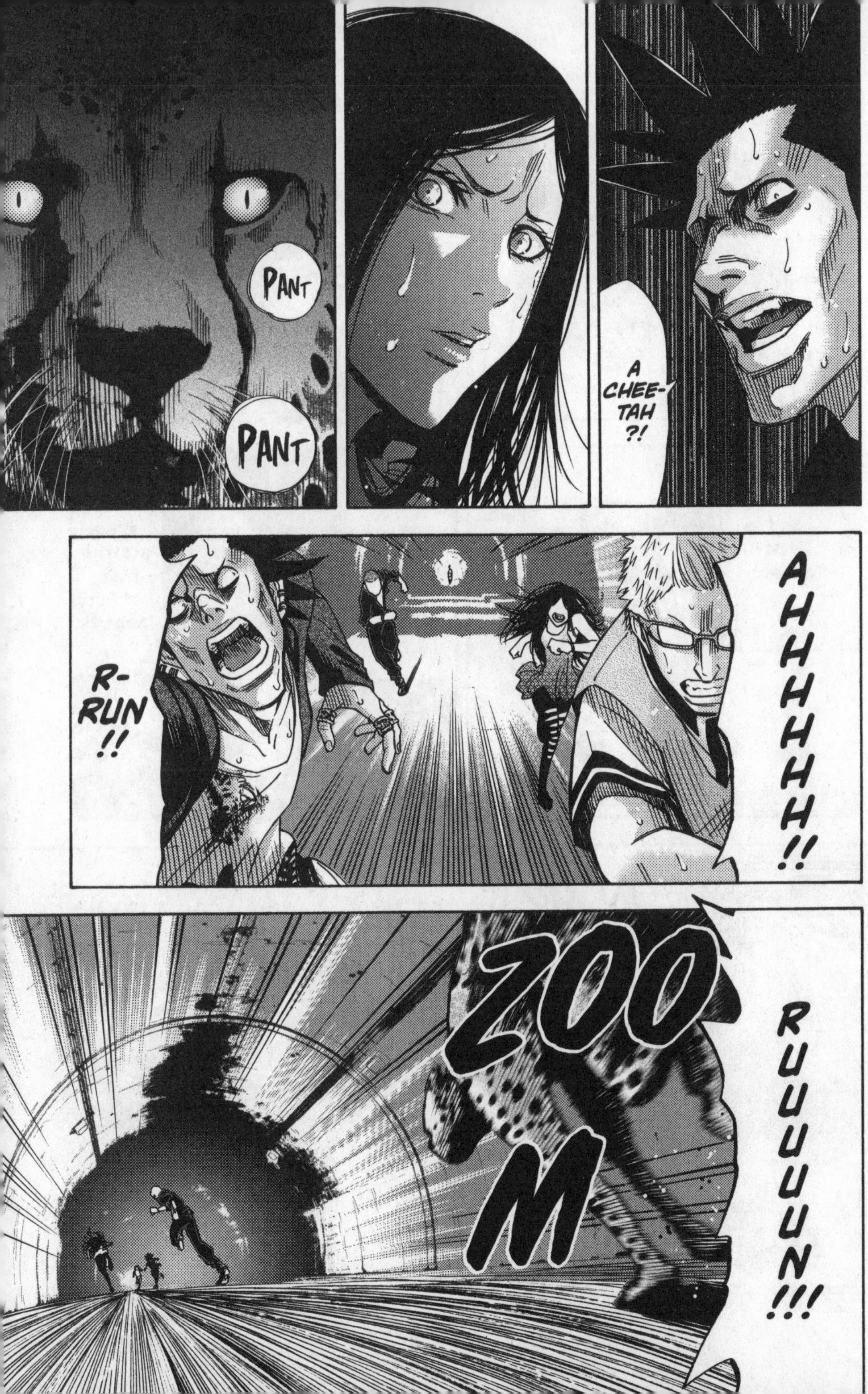
A CHEETAH?!
PANT
PANT
AHHHHHHH!!
R-RUN!!
RUUUUUN!!!
ZOOM

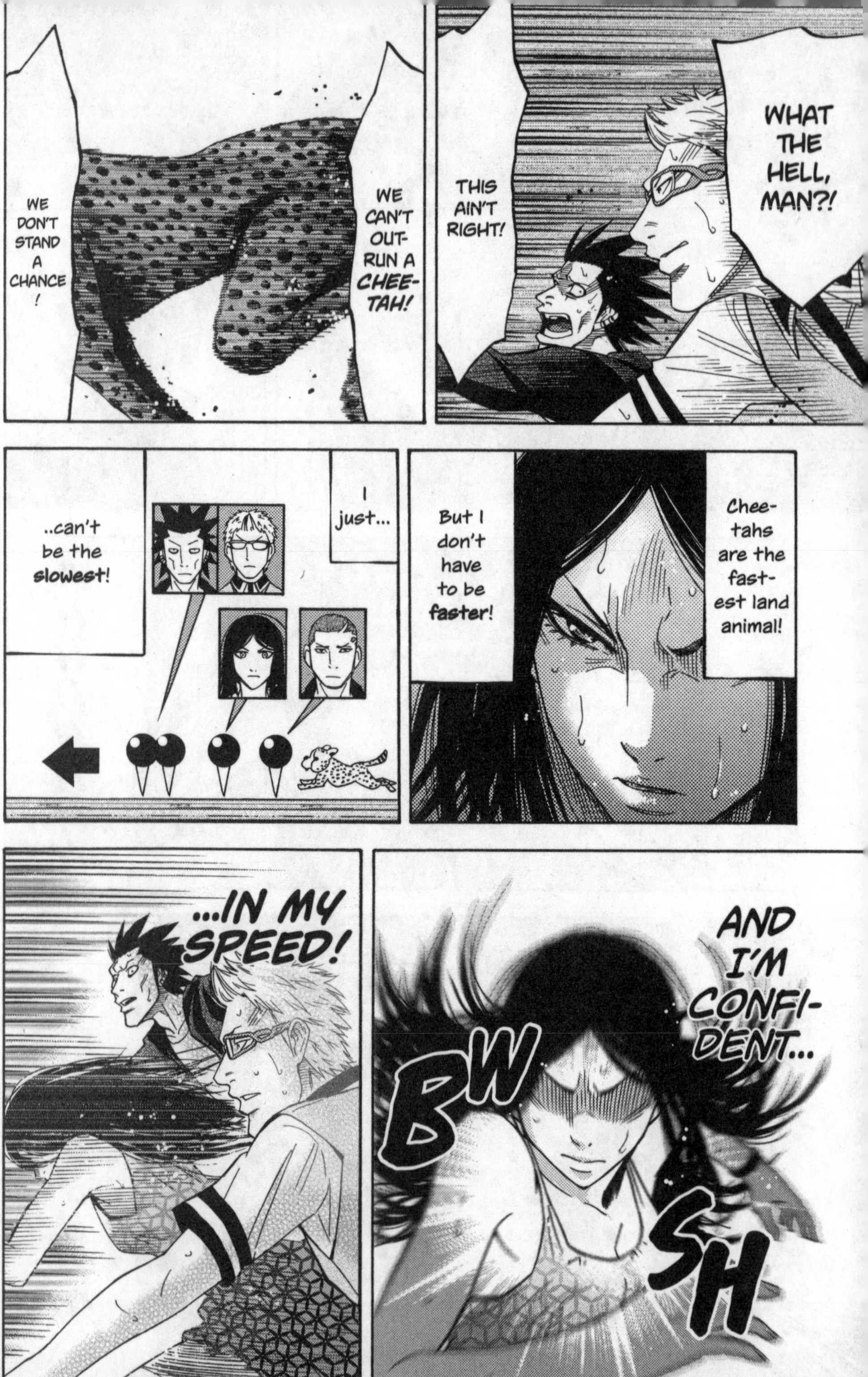
WHAT THE HELL, MAN?!
THIS AIN'T RIGHT!
WE CAN'T OUT-RUN A CHEE-TAH!
WE DON'T STAND A CHANCE!
Chee-tahs are the fast-est land animal!
But I don't have to be faster!
I just...
...can't be the slowest!
AND I'M CONFI-DENT...
BWSH
...IN MY SPEED!

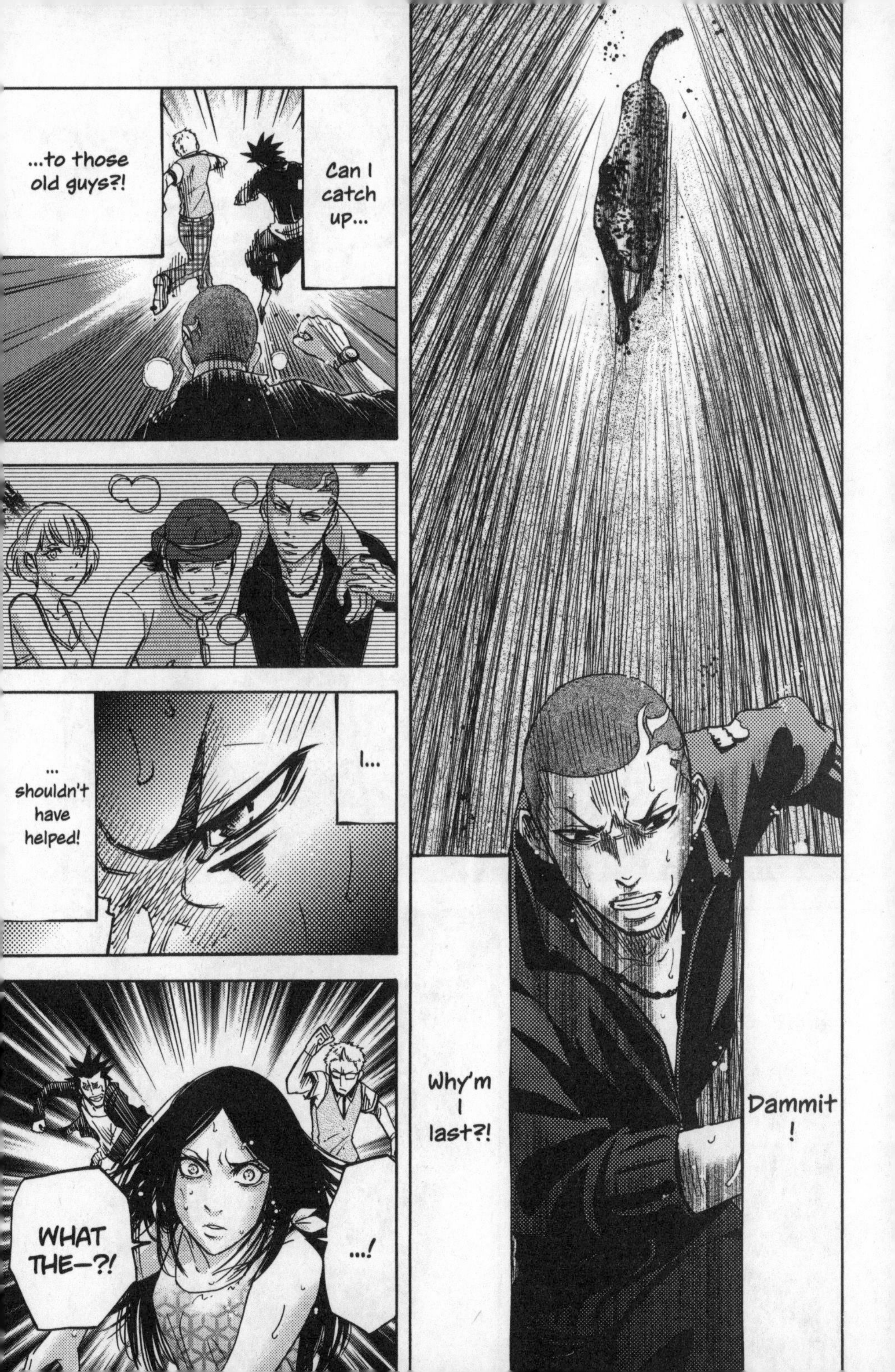
Dammit!
Why'm I last?!
Can I catch up...
...to those old guys?!
I...
...shouldn't have helped!
...!
WHAT THE—?!

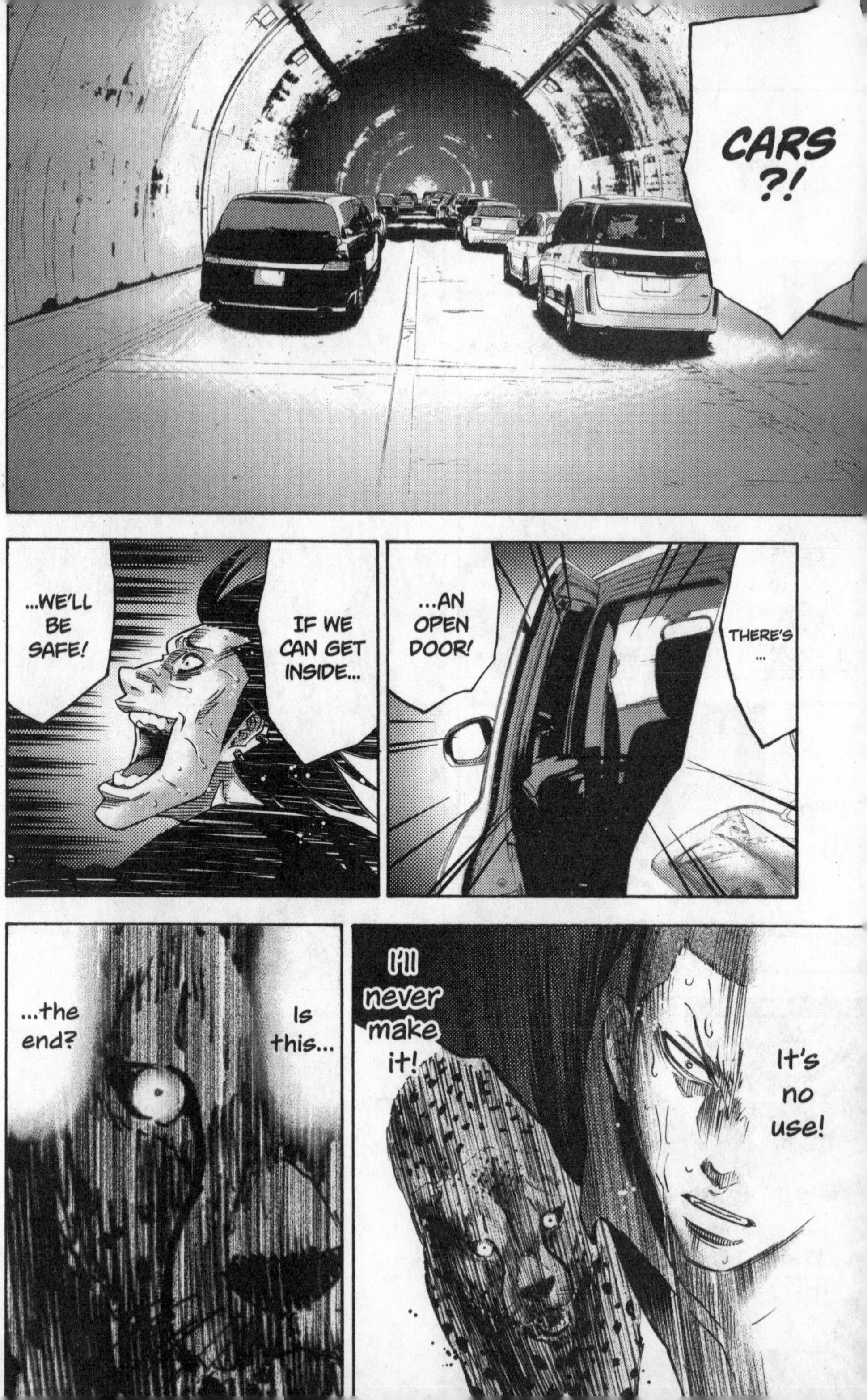
CARS ?!
THERE'S ...
...AN OPEN DOOR!
IF WE CAN GET INSIDE...
...WE'LL BE SAFE!
It's no use!
I'll never make it!
Is this...
...the end?

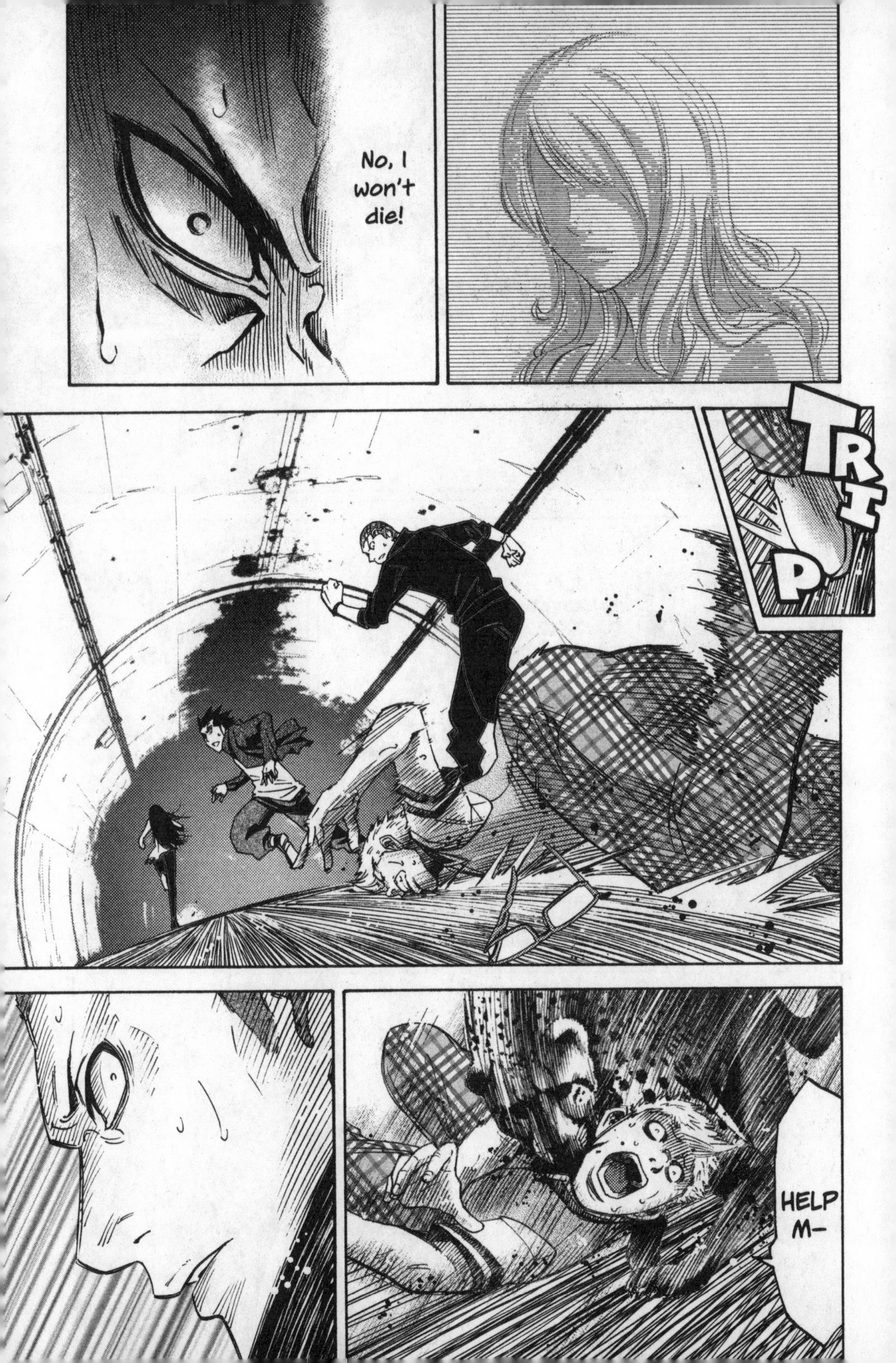
No, I won't die!
TRIP
HELP M–

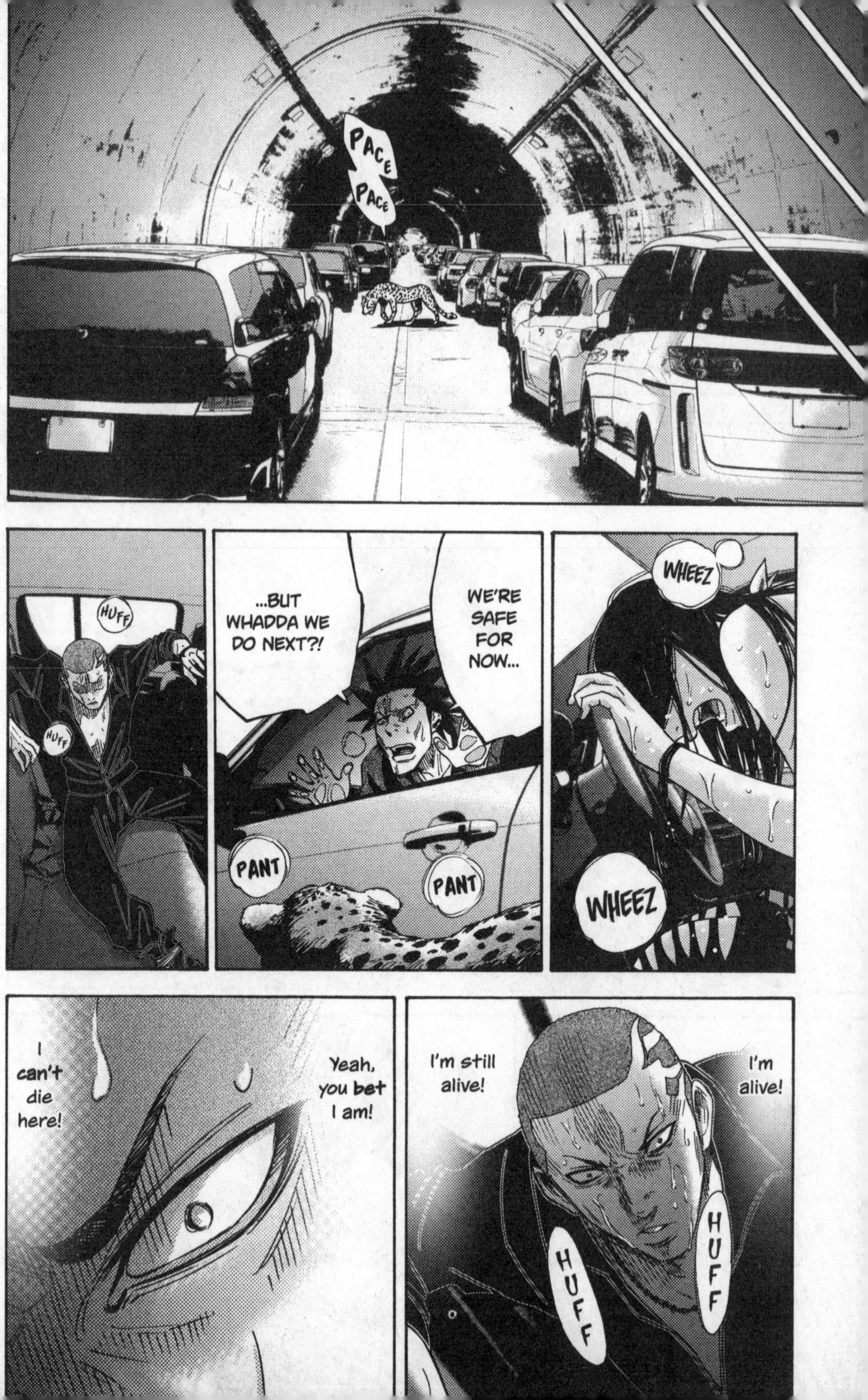
PACE PACE
WHEEZ
WHEEZ
WE'RE SAFE FOR NOW...
...BUT WHADDA WE DO NEXT?!
PANT
PANT
HUFF
HUFF
I'm alive!
I'm still alive!
HUFF
HUFF
Yeah, you **bet** I am!
I can't die here!

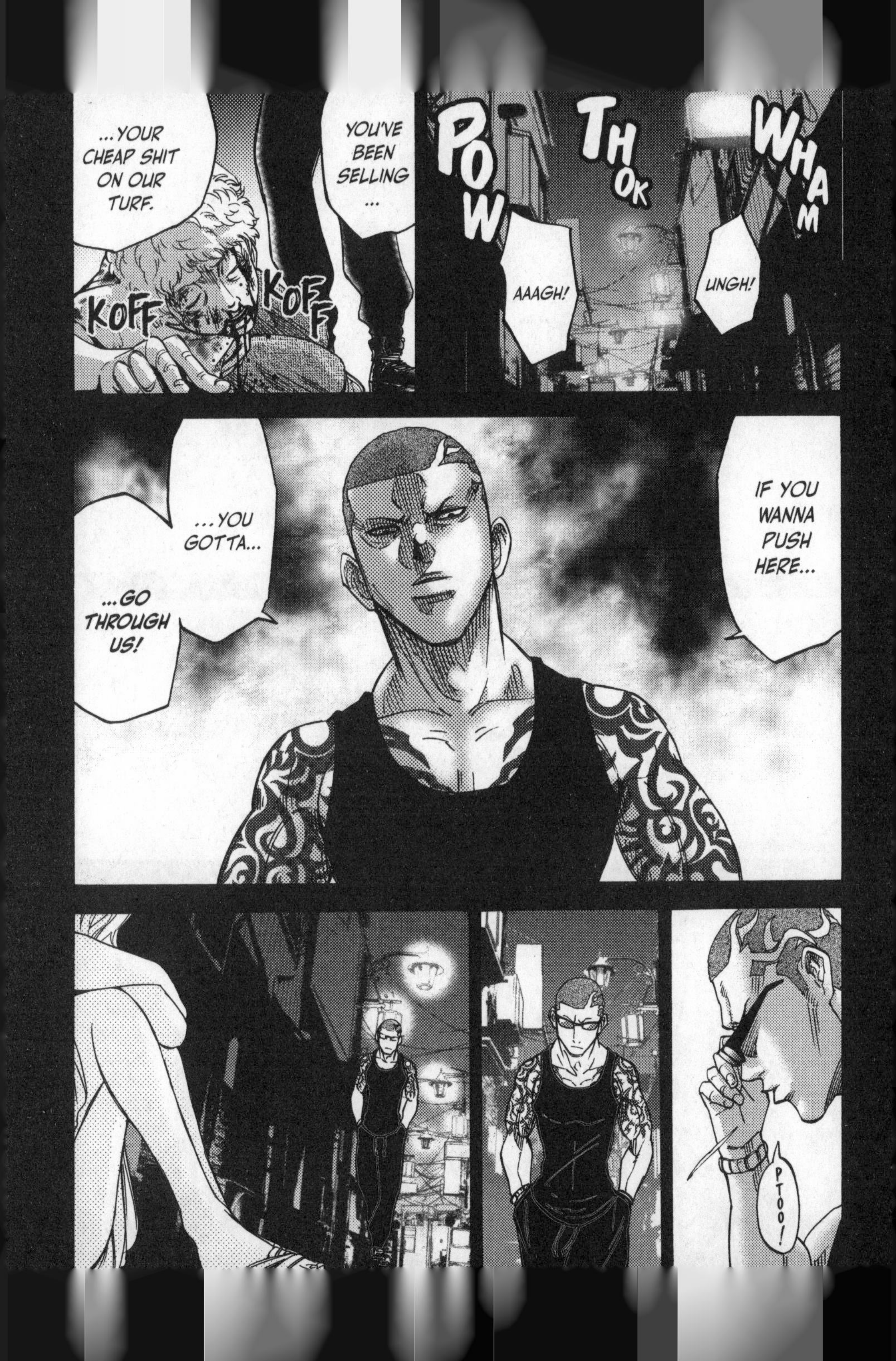
WHAM
THOK
POW
UNGH!
AAAGH!
YOU'VE BEEN SELLING...
...YOUR CHEAP SHIT ON OUR TURF.
KOFF
KOFF
IF YOU WANNA PUSH HERE...
...YOU GOTTA...
...GO THROUGH US!
PTOO!

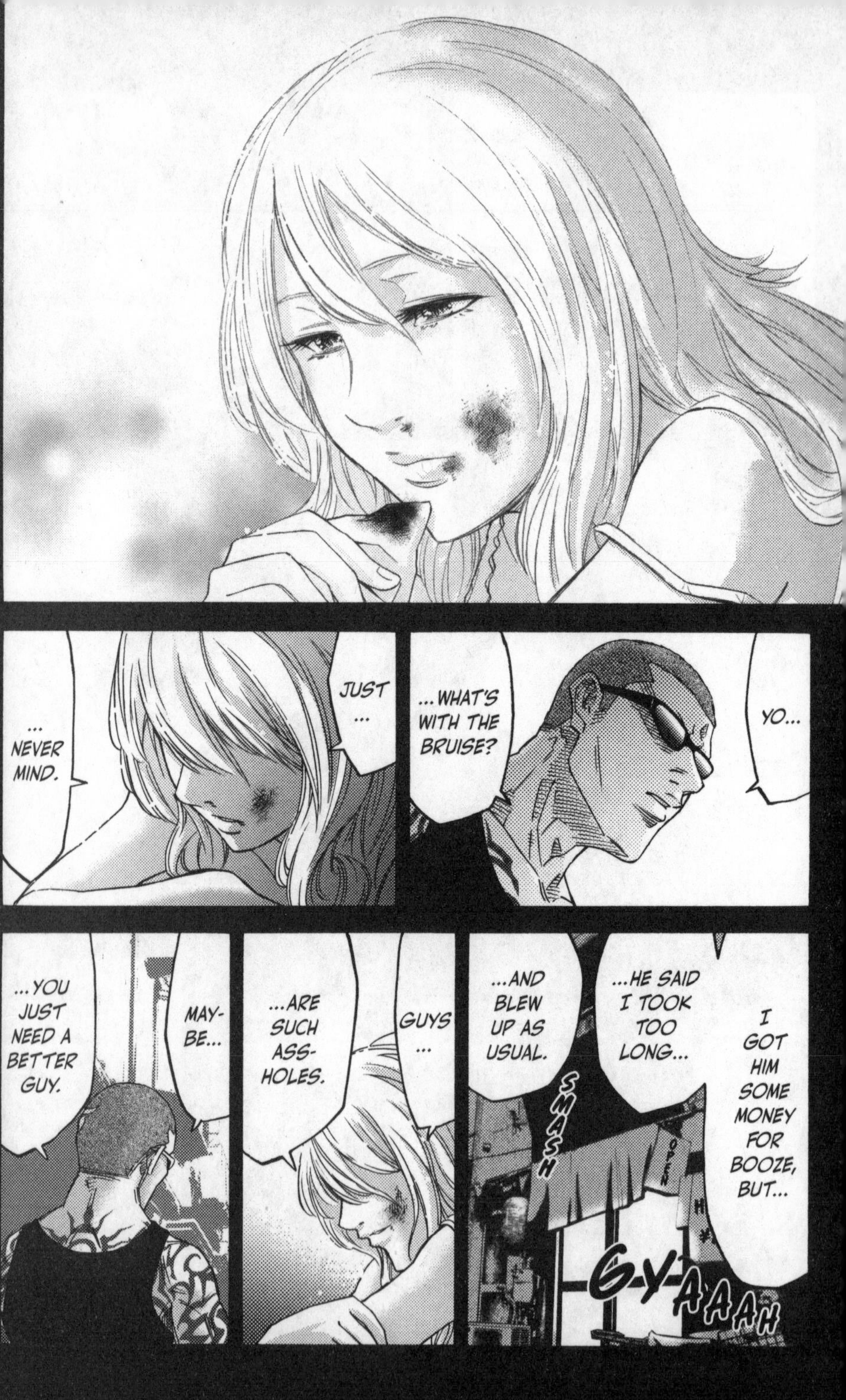
YO...
...WHAT'S WITH THE BRUISE?
JUST ...
... NEVER MIND.
I GOT HIM SOME MONEY FOR BOOZE, BUT...
...HE SAID I TOOK TOO LONG...
...AND BLEW UP AS USUAL.
SMASH
OPEN
GYAAAAH
GUYS ...
...ARE SUCH ASS-HOLES.
MAY-BE...
...YOU JUST NEED A BETTER GUY.

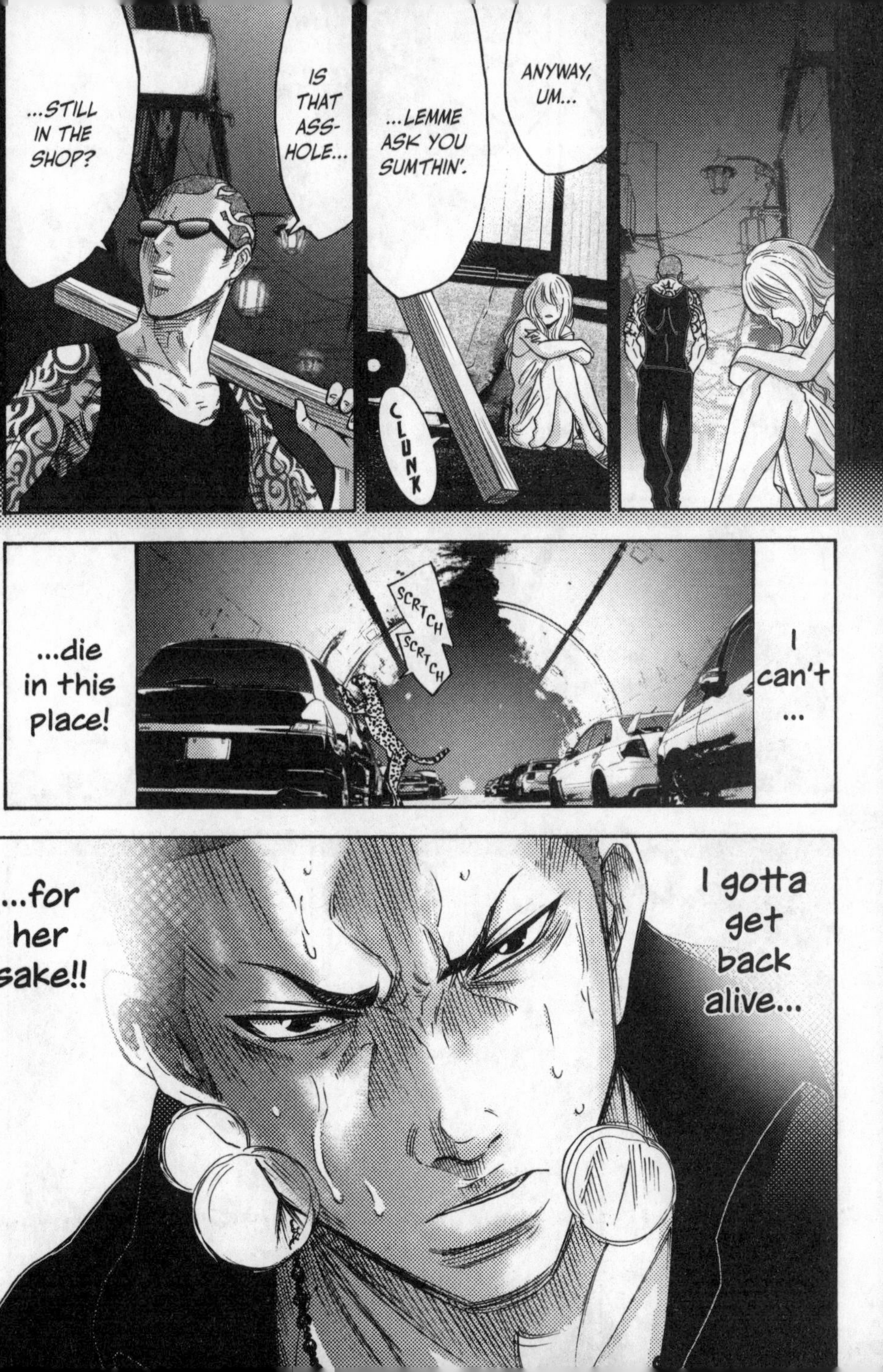

ANYWAY, UM...
...LEMME ASK YOU SUMTHIN'.
CLUNK
IS THAT ASS-HOLE...
...STILL IN THE SHOP?
I can't ...
SCRTCH SCRTCH
...die in this place!
I gotta get back alive...
...for her sake!!

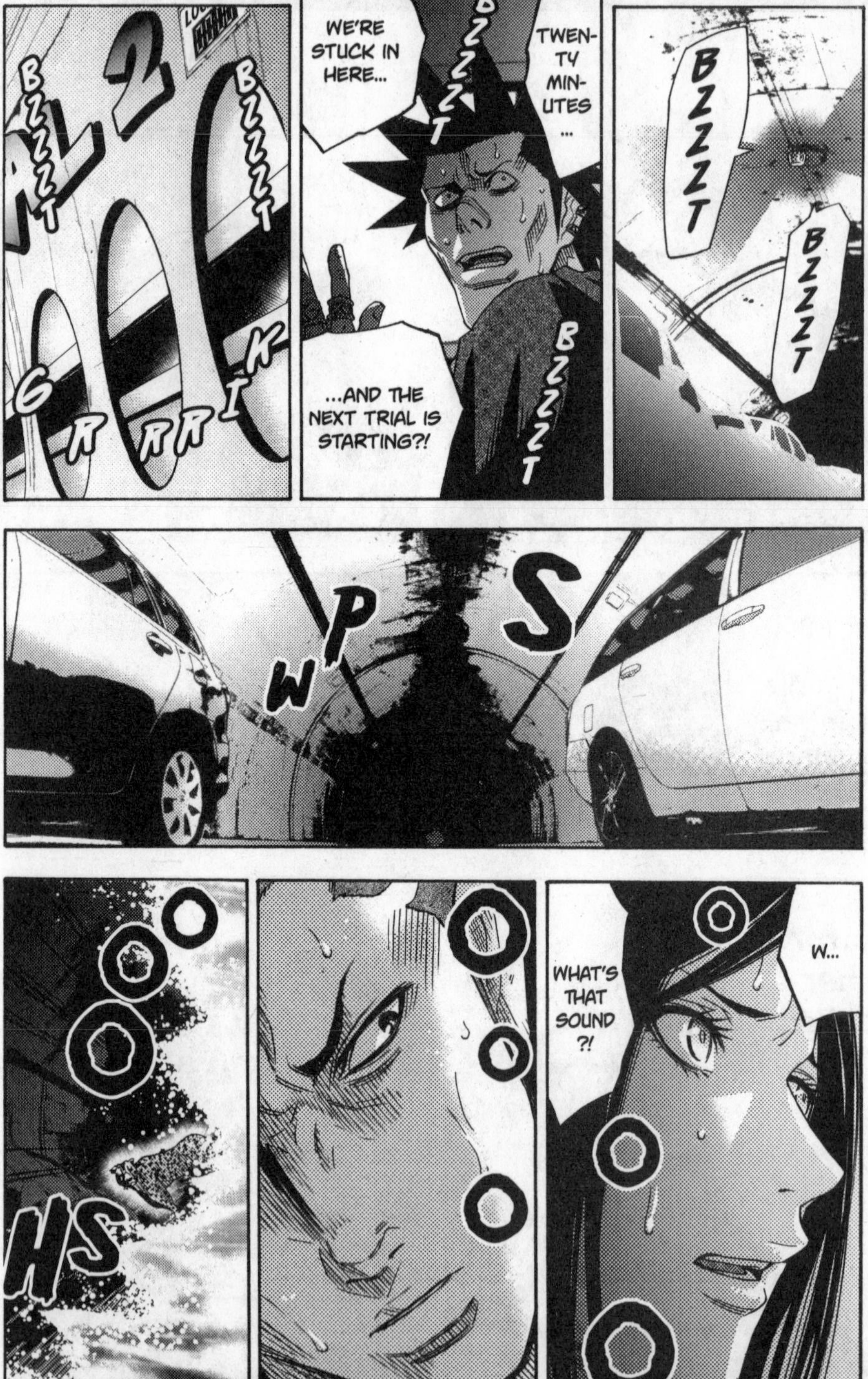
BZZZZT
BZZZZT
TWENTY MINUTES...
WE'RE STUCK IN HERE...
BZZZZT
...AND THE NEXT TRIAL IS STARTING?!
BZZZZT
BZZZZT
BZZZZT
GRRRIK
WPS
W...
WHAT'S THAT SOUND?!
HS

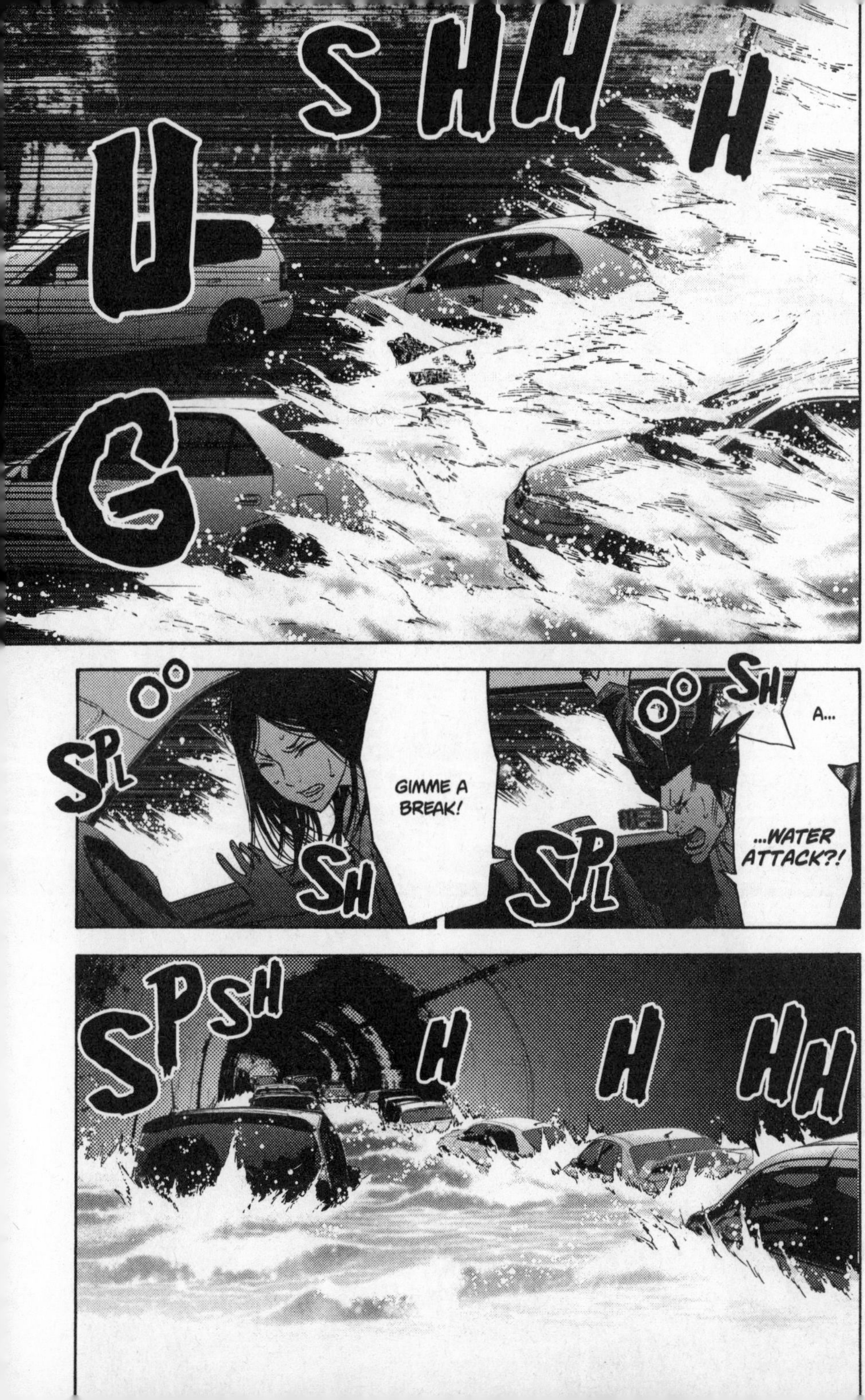
U SHHH
G
OO SH
A...
SPL
...WATER ATTACK?!
SPL OO
GIMME A BREAK!
SH
SPSH H H HH

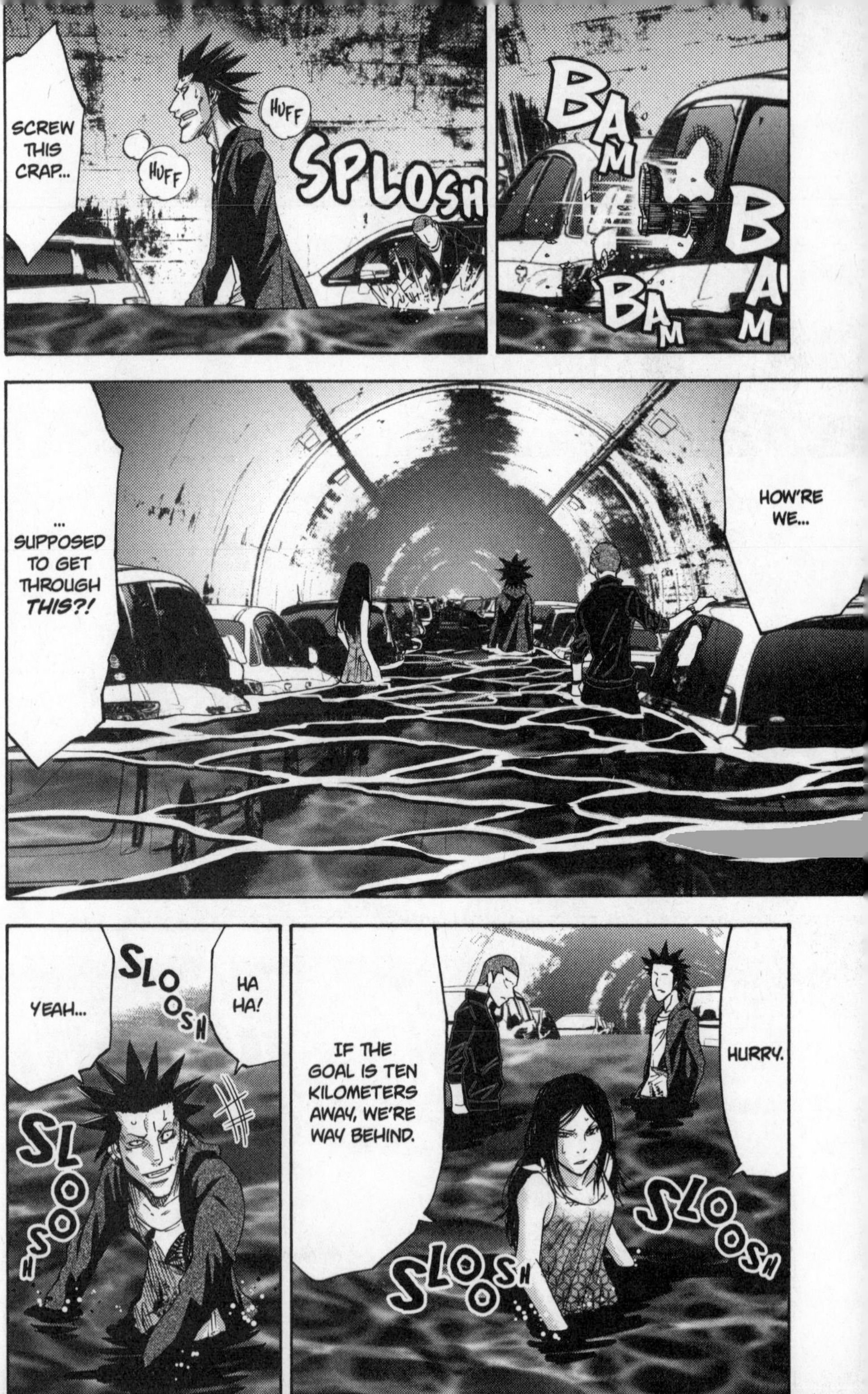
BAM
BAM
BAM
BAM
HUFF
SPLOSH
SCREW THIS CRAP...
HUFF
HOW'RE WE...
...SUPPOSED TO GET THROUGH *THIS?!*
HURRY.
IF THE GOAL IS TEN KILOMETERS AWAY, WE'RE WAY BEHIND.
SLOOSH
SLOOSH
HA HA!
SLOOSH
YEAH...
SLOOSH

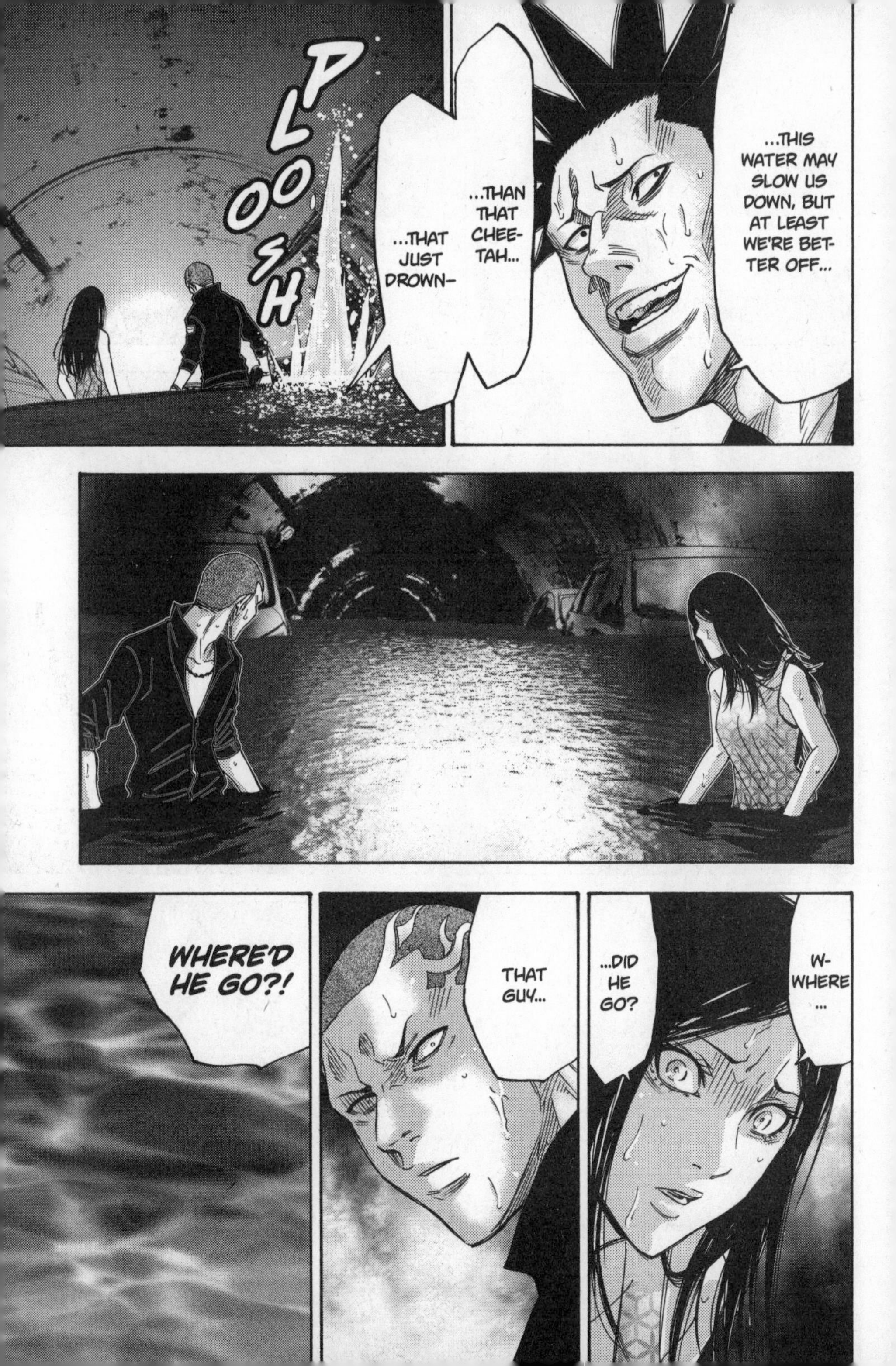
...THIS WATER MAY SLOW US DOWN, BUT AT LEAST WE'RE BET-TER OFF...
...THAN THAT CHEE-TAH...
...THAT JUST DROWN-
PLOOSH
W-WHERE...
...DID HE GO?
THAT GUY...
WHERE'D HE GO?!

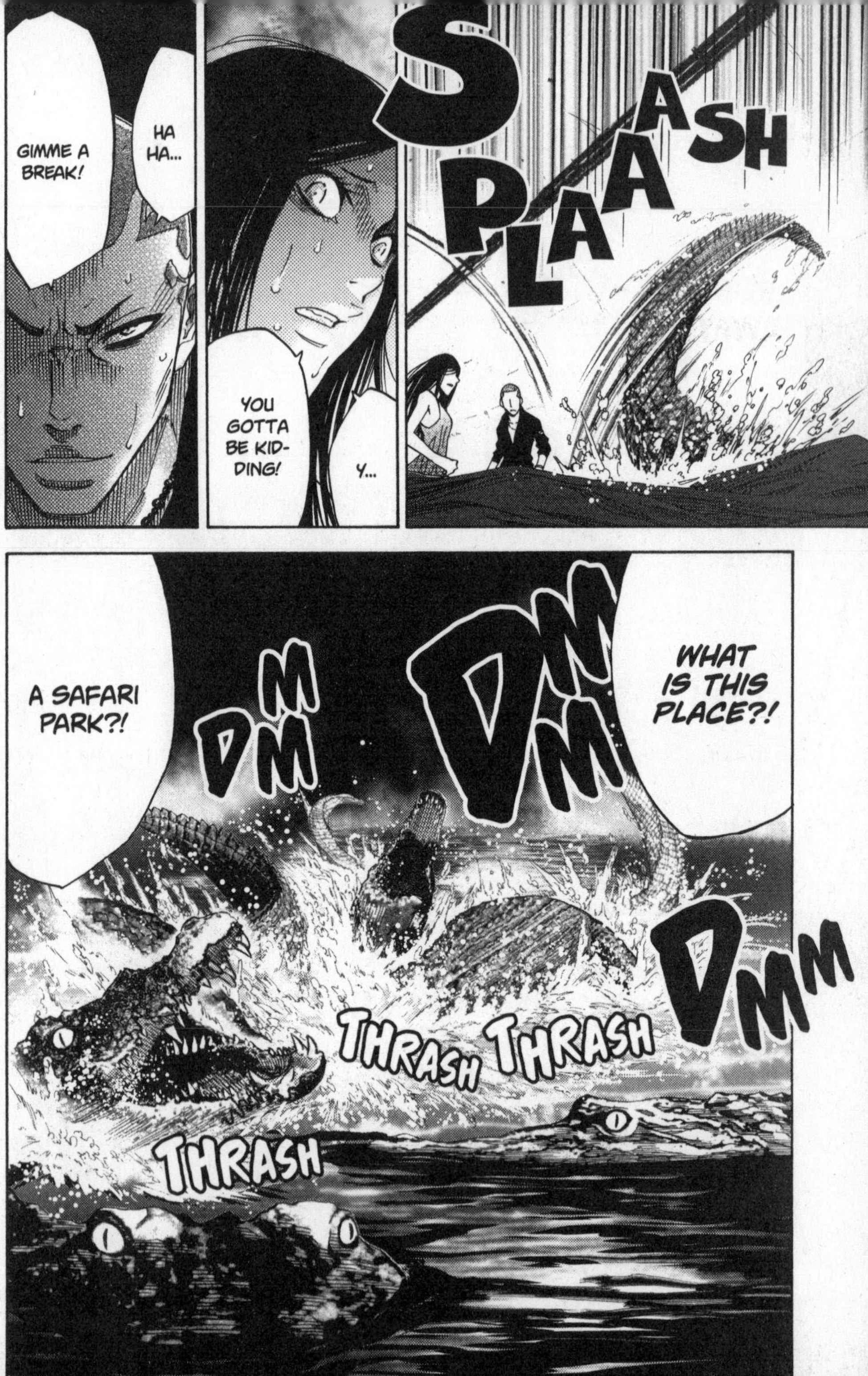
SPLAAASH
Y...
YOU GOTTA BE KID-DING!
HA HA...
GIMME A BREAK!
WHAT IS THIS PLACE?!
DMM DMM
DMM
A SAFARI PARK?!
DMM
THRASH THRASH
THRASH

SIDE STORY 2: Four of Clubs, Part 2

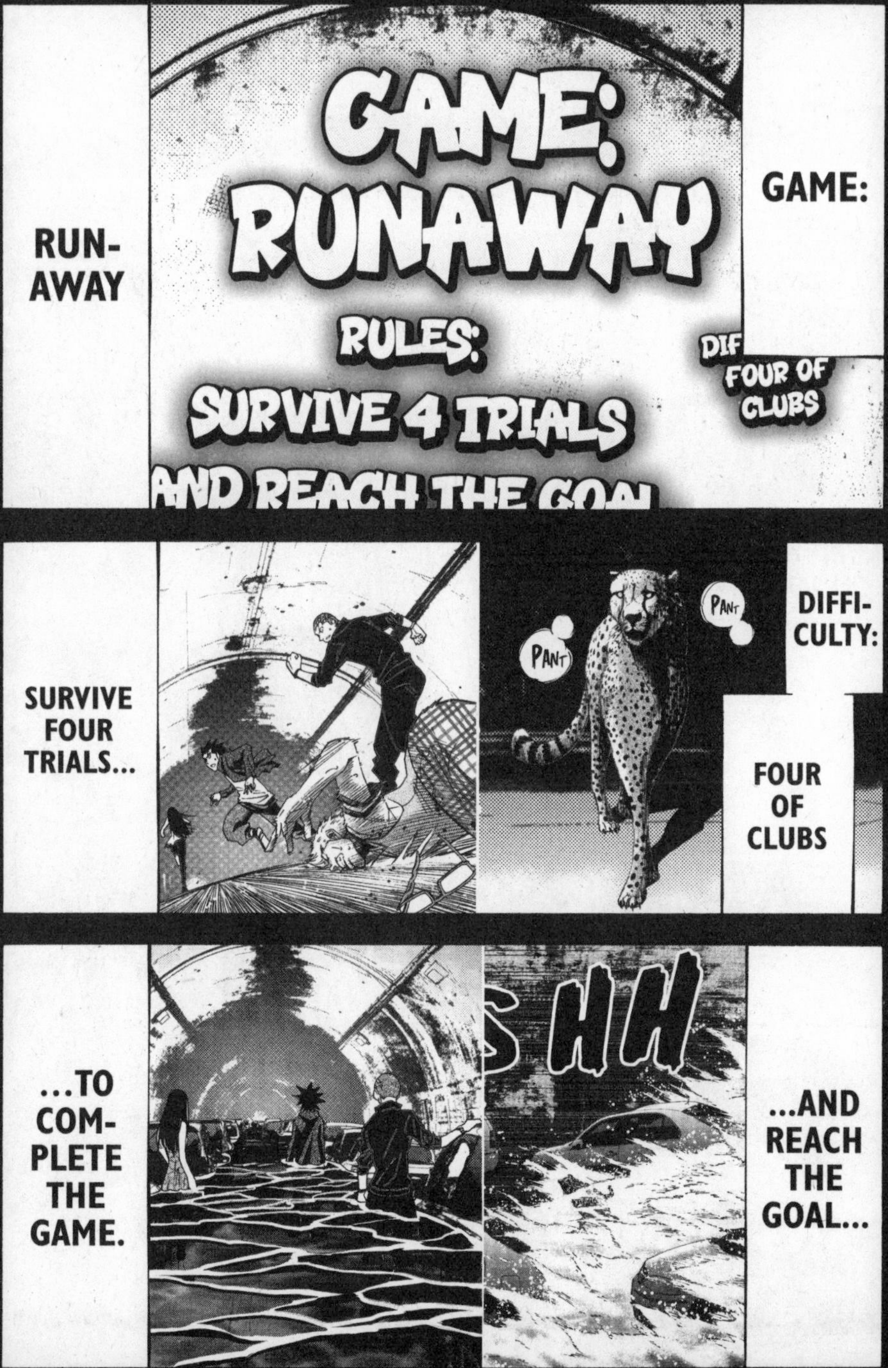
GAME:
GAME: RUNAWAY
RULES: SURVIVE 4 TRIALS AND REACH THE GOAL
DIF
FOUR OF CLUBS
RUN-AWAY
DIFFI-CULTY:
FOUR OF CLUBS
PANT
PANT
SURVIVE FOUR TRIALS...
...AND REACH THE GOAL...
SHH
...TO COM-PLETE THE GAME.

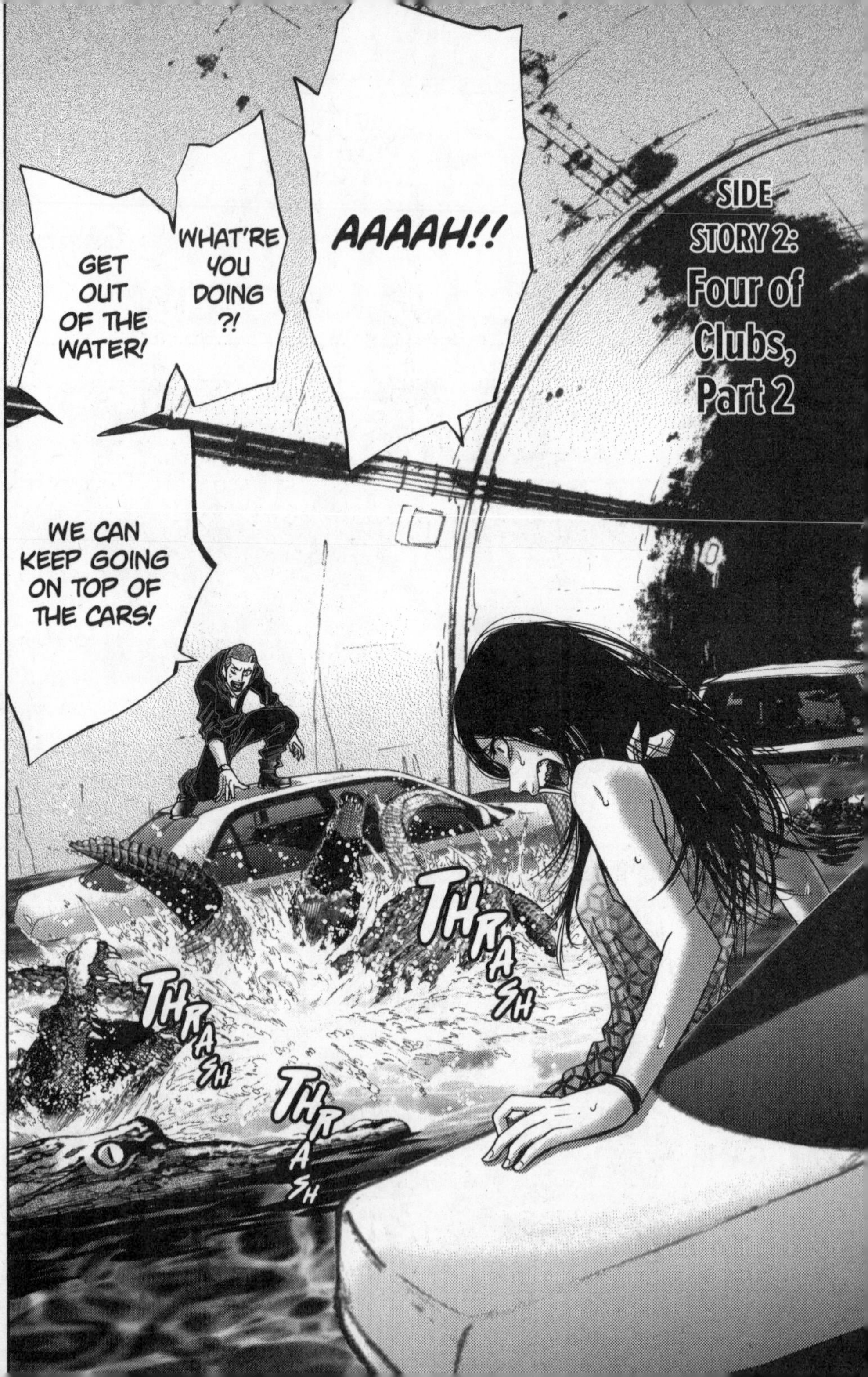
SIDE STORY 2: Four of Clubs, Part 2
AAAAH!!
WHAT'RE YOU DOING ?!
GET OUT OF THE WATER!
WE CAN KEEP GOING ON TOP OF THE CARS!
THRASH
THRASH
THRASH

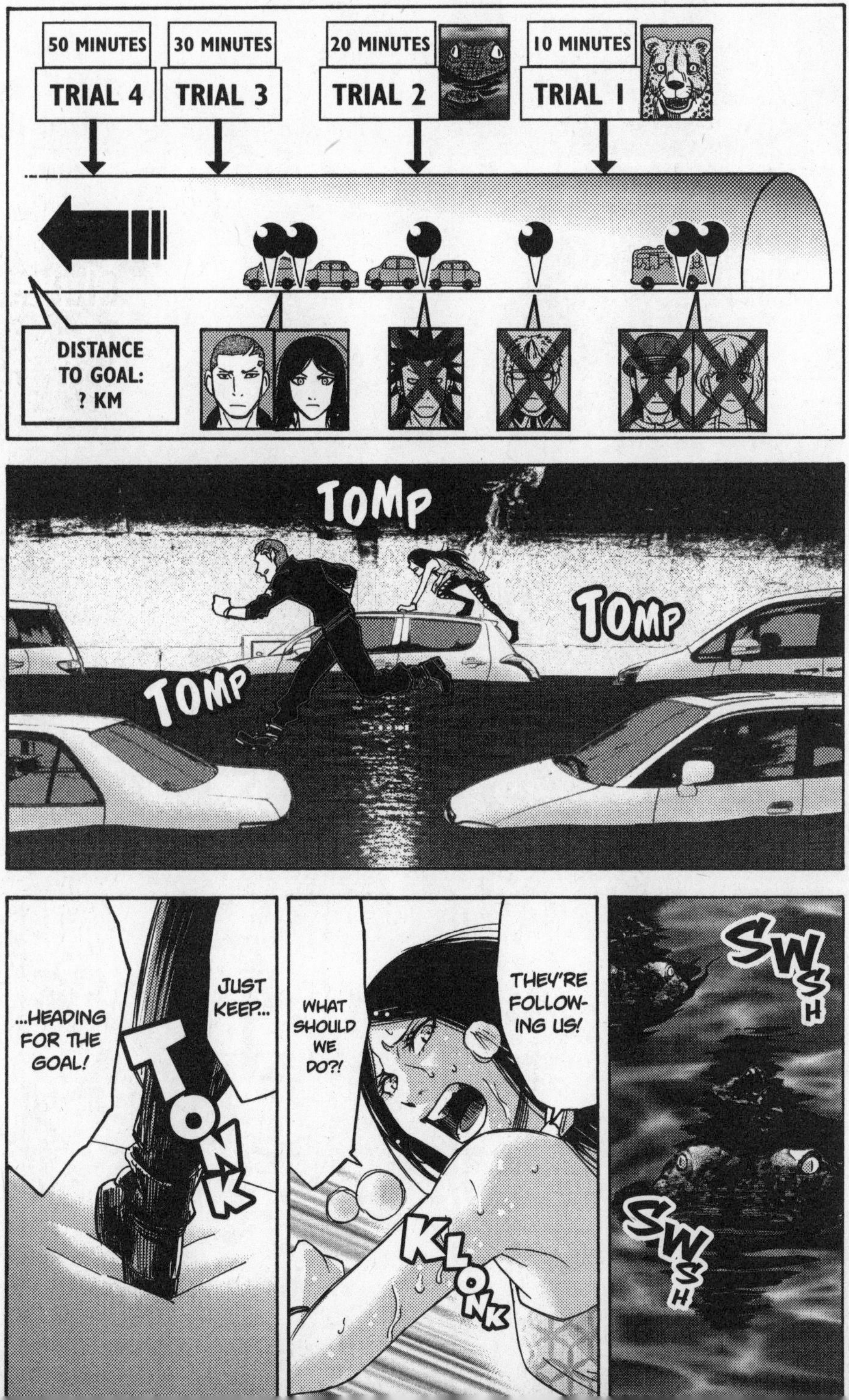
10 MINUTES
TRIAL 1
20 MINUTES
TRIAL 2
30 MINUTES
TRIAL 3
50 MINUTES
TRIAL 4
DISTANCE TO GOAL: ? KM
TOMP
TOMP
TOMP
SWSH
SWSH
THEY'RE FOLLOWING US!
WHAT SHOULD WE DO?!
KLONK
JUST KEEP...
...HEADING FOR THE GOAL!
TONK

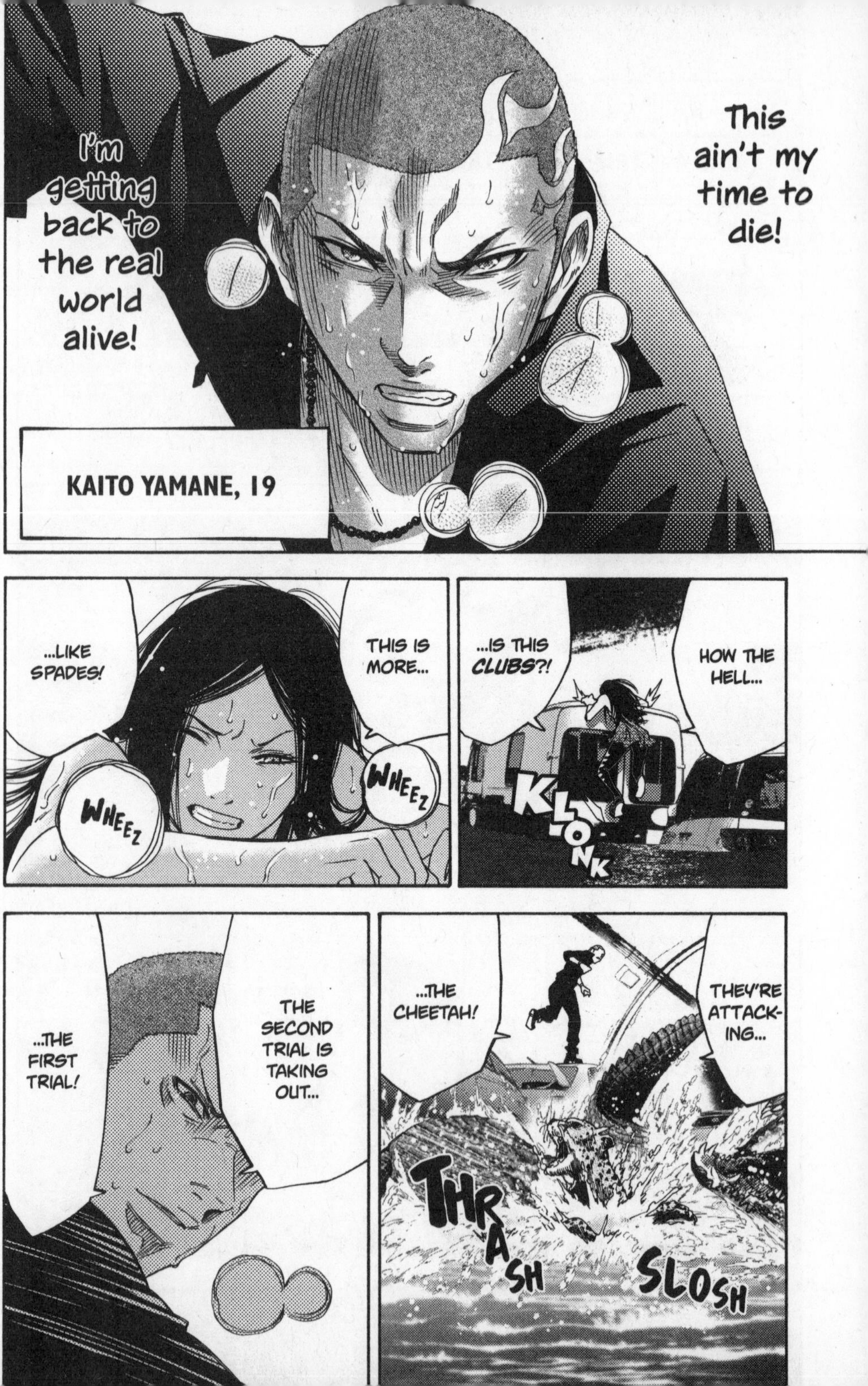
This ain't my time to die!
I'm getting back to the real world alive!
KAITO YAMANE, 19
HOW THE HELL...
...IS THIS CLUBS?!
KLONK
THIS IS MORE...
...LIKE SPADES!
WHEEZ
WHEEZ
THEY'RE ATTACKING...
...THE CHEETAH!
THRASH
SLOSH
THE SECOND TRIAL IS TAKING OUT...
...THE FIRST TRIAL!

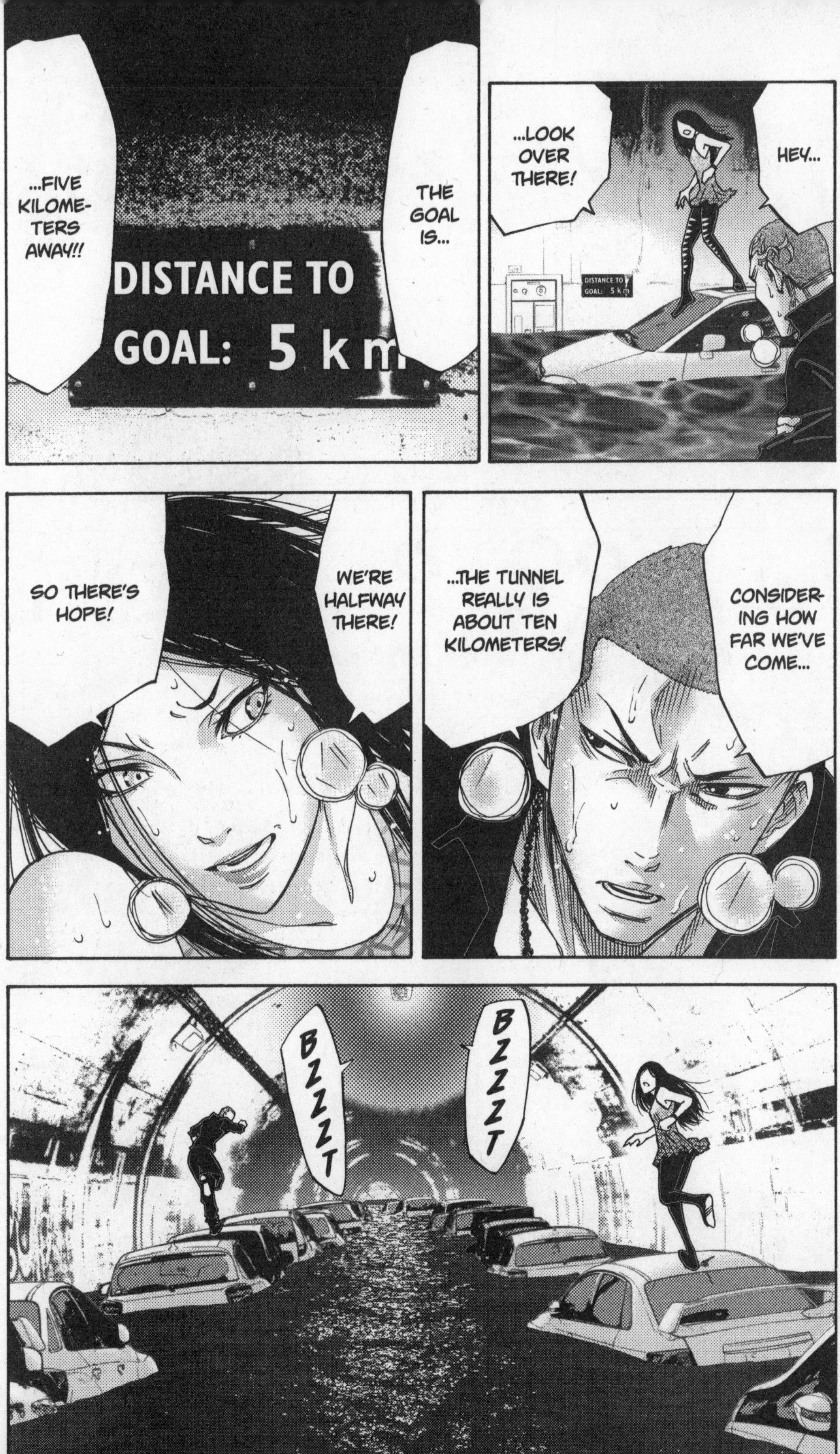
HEY...
...LOOK OVER THERE!
DISTANCE TO GOAL: 5 km
THE GOAL IS...
...FIVE KILOMETERS AWAY!!
DISTANCE TO GOAL: 5 km
CONSIDERING HOW FAR WE'VE COME...
...THE TUNNEL REALLY IS ABOUT TEN KILOMETERS!
WE'RE HALFWAY THERE!
SO THERE'S HOPE!
BZZZT
BZZZT

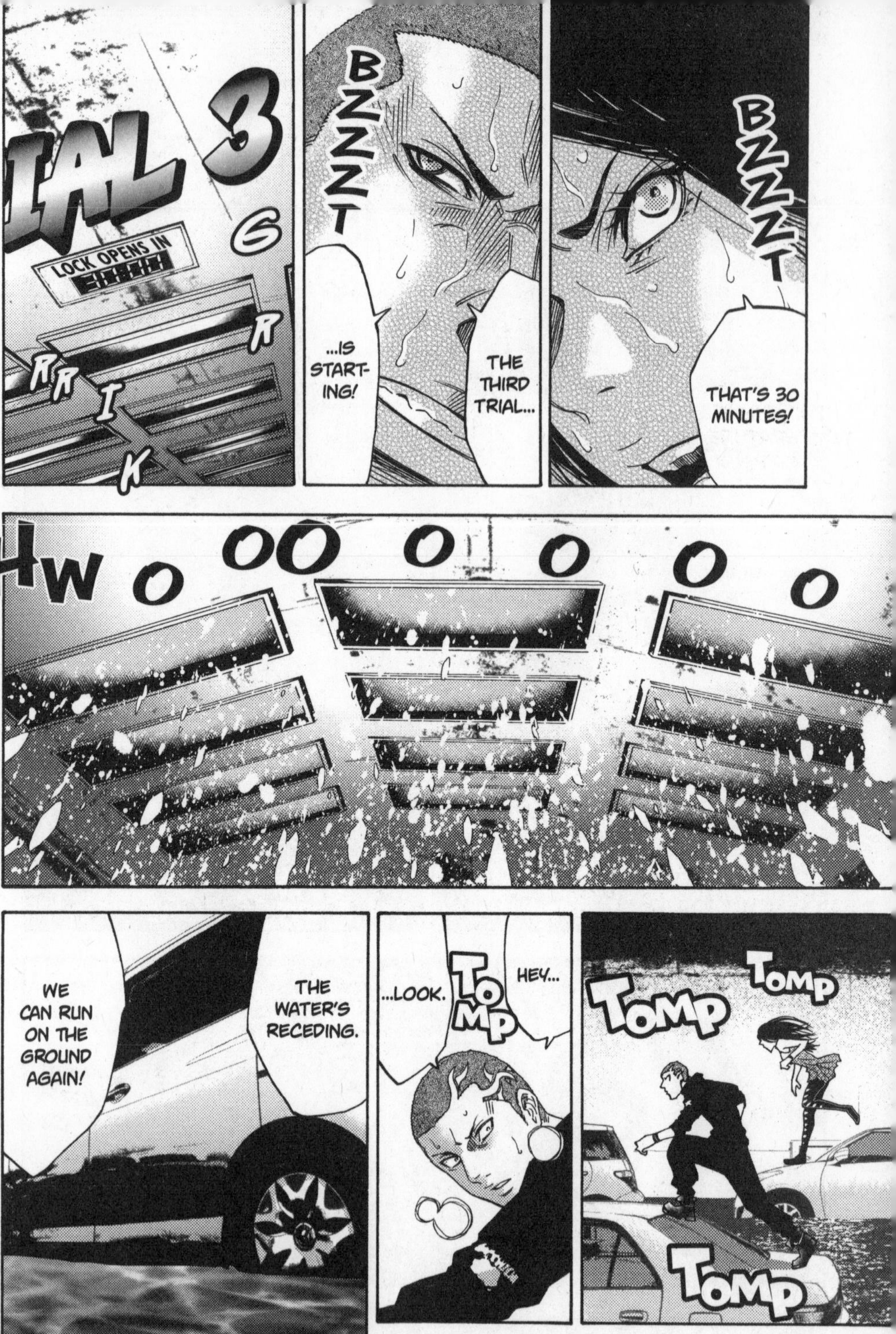
BZZZT
THAT'S 30 MINUTES!
BZZZT
THE THIRD TRIAL...
...IS STARTING!
IAL 3
G
LOCK OPENS IN
RRRIK
HWOOOOOOOOO
TOMP
TOMP
TOMP
HEY...
TOMP
...LOOK.
THE WATER'S RECEDING.
WE CAN RUN ON THE GROUND AGAIN!

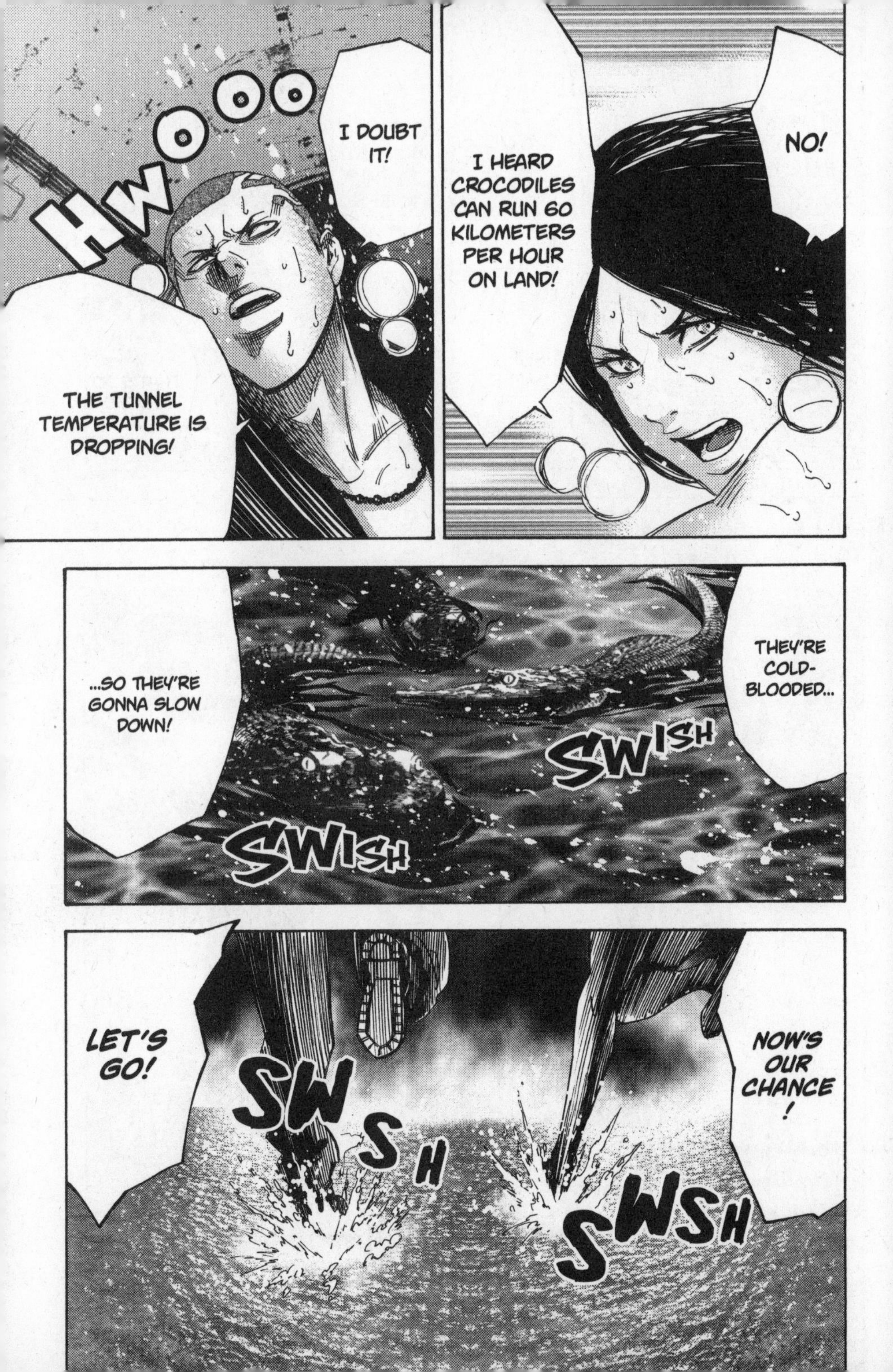
NO!
I HEARD CROCODILES CAN RUN 60 KILOMETERS PER HOUR ON LAND!
HWOOO
I DOUBT IT!
THE TUNNEL TEMPERATURE IS DROPPING!
THEY'RE COLD-BLOODED...
SWISH
...SO THEY'RE GONNA SLOW DOWN!
SWISH
NOW'S OUR CHANCE!
SWSH
LET'S GO!
SWSH

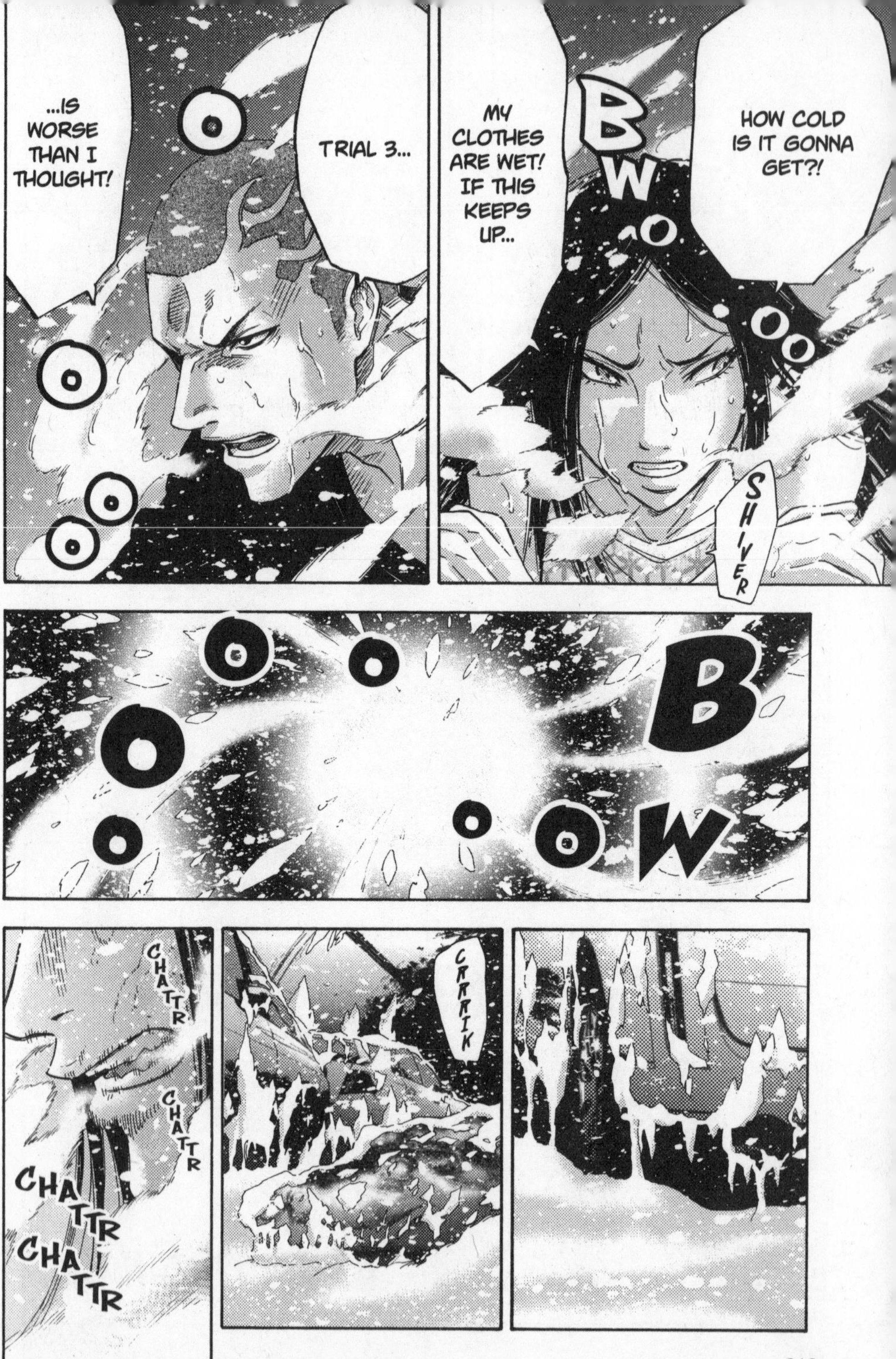
HOW COLD IS IT GONNA GET?!
BWOOO
MY CLOTHES ARE WET! IF THIS KEEPS UP...
SHIVER
TRIAL 3...
...IS WORSE THAN I THOUGHT!
OOOO
BOOOOOOW
CRRRIK
CHATTR
CHATTR
CHATTR
CHATTR

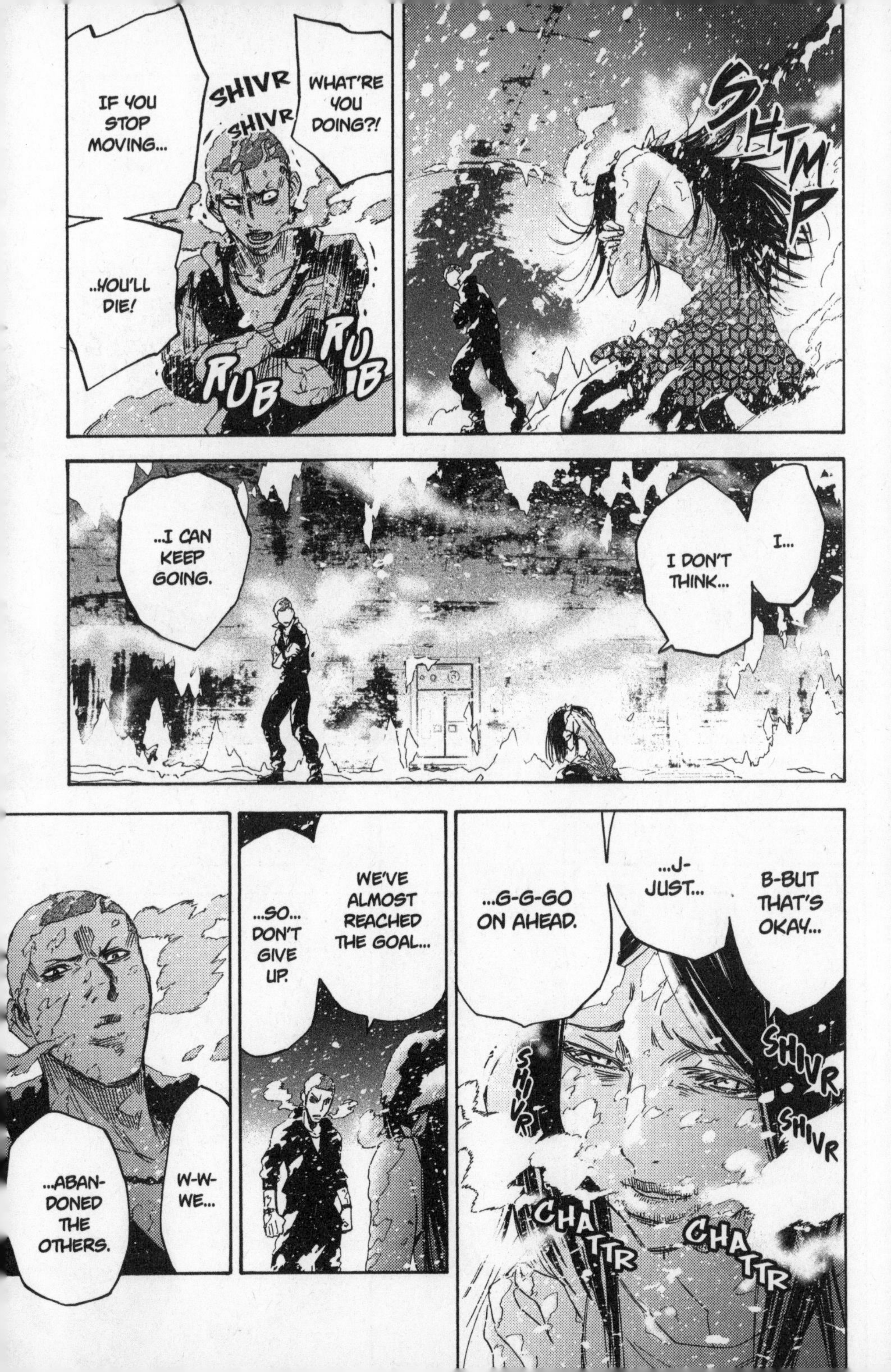
SHTMP
WHAT'RE YOU DOING?!
SHIVR SHIVR
IF YOU STOP MOVING...
...YOU'LL DIE!
RUB RUB
I... I DON'T THINK...
...I CAN KEEP GOING.
B-BUT THAT'S OKAY...
...J- JUST...
...G-G-GO ON AHEAD.
SHIVR SHIVR
SHIVR
CHATTR CHATTR
WE'VE ALMOST REACHED THE GOAL...
...SO... DON'T GIVE UP.
W-W-WE...
...ABAN-DONED THE OTHERS.

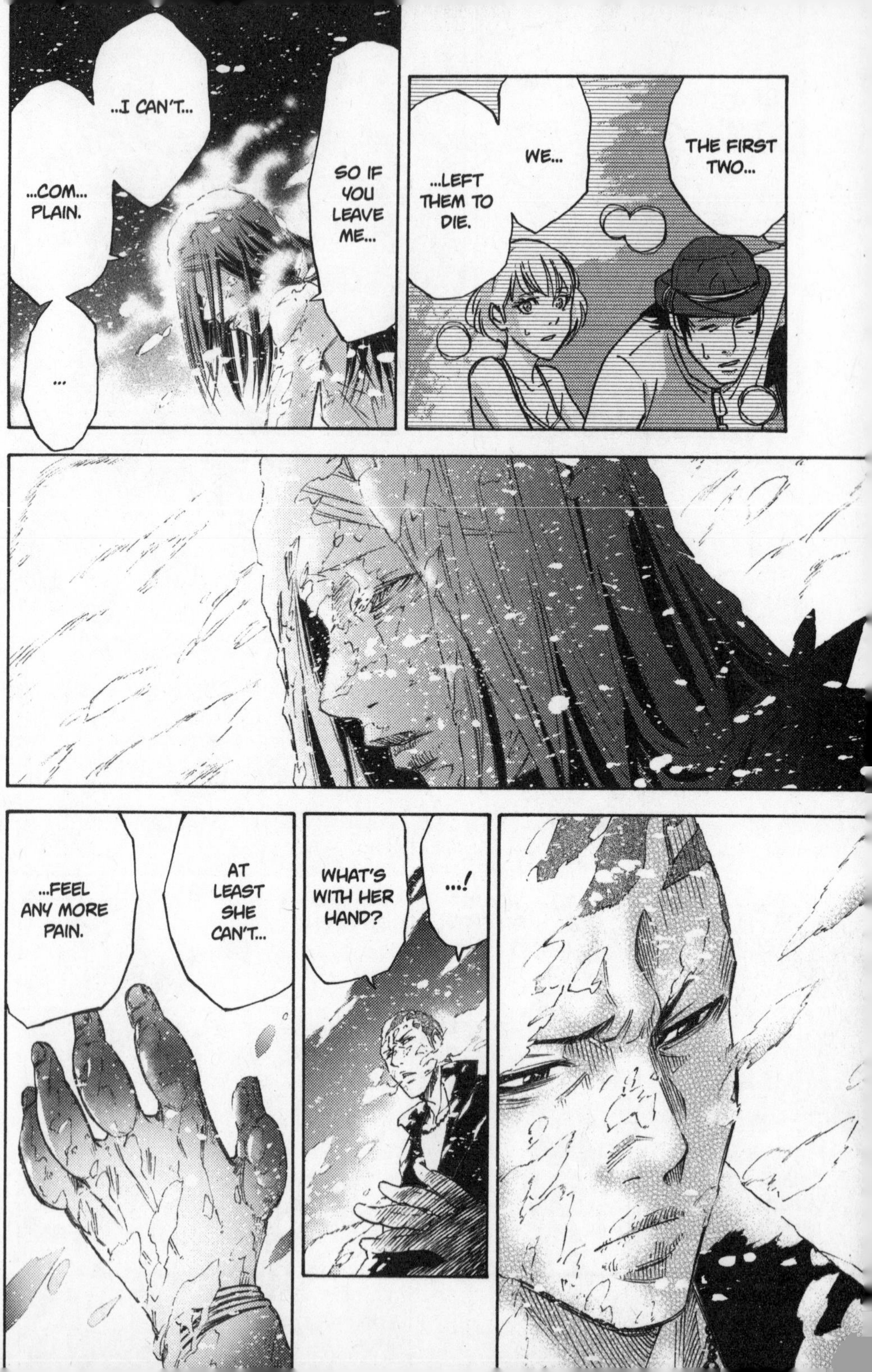
THE FIRST TWO...
WE...
...LEFT THEM TO DIE.
SO IF YOU LEAVE ME...
...I CAN'T...
...COM... PLAIN.
...
...!
WHAT'S WITH HER HAND?
AT LEAST SHE CAN'T...
...FEEL ANY MORE PAIN.

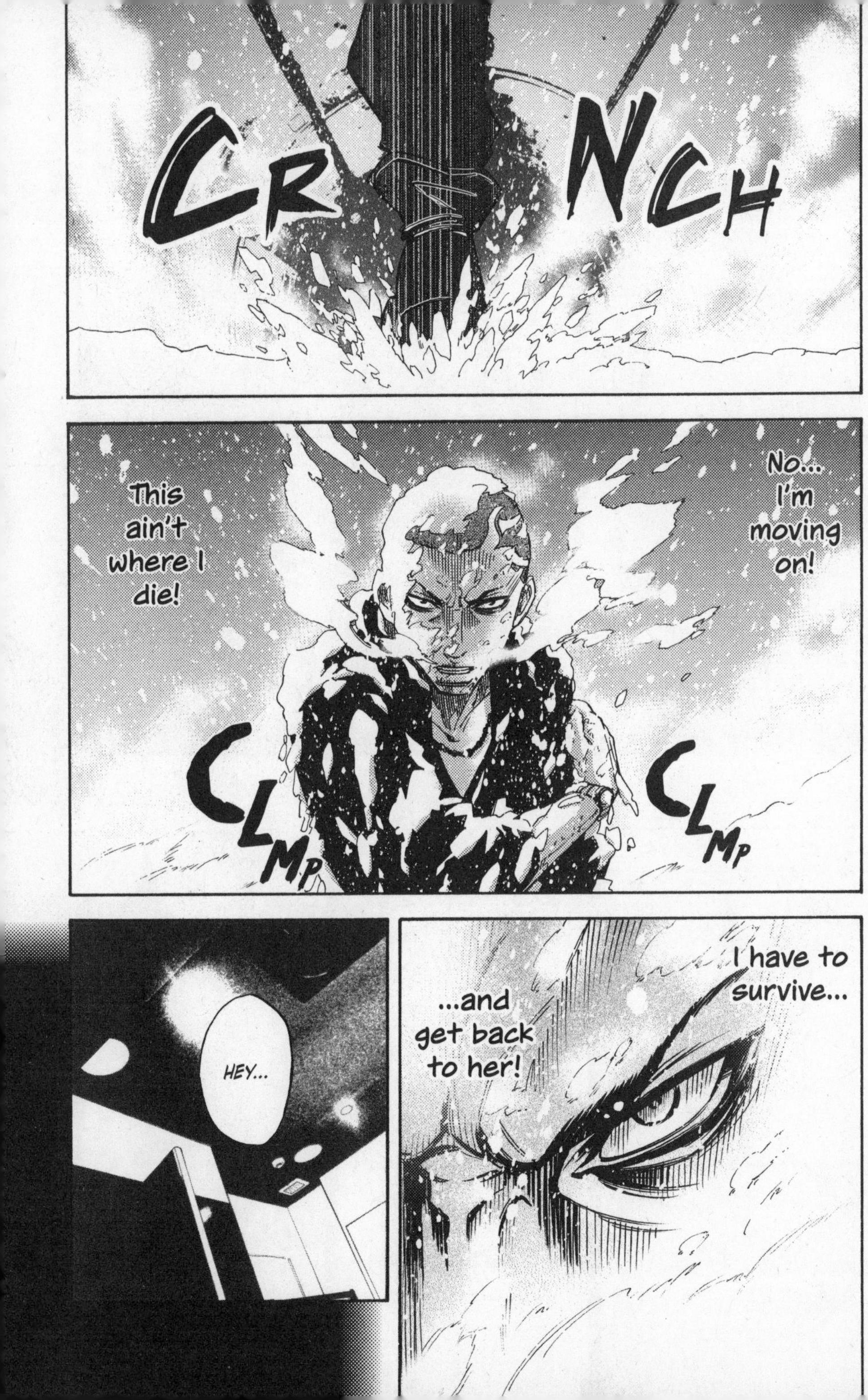
CRUNCH
No... I'm moving on!
This ain't where I die!
CLMP
CLMP
I have to survive...
...and get back to her!
HEY...

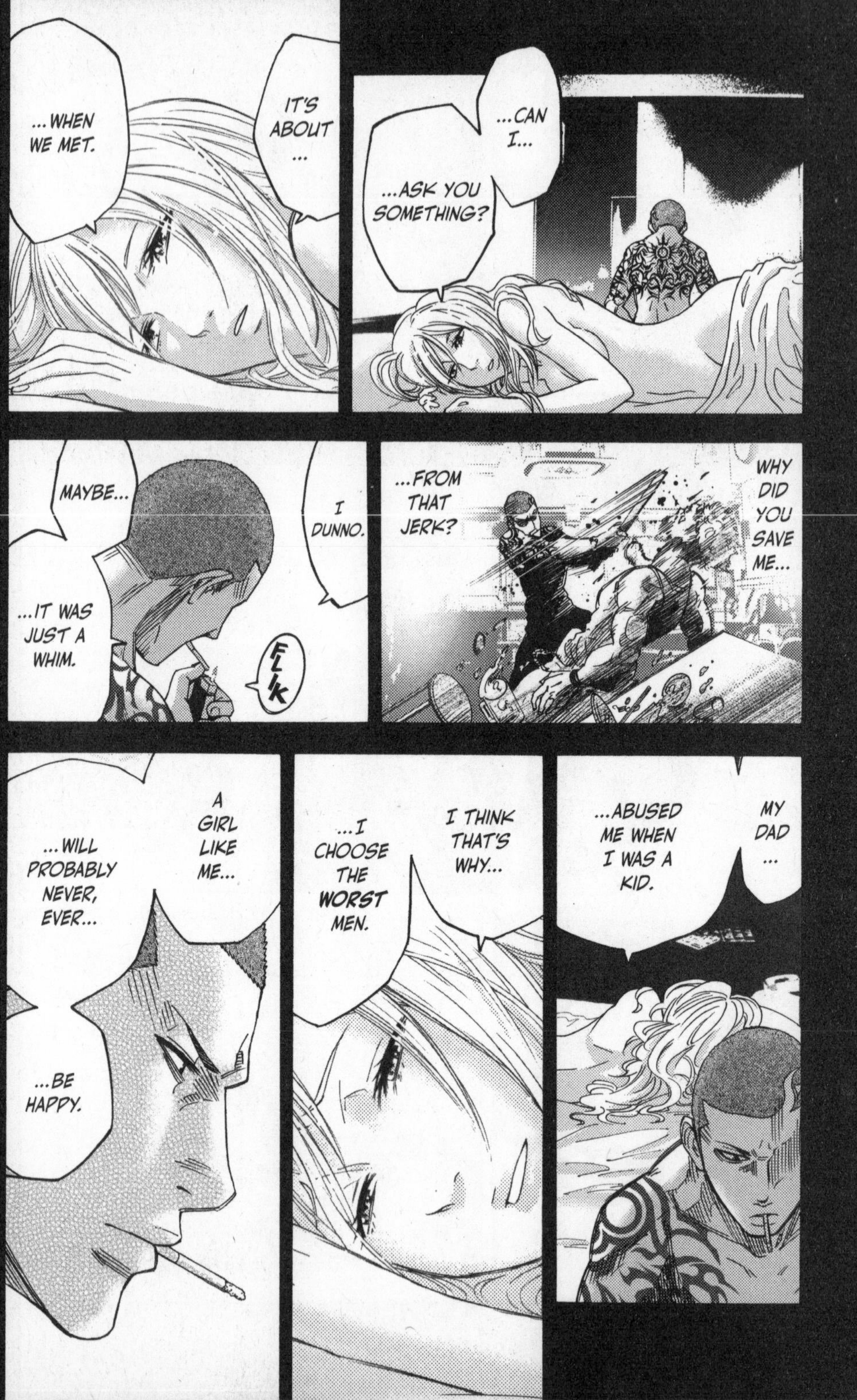
...CAN I...
...ASK YOU SOMETHING?
IT'S ABOUT ...
...WHEN WE MET.
WHY DID YOU SAVE ME...
...FROM THAT JERK?
I DUNNO.
MAYBE...
...IT WAS JUST A WHIM.
FLIK
MY DAD ...
...ABUSED ME WHEN I WAS A KID.
I THINK THAT'S WHY...
...I CHOOSE THE WORST MEN.
A GIRL LIKE ME...
...WILL PROBABLY NEVER, EVER...
...BE HAPPY.

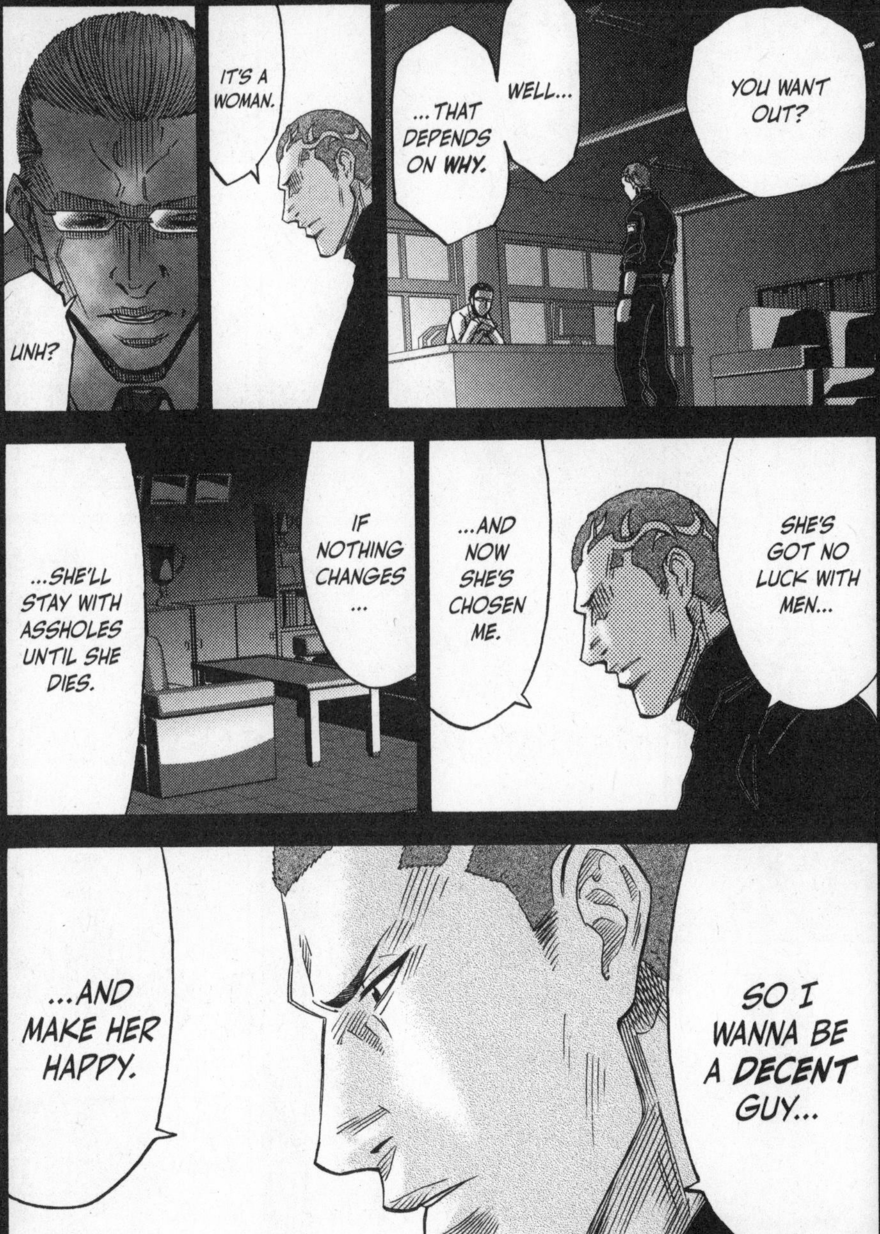
YOU WANT OUT?
WELL...
...THAT DEPENDS ON WHY.
IT'S A WOMAN.
UNH?
SHE'S GOT NO LUCK WITH MEN...
...AND NOW SHE'S CHOSEN ME.
IF NOTHING CHANGES ...
...SHE'LL STAY WITH ASSHOLES UNTIL SHE DIES.
SO I WANNA BE A DECENT GUY...
...AND MAKE HER HAPPY.

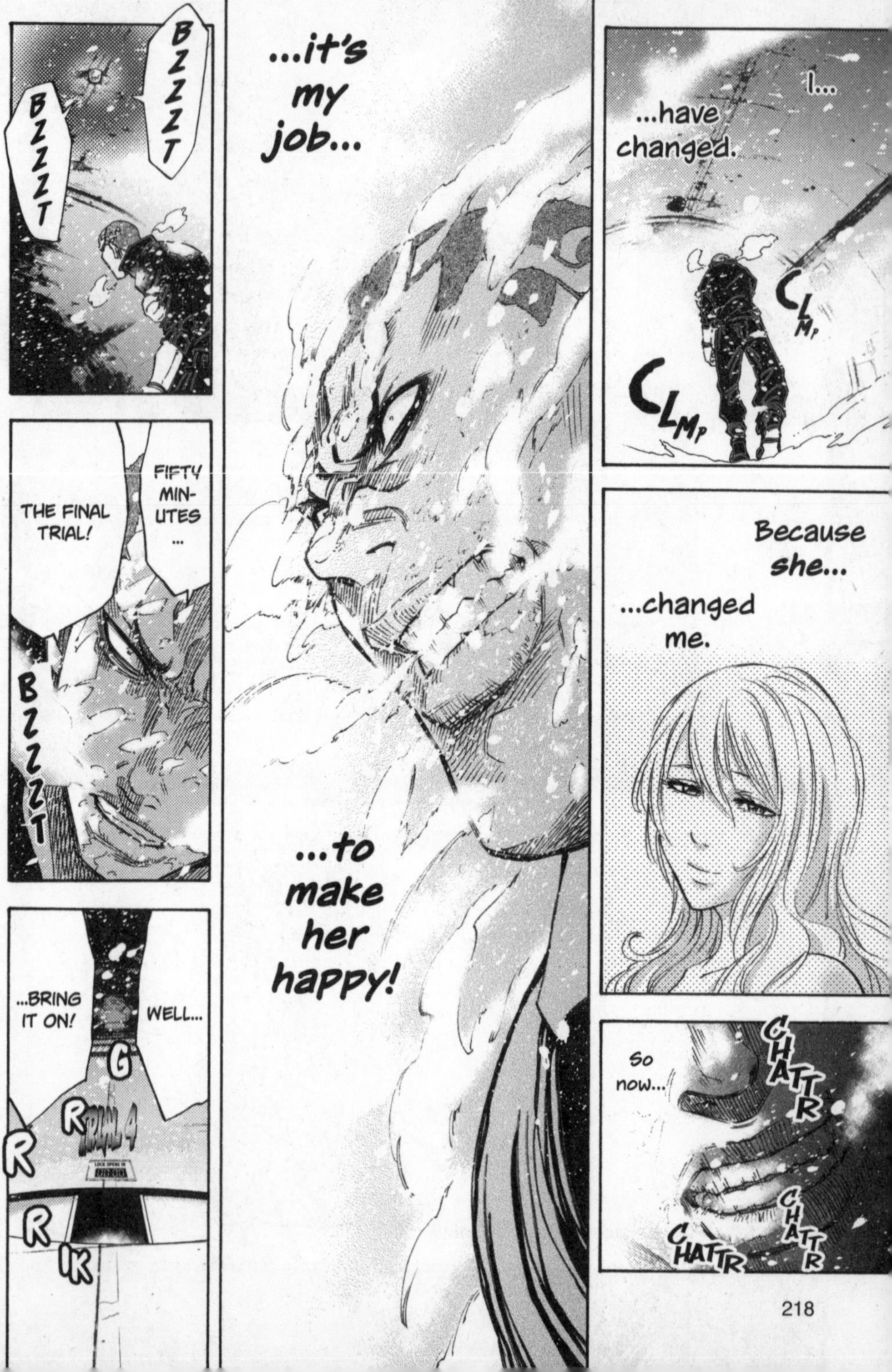

I...
...have changed.
CLMP
CLMP
Because she...
...changed me.
So now...
CHATTR
CHATTR
CHATTR
...it's my job...
...to make her happy!
BZZZT
BZZZZT
FIFTY MIN-UTES...
THE FINAL TRIAL!
BZZZZT
WELL...
...BRING IT ON!
GRRRRK
TRIAL 4
LOCK OPENS IN

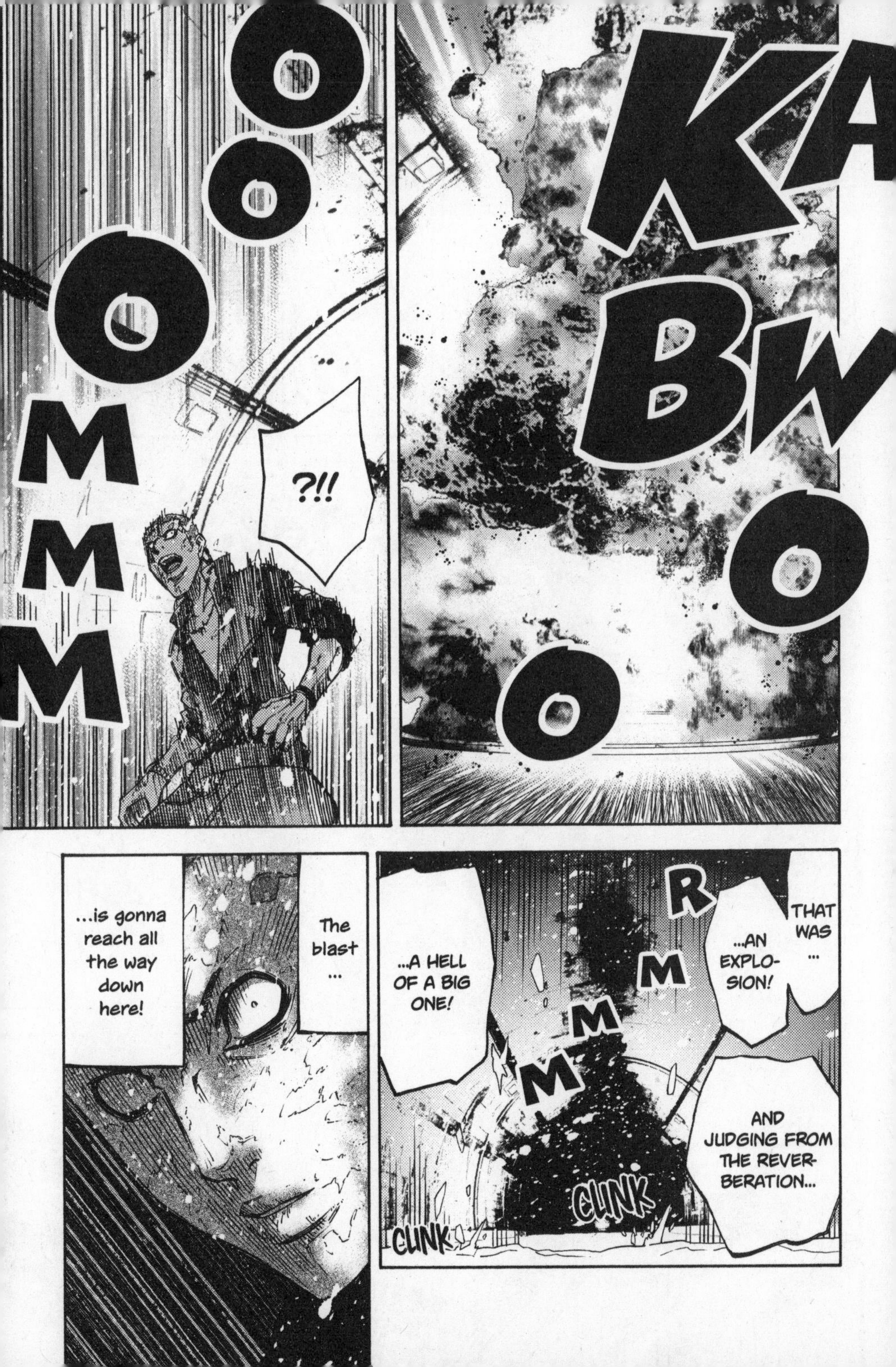
KABWOOO
OOOMMMM
?!!
THAT WAS...
...AN EXPLOSION!
RMMMM
...A HELL OF A BIG ONE!
AND JUDGING FROM THE REVERBERATION...
CLINK
CLINK
The blast...
...is gonna reach all the way down here!

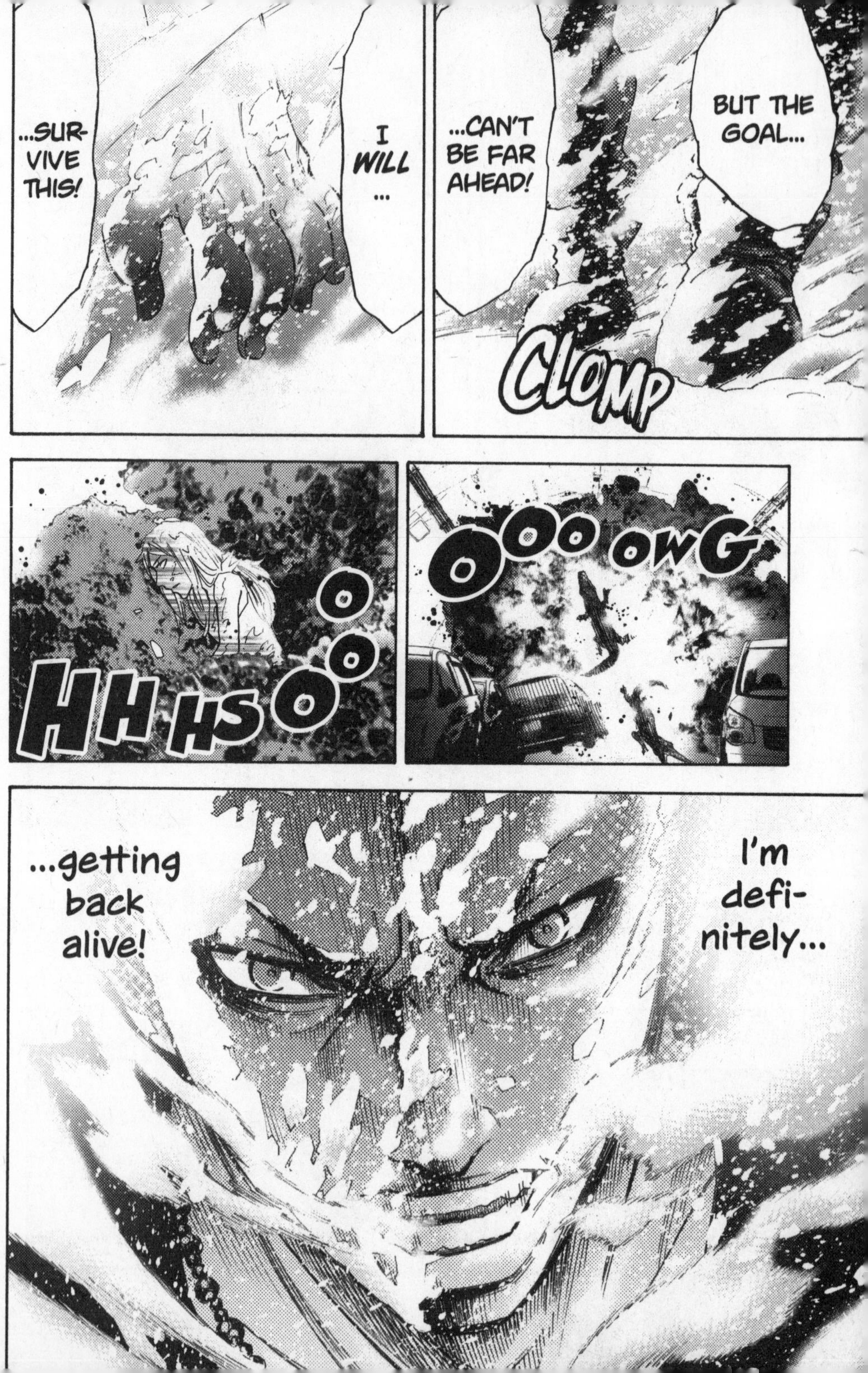
BUT THE GOAL...
...CAN'T BE FAR AHEAD!
CLOMP
I WILL...
...SURVIVE THIS!
OOOO OWG
HHHSOOOO
I'm definitely...
...getting back alive!

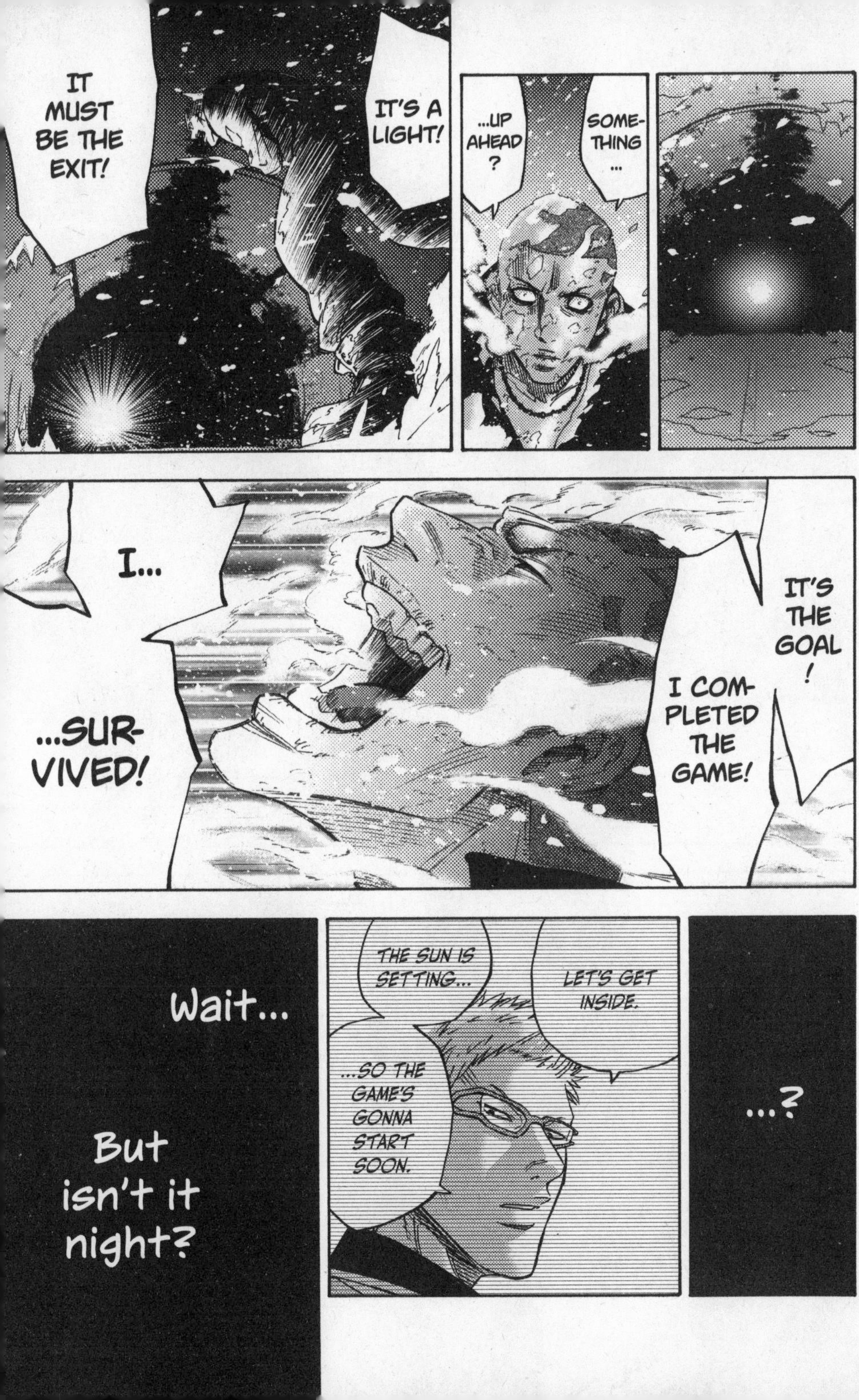
SOMETHING...
...UP AHEAD?
IT'S A LIGHT!
IT MUST BE THE EXIT!
IT'S THE GOAL!
I COMPLETED THE GAME!
I...
...SURVIVED!
...?
LET'S GET INSIDE.
THE SUN IS SETTING...
...SO THE GAME'S GONNA START SOON.
Wait...
But isn't it night?

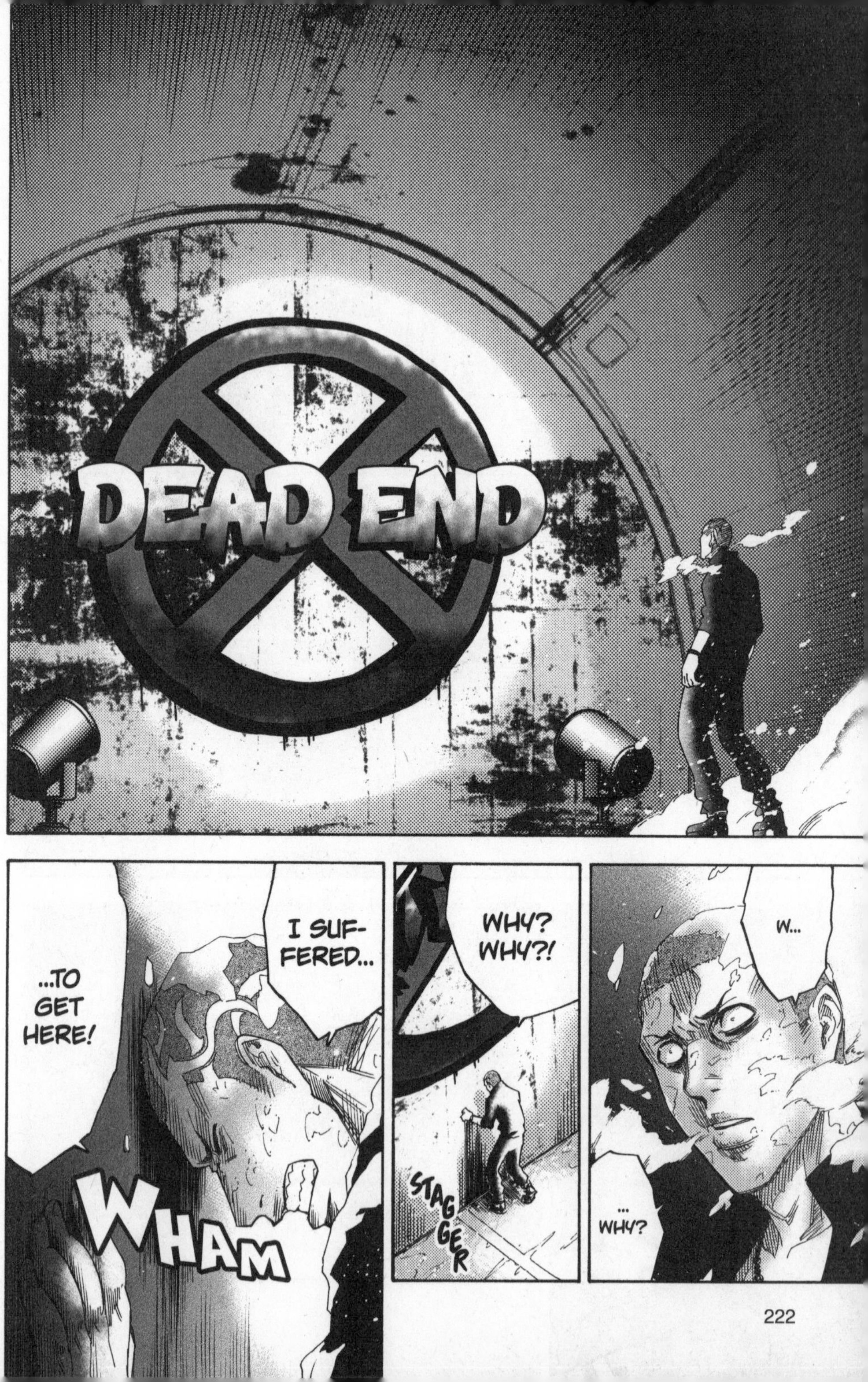
DEAD END
W...
...WHY?
WHY? WHY?!
STAGGER
I SUFFERED...
...TO GET HERE!
WHAM

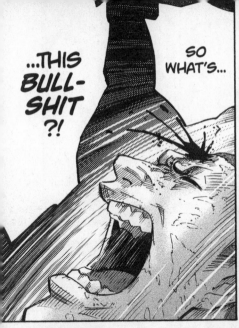

I SURVIVED...
...THE TRIALS!
I MADE IT THROUGH!
BAM
BAM
BAM
SO WHAT'S...
...THIS BULLSHIT?!
RULES:
SURVIVE 4 TRI
ND REACH THE
GWOOOOSH
No, wait...
Did I mess up somehow?!
RULES
RVIVE 4 T
EACH

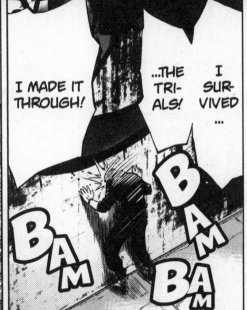

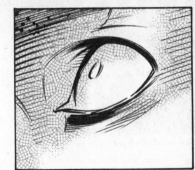

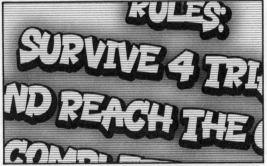

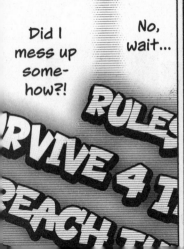

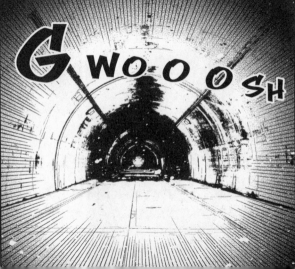

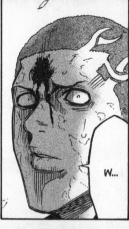

DMM
...!
DISTA
GOAL:
W...
VMMM
STANCE TO
AL: 10
WHAT DOES THAT MEAN?!
DMM
DMM
DMM
DMM
DISTANCE TO
GOAL: 10 km
Does that mean...
...that the first sign...
DISTANCE TO
GOAL km
THE DISTANCE IS RUBBED OUT!
DISTANCE TO
GOAL K
So this whole time...
...we were running away from the goal?!
STANCE TO
AL 0 K

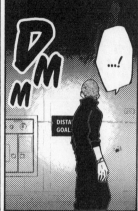

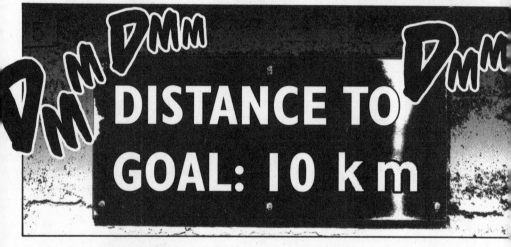

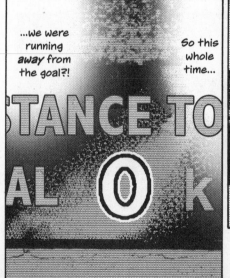

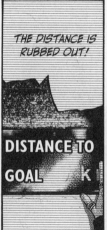

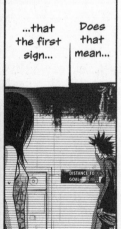

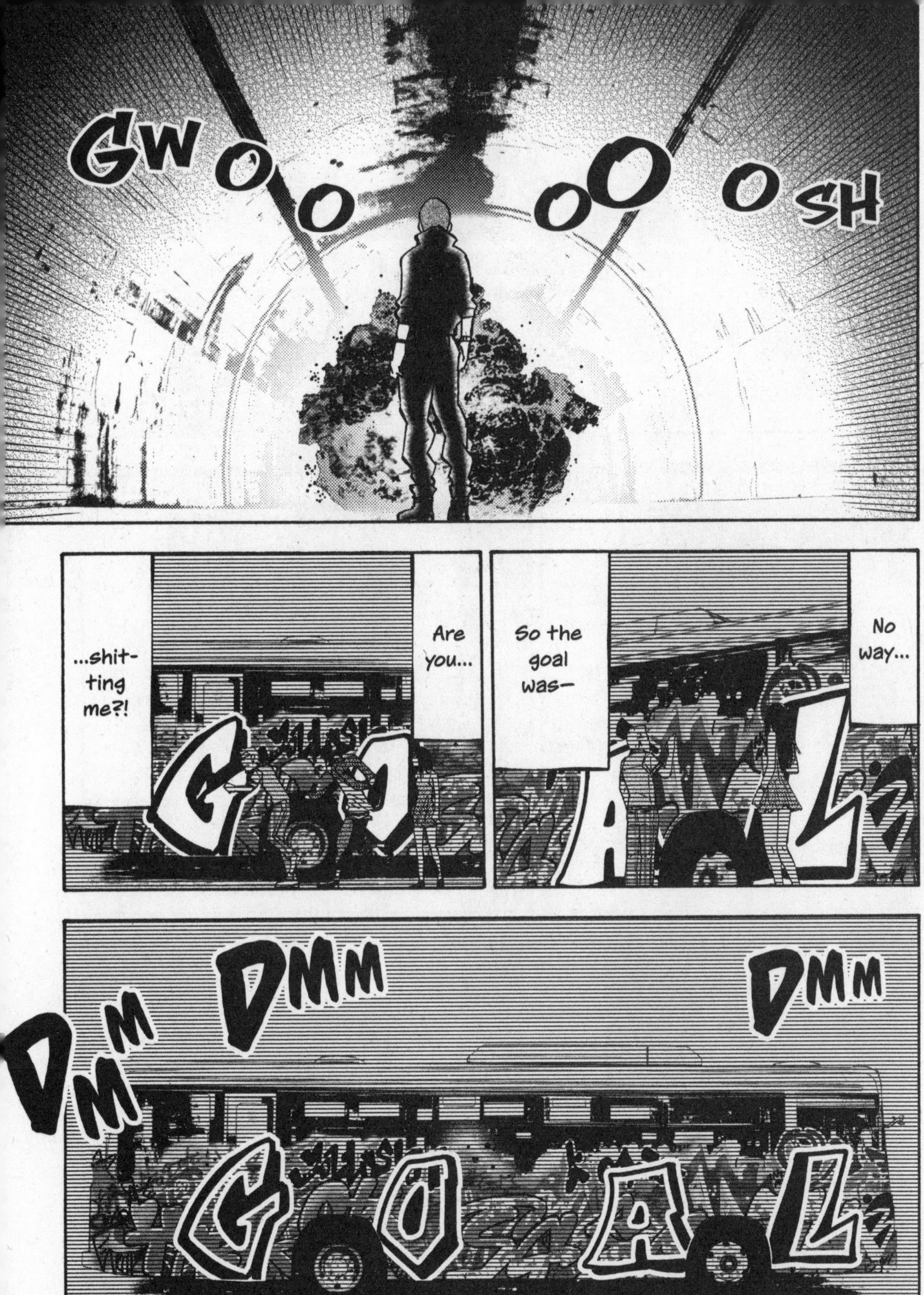
GWOOOOOSH
No way...
So the goal was—
Are you...
...shitting me?!
DMM
DMM
DMM
GOAL

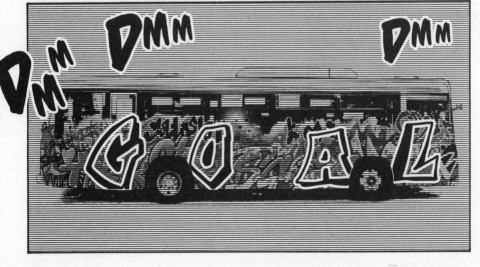

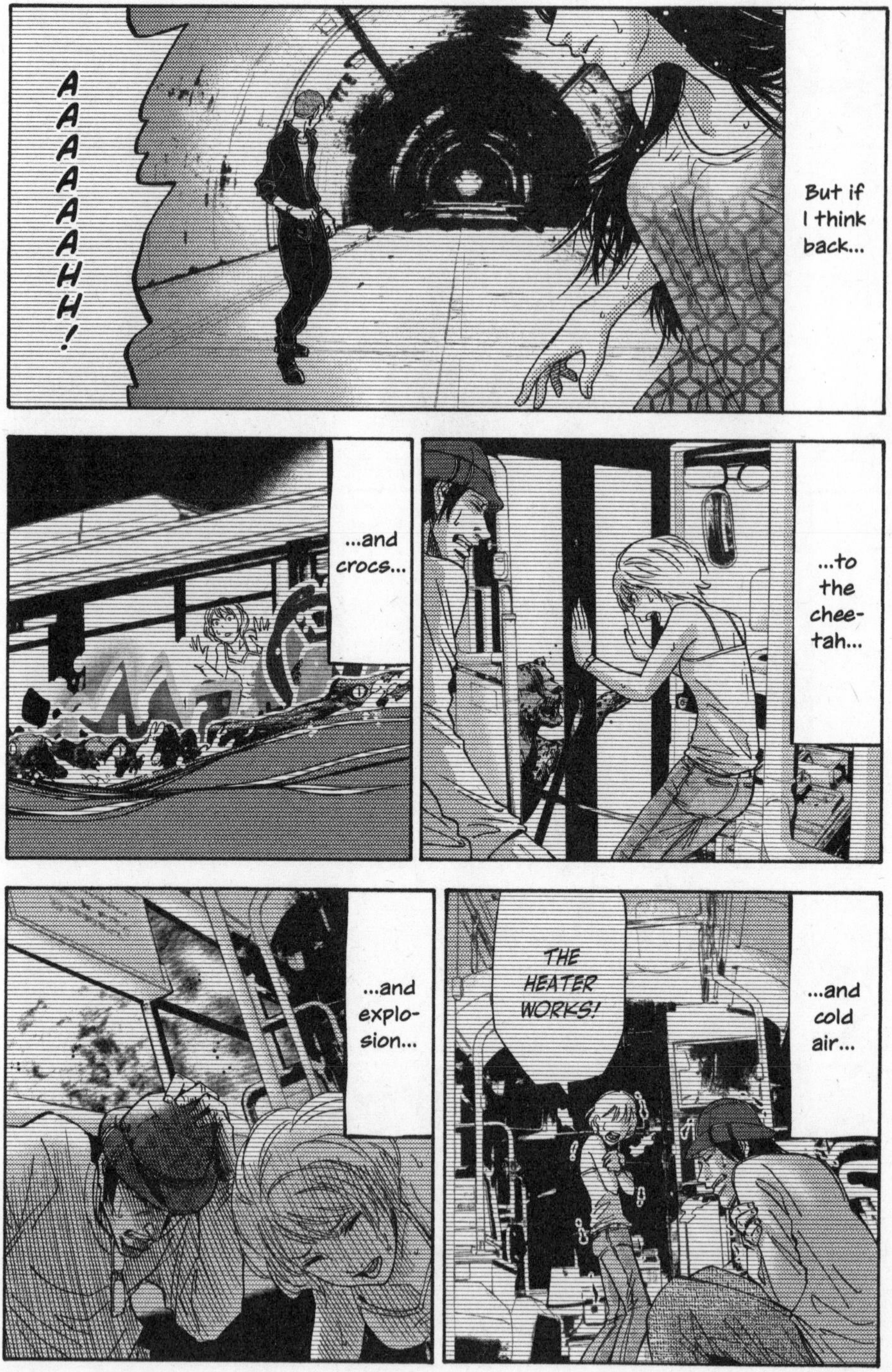
But if I think back...
AAAAAAAAHH!
...to the cheetah...
...and crocs...
...and cold air...
THE HEATER WORKS!
...and explosion...

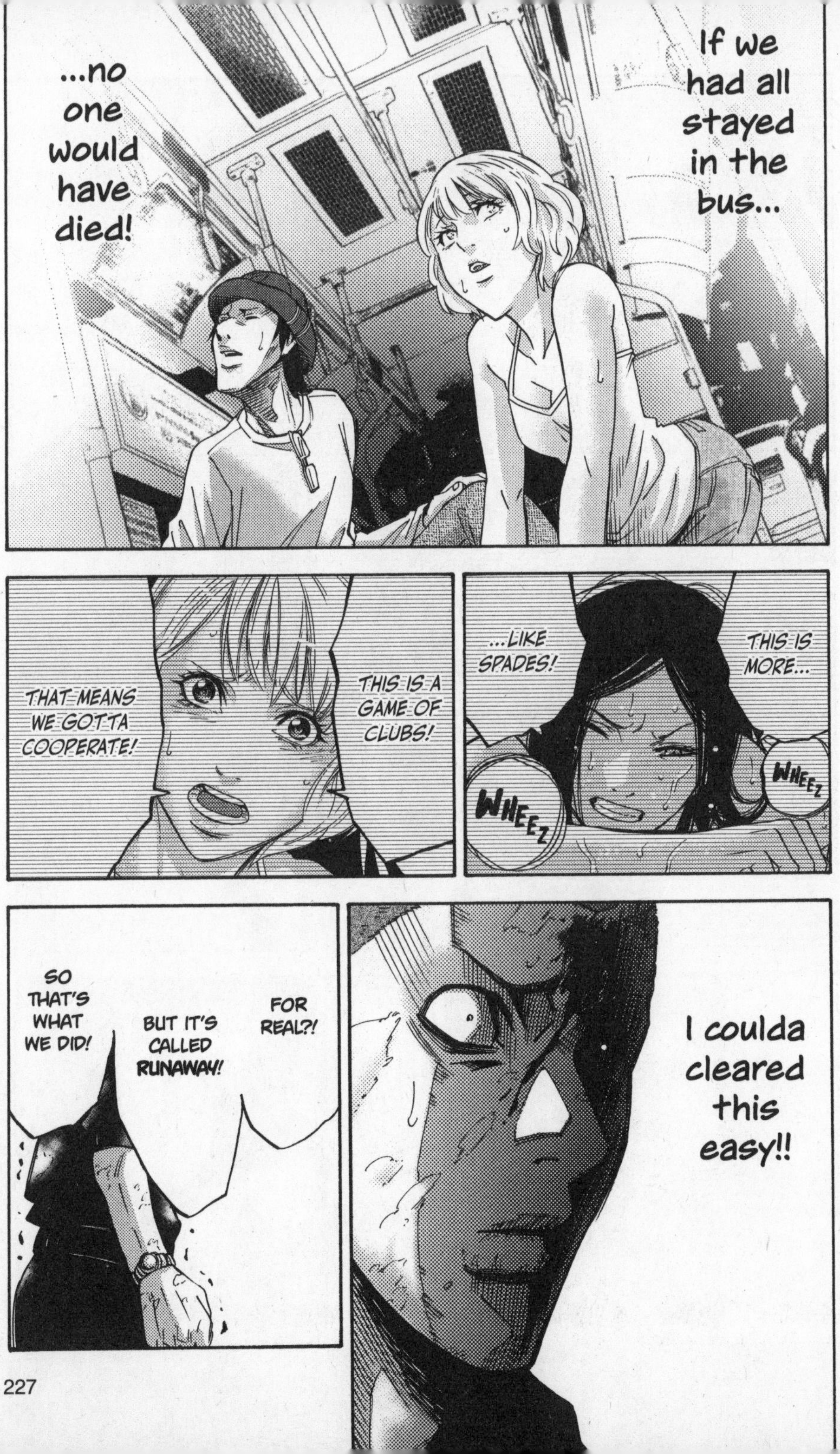
If we had all stayed in the bus...
...no one would have died!
THIS IS MORE...
...LIKE SPADES!
WHEEZ
WHEEZ
THIS IS A GAME OF CLUBS!
THAT MEANS WE GOTTA COOPERATE!
I coulda cleared this easy!!
FOR REAL?!
BUT IT'S CALLED RUNAWAY!
SO THAT'S WHAT WE DID!

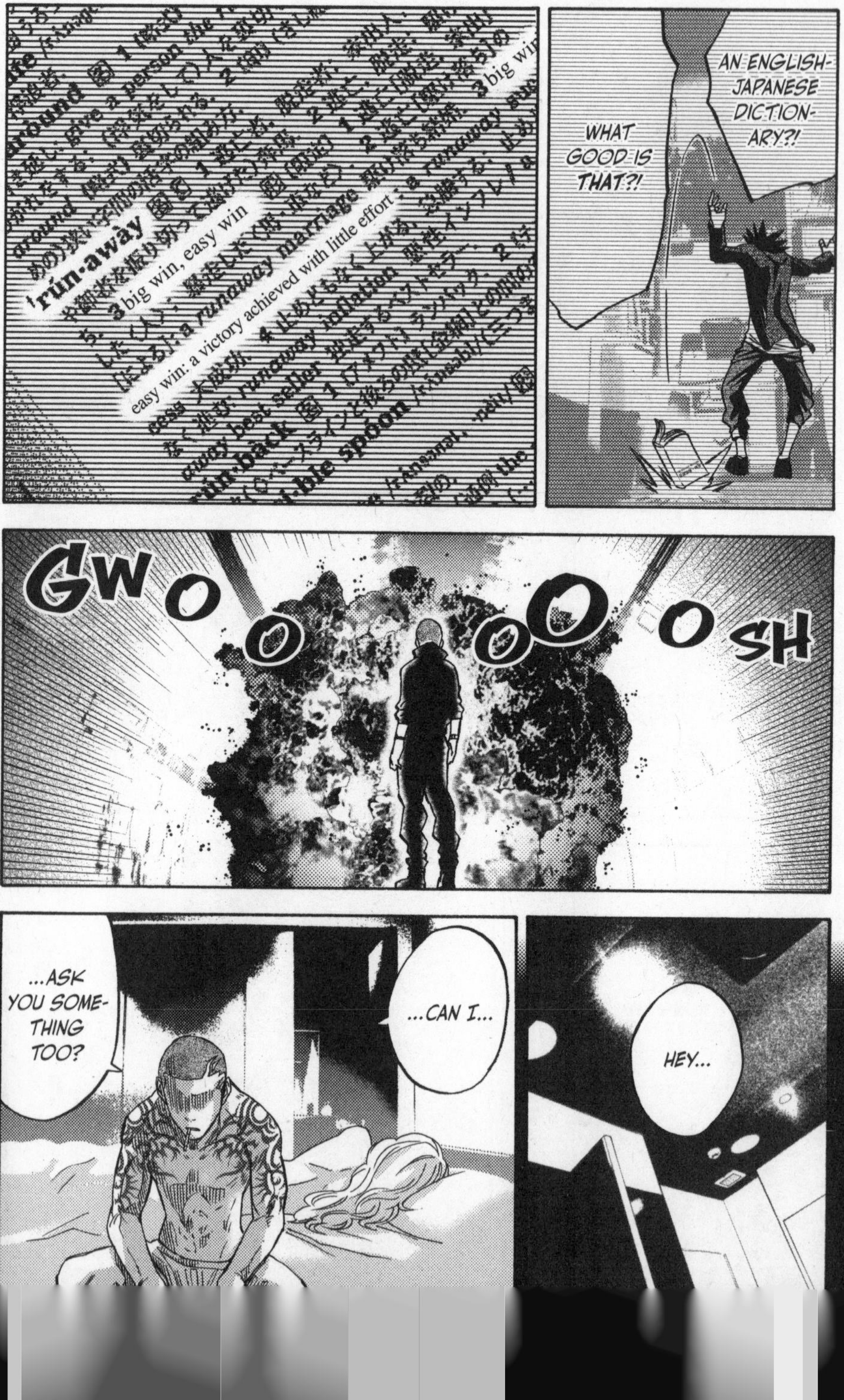
AN ENGLISH-JAPANESE DICTION-ARY?!
WHAT GOOD IS THAT?!
rún·away
3 big win, easy win
easy win: a victory achieved with little effort
GWOOOOOOOSH
HEY...
...CAN I...
...ASK YOU SOME-THING TOO?

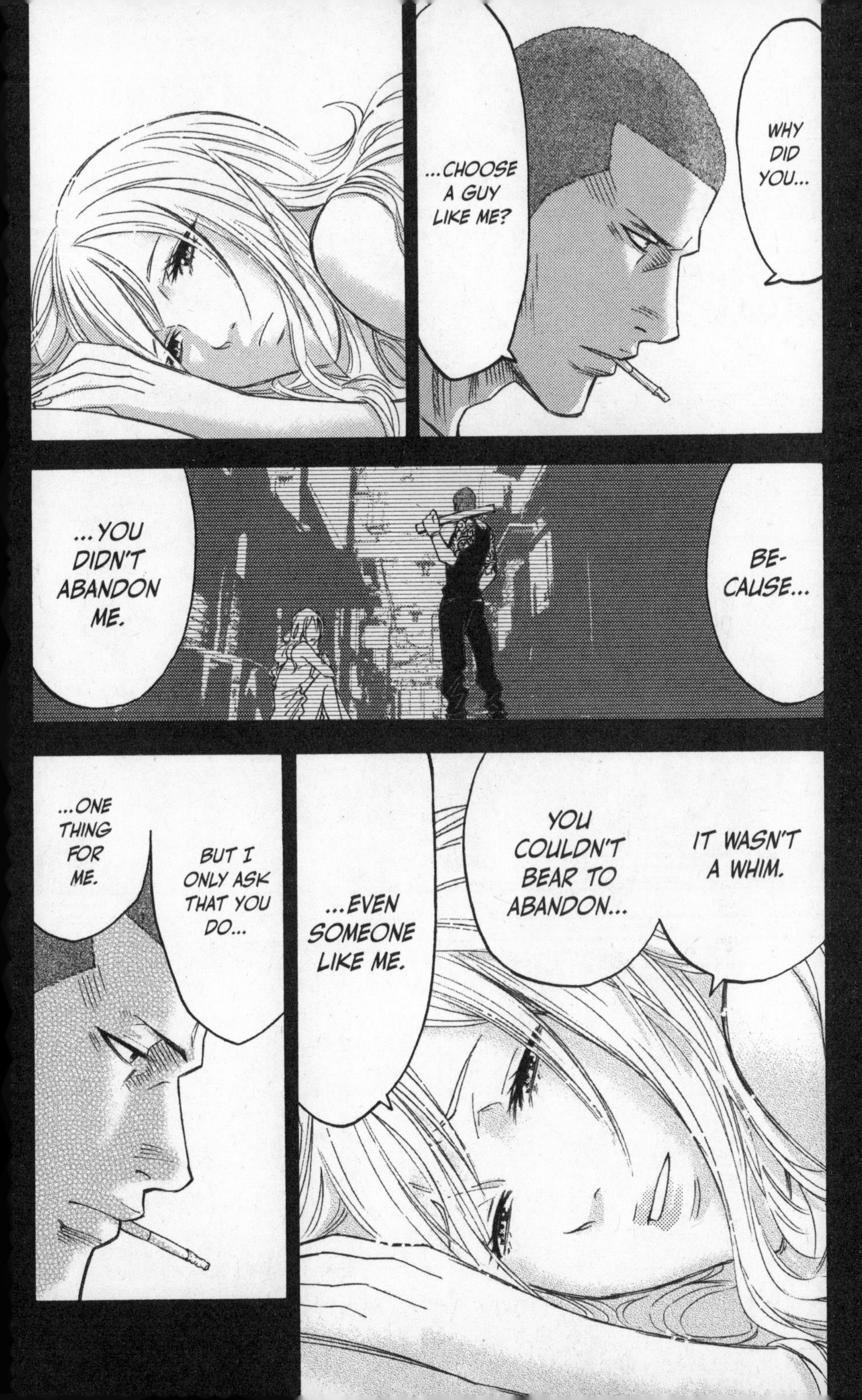
WHY DID YOU...
...CHOOSE A GUY LIKE ME?
BE-CAUSE...
...YOU DIDN'T ABANDON ME.
IT WASN'T A WHIM.
YOU COULDN'T BEAR TO ABANDON...
...EVEN SOMEONE LIKE ME.
BUT I ONLY ASK THAT YOU DO...
...ONE THING FOR ME.

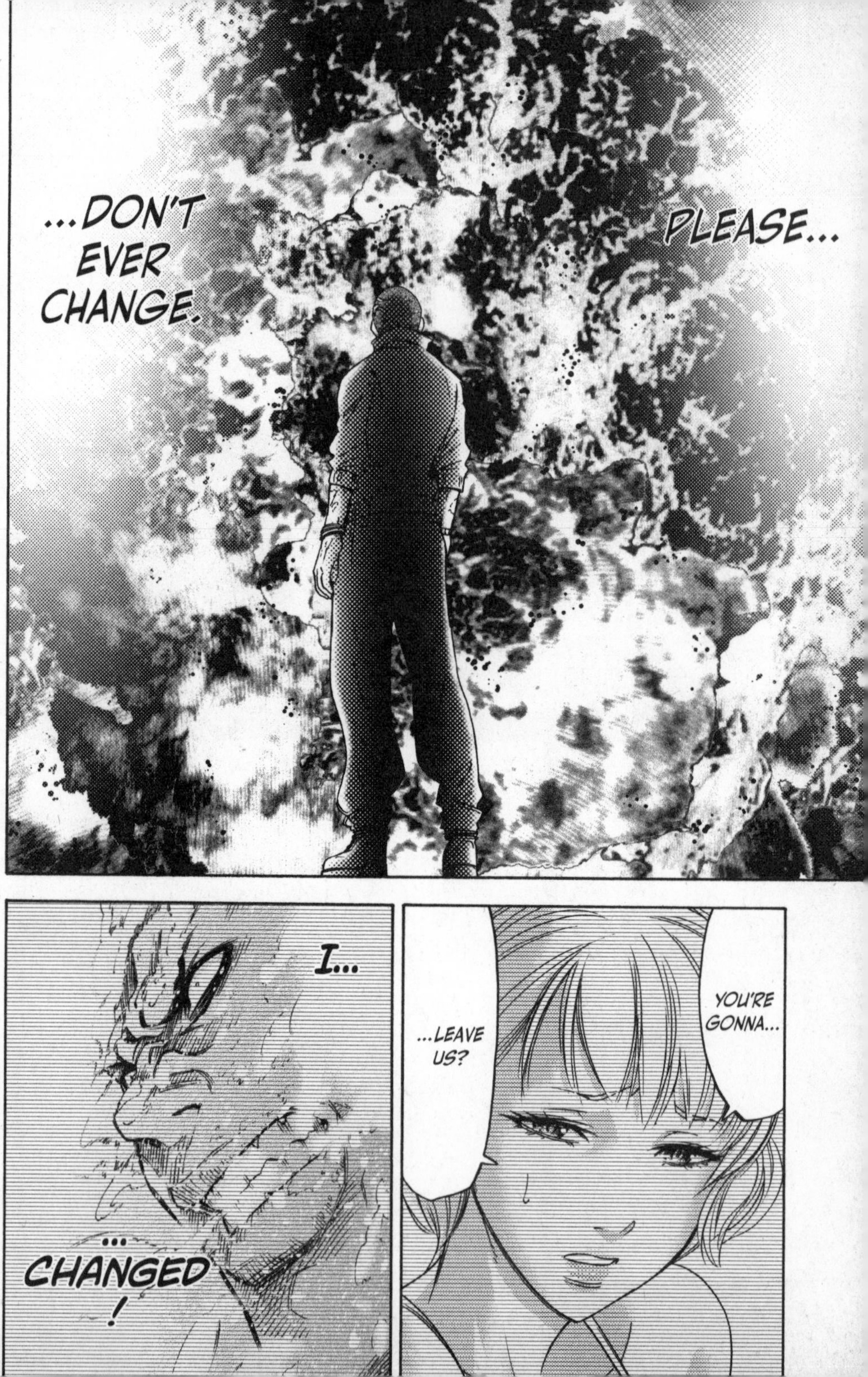
PLEASE...
...DON'T EVER CHANGE.
YOU'RE GONNA...
...LEAVE US?
I...
...CHANGED!

...I WAS JUST ANOTHER ASSHOLE.

IN THE END...

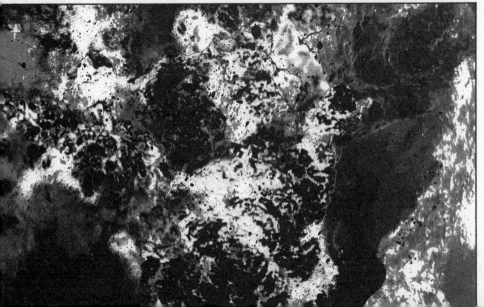

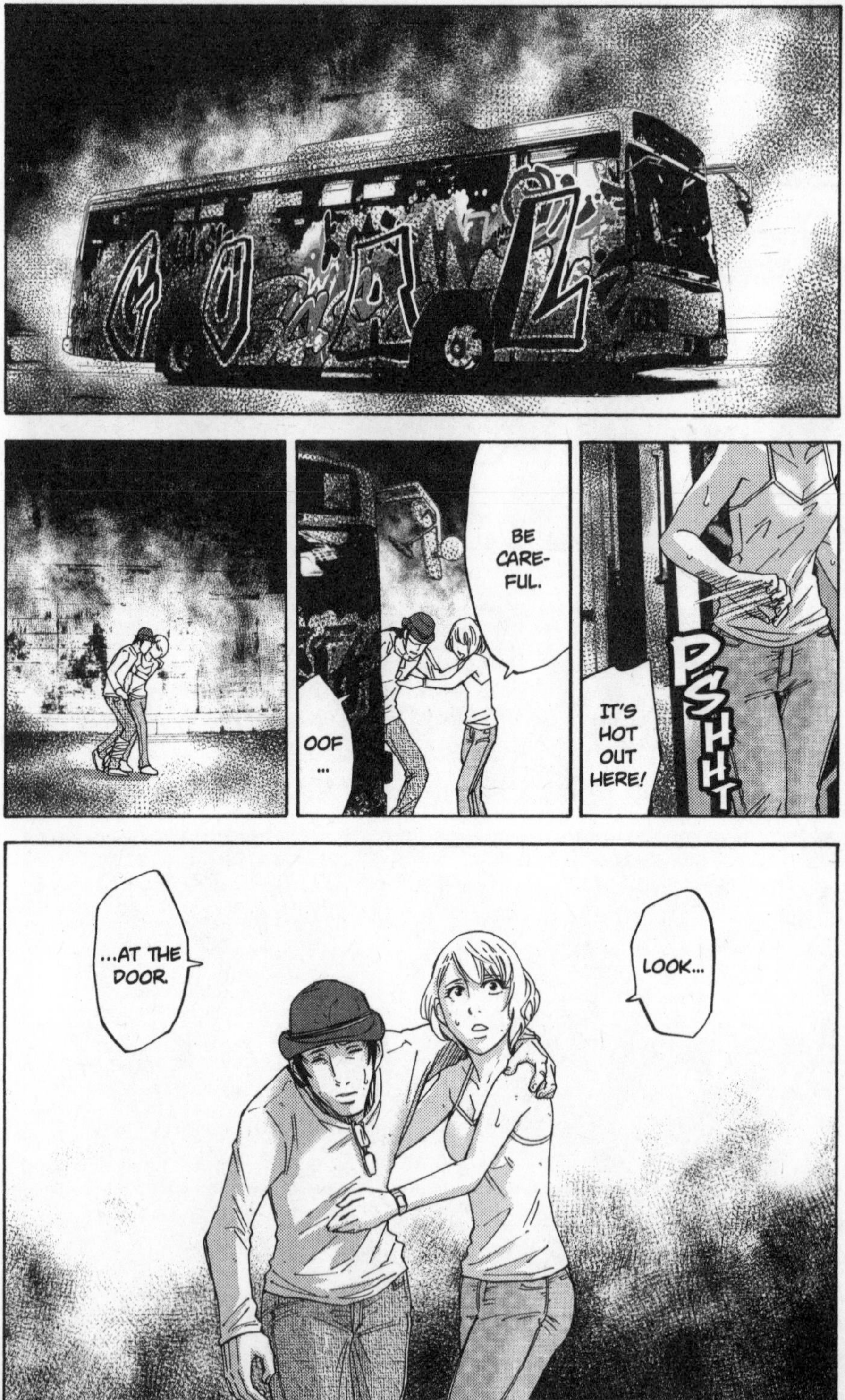
PSHHT
IT'S HOT OUT HERE!
BE CARE-FUL.
OOF ...
LOOK...
...AT THE DOOR.

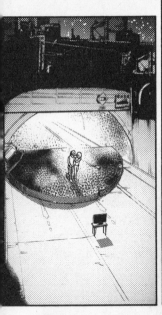

DID THE EXPLO- SION...

... KNOCK IT DOWN?

Congratulations
Game Complete

KRIK KRIK

KRIK

...COM- PLETE.

GAME...

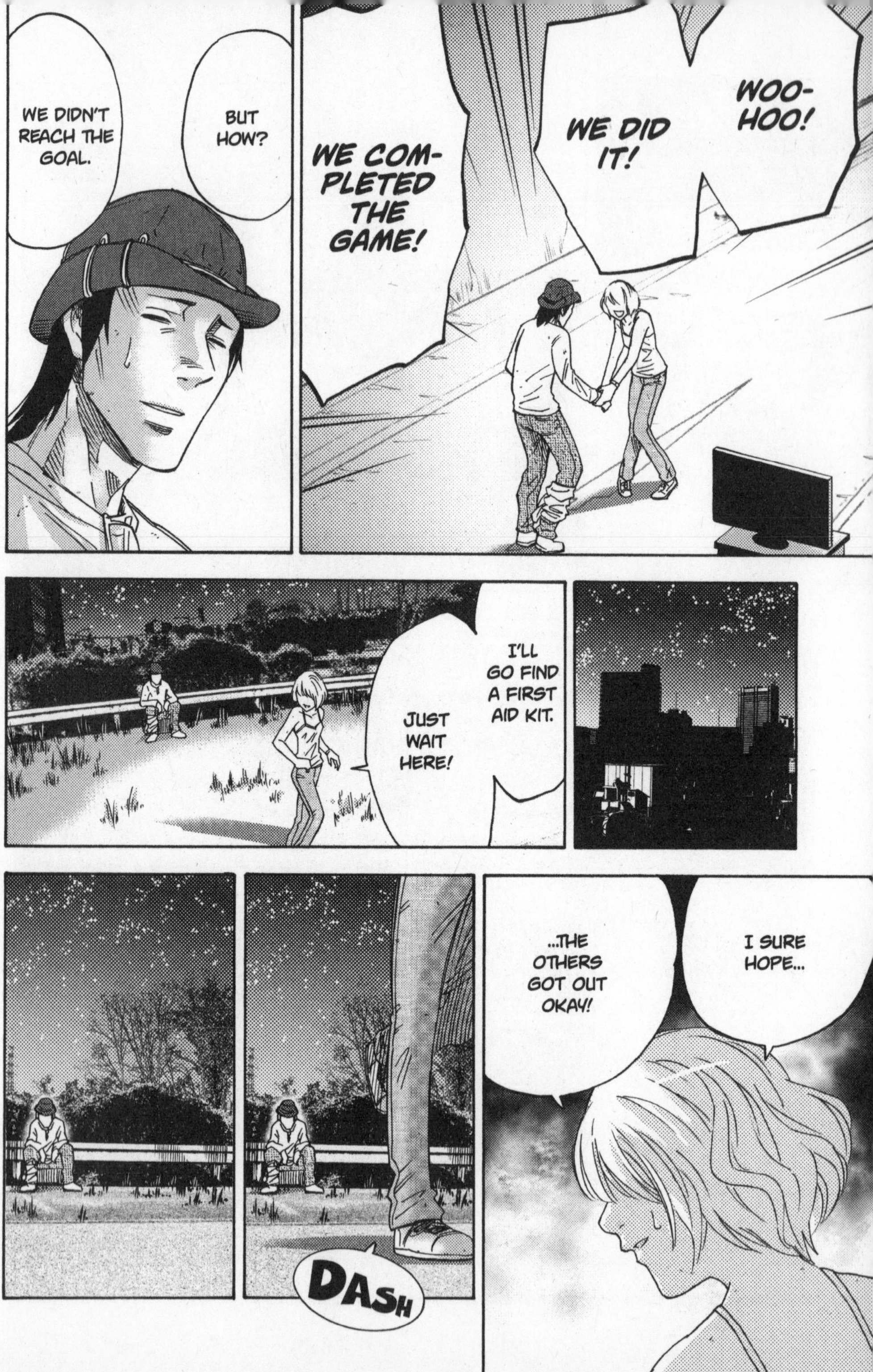
WOO-HOO!
WE DID IT!
WE COM-PLETED THE GAME!
BUT HOW?
WE DIDN'T REACH THE GOAL.
I'LL GO FIND A FIRST AID KIT.
JUST WAIT HERE!
I SURE HOPE...
...THE OTHERS GOT OUT OKAY!
DASH

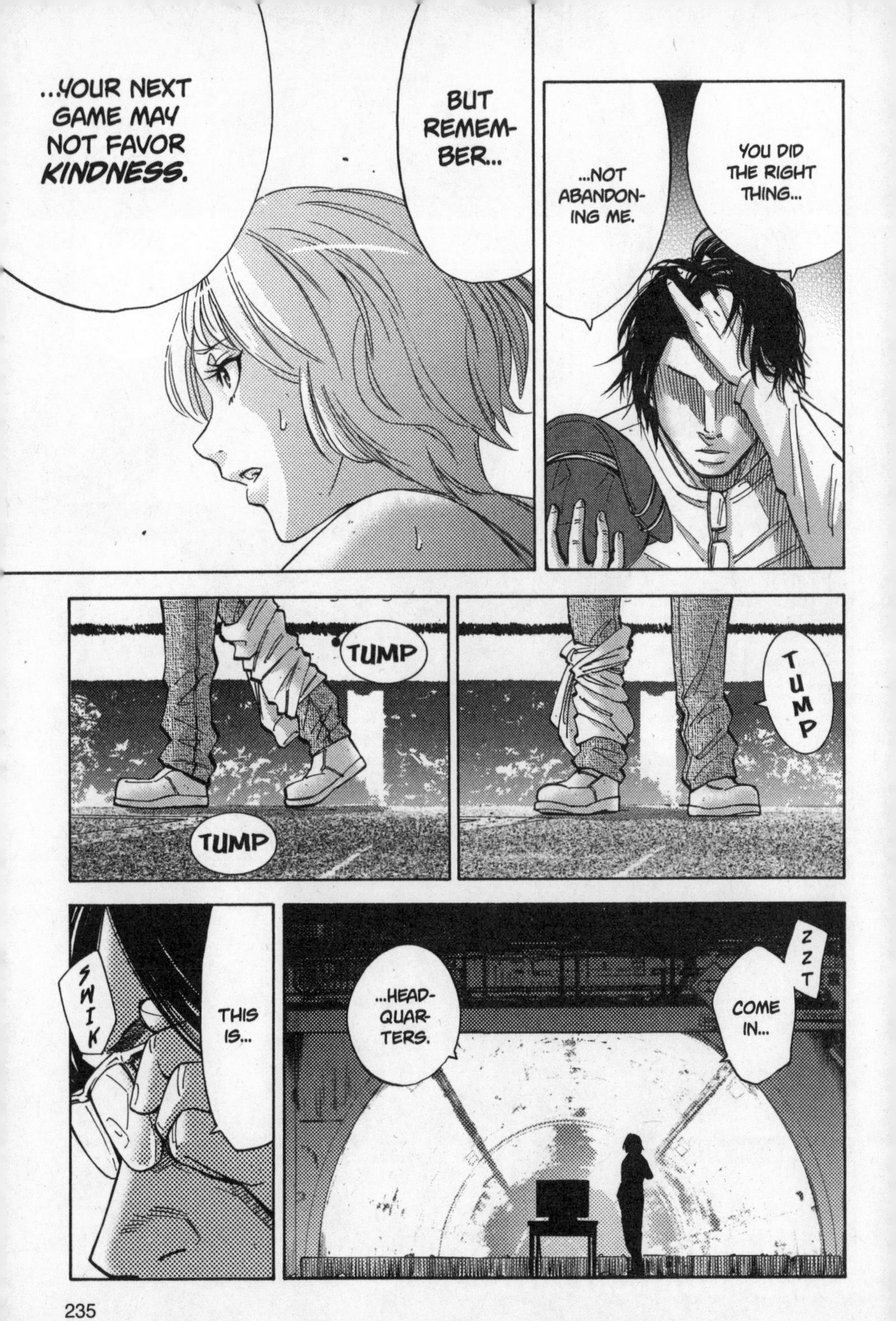

YOU DID THE RIGHT THING...
...NOT ABANDONING ME.
BUT REMEMBER...
...YOUR NEXT GAME MAY NOT FAVOR KINDNESS.
TUMP
TUMP
TUMP
ZZT
COME IN...
...HEADQUARTERS.
SWIK
THIS IS...

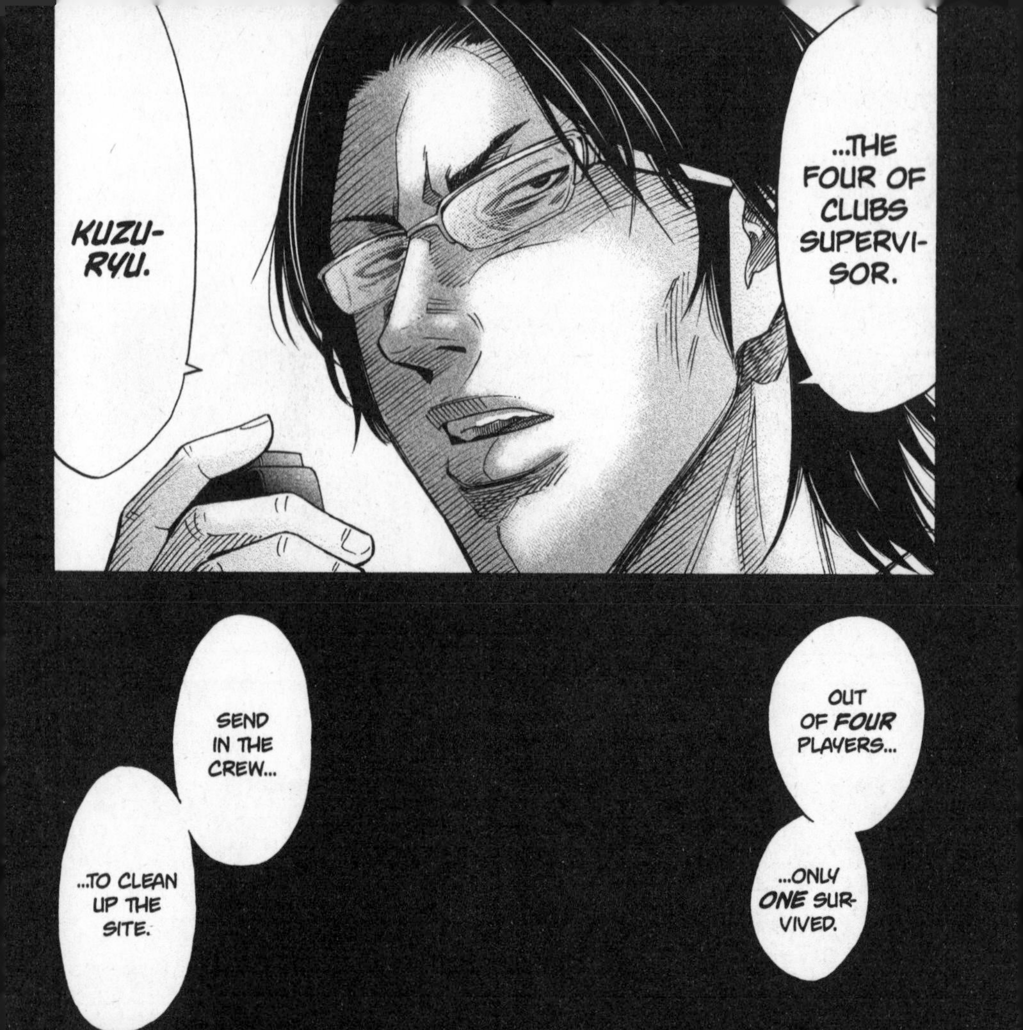
...THE FOUR OF CLUBS SUPERVISOR.
KUZURYU.
OUT OF *FOUR* PLAYERS...
...ONLY *ONE* SURVIVED.
SEND IN THE CREW...
...TO CLEAN UP THE SITE.

ALICE IN BORDERLAND

WE NOW RETURN TO THE MAIN STORY.

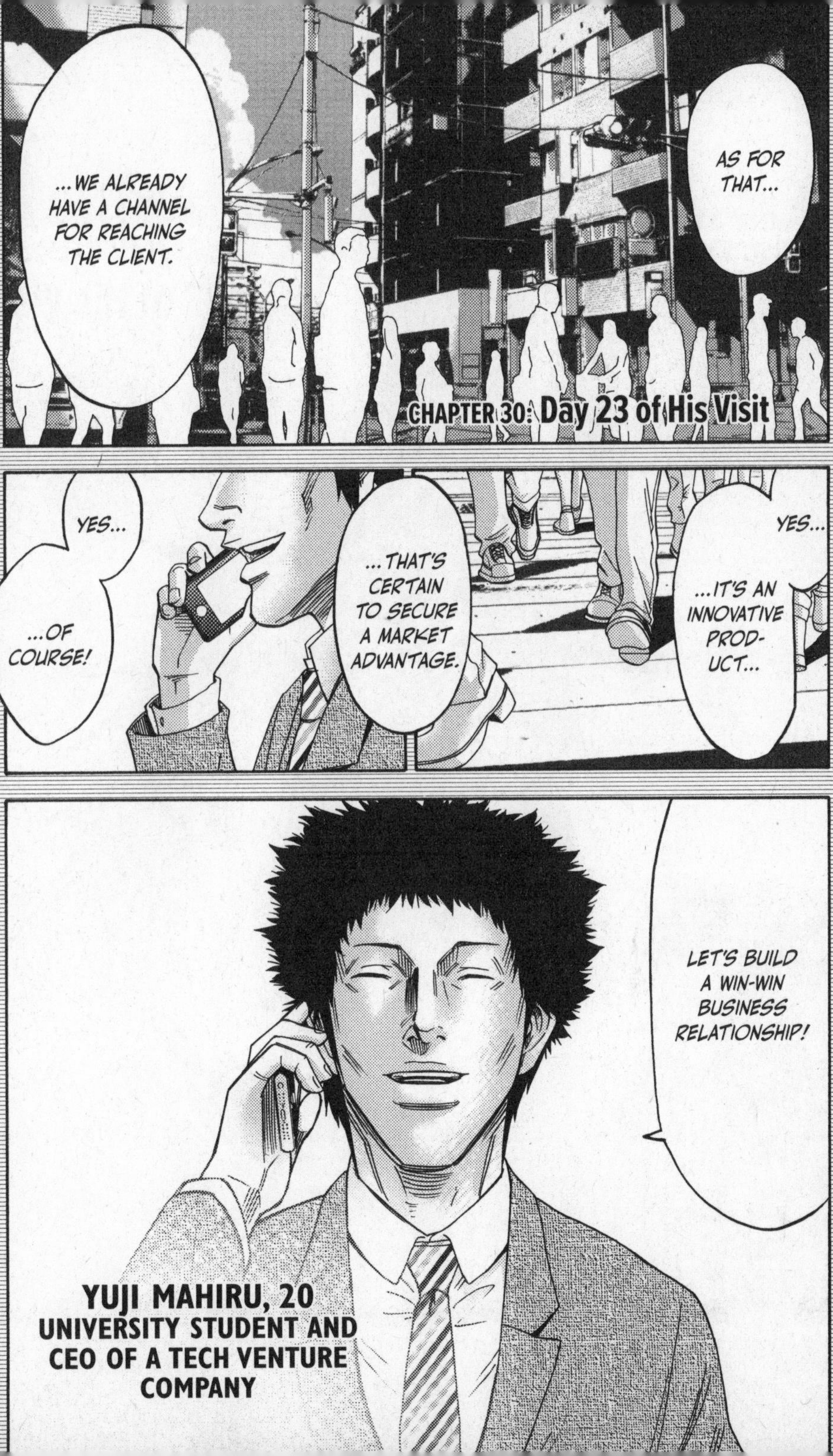
AS FOR THAT...
...WE ALREADY HAVE A CHANNEL FOR REACHING THE CLIENT.
CHAPTER 30: Day 23 of His Visit
YES...
...IT'S AN INNOVATIVE PROD-UCT...
...THAT'S CERTAIN TO SECURE A MARKET ADVANTAGE.
YES...
...OF COURSE!
LET'S BUILD A WIN-WIN BUSINESS RELATIONSHIP!
YUJI MAHIRU, 20
UNIVERSITY STUDENT AND CEO OF A TECH VENTURE COMPANY

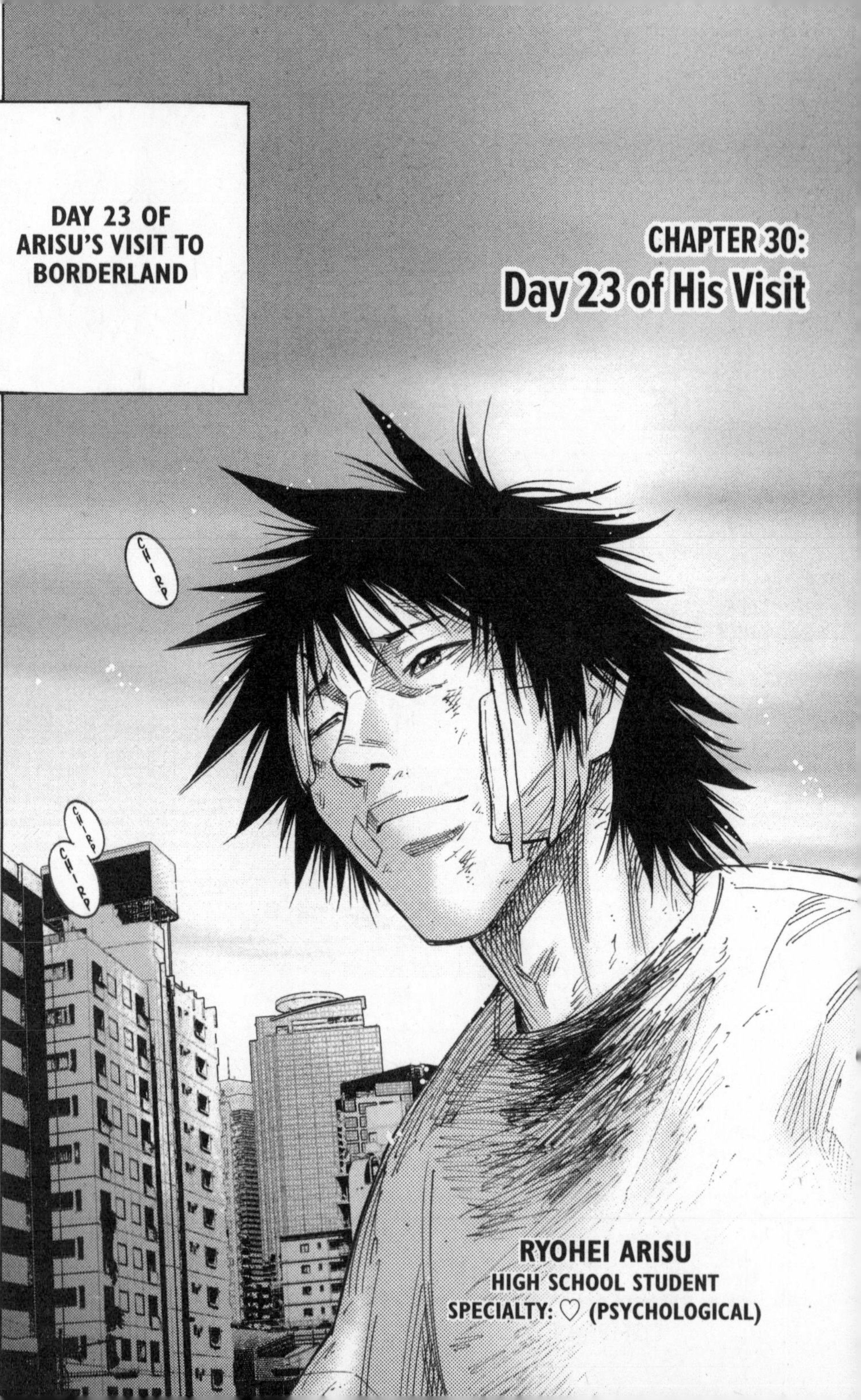
CHAPTER 30:
Day 23 of His Visit
DAY 23 OF ARISU'S VISIT TO BORDERLAND
CHIRP
CHIRP
CHIRP
RYOHEI ARISU
HIGH SCHOOL STUDENT
SPECIALTY: ♡ (PSYCHOLOGICAL)

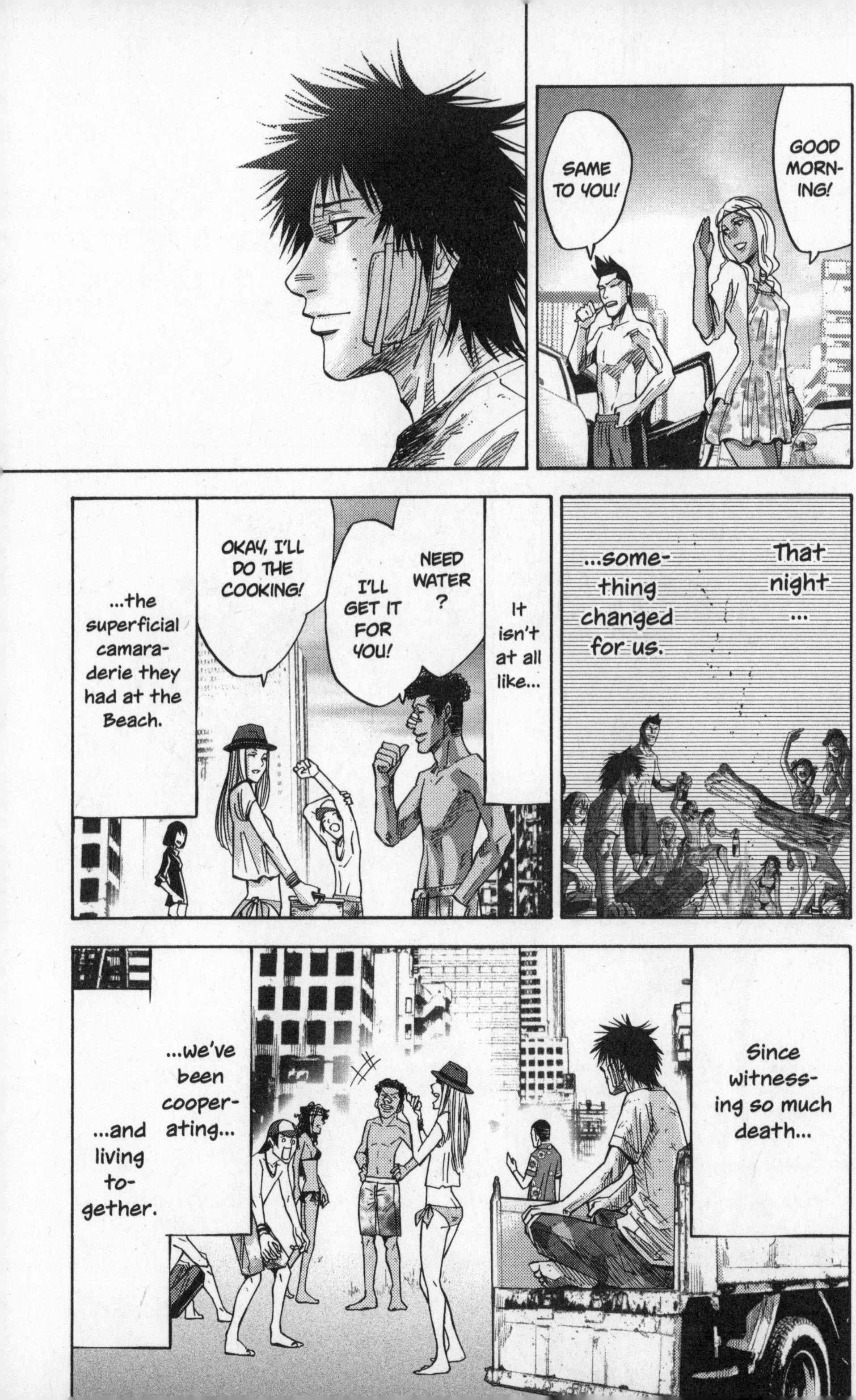
GOOD MORNING!
SAME TO YOU!
That night...
...something changed for us.
It isn't at all like...
NEED WATER?
I'LL GET IT FOR YOU!
OKAY, I'LL DO THE COOKING!
...the superficial camaraderie they had at the Beach.
Since witnessing so much death...
...we've been cooperating...
...and living together.

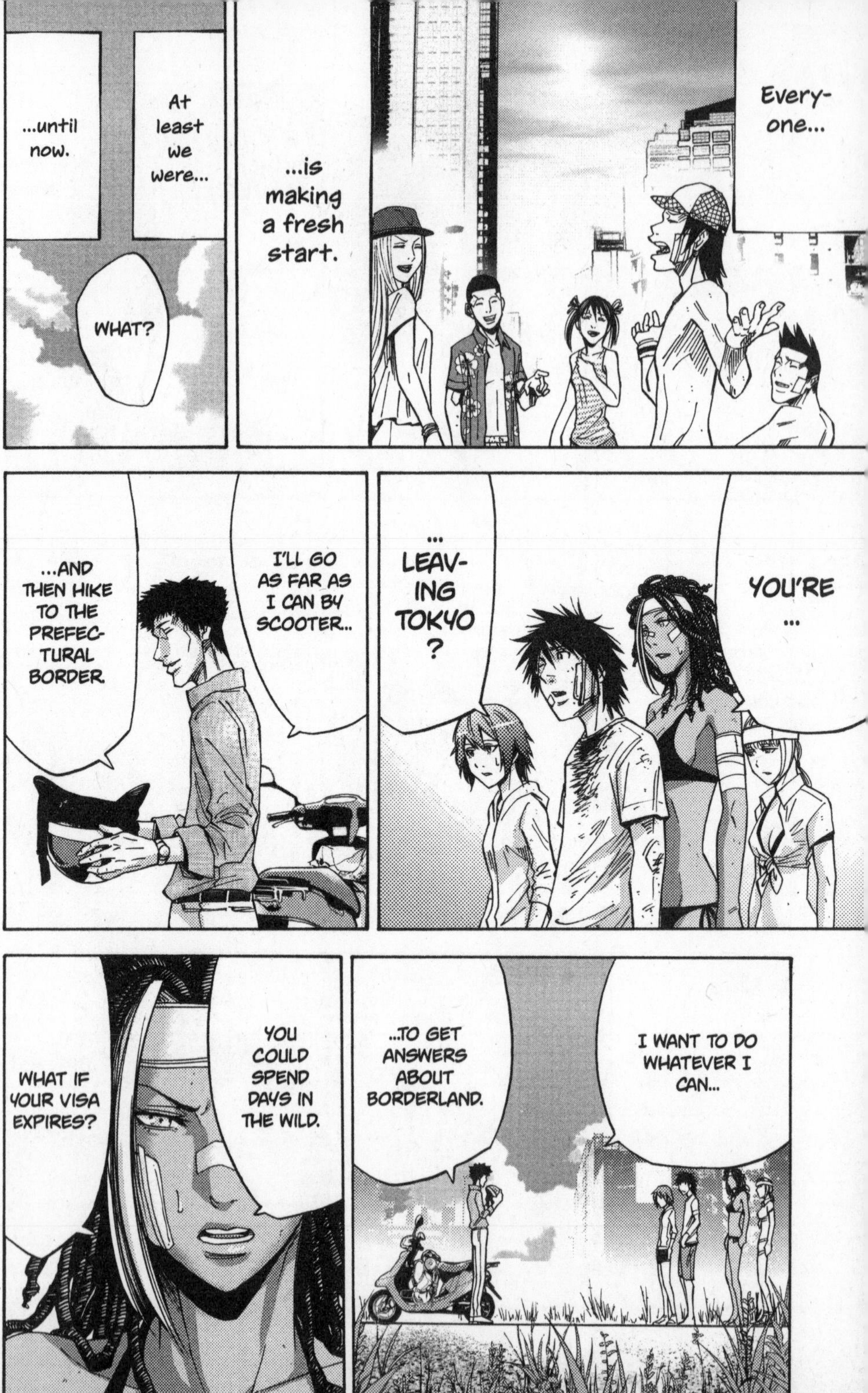
Every-one...
...is making a fresh start.
At least we were...
...until now.
WHAT?
YOU'RE ...
... LEAVING TOKYO?
I'LL GO AS FAR AS I CAN BY SCOOTER...
...AND THEN HIKE TO THE PREFECTURAL BORDER.
I WANT TO DO WHATEVER I CAN...
...TO GET ANSWERS ABOUT BORDERLAND.
YOU COULD SPEND DAYS IN THE WILD.
WHAT IF YOUR VISA EXPIRES?

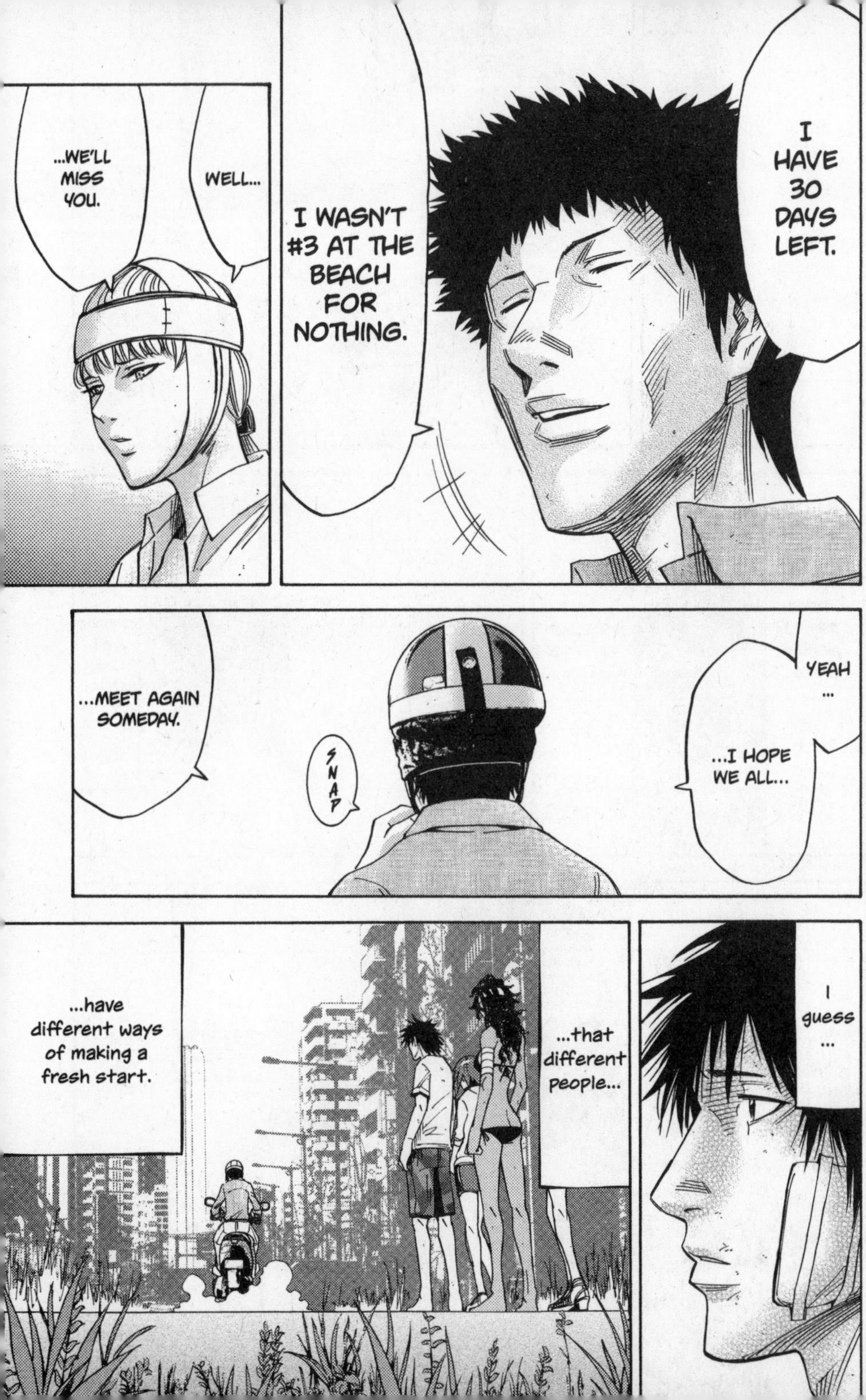
I HAVE 30 DAYS LEFT.
I WASN'T #3 AT THE BEACH FOR NOTHING.
WELL...
...WE'LL MISS YOU.
YEAH ...
...I HOPE WE ALL...
SNAP
...MEET AGAIN SOMEDAY.
I guess ...
...that different people...
...have different ways of making a fresh start.

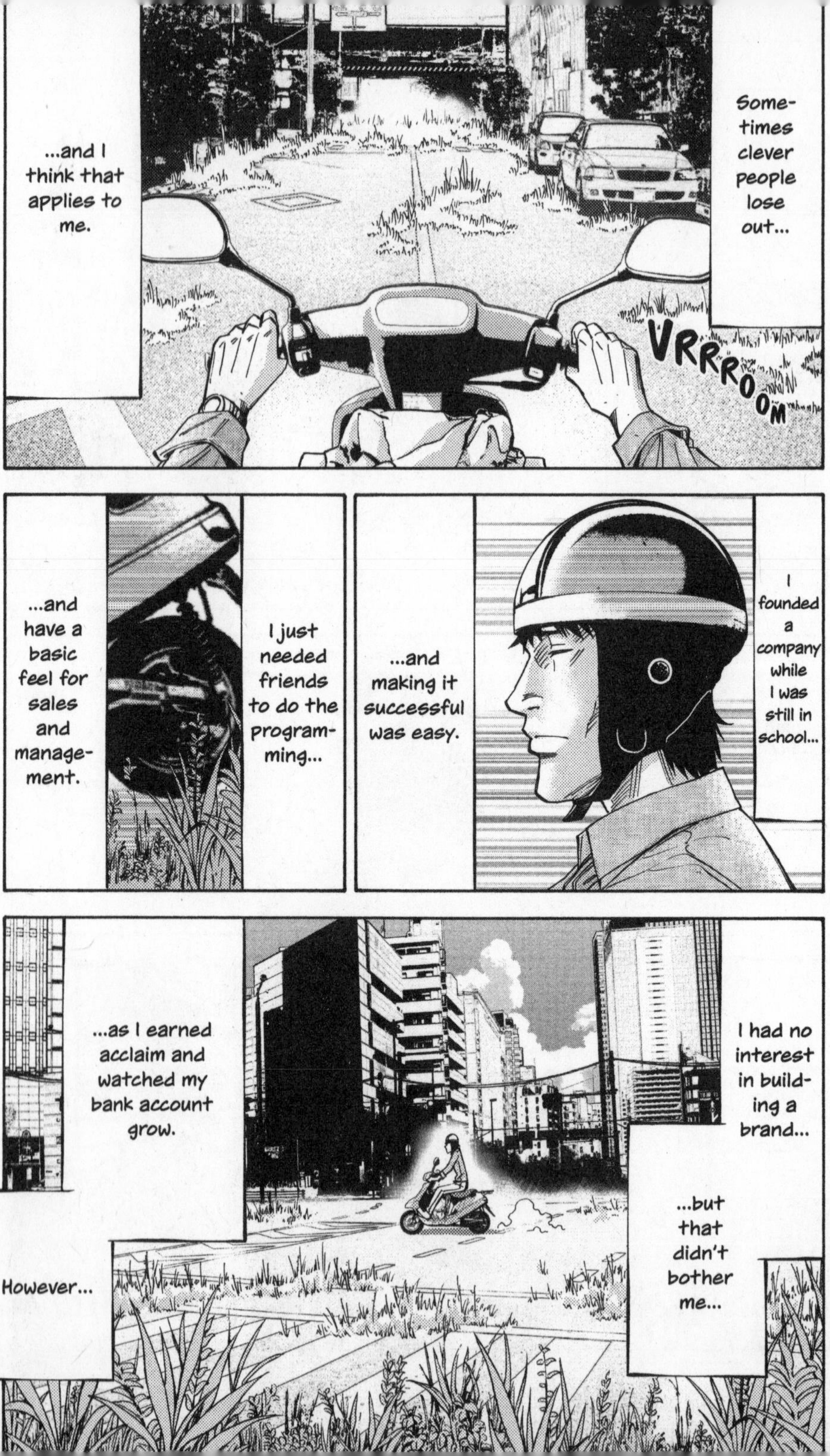
Some-times clever people lose out...
...and I think that applies to me.
VRRROOM
I founded a company while I was still in school...
...and making it successful was easy.
I just needed friends to do the programming...
...and have a basic feel for sales and management.
I had no interest in building a brand...
...as I earned acclaim and watched my bank account grow.
...but that didn't bother me...
However...

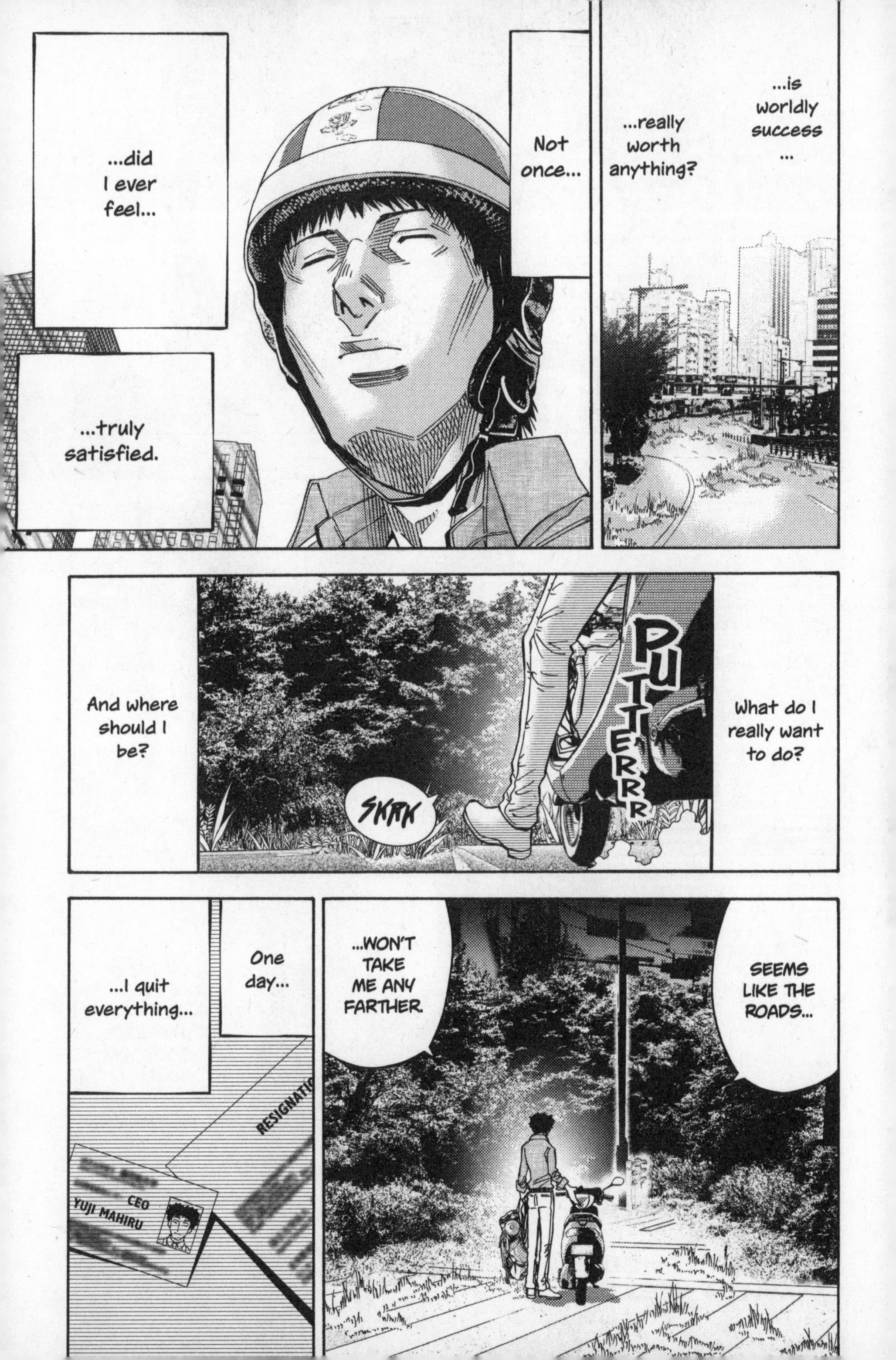
...is worldly success ...
...really worth anything?
Not once...
...did I ever feel...
...truly satisfied.
What do I really want to do?
PUTTERRR
SKRK
And where should I be?
SEEMS LIKE THE ROADS...
...WON'T TAKE ME ANY FARTHER.
One day...
...I quit everything...
CEO
YUJI MAHIRU

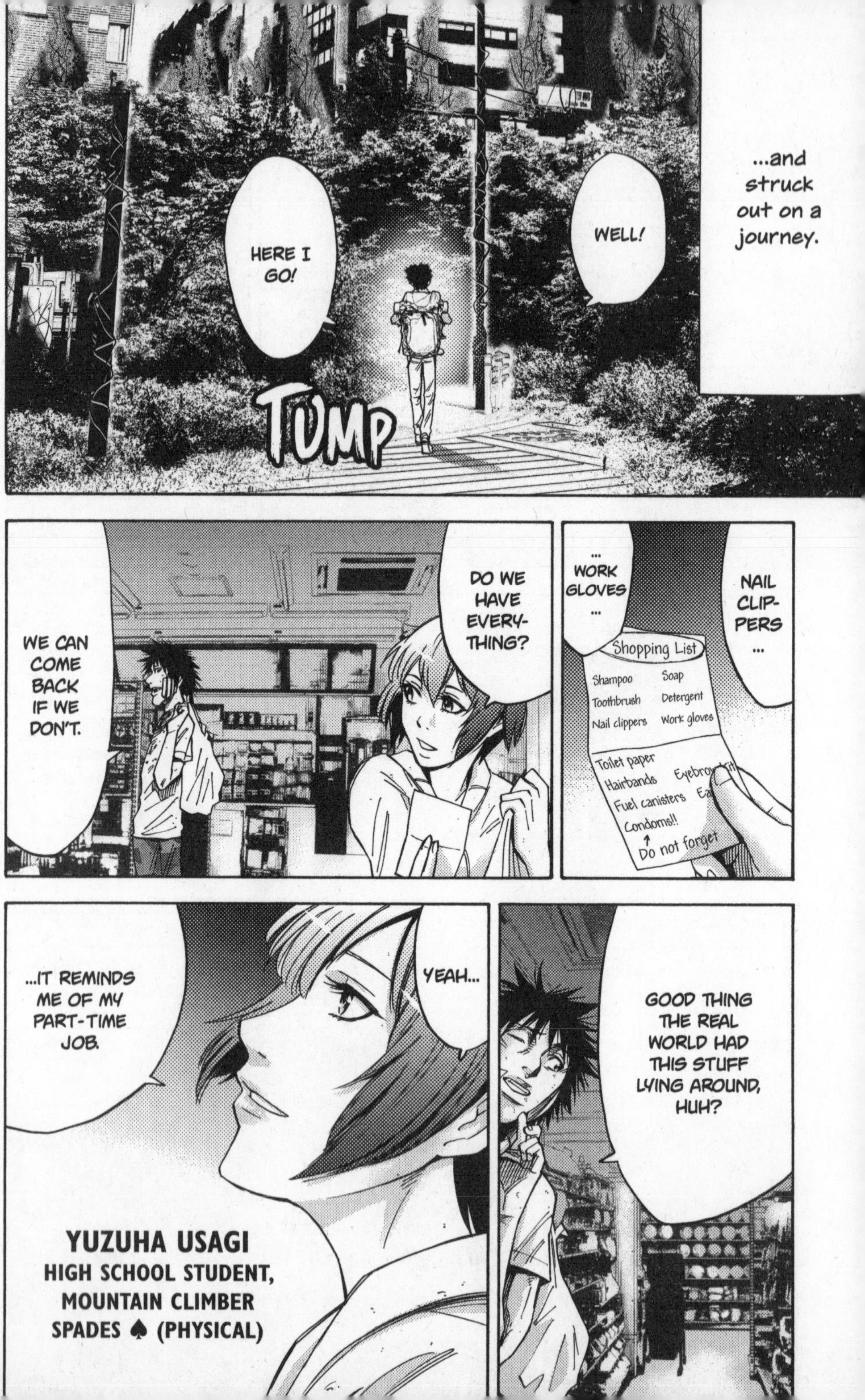
...and struck out on a journey.
WELL!
HERE I GO!
TUMP
NAIL CLIP-PERS ...
... WORK GLOVES ...
Shopping List
Shampoo Soap
Toothbrush Detergent
Nail clippers Work gloves
Toilet paper
Hairbands
Fuel canisters
Condoms!!
↑ Do not forget
DO WE HAVE EVERY-THING?
WE CAN COME BACK IF WE DON'T.
GOOD THING THE REAL WORLD HAD THIS STUFF LYING AROUND, HUH?
YEAH...
...IT REMINDS ME OF MY PART-TIME JOB.
YUZUHA USAGI
HIGH SCHOOL STUDENT, MOUNTAIN CLIMBER
SPADES ♠ (PHYSICAL)

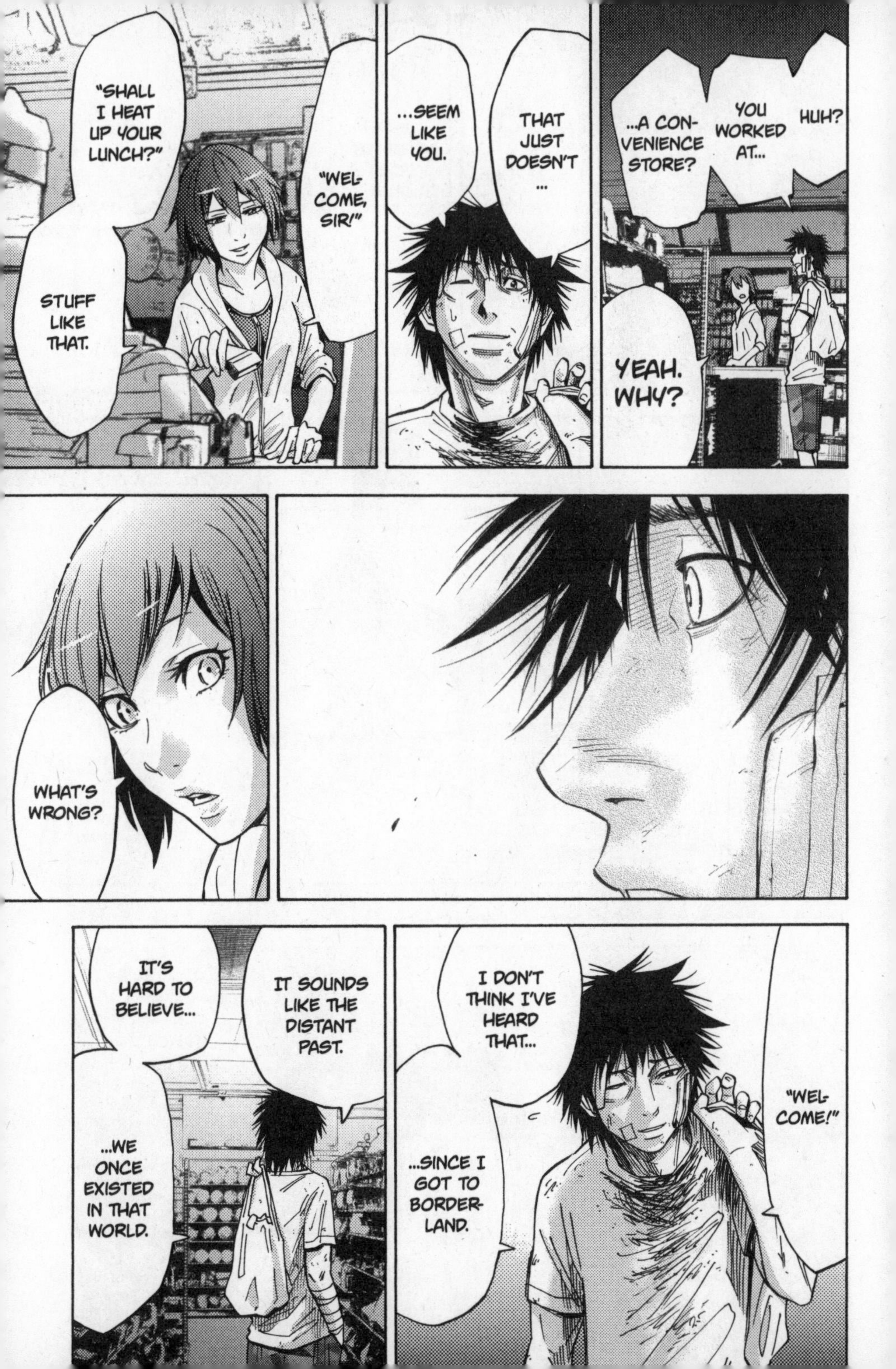
HUH?
YOU WORKED AT...
...A CONVENIENCE STORE?
YEAH. WHY?
THAT JUST DOESN'T ...
...SEEM LIKE YOU.
"WELCOME, SIR!"
"SHALL I HEAT UP YOUR LUNCH?"
STUFF LIKE THAT.
WHAT'S WRONG?
"WELCOME!"
I DON'T THINK I'VE HEARD THAT...
...SINCE I GOT TO BORDERLAND.
IT SOUNDS LIKE THE DISTANT PAST.
IT'S HARD TO BELIEVE...
...WE ONCE EXISTED IN THAT WORLD.

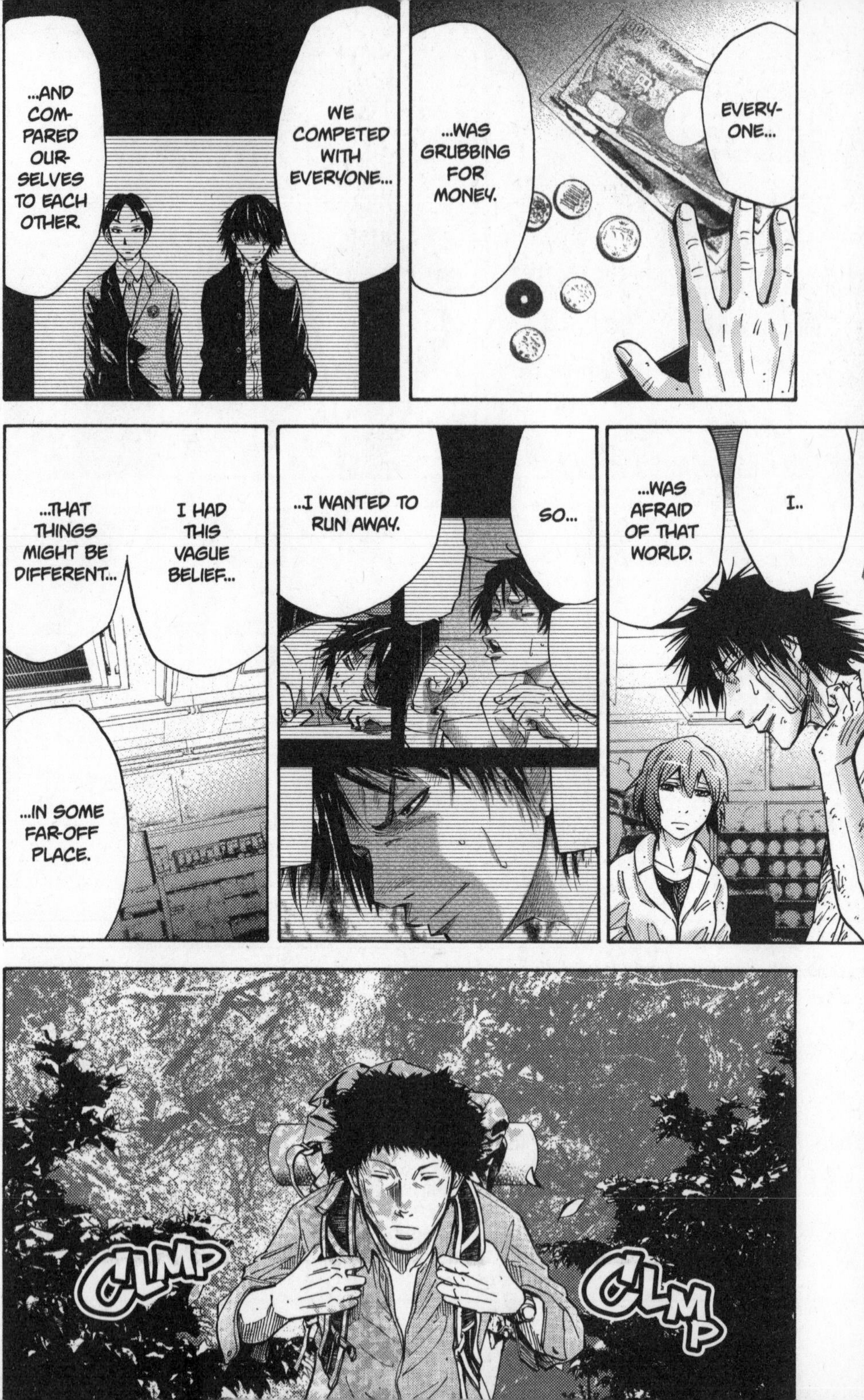
EVERY-ONE...
...WAS GRUBBING FOR MONEY.
WE COMPETED WITH EVERYONE...
...AND COM-PARED OUR-SELVES TO EACH OTHER.
I..
...WAS AFRAID OF THAT WORLD.
SO...
...I WANTED TO RUN AWAY.
I HAD THIS VAGUE BELIEF...
...THAT THINGS MIGHT BE DIFFERENT...
...IN SOME FAR-OFF PLACE.
CLMP
CLMP

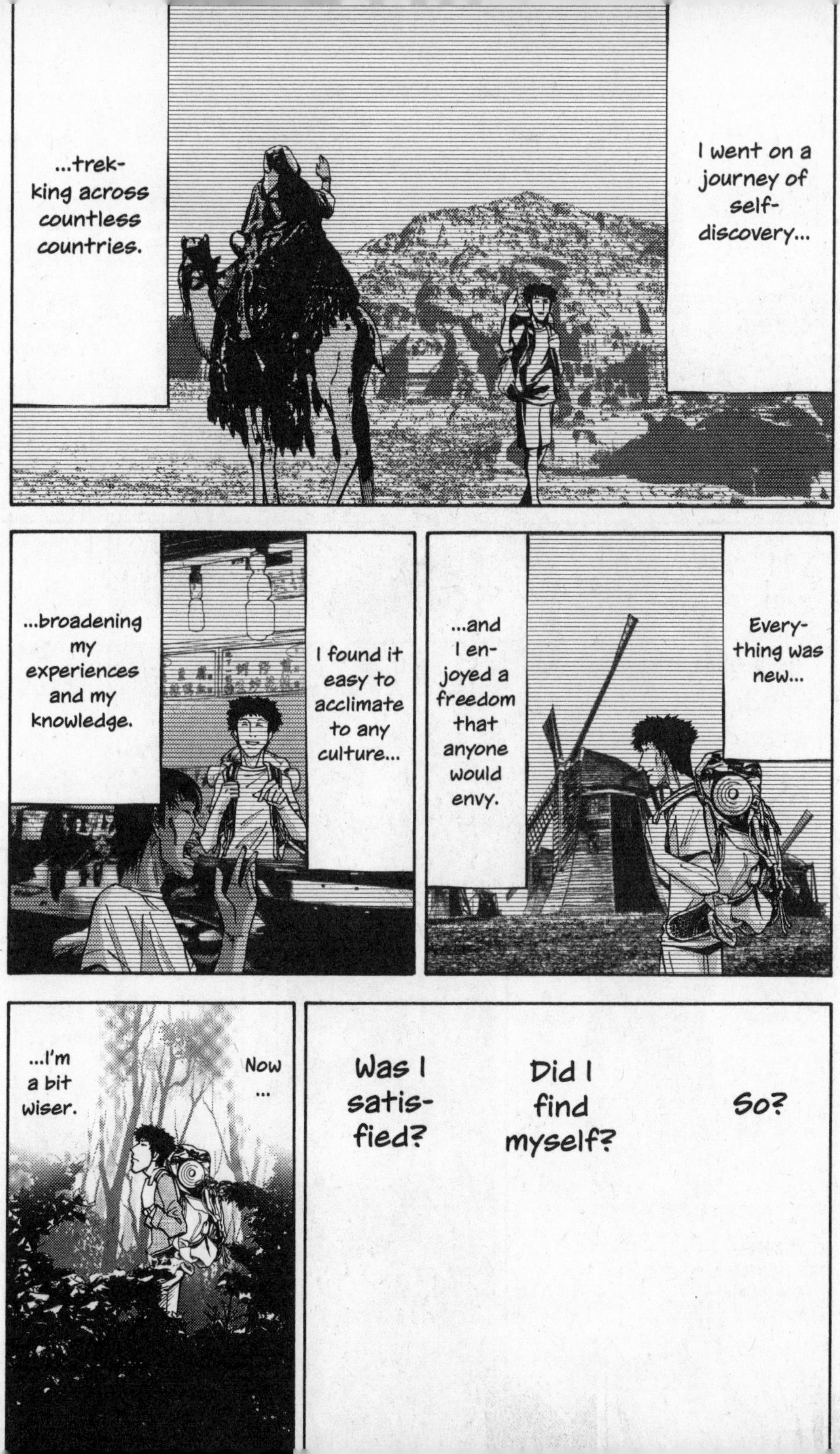
I went on a journey of self-discovery...
...trek-king across countless countries.
Every-thing was new...
...and I en-joyed a freedom that anyone would envy.
I found it easy to acclimate to any culture...
...broadening my experiences and my knowledge.
So?
Did I find myself?
Was I satis-fied?
Now...
...I'm a bit wiser.

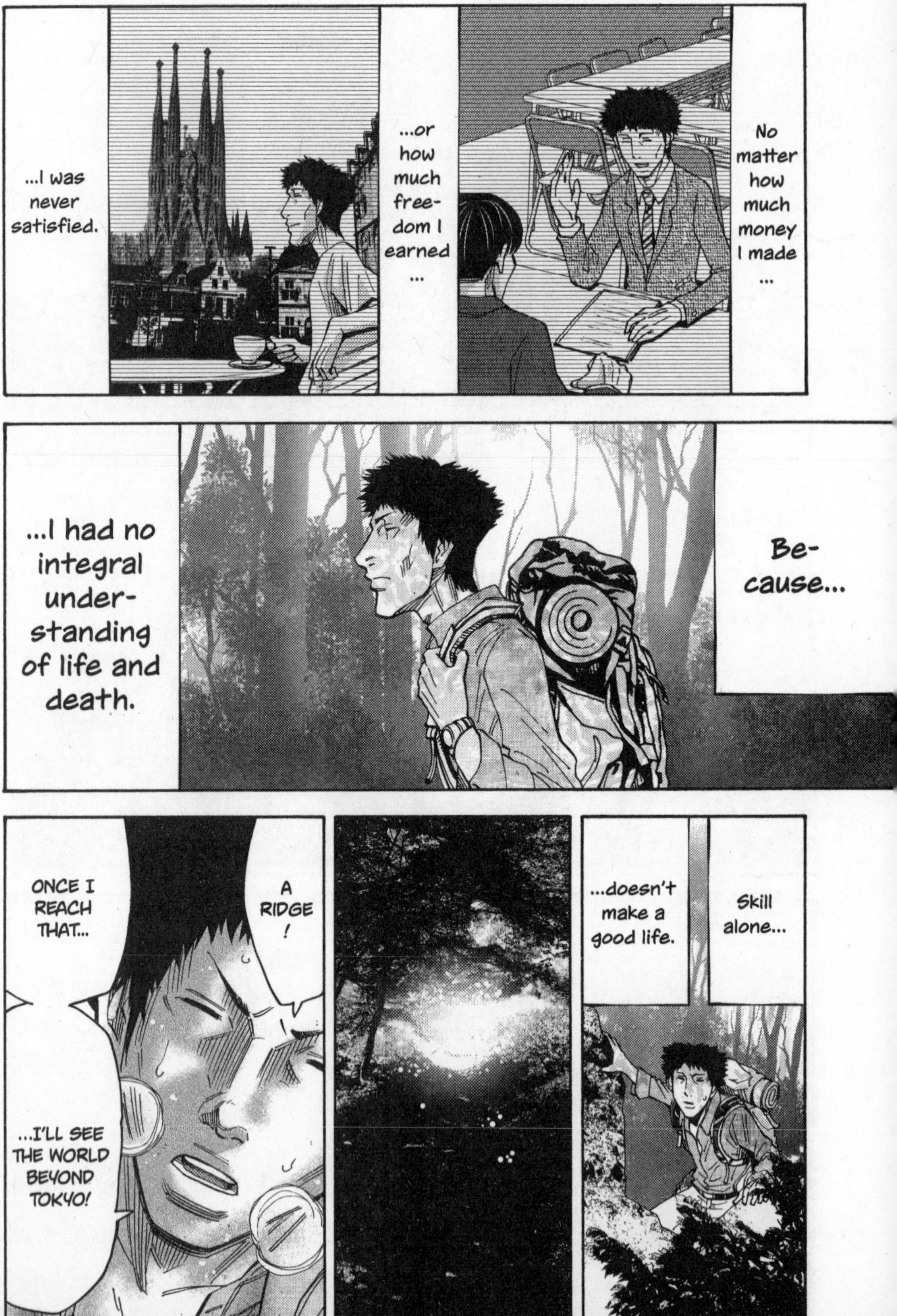
No matter how much money I made...
...or how much freedom I earned...
...I was never satisfied.
Because...
...I had no integral understanding of life and death.
Skill alone...
...doesn't make a good life.
A RIDGE!
ONCE I REACH THAT...
...I'LL SEE THE WORLD BEYOND TOKYO!

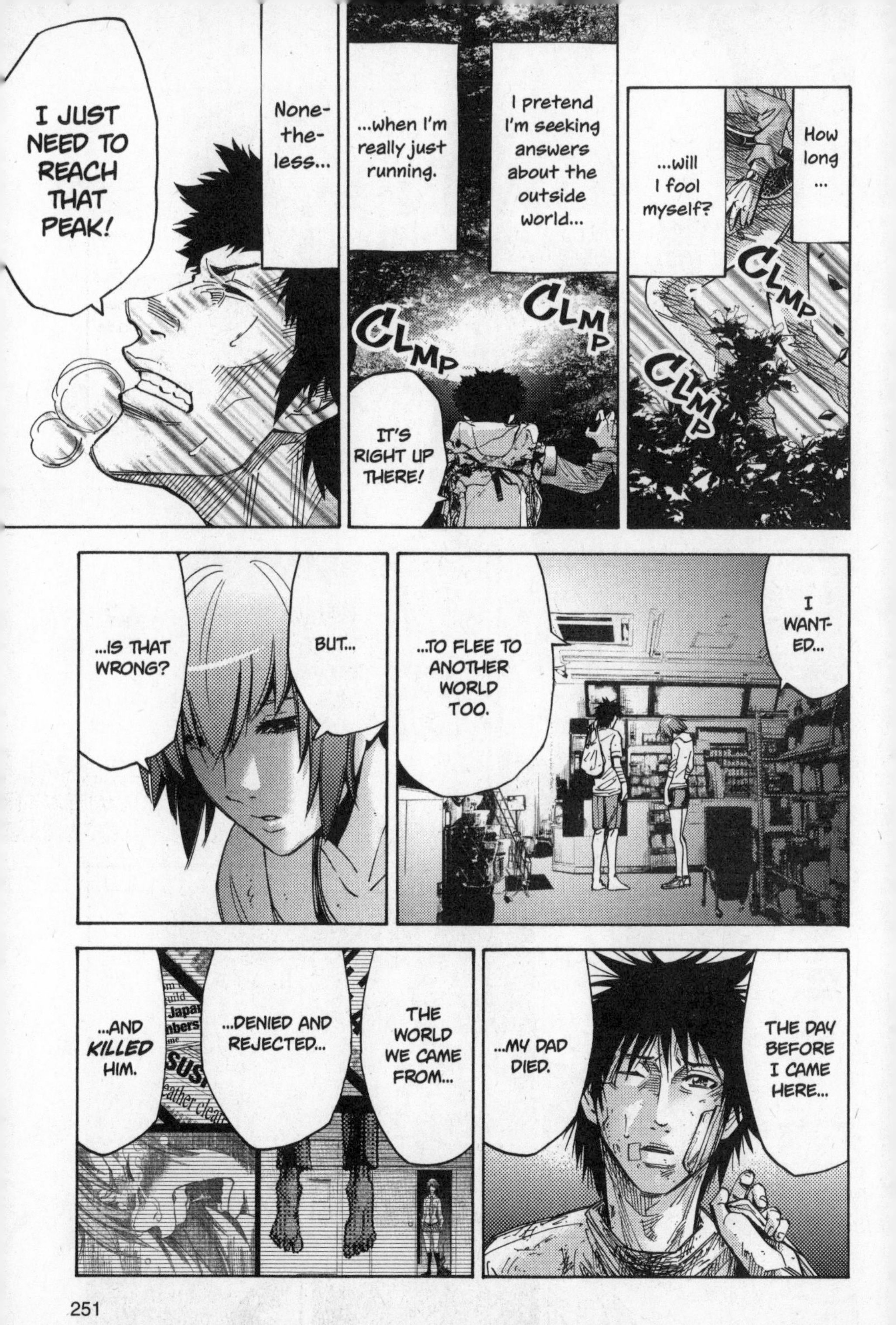
How long ...
...will I fool myself?
CLMP
CLMP
I pretend I'm seeking answers about the outside world...
...when I'm really just running.
CLMP
CLMP
IT'S RIGHT UP THERE!
None-the-less...
I JUST NEED TO REACH THAT PEAK!
I WANTED...
...TO FLEE TO ANOTHER WORLD TOO.
BUT...
...IS THAT WRONG?
THE DAY BEFORE I CAME HERE...
...MY DAD DIED.
THE WORLD WE CAME FROM...
...DENIED AND REJECTED...
...AND *KILLED* HIM.

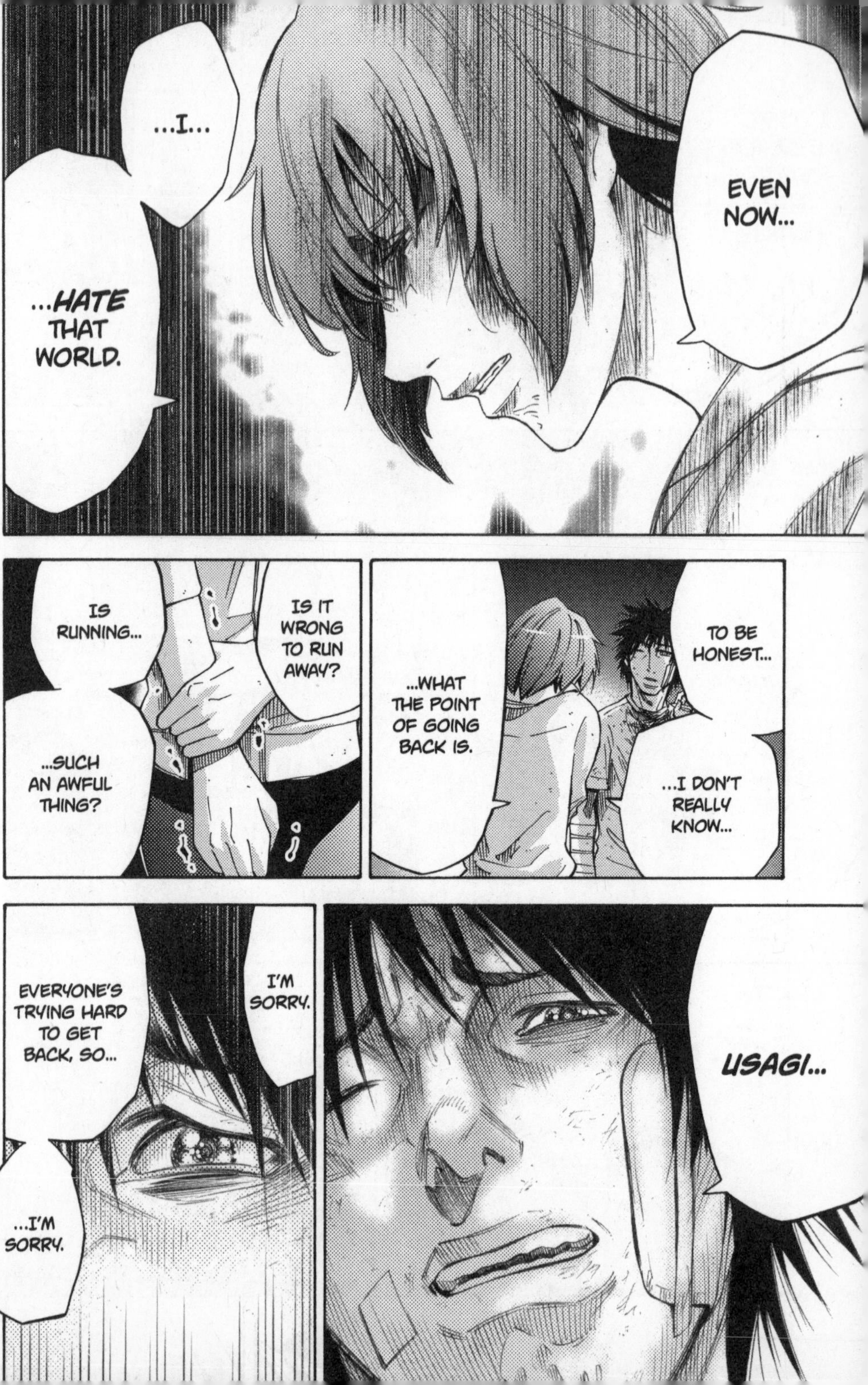
EVEN NOW...
...I...
...HATE THAT WORLD.
TO BE HONEST...
...I DON'T REALLY KNOW...
...WHAT THE POINT OF GOING BACK IS.
IS IT WRONG TO RUN AWAY?
IS RUNNING...
...SUCH AN AWFUL THING?
USAGI...
I'M SORRY.
EVERYONE'S TRYING HARD TO GET BACK, SO...
...I'M SORRY.

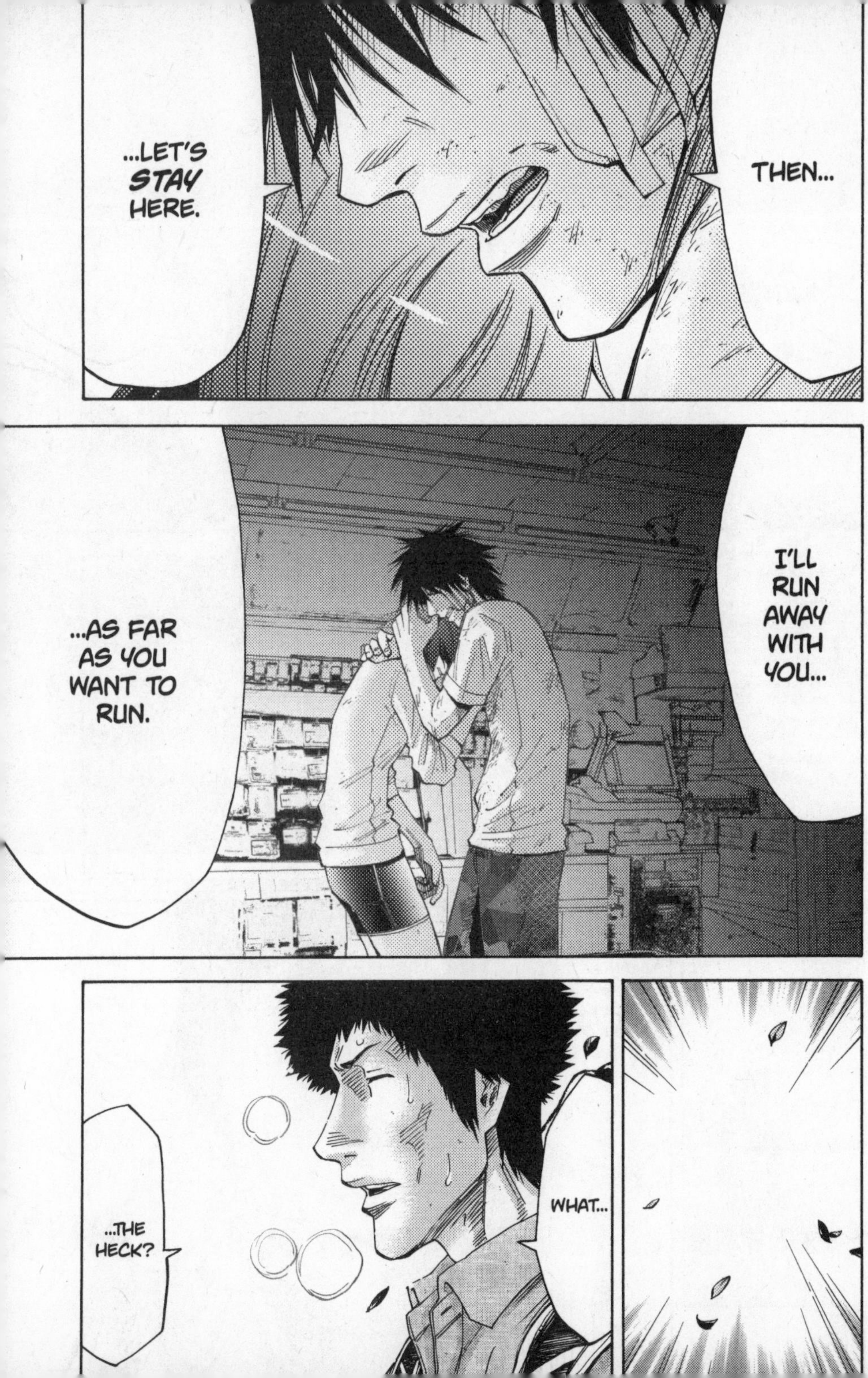
THEN...
...LET'S STAY HERE.
I'LL RUN AWAY WITH YOU...
...AS FAR AS YOU WANT TO RUN.
WHAT...
...THE HECK?

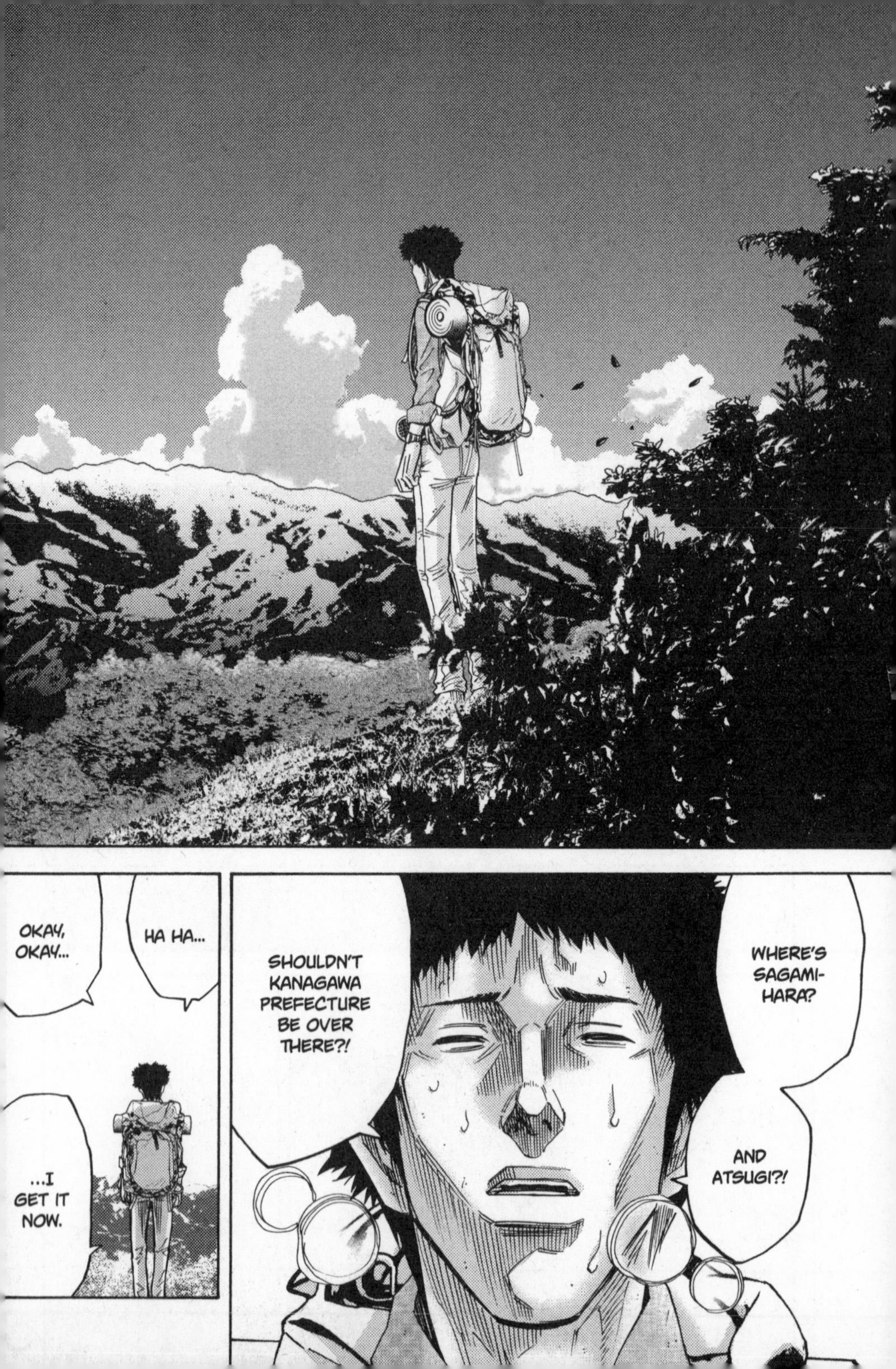
WHERE'S SAGAMI-HARA?
AND ATSUGI?!
SHOULDN'T KANAGAWA PREFECTURE BE OVER THERE?!
HA HA...
OKAY, OKAY...
...I GET IT NOW.

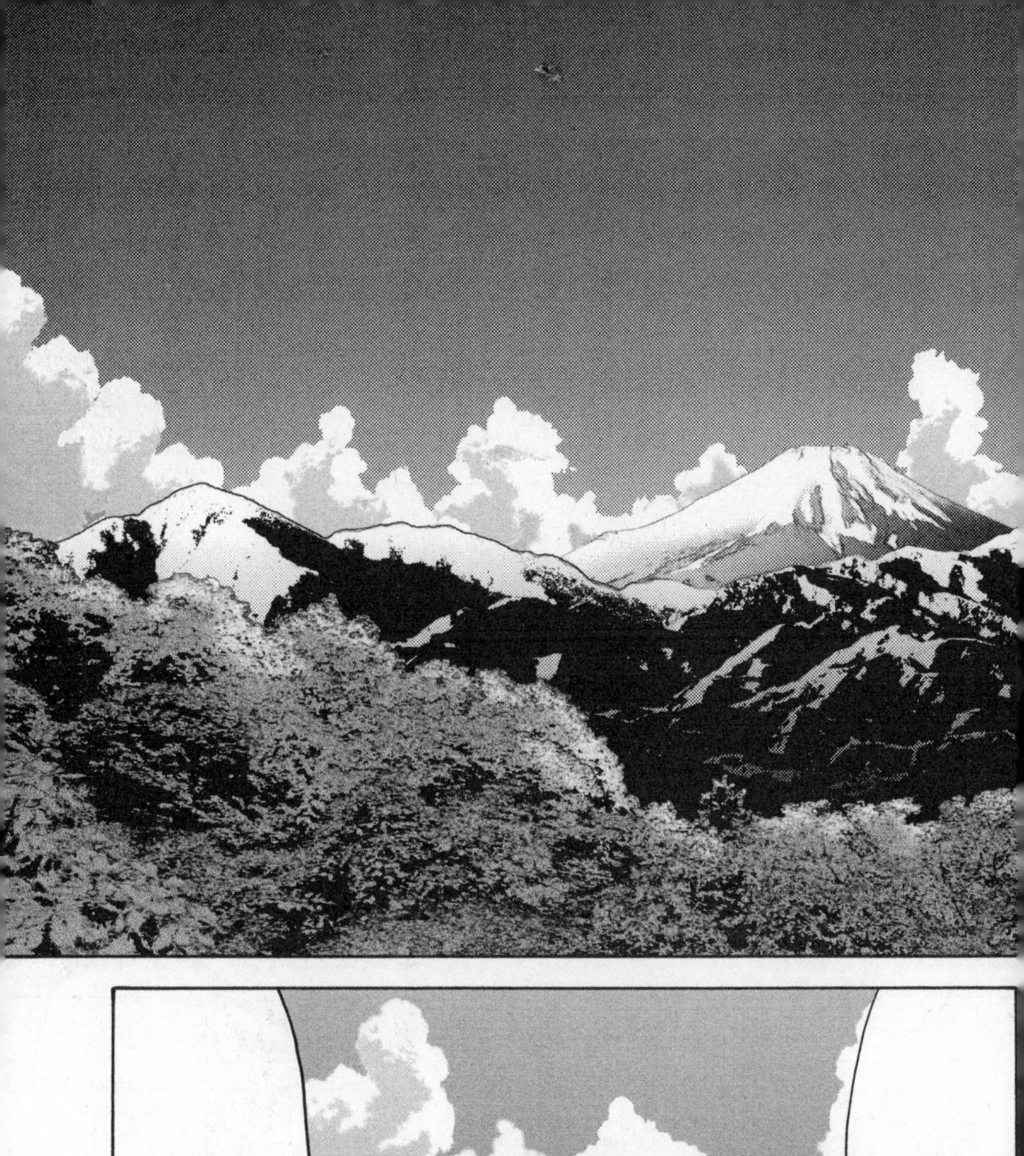

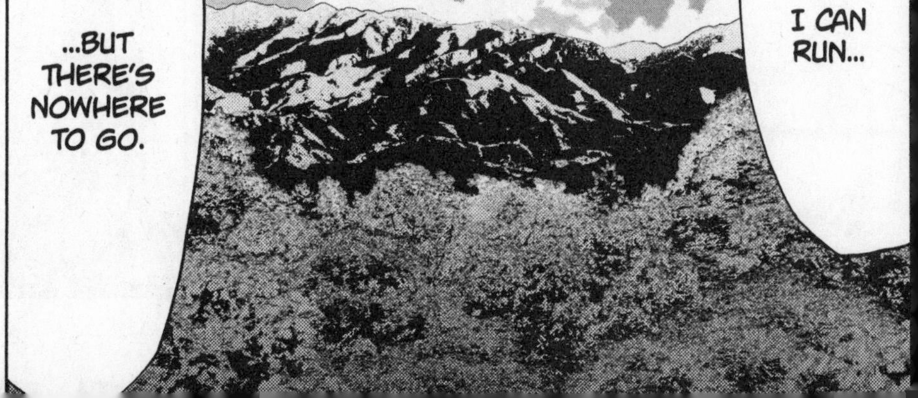
I CAN RUN...
...BUT THERE'S NOWHERE TO GO.

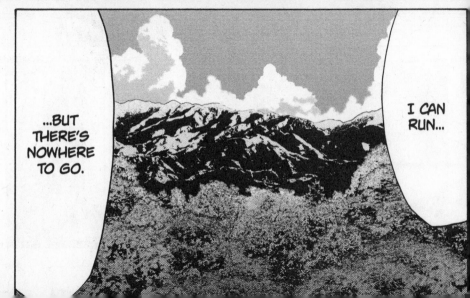

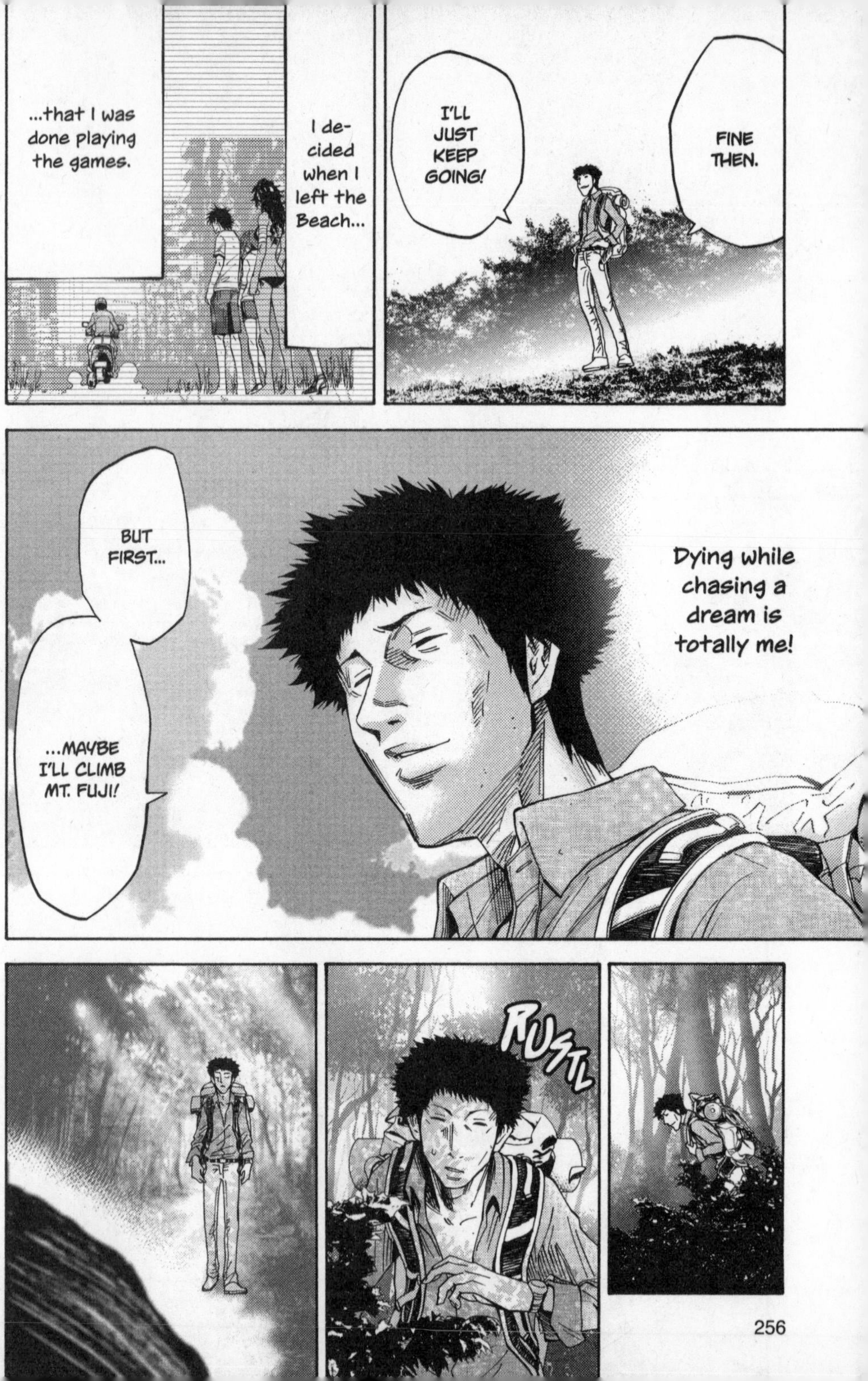
FINE THEN.
I'LL JUST KEEP GOING!
I de-cided when I left the Beach...
...that I was done playing the games.
Dying while chasing a dream is totally me!
BUT FIRST...
...MAYBE I'LL CLIMB MT. FUJI!
RUSTL

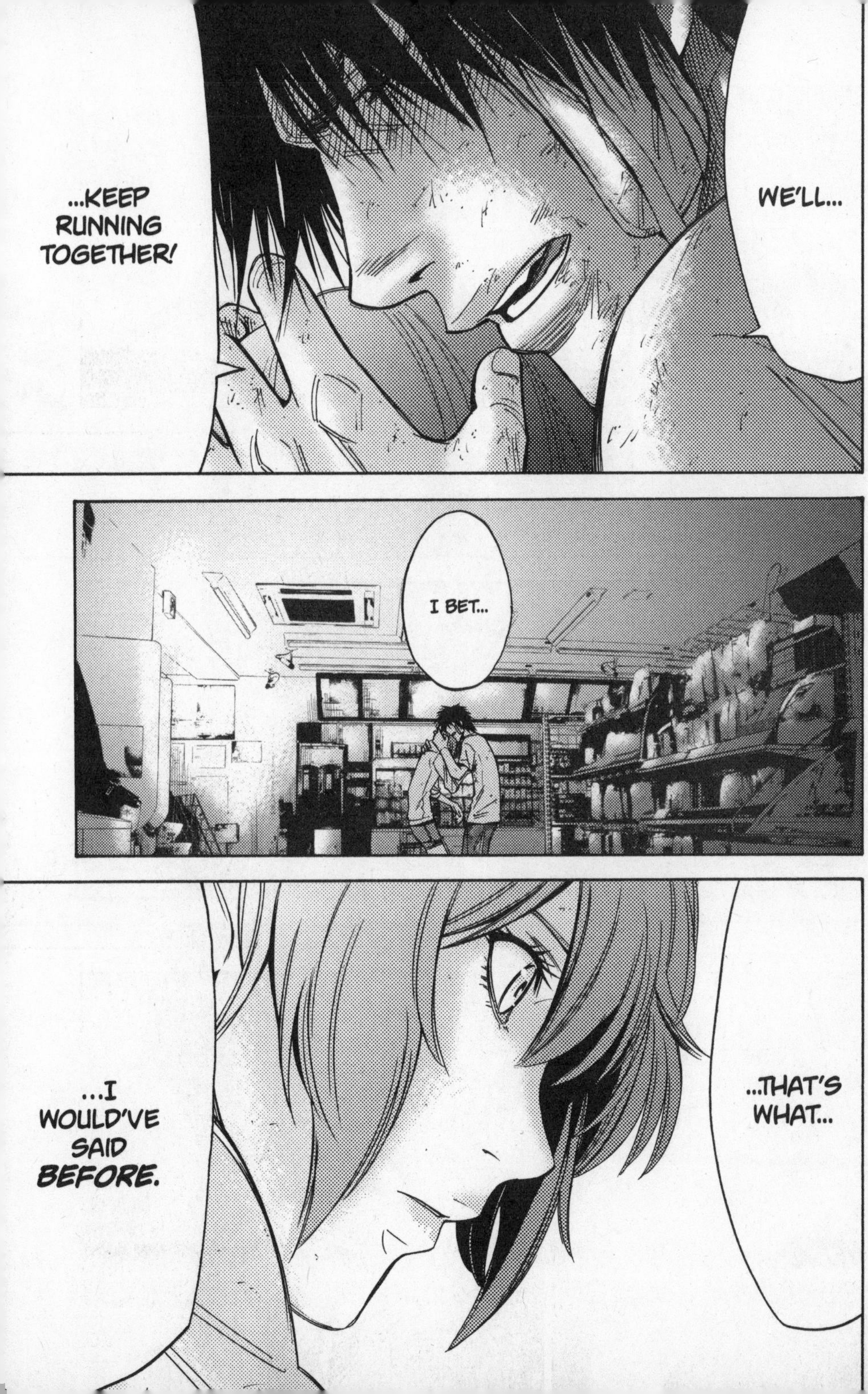
WE'LL...
...KEEP RUNNING TOGETHER!
I BET...
...THAT'S WHAT...
...I WOULD'VE SAID BEFORE.

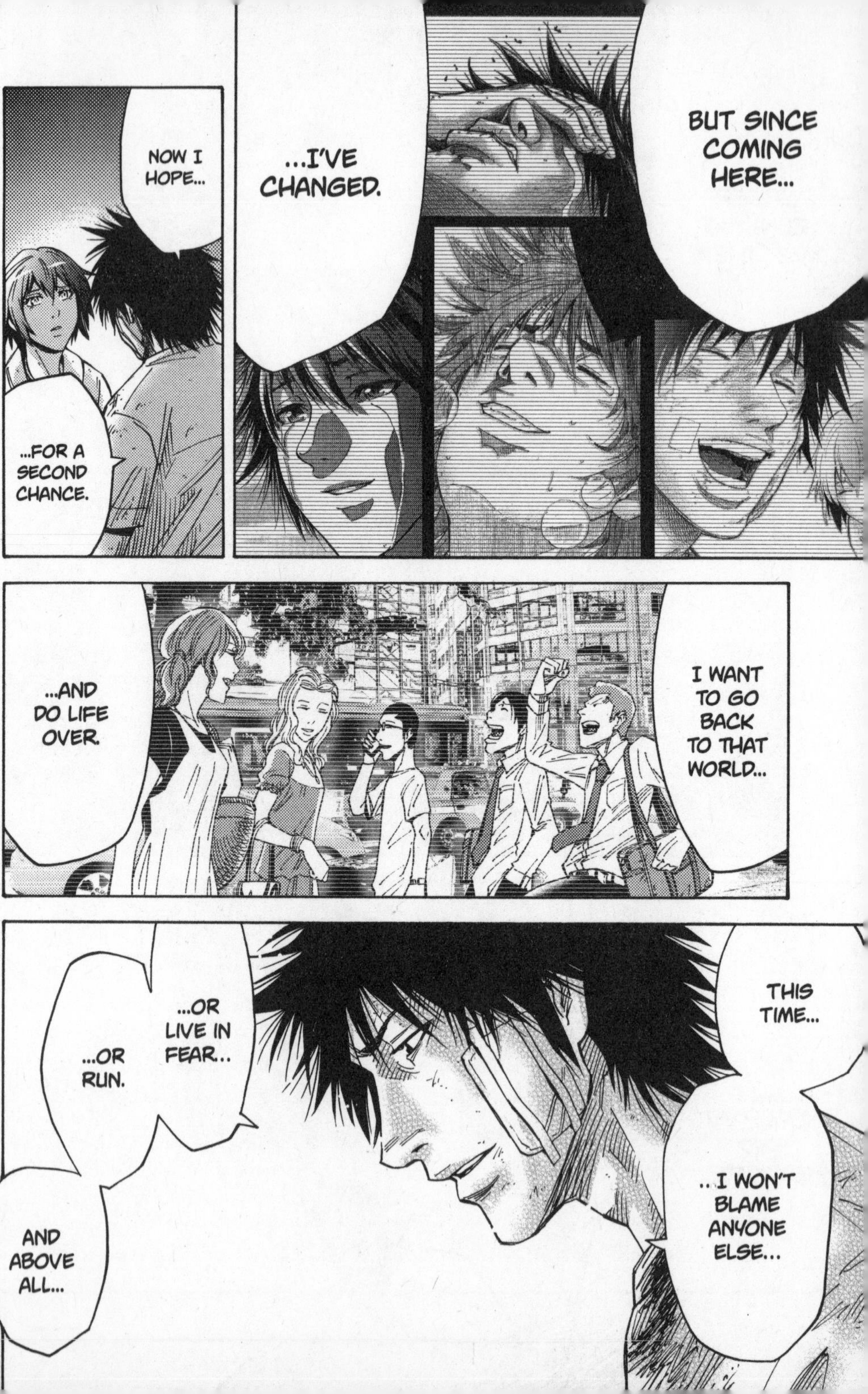
BUT SINCE COMING HERE...
...I'VE CHANGED.
NOW I HOPE...
...FOR A SECOND CHANCE.
I WANT TO GO BACK TO THAT WORLD...
...AND DO LIFE OVER.
THIS TIME...
...I WON'T BLAME ANYONE ELSE...
...OR LIVE IN FEAR...
...OR RUN.
AND ABOVE ALL...

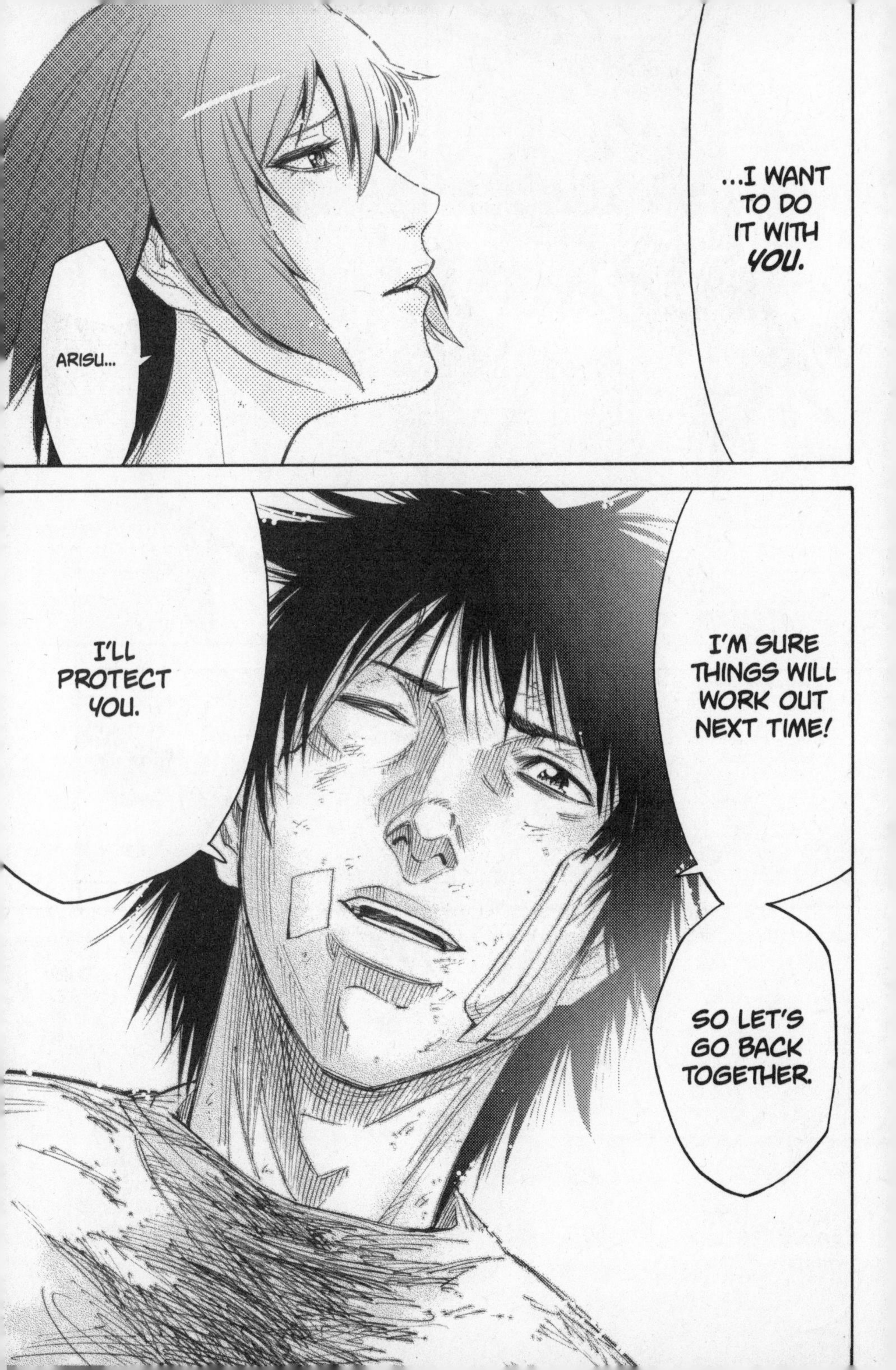
...I WANT TO DO IT WITH *YOU*.
ARISU...
I'M SURE THINGS WILL WORK OUT NEXT TIME!
SO LET'S GO BACK TOGETHER.
I'LL PROTECT YOU.

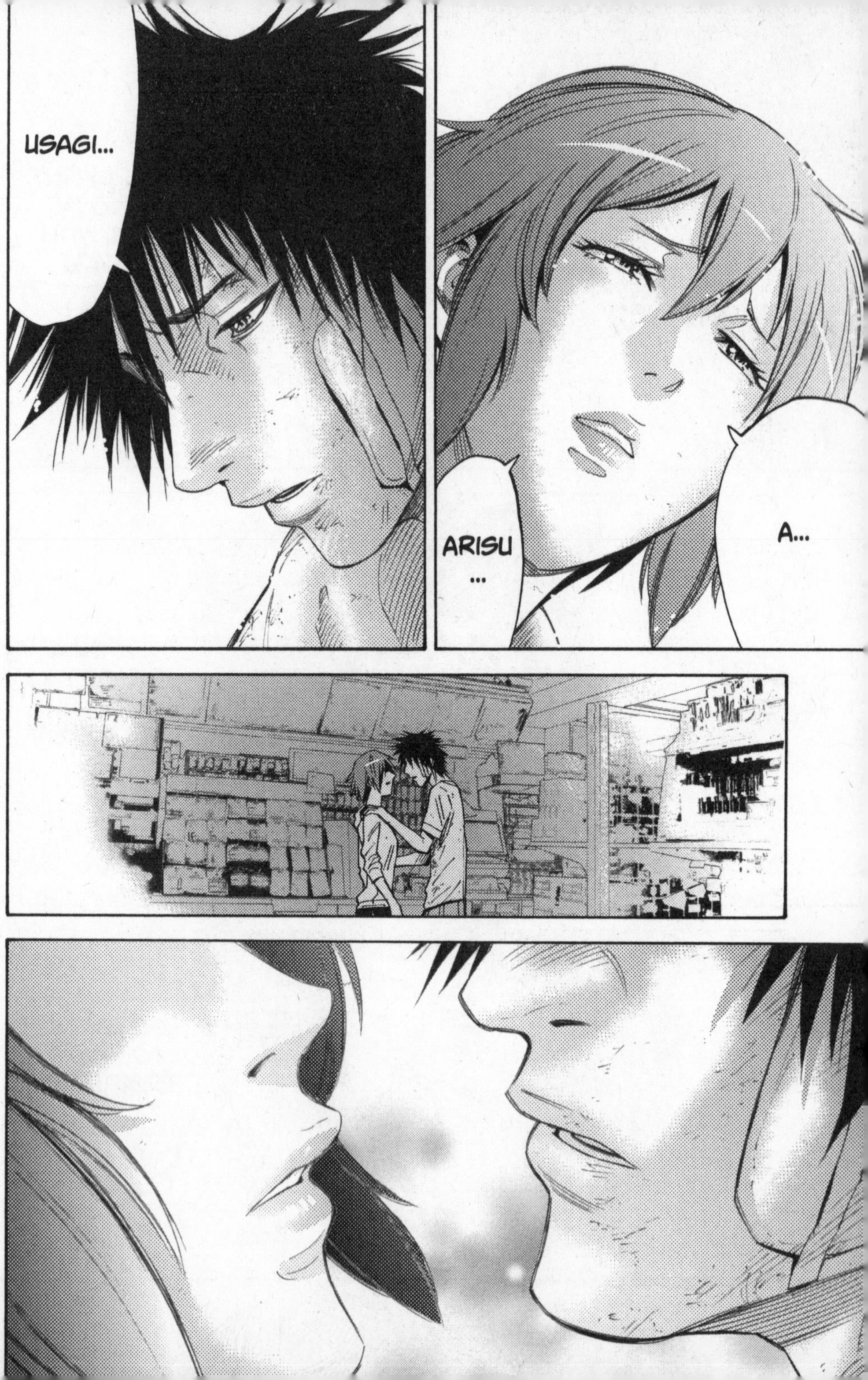
A...
ARISU ...
USAGI...

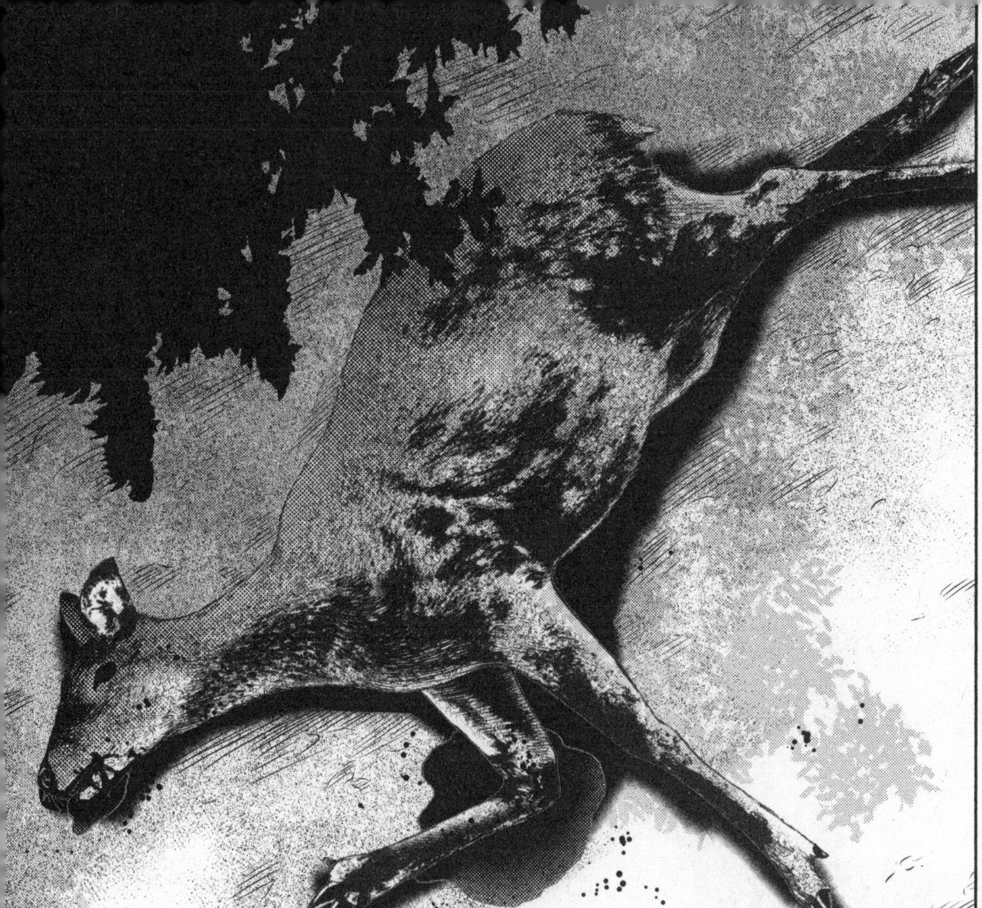
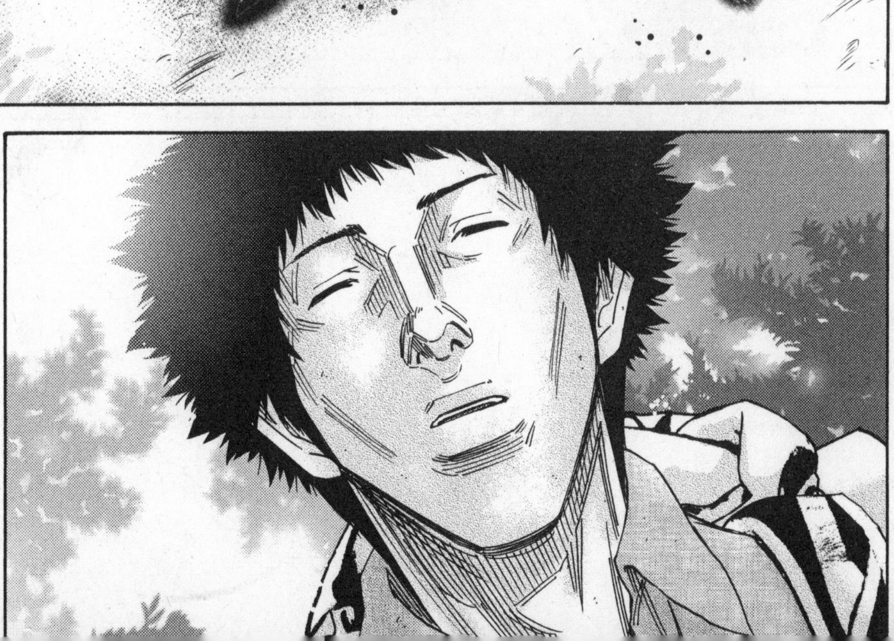

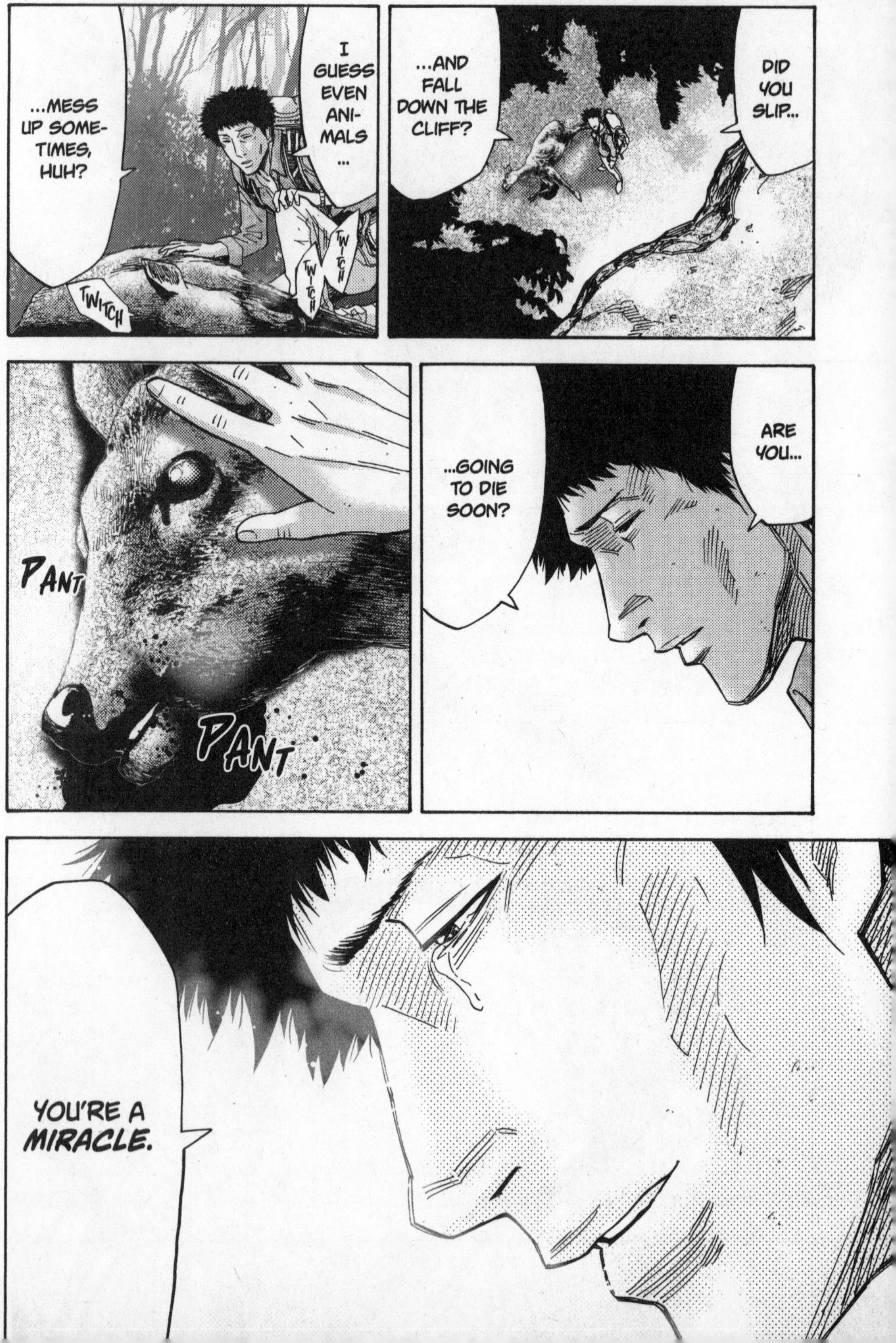
DID YOU SLIP...
...AND FALL DOWN THE CLIFF?
I GUESS EVEN ANIMALS...
...MESS UP SOMETIMES, HUH?
TWITCH
TWITCH
TWITCH
ARE YOU...
...GOING TO DIE SOON?
PANT
PANT
YOU'RE A MIRACLE.

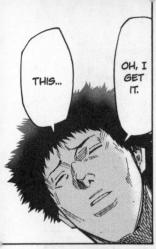

BUT WHY?
WHY...
...IS THIS SO BEAUTIFUL?
OH, I GET IT.
THIS...
...is life.
You try to live until the very end.
That itself is the gleam of life.

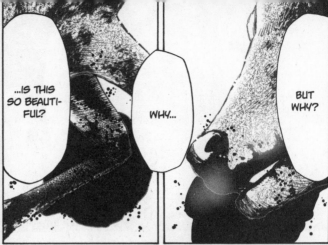

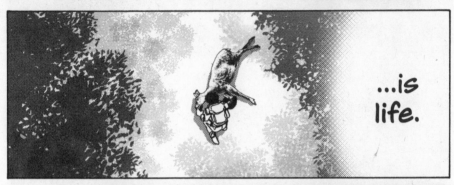

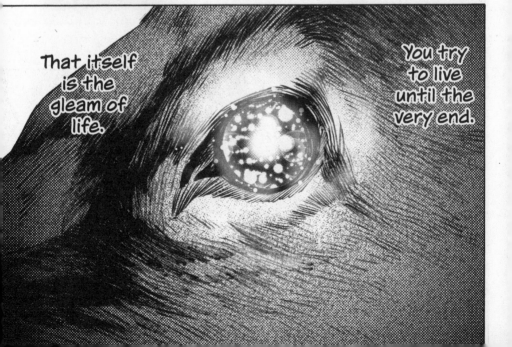

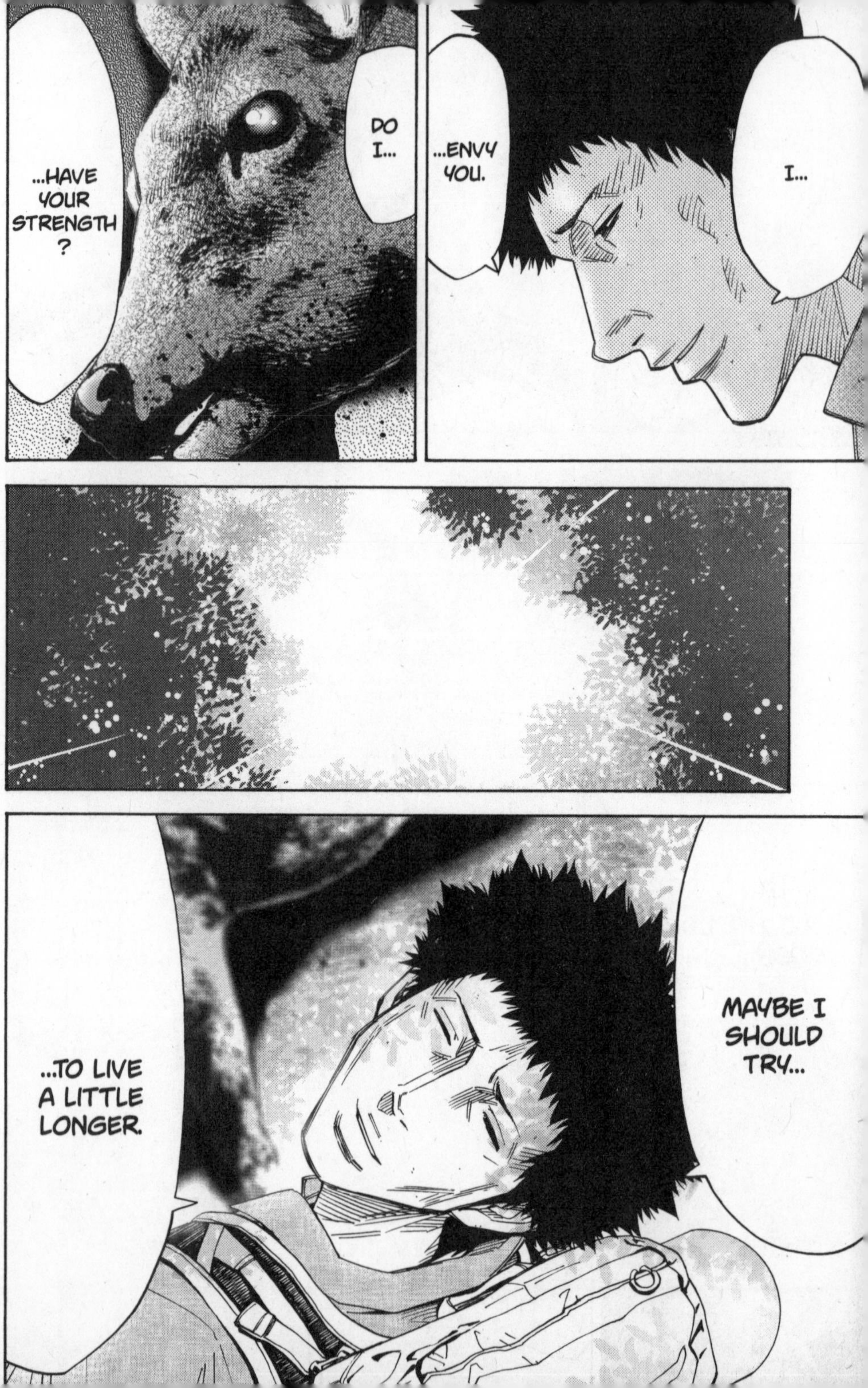
I...
...ENVY YOU.
DO I...
...HAVE YOUR STRENGTH?
MAYBE I SHOULD TRY...
...TO LIVE A LITTLE LONGER.

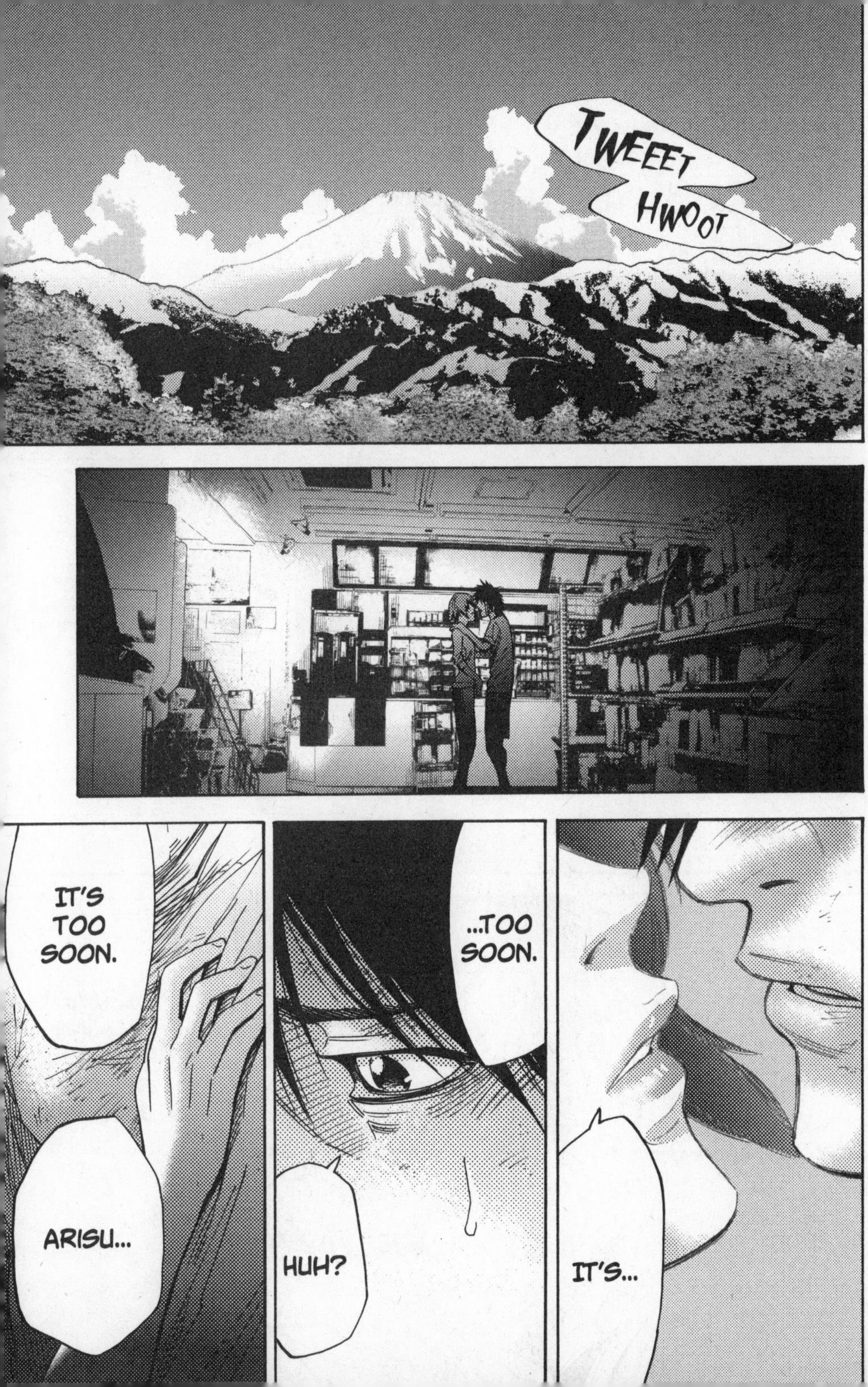
TWEEEET
HWOOT
IT'S...
...TOO SOON.
HUH?
IT'S TOO SOON.
ARISU...

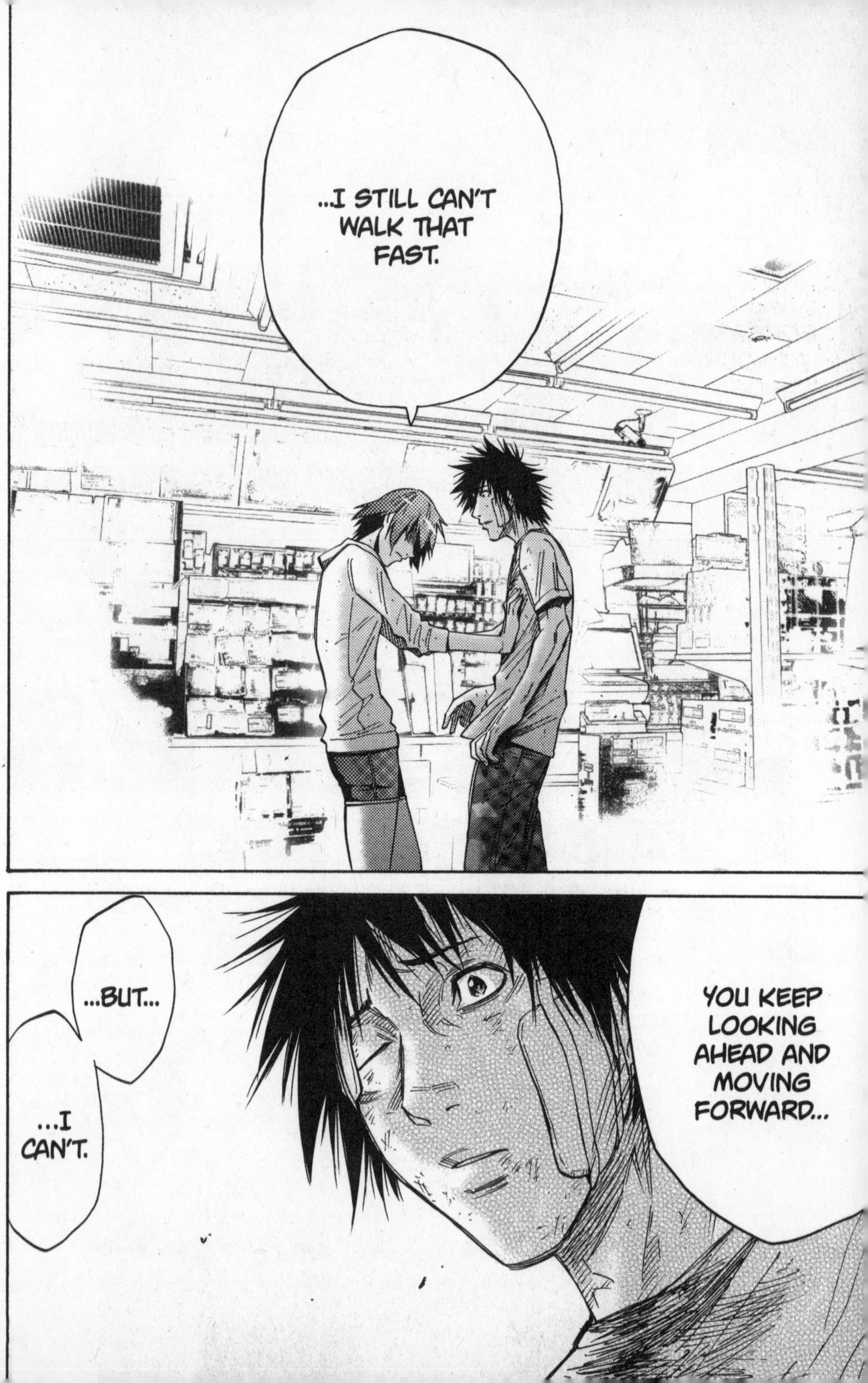
...I STILL CAN'T WALK THAT FAST.
YOU KEEP LOOKING AHEAD AND MOVING FORWARD...
...BUT...
...I CAN'T.

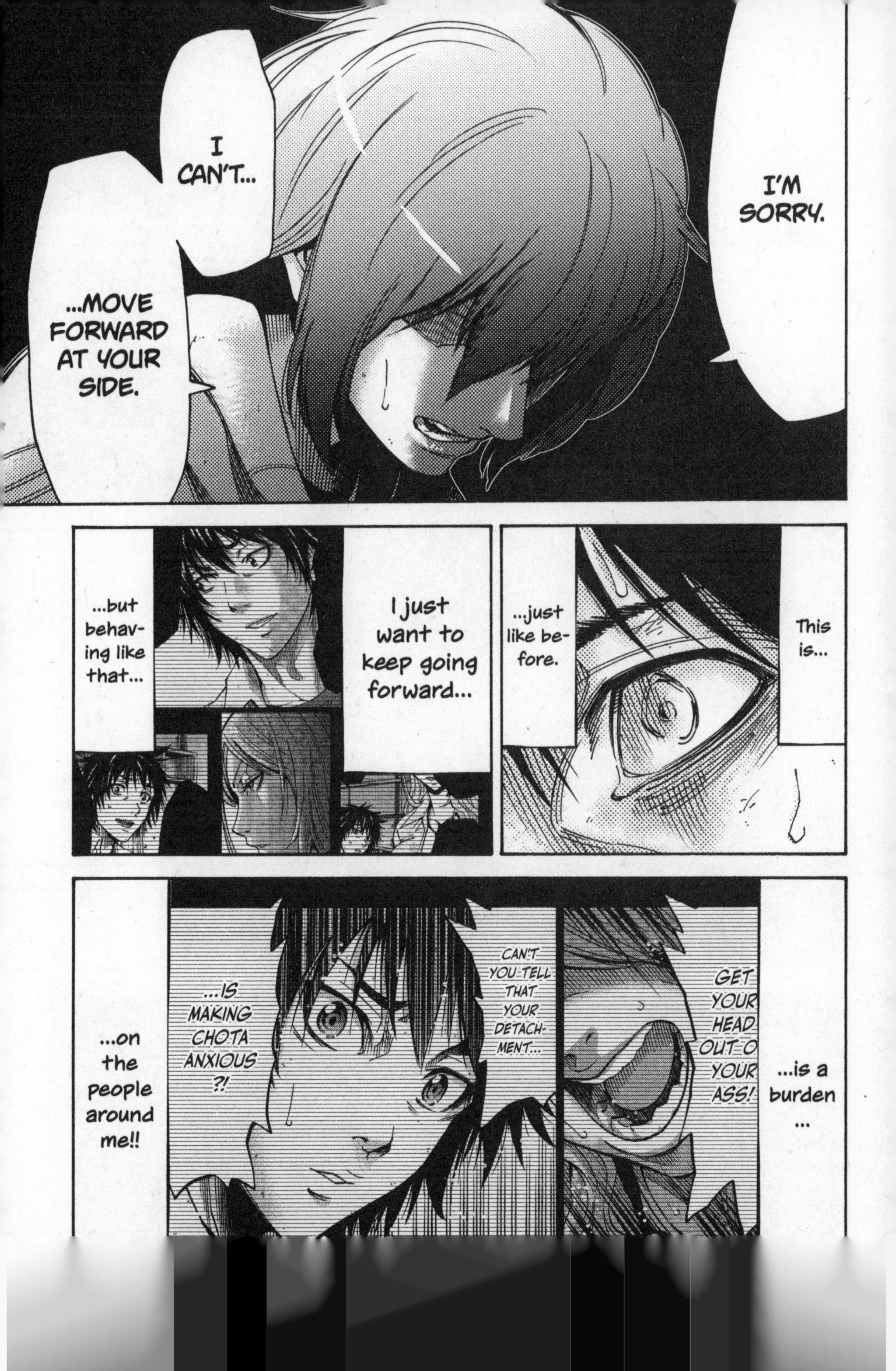
I'M SORRY.
I CAN'T...
...MOVE FORWARD AT YOUR SIDE.
This is...
...just like be-fore.
I just want to keep going forward...
...but behav-ing like that...
...is a burden ...
GET YOUR HEAD OUT O YOUR ASS!
CAN'T YOU TELL THAT YOUR DETACH-MENT...
...IS MAKING CHOTA ANXIOUS ?!
...on the people around me!!

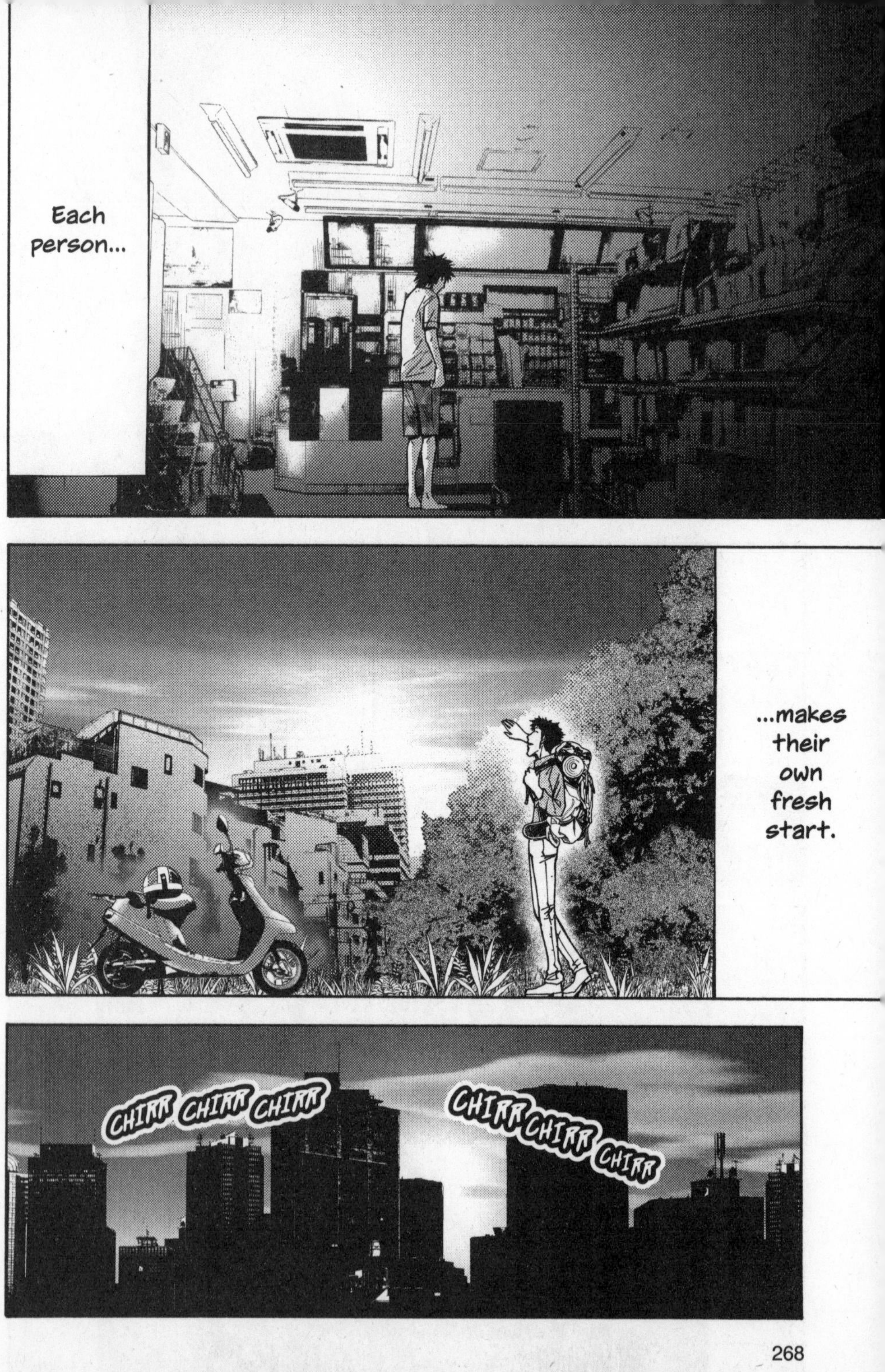
Each person...
...makes their own fresh start.
CHIRR CHIRR CHIRR
CHIRR CHIRR CHIRR

...

DAMN...

DAMN IT!!

AAARGH!!

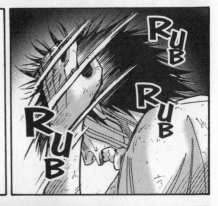

RUB

RUB

RUB

I've survived this bizarre and cruel world so far...

...but does that make me a saint?!

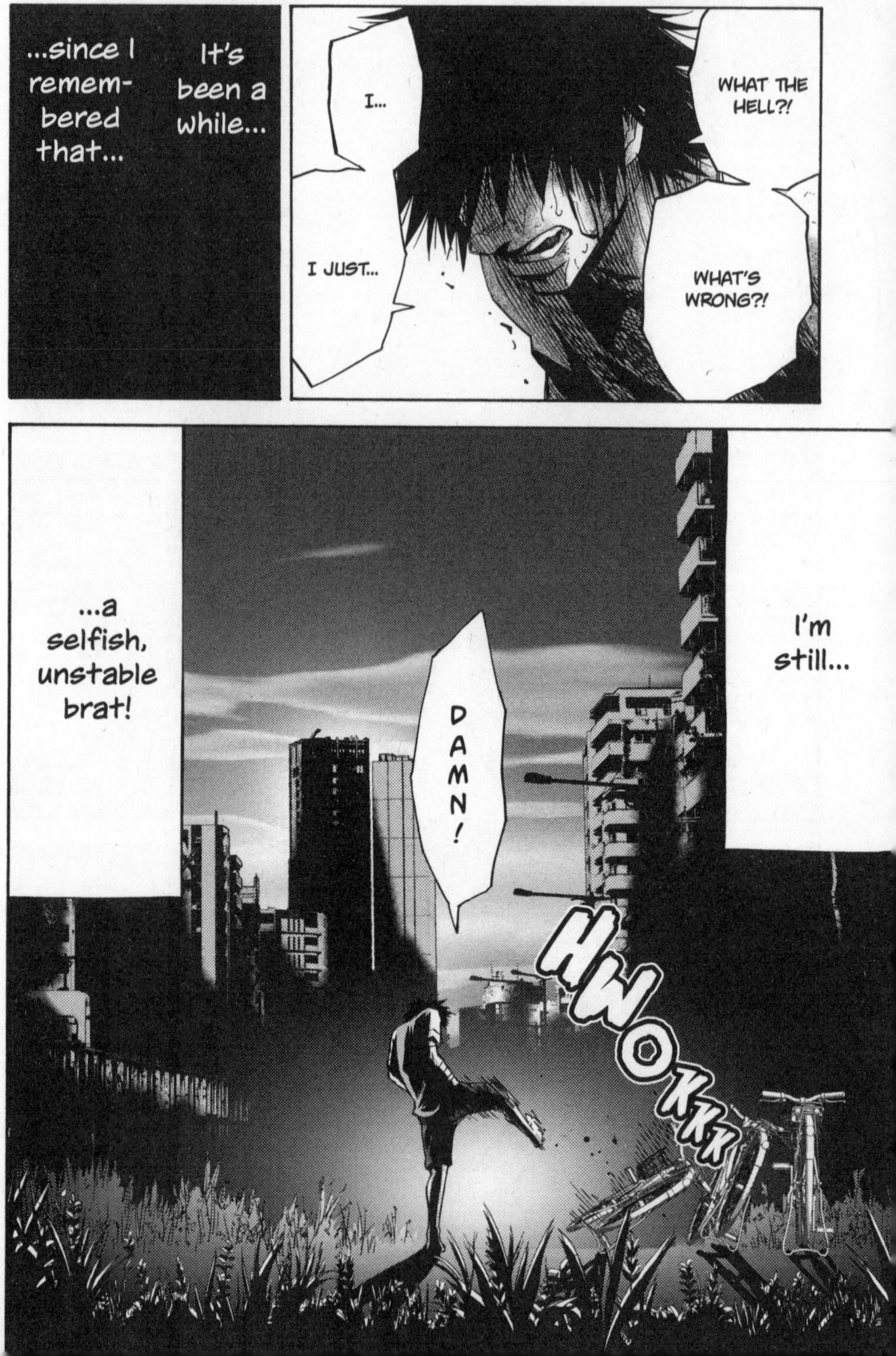
WHAT THE HELL?!
I...
WHAT'S WRONG?!
I JUST...
It's been a while...
...since I remembered that...
I'm still...
DAMN!
...a selfish, unstable brat!
HWOKKK

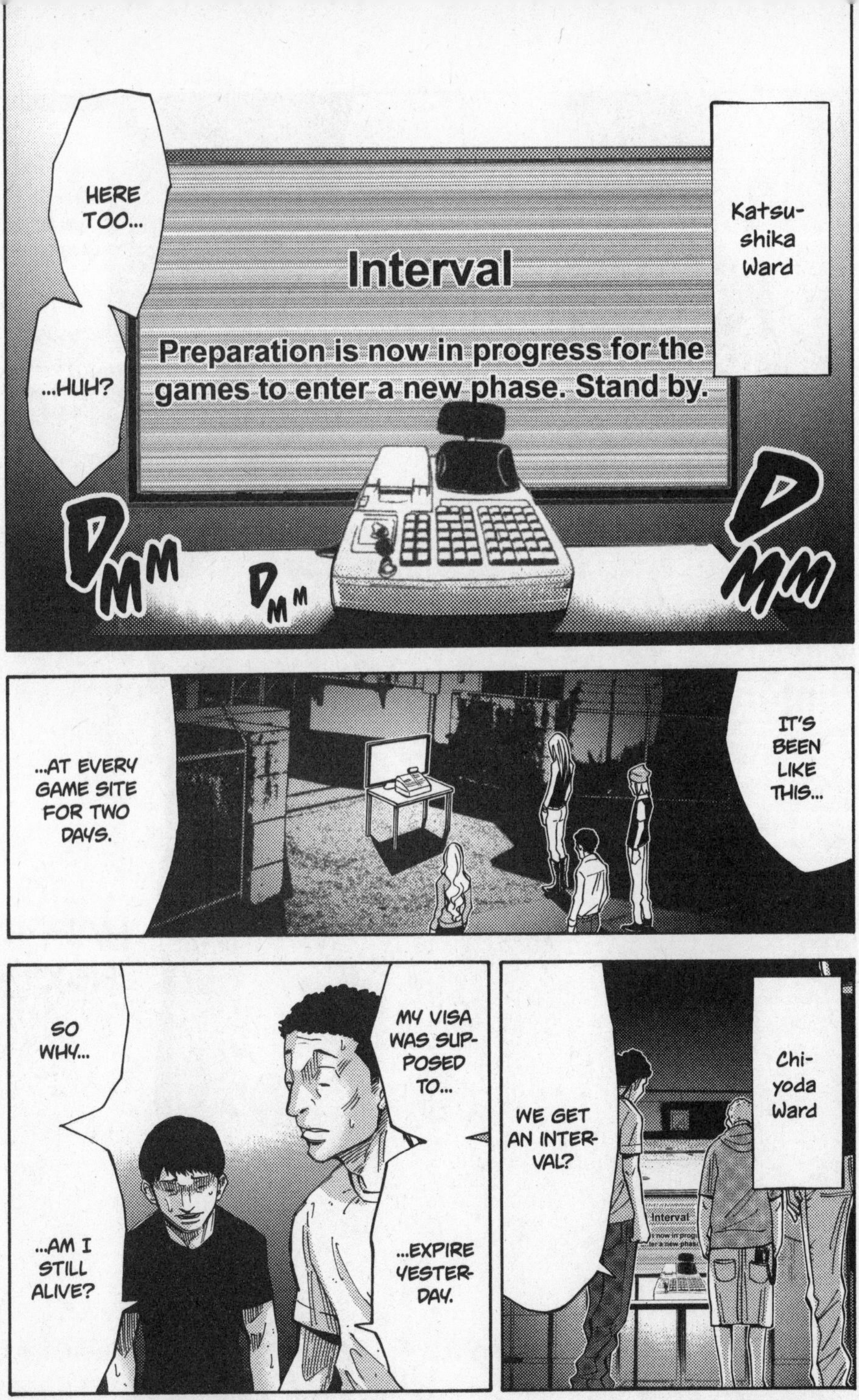
Katsu-
shika
Ward
HERE TOO...
Interval
Preparation is now in progress for the games to enter a new phase. Stand by.
...HUH?
DMMM
DMMM
DMMM
IT'S BEEN LIKE THIS...
...AT EVERY GAME SITE FOR TWO DAYS.
Chi-
yoda
Ward
WE GET AN INTER-VAL?
Interval
MY VISA WAS SUP-POSED TO...
...EXPIRE YESTER-DAY.
SO WHY...
...AM I STILL ALIVE?

CHAPTER 21: Interval

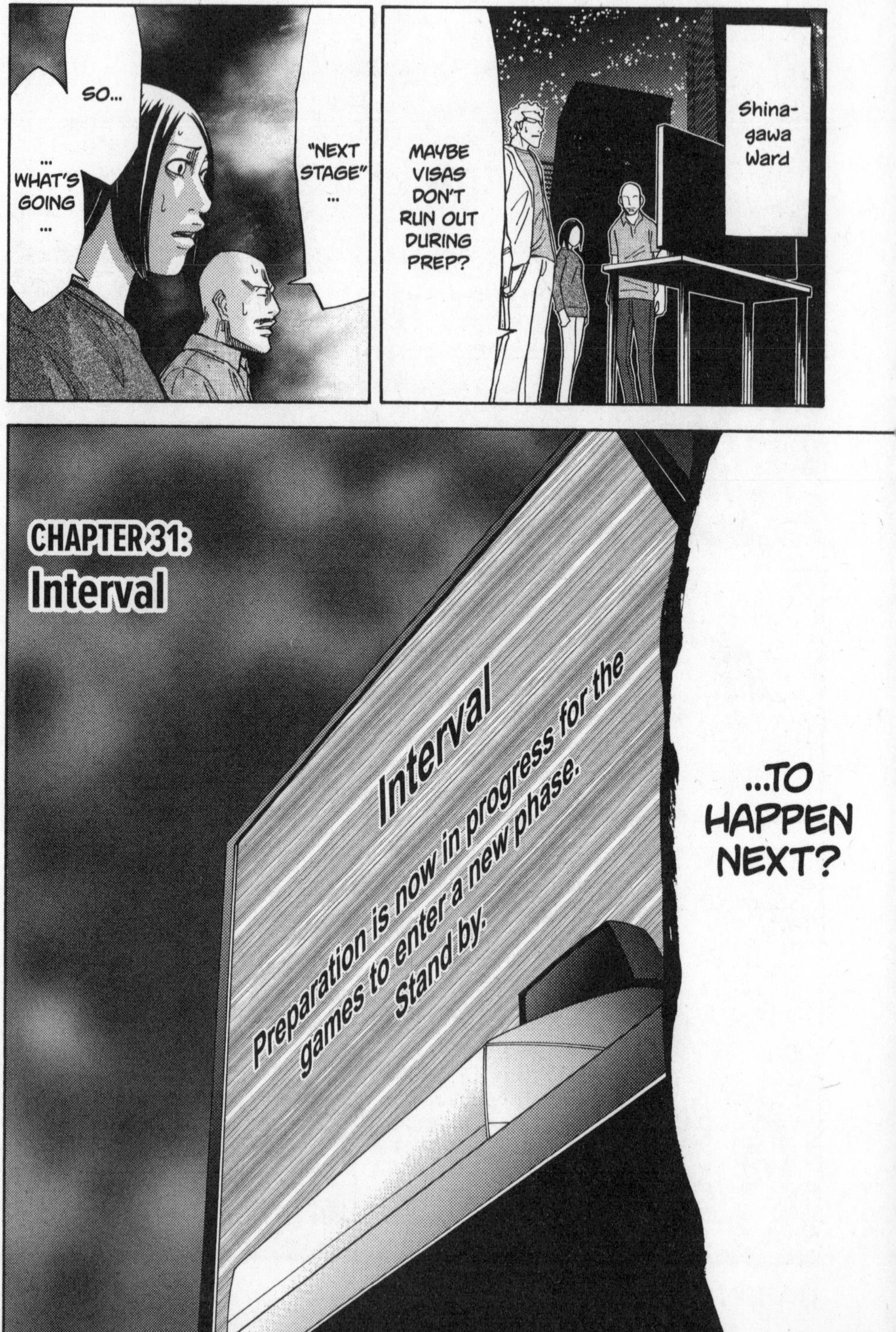
Shinagawa Ward
MAYBE VISAS DON'T RUN OUT DURING PREP?
"NEXT STAGE" ...
SO...
... WHAT'S GOING ...
CHAPTER 31:
Interval
Interval
Preparation is now in progress for the games to enter a new phase.
Stand by.
...TO HAPPEN NEXT?

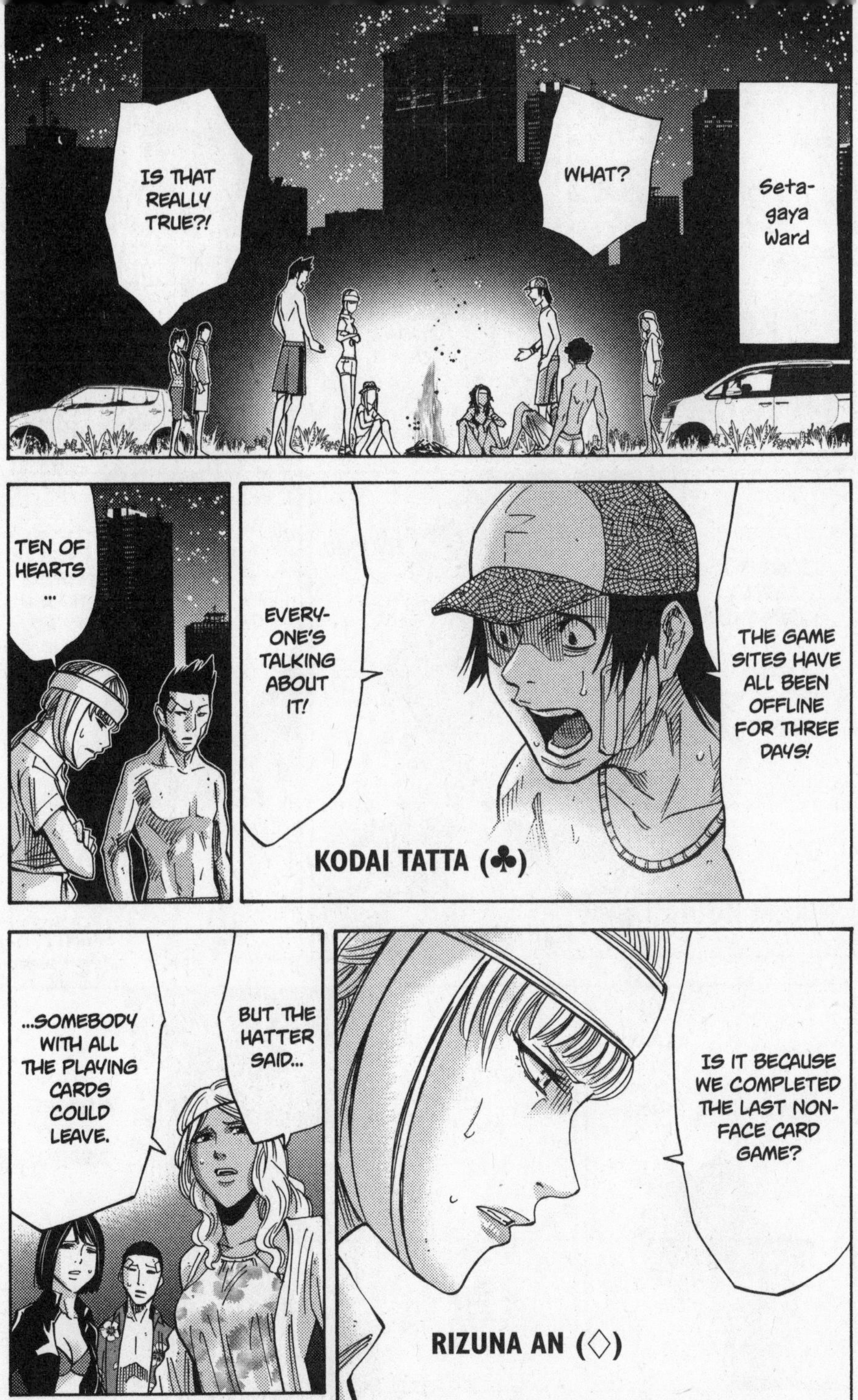

Seta-gaya Ward
WHAT?
IS THAT REALLY TRUE?!
THE GAME SITES HAVE ALL BEEN OFFLINE FOR THREE DAYS!
EVERY-ONE'S TALKING ABOUT IT!
KODAI TATTA (♣)
TEN OF HEARTS ...
IS IT BECAUSE WE COMPLETED THE LAST NON-FACE CARD GAME?
RIZUNA AN (♢)
BUT THE HATTER SAID...
...SOMEBODY WITH ALL THE PLAYING CARDS COULD LEAVE.

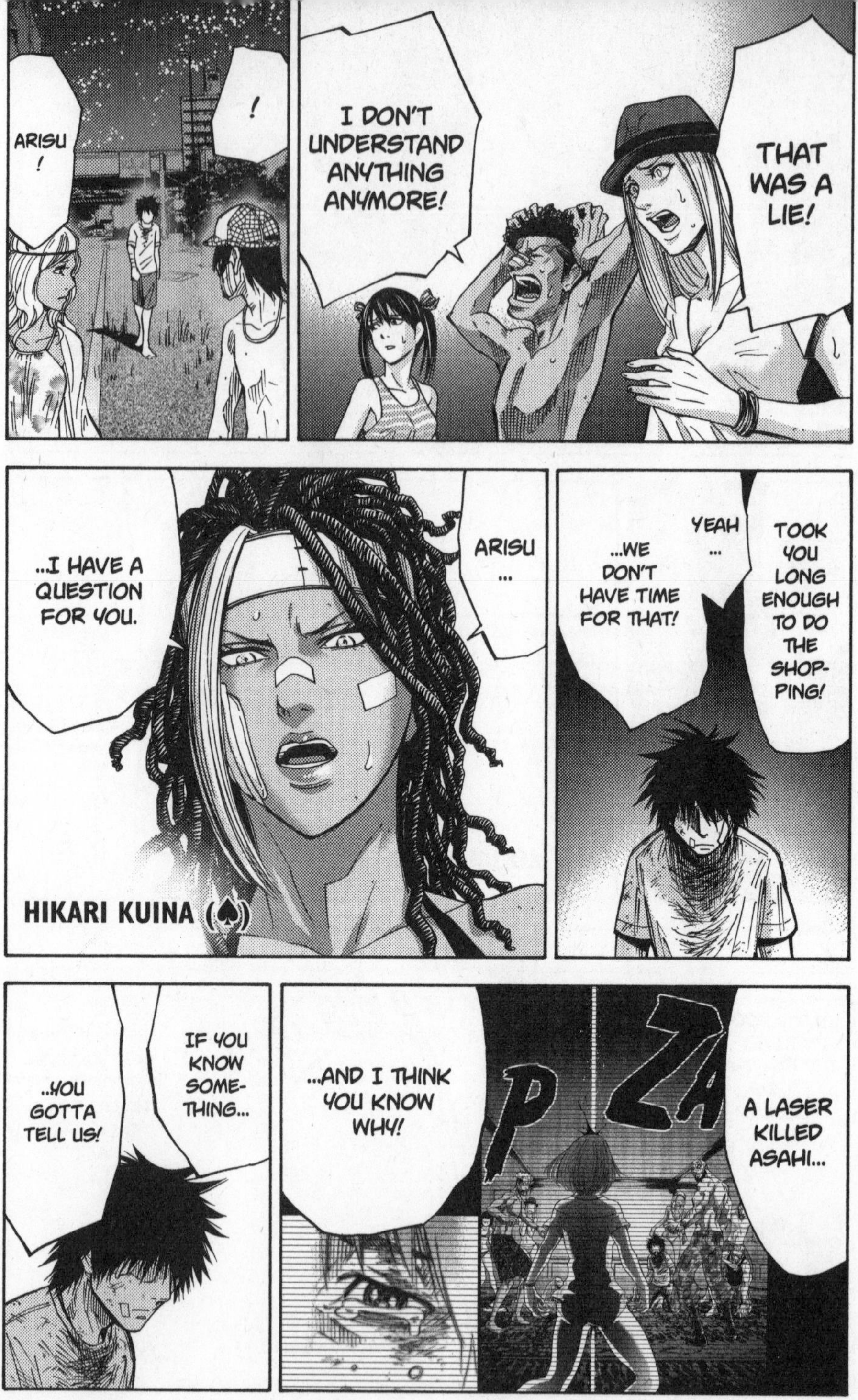
THAT WAS A LIE!
I DON'T UNDERSTAND ANYTHING ANYMORE!
!
ARISU!
TOOK YOU LONG ENOUGH TO DO THE SHOP-PING!
YEAH...
...WE DON'T HAVE TIME FOR THAT!
ARISU...
...I HAVE A QUESTION FOR YOU.
HIKARI KUINA (♠)
A LASER KILLED ASAHI...
ZAP
...AND I THINK YOU KNOW WHY!
IF YOU KNOW SOME-THING...
...YOU GOTTA TELL US!

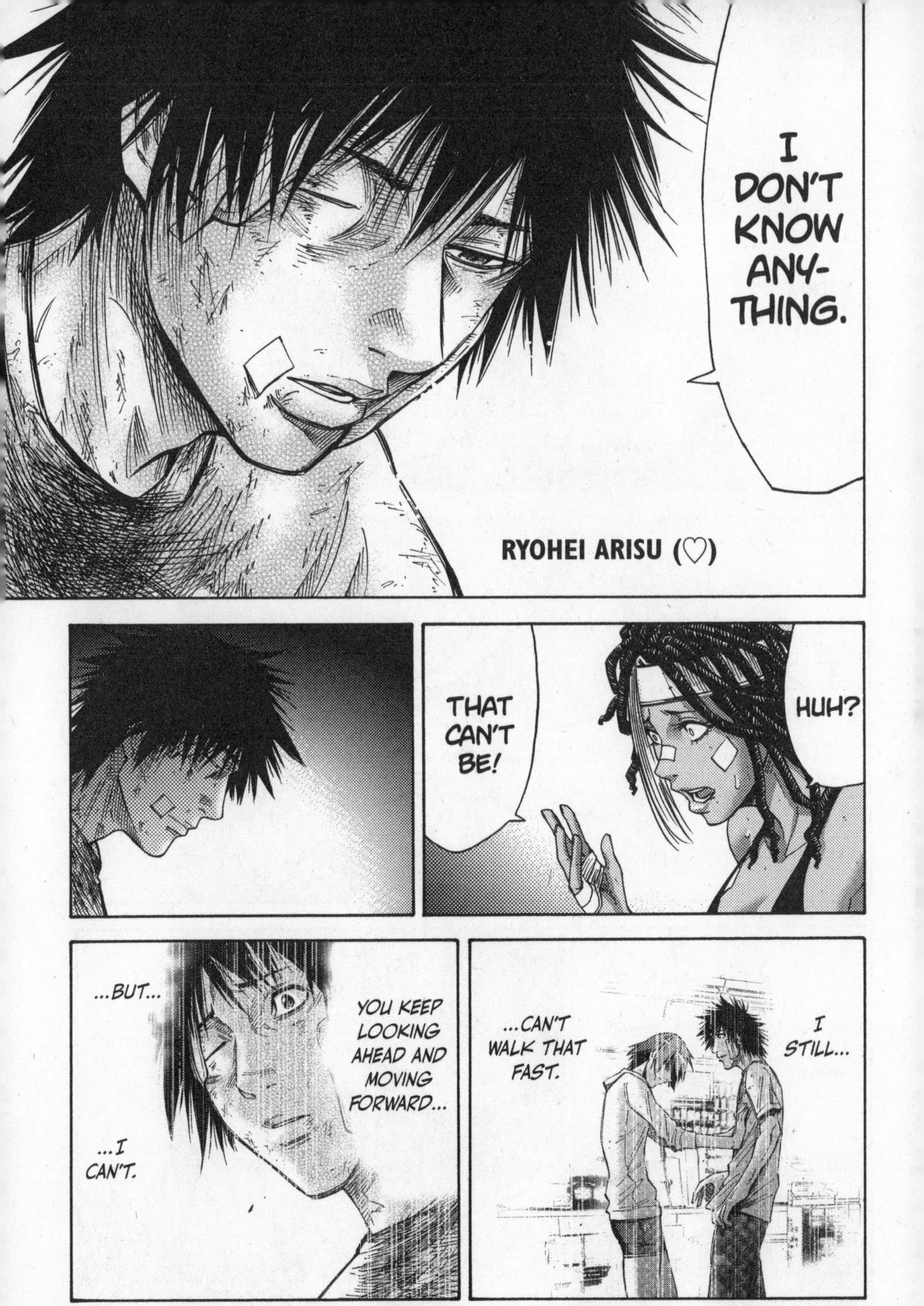
I DON'T KNOW ANY-THING.
RYOHEI ARISU (♡)
HUH?
THAT CAN'T BE!
I STILL...
...CAN'T WALK THAT FAST.
YOU KEEP LOOKING AHEAD AND MOVING FORWARD...
...BUT...
...I CAN'T.

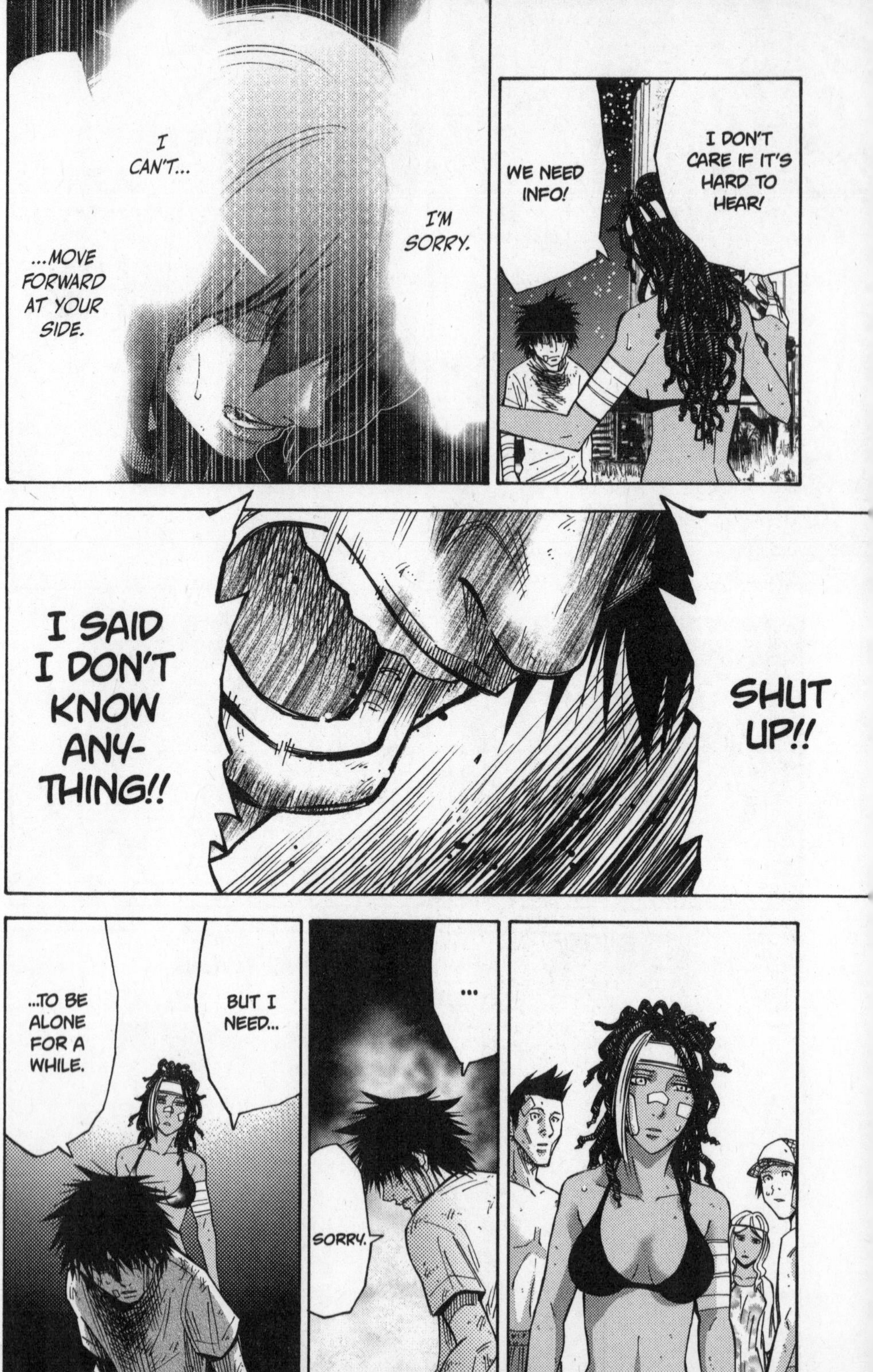
I DON'T CARE IF IT'S HARD TO HEAR!
WE NEED INFO!
I'M SORRY.
I CAN'T...
...MOVE FORWARD AT YOUR SIDE.
SHUT UP!!
I SAID I DON'T KNOW ANYTHING!!
...
SORRY.
BUT I NEED...
...TO BE ALONE FOR A WHILE.

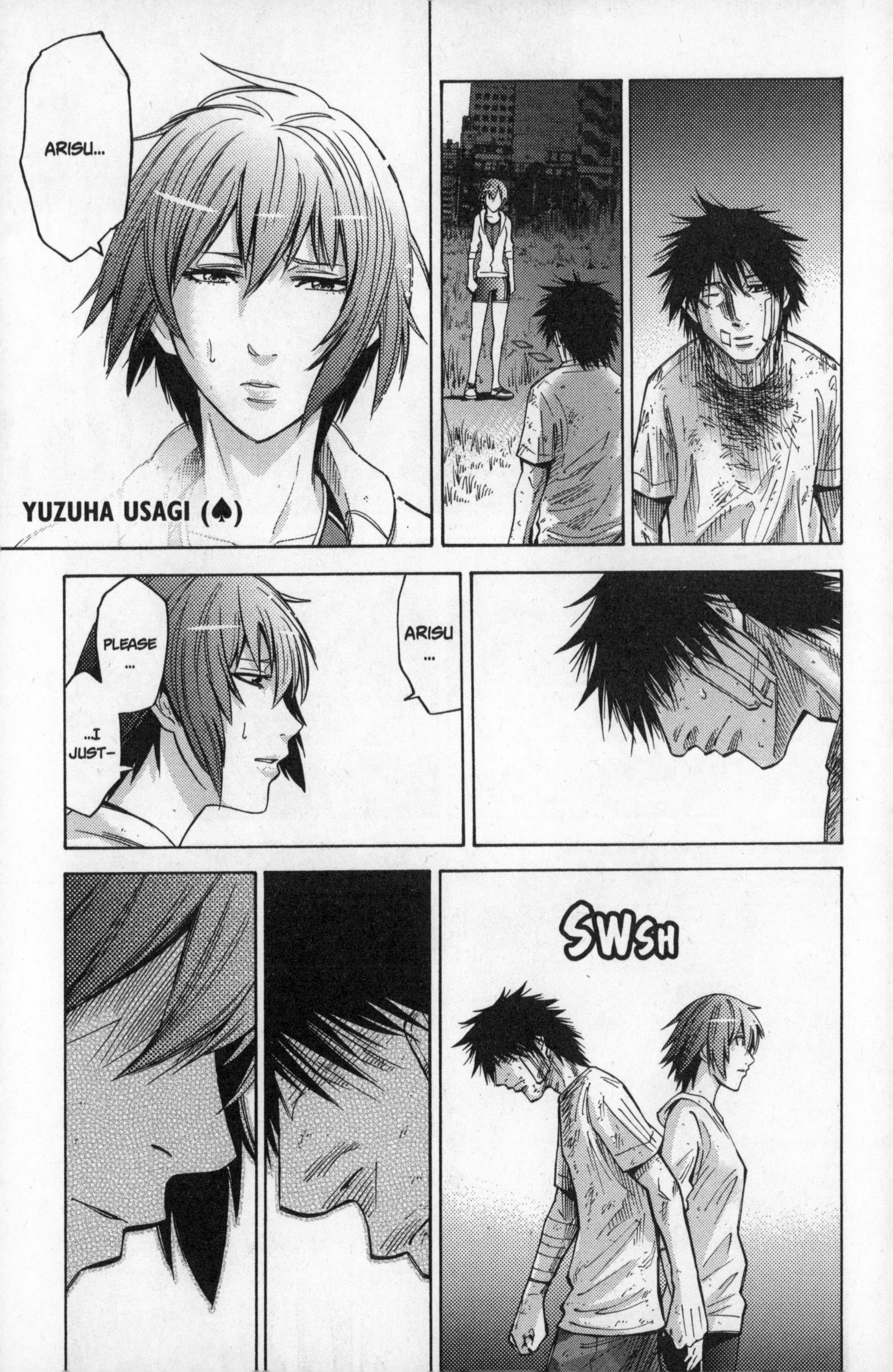
ARISU...
YUZUHA USAGI (♠)
ARISU ...
PLEASE ...
...I JUST-
SWSH

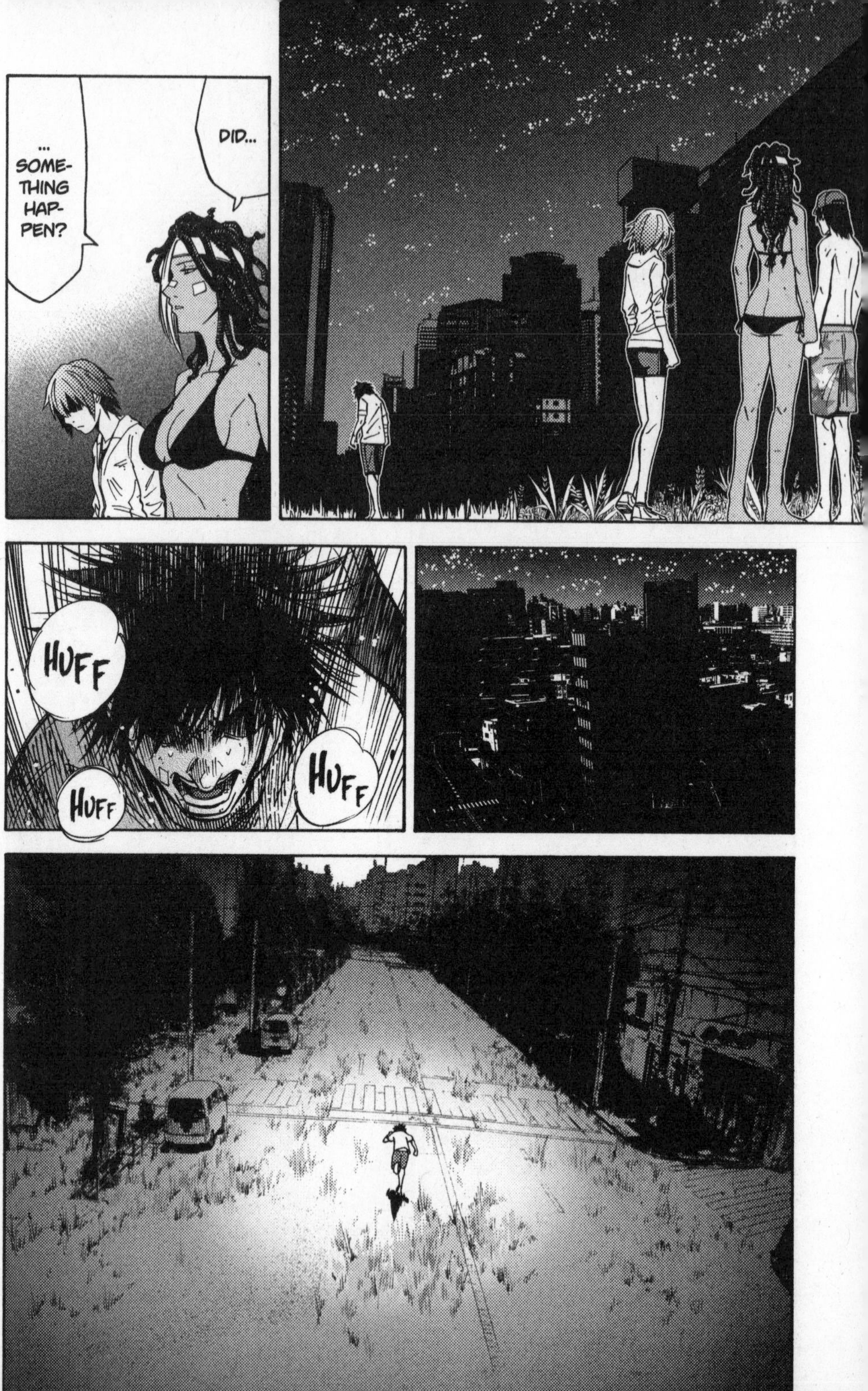
DID...
... SOME-THING HAP-PEN?
HUFF
HUFF
HUFF

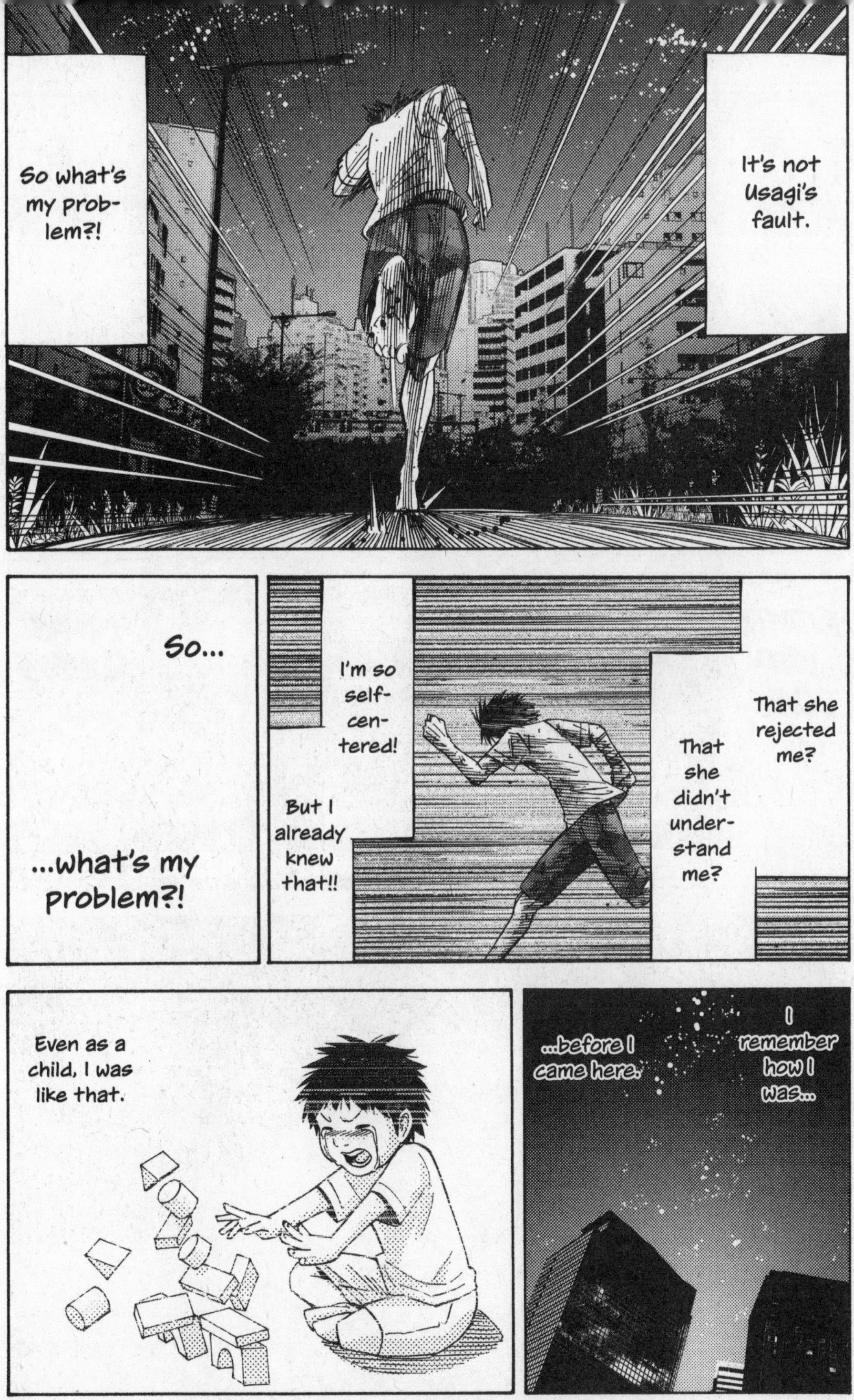
It's not Usagi's fault.
So what's my prob-lem?!
That she rejected me?
That she didn't under-stand me?
I'm so self-cen-tered!
But I already knew that!!
So...
...what's my problem?!
I remember how I was...
...before I came here.
Even as a child, I was like that.

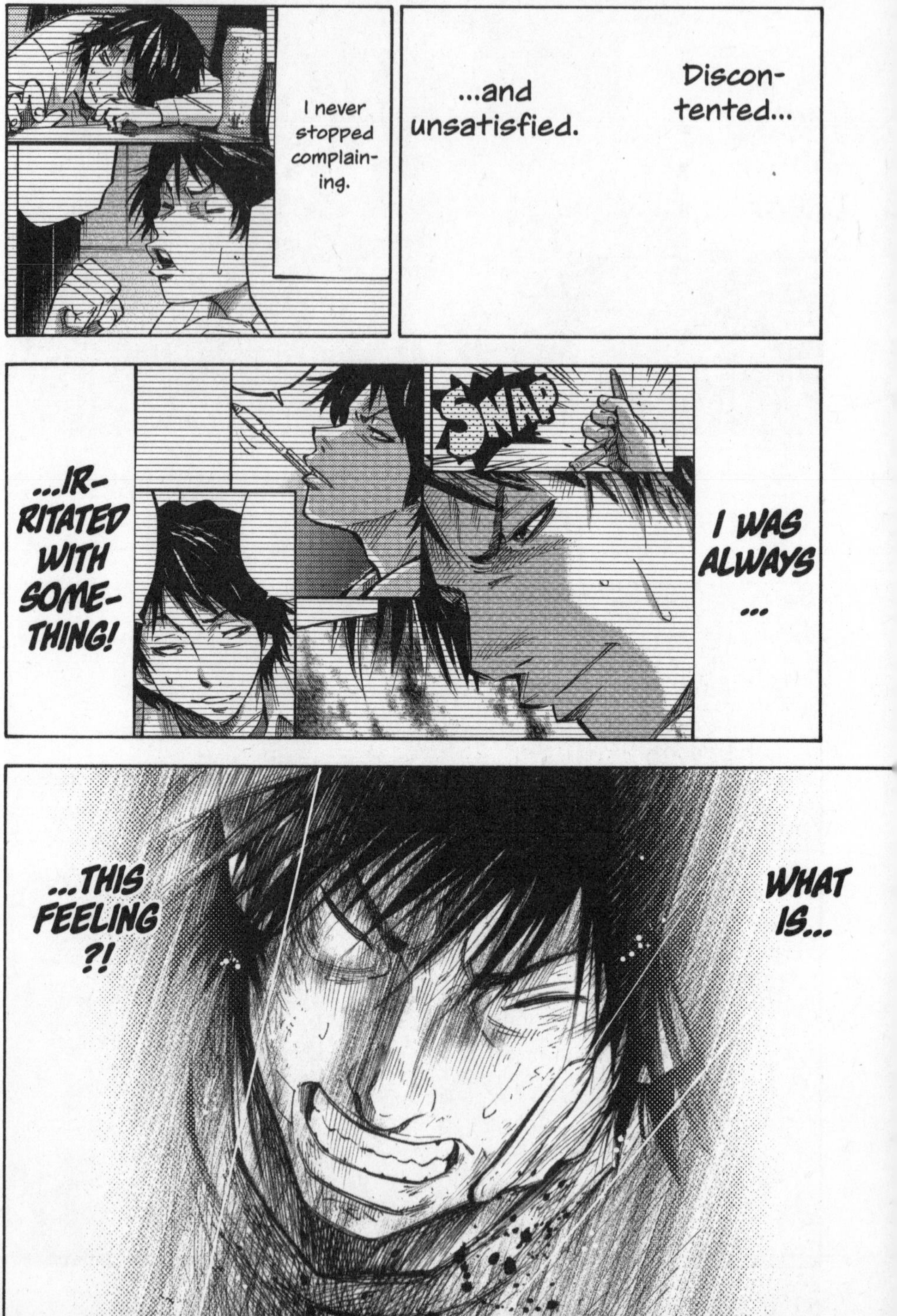
Discon-tented...
...and unsatisfied.
I never stopped complain-ing.
I WAS ALWAYS...
SNAP
...IR-RITATED WITH SOME-THING!
WHAT IS...
...THIS FEELING?!

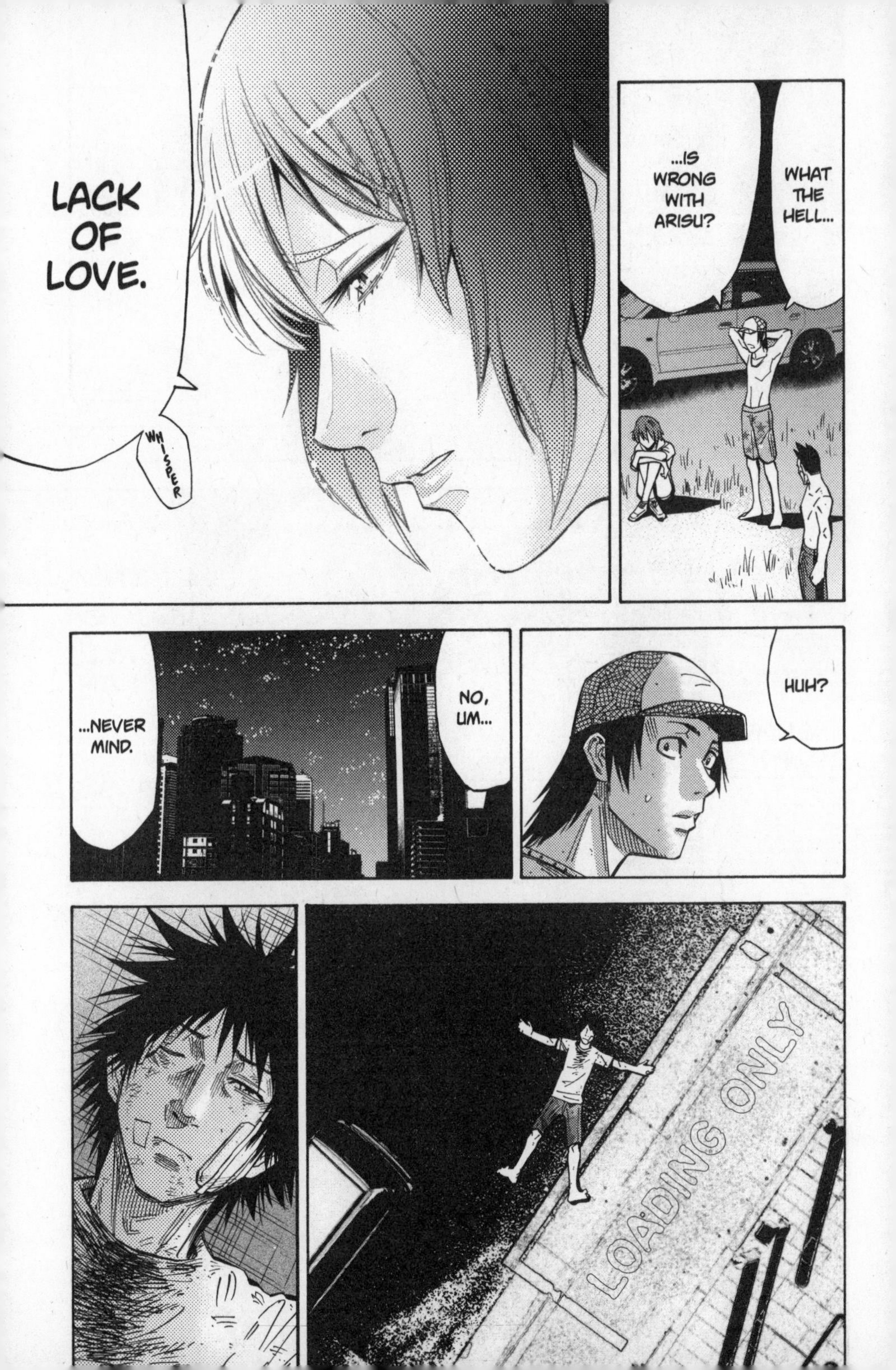
WHAT THE HELL...
...IS WRONG WITH ARISU?
LACK OF LOVE.
WHISPER
HUH?
NO, UM...
...NEVER MIND.
LOADING ONLY

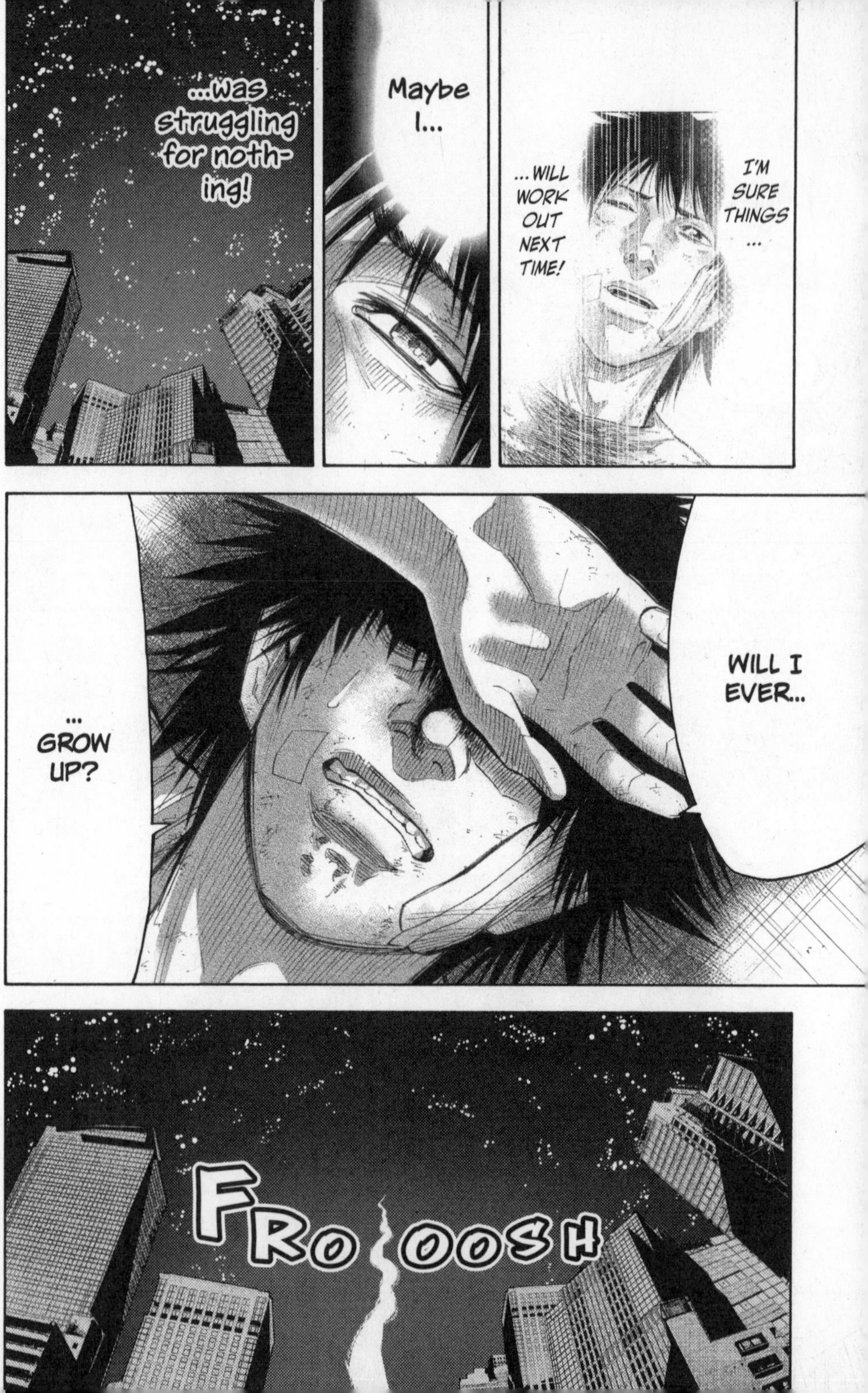
I'M SURE THINGS ...
...WILL WORK OUT NEXT TIME!
Maybe I...
...was struggling for nothing!
WILL I EVER...
... GROW UP?
FROOOSH

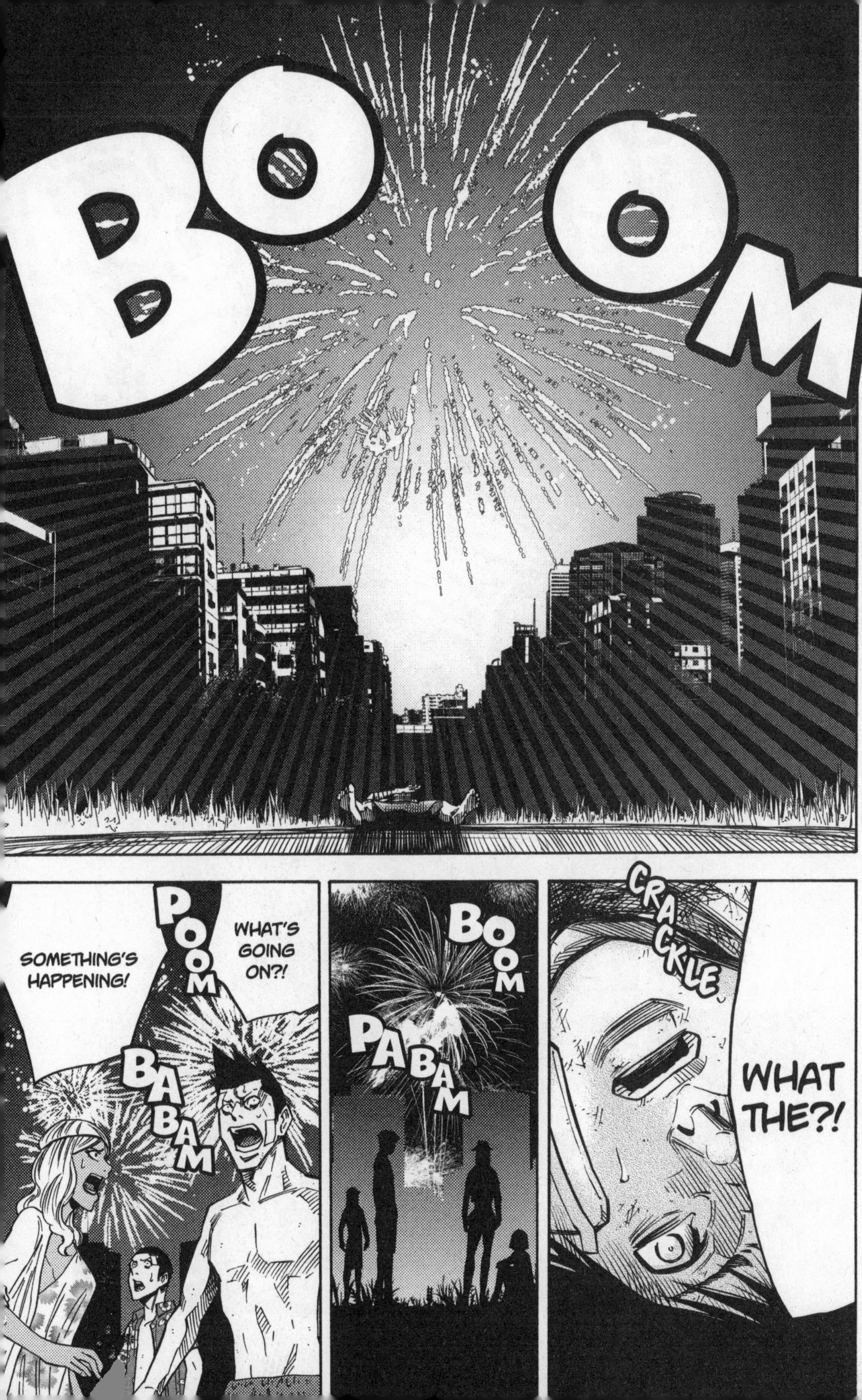
BOOM
CRACKLE
WHAT THE?!
BOOM
PABAM
WHAT'S GOING ON?!
POOM
SOMETHING'S HAPPENING!
BABAM

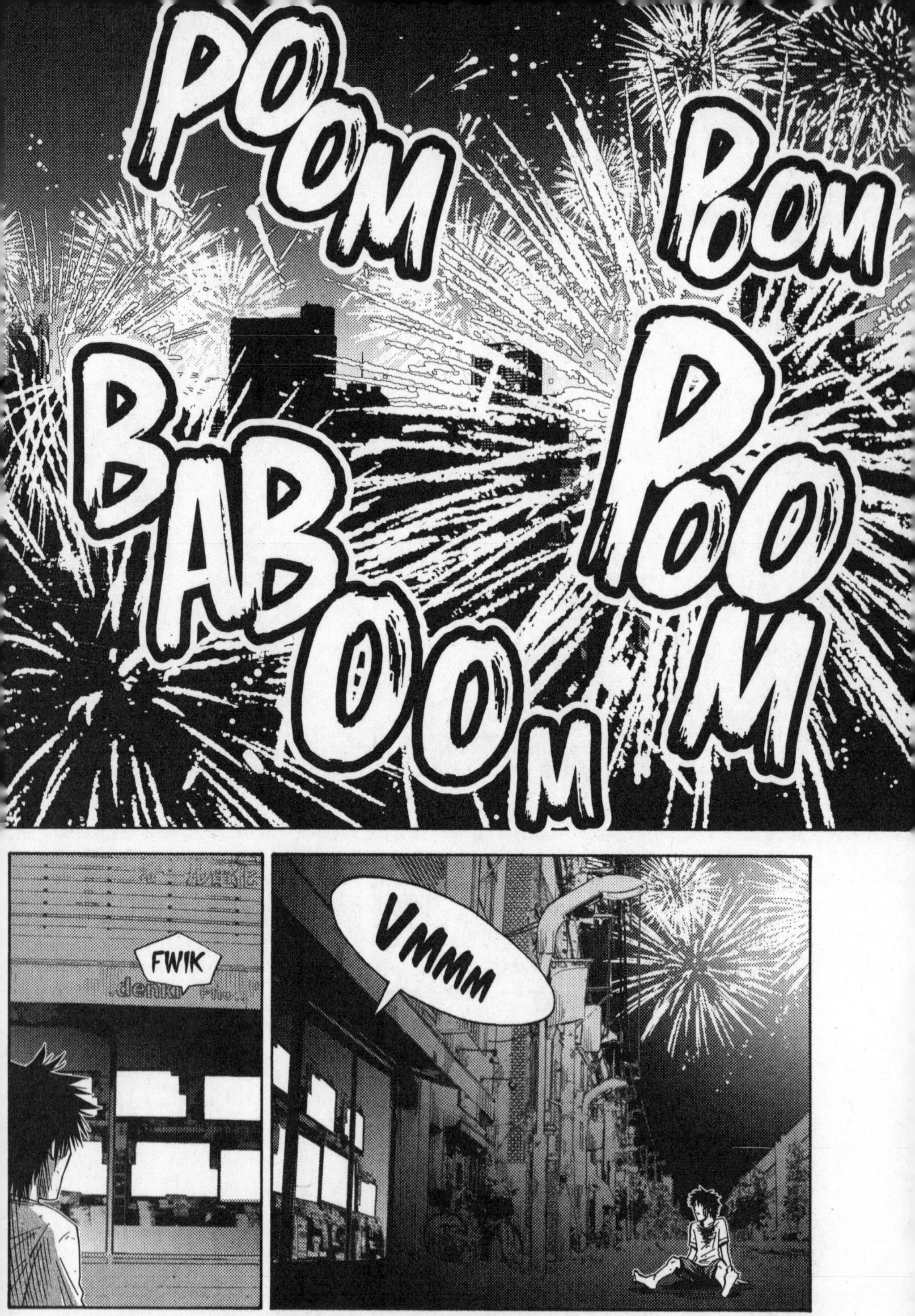
POOM
POOM
POOM
BABOOM
VMMM
FWIK

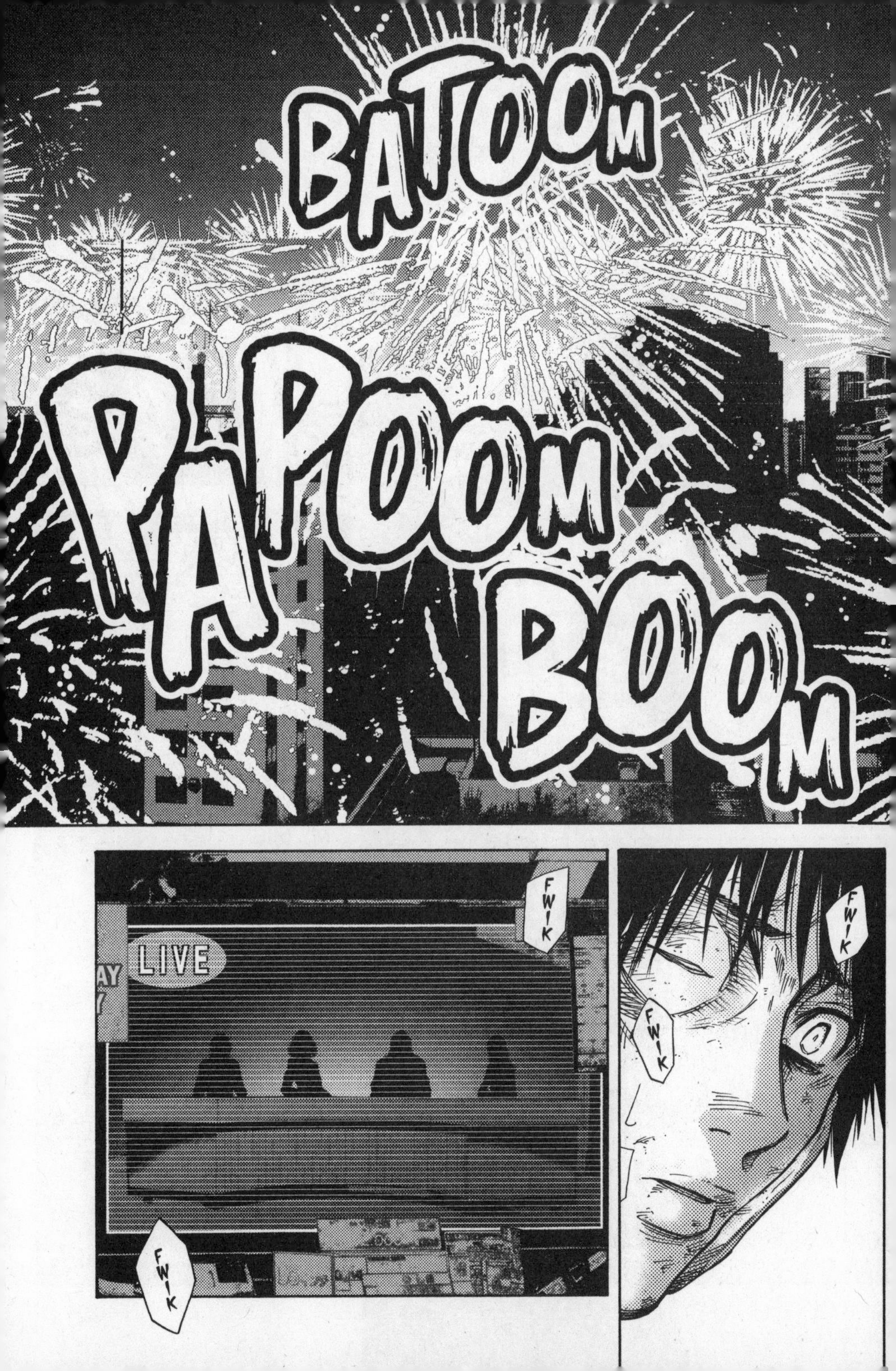
BATOOM
PAPOOM
BOOOM
FWIK
FWIK
FWIK
LIVE
FWIK

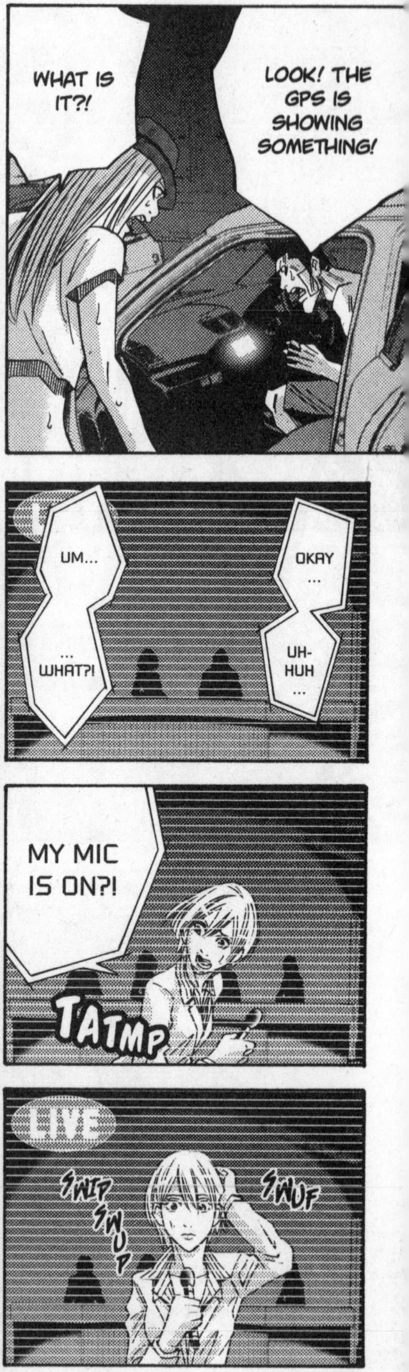
LOOK! THE GPS IS SHOWING SOMETHING!
WHAT IS IT?!
LIVE
OKAY ... UH-HUH ...
UM... ... WHAT?!
MY MIC IS ON?!
TATMP
LIVE
SWUF
SWIP SWUP
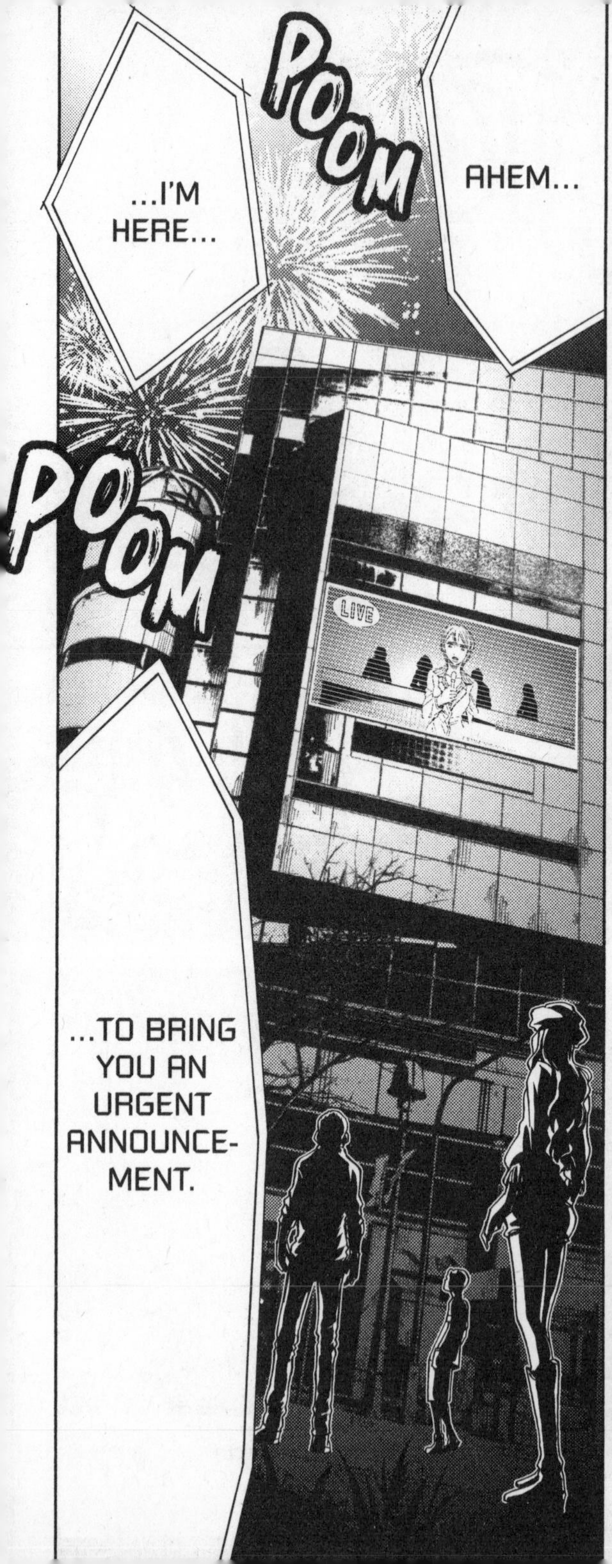
POOM
AHEM...
...I'M HERE...
POOM
LIVE
...TO BRING YOU AN URGENT ANNOUNCEMENT.

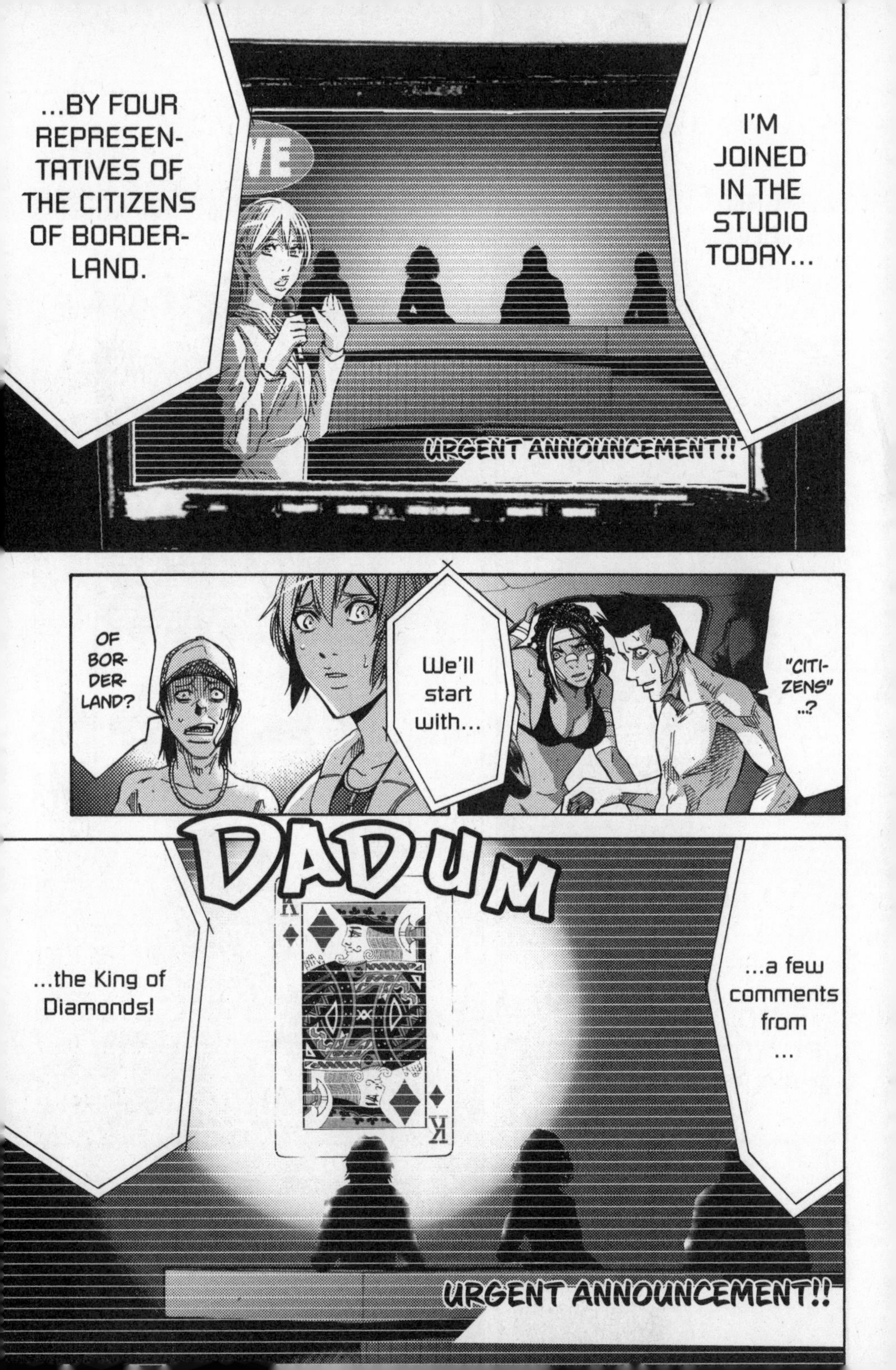
I'M JOINED IN THE STUDIO TODAY...
...BY FOUR REPRESEN-TATIVES OF THE CITIZENS OF BORDER-LAND.
URGENT ANNOUNCEMENT!!
"CITI-ZENS" ...?
We'll start with...
OF BOR-DER-LAND?
...a few comments from ...
DADUM
...the King of Diamonds!
URGENT ANNOUNCEMENT!!

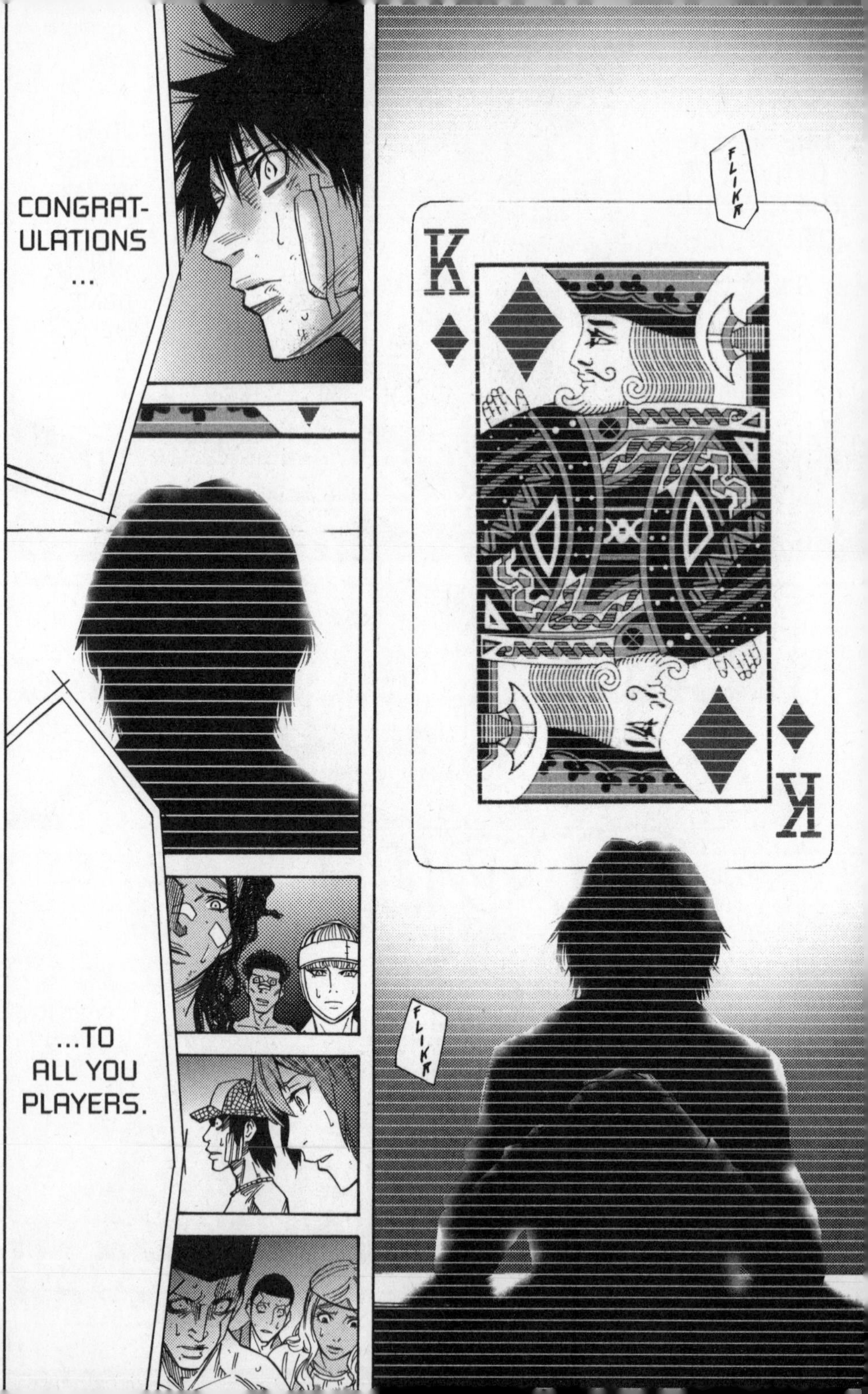
FLIKR
FLIKR
CONGRAT-
ULATIONS
...
...TO
ALL YOU
PLAYERS.

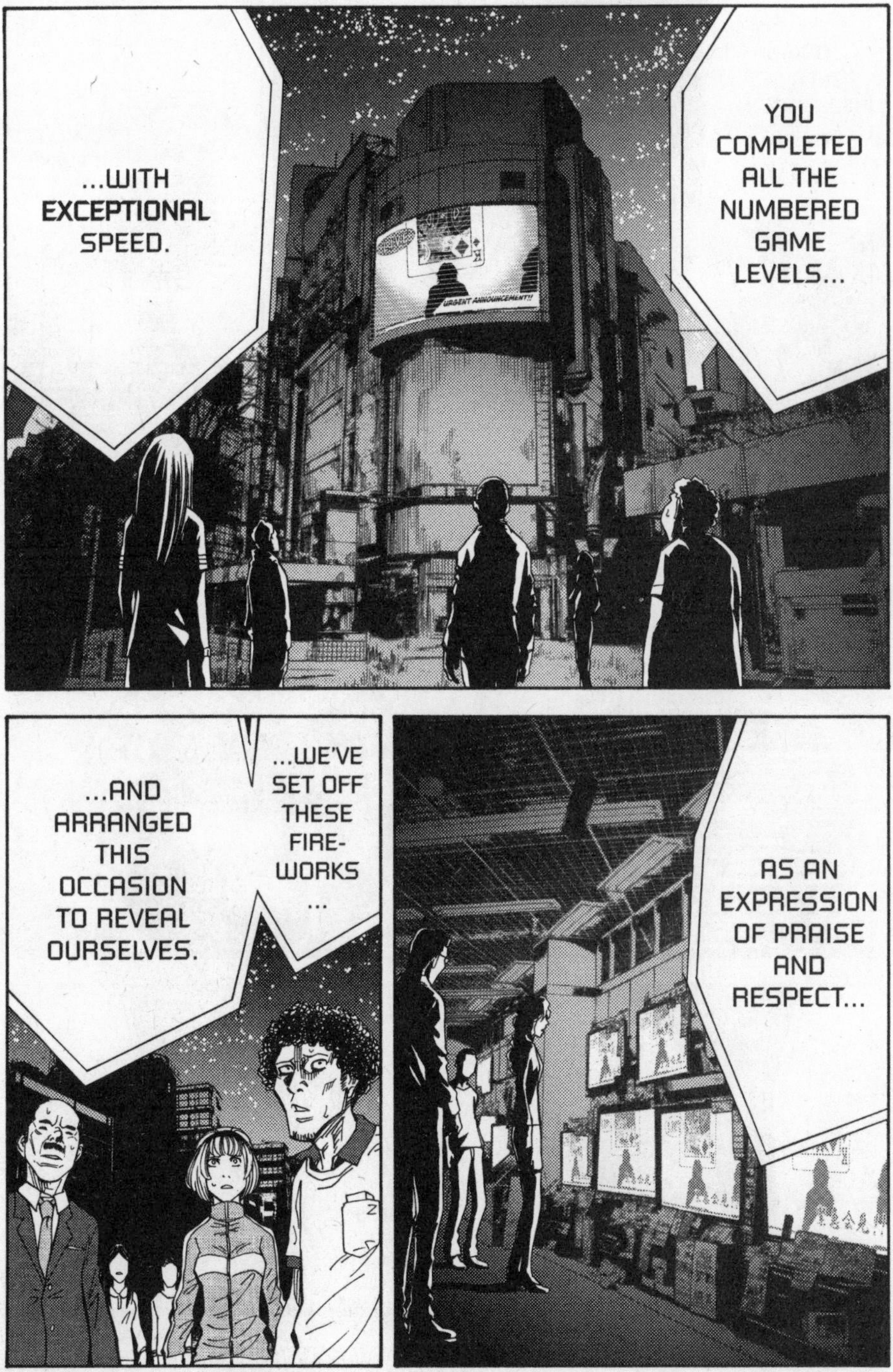
YOU COMPLETED ALL THE NUMBERED GAME LEVELS...
URGENT ANNOUNCEMENT!!
...WITH **EXCEPTIONAL** SPEED.
AS AN EXPRESSION OF PRAISE AND RESPECT...
...WE'VE SET OFF THESE FIRE-WORKS ...
...AND ARRANGED THIS OCCASION TO REVEAL OURSELVES.

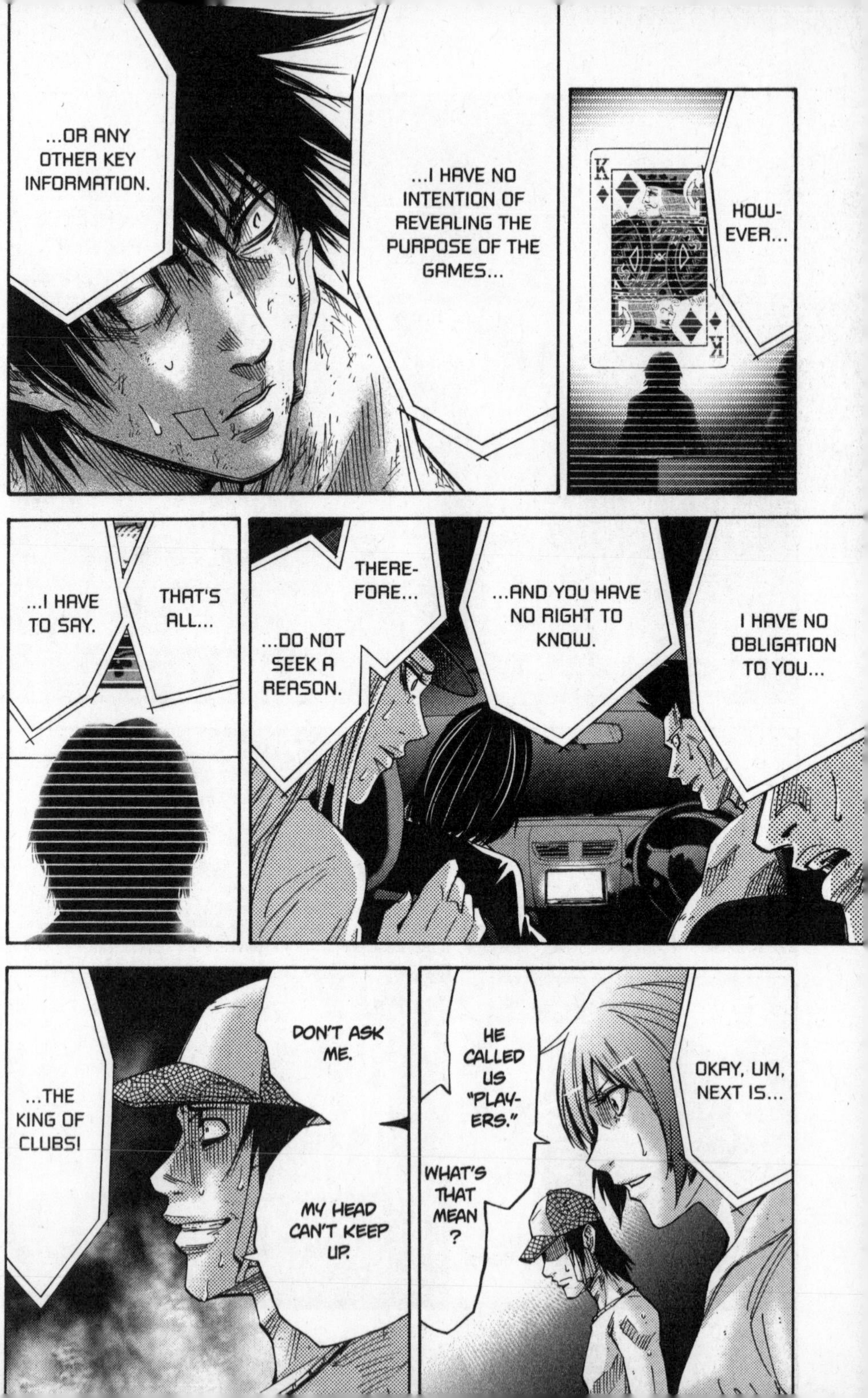
HOW-EVER...
...I HAVE NO INTENTION OF REVEALING THE PURPOSE OF THE GAMES...
...OR ANY OTHER KEY INFORMATION.
I HAVE NO OBLIGATION TO YOU...
...AND YOU HAVE NO RIGHT TO KNOW.
THERE-FORE...
...DO NOT SEEK A REASON.
THAT'S ALL...
...I HAVE TO SAY.
OKAY, UM, NEXT IS...
HE CALLED US "PLAY-ERS."
WHAT'S THAT MEAN ?
DON'T ASK ME.
...THE KING OF CLUBS!
MY HEAD CAN'T KEEP UP.

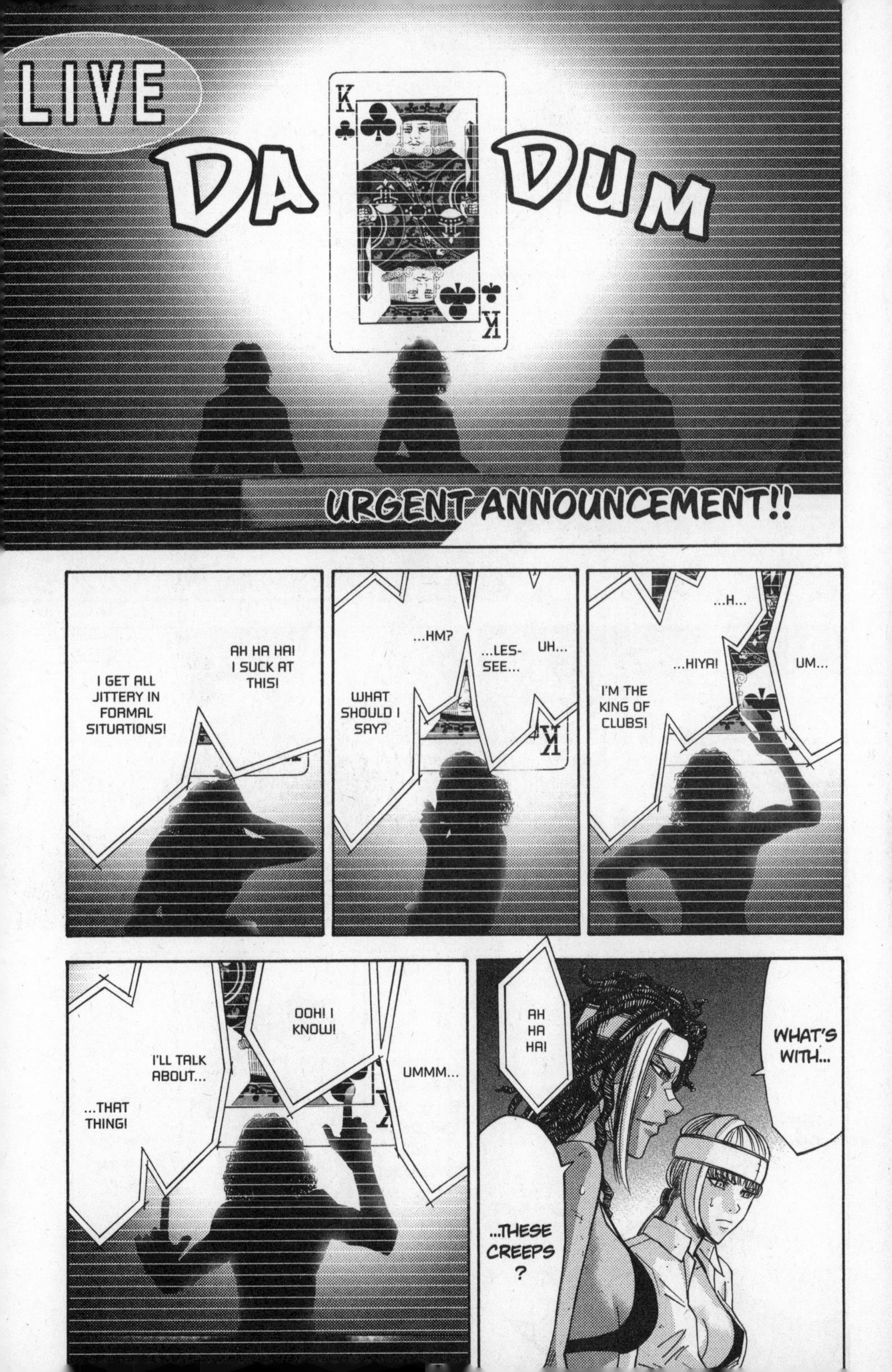
LIVE
DA DUM
URGENT ANNOUNCEMENT!!
...H...
UM...
...HIYA!
I'M THE KING OF CLUBS!
UH...
...LES-SEE...
...HM?
WHAT SHOULD I SAY?
AH HA HA! I SUCK AT THIS!
I GET ALL JITTERY IN FORMAL SITUATIONS!
WHAT'S WITH...
AH HA HA!
...THESE CREEPS?
UMMM...
OOH! I KNOW!
I'LL TALK ABOUT...
...THAT THING!

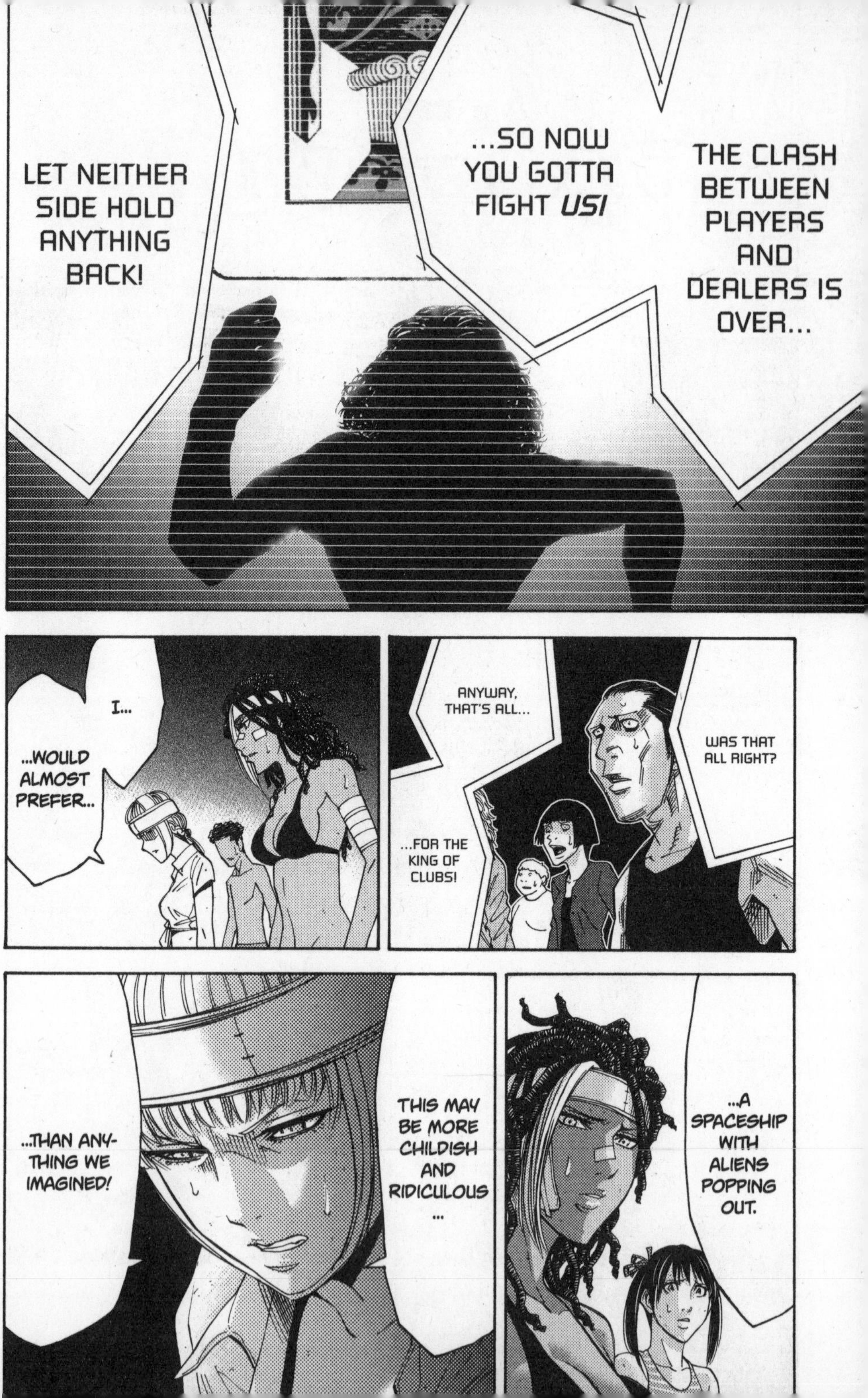
THE CLASH BETWEEN PLAYERS AND DEALERS IS OVER...
...SO NOW YOU GOTTA FIGHT US!
LET NEITHER SIDE HOLD ANYTHING BACK!
WAS THAT ALL RIGHT?
ANYWAY, THAT'S ALL...
...FOR THE KING OF CLUBS!
I...
...WOULD ALMOST PREFER...
...A SPACESHIP WITH ALIENS POPPING OUT.
THIS MAY BE MORE CHILDISH AND RIDICULOUS...
...THAN ANYTHING WE IMAGINED!

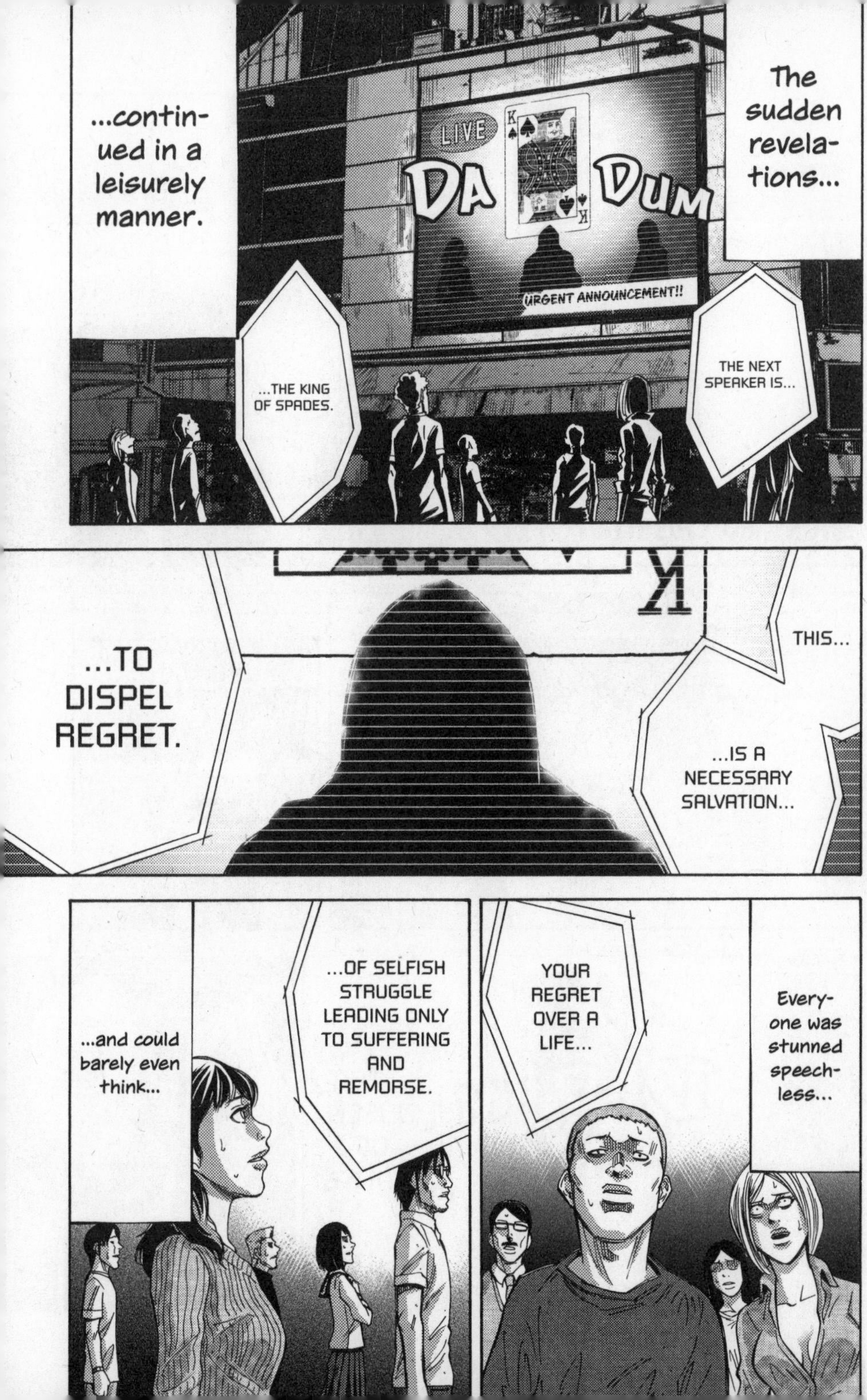
The sudden revelations...
THE NEXT SPEAKER IS...
LIVE
DA DUM
URGENT ANNOUNCEMENT!!
...THE KING OF SPADES.
...continued in a leisurely manner.
THIS...
...IS A NECESSARY SALVATION...
...TO DISPEL REGRET.
Everyone was stunned speechless...
YOUR REGRET OVER A LIFE...
...OF SELFISH STRUGGLE LEADING ONLY TO SUFFERING AND REMORSE.
...and could barely even think...

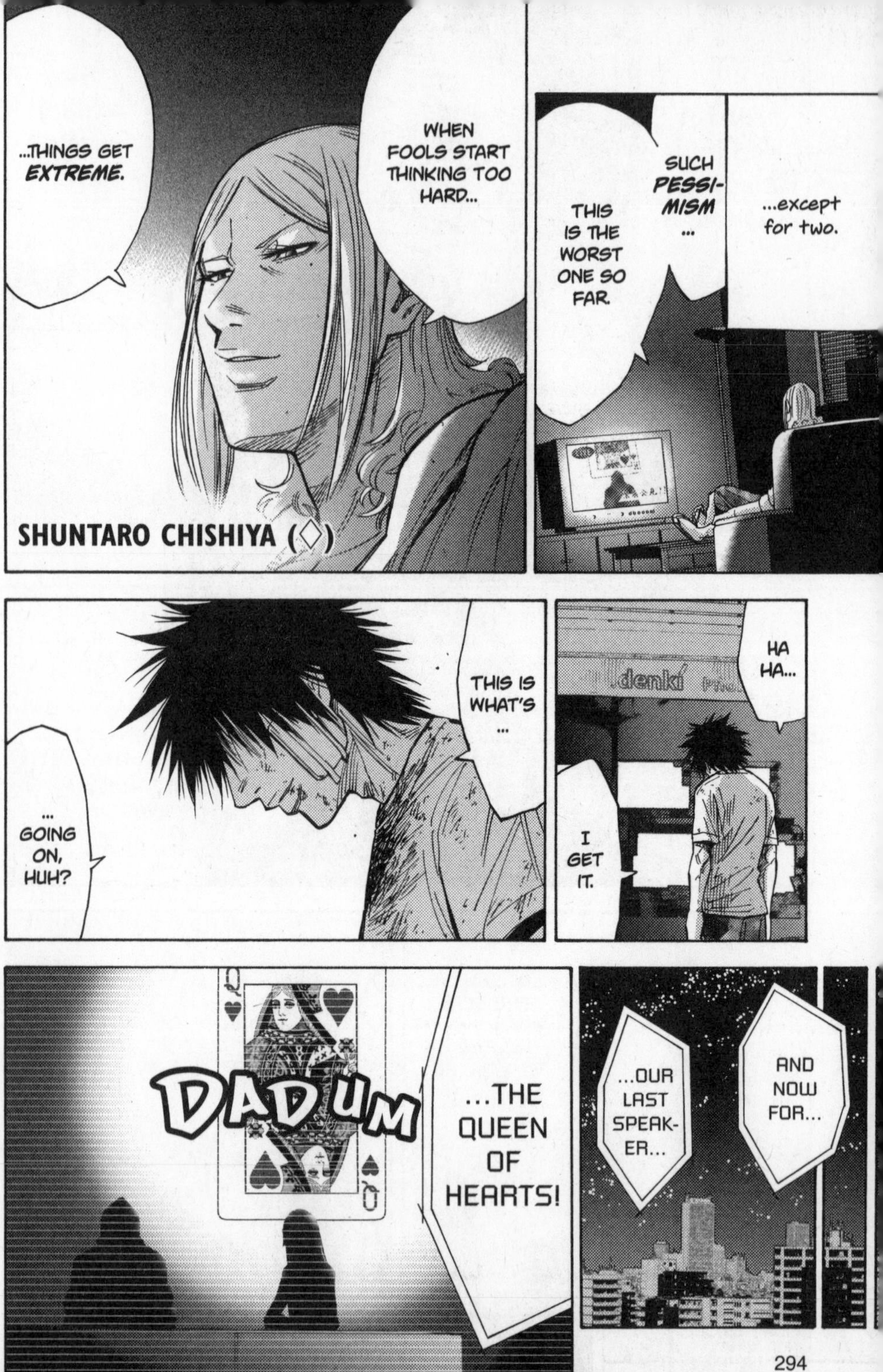
...except for two.
SUCH PESSIMISM...
THIS IS THE WORST ONE SO FAR.
WHEN FOOLS START THINKING TOO HARD...
...THINGS GET EXTREME.
SHUNTARO CHISHIYA (◊)
HA HA...
I GET IT.
THIS IS WHAT'S...
...GOING ON, HUH?
AND NOW FOR...
...OUR LAST SPEAKER...
...THE QUEEN OF HEARTS!
DADUM

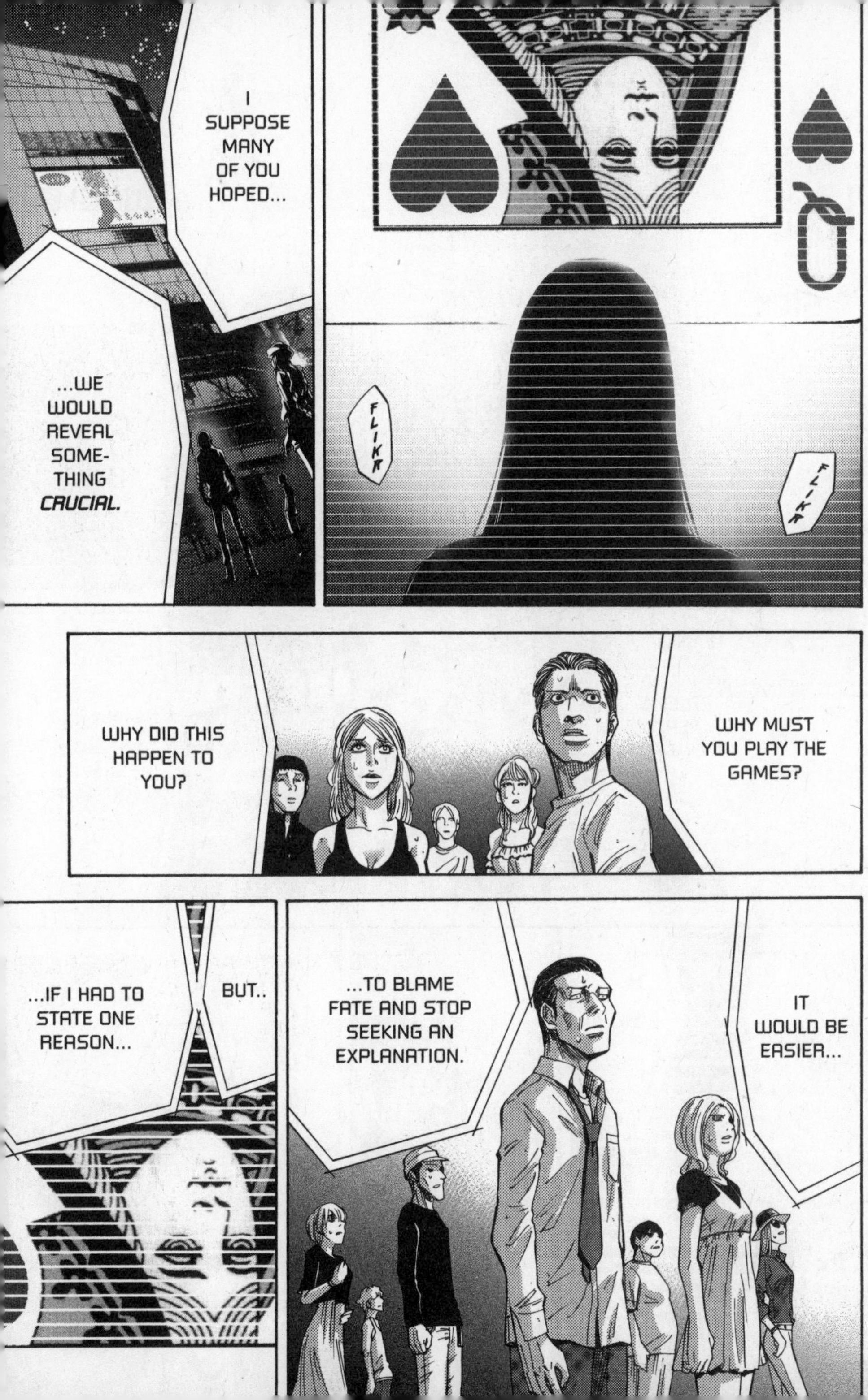
FLIKR
FLIKR
I SUPPOSE MANY OF YOU HOPED...
...WE WOULD REVEAL SOME-THING *CRUCIAL.*
WHY MUST YOU PLAY THE GAMES?
WHY DID THIS HAPPEN TO YOU?
IT WOULD BE EASIER...
...TO BLAME FATE AND STOP SEEKING AN EXPLANATION.
BUT..
...IF I HAD TO STATE ONE REASON...

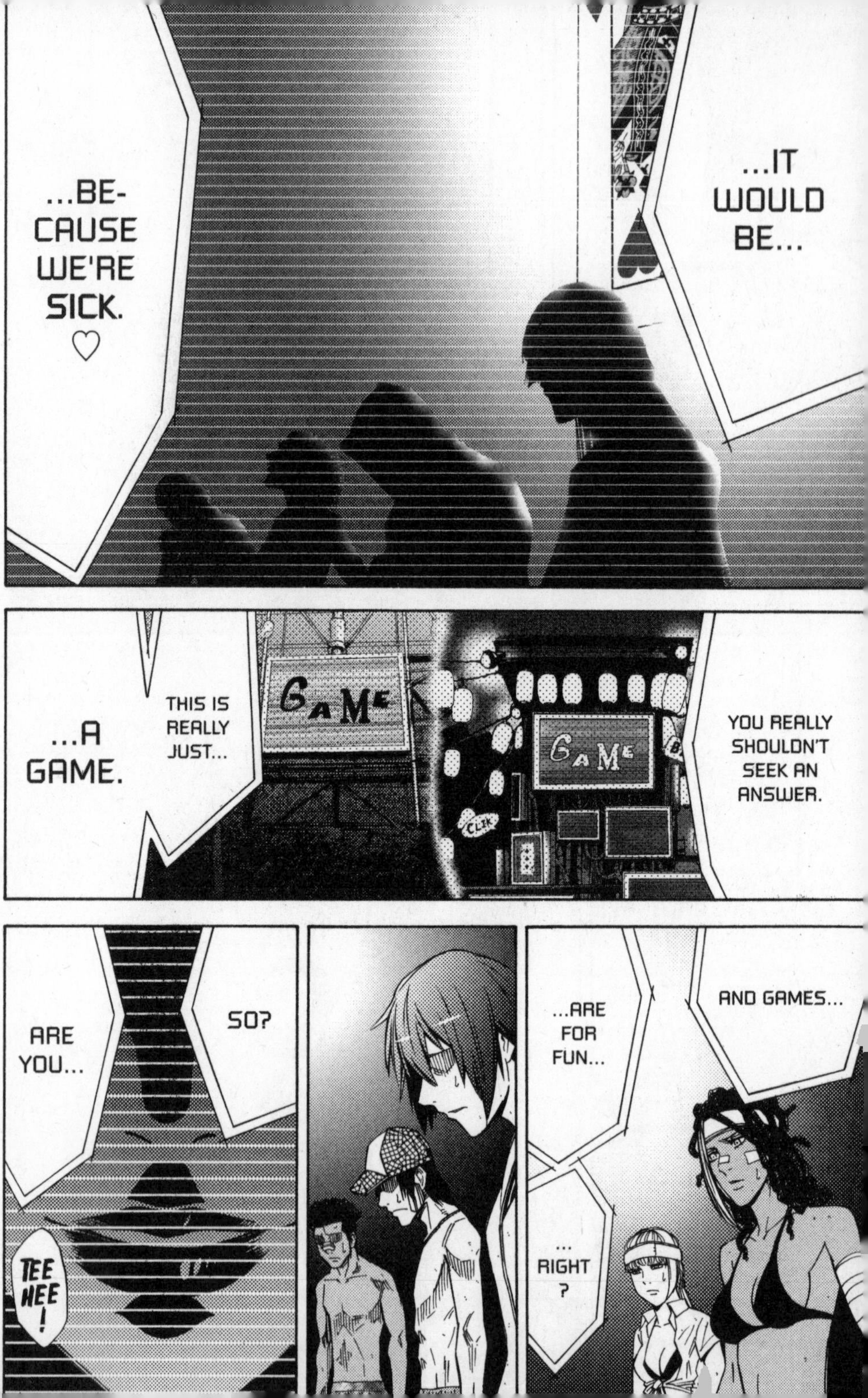
...IT WOULD BE...
...BE-CAUSE WE'RE SICK. ♡
YOU REALLY SHOULDN'T SEEK AN ANSWER.
GAME
GAME
CLIK
THIS IS REALLY JUST...
...A GAME.
AND GAMES...
...ARE FOR FUN...
...RIGHT?
SO?
ARE YOU...
TEE HEE!

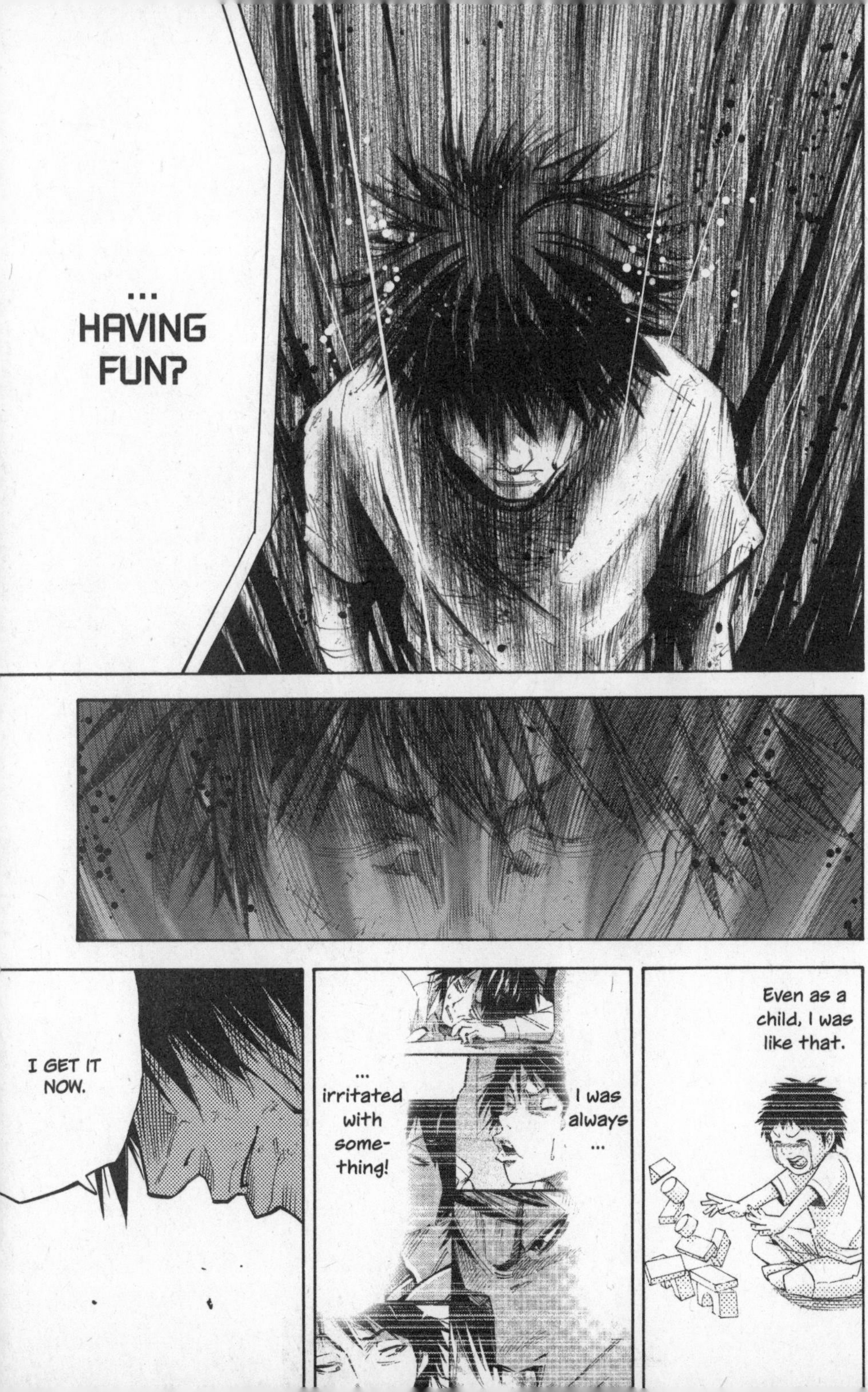
... HAVING FUN?
Even as a child, I was like that.
I was always ...
... irritated with something!
I GET IT NOW.

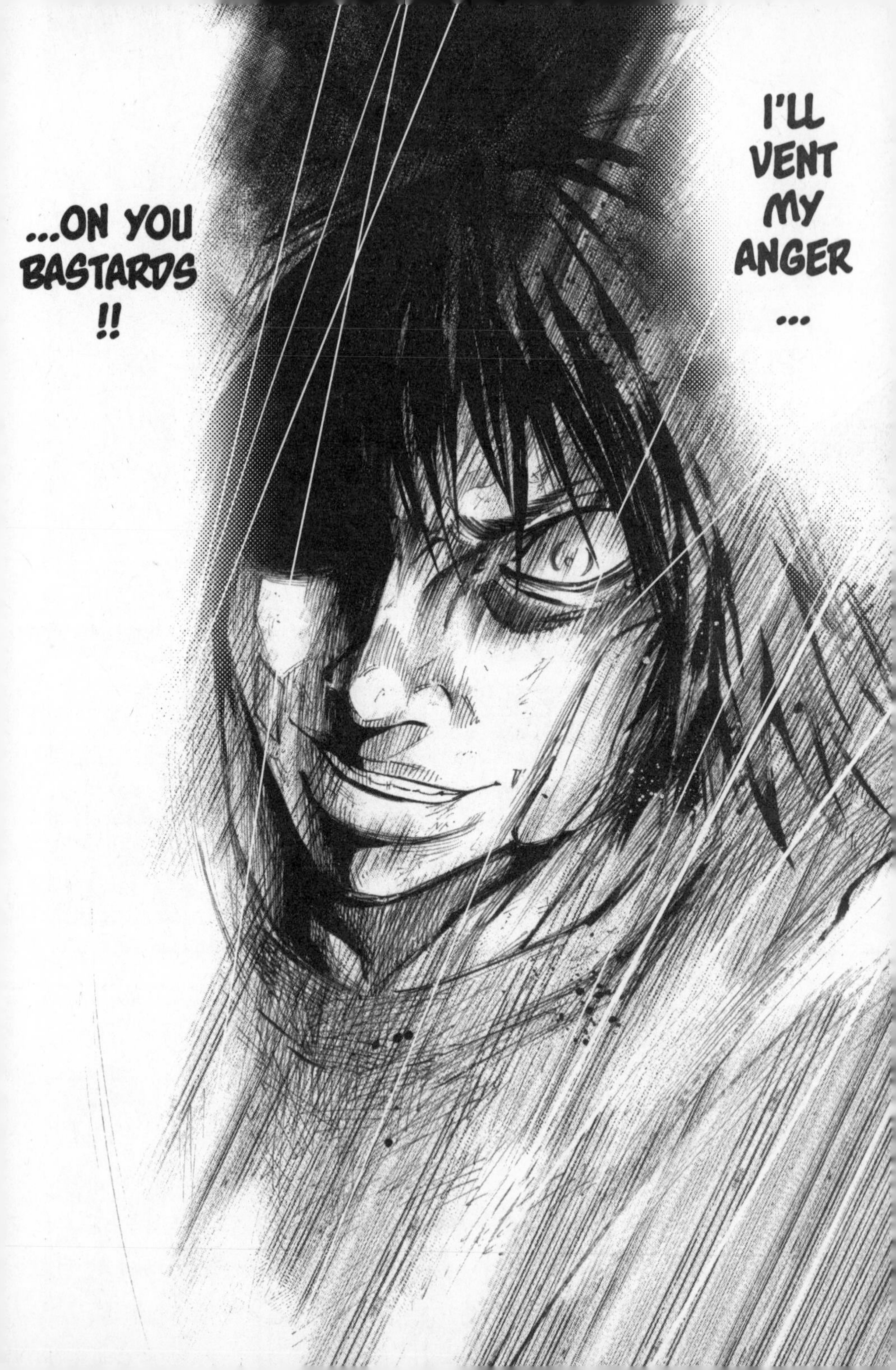
I'LL VENT MY ANGER ...
...ON YOU BASTARDS !!

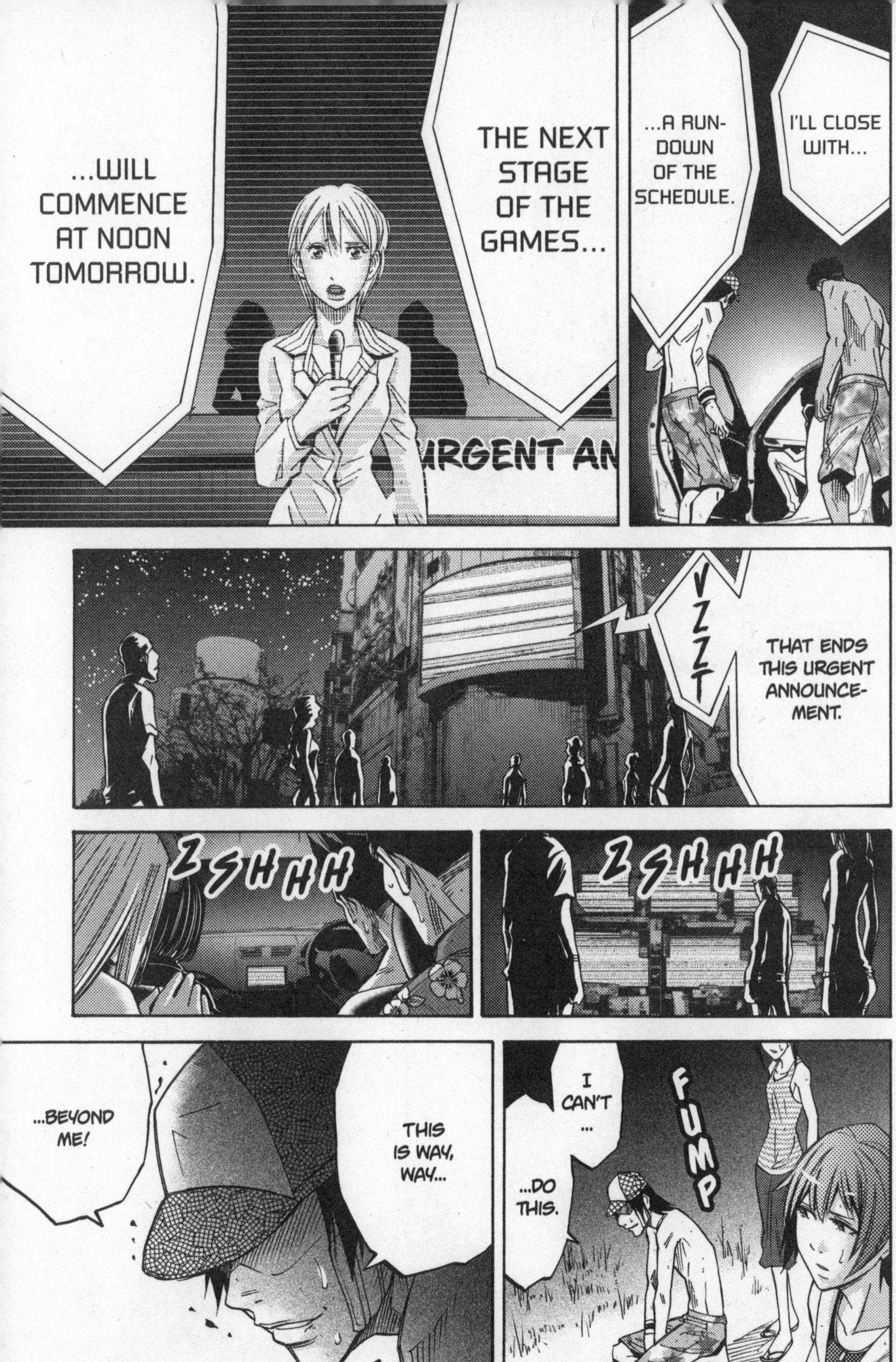
I'LL CLOSE WITH...
...A RUN-DOWN OF THE SCHEDULE.
THE NEXT STAGE OF THE GAMES...
...WILL COMMENCE AT NOON TOMORROW.
URGENT AN
VZZZT
THAT ENDS THIS URGENT ANNOUNCEMENT.
ZSHHHH
ZSHHHH
FUMP
I CAN'T...
...DO THIS.
THIS IS WAY, WAY...
...BEYOND ME!

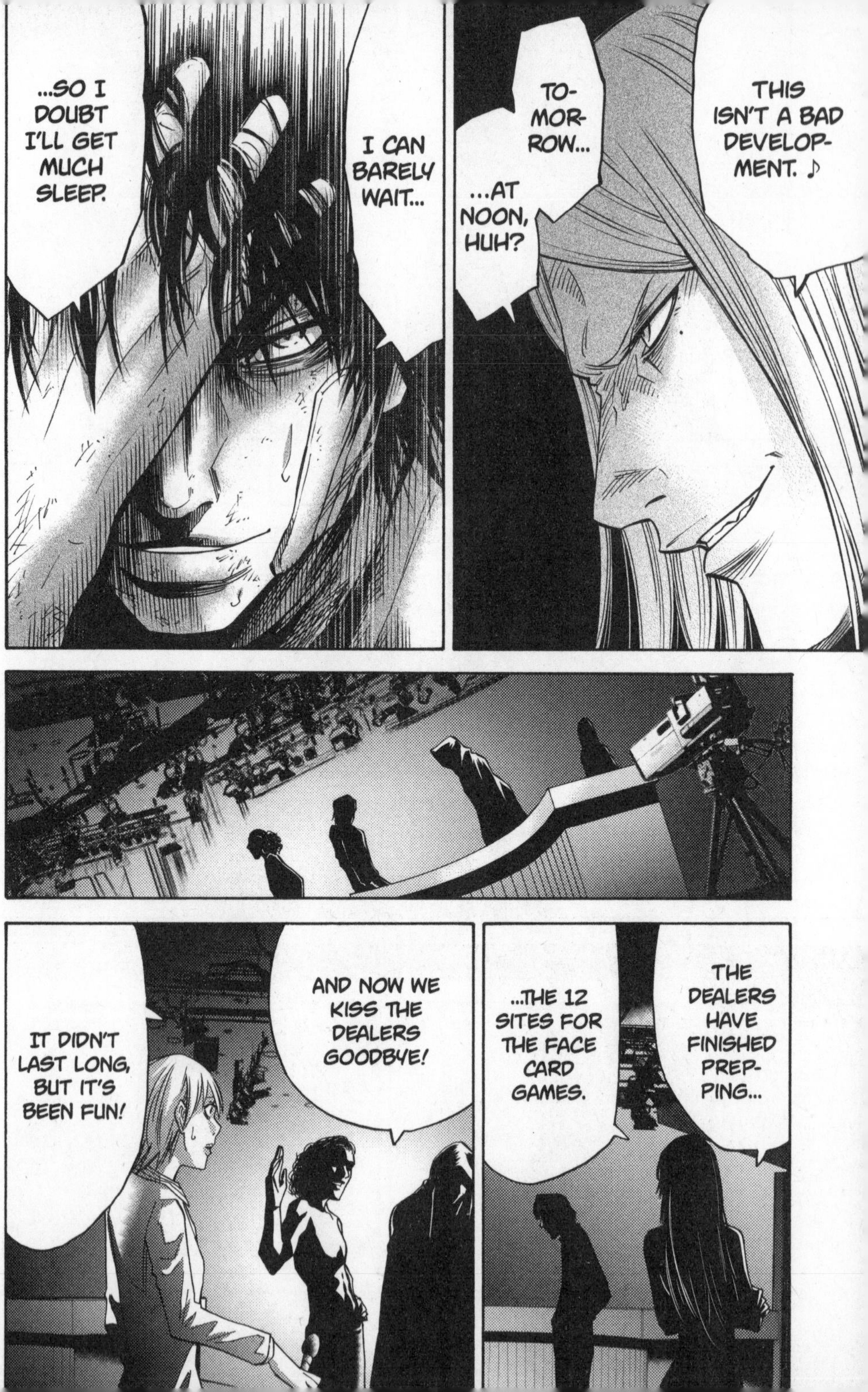
THIS ISN'T A BAD DEVELOPMENT. ♪
TOMORROW...
...AT NOON, HUH?
I CAN BARELY WAIT...
...SO I DOUBT I'LL GET MUCH SLEEP.
THE DEALERS HAVE FINISHED PREPPING...
...THE 12 SITES FOR THE FACE CARD GAMES.
AND NOW WE KISS THE DEALERS GOODBYE!
IT DIDN'T LAST LONG, BUT IT'S BEEN FUN!

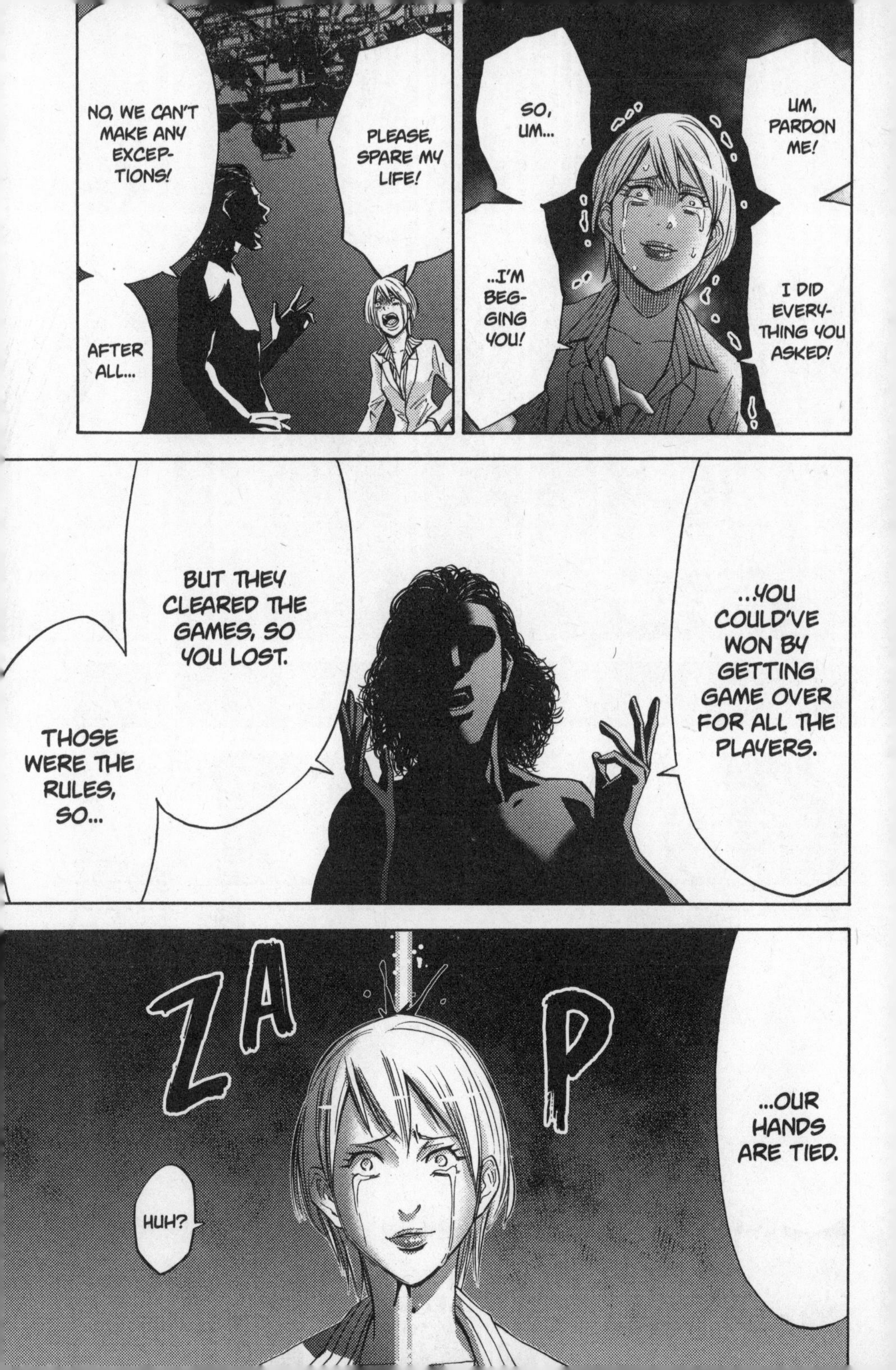
UM, PARDON ME!
SO, UM...
I DID EVERYTHING YOU ASKED!
...I'M BEGGING YOU!
PLEASE, SPARE MY LIFE!
NO, WE CAN'T MAKE ANY EXCEPTIONS!
AFTER ALL...
...YOU COULD'VE WON BY GETTING GAME OVER FOR ALL THE PLAYERS.
BUT THEY CLEARED THE GAMES, SO YOU LOST.
THOSE WERE THE RULES, SO...
...OUR HANDS ARE TIED.
ZAP
HUH?

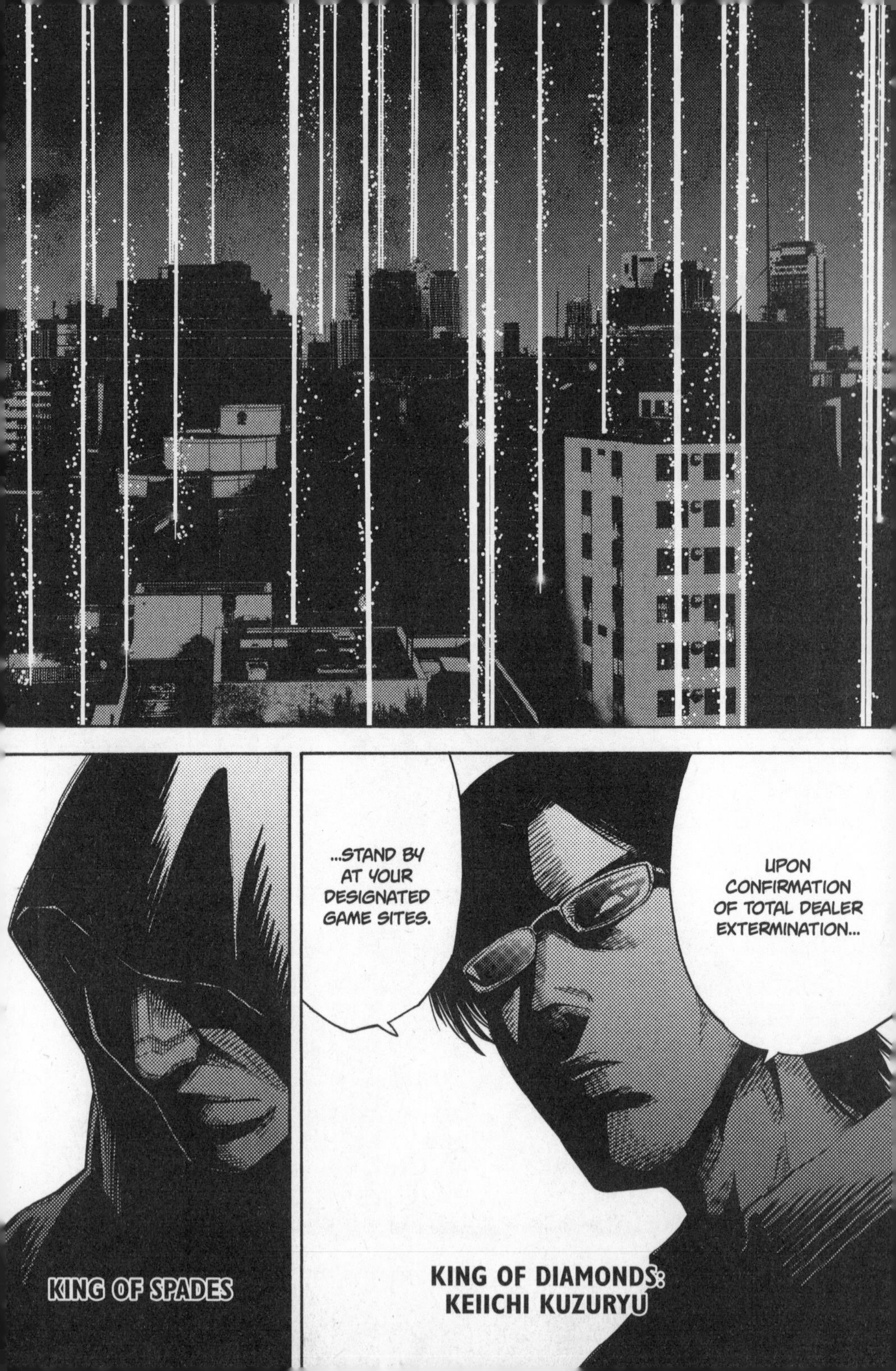
UPON CONFIRMATION OF TOTAL DEALER EXTERMINATION...
...STAND BY AT YOUR DESIGNATED GAME SITES.
KING OF DIAMONDS: KEIICHI KUZURYU
KING OF SPADES

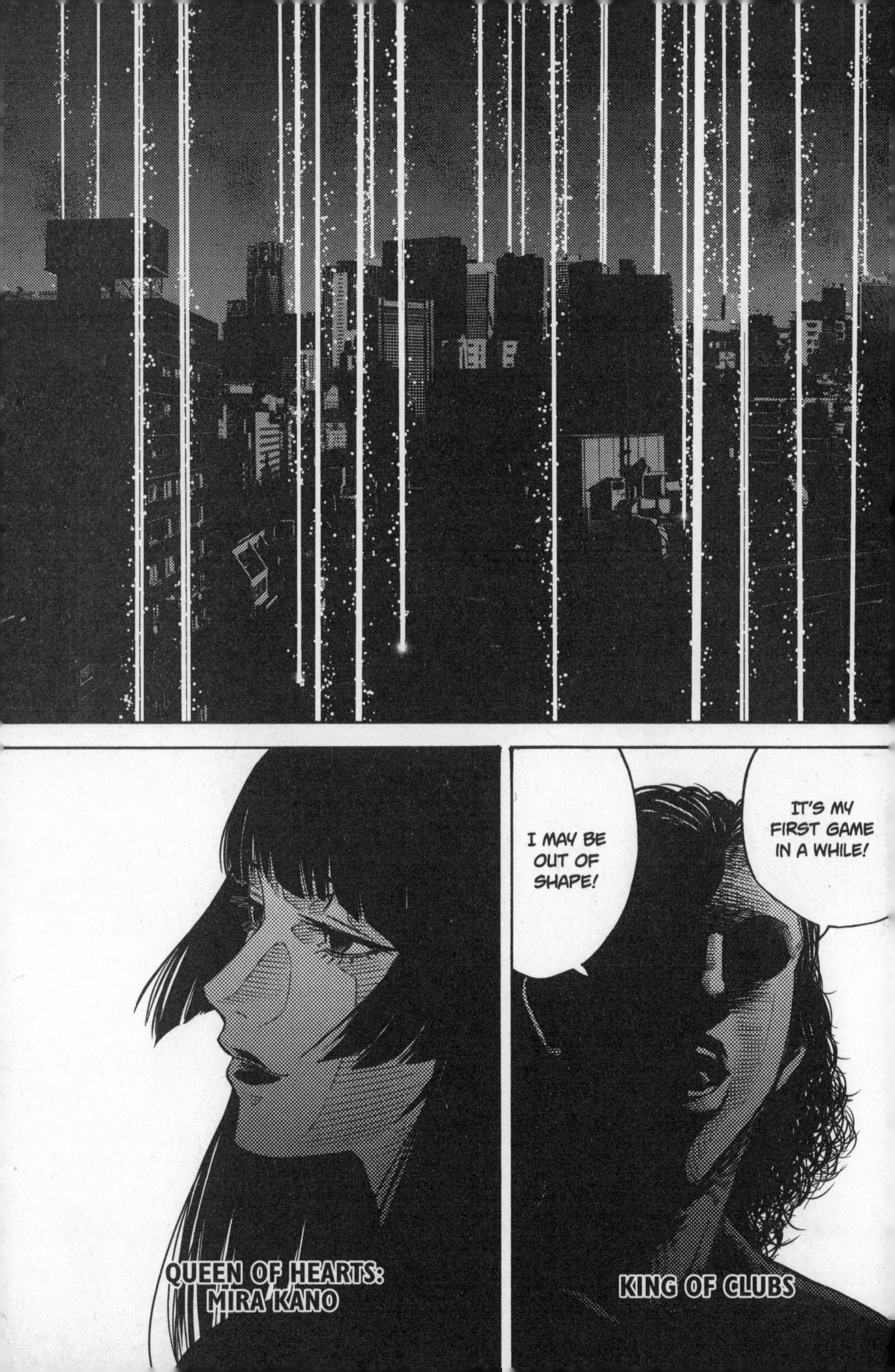
IT'S MY FIRST GAME IN A WHILE!
I MAY BE OUT OF SHAPE!
KING OF CLUBS
QUEEN OF HEARTS: MIRA KANO

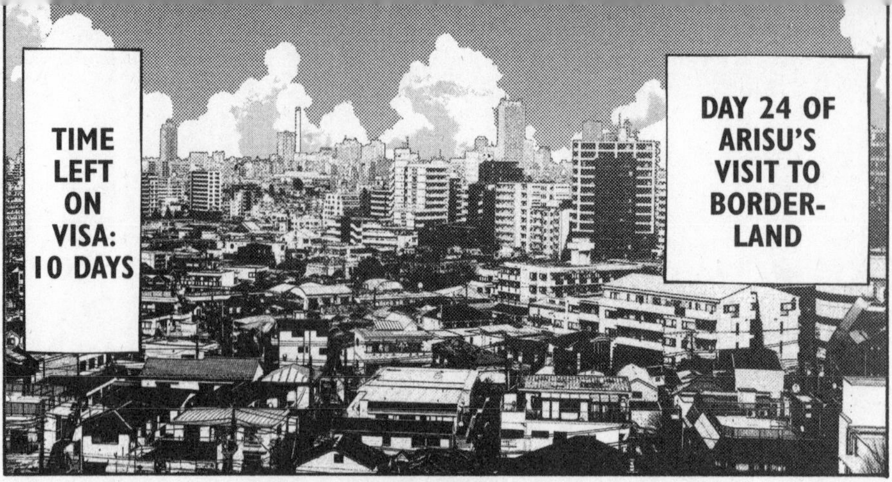
DAY 24 OF ARISU'S VISIT TO BORDER-LAND
TIME LEFT ON VISA: 10 DAYS

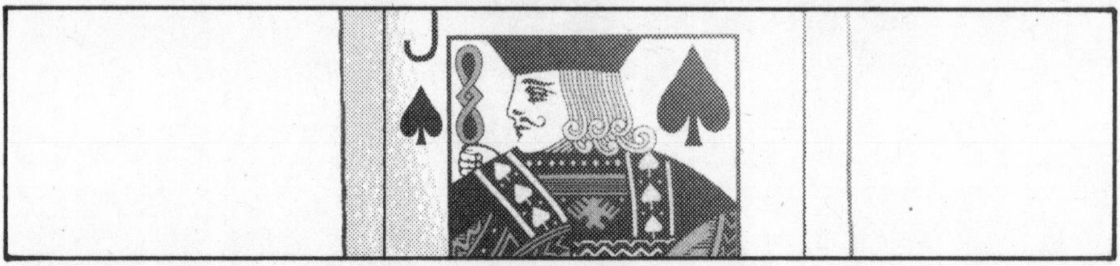

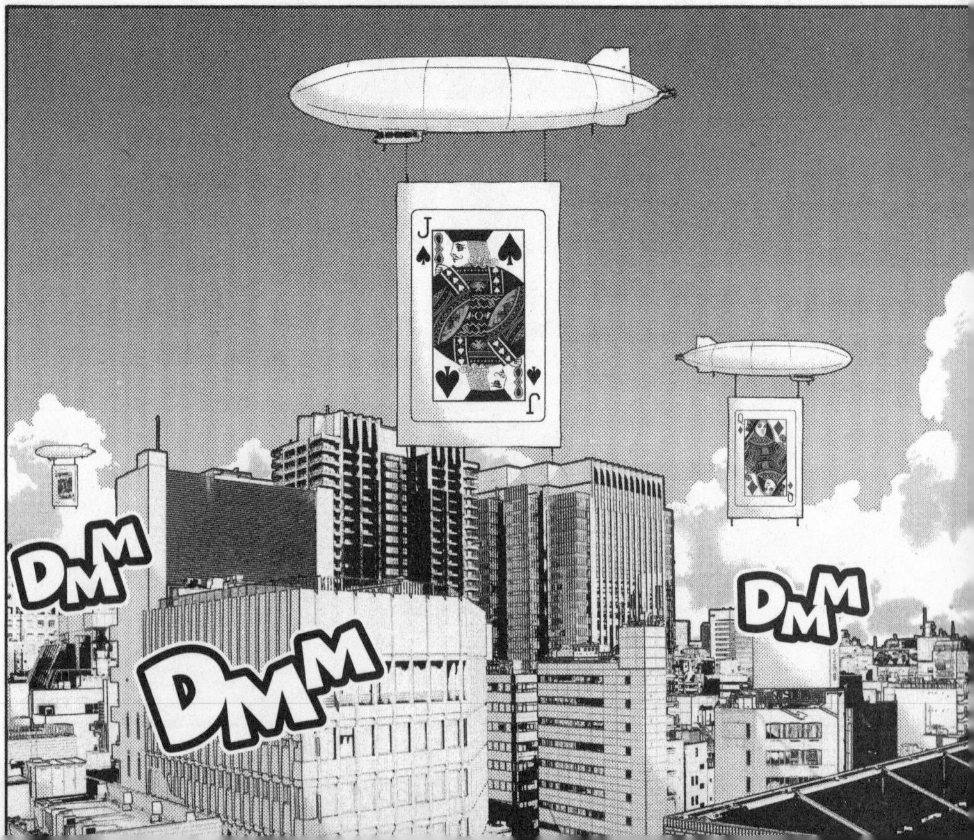
DMM
DMM
DMM

DAY 24 OF ARISU'S VISIT TO BORDER-LAND

SWIK

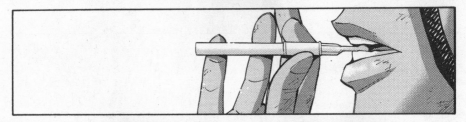

ZZZIP

The next stage begins.

Noon.

CHAPTER 32: Next Stage

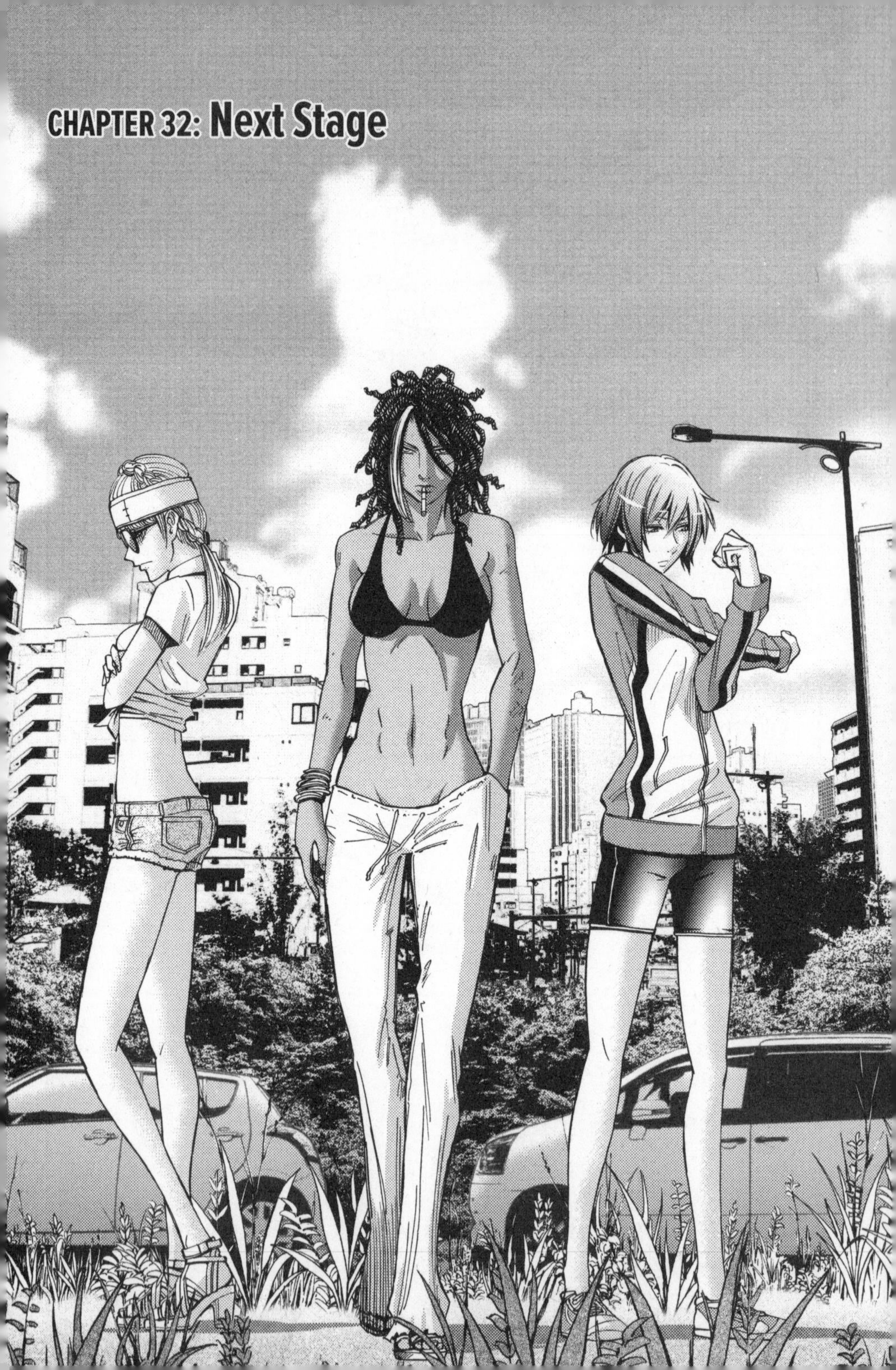

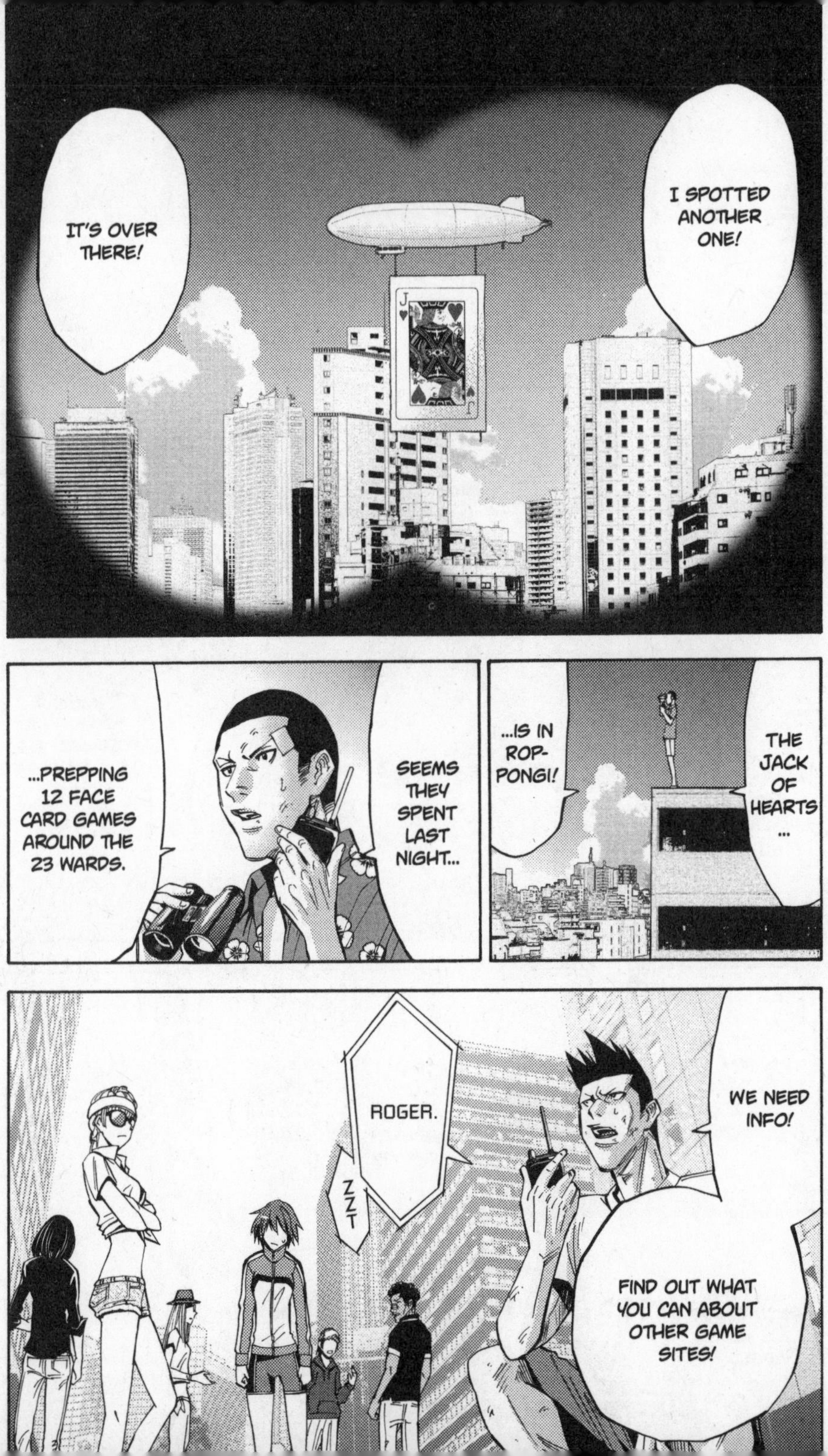
I SPOTTED ANOTHER ONE!
IT'S OVER THERE!
THE JACK OF HEARTS ...
...IS IN ROP-PONGI!
SEEMS THEY SPENT LAST NIGHT...
...PREPPING 12 FACE CARD GAMES AROUND THE 23 WARDS.
WE NEED INFO!
FIND OUT WHAT YOU CAN ABOUT OTHER GAME SITES!
ROGER.
ZZT

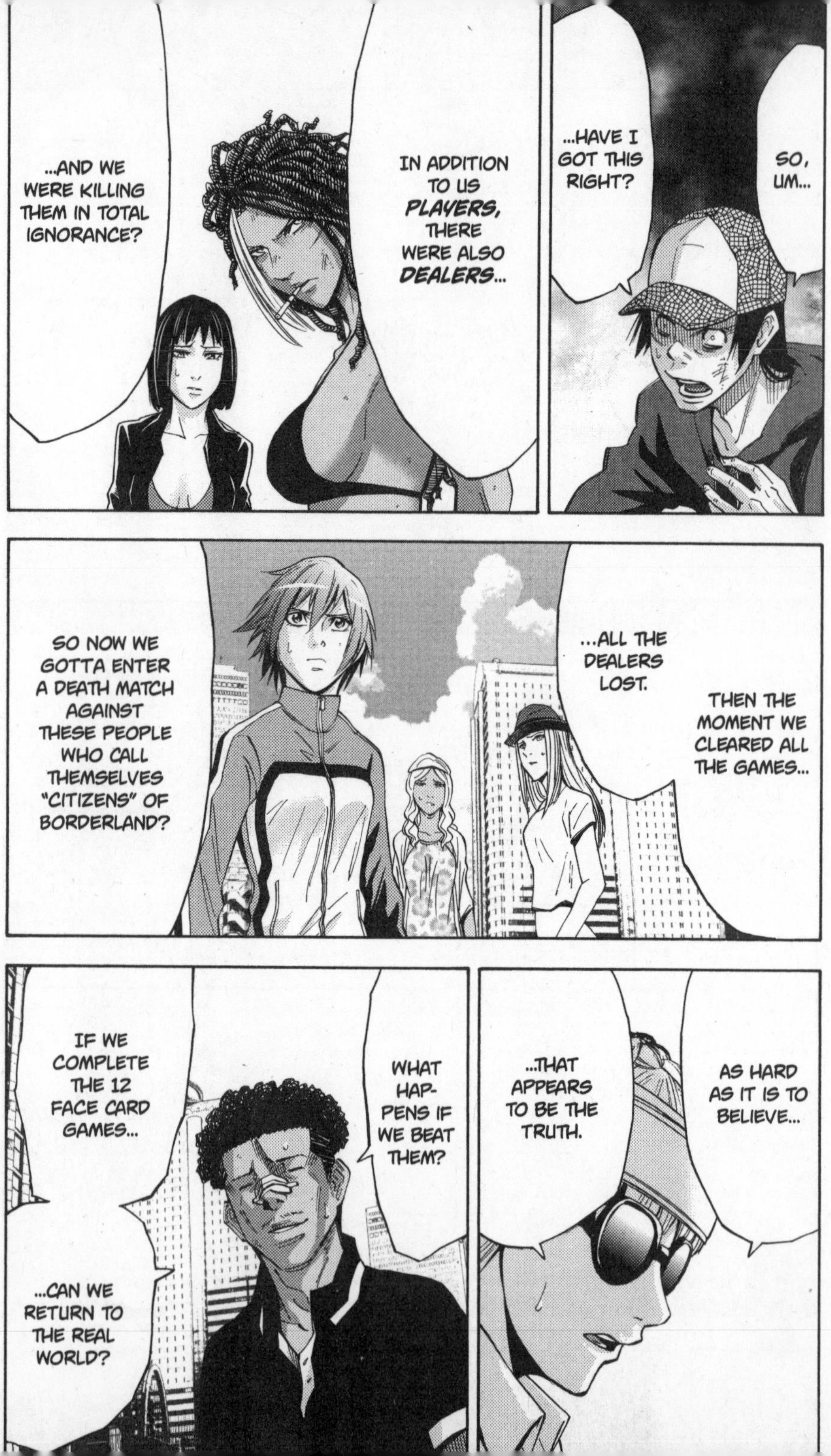
SO, UM...
...HAVE I GOT THIS RIGHT?
IN ADDITION TO US *PLAYERS*, THERE WERE ALSO *DEALERS*...
...AND WE WERE KILLING THEM IN TOTAL IGNORANCE?
THEN THE MOMENT WE CLEARED ALL THE GAMES...
...ALL THE DEALERS LOST.
SO NOW WE GOTTA ENTER A DEATH MATCH AGAINST THESE PEOPLE WHO CALL THEMSELVES "CITIZENS" OF BORDERLAND?
AS HARD AS IT IS TO BELIEVE...
...THAT APPEARS TO BE THE TRUTH.
WHAT HAP-PENS IF WE BEAT THEM?
IF WE COMPLETE THE 12 FACE CARD GAMES...
...CAN WE RETURN TO THE REAL WORLD?

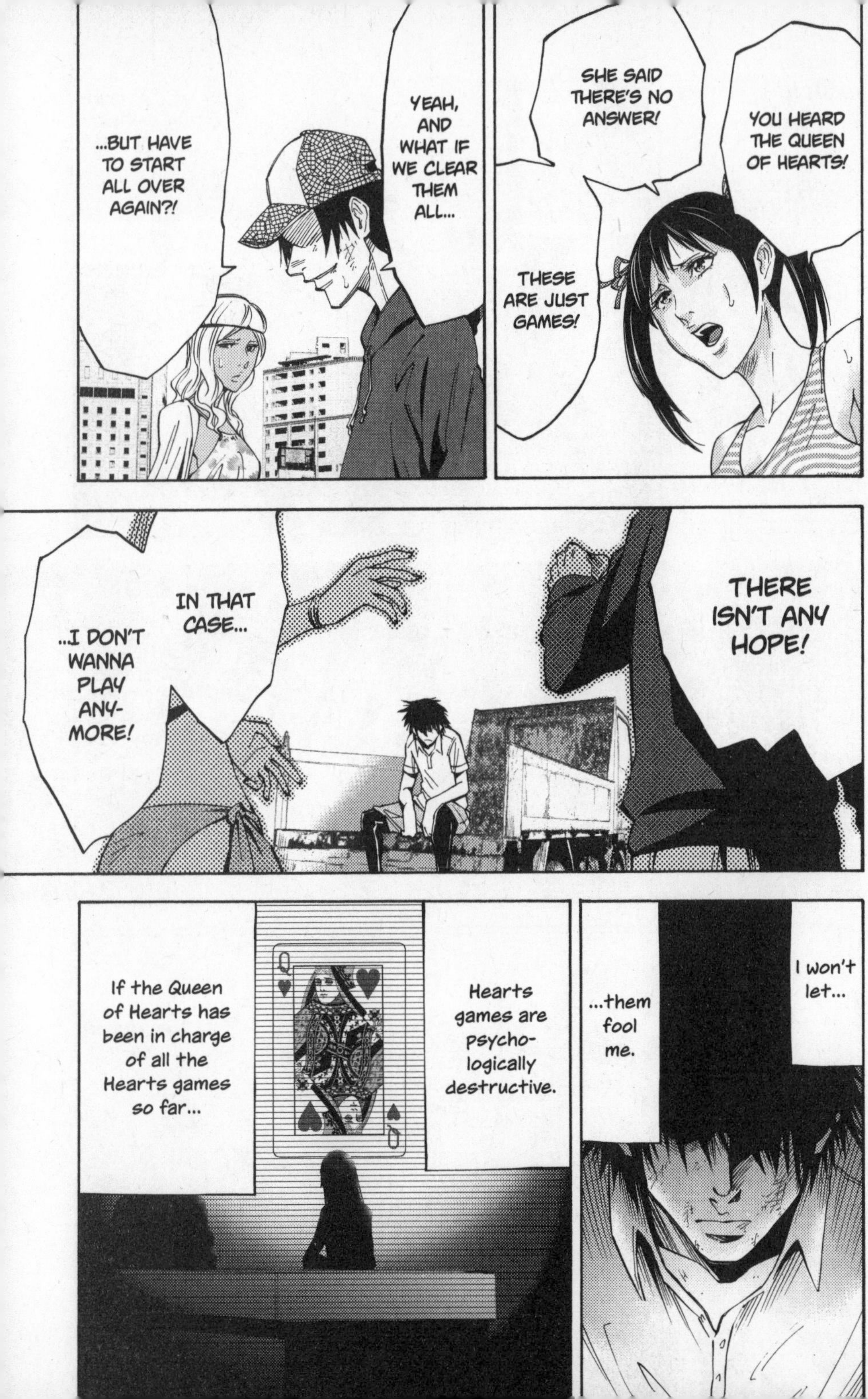
YOU HEARD THE QUEEN OF HEARTS!
SHE SAID THERE'S NO ANSWER!
THESE ARE JUST GAMES!
YEAH, AND WHAT IF WE CLEAR THEM ALL...
...BUT HAVE TO START ALL OVER AGAIN?!
THERE ISN'T ANY HOPE!
IN THAT CASE...
...I DON'T WANNA PLAY ANY-MORE!
I won't let...
...them fool me.
Hearts games are psycho-logically destructive.
If the Queen of Hearts has been in charge of all the Hearts games so far...

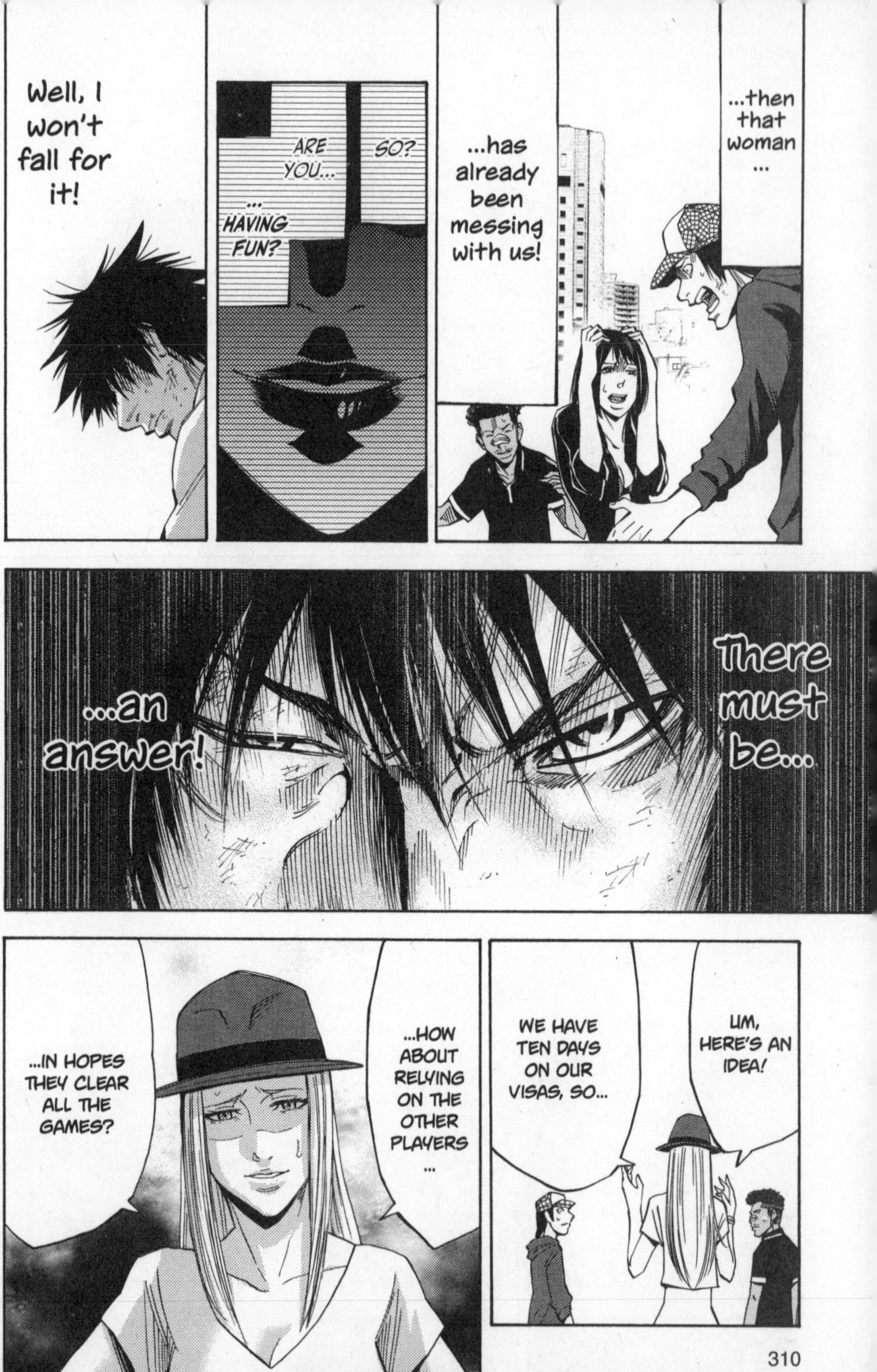
...then that woman...
...has already been messing with us!
SO?
ARE YOU...
...HAVING FUN?
Well, I won't fall for it!
There must be...
...an answer!
UM, HERE'S AN IDEA!
WE HAVE TEN DAYS ON OUR VISAS, SO...
...HOW ABOUT RELYING ON THE OTHER PLAYERS...
...IN HOPES THEY CLEAR ALL THE GAMES?

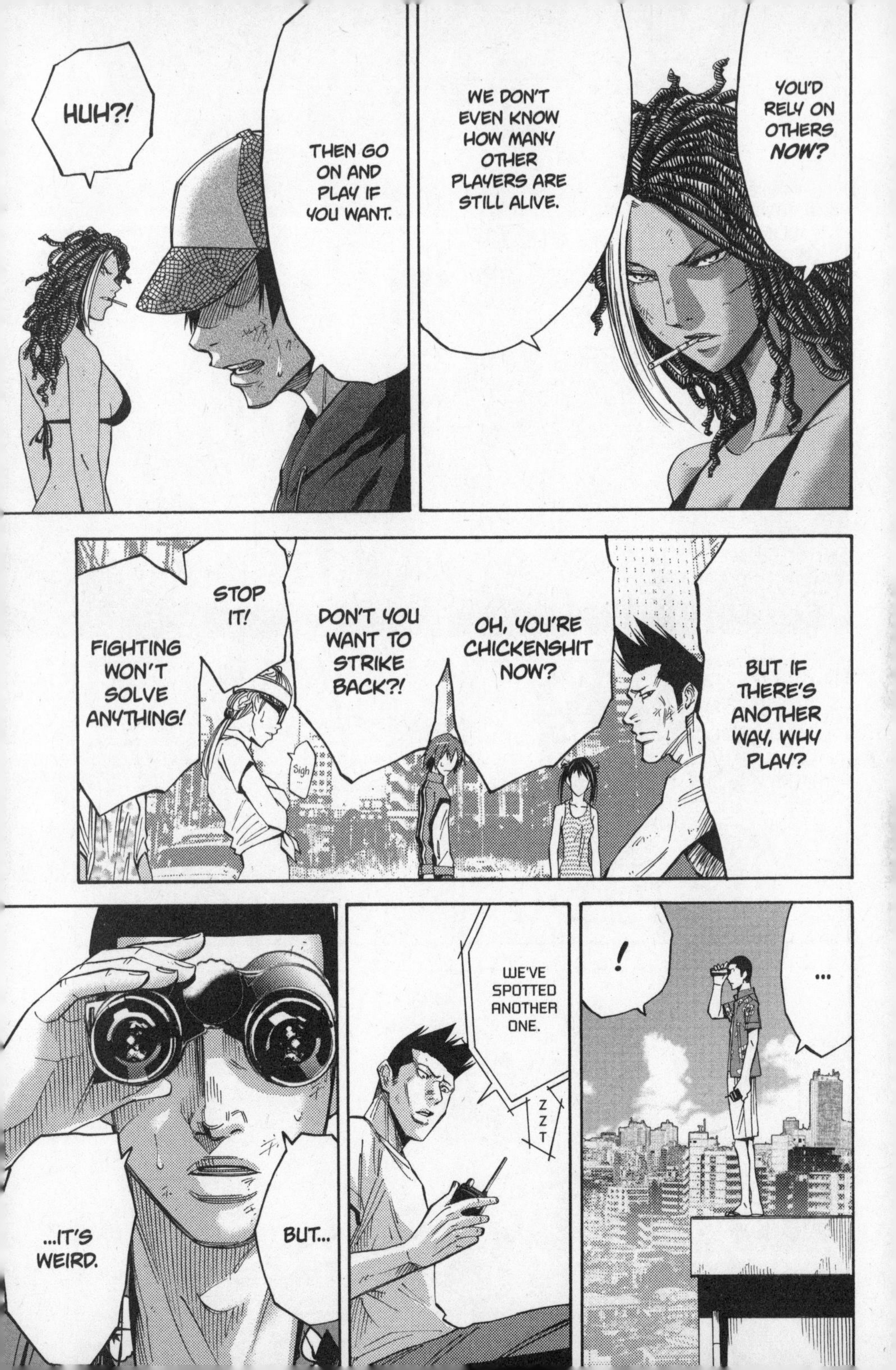
YOU'D RELY ON OTHERS NOW?
WE DON'T EVEN KNOW HOW MANY OTHER PLAYERS ARE STILL ALIVE.
THEN GO ON AND PLAY IF YOU WANT.
HUH?!
BUT IF THERE'S ANOTHER WAY, WHY PLAY?
OH, YOU'RE CHICKENSHIT NOW?
DON'T YOU WANT TO STRIKE BACK?!
STOP IT!
FIGHTING WON'T SOLVE ANYTHING!
Sigh...
...
!
WE'VE SPOTTED ANOTHER ONE.
ZZT
BUT...
...IT'S WEIRD.

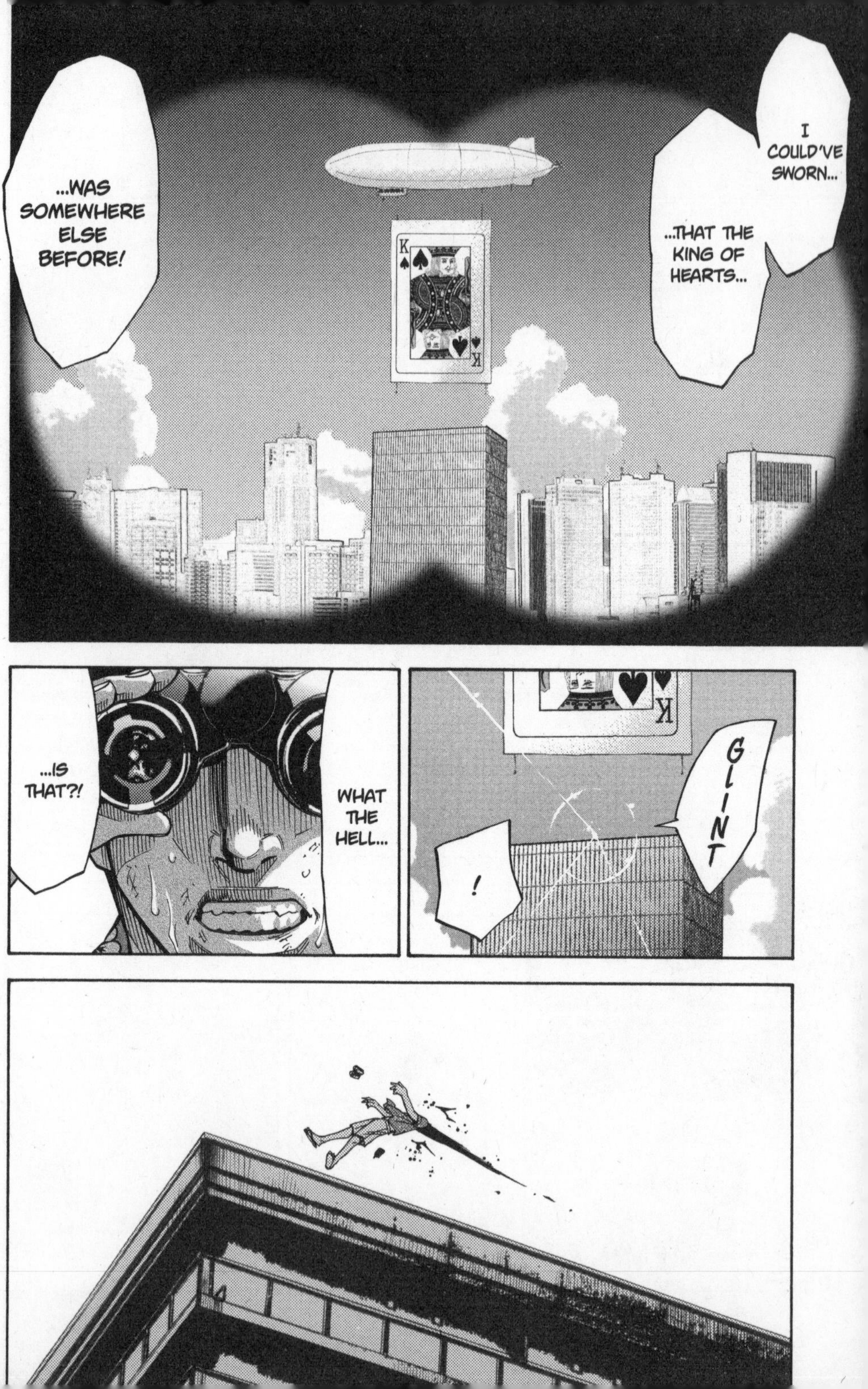
I COULD'VE SWORN...
...THAT THE KING OF HEARTS...
...WAS SOMEWHERE ELSE BEFORE!
GLINT
!
WHAT THE HELL...
...IS THAT?!

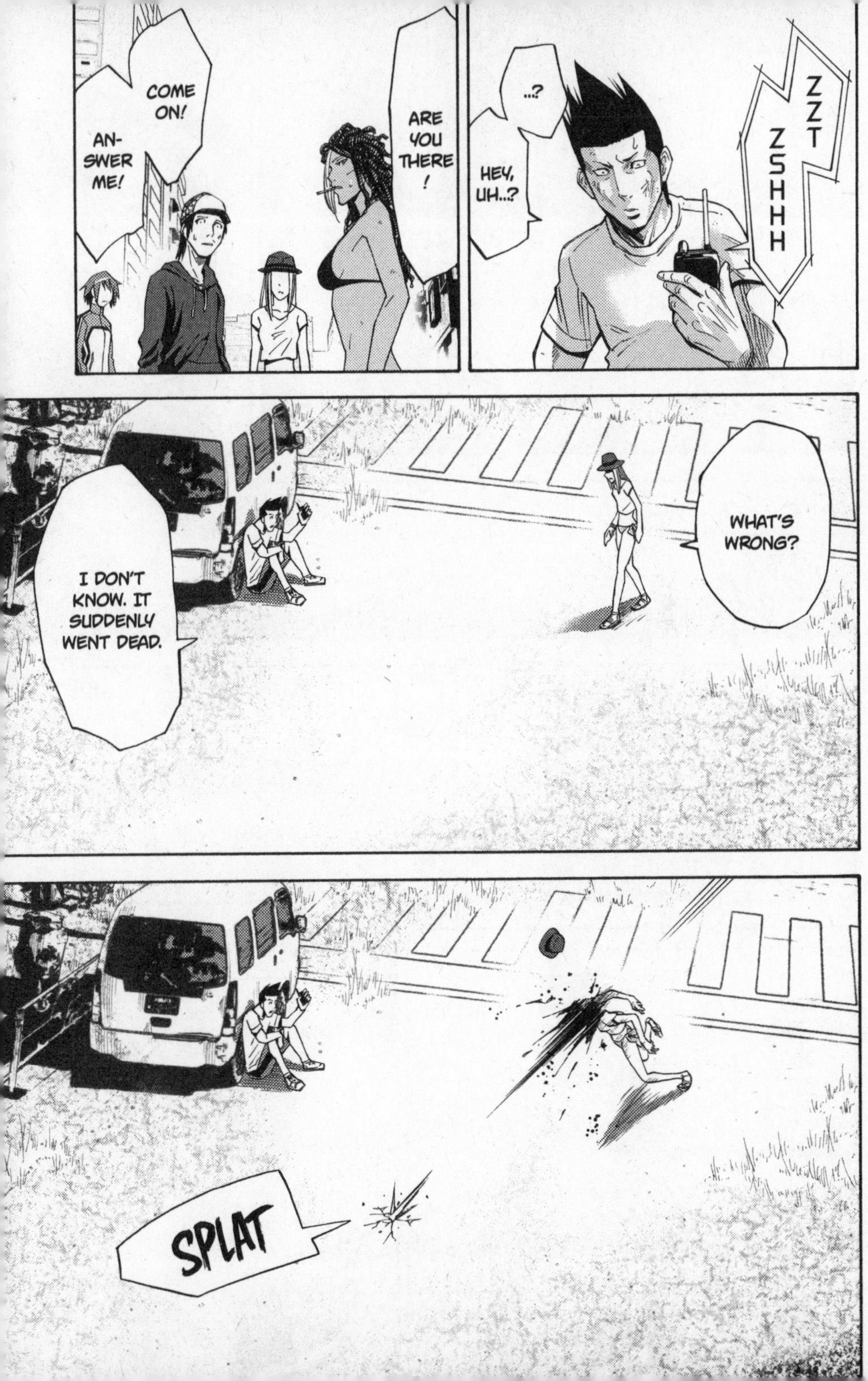

ZZT
ZSHHH
...?
HEY, UH..?
ARE YOU THERE!
COME ON!
AN-SWER ME!
WHAT'S WRONG?
I DON'T KNOW. IT SUDDENLY WENT DEAD.
SPLAT

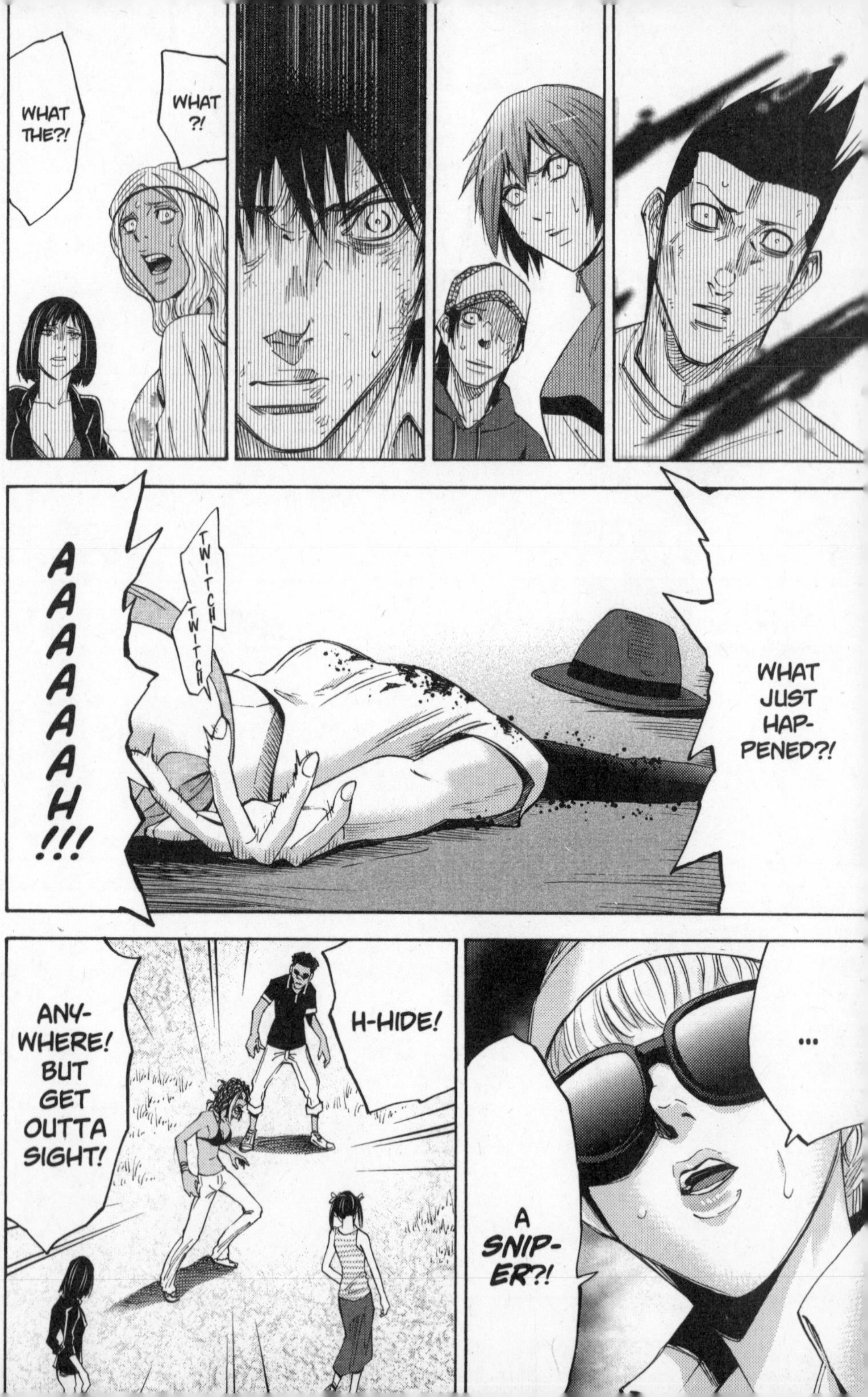
WHAT ?!
WHAT THE?!
WHAT JUST HAP-PENED?!
TWITCH TWITCH
AAAAAAAAH!!!
...
A SNIP-ER?!
H-HIDE!
ANY-WHERE! BUT GET OUTTA SIGHT!

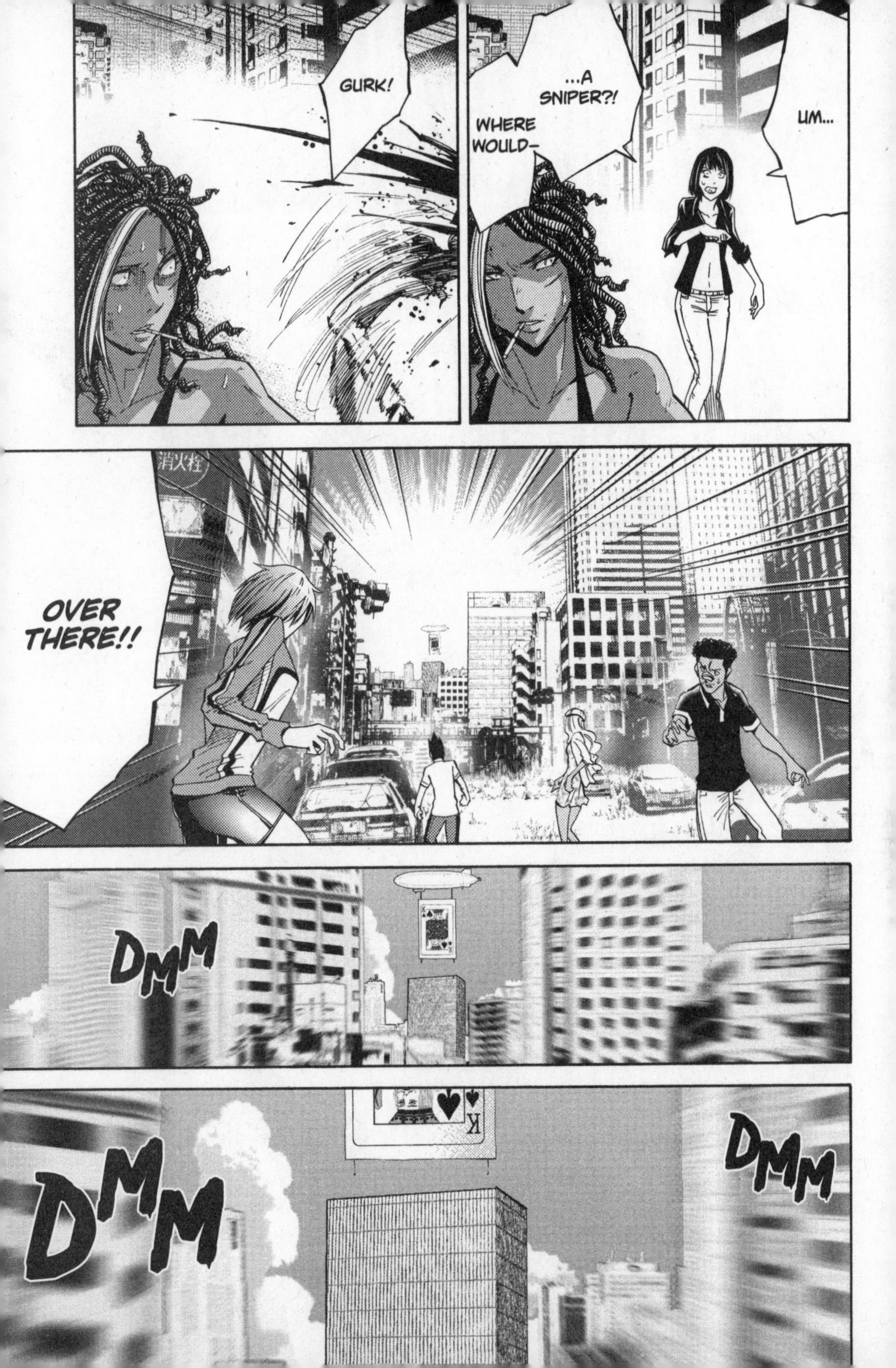
UM...
...A SNIPER?!
WHERE WOULD—
GURK!
OVER THERE!!
DMM
DMM
DMM

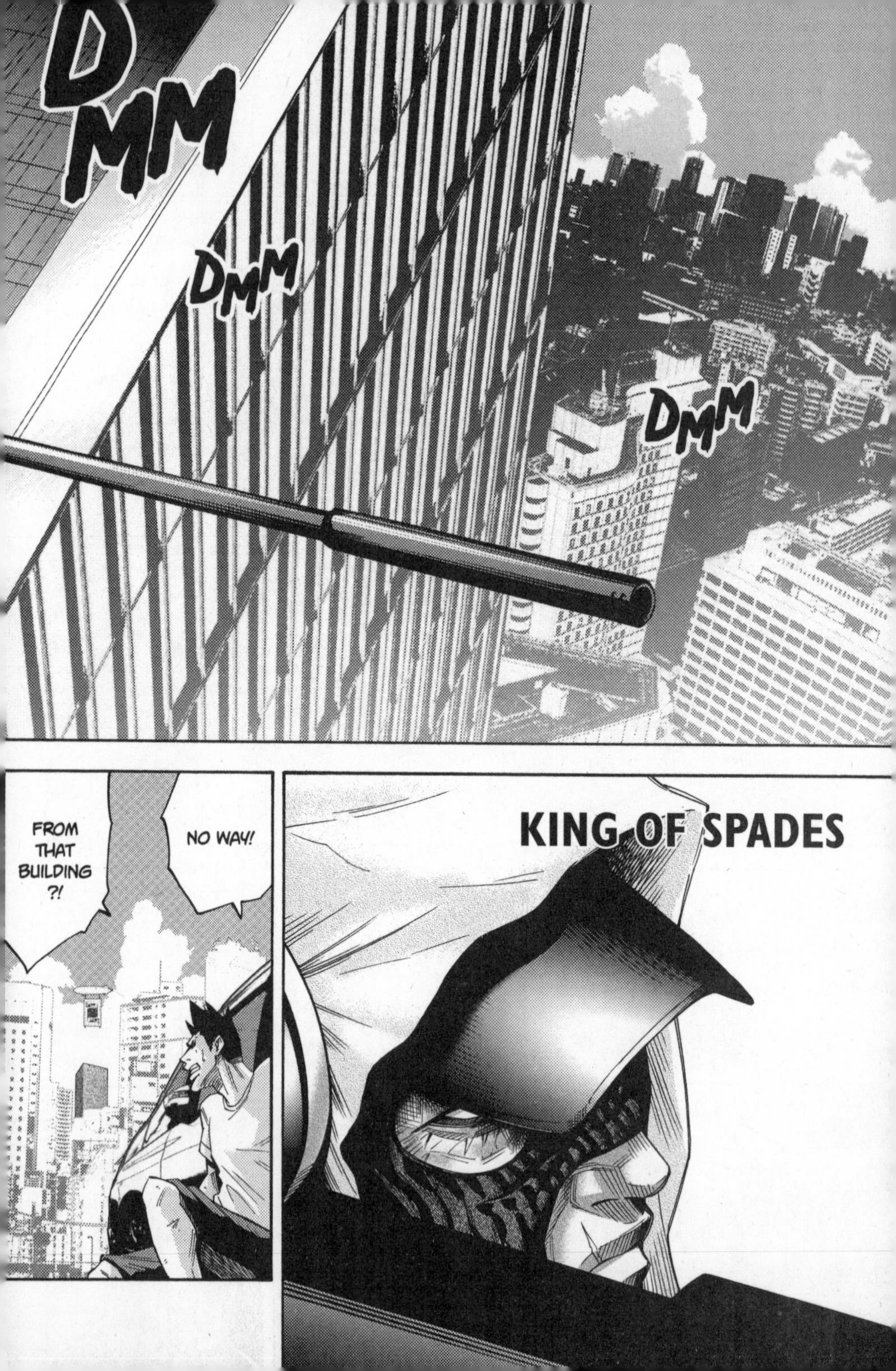
DMM
DmM
DmM
KING OF SPADES
NO WAY!
FROM THAT BUILDING ?!

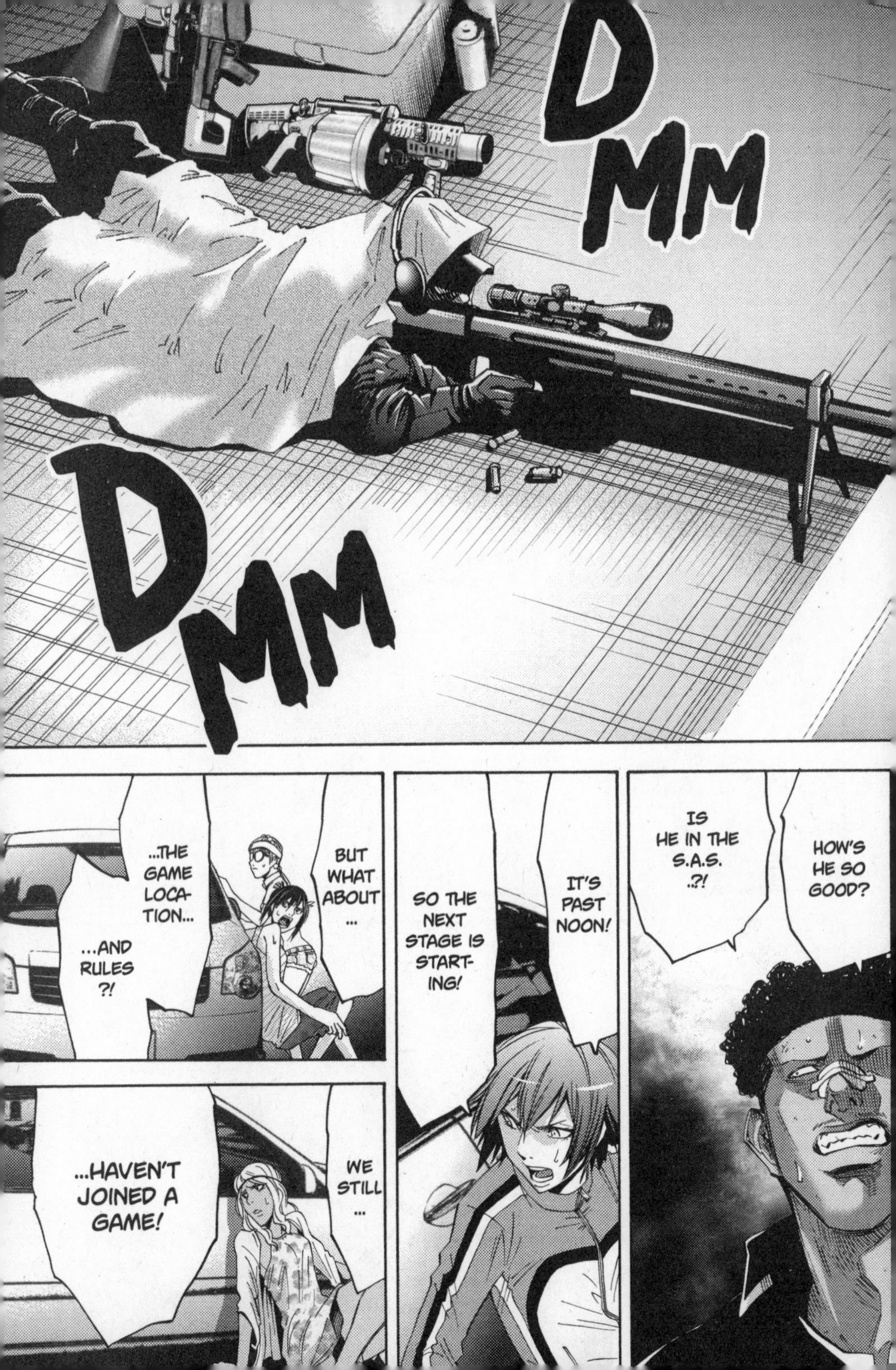
DMM
DMM
HOW'S HE SO GOOD?
IS HE IN THE S.A.S. ..?!
IT'S PAST NOON!
SO THE NEXT STAGE IS START-ING!
BUT WHAT ABOUT ...
...THE GAME LOCA-TION...
...AND RULES ?!
WE STILL ...
...HAVEN'T JOINED A GAME!

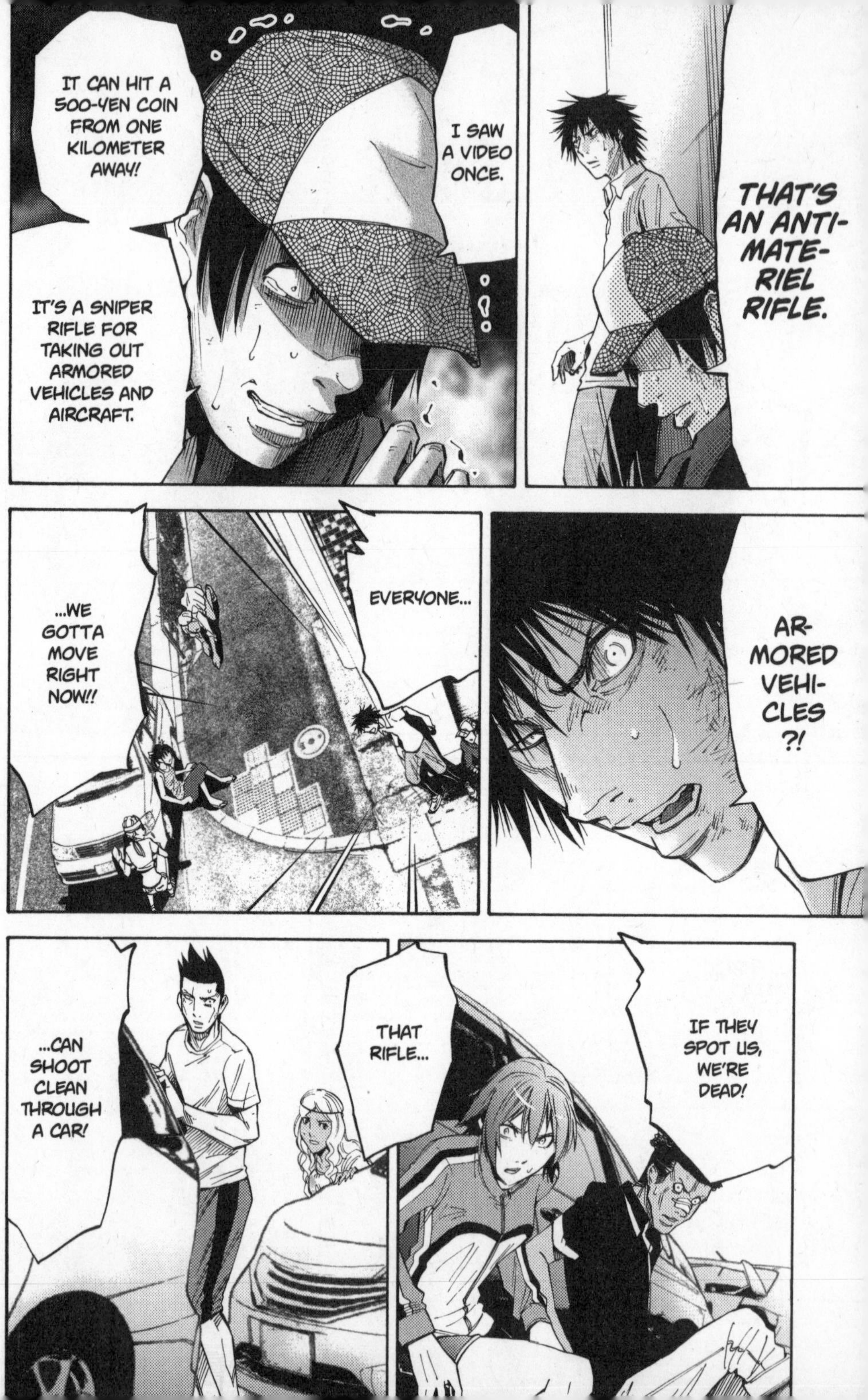
THAT'S AN ANTI-MATERIEL RIFLE.
I SAW A VIDEO ONCE.
IT CAN HIT A 500-YEN COIN FROM ONE KILOMETER AWAY!
IT'S A SNIPER RIFLE FOR TAKING OUT ARMORED VEHICLES AND AIRCRAFT.
ARMORED VEHICLES?!
EVERYONE...
...WE GOTTA MOVE RIGHT NOW!!
IF THEY SPOT US, WE'RE DEAD!
THAT RIFLE...
...CAN SHOOT CLEAN THROUGH A CAR!

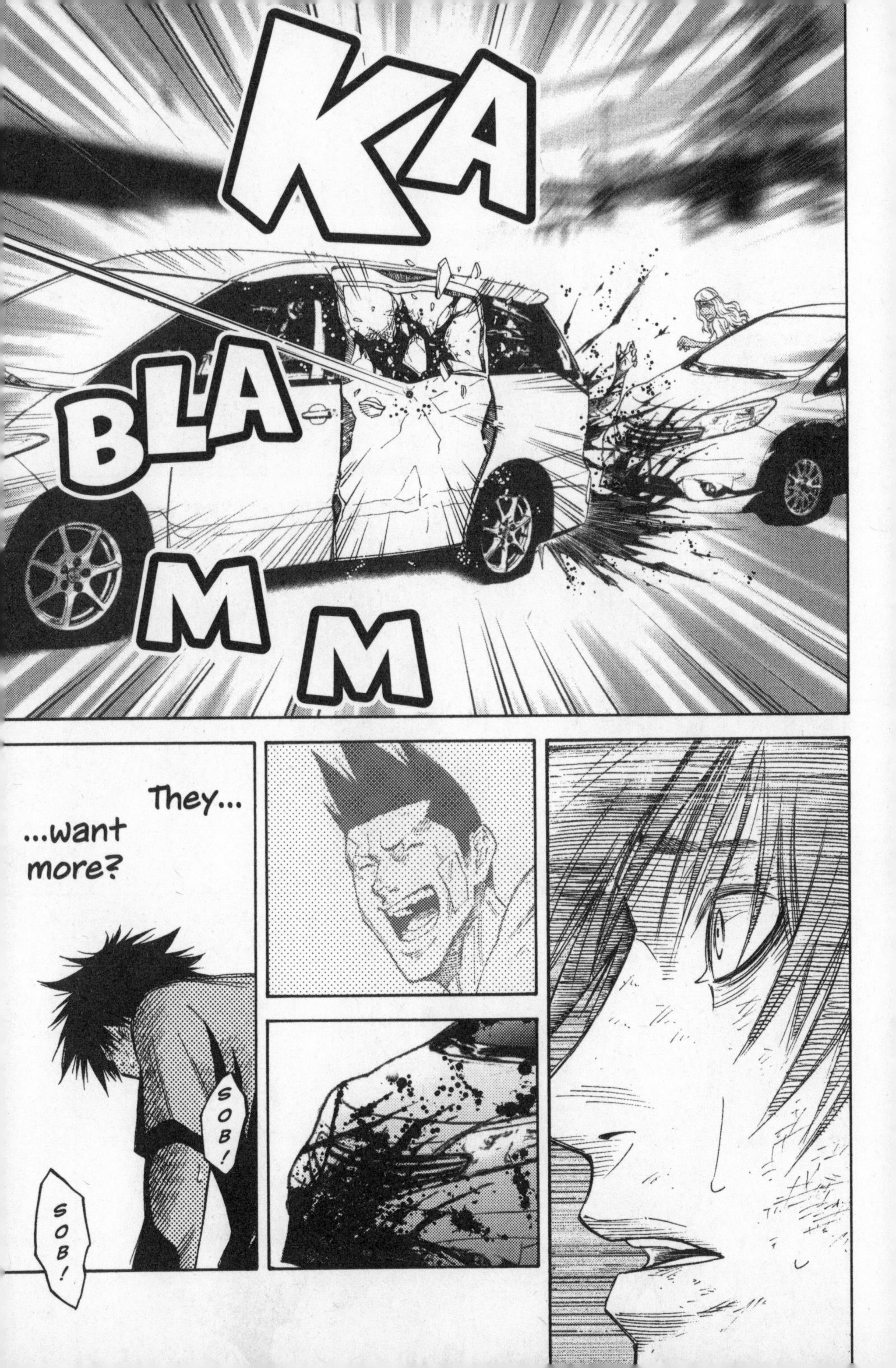
KA
BLA
M
M
They...
...want more?
SOB!
SOB!

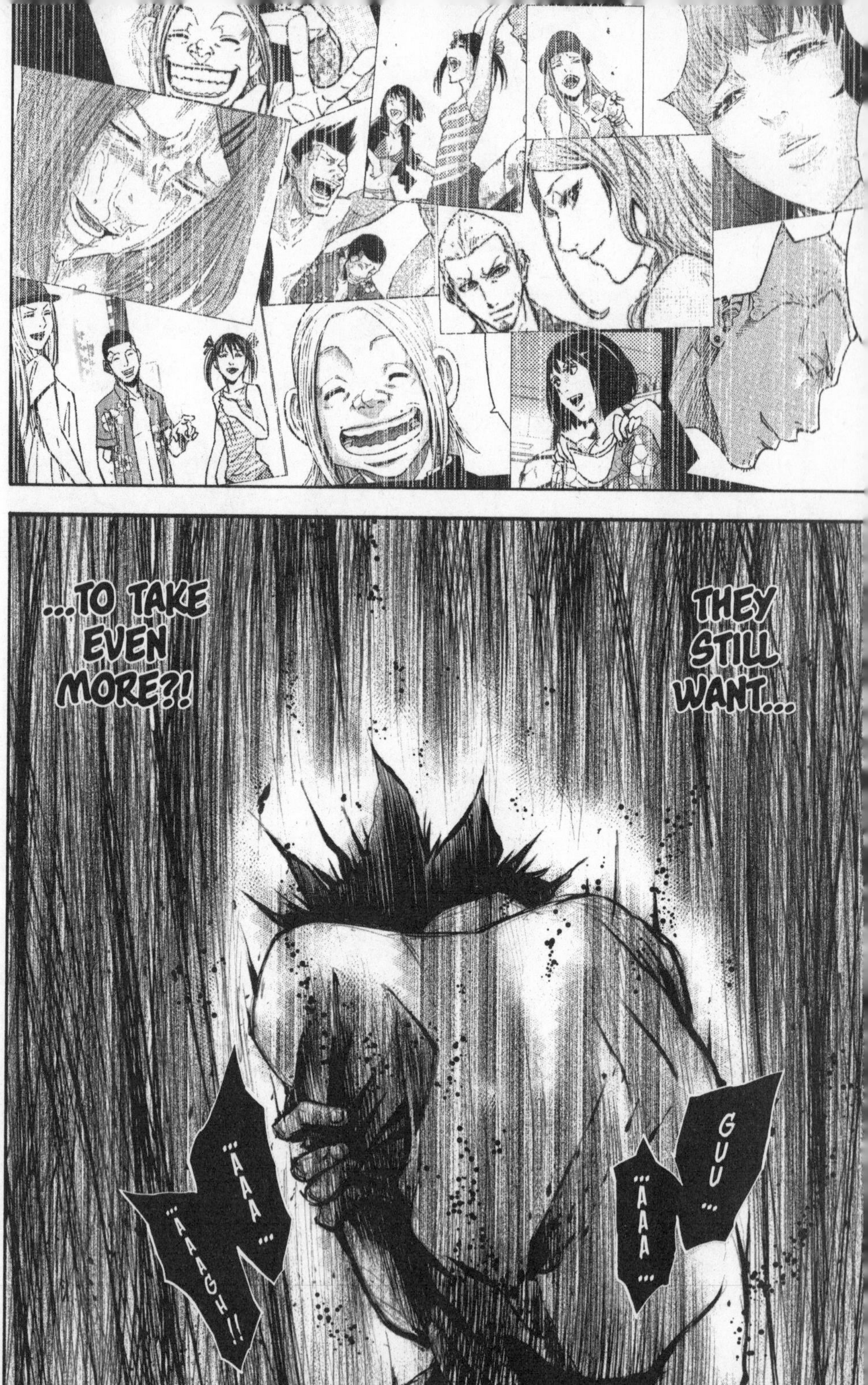
THEY STILL WANT...
...TO TAKE EVEN MORE?!
GUU... ...AAA...
...AAA... ...AAAGH!!

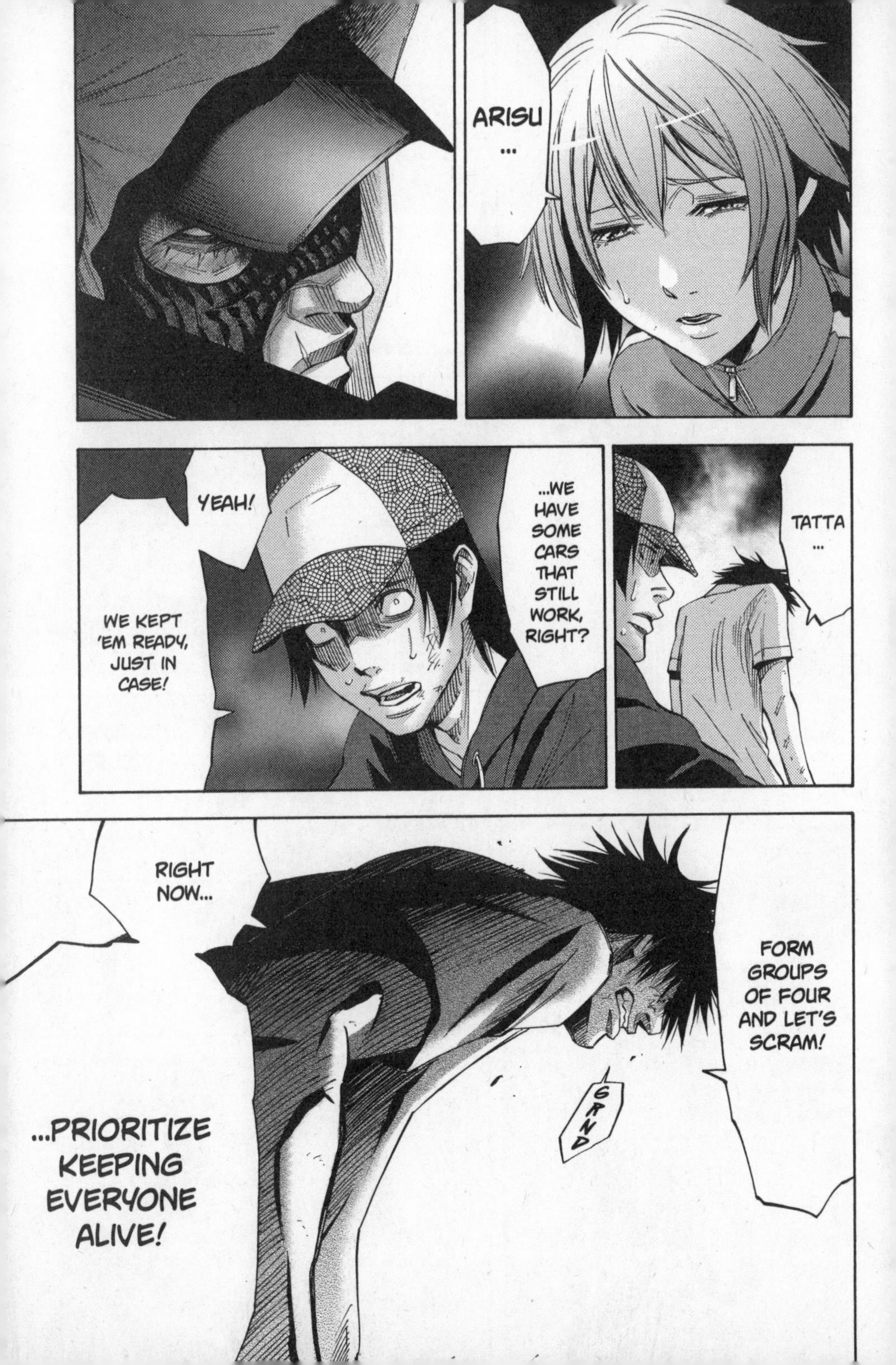
ARISU ...
TATTA ...
...WE HAVE SOME CARS THAT STILL WORK, RIGHT?
YEAH!
WE KEPT 'EM READY, JUST IN CASE!
FORM GROUPS OF FOUR AND LET'S SCRAM!
RIGHT NOW...
GRND
...PRIORITIZE KEEPING EVERYONE ALIVE!

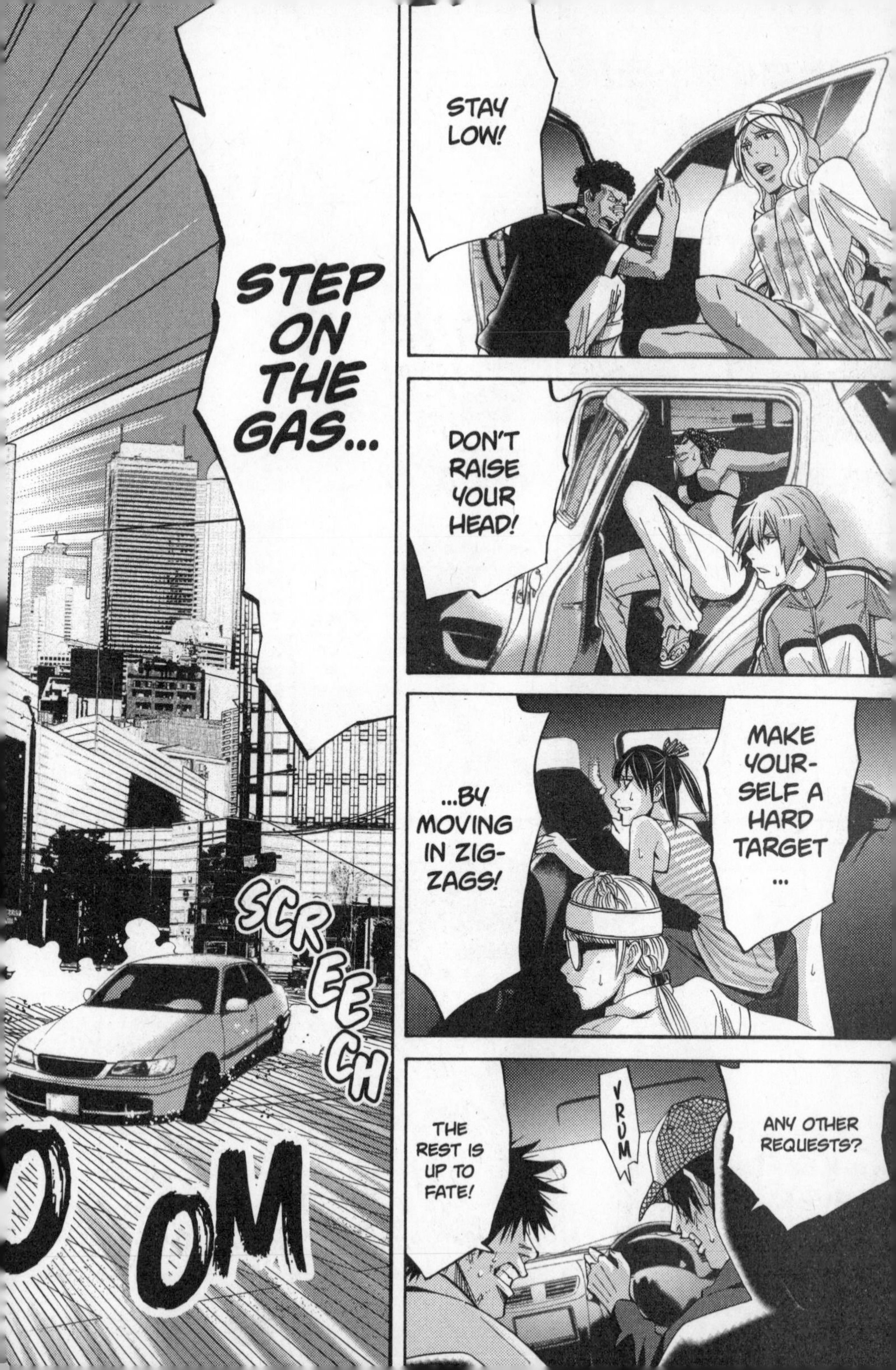
STAY LOW!
DON'T RAISE YOUR HEAD!
MAKE YOUR-SELF A HARD TARGET ...
...BY MOVING IN ZIG-ZAGS!
ANY OTHER REQUESTS?
VRUM
THE REST IS UP TO FATE!
STEP ON THE GAS...
SCREEECH
OOM

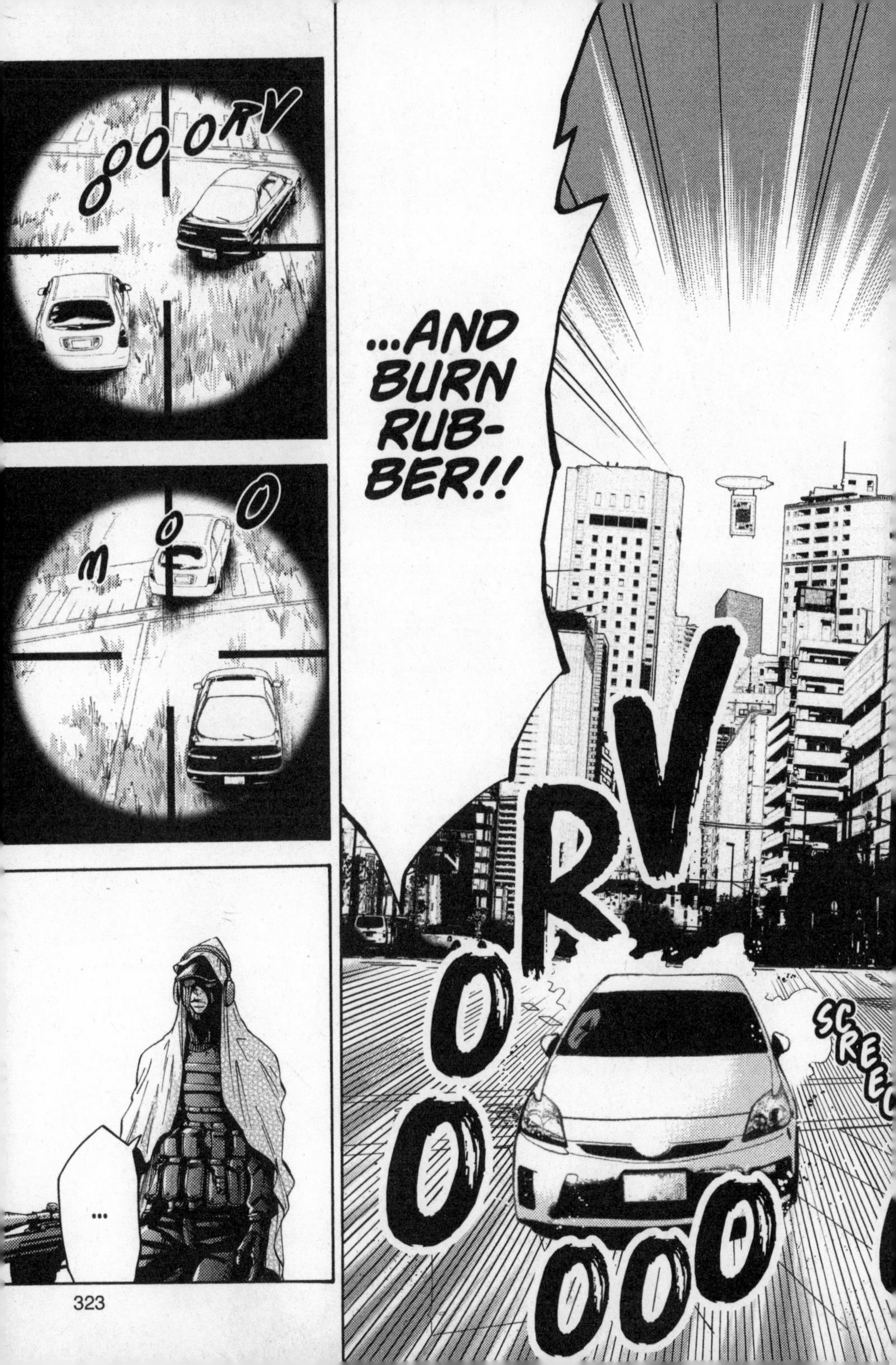
...AND BURN RUB-BER!!
SCREEC
...

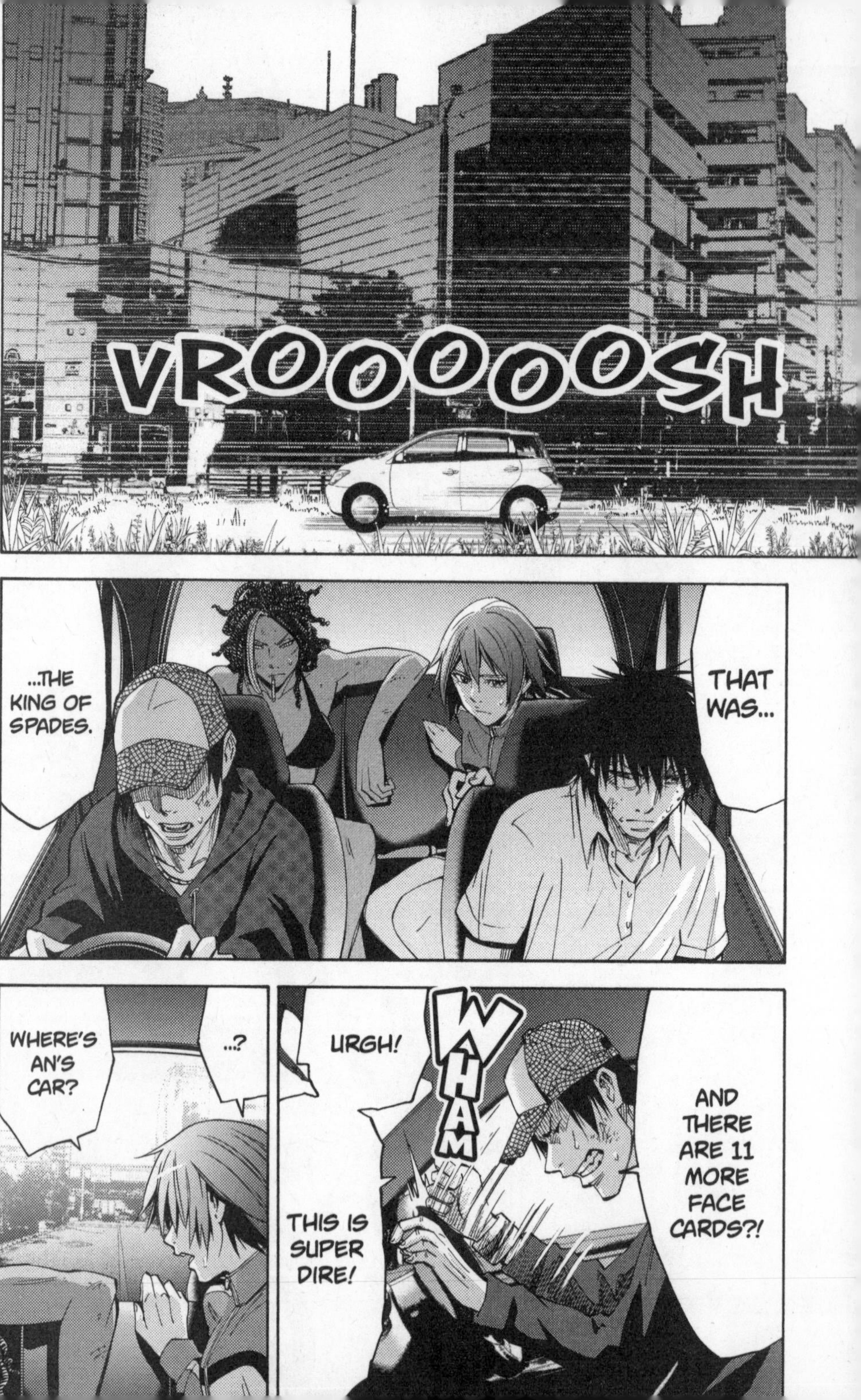
VROOOOOSH
THAT WAS...
...THE KING OF SPADES.
AND THERE ARE 11 MORE FACE CARDS?!
WHAM
URGH!
THIS IS SUPER DIRE!
...?
WHERE'S AN'S CAR?

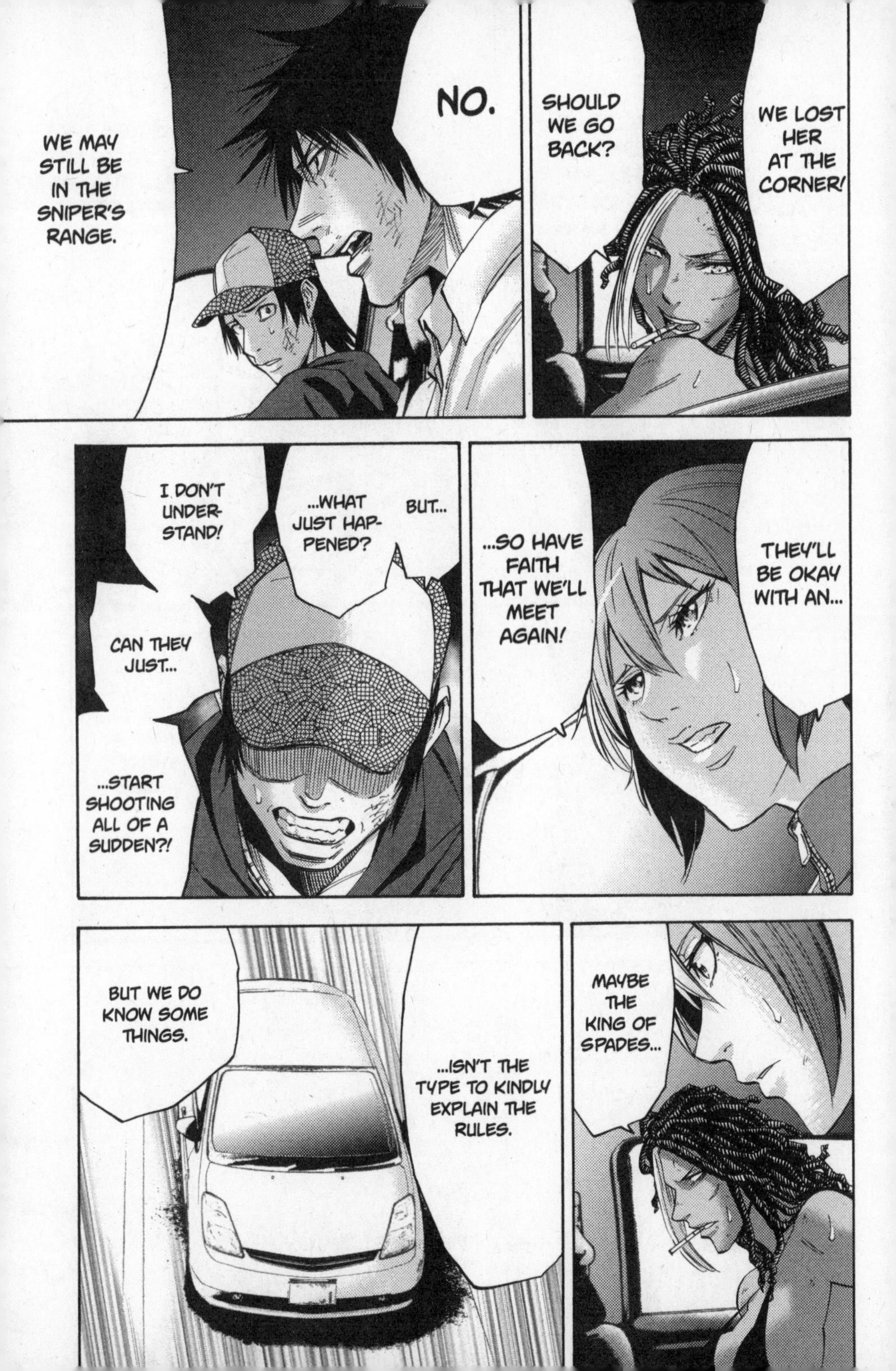
WE LOST HER AT THE CORNER!
SHOULD WE GO BACK?
NO.
WE MAY STILL BE IN THE SNIPER'S RANGE.
THEY'LL BE OKAY WITH AN...
...SO HAVE FAITH THAT WE'LL MEET AGAIN!
BUT...
...WHAT JUST HAP-PENED?
I DON'T UNDER-STAND!
CAN THEY JUST...
...START SHOOTING ALL OF A SUDDEN?!
MAYBE THE KING OF SPADES...
...ISN'T THE TYPE TO KINDLY EXPLAIN THE RULES.
BUT WE DO KNOW SOME THINGS.

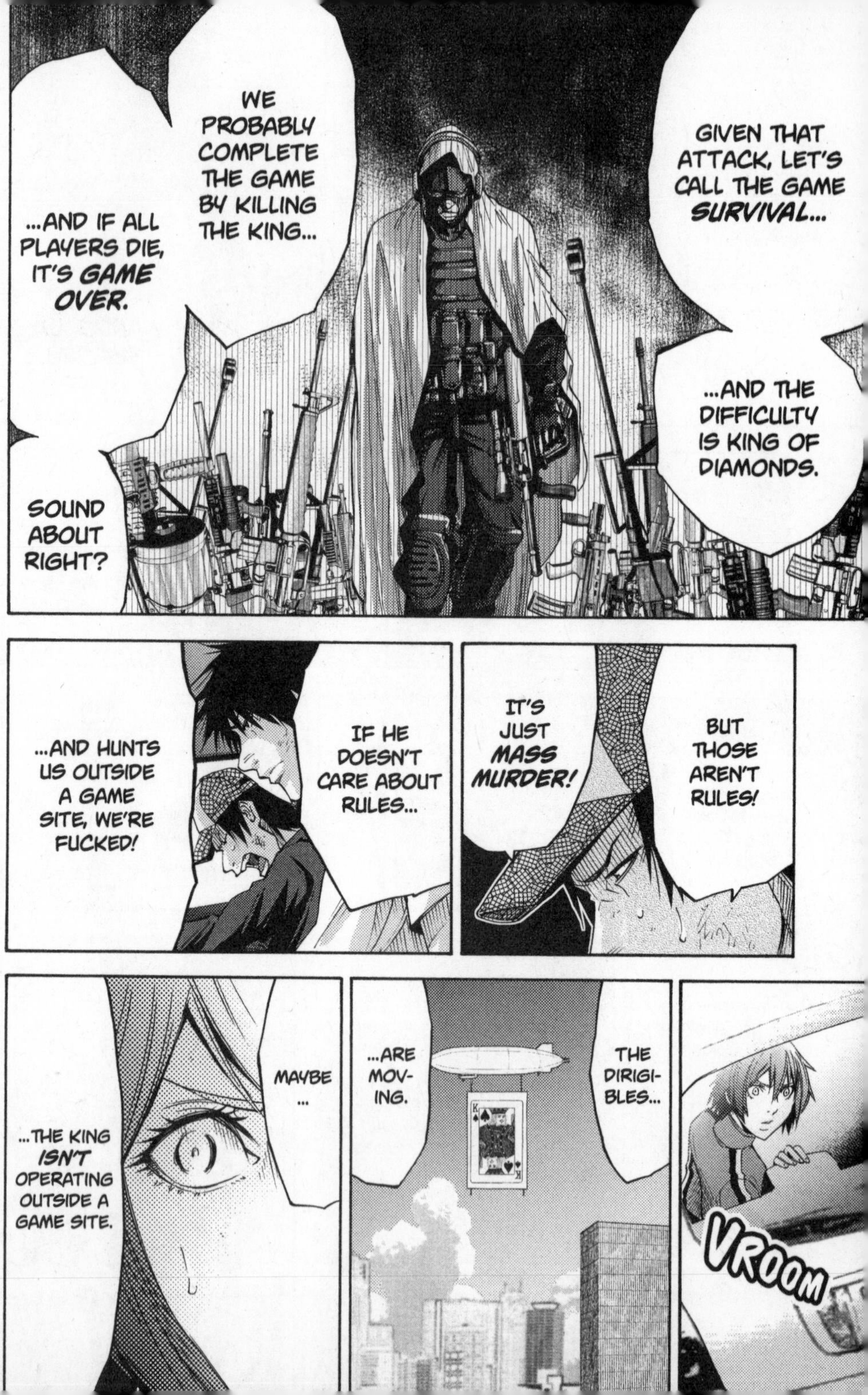
GIVEN THAT ATTACK, LET'S CALL THE GAME *SURVIVAL*...
...AND THE DIFFICULTY IS KING OF DIAMONDS.
WE PROBABLY COMPLETE THE GAME BY KILLING THE KING...
...AND IF ALL PLAYERS DIE, IT'S *GAME OVER*.
SOUND ABOUT RIGHT?
BUT THOSE AREN'T RULES!
IT'S JUST *MASS MURDER*!
IF HE DOESN'T CARE ABOUT RULES...
...AND HUNTS US OUTSIDE A GAME SITE, WE'RE FUCKED!
VROOM
THE DIRIGIBLES...
...ARE MOVING.
MAYBE...
...THE KING *ISN'T* OPERATING OUTSIDE A GAME SITE.

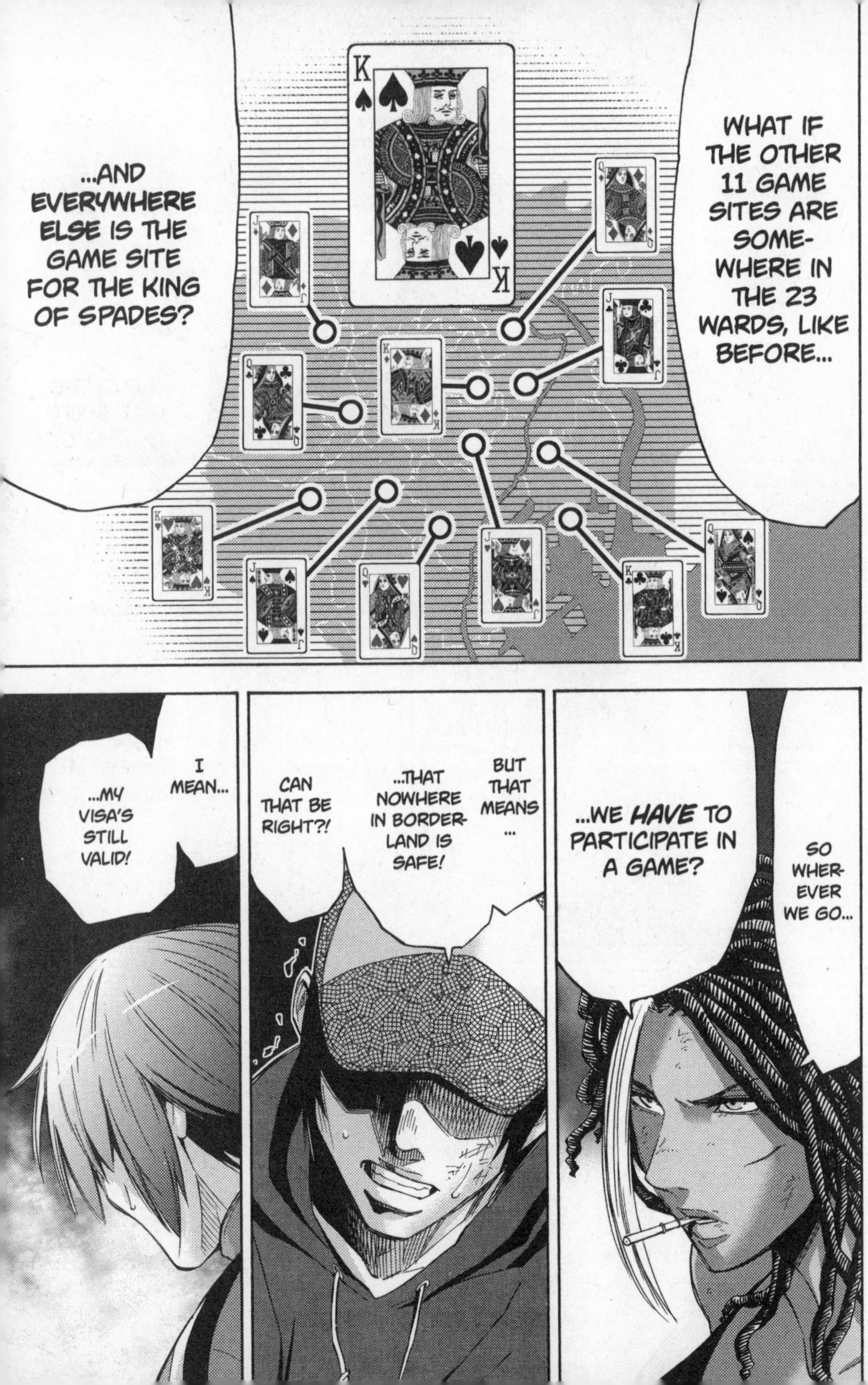
WHAT IF THE OTHER 11 GAME SITES ARE SOME-WHERE IN THE 23 WARDS, LIKE BEFORE...
...AND EVERYWHERE ELSE IS THE GAME SITE FOR THE KING OF SPADES?
SO WHER-EVER WE GO...
...WE *HAVE* TO PARTICIPATE IN A GAME?
BUT THAT MEANS ...
...THAT NOWHERE IN BORDER-LAND IS SAFE!
CAN THAT BE RIGHT?!
I MEAN...
...MY VISA'S STILL VALID!

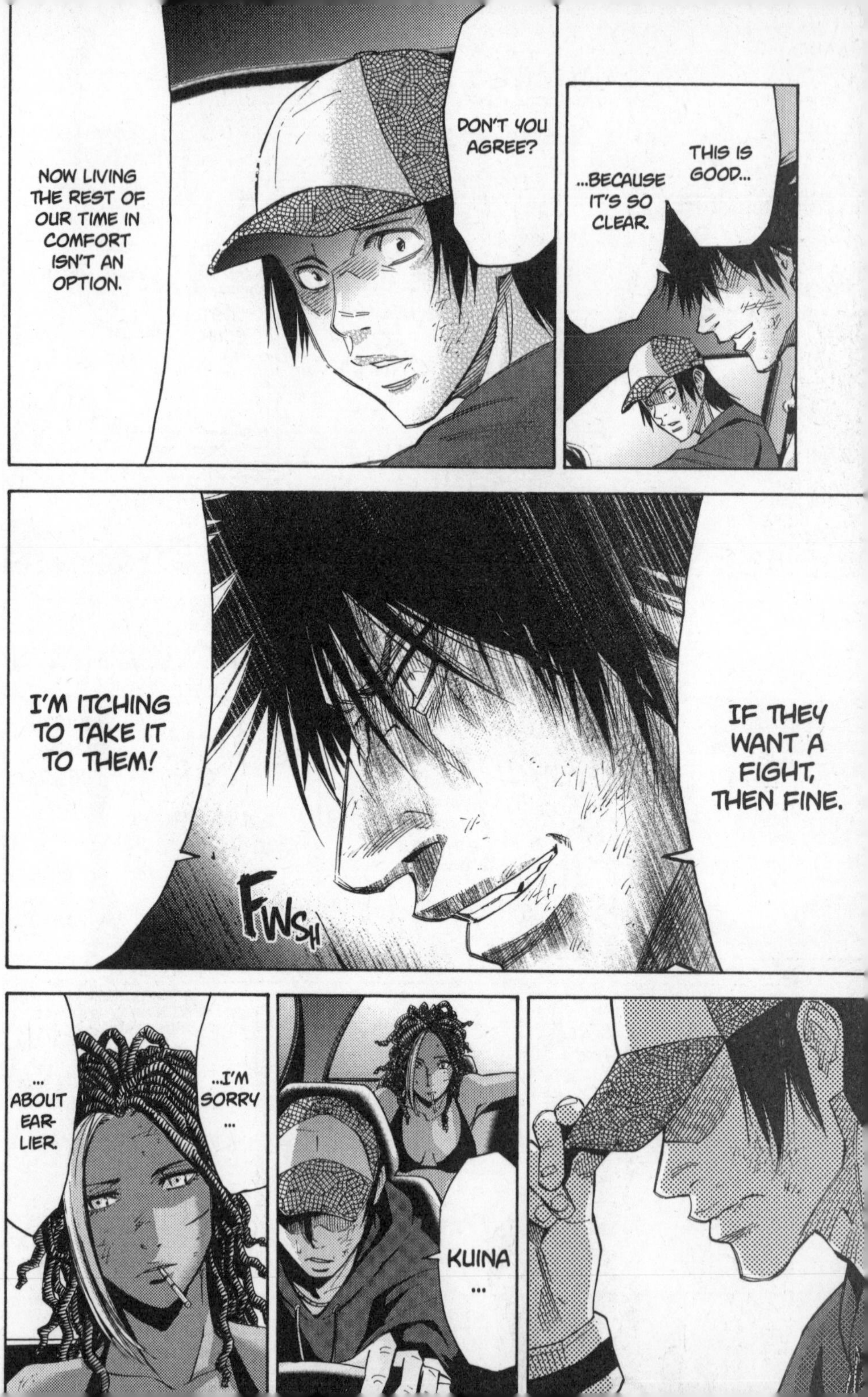
THIS IS GOOD...
...BECAUSE IT'S SO CLEAR.
DON'T YOU AGREE?
NOW LIVING THE REST OF OUR TIME IN COMFORT ISN'T AN OPTION.
IF THEY WANT A FIGHT, THEN FINE.
FWSH
I'M ITCHING TO TAKE IT TO THEM!
KUINA ...
...I'M SORRY ...
... ABOUT EAR-LIER.

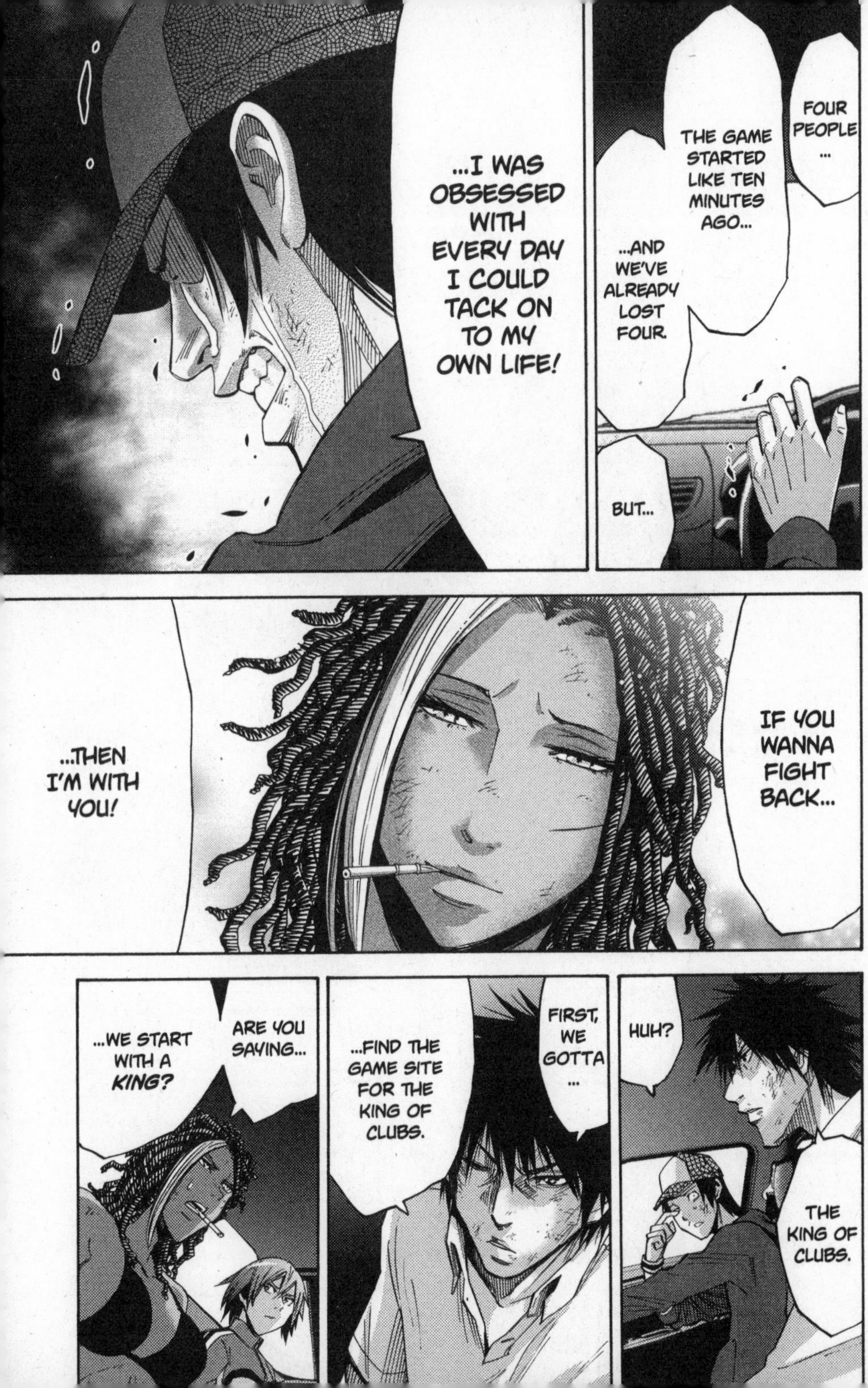
FOUR PEOPLE...
THE GAME STARTED LIKE TEN MINUTES AGO...
...AND WE'VE ALREADY LOST FOUR.
BUT...
...I WAS OBSESSED WITH EVERY DAY I COULD TACK ON TO MY OWN LIFE!
IF YOU WANNA FIGHT BACK...
...THEN I'M WITH YOU!
HUH?
THE KING OF CLUBS.
FIRST, WE GOTTA...
...FIND THE GAME SITE FOR THE KING OF CLUBS.
ARE YOU SAYING...
...WE START WITH A *KING*?

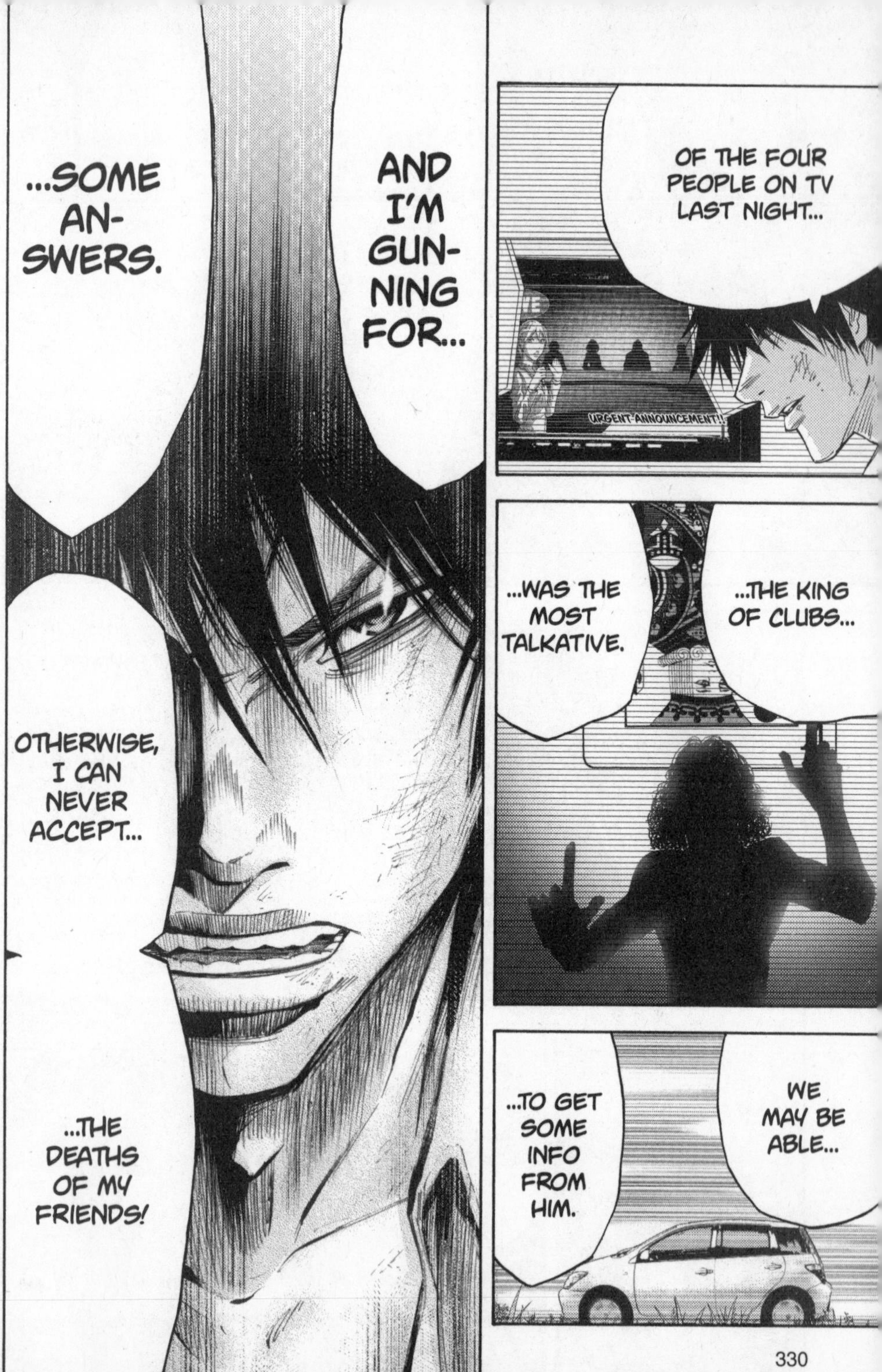
OF THE FOUR PEOPLE ON TV LAST NIGHT...
URGENT ANNOUNCEMENT!!
...THE KING OF CLUBS...
...WAS THE MOST TALKATIVE.
WE MAY BE ABLE...
...TO GET SOME INFO FROM HIM.
AND I'M GUN-NING FOR...
...SOME AN-SWERS.
OTHERWISE, I CAN NEVER ACCEPT...
...THE DEATHS OF MY FRIENDS!

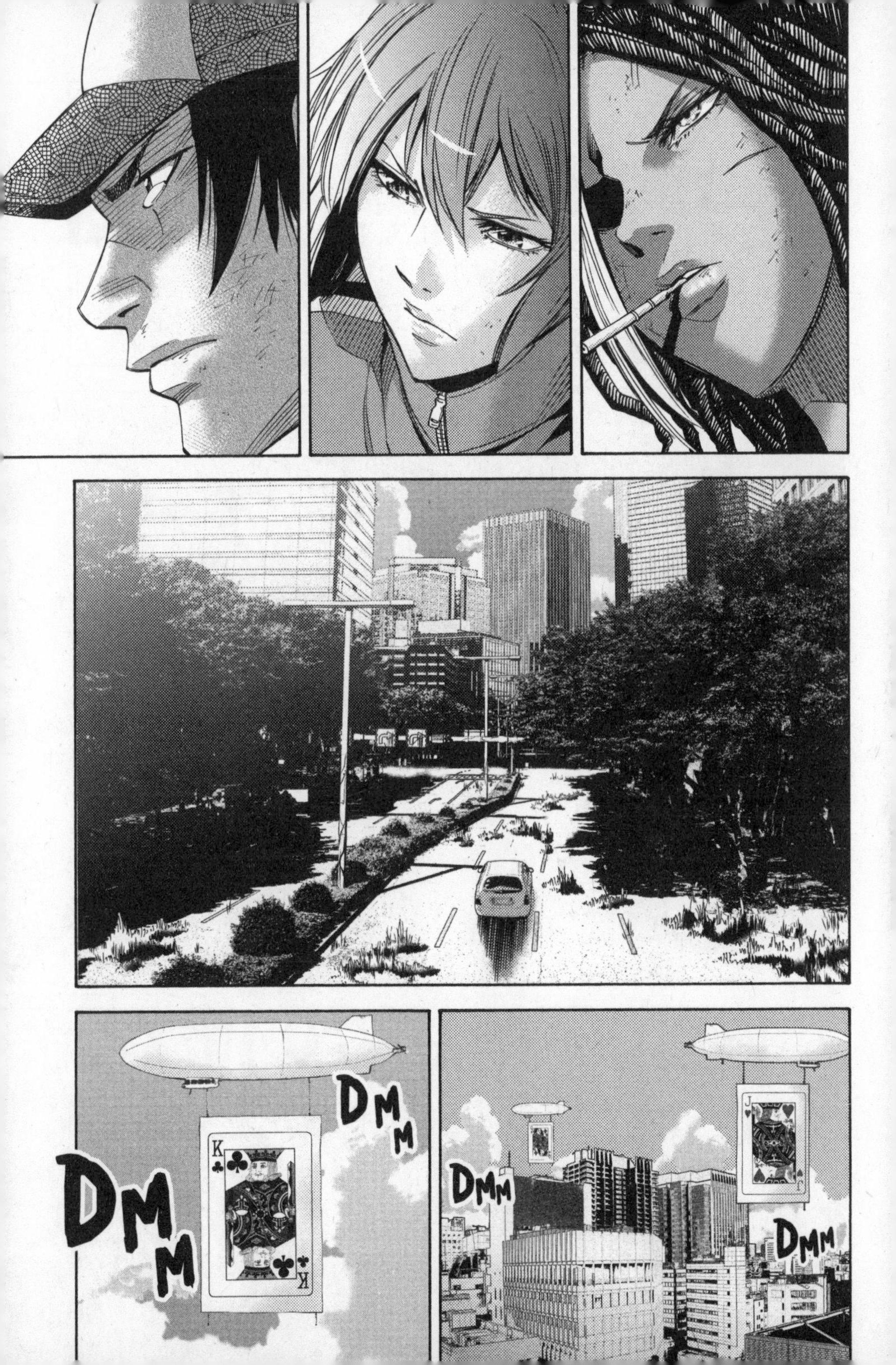
DMM
DMM
DMM
DMM

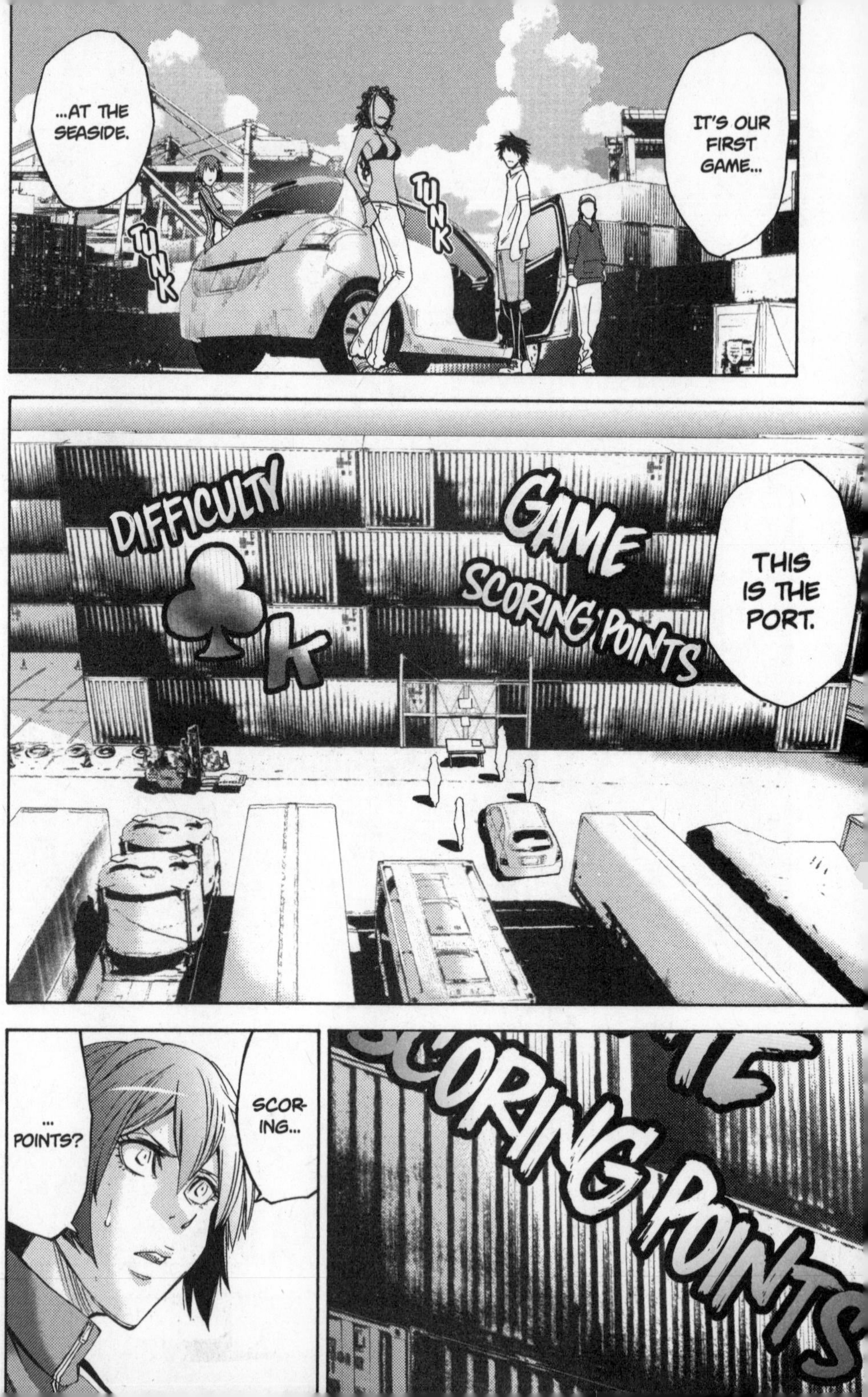
IT'S OUR FIRST GAME...
...AT THE SEASIDE.
TUNK
TUNK
THIS IS THE PORT.
GAME
SCORING POINTS
DIFFICULTY
K
SCORING POINTS
SCOR-ING...
...POINTS?

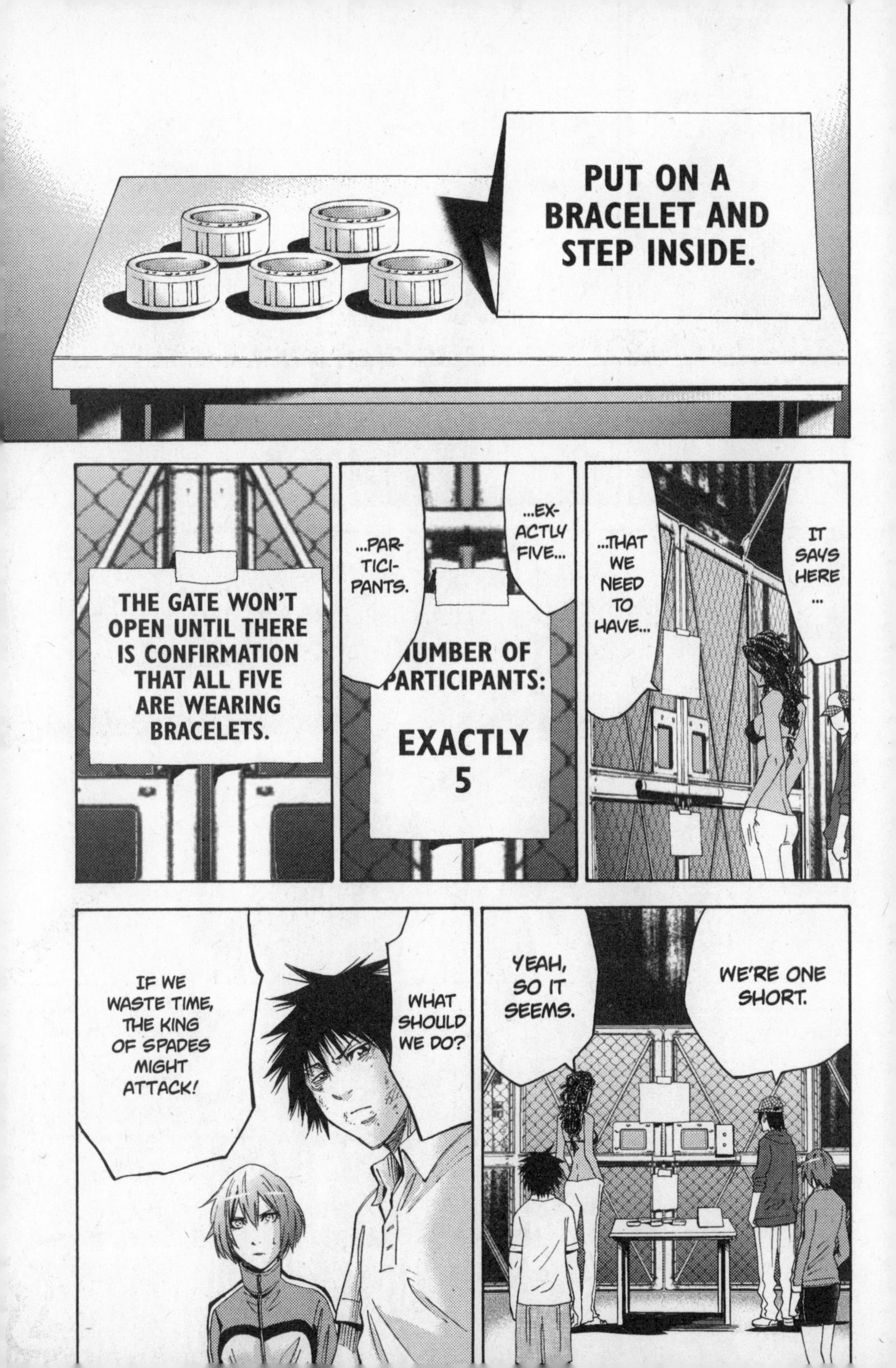
PUT ON A BRACELET AND STEP INSIDE.
IT SAYS HERE ...
...THAT WE NEED TO HAVE...
...EX-ACTLY FIVE...
...PAR-TICI-PANTS.
NUMBER OF PARTICIPANTS: EXACTLY 5
THE GATE WON'T OPEN UNTIL THERE IS CONFIRMATION THAT ALL FIVE ARE WEARING BRACELETS.
WE'RE ONE SHORT.
YEAH, SO IT SEEMS.
WHAT SHOULD WE DO?
IF WE WASTE TIME, THE KING OF SPADES MIGHT ATTACK!

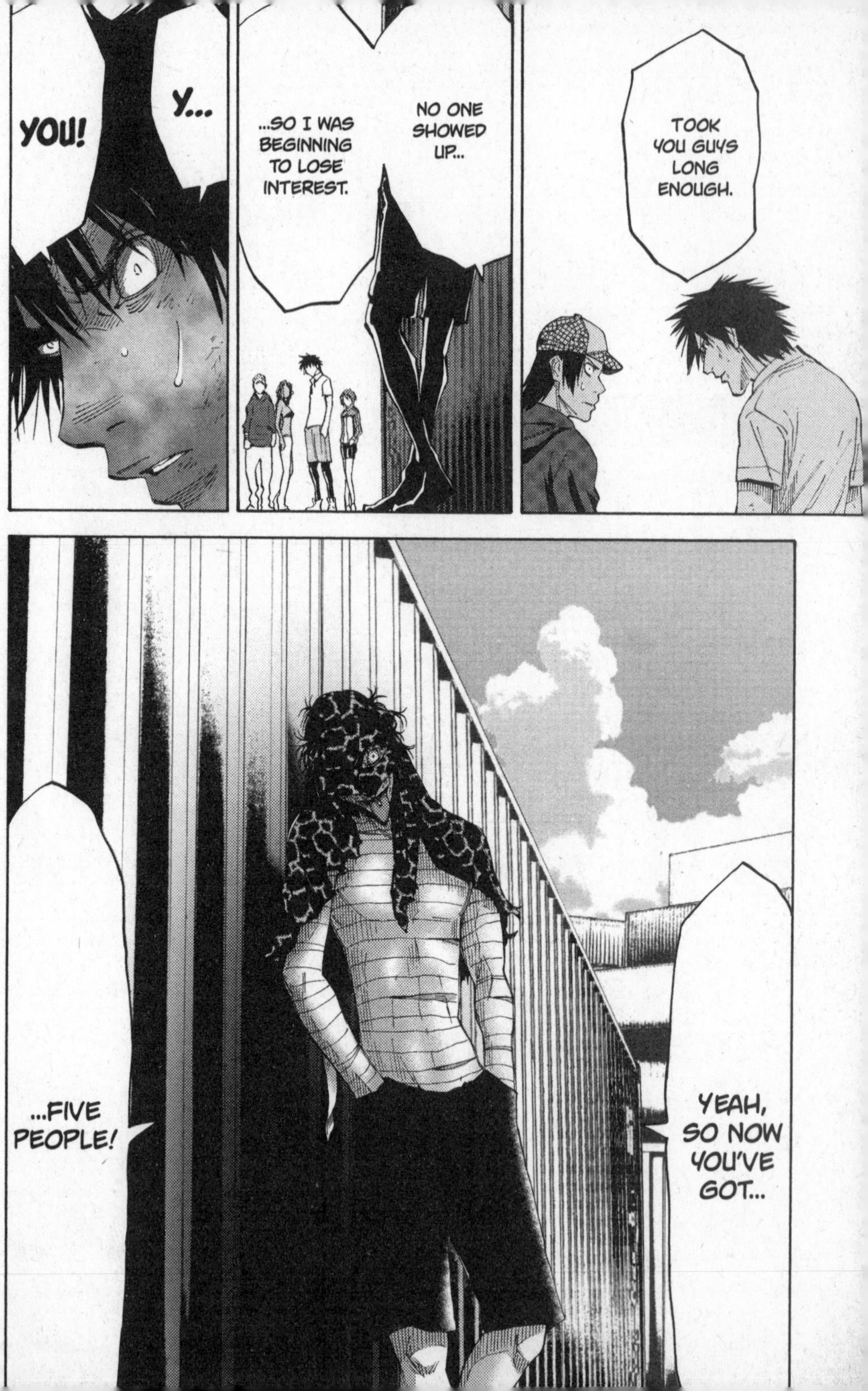
TOOK YOU GUYS LONG ENOUGH.
NO ONE SHOWED UP...
...SO I WAS BEGINNING TO LOSE INTEREST.
Y...
YOU!
YEAH, SO NOW YOU'VE GOT...
...FIVE PEOPLE!

I don't like the phrase "journey of self-discovery" because no matter how much you search, your self isn't out there in the world. Going on a journey isn't about finding yourself, it's about keeping yourself company. When you're all by yourself in an unknown world, you can have conversations with your inner self to your heart's content. Mahiru is me at 33.

— HARO ASO

HARO ASO

In 2004, Haro Aso received *Shonen Sunday's* Manga
College Award for his short story "YUNGE!" After the
success of his 2007 short story "Onigami Amon,"
Aso got the chance to start a series of his own—
2008's *Hyde & Closer*. In 2010, his series *Alice in
Borderland* began serialization in *Shonen Sunday S*
and is now a Netflix live-action drama. *Zom 100:
Bucket List of the Dead* is his follow-up series.

ALICE IN BORDERLAND

VOLUME 4
VIZ SIGNATURE EDITION

STORY AND ART BY
HARO ASO

English Translation & Adaptation JOHN WERRY
Touch-Up Art & Lettering ERIKA MILLIGAN
Design ALICE LEWIS
Editor PANCHA DIAZ

IMAWA NO KUNI NO ALICE Vols. 7–8
by Haro ASO
© 2011 Haro ASO
All rights reserved.
Original Japanese edition published by SHOGAKUKAN.
English translation rights in the United States of America, Canada, the United Kingdom,
Ireland, Australia, and New Zealand arranged with SHOGAKUKAN.

Printed in Canada

Published by VIZ Media, LLC.
P.O. Box 77010
San Francisco, CA 94107

10 9 8 7 6 5 4 3 2 1
First printing, December 2022

VIZ MEDIA   VIZ SIGNATURE
viz.com   vizsignature.com

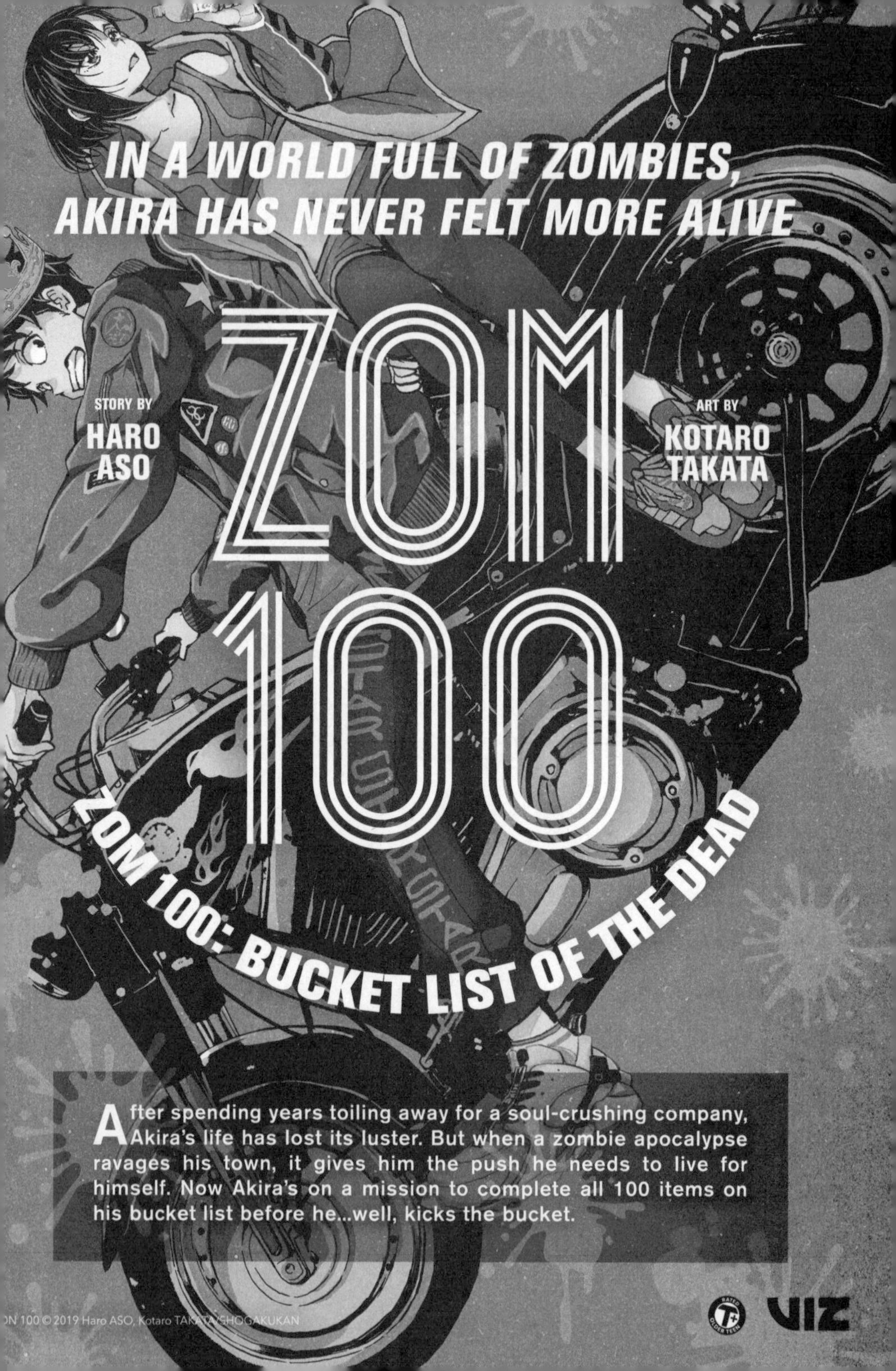
IN A WORLD FULL OF ZOMBIES, AKIRA HAS NEVER FELT MORE ALIVE
STORY BY
HARO ASO
ZOM 100
ART BY
KOTARO TAKATA
ZOM 100: BUCKET LIST OF THE DEAD
After spending years toiling away for a soul-crushing company, Akira's life has lost its luster. But when a zombie apocalypse ravages his town, it gives him the push he needs to live for himself. Now Akira's on a mission to complete all 100 items on his bucket list before he...well, kicks the bucket.
N 100 © 2019 Haro ASO, Kotaro TAKATA/SHOGAKUKAN
RATED T+ OLDER TEEN
VIZ

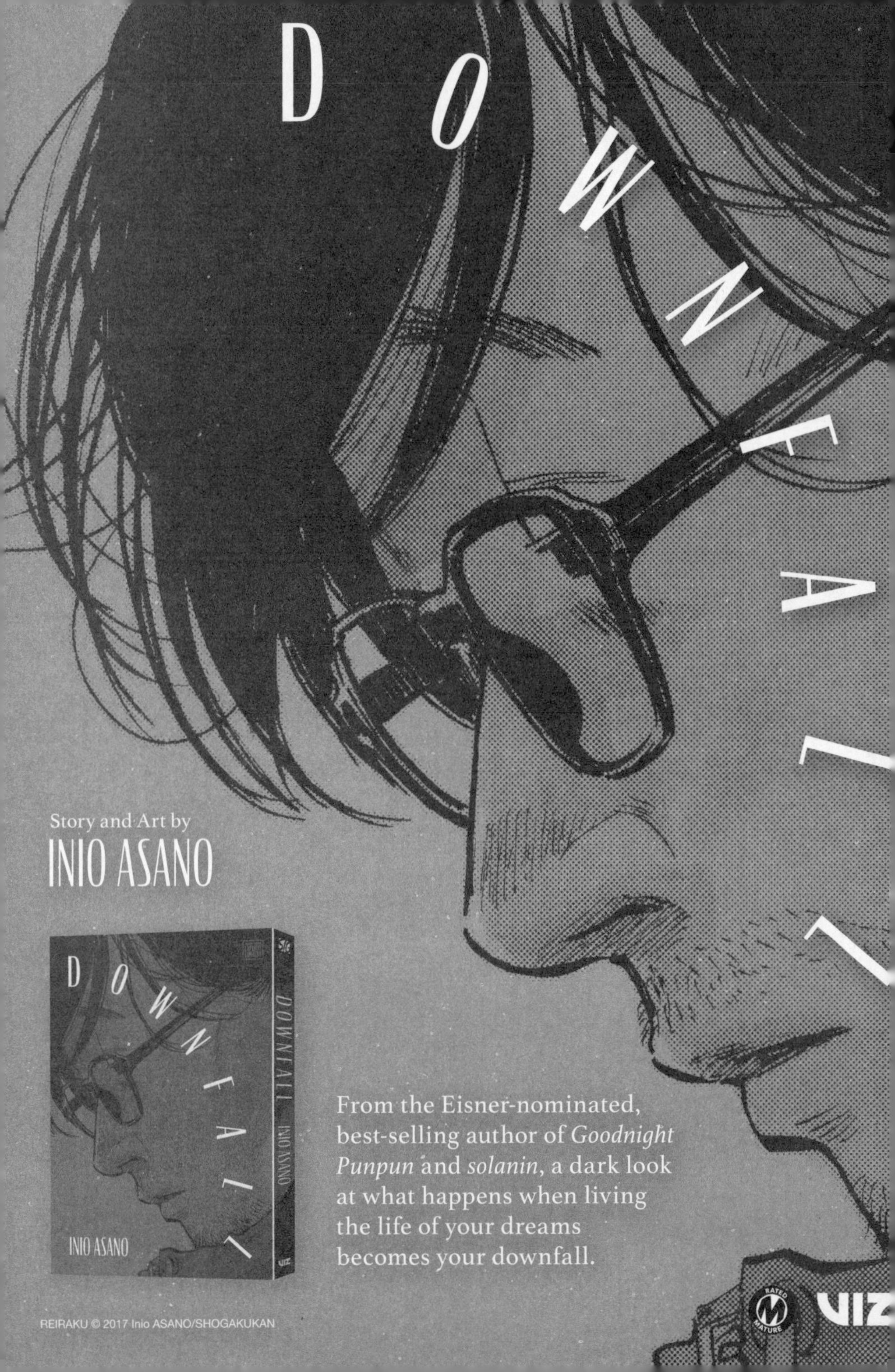
DOWNFALL
Story and Art by
INIO ASANO
DOWNFALL
INIO ASANO
From the Eisner-nominated, best-selling author of *Goodnight Punpun* and *solanin*, a dark look at what happens when living the life of your dreams becomes your downfall.
RATED MATURE
VIZ
REIRAKU © 2017 Inio ASANO/SHOGAKUKAN

THE DRIFTING CLASSROOM
PERFECT EDITION
by KAZUO UMEZZ

Out of nowhere, an entire school vanishes, leaving nothing but a hole in the ground. While parents mourn and authorities investigate, the students and teachers find themselves not dead but stranded in a terrifying wasteland where they must fight to survive.

COMPLETE IN 3 VOLUMES

VIZ

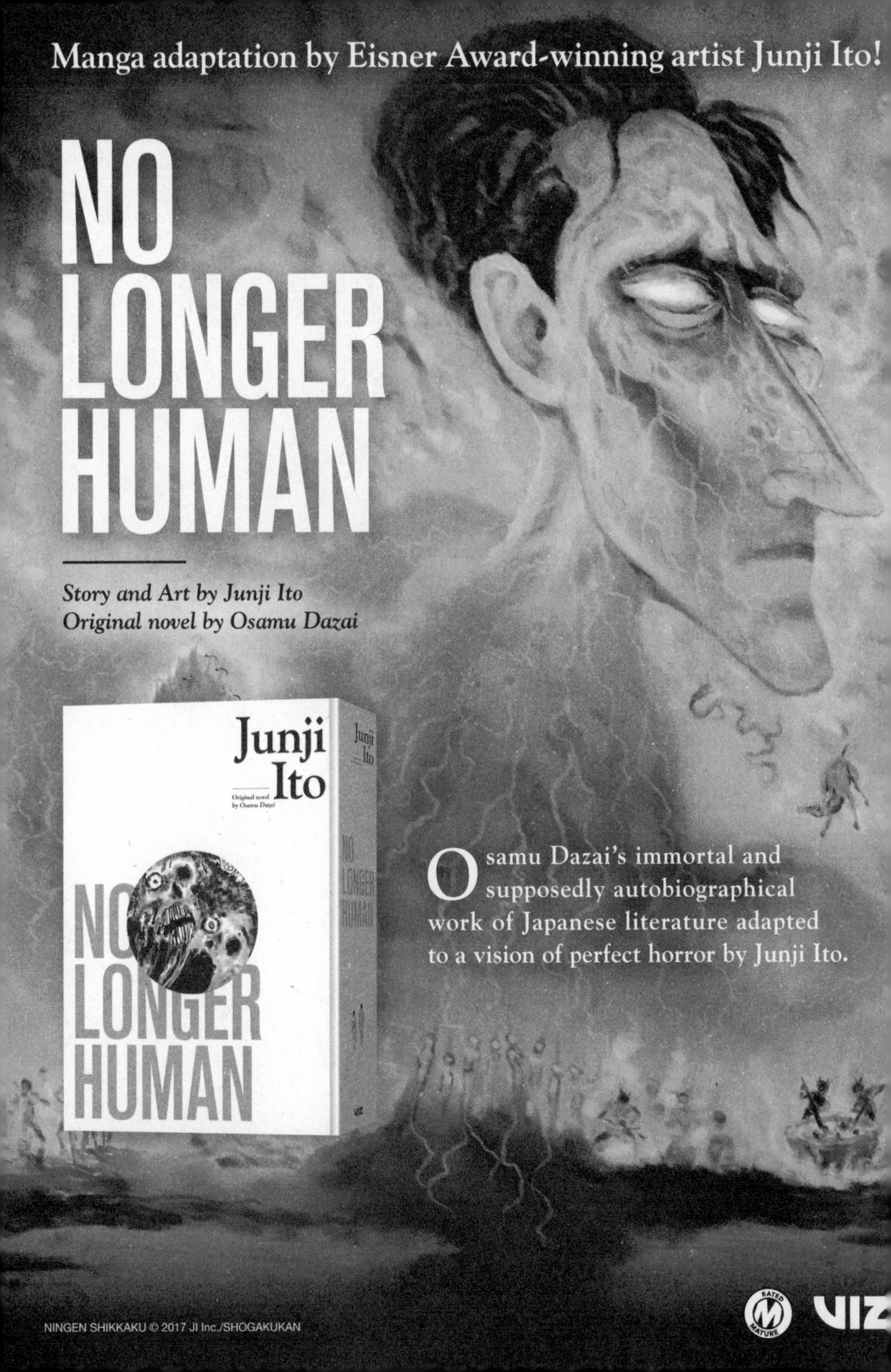
Manga adaptation by Eisner Award-winning artist Junji Ito!
NO LONGER HUMAN
Story and Art by Junji Ito
Original novel by Osamu Dazai
Junji Ito
Original novel by Osamu Dazai
NO LONGER HUMAN
Junji Ito
NO LONGER HUMAN
VIZ
Osamu Dazai's immortal and supposedly autobiographical work of Japanese literature adapted to a vision of perfect horror by Junji Ito.
RATED M MATURE
VIZ
NINGEN SHIKKAKU © 2017 JI Inc./SHOGAKUKAN

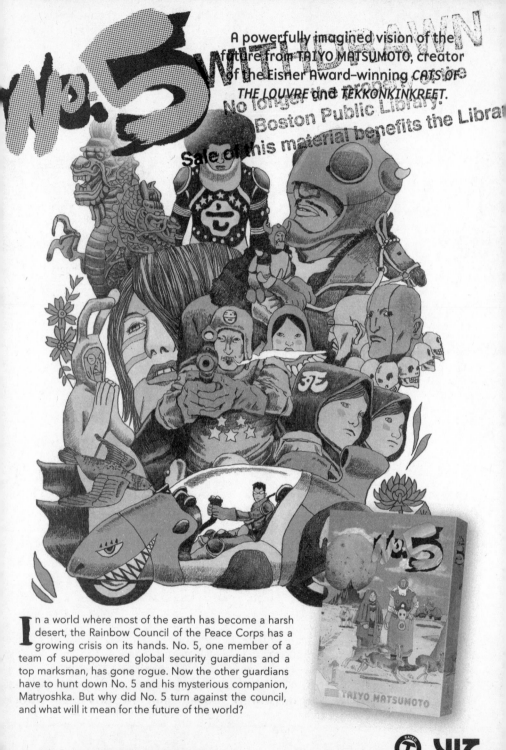

No. 5

A powerfully imagined vision of the future from TAIYO MATSUMOTO, creator of the Eisner Award–winning *CATS OF THE LOUVRE* and *TEKKONKINKREET*.

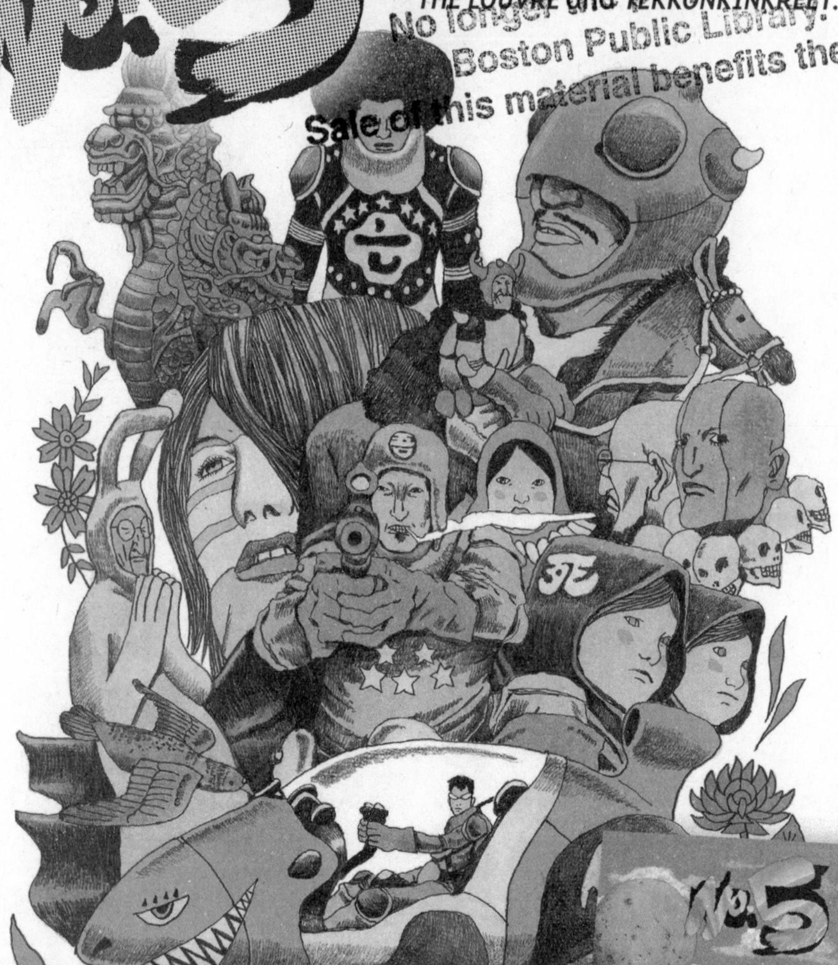

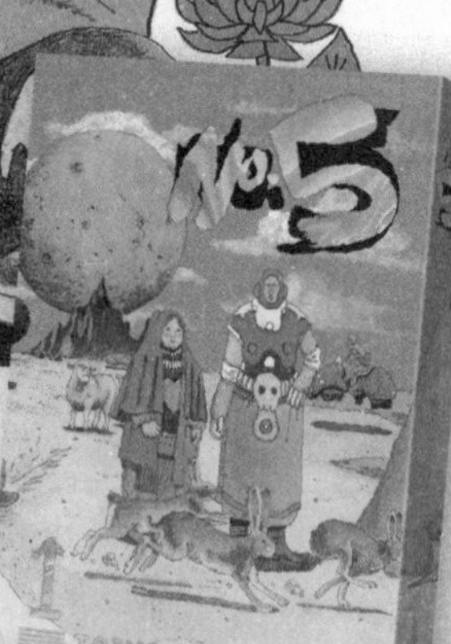
No. 5
TAIYO MATSUMOTO

In a world where most of the earth has become a harsh desert, the Rainbow Council of the Peace Corps has a growing crisis on its hands. No. 5, one member of a team of superpowered global security guardians and a top marksman, has gone rogue. Now the other guardians have to hunt down No. 5 and his mysterious companion, Matryoshka. But why did No. 5 turn against the council, and what will it mean for the future of the world?

RATED T TEEN

VIZ

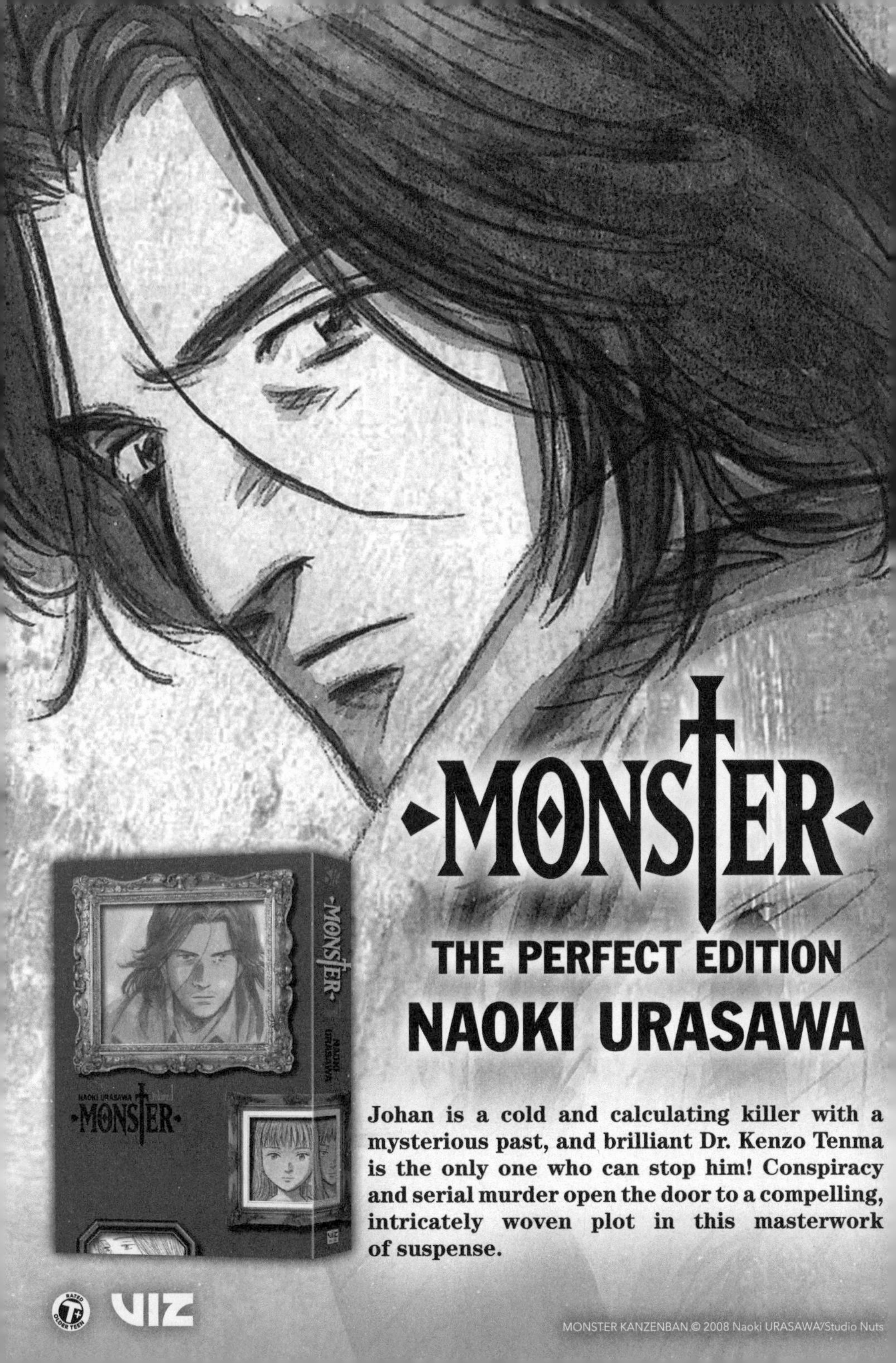
MONSTER
THE PERFECT EDITION
NAOKI URASAWA
Johan is a cold and calculating killer with a mysterious past, and brilliant Dr. Kenzo Tenma is the only one who can stop him! Conspiracy and serial murder open the door to a compelling, intricately woven plot in this masterwork of suspense.
VIZ
MONSTER KANZENBAN © 2008 Naoki URASAWA/Studio Nuts

THIS IS THE LAST PAGE

This book reads from right to left.

Turn the book over and start reading from the other side.

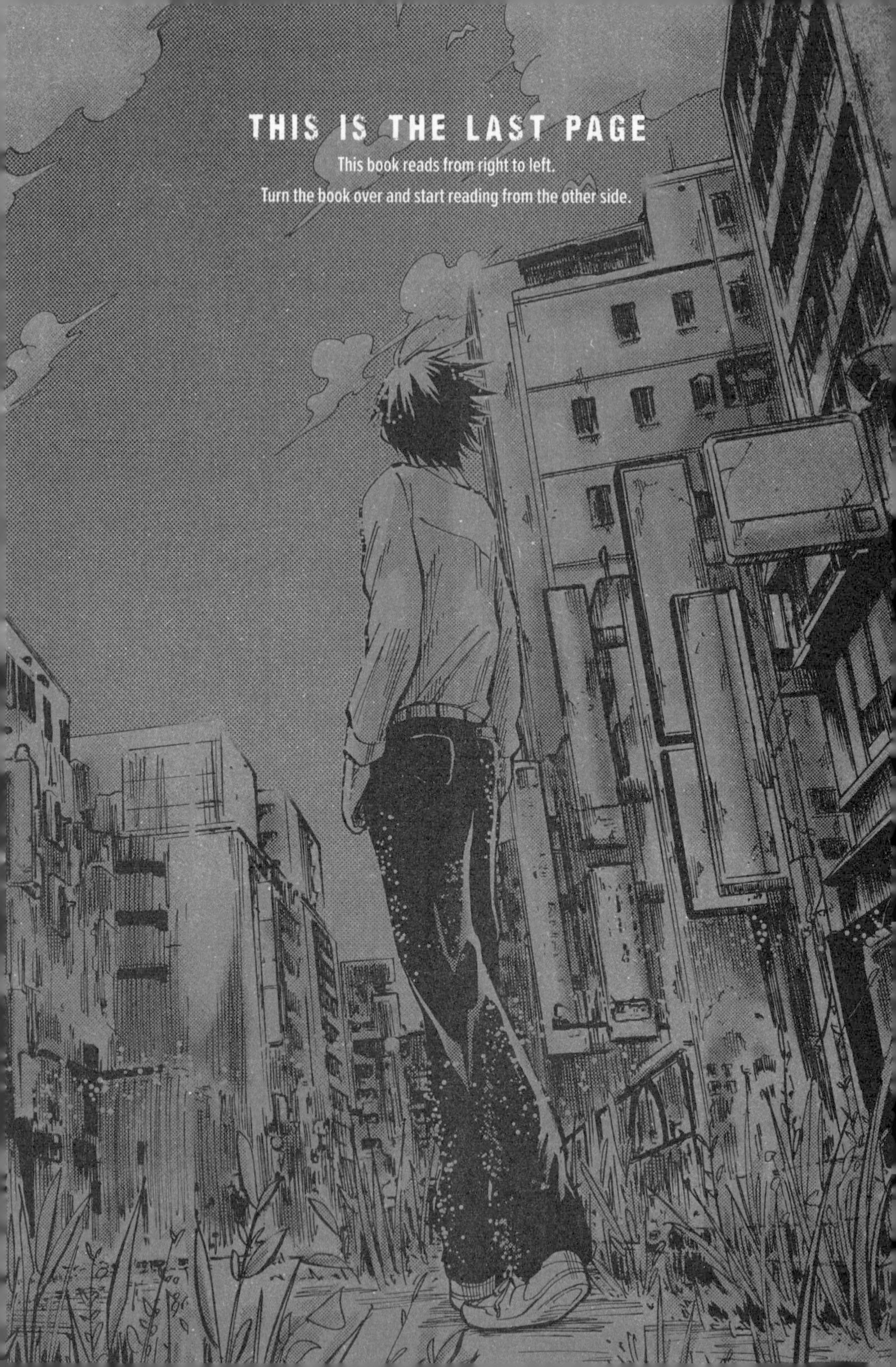